Landmark Legislation 1774–2012

Second Edition

*To my wife, Barbara; our four children—Jonathan,
Melanie, Jennifer, and David; and their families, with love*

Landmark Legislation 1774–2012

Major U.S. Acts and Treaties

Second Edition

Stephen W. Stathis

Los Angeles | London | New Delhi
Singapore | Washington DC

Los Angeles | London | New Delhi
Singapore | Washington DC

FOR INFORMATION:

CQ Press
An Imprint of SAGE Publications, Inc.
2455 Teller Road
Thousand Oaks, California 91320
E-mail: order@sagepub.com

SAGE Publications Ltd.
1 Oliver's Yard
55 City Road
London EC1Y 1SP
United Kingdom

SAGE Publications India Pvt. Ltd.
B 1/I 1 Mohan Cooperative Industrial Area
Mathura Road, New Delhi 110 044
India

SAGE Publications Asia-Pacific Pte. Ltd.
3 Church Street
#10-04 Samsung Hub
Singapore 049483

Developmental Editor: Sanford Robinson
Production Editor: David. C. Felts
Typesetter: C&M Digitals (P) Ltd.
Copyeditor: Kate Macomber Stern
Proofreader: Bonnie Moore
Indexer: Wendy Allex
Cover Designer: Anthony Paular
Marketing Manager: Carmel Schrire

Printed in the United States of America

Library of Congress Cataloging-in-Publication Data

Stathis, Stephen W.

Landmark legislation 1774–2012 : major U.S. acts and treaties / Stephen W. Stathis.—Second edition.

p. cm.
Includes bibliographical references and index.

ISBN 978-1-4522-9230-4

1. United States. Congress—History. 2. Legislation—United States—History. I. Title.

JK1021.S733 2003
348.73′2—dc23   2013029374

This book is printed on acid-free paper.

14 15 16 17 18 10 9 8 7 6 5 4 3 2 1

Contents

Contents

Preface

Since its inception, the U.S. Congress has served as a barometer of the mood of the country, and its members have given voice to the various interests of the nation. Despite a history of being innovative, responsive, and increasingly open to the people, Congress also has been seen by some as remote, irrelevant, and difficult to understand, and it has been an easy target for criticism. Especially in recent decades, many have doubted and sometimes made light of the role of Congress in the determination of national policy and the operation of the federal government.

Landmark Legislation 1774–2012 seeks to improve understanding of the work of Congress by highlighting its most significant accomplishments. Congress is the crucible in which interests clash, ideas contend, and compromises are forged. Three recurring themes have dominated its work over the past two centuries: (1) Congress is an institution in which ideas can be initiated and allowed to incubate while its members try to reach consensus; (2) Congress responds to what the American people want from the federal government and what they think it should do; and (3) Congress stops legislation it sees as inappropriate, slows the legislative process to permit public support to build, and uses its oversight powers to ensure enforcement of its policies.

Since 1789, more than 12,000 individuals have served as legislators in the halls of Congress. Their contributions are deeply etched in the legislative proposals that have been introduced, without interruption, since the first session of the First Congress. Although many of those ideas, on their face, were clearly impractical, the observations, suggestions, and propositions provide a meaningful barometer of

prevailing perspectives and pressures, a stimulus for positive action, and the substance of what may become law.

Nearly 46,000 public acts have been approved by Congress, submitted to the president for his approval, and signed into law since the First Congress convened. Many of these enactments represent momentary needs or fleeting passions, while others provide a glimpse of the continually changing texture of the national fabric. Only a relatively few, however, have withstood the test of history or so dramatically altered the perception of the role of government that they may be considered of enduring importance.

Landmark Legislation documents Congress's most momentous accomplishments in determining the national policies to be carried out by the executive branch, in approving appropriations to support those policies, and in fulfilling its responsibility to ensure that such actions are being implemented as intended. Also included are landmark laws relating to the federal judiciary and notable treaties. Although some laws characterized as landmark have declined in importance or been forgotten over time, when passed they represented a recognition of needed action and guidance to administrative entities, a significant departure from previous policy, a creative response to an emergency, or a solution to a long-standing national concern.

Evaluating the relative significance of an enactment with others in a given field and determining the precedents they set has proved an extraordinary exercise. The *U.S. Congressional Serial Set*, published by Congress, provides invaluable insight into the proceedings of the legislative branch. This largely forgotten collection of congressional documents, reports, legislative journals, executive journals of the Senate, and reports made to Congress by the executive branch is a treasure trove that serves as the starting point for serious research on the institution. Equally valuable are the *Annals of Congress, Register of Debates, Congressional Globe, Congressional Record,* committee hearing transcripts, committee prints, *Congressional Directory,* and *Biographical Directory of the United States Congress.* These diverse published sources are supplemented by the vast holdings of congressional papers in the National Archives.

Complementing these primary sources are a broad range of biographies of congressional personalities and general and specialized works on American history and politics that proved to be extremely useful in drawing conclusions and making judgments. Also, I consulted specialists in each of the various areas of expertise within the Congressional Research Service (CRS) of the Library of Congress, as well as scholars throughout the academic community. Their insights were invaluable in preparing *Landmark Legislation.*

Although some major laws and treaties no doubt have been inadvertently omitted, this volume seeks to illuminate the extremely important role Congress has assumed in shaping the political and historical character of the American republic. It shows how and why Congress enlarged the responsibilities of the federal establishment and portrays the institutional development of a national government, the changing pattern of federal-state relations, and the continuing redefinition of constitutional rights. In doing so, it sheds light on how the actions of Congress affect each citizen of the United States and on how Congress does its job.

The accompanying bibliographic selections focus not only on the unique and important role of Congress in formulating major policy changes but also on the forces prompting consideration and adoption of laws. The range of available materials shows that many fields of congressional inquiry await efforts by the scholarly community to provide an intellectual framework for understanding the inner workings of the American legislative process. Much of America's congressional heritage remains unexamined and unexplored.

The numerous possibilities for scholarly inquiry offer rich opportunities for future generations of scholars. Although much of the work will necessitate extensive primary research in the vast collections of published and unpublished records of Congress, future scholars will be able to portray far more accurately and fully, and with greater insight, the deliberations and the decisions that demonstrate the framers' wisdom in creating the U.S. legislative framework. The basis of that framework is patient deliberation, with adequate allowance for every member and every viewpoint to be heard and considered. The deliberate pace the framers ensured has allowed maximum opportunity for the people's voices to be heard through their representatives in Congress.

This study was first proposed more than four decades ago by Frederick H. Pauls, then chief of the Government Division of the Congressional Research Service (CRS). Under his guidance, and with the assistance of Christopher Dell, I produced an abbreviated version of this work as a Congressional Research Service (CRS) report in 1982. The first edition of *Landmark Legislation* was originally suggested by Roger H. Davidson and benefitted from his continuing enthusiasm and insightful suggestions. I also wish to acknowledge with appreciation the steady encouragement, support, and sound advice of Daniel P. Mulhollan, former director of CRS; W. Ralph Eubanks, director of the Library of Congress publishing office; and David Tarr, executive editor of CQ Press, without whom the first edition would not have been brought to completion. I am equally indebted to Doug Goldenberg-Hart, former senior reference acquisitions editor of SAGE/CQ Press, for his encouragement and support of a second edition of *Landmark Legislation.* A special thanks to SAGE/CQ Press production editor David C. Felts for the time and talent he devoted to this book, and copy editor Kate Stern, whose impeccably high standards markedly improved the manuscript.

The first edition benefitted enormously from the exceptional editorial skills and gift for the English language, as well as the sophisticated historical perspective, of longtime colleague and friend Thomas H. Neale. The time and attention he generously gave to the text, both editorially and as a contributor, were especially appreciated, as were his continuous expressions of encouragement. Christopher Davis, also a CRS colleague and friend, was equally generous with his time and editorial skills during the preparation of this second edition. A significant number of other colleagues at CRS, as well as hundreds of scholars who have painstakingly chronicled the various enactments and treaties covered in this volume, likewise are just as deserving of special appreciation. Many details and nuances would certainly have been overlooked without their penetrating perceptivity.

This book is dedicated with loving appreciation to my wife, Barbara; our four children—Jonathan, Melanie, Jennifer, and David; and their families. Barbara, as usual, has endured all the frustrations inevitably accompanying such a project, read and proofed the text in its entirety, and offered numerous beneficial editorial suggestions. Her love, support, and patience cannot adequately be expressed in words. For more than four decades she has steadfastly supported my career as an historian and expanded my horizons far beyond what I had ever dreamed possible.

Stephen W. Stathis
Annandale, Virginia

About the Author

Stephen W. Stathis was, for nearly four decades, a specialist in American National Government for the Congressional Research Service (CRS) of the Library of Congress. Stathis, who specializes in the history of Congress, held both research and managerial positions at CRS. He is the author of the first edition of *Landmark Legislation* (2003) and *Landmark Debates in Congress: From the Declaration of Independence to the War in Iraq* (2009).

Introduction

During the eleven years between the signing of the Declaration of Independence in 1776 and the convening of the Constitutional Convention of 1787, the Continental Congress and its successor under the Articles of Confederation tried to hold together the loose association of the thirteen states that had broken from Great Britain. Ratification of the Articles of Confederation, the first effort by Americans to provide a written constitution for the "United States of America," was completed early in 1781, more than three years after their adoption by the Continental Congress.

Under the articles, the states retained control over the most essential governmental functions, and Congress—in which each state had an equal vote—was the sole instrument of national government. In their attempt to avoid anything like the system under which Great Britain had ruled her colonies, the colonists arguably left their own government too weak to perform its functions and duties. Almost from the outset, the confederation was beset with serious problems. These, for the most part, resulted from basic defects in the articles themselves, which failed to give Congress control over taxation and trade, made no provision for a federal executive or judiciary, and failed to provide the confederation any sanctions through which it might enforce its decisions.

Even as the inadequacies of the Articles became apparent, the unanimous consent required for amendments proved impossible to obtain. As a consequence, the states had to take responsibility for settling many of their common problems. In March 1785, delegates from Virginia and Maryland met first in Alexandria, Virginia, and then at Mount Vernon, hoping to settle disputes relating to the navigation of the Chesapeake Bay and the Potomac River. The success of the latter meeting led Virginia to issue an invitation to all the states to meet in Annapolis, Maryland, the following year to consider commercial reforms.

The achievement of the twelve delegates from Delaware, New Jersey, New York, Pennsylvania, and Virginia who met in Annapolis on September 11–14, 1786, was not readily apparent. The only resolution adopted called for a general meeting of delegates from all thirteen states in Philadelphia the following May to consider what steps were "necessary to render the constitution of the Federal Government adequate to the exigencies of the Union." James Madison and Alexander Hamilton persuaded their fellow delegates to adopt a report that described the state of the Union as "delicate and critical."[1] In February 1787, Congress endorsed the need for a convention in Philadelphia that could revise the Articles of Confederation and "render the federal Constitution adequate to the exigencies of Government and preservation of the Union."[2] By early May 1787, only Rhode Island had failed to respond to the calls from Annapolis and Philadelphia, and most of the fifty-five men who would become the framers of the U.S. Constitution were on their way to Philadelphia to establish a new form of government.

The framers' historic effort was designed to "form a more perfect Union, establish justice, insure domestic tranquility, provide for the common defense, promote the general welfare, and secure the blessings of liberty to ourselves and our posterity."[3] It represented a second, and more successful, attempt of Americans to develop a constitution that would be flexible, yet strong enough to meet the long-term legislative, administrative, and judicial needs of the new nation.

Intent of the Framers and the Powers of Congress

The Constitution and the Declaration of Independence were to become fundamental testaments of free government in the United States. Throughout American history, the interplay of the system crafted in Philadelphia has often prompted the question, "What was the intent of the framers?" Ironically, even the framers frequently did not agree and often had different conceptions about the new government they were creating. A reading of the proceedings in Philadelphia, however, shows a clear intent on the part of the framers to make Congress the major source of policy initiatives and proposals.

In designing Congress, the framers were influenced by both the successes and the failures of the Continental and Confederation Congresses. In particular, the Constitutional Convention of 1787 favored the principle of separation of powers, which reflected the concern of the founders with the relative powerlessness of Congress under the Articles of Confederation. Although the articles had not separated the legislative, executive, and judicial functions, most state governments at the time consisted of three branches. Most of the delegates to the Constitutional Convention had experience as members of the ineffective Continental Congress or their state legislatures, which were generally more powerful. The legislative branch, with which most delegates most closely identified, was the first branch discussed in depth during the constitutional debates and the first to be established by the Constitution. The framers devoted more than twice as much attention to the responsibilities of Congress than to the other two branches combined. Much is left unstated in the Constitution regarding the executive and judicial branches, but few details are spared when Congress is discussed.

The framers intended Congress to be a representative body, responsive to the demands of voters and constituents, reflecting local interests, yet responsible for making laws for the American people collectively. James Madison and the other statesmen who framed the Constitution acknowledged that in a "republican government" such as the one they had created, the "legislative authority necessarily predominates."[4] Congress, in Madison's mind, had the obligation "to refine and enlarge the public views" and needed "wisdom" to "discern the true interest of their country." The members' "patriotism and love of justice" should be such that they will be "least likely to sacrifice it to temporary or partial considerations."[5] "Nearly all legislation," Supreme Court justice Louis Brandeis observed in 1921, "involves a weighing of public needs as against private desires; and likewise a weighing of relative social values."[6] In creating a representative assembly as the structure within which the government considered its decisions, formulated policy, and enacted laws, the framers ensured that institutional restraints would operate not only to promote the primacy of the deliberative processes but also to allow the constraints of political reality to flourish.

Seeking to correct the deficiencies of the Articles of Confederation, as well as to enlarge the authority of Congress in dealing with both foreign and domestic matters, the framers invested Congress with tremendous power. The Constitution mandated that Congress make all laws, specifically those "necessary and proper" for exercising the powers granted to it, and execute the powers granted to the other branches. Article I, Section 8 of the Constitution enumerates eighteen powers entrusted to Congress.[7] Congress also was given almost unlimited power to control the expenditures of the executive branch through the appropriations process. In addition, Congress was given the responsibility of supervising the administration of the executive and judicial branches and the implicit responsibility of representing and informing the people. The legislative primacy of Congress also appears in the provisions for amending the Constitution (Article V), which call for approval by two-thirds of each house of Congress and ratification by three-fourths of the states.[8] The role of the president and the Supreme Court in this latter process was limited to whatever informal influence they might exert.

Constraining the Powers of Congress

The framers were fearful that Congress might abuse its power, as had many of the state legislatures during the Confederation period, and, as a consequence, attempted by several means to constrain that power. One remedy was "to divide the legislature into different branches; and to render them, by different modes of election and different principles of action, as little connected with each other as the nature of their common functions and their common dependence on society will admit."[9] A bicameral legislature provided a vital check, each house being able to counteract the other.

Each chamber was granted certain exclusive powers. The House of Representatives was delegated the responsibility of choosing a president when no clear electoral winner emerged. The Constitution also provided that tax legislation must originate in the House, as must impeachment proceedings against a president or other federal officials. The Senate was given authority to ratify treaties; approve presidential nominations to the Supreme Court, cabinet positions, and ambassadorships; and conduct impeachment trials.

The House of Representatives was intended to be the most immediately responsive element of the government. By virtue of their biannual election, representatives would be mindful of public opinion. The House, as James Madison explained in *Federalist* No. 52, was to have "an immediate dependence on, and an intimate sympathy with, the people."[10] Conversely, senators, who were selected by the state legislatures until 1913, when the Seventeenth Amendment provided for popular election, historically enjoyed greater independence because of their six-year terms. The Senate was envisioned by Madison as a safeguard against impulsive action, "until reason, justice, and truth can regain their authority over the public mind."[11]

The chief constraint the framers placed on congressional power was the tripartite governmental system, each element having the means to check and balance the other. Under this system of separated powers, Congress was not to have absolute control over the legislative process. Article I, Section 7 stipulated that the president must sign legislation, thus approving it, for it to become law, and that a presidential veto could be overridden only by a two-thirds vote of each house of Congress. If, however, the president took no action on a bill that had been presented, it could become law without his signature after ten days, provided Congress has not adjourned during the period. The failure of the president to sign a bill under these circumstances, with the intention that it not become law, is known as the "pocket veto." Other legislative responsibilities imposed on the president by Article II, Section

3 required him to provide Congress "information of the state of the Union, and recommend to their consideration such measures as he shall judge necessary and expedient"; to convene either or both houses of Congress into session "on extraordinary occasions"; and to adjourn them to a time of his choosing if they could not reach agreement on adjournment.

Performance of Congress in Expectation and Practice

Many observers, especially during the past century, asserted, or even presumed, the president's primacy in the policy-making process in general and in the legislative process in particular. An examination of legislative accomplishments throughout the decades, however, clearly indicates that Congress has maintained a much more persistent and crucial role in achieving these accomplishments than conventional wisdom often allows. A more careful consideration of the activity involved in national lawmaking reveals a much more complex process, one in which Congress has always played, and continues to play, a part not only central, but also vital, in the initiation, development, and establishment of policy.

One reason that the continuing centrality of Congress to the legislative policy-making process has been overlooked or minimized is the deliberative and representative nature of America's constitutional system. Legislation involves Congress as well as a wide variety of other actors, especially the president. The saliency of presidential involvement in the constitutional system is reinforced by the tendency of Congress, observable throughout U.S. history, to find occasion and means to delegate its functions. In assessing the operation of the system, however, these circumstances have arguably been overemphasized.

Delegation of Power and Its Control

Nearly two centuries ago, Chief Justice John Marshall wrote that "the legislature makes, the executive executes, and the judiciary construes the law." Congress, Marshall declared, must keep to itself "powers which are strictly and exclusively legislative."[12] Congress cannot relinquish its responsibility for creating executive departments and agencies, authorizing and regulating their activities, overseeing their work, reviewing their performance, and holding them accountable. Despite Marshall's admonition, Congress has, over time, delegated a significant portion of its legislative power to the president, executive agencies, and independent regulatory commissions.

Congress, however, also exercises a variety of means to check these delegations of authority. Operational guidelines are often established during the development of laws, and customs and traditions have evolved to confine executive discretion. Also, Congress, through the appropriations process and its oversight function, is continually able to review the operations and policies of the various agencies and influence their future direction. Through its oversight activities, Congress seeks to ensure that legislation is faithfully, effectively, and economically administered; internal management controls are adequate and effective; abuses of administrative discretion or improper conduct are discovered and corrected; and executive branch officials are held accountable for the use of public funds and for administrative shortcomings.

Also, when the courts have found that Congress has gone too far in delegating power, they have voided such actions. For example, the Line Item Veto Act, a majority of the U.S. Supreme Court held in 1998, was unconstitutional because it allowed the president effectively to rewrite bills he had already signed into law.[13] Although the power of the courts to review the constitutionality of federal and state legislative enactments is nowhere expressly conveyed, the concept was utilized in colonial times and assumed by the framers in the Constitutional Convention and by the members of the state ratifying conventions. The Supreme Court, however, did not until 1803, in *Marbury v. Madison,* expressly assert and exercise its power to strike down an act of Congress it considered inconsistent with the Constitution.[14]

Presidential and Congressional Legislation

Especially in the course of the past century, many scholars, as well as the press and electronic media, have viewed the president, not Congress, as the prime mover of the legislative process. The limitations of this presidential role have received less emphasis. The Constitution is silent on the extent of participation by the president and his subordinates in the legislative process once a measure is proposed. Although the president's recommendations carry great weight, he may not introduce legislation or compel Congress to act on his proposals. To win votes for a proposal, the president must make clear what the likely effects of the bill will be and provide a rationale that will secure support.

As Lawrence H. Chamberlain observed in *The President, Congress, and Legislation,* the "concept of presidential domination in legislation comes in part from the tendency of the press to magnify his every action." While the president's deeds are broadcast to the nation through a multitude of media sources, the accomplishments of Congress receive relatively little coverage. "It is easier," Chamberlain reasoned, "to follow the moves of one man than it is to trace the day-to-day developments of multitudinous committees, not to mention individual congressmen."[15]

Even when Congress has worked on a bill for months, and an administration has had only a limited role in its development, the president may receive much of the credit for its enactment. If a president decides to support a piece of legislation through a special message to Congress, a public statement, a White House conference, a radio or television appeal, or the efforts of his representatives, the proposal quickly becomes identified with the president regardless of its origin. Even if the president waits to comment on the merits of a bill until after it is signed into law, his limited association with the legislation often captures the spotlight. The same is the case when Congress overrides a presidential veto. This tendency to magnify the importance of the president, while frequently overlooking the role of Congress, distorts the history of the American legislative process.

In the final analysis, it is often difficult to weigh the relative influence of Congress and the president in the legislative process and accurately gauge the continual and influential activities of outside interests. The assumption, however, should not be made that during those periods when a president becomes "unusually active" in the process, Congress has relinquished its constitutional responsibility. "Despite the well-organized rise of the president as chief legislator, empirical research" by scholars has "consistently found that Congress is responsible for most proposed legislation, and a large share of enacted programs, either on its own or working in conjunction with the president."[16]

Although presidents since Franklin D. Roosevelt have established much of the legislative agenda for Congress, the issues and ideas endorsed by the White House often have been germinating in Congress for a considerable period of time. Changing conditions within the nation or abroad may thrust to the forefront a legislative idea that has lain dormant for years or decades, or a presidential administration may breathe new life into a proposal whose time had supposedly passed. Also, Congress is one of the most fertile springs for presidential initiatives. "Difficult as it may be to determine the origin of a policy initiative, to identify the parent of an idea," presidential scholar Mark A. Peterson writes, "it is evident that a large bulk of what becomes 'presidential' first met the legislative light of day as 'congressional.'"[17] Often, by the time a proposal appears in a presidential message or speech, the president's position has been significantly modified to take into consideration difficulties particular provisions face on Capitol Hill. As a consequence, proposals sent to the Congress frequently represent modifications of the president's preferences. Furthermore, much of the legislation considered by Congress is of little concern to the president or his administration.

Genesis of Legislation

Often, neither Congress nor the president would push a particular piece of legislation if it were not for the external influences of society at large. The ideas and pressure for much of the legislation approved by Congress and signed into law by the president originate at neither end of Pennsylvania Avenue. Individuals from virtually every walk of life have originated, and assisted in, the formulation of legislative initiatives that have dramatically begun, altered, or displaced a governmental policy. Ideas for legislative initiatives are brought to the attention of members of Congress by

- the president in his annual State of the Union message, where he sets out his agenda for the coming year, as well as in other speeches,

messages, interviews, and press conferences, and through the White House congressional liaison office;
- members of the president's cabinet and other executive branch officials and personnel responsible for the administration of governmental policies;
- state and local officials;
- lobbyists for interest groups such as the business community, trade organizations, labor unions, and professional associations;
- academics, independent policy specialists, and members of think tanks and consulting groups;
- technical advisers representing universities and other private and government research organizations;
- the media;
- congressional staff; and
- private citizens.

Much of the credit for legislation must be given to the individuals or groups most directly interested in the specific results of the proposal. Nevertheless, only Congress can transform an idea into a bill that may become law.

Congress continues, as it has since 1789, to be an incubator for legislative proposals. A continuous exposure to legislative ideas has allowed Congress to remain a vigorous institution and an integral partner in the constitutional system. On Capitol Hill, proposals are procedurally introduced, subjected to committee hearings, debated on the House and Senate floor, and approved, before being sent to the White House for the president's signature. During the process of developing original or amendatory legislation, which often spans a number of years and several Congresses, the merits of a proposal may become the topic of national debate, and the proposal may be modified or significantly altered.

Accomplishment of Legislation

While the framers devoted great detail to Congress's legislative responsibilities, they said little about how Congress should organize itself, except that the Speaker, the presiding officer of the House of Representatives, should be elected and that the vice president, or the president pro tempore in his absence, should preside over the Senate. The Constitution's brevity in this regard has allowed Congress the freedom to "change over time" and transform itself "from an informal, non-specialised representative and legislative assembly, attempting to fulfill the republican aspirations of post-revolutionary Americans, into a complex, highly specialised, rather bureaucratic institution which acts . . . like a complete government intervening in all policy areas and at every stage of the policy-making process." Congress's ability to change its internal structure and procedures has enabled it to respond for more than two centuries to "political, economic, and social changes which transformed the nature of problems facing constituents, and thus the public policies they were willing to support."[18] This transformation is most dramatically demonstrated in Congress's legislative accomplishments.

Congress, Lawrence H. Chamberlain argued, is better suited to deal with the "long germinative period detectable in the genesis of most laws" than is any other agency in America's democracy. Its composition, organization, and accessibility, "coupled with its ever-changing personnel, tends to guarantee a maximum responsiveness to varied but always moving currents of thought." A close examination of the official records of Congress reveals that individual senators and representatives frequently make a "substantial contribution" in "locating the weaknesses and gaps in our legislative fabric and initiating action to fill the breach." Were it not for "their persistent efforts and their unwillingness to give up in the face of administration indifference or hostility it is probable" that the enactment of many important laws would have been delayed much longer and "their content would have been much less definite."[19]

Although the legislative initiative has "shifted many times between the legislative and executive branches, the U.S. Congress remains virtually the only national assembly in the world that drafts in detail the laws it passes instead of simply debating and ratifying measures prepared by the government in power."[20] "In the United States," Chamberlain observed, "legislation is characteristically a collegial process in which the role of the Congress is no less important than that of the President."[21] Chamberlain's observations, penned nearly

seventy years ago, remain applicable today. In examining the origin of federal legislation over more than two centuries, landmark enactments have been approved during periods of comparative calm as well as during the stress of a national emergency. They have also gained acceptance when nonactivist presidents have occupied the Oval Office as well as strong ones.

A 2000 study of the most important laws enacted in the last half of the twentieth century credits Congress with "calling upon the federal government to tackle a bold agenda worthy of the world's greatest democracy, and providing the statutory authority to act." Survey responses from 450 history and political science professors, who were asked to select the government's greatest achievements of the past half century, "reflect a stunning level of bipartisan commitment." "Great endeavors appear to require equally great consensus."[22] The lessons of achievement, the study concluded, are:

> No one party, Congress, or president can be credited with any single achievement. Even Medicare, which was a signature accomplishment of the Great Society, and the Marshall Plan, which centered in a burst of legislation during the Truman administration, had antecedents in earlier Congresses and administrations. Rather, achievement appears to be the direct product of endurance, consensus, and patience.[23]

The report "suggests that the federal government did more than aim high," it "often succeeded in changing the nation and the world." Three important themes underlie the government's greatest achievements: (1) a "coherent policy strategy," (2) a conscious effort to take the "moral high ground despite significant resistance," and (3) a "readiness to intervene where the private and nonprofit sectors simply would not."[24]

Notes

1. *Journals of the Continental Congress, 1774–1789,* ed. Worthington Chauncey Ford and Roscoe R. Hill (Washington, D.C.: U.S. Government Printing Office, 1904–1937), 31:680.

2. *Journals of the Continental Congress* 32 (1787): 74.

3. *U.S. Constitution,* preamble.

4. Benjamin Fletcher Wright, ed., *The Federalist* (Cambridge, Mass.: Belknap Press of Harvard University Press, 1966), No. 51, 356.

5. Wright, *The Federalist,* No. 10, 134.

6. *Truax v. Corrigan,* 257 U.S. 312, 357 (1921).

7. These include the authority to tax, spend, and borrow; to regulate foreign and interstate commerce; to admit new states; to establish uniform naturalization and bankruptcy standards; to coin money, regulate its value, and fix the standard of weights and measures; to establish post offices and post roads; to develop copyright protections; to create federal courts of lesser authority than the U.S. Supreme Court, which was specifically provided for; to maintain a defense establishment; and to declare war.

8. Article V of the Constitution also provides that "the Legislatures of two-thirds of the several States" may "call a convention for proposing amendments."

9. Wright, *The Federalist,* No. 51, 357.

10. Wright, *The Federalist,* No. 52, 361.

11. Wright, *The Federalist,* No. 63, 415.

12. *Wayman v. Southard,* 23 U.S. (10 Wheaton), 41, 44 (1825).

13. *Clinton v. City of New York,* 524 U.S. 417 (1998).

14. *Marbury v. Madison,* 5 U.S. 137 (1803).

15. Lawrence H. Chamberlain, *The President, Congress, and Legislation* (New York: Columbia University Press, 1946), 15.

16. Mark A. Peterson, "Legislative Initiative," in *The Encyclopedia of the United States Congress,* ed. Donald C. Bacon, Roger H. Davidson, and Morton Keller (New York: Simon and Schuster, 1995), 3:1275.

17. Mark A. Peterson, *Legislating Together: The White House and Capitol Hill from Eisenhower to Reagan* (Cambridge, Mass.: Harvard University Press, 1990), 33, 35.

18. Michael Foley and John E. Owens, *Congress and the Presidency: Institutional Politics in a Separated System* (Manchester, England: Manchester University Press, 1996), 13.

19. Chamberlain, *The President, Congress, and Legislation,* 463.

20. Roger H. Davidson, Walter J. Oleszek, and Frances E. Lee. *Congress and Its Members,* 13th ed. (Los Angeles: SAGE/CQ Press, 2012), 8.

21. Chamberlain, *The President, Congress, and Legislation,* 15.

22. Paul C. Light, "Government's Greatest Achievements of the Past Half Century," *Reform Watch,* No. 2 (November 2000): 1, 4. See also Paul C. Light. *Government's Greatest Achievements: From Civil Rights to Homeland Defense.* (Washington, D.C.: Brookings Institution Press, 2002), 2, 46, 63–64.

23 Light, "Government's Greatest Greatest Achievements of the Past Half Century," 11.

24. Light, "Government's Greatest Greatest Achievements of the Past Half Century," 1, 12.

Finder's Guide

The Finder's Guide will help readers track legislation and treaties by major policy areas and national issues. Beginning with the First Congress, CQ Press editors assigned each summary entry in the book to at least one of forty-one categories and in many cases to several where the law or treaty had multiple purposes. Within each category, the entries are arranged chronologically by Congress. The Finder's Guide is intended to supplement the more detailed subject index found at the back of the volume by helping a reader track, for example, national security or continental development laws and treaties over the one hundred twelve Congresses surveyed. Because legislation often overlaps many areas, the categories are not neatly compartmentalized but will provide a road map in major areas on which Congress has legislated. An alphabetical list of categories follows. In the Guide pages, categories are grouped together in related areas such as law and justice issues or federal state relationships.

Agriculture

Civil Liberties

Communication, Information Technology

Congress

Continental Development, Union Expansion

Criminal Justice, Law Enforcement

District of Columbia

Economic Competition and Controls; Antitrust

Economic Development

Education

Elections, Campaign Finance

Energy, Power, Nuclear Development

Federalism

Financial Regulation and Banking

Foreign Affairs

General Commerce, Bankruptcy

Government Finance and Institutions, Coinage and Currency, Taxes and Expenditures

Government Organization, Operations

Health, Consumer Safety

Housing

Human Services, Welfare

Immigration, Naturalization, Citizenship

Indian Affairs

Judiciary

Labor

National Security

Natural Resources and Public Works

Parks and Recreation

Revenue: Taxes and Tariffs

Science and Space

Slavery, Civil Rights, Voting Rights

Territories

Trade

Transportation

Urban Assistance

Continental Congress
September 5, 1774, to March 2, 1781

United States in Congress Assembled
March 2, 1781, to October 10, 1788

First Continental Congress—September 5, 1774, to
October 26, 1774

Second Continental Congress—May 10, 1775, to March
2, 1781

United States in Congress Assembled—March 2, 1781,
to October 10, 1788

Historical Background

Most of the delegates who assembled in Philadelphia, Pennsylvania, on September 5, 1774, for the First Continental Congress were instructed to focus on the redress of specific grievances against the Crown. As representatives of Great Britain's North American colonies, most thought that they could quickly "reestablish satisfactory, if not harmonious, relations with England." The delegates "were established social, economic, and political leaders in their home colonies, and most had served in colonial legislatures that had struggled successfully to overturn earlier programs and policies of the king and Parliament. Most assumed their earlier experiences of successful conflict resolution within the existing imperial structure would be repeated."[1] The colonies had balked for more than a decade at policies designed to reduce British war debt, cover the expenses of an expanding empire, and "rationalize" the historically loose and ad hoc relationship between Britain and her North American colonies. The purpose of the Philadelphia assemblage was neither revolution nor independence from England.

The need, however, for an ongoing representative assembly quickly became clear. Over the next fifteen years, Congress (as the First Continental Congress, 1774; the Second Continental Congress, 1775–1781; and the United States in Congress Assembled, 1781–1788) would serve as the sole organ of American government. Congress was responsible for setting war aims, organizing and provisioning the army and navy, conducting foreign relations, and settling, when possible, squabbles between states. While victory in the American Revolution cannot be properly attributed to Congress, its contributions were indispensable. It articulated, nurtured, and sustained committed patriots, who were often a minority; it supported the armies, however unevenly; and it bound the states, albeit loosely.

The failures of Congress did not result from lack of zeal, vigor, or intelligence on the part of its delegates, who were, on the average, some of the most able public men ever to emerge from American society. Most of Congress's failings were attributable to a simple lack of power. This group of men, whose interests varied greatly and whose number seldom exceeded forty, were responsible for carrying out the legislative, executive, and, to a lesser extent, judicial functions of the nation. Their achievements were attained under the most adverse circumstances by a body that chose to limit severely its own authority. Before 1781, Congress did not even arm itself with enough power to pass legislation that would be binding as law on the states as a whole.

The Intolerable Acts of 1774 accentuated the differences between Britain and the colonies, rallied the other twelve colonies to the plight of Massachusetts, and created the emergency that prompted the assemblage at Carpenter's Hall in Philadelphia. Four of the five acts were designed to punish Boston for leading colonial resistance against the 1773 Tea Act, which Parliament had approved to shore up the faltering East India Company and to reinforce royal authority at the expense of popular liberty. The Quebec Act, the fifth act, was also resented in the colonies. First, it extended Quebec's boundaries to the Ohio and Mississippi Rivers, indicating that Britain intended to prohibit further westward settlement. Second, it reestablished French civil law in Quebec and extended full tolerance of Roman Catholicism to the province. The British had found particularly galling the Boston Tea Party of 1773, when a mob disguised as Indians boarded three tea-carrying ships and dumped their cargoes into the harbor.

Before approving a Declaration of Rights on October 14, 1774, Congress debated whether colonial rights should be based upon the law of nature or on the English constitution. The declaration reviewed the British measures deemed obnoxious and articulated the fundamental rights of the colonies, which were held to be "life, liberty, property" and participation in provincial legislatures. A plan, the Continental Association of 1774, subsequently developed a rigid policy of nonimportation, nonconsumption, and nonexportation with Britain until the grievances identified were redressed. The provisions were to be uniformly applicable throughout the colonies and "emphasized the question of allegiance." The association made it more difficult to remain neutral "as the Continental Congress was steered in the direction of independence, and the British government made plain its intention of continuing a policy of coercion."[2]

Conflict erupted in April 1775, when General Thomas Gage, the British military governor of Massachusetts appointed to enforce the Intolerable Acts, ordered the seizure of the military supplies of the Massachusetts Provincial Congress at Concord. Apprised of the plan, Paul Revere, William Dawes, and Samuel Prescott set out to warn Concord. At dawn the following morning, sixty to seventy armed Minutemen confronted seven hundred British troops at Lexington. When the skirmish ended, eight Americans lay dead. By the time the British reached Concord, six miles

away, the rebel military supplies had been removed and British forces were compelled to retreat to Boston, under steady fire from Massachusetts militia. By the end of the day, seventy-three British and forty-nine Americans had lost their lives.

Following Lexington and Concord, a force of Massachusetts militia, aided by a growing number of volunteers from other New England colonies, set up a loose cordon around Boston, confining British troops to the city. They fortified Breed's Hill, opposite Boston on the Charlestown Peninsula. Ultimately, the British troops dislodged the American forces at great cost in a bloody assault on June 17, 1775. Mistakenly known as the Battle of Bunker Hill, this clash further galvanized colonial opinion in favor of armed resistance. Soon military action spread to several points up and down the Atlantic Coast, and in ensuing weeks some sixteen thousand militiamen from various colonies came to the aid of Boston as American colonial legislatures began to arm for an all-out war. Prior to the clashes at Lexington, Concord, and Boston, the American colonies had begun to assume many of the duties of self-government, expelling their royal governors and other colonial officials, establishing new legislatures (usually in the form of provisional conventions), and adopting new constitutions in place of their colonial charters. When representatives of the thirteen colonies met on May 10, 1775, to convene the Second Continental Congress, the need for regular military forces was apparent if the colonists were to stand up to the British. On June 14, 1775, Congress authorized ten companies of expert riflemen to assist the New England provincial forces gathered near Boston and named a five-member committee to draft administrative rules for the army. A day later, Congress unanimously voted to appoint Colonel George Washington of Virginia to command all the "Continental" forces.

Even after the initial armed clashes, Congress made another attempt to settle their grievances with King George III, in the conciliatory Olive Branch Petition. While asserting a desire for a reconciliation that would restore harmony and end further hostilities, Congress adopted a Declaration Setting Forth the Causes and Necessities for Taking Up Arms, which enumerated the reasons that the colonists had been stirred to action. Later in July 1775, Congress established a continental postal system, recognizing that the "critical situation of the colonies" required a "speedy and secure conveyance of Intelligence from one end of the Continent to the other."

That August, London responded to the Olive Branch Petition by proclaiming a state of rebellion in America. During the latter part of 1775, Congress turned its attention to creating a navy and a Marine Corps by voting to outfit four armed ships, raise two battalions of Marines, and adopt "Rules for the Regulation of the Navy of the United Colonies." A concerned Congress also watched as Americans suffered defeats at Quebec City, Norfolk, Virginia, and Falmouth (Portland), Maine, and struggled with the reality that many Americans remained uncommitted to either war or independence at year's end.

In January 1776, Thomas Paine published *Common Sense,* the first effective presentation of the American cause. Within three months, its circulation reached 120,000, and sentiment for independence began to grow as colonial assemblies openly discussed the question. In the field, the failed campaign to seize Quebec was somewhat compensated for in March 1776, when British troops evacuated Boston, which had been rendered untenable by Washington's placement of heavy artillery on Dorchester Heights. On June 7, Richard Henry Lee of Virginia offered a resolution in Congress that "these United Colonies are, and of right ought to be, free and independent States." A five-member committee was appointed to prepare a declaration of independence. A draft declaration, largely the work of Thomas Jefferson, was presented to Congress on June 28. Lee's resolution was adopted on July 2. Attention then shifted to consideration of Jefferson's draft. Much of his original writing was retained, but forty additions and extensive cuts reduced it by a quarter. On July 4, copies were ordered printed and sent to the states and commanding officers of the continental troops. The summer of 1776 proved that the American revolution would not be easily quelled.

For much of the remainder of 1776, the Continental Army met with repeated defeats. In August, a British army defeated Washington's troops at the Battle of Long Island, and the American army was forced to evacuate New York, narrowly escaping entrapment. After a prolonged retreat, Washington stabilized the situation when he launched a successful surprise attack at Trenton, New Jersey, the day after Christmas. Within days, he crossed the Delaware River and followed the victory at Trenton with another near Princeton.

The campaigns of 1777 included both triumph and defeat for the Americans. In the north, a two-pronged British invasion of New York from Canada failed when an expedition was repelled at Fort Stanwix in the Mohawk Valley and when General John Burgoyne's invasion force from Canada was defeated and forced to surrender at Saratoga in October. The first major American victory contributed to France's subsequent recognition of the United States. Further south, fifteen thousand British troops under the command of Sir William Howe sailed from New York, landed in the Chesapeake Bay in August, and marched on Philadelphia. Washington, who had determined Howe's objective, attempted to block the advance but was defeated at Brandywine Creek. Congress evacuated Philadelphia on September 13, moving first to Lancaster and then settling west of the Susquehanna River, at York, where members were to remain until June 1778. The British occupied Philadelphia on September 26 and repelled an American counterattack at Germantown on October 4. Washington's army took up winter quarters at nearby Valley Forge.

Congress in November 1777, after more than a year of intermittent debate, adopted a plan for uniting the states. The Articles of Confederation and Perpetual Union established a unicameral Congress that possessed neither the power to tax nor the authority to effectively regulate interstate or foreign commerce. In the view of most observers, the articles were the best that could be achieved, given the "difficulty of combining in one general system the various sentiments and interests of a continent divided into so many sovereign and independent communities."

The inherent flaws of the articles brought the nation close to bankruptcy and internal chaos within a few years, and growing sentiment for their revision ultimately led to the Constitutional Convention of 1787. The importance of the articles should not, however, be underestimated. They preserved the Union until a more efficient system could be established, embraced many of the ideas that ultimately appeared in the Constitution, and afforded the state delegates invaluable experience in establishing an operational and diplomatic framework for government. The struggle to gain ratification of the articles took more than four years as several smaller states successfully sought to insert a provision making western lands a common possession of all the states.

On December 17, 1777, France formally recognized the independence of the United States. The following February, the two nations concluded treaties of alliance and amity and commerce that were ratified by Congress in May. The Treaty of Alliance provided that neither country would make a separate peace with Great Britain without the other's consent and that peace would not be possible until an agreement was reached securing independence for the United States. The Treaty of Amity and Commerce granted most-favored-nation trading privileges to American shippers. As anticipated, the alliance precipitated war between France and Great Britain.

In the summer of 1778, the conflict shifted to New York and the Northeast, as the British evacuated Philadelphia. Washington followed the British army, which marched overland to New York, and attacked his opponents, now commanded by Sir Henry Clinton, on June 28, 1778. In this fierce battle, fought in sweltering heat, Washington came close to crushing Clinton, but as night fell, Clinton was able to continue his escape to New York. In 1779, the South became the principal theater of operations, as the British overran Georgia and South Carolina. In the West, Kentucky frontiersmen, under the command of George Rogers Clark, were successful in seizing British posts in the Illinois country. Despite subsequent victories at Kings Mountain, North Carolina, and Cowpens, South Carolina, little hope existed of an overall American victory. By 1781, the British either controlled or had blockaded every American port except Boston and Newport; Congress was unable to raise either money or troops; and the French, who had joined the war, continued to be preoccupied with action in the West Indies and other theaters.

Not until fall 1781 did the French and American allies take the offensive together, for the first time, at the mouth of the Chesapeake Bay. For six weeks, the French fleet commanded by Admiral Comte de Grasse and an allied army of more than twenty thousand under the joint command of Washington, the Marquis de Lafayette, and the Comte de Rochambeau laid siege to Yorktown, Virginia, as an entrapped General George Cornwallis and nearly ten thousand British troops waited in vain for aid or evacuation. A British fleet sent to support Cornwallis was defeated by de Grasse off the Virginia Capes on September 5, sealing the fate of Cornwallis's army. The combined French-American army then pressed the siege of Yorktown, gaining a British surrender on October 19 and bringing to a close major military operations in the American Revolutionary War.

Nearly two years passed before a peace treaty was signed, but the American victory at Yorktown essentially concluded the war. A preliminary peace treaty between the United States and Great Britain was signed in Paris in November 1782, and the definitive Treaty of Paris was signed on September 2, 1783. While several of the nine article agreements proved difficult for the American Congress to enforce, the treaty formally ended the war and granted the United States control of the continent from the Atlantic Coast to the Mississippi River.

Several months before the victory at Yorktown, and several weeks prior to ratification of the Articles of Confederation on March 1, 1781, Congress began to establish the new government by creating the Departments of Foreign Affairs, Finance, War, and Marine under secretaries selected by Congress. Three of the four departments—Foreign Affairs, Finance, and War—attained varying levels of success, while the Department of Marine was never organized. Robert Morris, the first superintendent of finance, brought a measure of stability to the nation's finance, secured foreign loans, and made Treasury operations considerably more effective. His first proposal, a national bank, was chartered by Congress in December 1781. During the final months of the Revolutionary War, the Bank of North America supplied vital financial aid to the government.

Given the pressing business of the war, Congress took no action on a new flag when the Declaration of Independence was signed. Even when Congress acted, news about it spread only gradually and the "Union Jack in the old Continental Colors give way to the first official flag of the United States."[3] Adoption of a national seal took longer: Six years, three committees, and the combined efforts of fourteen men were needed to complete the task. Today, the appearance of the Great Seal of the United States remains as decreed by Congress in 1782.

A more urgent issue was the distribution of western lands. With the passage of Land Ordinance of 1785, Congress established a method for surveying and selling land in the Northwest Territory; created land reserves for revolutionary veterans, for many others who aided the American cause, and for U.S. government use; and provided the first government support of education. The ordinance remained the basis for public land policy until the Homestead Act of 1862. Also in 1785, Congress adopted the dollar as the monetary unit of the United States. Previously, the Spanish dollar had been widely employed as the standard of value. Although, the decimal system was never actually used during the Continental period, it was subsequently incorporated by the Coinage Act of 1792.

By 1786, Congress's need for independent sources of revenue and the limitations of the Articles of Confederation pointed to the need for significant changes in the charter. In September, delegates from five states—Delaware, New Jersey, New York, Pennsylvania, and Virginia—assembled in Annapolis, Maryland, to discuss questions of interstate commerce. Although the Annapolis Convention took no action, its report described the state of the Union as "delicate and critical," recommending that all thirteen states meet in Philadelphia the following May "to devise such further provisions as shall appear to them necessary to render the constitution of the Federal Government adequate to the exigencies of the Union."

In February 1787, Congress endorsed the proposed convention to revise and amend the articles. That summer, while the Constitutional Convention of 1787 in Philadelphia was writing the obituary of one government and birthing another, the Continental Congress, then in session in New York, set in place what has been characterized as the "most constructive and influential legislative act in American history."[4] The Northwest Ordinance established a process for expanding the Union. It created the Northwest Territory (an area that today includes Illinois, Indiana, Michigan, Ohio, Wisconsin, and part of Minnesota), provided for its government, and banned slavery in the territory. Despite the controversial nature of several of its provisions, particularly regarding the question of slavery, the ordinance

passed with ease. The precarious economic condition of the Treasury dictated the need for the immediate sale of western lands, and the government had in hand an offer from the Ohio Company to purchase a million-acre block.

While many of the delegates that assembled in Philadelphia in the summer of 1787 were prepared to follow the instructions of Congress to revise the existing Articles of Confederation, those in favor of more drastic reform prevailed. The decision by the convention to create a new national government consisting of three branches—legislative, executive, and judicial—represented a broad acceptance of the separation of powers. Unlike its predecessors, the new national legislature was to be bicameral, mirroring the two-house pattern established by ten of the thirteen colonial legislatures. Ten days after the convention adjourned on September 17, Congress submitted the new Constitution drafted by the convention to the states for their consideration. During the next ten months, eleven of the thirteen original states ratified the Constitution, and the remaining two, North Carolina and Rhode Island, agreed in November 1789 and May 1790, respectively. Congress declared the Constitution ratified on September 13, 1788, and conducted its last official work a month later. The following spring the president and vice president of the United States and members of the First Congress began their service under the new government.

William Pitt (first earl of Chatham) gave the Continental Congress what was perhaps its greatest tribute when, during the course of debate in the British House of Lords on the conflict between America and Britain, he said:

> When your lordships look at the papers transmitted to us from America; when you consider their decency, firmness, and wisdom, you cannot help but respect their cause and wish to make it your own. For myself, I must declare and avow, that in all my reading and observation . . . and I have studied and admired the master states of the world—that for solidity of reasoning, force of sagacity, and wisdom of conclusion, under such a complication of difficult circumstances, no nation, or body of men, can stand in preference to the general congress at Philadelphia.[5]

Major Resolutions and Treaties

Declaration and Resolves of the First Congress. Denounced the Coercive Acts (Intolerable Acts) and the Quebec Act as "impolitic, unjust, and cruel, as well as unconstitutional, and most dangerous and destructive of American rights." Declared that colonists had the right to "life, liberty, and property," to "participate in their legislative council," and "to a free and exclusive power of legislation in their several provincial legislatures . . . subject only to the negative of the sovereign." Enumerated the parliamentary acts that had to be repealed "in order to restore harmony between Great Britain and the American colonies." Approved October 14, 1774 (*Journals of the Continental Congress,* vol. 1, pp. 63–73).[6]

Continental Association of 1774. Declared to the people of Great Britain that the American colonies sought to obtain redress of grievances that "threatened destruction to the lives, liberty, and property of his majesty's subjects, in North America." Stated "that a non-importation, non-consumption, and non-exportation agreement, faithfully adhered to, will prove the most speedy, effectual, and peaceable measure." Declared that the colonies would cease importation of British goods; discontinue the slave trade; institute a nonconsumption of British goods policy; and suspend all exports to Great Britain, Ireland, and the West Indies. Called on each county, city, and town to select a committee to observe the conduct of all persons regarding the association, prohibit trade with those violating or not acceding to the association, and publicize their actions in the local papers so they might "be publicly known, and universally condemned as the enemies of American liberty." Approved October 20, 1774 (*Journals of the Continental Congress,* vol. 1, pp. 75–80).

Army Authorized. Resolved that "six companies of expert riflemen, be immediately raised in Pennsylvania, two in Maryland, and two in Virginia," to join the army near Boston where they would be "employed as light infantry, under the command of the chief Officer in that army." Specified that each company "consist of a captain, three lieutenants, four sergeants, four corporals, a drummer or trumpeter, and sixty-eight privates." Named a five-member committee to draft rules and regulations for the army. Approved June 14, 1775 (*Journals of the Continental Congress,* vol. 2, pp. 89–90).

Olive Branch Petition. Stated the attachment of the American colonists to the king, expressed a desire for harmony to be restored with Great Britain, reiterated the complaints of the colonists, and begged the king to prevent further hostile action against the colonies until a reconciliation could be worked out. Approved July 5, 1775 (*Journals of the Continental Congress,* vol. 2, p. 127).[7]

Declaration Setting Forth the Causes and Necessities of Taking Up Arms. Declared in a petition to the king that the cause of the American colonies "is just," "Our union is perfect," and "Our internal resources are great, and, if necessary, foreign assistance is attainable." Declared that the arms the colonists had been compelled to assume were taken up "with unabating firmness and perseverance," to preserve their liberties. Declared the colonists did not desire "to dissolve that Union which has so long and so happily subsisted between us, and which we sincerely wish to see restored." Approved July 6, 1775 (*Journals of the Continental Congress,* vol. 2, pp. 127–157).

Postal Service Established. Provided for the appointment of a postmaster general for the united colonies, with the power to appoint a secretary and comptroller and a "line of posts [to] be appointed under the direction of the Postmaster general, from Falmouth in New England to Savannah in Georgia, with as many posts as he shall think fit." Approved July 26, 1775 (*Journals of the Continental Congress,* vol. 2, pp. 208–209).

Navy Authorized. Provided for the creation of a three-member committee to prepare an estimate of fitting out two ships that could intercept British vessels "laden with warlike stores and other supplies for our enemies" and "contract with proper persons" to outfit the vessels. Approved October 13, 1775 (*Journals of the Continental Congress,* vol. 3, pp. 293–294). Provided for the expansion of the committee to seven members and the outfitting of two additional "armed vessels" that could be employed in the "protection and defense of the united Colonies." Approved October 13, 1775

(*Journals of the Continental Congress,* vol. 3, p. 311). Adopted the "Rules for the Regulation of the Navy of the United Colonies." Approved November 28, 1775 (*Journals of the Continental Congress,* vol. 3, pp. 378–387).[8]

Marine Corps Authorized. Provided for two battalions of Marines to be raised consisting of "good seamen, or so acquainted with maritime affairs as to be able to serve to advantage by sea when required . . . during the present war between Great Britain and the colonies." Approved November 10, 1775 (*Journals of the Continental Congress,* vol. 3, p. 348).

Vote for Independence. Declared that the "United Colonies are, and, of right ought to be, Free and Independent States; that they are absolved from all allegiance to the British crown, and that all political connexion [*sic*] between them, and the state of Great Britain, is, and ought to be totally dissolved." Approved July 2, 1776 (*Journals of the Continental Congress,* vol. 5, p. 507).

Declaration of Independence. Provided the theoretical basis for the colonies to separate from Great Britain based upon truths held "to be self-evident, that all men are created equal, that they are endowed by their Creator with certain unalienable Rights, that among these, are Life, Liberty, and the pursuit of Happiness." Presented a "history of repeated injuries and usurpations," by the king, "all having in direct object the establishment of an absolute Tyranny over" the colonies. Renounced formally all ties with Great Britain. Pledged that "with a firm reliance on the protection of divine Providence" the signers committed their "Lives," "Fortunes," and "sacred Honor" to the support of the declaration. Approved July 4, 1776 (*Journals of the Continental Congress,* vol. 5, pp. 510–515).

Flag of United States. Resolved that the flag of the United States "be thirteen stripes, alternate red and white: that the union be thirteen stars, white in a blue field, representing a new constellation." Approved June 14, 1777 (*Journals of the Continental Congress,* vol. 8, p. 464).

Articles of Confederation and Perpetual Union. Provided for a confederacy called "The United States

of America" based on "firm league of friendship" that allowed each state to retain much of "its sovereignty, freedom and independence." Established a single organ of government—a Congress—with each state having one vote. Provided for freedom of speech and debate in Congress and immunity for its members from arrest. Empowered Congress to conduct foreign affairs, make war and peace, send and receive ambassadors, make treaties (except commercial agreements), settle disputes between the states, regulate the coinage of money and its value, fix the standard of weights and measures, regulate Indian affairs, establish and regulate post offices, borrow money on the credit of the United States, and maintain an army and navy. Required Congress to publish a journal of its proceedings. Denied Congress the authority to make treaties that prohibited imports or exports or to forbid a state from imposing retaliatory taxes. Denied Congress the power to fix the western boundaries of states (this provision was removed from the articles prior to ratification). Delegated to the states responsibility for raising land forces and taxes (which were to be based on land values with improvements). Approved November 15, 1777 (*Journals of the Continental Congress,* vol. 9, pp. 907–925). Ratified March 1, 1781.

Treaty of Amity and Commerce between the United States and France. Recognized the United States as an independent nation. Established most-favored-nation trading privileges between the United States and France, which provided that any commercial privileges one signatory might grant to another nation would immediately accrue to the other signatory. Reduced the contraband list of materials that neutral ships could carry without being seized by belligerents, and stipulated that noncontraband enemy goods transported on neutral ships were immune from capture. Concluded February 6, 1778. Ratified May 4, 1778 (*Journals of the Continental Congress,* vol. 11, pp. 421–444).

Treaty of Alliance between the United States and France. Provided that if war broke out between France and Great Britain as a result of the Treaty of Amity and Commerce, France and the United States would fight together until American independence was "formally, or tacitly assured" by treaty, and neither would "conclude either truce or peace with Great Britain" without the "formal consent" of the other. Declared the purpose of the alliance was to "maintain effectually the liberty, sovereignty, and independence" of the United States. Guaranteed that the United States would retain all the "Northern Parts of America" taken from England and all other "conquests" made in the war except those in the West Indies. Guaranteed that France would not seek to gain control of any North American territory held by Great Britain prior to 1763 and that the United States would uphold French possessions in the Western Hemisphere as well as any new ones it might acquire in the war. Concluded February 6, 1778. Ratified May 4, 1778 (*Journals of the Continental Congress,* vol. 11, pp. 448–453).

Department of Foreign Affairs. Provided for the establishment of a Department of Foreign Affairs, "to be kept always in the place where Congress shall reside." Provided for a secretary of foreign affairs responsible for maintaining the books and papers of the department, receiving and reporting all applications of foreigners, corresponding with American and other foreign ministers, reporting to Congress, and attending its sessions "to be better informed of the affairs of the United States." Approved January 10, 1781 (*Journals of the Continental Congress,* vol. 19, pp. 42–44).

Department of Finance. Provided for the establishment of a Department of Finance headed by a superintendent of finance responsible for examining the "state of the public debt, the public expenditures, and the public revenue"; reporting plans for "improving and regulating finances, and for establishing order and economy in the expenditure of public money"; directing the financial plans adopted by Congress; managing all individuals procuring supplies for public service or expending public funds; and compelling the payment of monies owed to the United States. Approved February 7, 1781 (*Journals of the Continental Congress,* vol. 19, p. 126).

Department of War. Provided for the establishment of a Department of War headed by a secretary at war responsible for maintaining records of troops, military stores, and equipment; preparing estimates for recruiting and paying the army; gathering and providing information for Congress; and transmitting the orders of Congress to the military establishment. Approved

February 7, 1781 (*Journals of the Continental Congress,* vol. 19, pp. 126–127).

Department of Marine. Provided for a Department of Marine headed by a secretary of marine responsible for preparing a report to Congress on the state of the navy that included a register of officers and naval and other supplies belonging to that department; preparing a report for the superintendent of finance on the estimated cost of maintaining the navy; gathering and providing information to Congress; and transmitting the orders of Congress to the naval establishment. Approved February 7, 1781 (*Journals of the Continental Congress,* vol. 19, pp. 127–128).

Bank of North America. Provided for the establishment of the first government-incorporated bank in U.S. history. Fixed the initial capital of the bank at $400,000, which could be increased to $10 million. Authorized the superintendent of finance to examine the finances of the bank at any time. Approved May 26, 1781 (*Journals of the Continental Congress,* vol. 20, pp. 545–548). Chartered December 31, 1781 (*Journals of the Continental Congress,* vol. 21, pp. 1187–1190).

Great Seal of the United States. Decreed the "device for an armorial achievement and reverse of the great seal of the United States in Congress assembled." Approved June 20, 1782 (*Journals of the Continental Congress,* vol. 22, pp. 338–339).

Treaty of Paris (1783). Formally ended the American Revolutionary War, confirmed British recognition of American independence, and provided for the withdrawal of British forces from U.S. territory. Granted to the United States territorial cessions that extended from the Atlantic Ocean to the Mississippi River and from Canada to Spanish Florida at the 31st parallel. Accorded the United States fishing rights off the coasts of Newfoundland and Nova Scotia. Validated all private prewar debts owed to British creditors by American citizens. Pledged Congress to encourage state legislators to restore fully the rights and property of Loyalists, and prohibited future confiscations and persecutions of Loyalists. Permitted both nations to have free navigation of the Mississippi River. Concluded September 3, 1783. Ratified January 14, 1784 (*Journals of the Continental Congress,* vol. 26, pp. 22–31).

Land Ordinance of 1785. Provided for a rectangular system of survey for the Northwest Territory that divided the land into townships of thirty-six square mile sections and sections of 640 acres. Established land offices at convenient points in the West to sell the land, and set the price of the land at no less than a dollar an acre. Created three land reserves in Ohio for Revolutionary War veterans, and granted a total of 85,120 acres to individuals and groups that had aided the American war effort. Reserved four sections of each township for the U.S. government and one section for the maintenance of public schools. Approved May 20, 1785 (*Journals of the Continental Congress,* vol. 28, pp. 375–381).

Decimal System of Currency. Resolved that the "money unit of the United States of America would be one dollar," with the smallest coin consisting of copper of which two hundred would be equal to a dollar, and that the value of the several pieces were "to increase in a decimal ratio." Approved July 6, 1785 (*Journals of the Continental Congress,* vol. 29, p. 500).

Northwest Ordinance. Created the Northwest Territory, to be administered by a governor, secretary, and three judges appointed by Congress until the population of the territory reached five thousand free male adults, at which time it could elect a bicameral legislature and a nonvoting member of the House of Representatives. Provided that when a designated area of the territory attained a population of sixty thousand free inhabitants, it could apply to become a state by complying with specified requirements. Required that the territory be divided into at least three, but not more than five, states. Prohibited slavery within the territory, declared that no law could be enacted that would impair a good-faith contract, and guaranteed religious freedom, right of trial by jury, and support of public education. Approved July 13, 1787 (*Journals of the Continental Congress,* vol. 32, pp. 334–343).

Proposed Constitution of the United States Sent to the States for Ratification. Resolved that the report of the Constitutional Convention together with the proposed Constitution "be transmitted to the several legislatures in Order to be submitted to a convention of Delegates chosen in each state by the people thereof in conformity to the resolves the Convention made."

Approved September 28, 1787 (*Journals of the Continental Congress,* vol. 33, p. 549).

Constitution Ratified. Declared that the Constitution had been ratified by a sufficient number of states (eleven) to put it into operation. Stipulated that on the first Wednesday in January presidential electors be appointed in the several states, on the first Wednesday in February the electors assemble in their respective states and vote for a president, and on the first Wednesday in March Congress should convene. Approved September 13, 1778 (*Journals of the Continental Congress,* vol. 34, p. 523).

Notes

1. Calvin Jillson and Rick K. Wilson, *Congressional Dynamics: Structure, Coordination, and Choice in the First American Congress, 1774–1789* (Stanford, Calif.: Stanford University Press, 1994), 17.

2. Merrill Jensen, *The Articles of Confederation* (Madison, Wis.: University of Wisconsin Press, 1953), 64.

3. Whitney Smith, *The Flag Book of the United States,* rev. ed. (New York: William Morrow and Company, 1975), 54–55.

4. Leonard W. Levy, "Northwest Ordinance (1787)," in *Encyclopedia of the American Constitution,* 2d ed., ed. Leonard W. Levy and Kenneth L. Karst (New York: Macmillan Reference USA, 2000), 4:1829.

5. *Celebrated Speeches of Chatham, Burke, and Erskine* (Philadelphia, Pa.: Desilver, Thomas, and Company, 1852), 32.

6. *Journals of the Continental Congress: 1774–1789,* ed. Worthington Chauncey Ford and Roscoe R. Hill (Washington, D.C.: U.S. Government Printing Office, 1904–1937).

7. For the text of the Olive Branch Petition, see *Journals of the Continental Congress* 1(1774): 158–162.

8. Nathan Miller, in his history of the U.S. Navy, states: "On October 13, 1775, Congress took a step that the U.S. Navy today regards as marking its official birth." Nathan Miller, *The U.S. Navy: A History,* 3d ed. (Annapolis, Md.: Naval Institute Press, 1997), 16. Other scholars do not identify a specific action by the Continental Congress that constituted the birth of the U.S. Navy. They instead suggest these events together mark the beginning of America's naval force. See Stephen Howarth, *To Shining Sea: A History of the United States Navy, 1775–1991* (New York: Random House, 1991), 7; and Dudley W. Knox, *A History of the United States Navy* (New York: G. P. Putnam's Sons, 1948), 10–11.

First Congress
March 4, 1789, to March 3, 1791

First session—March 4, 1789, to September 29, 1789
Second session—January 4, 1790, to August 12, 1790
Third session—December 6, 1790, to March 3, 1791
(First administration of George Washington,
    1789–1793)

Historical Background

The Articles of Confederation, drawn up in reaction to the monarchical rule of Great Britain over its American colonies, protected the individual states by eschewing a central government and executive power. In turn, the U.S. Constitution sought to correct the weak institutional structure established by the Articles. It attempted to create a president strong enough to stand up to an aggressive legislature but not so commanding as to become a despot.

The Constitution is a work in progress, with corrections and additions made to it over time. For example, a fundamental flaw in the presidential selection process became apparent in the first presidential election, in 1789. While the election of Revolutionary War hero George Washington to be president was widely supported and expected, the system could have resulted in his defeat. The Constitution provided that the electors cast two votes for president, with the candidate receiving the majority of the vote becoming president and the candidate receiving the second largest number becoming vice president. Because no distinction was made in the balloting for president and vice president, the election could result in a tie, which would require the House of Representatives to decide the outcome, or it could result in the intended vice president being elected president and vice versa. Alexander Hamilton,

seeing the potential problem and disliking John Adams, who had emerged as the leading contender for vice president, directed votes away from Adams and toward other candidates. Washington thus won the presidency with sixty-nine electoral votes and Adams the vice presidency with thirty-four electoral votes. The presidential election process subsequently was changed in 1804. *(Twelfth Amendment, p. 31)*

President Washington made few legislative suggestions and refrained from disclosing his views on matters being considered by Congress. "His power over lawmaking, as he saw it," Douglas Southall Freeman has observed, "was confined to his veto."[1] In the absence of Washington taking the initiative, three men assumed the lead in guiding Congress: Rep. James Madison of Virginia, Secretary of the Treasury Alexander Hamilton, and Secretary of State Thomas Jefferson. During the formative months of the First Congress, Madison was virtually the only member of Congress who possessed the combined political talents and imagination that the process of institution building demanded.

Of the few hundred public bills introduced during the First Congress, 118 were enacted into law. Most of the public bills dealt with the establishment of the new government and its relations with the states and with matters of defense or foreign policy. The first law signed by President Washington prescribed the oath to be taken by senators, representatives, members of state legislatures, and all federal and state executive and judicial officers. (The oath required of the president is prescribed in Article II, Section 1 of the Constitution.)

In ratifying the Constitution, six states had suggested amendments to safeguard individual rights. Many legislators elected to the First Congress arrived in New York prepared to vote to adopt these constitutional amendments. Although Madison had opposed a bill of rights both before and during ratification, when a national consensus emerged favoring one, he decided to draft it himself. Madison in June 1789 proposed twelve amendments to the Constitution, ten of which, known collectively as the Bill of Rights, were ratified by the requisite number of states by December 1791. The two proposed amendments that did not become part of the Bill of Rights prescribed the ratio of members in the House of Representatives and specified that no law varying the compensation of members would be effective until after an intervening election of representatives. More than two centuries later, on May 7, 1992, the congressional pay proposal was ratified, and it became the Twenty-seventh Amendment to the Constitution. *(Twenty-seventh Amendment, p. 406)*

By adopting the Bill of Rights and enacting the Judiciary Act of 1789, which established the federal judiciary, Congress completed the work of the Constitutional Convention and helped to secure the legacy of the American Revolution. The First Congress also devoted considerable attention to establishing the executive departments authorized in the Constitution. While the Northwest Ordinance laid the foundation for future trade and diplomatic exchange with Indian tribes, the Trade and Intercourse Act of 1790 established the rules governing that relationship.

To ease the economic burdens of the new nation, Congress authorized a tariff on imported goods to raise revenue and passed legislation providing for a national bank. The first important legislation of the new government, the Tariff Act of 1789, was passed only days after the First Congress reached a quorum. It provided what the Articles of Confederation lacked and the new one badly needed—a regular, assured source of revenue. Initially, it produced most of the government's total annual revenue. The concept of a central national bank grew out of Secretary of the Treasury Alexander Hamilton's belief that the government needed a repository for federal funds and an entity to act as its fiscal agent.

A bitter debate preceded approval of a plan for the federal government to pay off the entire foreign and domestic debt and to assume the Revolutionary War debts of the states. The strongest opposition to the plan was centered on the assumption aspect of the bill because some states had already paid a significant portion of their Revolutionary War debt while others had paid relatively little. The New England states, with the largest war debts, generally favored assumption while the southern states, which largely had arranged to pay off their debts, were against the plan. In mid-May 1790, the impasse was settled, according to Jefferson, when he and Madison agreed to support assumption in return for Hamilton's securing northern support for locating the nation's capital permanently on the banks of the Potomac.

Far less controversial were bills creating the office of postmaster general, providing for the first decennial census, authorizing the first patent and copyright laws, establishing a uniform rule of naturalization, and instituting the first internal revenue law (Whiskey Tax). In 1794, growing resentment against the tax, which was particularly unpopular among small farmers in western states, ignited the so-called Whiskey Rebellion in western Pennsylvania. The uprising provoked the first occasion for a president to call out the militia to suppress an insurrection against the authority of the federal government. Although the revolt was quickly suppressed, increased opposition to the tax in the South and West in 1801 led to the act's repeal. Late in the First Congress, Vermont settled a long-standing dispute with New York over land grants and was admitted to the Union as the fourteenth state. A bill admitting Kentucky was also approved.

Major Acts

Oath of Office for Federal and State Officials. Prescribed, as required by the Constitution, the oath of allegiance to be sworn by senators, representatives, members of state legislatures, and all federal and state executive and judicial officers. Designated the time and manner of administering the oath. Approved June 1, 1789 (1 Stat. 23–24).

Tariff Act of 1789. Established duties on thirty imported commodities as a means of financing government obligations and retiring the national debt. Most imported goods were subject to a 5 percent ad valorem duty, which meant that they were taxed at 5 percent of their value. The act also listed a number of specific duties on particular items regardless of their value. The mixing of ad valorem and specific duties would become the standard practice of U.S. trade acts. The overall level of the taxes averaged about 8 percent. Approved July 4, 1789 (1 Stat. 24–27).

Department of State. Established the Department of Foreign Affairs and defined the duties and responsibilities of the secretary of foreign affairs. Approved July 27, 1789 (1 Stat. 28–29). Name changed to the Department of State on September 15, 1789 (1 Stat. 68–69).

Department of War. Established the Department of War and defined the duties and responsibilities of the secretary of war. Approved August 7, 1789 (1 Stat. 49–50).

Department of the Treasury. Established the Department of the Treasury, designated the principal officers to be appointed by the secretary of the Treasury, and defined duties and responsibilities of these officers as well as those of the secretary. Approved September 2, 1789 (1 Stat. 65–67).

Office of Postmaster General. Provided for the temporary appointment of a postmaster general, created positions for assistants or clerks and deputies that the postmaster general might appoint, and confirmed existing post office regulations as provided under the Articles of Confederation. The postmaster general was to "be subject to the President of the United States in performing the duties of his office, and in forming contracts for transporting of the mail." Approved September 22, 1789 (1 Stat. 70).

Judiciary Act of 1789. Implemented Article III, Section 1 of the Constitution by organizing the federal judiciary. Provided for a Supreme Court consisting of a chief justice and five associate justices, three circuit courts composed of two Supreme Court justices and a district court judge, and thirteen district courts, corresponding roughly to state boundaries, with a judge for each. Also established the office of attorney general. Approved September 24, 1789 (1 Stat. 73–93).

Bill of Rights (First Ten Amendments). Amendment I provided for the freedom of religion, speech, and the press and "the right of people peaceably to assemble, and to petition the government for redress of grievances." Amendment II guaranteed the right of the people to bear arms. Amendment III forbade the government from quartering troops in private homes in times of peace without the consent of the owner and in times of war only as prescribed by law. Amendment IV protected the people against unreasonable searches and seizures. Amendment V outlawed double jeopardy and the deprivation of life, limb, and property without due process of law. Amendments VI and VII guaranteed the right to a speedy and impartial jury trial and the right to defense counsel, respectively. Amendment VIII prohibited excessive bail or fines as well as cruel and unusual punishment. Amendment IX declared that the enumeration of rights presented in the Constitution could "not be construed to deny or disparage others retained by the people." Amendment X declared that "powers not delegated to the United States by the Constitution, nor prohibited by it to the States, are reserved to the States, or to the people." Proposed September 29, 1789 (1 Stat. 97–98). Ratified by requisite number of states December 15, 1791.[2]

First Federal Census. Article I, Section 2, Clause 3 of the Constitution stipulates that representatives "shall be apportioned among the several States . . . according to their representative numbers" and provides for a decennial census to furnish the necessary basis for such apportionment. With this act the United States became the first nation to provide by law for the periodic enumeration of its people. Approved March 1, 1790 (1 Stat. 101–103).

Uniform Rule of Naturalization. Established a uniform rule for naturalization for white free persons who had resided within the limits and under the jurisdiction of the United States for at least two years. Approved March 26, 1790 (1 Stat. 103–104). *(Naturalization Act of 1795, p. 18)*

Patent Act of 1790. Gave an examining board, consisting of the secretary of state, the secretary of war, and the attorney general the authority to grant a patent for 14 years, if they deemed an "invention or discovery sufficiently useful and important." Required applicants to file a specification in writing, a drawing, and a model if possible. Approved April 10, 1790 (1 Stat. 109–112).

First Copyright Law. Provided for the protection of plays, maps, and books for fourteen years with the right of renewal for another fourteen years. Protection was granted only to U.S. citizens and residents. Required that the title page of the work being copyrighted, be deposited in the clerk's office of the local U.S. district court, a notice be placed in a newspaper within two months after publication, and a copy deposited with the secretary of state within six months of publication. Approved May 31, 1790 (1 Stat. 124–126). *(1831 Revision of the Copyright Act, p. 62)*

Permanent Seat of Government. Established the permanent seat for the national government, beginning in 1800, in a district ten miles square on the banks of the Potomac River. Until that time, the capital would be Philadelphia, Pennsylvania. Provided rules for the purchase of land or the acceptance of grants of land on which to construct buildings for the housing of Congress, the president, and other public offices of the federal government. Approved July 16, 1790 (1 Stat. 130).

Trade and Intercourse Act of 1790. Required every person who traded with the Indian tribes to have a government-issued license. Required traders to post a bond of $1,000 to guarantee faithful observance of federal laws and regulations. Authorized the recall of such licenses if a person broke any of the regulations or restrictions. Declared the purchase of lands from the Indians invalid unless made by a public treaty with the United States. Provided punishments for murder and other crimes committed by whites against Indians. Approved July 22, 1790 (1 Stat. 137–138).

Funding and Assumption Act of 1790. Provided for the payment of the nation's foreign and domestic debt by allowing creditors to exchange their securities for government bonds, which would be paid off through the use of a certain portion of the government's annual revenues. Permitted the federal government to assume the debts incurred by the states as a result of their participation in the Revolutionary War. Approved August 4, 1790 (1 Stat. 138–144).

Kentucky Admitted to the Union. Declared that the state of Kentucky was to be admitted into the Union on June 1, 1792 "as a new and entire member of the United States." Approved February 4, 1791 (1 Stat. 189).

Vermont Admitted to the Union. Declared that the state of Vermont was to be admitted into the Union on March 4, 1791 "as a new and entire member of the United States." Approved February 18, 1791 (1 Stat. 191).

First Bank of the United States. Incorporated the Bank of the United States, a national bank, with a capital stock of $10 million. Provided for the bank to serve as a depository for government funds, serve as an agent for collecting taxes, and issue notes, redeemable in specie and acceptable in the payment of taxes. Specified how its directors were to be selected, the disposition of dividends, and the method of advancing and lending its money. Achieved government supervision of its operations by requiring the directors to supply frequent statements to the secretary of the Treasury. Approved February 25, 1791 (1 Stat. 191–196).

Whiskey Act (First Internal Revenue Law). Created fourteen revenue districts and a tax of twenty to thirty cents a gallon on imported distilled liquors, as well as those distilled in the United States. Approved March 3, 1791 (1 Stat. 199–214).

Notes

1. *George Washington: A Biography*, vol. 6, *Patriot and President* (Clifton, N.J.: Augustus M. Kelly Publishers, 1975), 221.

2. U.S. Senate, *The Constitution of the United States of America: Analysis and Interpretation*, 108th Cong., 2d sess., 2004, S. Doc. 108–17, 25, n. 2.

Second Congress
March 4, 1791, to March 3, 1793

First session—October 24, 1791, to May 8, 1792
Second session—November 5, 1792, to March 2, 1793
Special session of the Senate—March 4, 1791
(First administration of George Washington,
    1789–1793)

Historical Background

Embryonic political parties began to emerge as philosophical differences intensified over the role of the federal government in domestic as well as foreign policy. As a result, the Second Congress saw a drop in productivity, especially in comparison with the ambitious efforts of the First Congress to organize the new government. The Second Congress, however, did clarify presidential succession, establish the first U.S. Mint in Philadelphia and a coinage system, and create the mechanism for slave owners to recover fugitive slaves. Because the framers left unanswered what would happen if both the president and vice president were unable to discharge their duties, that responsibility was left to Congress. The Presidential Succession Act of 1792 was the first legislative attempt to extend the succession line. Although there had been earlier discussions of a national mint, no legislation had been put in place for an actual coinage facility. The Fugitive Slave Act of 1793 provided for the extradition of criminals and escaped slaves.

With the passage of the Post Office Act of 1792, procedures were established that would facilitate the rapid expansion of mail service throughout the nation. The Post Office Act also allowed newspapers to be sent by mail for the first time, significantly hastening the further development of the press as an important means of communication in the United States. This enactment, however, was limited to two years. It would be up to the next Congress to make the postal system a permanent part of the government.

On April 5, 1792, Washington, after consulting with Attorney General Edmund Randolph, Secretary of State Thomas Jefferson, and Secretary of War Henry Knox, decided to cast the first presidential veto. He argued that under the proposed congressional apportionment act some states would have been allocated more representatives than one for every 30,000 people, which violated Article I, Section II of the Constitution. Congress responded by passing a revised apportionment act, which increased the number of residents each House member would represent.

During his first term as president, George Washington worked with Secretary of War Henry Knox on a plan to reorganize and strengthen the militia. Congress, after considerable debate, approved two militia acts. The first established a president's right to call out the militia. The second assigned responsibility for organizing and maintaining the militias to the states, with almost no standards, minimum training requirements, or federal oversight. While the latter did create the nation's first national conscription, it fell far short of creating the adequate defense force the president had sought.

Objections to delays in processing patent petitions and a narrow interpretation of the 1790 Patent Act led to passage of a new patent law. The drafting of the 1793 act is largely attributed to Thomas Jefferson, who was at the time secretary of state and therefore intimately involved in the administration of the 1790 Act. The act is notable for its definition of what constitutes patentable subject matter in the United States, a definition that continues today largely unchanged.

George Washington was reelected for a second term as president in 1792 by a unanimous electoral vote of 132. Federalist John Adams was reelected vice president, but he faced a challenger in a partisan contest. Democratic-Republicans chose George Clinton as their candidate for vice president. (Members of the opposition party to the Federalists were variously known as Democratic-Republicans, Jeffersonian Democrats, and Jeffersonian Republicans.) Given that the framers did not anticipate the formation of organized political parties, the election thus deviated from the Constitution's conception of the presidential selection process. Adams received seventy-seven electoral votes; Clinton, fifty. The presidential election, with party-backed candidates, proved a harbinger of the future.

Major Acts

Postal Act of 1792. Authorized the postmaster general to appoint postmasters and enter into contracts for the transportation of mail over routes established by Congress. Established postage rates and operational rules and regulations. Designated post roads on which the government had the monopoly of carrying mail. Provided penalties for obstructing or retarding mail deliveries; unlawfully opening, secreting, or embezzling mail; and stealing a letter or package, robbing a post office, or holding up a postal carrier. Allowed newspapers to be sent in the mail for the first time. Approved February 20, 1792 (1 Stat. 232–239).

Presidential Succession Act of 1792. Provided that if the president and vice president were both removed, resigned, or died in office, the president pro tempore of the Senate (followed by the Speaker of the House) was to act as president until the disability was removed or a president elected. Approved March 1, 1792 (1 Stat. 239–241).

Coinage Act of 1792. Authorized establishment of the first U.S. Mint, to be constructed in Philadelphia, Pennsylvania, and prescribed a decimal system of coinage: eagles, dollars, dismes, and cents. The eagle

was to contain 247.50 grains of pure gold. The dollar was to contain 371.25 grains of pure silver. "The proportional value of gold to silver in all coins" was to be "fifteen to one." Provided for a director, an assayer, a chief coiner, an engraver, and a treasurer as officers of the mint. Authorized the director to employ as many clerks, workmen, and servants as was deemed necessary. Prescribed the duties and salaries of mint employees. Approved April 2, 1792 (1 Stat. 246–251).

First Apportionment Act. Increased the ratio from one House member for every 30,000 residents, the proportion set by the Constitution, to one for every 33,000 residents. Increased the number of seats in the House of Representatives from 69 to 105. Approved April 14, 1792 (1 Stat. 253).

First Militia Act of 1792. Authorized the president to call out the militias of the states, "whenever the United States shall be invaded, or be in imminent danger of invasion from any foreign nation or Indian tribe." Authorized the president to call the militias into federal service "whenever the laws of the United States shall be opposed or the execution thereof obstructed, in any state, by combinations too powerful to be suppressed by the ordinary course of judicial proceedings, or by the powers vested in the marshals by this act." Approved May 2, 1792 (1 Stat. 264–265).

Second Militia Act of 1792. Provided for the organization of the state militias. Required "each and every free able-bodied white male citizen" between the ages of eighteen and forty-five to serve in a state militia. Required militia members to arm themselves at their own expense. Exempted the president, vice president, judicial and executive officers of the government, members of Congress and their officers, post-officers, custom house officials, stagecoach drivers, ferry boatmen, ship pilots, and mariners from having to serve. Approved May 8, 1792 (1 Stat. 271–274).

Fugitive Slave Act of 1793. Empowered slave owners, or their agents, to seize and return a fugitive slave to servitude by presenting an affidavit of ownership to specified state or state officials, who were required to enforce the law. Imposed a fine of $500 on anyone interfering with the return of a fugitive slave. Approved

February 12, 1793 (1 Stat. 302–305). *(For subsequent amendments, see Fugitive Slave Act, p. 86)*

Patent Act of 1793. Replaced the three-member board created by the first Patent Act of 1790 with an administrative structure that was responsible for examining the merits of patent petitions. Defined a patent as "any new and useful art, machine, manufacture or composition of matter." Required the applicant to register with the secretary of state, pay a fee, provide a short description and model of their invention, and affirm that they believed they were the first and true inventor. Approved February 21, 1793 (1 Stat. 318–323).

Third Congress
March 4, 1793, to March 3, 1795

First session—December 2, 1793, to June 9, 1794
Second session—November 3, 1794, to March 3, 1795
Special session of the Senate—March 4, 1793
(Second administration of George Washington,
        1793–1797)

Historical Background

During George Washington's second term as president, foreign wars and violent political confrontations were ongoing. American citizens were forbidden by the Neutrality Act of 1794 to aid a foreign power. On February 1, 1793, France had declared war on Great Britain, Spain, and Holland. Washington kept the United States out of the war with his April 22, 1793, declaration that the United States was "friendly and impartial toward the belligerent powers." The Neutrality Act served to reinforce Washington's proclamation. In March 1794, in response to repeated attacks on American merchant ships by the Barbary pirates, a law was enacted to establish a naval force to protect American shipping.

The Eleventh Amendment to the U.S. Constitution exempting a state from being sued by a citizen of another state in federal court was ratified in 1795. It nullified the 1793 U.S. Supreme Court decision in *Chisholm v. Georgia,* which upheld the right of a citizen of one state to sue another state. The courts as well as constitutional scholars, however, continue today, as they have for two centuries, to debate the question of the breadth of state immunity from lawsuits. Although the United States did not have the power to end the international slave trade, it did have the power to regulate it. In March 1794, Congress prohibited the use of

any U.S. port or shipyard to outfit or build a ship for the purpose of transporting slaves. The Constitution gave Congress the power to "establish post offices and post roads," but it was not until the Postal Act of 1794 that the American postal service was permanently established as a part of the government. Prior to this act, the postmaster had to go before each Congress to gain authorization to continue the service.

The Naturalization Act of 1795 reflected the feeling that the government needed to tighten its naturalization policy and that more than two years were needed to determine the desirability of a particular individual being granted citizenship. Under the new act, the period of residency was extended to five years and the potential applicant had to renounce allegiance to another nation and any hereditary or nobility titles. The act also prohibited state naturalization laws and established Congress's exclusive control over citizenship.

Major Acts

Eleventh Amendment. Removed from the jurisdiction of state courts any suit in law or equity commenced or prosecuted against one state of the United States by citizens of another state or by citizens or subjects of any foreign state. Proposed March 4, 1794 (1 Stat. 402). Ratified by requisite number of states February 7, 1795.[1]

Slave Trade Act of 1794. Prohibited the building, fitting out, equipping, or loading of a vessel within American borders for slave trading. Required ships sailing from the United States, even if a foreign registry, to "give bond with sufficient sureties, to the treasurer of the United States, that none of the natives of Africa, or any other foreign country or place, shall be taken on board … to be transported or sold as slaves in any other foreign place." Imposed a fine of $2,000 for outfitting a ship and fine of $200 for an individual working on such a ship. Provided for confiscation of ships and for half of fines to be given to informers. Approved March 22, 1794 (1 Stat. 347–349).

Naval Act of 1794. Appropriated $600,000 to construct and man four frigates of forty-four guns and two of thirty-six guns. Empowered the president to fix the pay of the petty officers, midshipmen, seamen, ordinary seamen, and marines. Specified what the daily ration would be of the crews of the six frigate navy. Approved March 27, 1794 (1 Stat. 350–351).

Postal Act of 1794. Established the Post Office as a permanent part of the government. Authorized the appointment of the first letter carriers. Prohibited anyone other than the postmaster, his deputies, or persons employed by them, from establishing a private service that would compete with the postal service. Authorized magazines and pamphlets to be mailed for the first time, if "the mode of conveyance, and the size of the mails, will admit of it." Approved May 8, 1794 (1 Stat. 354–366).

Neutrality Act of 1794. Forbade U.S. citizens from enlisting in the militaries of any foreign power or giving aid to any hostile force, and prohibited the fitting out of foreign vessels in American ports that were to be employed in hostilities. Levied a fine of $2,000 and three years imprisonment for persons enlisting with a foreign power and a fine of $1,000 and one year imprisonment for helping fit a foreign war vessel. Stipulated that persons within the territory or jurisdiction of the United States who participated in a military expedition against a friendly nation would be subject to a fine of $3,000 and three years imprisonment. Approved June 5, 1794 (1 Stat. 381–384).

Naturalization Act of 1795. Repealed the Uniform Rule of Naturalization (1790). Required that aliens reside in the United States for at least five years, renounce any hereditary titles or titles of nobility, and renounce forever allegiance to any foreign prince, potentate, state, or sovereignty to be eligible for citizenship. Declared that aliens could only become naturalized on these conditions "and not otherwise." Approved January 29, 1795 (1 Stat. 414–415). (*Naturalization Act [First of the Alien and Sedition Acts], p. 23; Naturalization Act of 1802, p. 28*)

Note

1. U.S. Senate, *The Constitution of the United States of America: Analysis and Interpretation,* 108th Cong., 2d sess., 2004, S. Doc. 108–17, 27–28, n. 3.

Fourth Congress
March 4, 1795, to March 3, 1797

First session—December 7, 1795, to June 1, 1796
Second session—December 5, 1796, to March 3, 1797
Special session of the Senate—June 8, 1795, to
    June 26, 1795
(Second administration of George Washington,
    1793–1797)

Historical Background

The potential for war with Great Britain loomed during the latter part of George Washington's second term. The British refused to evacuate forts in the Northwest Territory, encouraged Indian attacks on American settlers, and seized U.S. merchant vessels and impressed their crews. War was averted when a delegation headed by John Jay, chief justice of the United States, successfully completed negotiations with England. However, once the terms of the Jay Treaty became known, protests arose all over the country. The Senate advised ratification of the treaty in 1795 following a highly partisan debate. Congress subsequently agreed to pay the dey of Algiers approximately $800,000 and a yearly tribute of $24,000 to ransom American seamen captured by the Barbary pirates. In separate action, the president was authorized to appoint two agents to investigate all impressments and detentions of American seamen.

Pinckney's Treaty, cleared by the Senate in 1796, resolved a variety of diplomatic questions between Spain and the United States that had persisted since the American Revolution. It granted the United States the Southwestern Territory north of 31° latitude and free navigation of the Mississippi River. As a consequence of the treaty, commercial relations were established between the two countries. Under its terms, the British agreed to evacuate frontier forts in the American Northwest; such issues as boundary disputes, payment of pre–Revolutionary War debts to the British, and British compensation for illegal maritime seizures were to be referred to joint arbitral commissions. The treaty did not, as some had hoped, address such questions as the impressment of seamen, abducted American slaves, and the British incitement among Indian tribes. When terms of the treaty became known, Jeffersonian Republicans condemned it as a sellout to Britain. Even after the Senate narrowly advised ratification of the treaty in 1795 following a highly partisan debate, opponents refused to give up their fight, unsuccessfully seeking to have the House withhold funds to carry out the treaty. The treaty maintained the peace with Great Britain, and within a year after losing the support of Great Britain, the Indians of the Northwest ceded most of Ohio to the United States.

A desire to reduce the public debt prompted passage of the Land Act of 1796. During House debate on the debt, the idea was introduced to place the purchase of public lands within the reach of average citizens. By surveying part of the land and dividing it into small tracts of 160 acres, more people would have an opportunity to purchase land and settle in the West. The Senate, however, failed to concur, and a measure far more favorable to speculators was enacted. The act raised the price of land from $1 an acre under the Ordinance of 1785 to $2 an acre, and it provided for local land offices in Cincinnati, Ohio, and Pittsburgh, Pennsylvania. Approximately half the land was to be sold in large tracts (5,120 acres) and the rest in smaller tracts (640 acres).

In his December 1795 annual message, President Washington urged approval of measures that would protect Indians from injustices inflicted by "the lawless part of our frontier inhabitants" and would "supply the necessities of the Indians on reasonable terms." Congress responded with the Indian Trade and Intercourse Act of 1796, which established a boundary between the settlers and the Indians and satisfied many other concerns of the president. The nomination of John Rutledge, Washington's selection to succeed John Jay as chief justice, was rejected 10–14 by the Senate. Rutledge had fallen into disfavor because of a speech denouncing the Jay Treaty after its ratification by the Senate. Congress approved legislation admitting Tennessee into the Union on June 1, 1796.

Despite his popularity, George Washington declined to run for a third term as president, thus setting a precedent that would endure for nearly 150 years. (A constitutional amendment limiting presidents to two terms was ratified in 1951.) Throughout his tenure, Washington was mindful of the symbolic importance of what he did and sought to establish the legitimacy of the office he occupied and the government he served. He left to his predecessors a firm foundation to preside from as well as an exalted standard to live up to. (*Twenty-second Amendment, p. 279*)

However, one legacy of Washington's quickly fell by the wayside; that is, his efforts to remain nonpartisan. In the first competitive presidential election in American history, Vice President John Adams, backed by the Federalists, in 1796 bested former secretary of state Thomas Jefferson, who was supported by the Democratic-Republicans, with a three-vote (seventy-one to sixty-eight) electoral vote win. Jefferson thus became Adams's vice president.

Major Acts and Treaties

Jay Treaty (Anglo-American Treaty of Amity, Commerce, and Navigation). Provided for withdrawal of British military forces from six frontier forts in American territory on or before June 1, 1796. Allowed U.S. vessels to enter British East Indian ports on a nondiscriminatory basis and opened West Indian trade to U.S. vessels not exceeding seventy tons, providing they did not carry such staples as cotton, sugar,

and molasses. Created joint commissions to adjudicate pre–Revolutionary War debts, the northeast boundary question, and compensation for illegal maritime seizures. Concluded November 19, 1794 (8 Stat. 116–132). Ratification advised by the Senate June 24, 1795.[1]

Treaty of Peace and Amity with Algiers. Provided for the payment to the dey of Algiers of approximately $800,000 and $24,000 in yearly tribute to ransom American seamen captured by the Barbary pirates. Concluded September 5, 1795 (8 Stat. 133–137). Ratification advised by the Senate March 2, 1796.[2]

Pinckney's Treaty (Treaty of San Lorenzo). Recognized the boundary claims of the United States as being the Mississippi River on the west and the 31° latitude on the south, established commercial relations with Spain, and guaranteed free navigation of the Mississippi River by American citizens. Concluded October 27, 1795 (8 Stat. 138–153). Ratification advised by the Senate March 3, 1796.[3]

Land Act of 1796. Provided for the appointment of a surveyor general "to engage a sufficient number of skilful surveyors, as his deputies," to "survey and mark the unascertained outlines of the lands lying northwest of the river Ohio, and above the mouth of the river Kentucky, in which the titles of the Indian tribes have been extinguished." Required that each sale consist of at least 640 acres, at a minimum of $2 per acre, payable in one year. Established local land offices in Cincinnati, Ohio, and Pittsburgh, Pennsylvania. Approved May 18, 1796 (1 Stat. 464–469).

Indian Trade and Intercourse Act of 1796. Established a boundary line between the United States and various Indian tribes. Prohibited settlers from driving livestock onto Indian lands. Required that an individual be issued a passport before traveling into Indian country and that Indian traders be licensed. Prohibited purchase of Indian lands, except by treaty or convention. Provided for Indian agents to reside among the friendly tribes "to secure the continuance of their friendship" and to furnish them "with useful domestic animals, and implements of husbandry, and with goods or money." Provided that Indians who crossed over into the states or territories would have tribal annuities withheld. Approved May 19, 1796 (1 Stat. 469–474).

Relief and Protection of American Seamen. Authorized the president to appoint two or more agents, one of whom would reside in Great Britain and the other in whichever port the president directed, to investigate impressments and detentions of American seamen and through legal means to obtain their release. Approved May 28, 1796 (1 Stat. 477–478).

Tennessee Admitted to the Union. Declared that Tennessee was "one of the United States of America, on an equal footing with the original States." Approved June 1, 1796 (1 Stat. 491–492).

Notes

1. *Journal of the Executive Proceedings of the Senate* (Washington, D.C.: Duff Green, 1828), 1:184–187.
2. *Journal of the Executive Proceedings of the Senate,* 1:202–203.
3. *Journal of the Executive Proceedings of the Senate,* 1:203.

Fifth Congress
March 4, 1797, to March 3, 1799

First session—May 15, 1797, to July 10, 1797
Second session—November 13, 1797, to July 16, 1798
Third session—December 3, 1798, to March 3, 1799
Special sessions of the Senate—March 4, 1797; July 17,
    1798, to July 19, 1798
(Administration of John Adams, 1797–1801)

Historical Background

John Adams, who served as George Washington's vice president, became president in 1797. Efforts at a reconciliation between the Federalists and the Democratic-Republicans collapsed due to renewed foreign policy differences. France, angered by the Jay Treaty with Great Britain, broke off commercial relations with the United States in May 1797 and refused to receive the U.S. minister. Furthermore, French privateers continued to harass American merchant ships. A three-member U.S. commission dispatched to France with orders to secure a treaty of commerce and amity was presented with an unofficial request for a U.S. loan to France and for a bribe of $240,000. The U.S. commissioners rejected the proposal, which ushered in an undeclared naval war with France, lasting from 1798 to 1800.

The XYZ Affair aroused anti-French opinion in the United States. The Federalist-dominated Fifth Congress, acting on Adams's recommendation, began to make preparations for war. After considerable debate, Congress created a Department of the Navy, and a Marine Corps was authorized. The Federalist majority also secured passage of the Alien and Sedition Acts of 1798, designed to suppress political opposition to the administration's foreign policy and to restrain aliens and citizens whose loyalty to the Federalists was questioned. The first of the four acts, the Naturalization Act, which extended the residency requirement for citizenship from five years to fourteen years, was repealed in 1802. The second, the Alien Friends Act, which was limited to two years, authorized the president to deport aliens regarded as dangerous to the "peace and safety of the United States." The third, the Alien Enemies Act, authorized the president to arrest, imprison, and deport "all natives, citizens, denizens, or subjects of a hostile nation or government" in time of war. It was the only one of the four to gather strong Republican support as a clearly defensive measure in time of declared war. The fourth, the Sedition Act, provided fines and imprisonment of citizens or aliens who combined or conspired to oppose the execution of federal laws, interfered with an officer of government in the discharge of his duties, or engaged in or abetted "insurrection, riot, unlawful assembly, or combination." Although President Adams did not request the acts, enforcement of the fourth act resulted in the conviction of ten Democratic-Republicans, two newspaper editors, and a political writer. This action ultimately brought about a broader definition of freedom of the press.

The Logan Act of 1799, restricting diplomatic relations by private citizens, was prompted by the efforts of Dr. George Logan of Pennsylvania, a Republican and Quaker, who traveled to Paris in 1789 to negotiate with French officials in an effort to try and defuse tensions between the United States and France. A yellow fever epidemic prompted the first federal public health law. The Quarantine Act of 1799 authorized federal officials to assist states in the execution of their quarantine laws, and established the first federal inspection system for maritime quarantines.

Major Acts

Mississippi Territory. Created the Mississippi Territory, which covered land within 32° 28' latitude on the north, 31° north latitude on the south, the Mississippi River on the west, and the Chattahoochee River on the east. Approved April 7, 1798 (1 Stat. 549–550).

Naval Armament for the Protection of American Commerce. Authorized the president to cause to be built, purchased, or hired as many as twelve naval vessels, to be fitted out with no more than twenty-two guns apiece, and to appoint the officers and men for the service of said vessels, to be used for the nation's defense. Approved April 27, 1798 (1 Stat. 552).

Department of the Navy. Established the Department of the Navy, directed by a new cabinet officer, the secretary of the navy, whose duties included procurement of naval stores and materials as well as construction, armament, equipment, and employment of vessels of war. Approved April 30, 1798 (1 Stat. 553–554).

Naturalization Act (first of the Alien and Sedition Acts). Amended the Naturalization Act of 1795 to provide that no alien could become a citizen unless he declared his intention five years in advance. Upon this declaration, an alien had to prove fourteen years of residence within the United States and five years of residence within the state where he applied for citizenship. Mandated that all aliens register with the clerk of their district court. Approved June 18, 1798 (1 Stat. 566–569). Repealed April 14, 1802 (2 Stat. 153–155). *(Naturalization Act of 1795, p. 18; Naturalization Act of 1802, p. 28)*

Alien Friends Act (second of the Alien and Sedition Acts). Authorized the president to order the deportation of aliens adjudged to be undesirable and to require the licensing of certain other aliens for a two-year period. Allowed deported aliens to take with them what personal property it was convenient to remove and to retain control over the disposition of property left behind. Approved June 25, 1798 (1 Stat. 570–572).

Alien Enemies Act (third of the Alien and Sedition Acts). Empowered the president, in the case of war or threatened invasion, to arrest, imprison, or banish aliens subject to an enemy power. Provided that such aliens, if not chargeable with crimes against the public safety, would be allowed to leave the country. Provided that all courts of criminal jurisdiction could receive and hear complaints against suspected alien enemies. Approved July 6, 1798 (1 Stat. 577–578).

Marine Corps Act. Organized the Marine Corps into a distinct military service of the U.S. government and provided the basis for assigning duties to the new corps. Remained the legal authority for Marine Corps missions for 149 years, with minor changes. Approved July 11, 1798 (1 Stat. 594–596).

Sedition Act (fourth of the Alien and Sedition Acts). Made it a high misdemeanor "to unlawfully combine" to oppose legal measures of the government, to interfere with an officer in the discharge of his duty, to engage in or abet "insurrection, riot, or unlawful assembly or combination, whether such conspiracy . . . shall have the proposed effect or not." Provided that anyone found guilty of a high misdemeanor was to be punished by a fine of not more than $5,000 and up to five years in prison. Imposed a fine of not more than $2,000, and a prison term of not more than two years, on persons convicted of publishing "any false, scandalous and malicious writing." Set an expiration date on the act of March 3, 1801. Approved July 14, 1798 (1 Stat. 596–597).

Logan Act. Made it a high misdemeanor subject to fine and imprisonment for any U.S. citizen to carry on unauthorized "verbal or written correspondence or intercourse with any foreign government," with "an intent to influence the measures or conduct of any foreign government," regarding "any disputes or controversies with the United States, or defeat the measures of the government of the United States." Imposed a fine of not more than $5,000, and a prison term of not less than six months or more than three years for violation of the act. Exempted individual citizens or their lawful agents to obtain redress from foreign governments for any injuries sustained from such government. Approved January 30, 1799 (1 Stat. 613).

First National Quarantine Act. Empowered the secretary of the Treasury to make regulations governing cooperation between federal revenue officers, the government, and state health officials. Required customs officials and the masters and crew of revenue cutters to conform to the quarantine and health laws of the state, and to aid in their execution as directed by the secretary of the Treasury. Specified how maritime quarantines were to be handled in a variety of different circumstances. Provided for the removal of public offices and the Supreme Court in case of the prevalence of a contagious disease or epidemic. Approved February 25, 1799 (1 Stat. 619–621).

Sixth Congress
March 4, 1799, to March 3, 1801

First session—December 2, 1799, to May 14, 1800
Second session—November 17, 1800, to March 3, 1801
(Administration of John Adams, 1797–1801)

Historical Background

Unstable economic conditions and widespread speculation prompted Congress to enact the first state bankruptcy law in April 1800. One of the chief complaints of the federal land system prior to 1800 was that it encouraged the purchase of land by speculators and inhibited the acquisition of farm tracts by settlers. The Harrison Land Act of 1800 was designed to facilitate individual purchases of land on easy financial terms. Days later, responding to rapid increases in settlement, Congress divided the Northwest Territory, with the western part of the region becoming the Territory of Indiana. To strengthen the prohibition on Americans participating in the African slave trade, fines for importing slaves were dramatically increased and Americans were barred from being involved in any way with ships involved in the trade.

Congress also provided for the federal government's permanent relocation to Washington, D.C., and the purchase of books for a congressional library—the Library of Congress. In April 1801, an organic act officially organized the District of Columbia and placed the entire federal territory, including the cities of Washington, Georgetown, and Alexandria under the exclusive control of Congress.

John Adams's final two years in office were marked by growing antagonism between the Federalists and the Jeffersonian Republicans. The president was further troubled by a growing schism, led by Alexander Hamilton, within the ranks of his own Federalist supporters. Although Adams ultimately prevailed in the conflict with Hamilton for control of public policy, their struggle contributed to the Federalists' loss of both the presidency and Congress in the election of 1800.

Thomas Jefferson's election on the thirty-sixth ballot by the House of Representatives on February 17, 1801, resolved one of the great constitutional-political crises in U.S. history. Although Aaron Burr had sought the vice presidency, he received the same number of electoral votes (seventy-three) as fellow Jeffersonian-Republican Thomas Jefferson. Thus the House was constitutionally required to elect the president. To avoid a repeat of a tie vote, the Twelfth Amendment was ratified in time for the 1804 election. *(Twelfth Amendment, p. 31)*

With enactment of the Judiciary Act of 1801, the Federalists sought to entrench themselves in government for the foreseeable future. During the concluding weeks of his presidency, Adams filled all the new posts created by the act through midnight appointments. The Judiciary Act would be repealed in 1802. *(Repeal of Judiciary Act of 1801, p. 28)*

Major Acts

First Federal Bankruptcy Law. Established federal guidelines for the creation and administration of bankruptcy proceedings throughout the United States. Asserted federal law over state bankruptcy laws. Applied only to merchants, bankers, brokers, factors, underwriters, and marine insurers who owed a minimum of $1,000. Allowed only involuntary bankruptcy by their creditors. Approved April 4, 1800 (2 Stat. 19–36). Repealed December 19, 1803 (2 Stat. 248).

Establishment of the Library of Congress. Authorized the purchase of such books as might be necessary for a congressional library (Library of Congress) in Washington, and a "suitable apartment for containing them." Appropriated $5,000 to carry out the provisions of the act. Approved April 24, 1800 (2 Stat. 56, Sec. 5).

Making Provision for Removal of Government to Washington. Provided for the removal of the government to the city of Washington, furnishings for the president's house, accommodations in the new capital for the secretaries of the four executive departments, and construction of additional "footways." Approved May 7, 1800 (2 Stat. 55, Sec. 1–4).

Indiana Territory Created. Northwest Territory Divided. Divided the Northwest Territory into the Indiana Territory, which included everything west of approximately the western border of present-day Ohio, and the Northwest Territory. Approved May 7, 1800 (2 Stat. 58–60).

Slave Trade Act of 1800. Prohibited American ships from participating in the slave trade, and any American citizen or resident alien from serving "on board any foreign ship or vessel . . . employed in the slave trade." Subjected American sailors found on slave ships to a $2,000 fine and two years imprisonment. Authorized all "commissioned vessels of the United States to seize and take vessels employed" in the trade, with the crew receiving the proceeds from the sale of the ship and goods aboard. Gave informants a right to the entire value of any ship condemned under the act. Approved May 10, 1800 (2 Stat. 70–71).

Harrison Land Act of 1800. Reduced the minimum amount of public land that might be purchased from 640 acres to 320 for a minimum of $2 per acre, and introduced a credit feature. Required one-fourth of the price of the land to be paid within 40 days, another one-fourth within two years, another within three years, and the final within four years. Provided for the unpaid balance to incur 6 percent interest. Provided an 8 percent discount for cash payments. Established four western land offices. Approved May 10, 1800 (2 Stat. 73–78).

Judiciary Act of 1801 (Midnight Judges Act). Increased the number of district courts to twenty-one, established six circuit courts to be staffed by sixteen new and separate circuit judges, and provided for additional marshals, attorneys, clerks, and bailiffs. Reduced the number of U.S. Supreme Court justices from six to five. Approved February 13, 1801 (2 Stat. 89–100). Repealed March 8, 1802 (2 Stat. 132).

District of Columbia Organic Act. Formally incorporated the land ceded to the federal government by Virginia and Maryland into the District of Columbia. Established two counties in the District—Washington County on the east side of the Potomac River (formerly Maryland) and Alexandria County (formerly Virginia, on the west of the Potomac River). Established a circuit court for the District consisting of a chief judge and two assistant judges. Provided a marshal, attorney, clerks, justices of the peace, register of wills, and judges of the orphans' court for the District. Stipulated that the common law of both Maryland and Virginia would remain in force within the District. Approved February 27, 1801 (2 Stat. 103–108).

Seventh Congress
March 4, 1801, to March 3, 1803

First session—December 7, 1801, to May 3, 1802
Second session—December 6, 1802, to March 3, 1803
Special session of the Senate—March 4, 1801, to
      March 5, 1801
(First administration of Thomas Jefferson, 1801–1805)

Historical Background

Thomas Jefferson's election as president set an important precedent in the life of the new government of the United States: the orderly and constitutional transfer of power from one party to another without a bitter struggle. This was accomplished notwithstanding controversy and the politically charged atmosphere surrounding the Electoral College misfire that led to Jefferson's election by the House of Representatives.

Jefferson's inaugural ceremony, the first in the new federal city of Washington, D.C., was conducted in the recently completed Senate wing of the U.S. Capitol. In the home of what he called the "Great Council of the Nation." Jefferson declared that the recently established government of the United States represented the "world's best hope." While as president Jefferson was respectful of Congress, he "exercised influence on legislation which has rarely been matched in presidential history and which probably went considerably beyond his own original expectations." Jefferson "acted chiefly through the congressional leaders of his own party, whom he treated with due respect and relied on for counsel."[1]

By these means, Jefferson secured a repeal of the Federalist-sponsored Judiciary Act of 1801, the most controversial question before the Seventh Congress, and a repeal of the Naturalization Act of 1798, which had made qualifying for citizenship far more difficult for resident aliens. In other action, the United States Military Academy was established at West Point, a new Judiciary Act was enacted, an annual appropriation was provided for the reduction of the national debt, and a plan was drawn up whereby most states would subsequently be admitted to the Union. The process for admitting new states called for residents of a territory desiring statehood to first petition Congress. If Congress concurred, an "enabling act" would be passed authorizing a convention to draft a state constitution, providing for election of convention delegates, and, in certain instances, stipulating conditions on the convention and new state. The constitution had to be ratified by popular vote and submitted to Congress. The House and Senate then would pass a joint resolution declaring the state admitted to the Union. This new mechanism allowed Congress to reaffirm its authority over territorial possessions by providing a transition period during which the people could school themselves in the democratic tradition of drafting a constitution and organizing a government. Ohio became the first state admitted to the Union through an enabling act.

Jefferson was the benefactor of John Adams's lengthy and successful effort to obtain a peace settlement with France. On September 30, 1800, an American diplomatic mission had signed a convention with the French government, and Adams submitted the Treaty of Mortefontaine to the Senate on December 16, 1800. Only after the Senate had expunged the second article of the convention, and the French government approved the change, was final action taken by the Democratic-Republican–controlled Senate on December 19, 1801, nearly ten months after Adams left office.

Shortly after he assumed the presidency, Jefferson learned that Napoleon Bonaparte, emperor of France, was in the process of acquiring the Louisiana Territory from Spain. Alarmed at the prospect of France controlling the strategic port of New Orleans, Jefferson sent James Monroe to help Secretary of State Robert R. Livingston convince the French government to sell the port to the United States. Monroe and Livingston were authorized by Congress to offer up to $2 million to purchase the east bank of the Mississippi. Jefferson secretly advised them to offer over $10 million for New Orleans and West Florida. Initially, Napoleon resisted, but for a variety of reasons changed his mind in April 1803 and instructed his foreign minister, Charles-Maurice de Talleyrand-Périgord, to offer the entire Louisiana Territory to the United States. On April 30, Monroe and Livingston, acting on their own, signed a treaty whereby the United States agreed to buy Louisiana for $15 million, with $12 million paid to France and $3 million paid to United States citizens who had outstanding claims against France. The purchase agreement, dated April 30, was signed May 2, 1803. The treaty was submitted to the Senate in the Eighth Congress.

In his Annual Message of December 15, 1802, President Jefferson called for a review of the nation's militia instruction based on the premise that the militia should be "our general reliance for the great and sudden emergencies." Although Congress was in no mood to centralize the nation's military power in the executive branch, it did pass legislation three months later authorizing the president to require state executives to hold in readiness up to 80,000 militia.

Congress, in 1803, instituted new fines for people who brought newly imported slaves into states that banned the international slave trade. A penalty was levied for each and every individual imported and ship captains were held responsible for violations. The intent was to prevent people who might bring in Africans by claiming they were not slaves but servants or indentured servants, or claim that they were not actually African but Caribbean.

Major Acts and Treaties

Convention of 1800 (Treaty of Mortefontaine). Provided for a "firm, invincible, and universal . . . peace between the French Republic, and the United States of America." Released the United States from its 1778 Treaty of Alliance with France (already unilaterally abrogated by the United States in 1798) and France from American claims totaling $20 million for damage done to American commerce by French vessels. Concluded September 30, 1800. Ratified as amended by the French government on July 31, 1801 (8 Stat. 178–195). Ratification advised by the Senate December 19, 1801.[2]

Repeal of Judiciary Act of 1801. Repealed the Judiciary Act of 1801 (2 Stat. 89–100). Approved March 8, 1802 (2 Stat. 132). *(Judiciary Act of 1801, p. 26)*

U.S. Military Academy at West Point. Authorized the establishment of the United States Military Academy at West Point in the state of New York. Initially, the academy's sole function was to train engineers. The academy formally opened on July 4, 1802. Approved March 16, 1802 (2 Stat. 137, Sec. 27).

Naturalization Act of 1802. Repealed the Naturalization Act of 1798, the first of the Alien and Sedition Acts (1 Stat. 566–569). Reduced the period of residence required for full citizenship from fourteen to five years, and reestablished the other provisions of the Naturalization Act of 1795. Required prospective citizens to give three years notice of their intent to renounce previous citizenship, swear or affirm support of the Constitution, renounce all titles of nobility, and demonstrate themselves to be of "good moral character." Allowed children of naturalized citizens, who were under 21 when their parents were naturalized, to be considered citizens. Approved April 14, 1802 (2 Stat. 153–155). *(Naturalization Act of 1795, p. 18; Naturalization Act (First of the Alien and Sedition Acts), p. 23)*

Judiciary Act of 1802. Restored the number of Supreme Court justices to six, and reduced the number of circuit courts from sixteen to six. Each of the circuit courts was to be headed by a Supreme Court justice. Approved April 29, 1802 (2 Stat. 156–167).

Appropriations for Extinguishing the Public Debt. Provided an annual appropriation of $7.3 million for the redemption of the public debt of the United States. Approved April 29, 1802 (2 Stat. 167–170).

First Enabling Act. Authorized the people of the eastern division of the Northwest Territory to hold a convention and frame a constitution to become a state. Approved April 30, 1802 (2 Stat. 173–175).

Ohio Admitted to the Union. Accepted the conditions agreed upon by an Ohio convention of November 29, 1802, admitting Ohio "into the Union on an equal footing with the original States." Approved February 19, 1803 (2 Stat. 201–202). By this action, Congress did not, however, declare Ohio a member of the Union. President Dwight D. Eisenhower signed legislation resolving confusion and controversy over the exact date Ohio was admitted to the Union. Congress determined that the date should be March 1, 1803, because this was the "date upon which the first Ohio State Legislature was seated, when the first Governor took office, and upon which Ohio might be said to have begun functioning as a State."[3] Approved August 7, 1953 (P.L. 83–204; 57 Stat. 407).

Loan to Purchase New Orleans. Authorized the president to borrow $2 million for the purchase of the port of New Orleans and West Florida. Approved February 26, 1803 (2 Stat. 202).

Slave Trade Act of 1803. Established a penalty of $1,000 for each person brought to the United States on a ship with the intention of selling that person as a slave. Placed responsibility on the captain of any vessel transporting slaves. Prohibition applied to any "negro, mulatto, or other person of color" introduced as a slave, whether from Africa or the Caribbean. Charged customs and revenue officials with enforcement. Approved February 28, 1803 (2 Stat. 205–206).

Militia Act of 1803. Authorized the president to require "the executives of such states as he may deem expedient . . . to organize, arm, and equip" up to 80,000 militia. Appropriated $1.5 million to pay and sustain the troops, to purchase of military stores, and to defraying other expenses. Appropriated $25,000 for erecting military arsenals in the West. Approved March 3, 1803 (2 Stat. 241).

Notes

1. Dumas Malone, *Jefferson and His Time*, vol. 4, *Jefferson the President: First Term, 1801–1805* (Boston: Little, Brown and Company, 1970), xviii, 21.

2. *Journal of the Executive Proceedings of the Senate* (Washington, D.C.: Guff Green, 1828), 1:398–399.

3. U.S. Senate, *Admitting the State of Ohio to the Union*, 83d Cong., 1 sess., 1953, S. Rept. 720, 2.

Eighth Congress
March 4, 1803, to March 3, 1805

First session—October 17, 1803, to March 27, 1804
Second session—November 5, 1804, to March 3, 1805
(First administration of Thomas Jefferson, 1801–1805)

Historical Background

Although President Thomas Jefferson initially believed that he lacked the authority to acquire foreign territory because the U.S. Constitution contained no provision for such action, he ultimately arranged, without legislative sanction, the purchase of the Louisiana Territory from the French government in 1803 for $15 million, $3.75 million of which went to France's American creditors. Some have characterized this acquisition as the "greatest real estate deal in history." The Louisiana Purchase removed the threat of another nation establishing a colonial empire west of the Mississippi River, doubled the size of the United States (adding 828,000 square miles), significantly enhanced the nation's natural resources, ensured its continued commercial expansion, and guaranteed room for expansion. It also set a precedent for the United States to acquire territory by treaty and paved the way for the expansion of executive power. The "noble bargain," as Jefferson called it, has been viewed as the foremost accomplishment of his presidency.

Jefferson endorsed the National Bank Act of 1804, even though he had opposed Federalist demands under Presidents George Washington and John Adams for a stronger, more centralized national financial structure. An upturn in economic conditions coupled with growing dissatisfaction with the Bankruptcy Act of 1800 brought about that law's repeal in 1803.

The Senate formally advised ratification of the Louisiana Purchase Treaty by a vote of 24–7 on October 20, 1803, and on the last day of the month President Jefferson signed legislation formally authorizing him to take possession and occupy the territory ceded by France. A separate bill, also signed on October 31, provided for $11,250,000 in stock to pay for the purchase. Five months later, Congress provided for the creation of territorial governments for the newly acquired purchase. Initially, the vast land acquired from France was divided into the Territory of Orleans and the District of Louisiana. Then in March 1803, the District of Louisiana became the Territory of Louisiana.

Other measures provided for a division of the Indiana Territory to allow for creation of the Michigan Territory, and fundamental changes in land policy to address a popular demand that no interest payments be charged until payments became due. A second concession in the Land Act of 1804 reduced the minimum amount of land a settler had to purchase.

Congress proposed the Twelfth Amendment to provide for separate balloting by electors for president and vice president, thus avoiding the possibility of another constitutional crisis, as occurred in the election of 1800. Ratification of the amendment by the requisite number of states required less than a year and made it effective in time for the 1804 election. In that election, Jefferson received 162 electoral votes for president, and Charles C. Pickney captured 14 votes. George Clinton became vice president by an identical vote over Federalist Rufus King.

Major Acts and Treaties

Louisiana Purchase Treaty. Provided that France cede all of Louisiana to the United States for 80 million francs (about $15 million), including 20 million francs for assumption of American claims against France.

Its boundaries to the west and south were not specified, but were generally considered to embrace the Isles of Orleans on the east bank of the Mississippi River and the vast area between the river, the Rocky Mountains, and the Spanish possessions in the Southwest. Concluded April 30, 1803 (8 Stat. 200–213). Ratification advised by the Senate October 20, 1803.[1]

Authority of the United States in Louisiana Established. Authorized the president to take possession of the territory ceded by France to the United States on April 13, 1802, and employ the armed forces to maintain the territory as he might deem necessary. Stipulated that until Congress should provide for a permanent government, all "military, civil and judicial powers" should be vested in such persons and exercised in such manner as the president directed in order to maintain and protect the "inhabitants of Louisiana in the free enjoyment of their liberty, property and religion." Approved October 31, 1803 (2 Stat. 245).

Stock Created to Pay for Louisiana Purchase. Authorized the secretary of the Treasury to create $11,250,000 in stock certifications to finance the Louisiana Purchase. Approved October 31, 1803 (2 Stat. 245–247).

Repeal of Bankruptcy Act of 1800. Provided for the repeal of the Bankruptcy Act of 1800, which had "established a uniform system of bankruptcy throughout the United States." Approved December 19, 1803 (2 Stat. 248).

Second National Bank Act. Supplemented the National Bank Act of 1791 by authorizing bank officials to establish offices of discount and deposit in any part of the territories or dependencies of the United States. Approved March 23, 1804 (2 Stat. 274).

Land Act of 1804. Reduced the minimum amount of land that could be purchased from 320 acres to 160 acres. Introduced a credit feature by which one-fourth of the purchase price was required at the time of purchase and the balance was payable in annual installments over six years. Abolished interest on installments until they became due. Provided for additional land offices in the areas being opened for sale. Approved March 26, 1804 (2 Stat. 277–283).

Territory of Orleans and District of Louisiana. Created the Territory of Orleans and District of Louisiana by dividing the Louisiana Territory into two territories. Vested executive power over the Territory of Orleans in a governor selected by the president, and legislative power in the governor and a thirteen-member legislative council also appointed by the president. Vested judicial power in a superior court, and such inferior courts and justices of the peace as the legislature might establish. Provided for a presidentially appointed secretary for the territory to record and preserve all "papers and proceedings of the executive." Prohibited importation of slaves into the Territory of Orleans except by citizens who were their bona fide owner. Extended the executive power in the governor of Indiana Territory to the District of Louisiana. Granted to the governor and judges of the Indiana Territory authority to establish inferior courts and prescribe their jurisdiction and duties, and to make laws deemed conducive to the good of the inhabitants. Approved March 26, 1804 (2 Stat. 283–289).

Twelfth Amendment. Provided for separate voting by electors for president and vice president. The person receiving a majority of the votes for the office of president would be president and the person receiving a majority of the votes for vice president would be vice president. If no candidate received a majority, then the House, voting by state, with each state casting a single vote, would elect the president. The Senate voting per capita would elect the vice president. Proposed December 9, 1803 (2 Stat. 306). Ratified by requisite number of states June 15, 1804.[2]

Michigan Territory. Created the Michigan Territory by dividing the Indiana Territory into two separate governments. Provided for all of the Indiana Territory lying "north of a line drawn east from the southerly bend or extreme of Lake Michigan, until it shall intersect Lake Erie, and east of a line drawn from the said southerly bend through the middle of said lake to its northern extremity, and thence due north to the northern boundary of the United States," to become part of the Michigan Territory. Established for the new territory a government similar in all respects to that of the Indiana Territory. Designated Detroit as the seat of new government. Approved January 11, 1805 (2 Stat. 309–310).

District of Louisiana Made a Territory. Provided for the creation of the Territory of Louisiana (previously called the District of Louisiana). Vested executive power over the Territory of Louisiana in a governor selected by the president. Provided for a presidentially appointed secretary for the territory "to record and preserve all the papers and proceedings of the executive." Vested legislative power in the governor and three presidentially appointed judges. Provided for all criminal prosecutions to be "by a jury of twelve good and lawful men of the vicinage." Provided for the appointment of three judges who possessed the "same jurisdiction which is possessed by the judges of the Indiana territory." Approved March 3, 1805 (2 Stat. 331–332).

Notes

1. *Journal of the Executive Proceedings of the Senate* (Washington, D.C.: Guff Green, 1828), 1:430.

2. U.S. Senate, *Constitution of the United States of America: Analysis and Interpretation,* 108th Cong., 2d sess., 2004, S. Doc. 108–17, 28, n. 4.

Ninth Congress
March 4, 1805, to March 3, 1807

First session—December 2, 1805, to April 21, 1806
Second session—December 1, 1806, to March 3, 1807
Special session of the Senate—March 4, 1805, to March 5, 1805
(Second administration of Thomas Jefferson, 1805–1809)

Historical Background

On March 4, 1805, Thomas Jefferson began his second term as president. In his inaugural address, Jefferson called for Congress to approve a constitutional amendment authorizing the distribution of excess funds among the states for "rivers, canals, roads, arts, manufactures, education, and other great objects." Although the Ninth Congress did not act on his proposal, the question of internal improvements continued to occupy considerable attention. Jeffersonian Republicans soon would align themselves against the practice of constructing roads and waterways at federal expense, but in 1806 the Jefferson administration successfully promoted legislation to construct a national road from Cumberland, Maryland, to the Ohio River. The National Turnpike was to become an important route for immigrants to the Northwest until 1840.

Creation of the office of superintendent of Indian trade, the historical forerunner of the commissioner of Indian affairs, was a milestone in how the government dealt with Indian affairs. The act separated nonmilitary affairs from military concerns, even though both continued to operate out of the War Department, and established government trading posts where goods of all kinds were made available to the Indians in exchange for furs and skins.

Jefferson unsuccessfully sought to halt the harassment of American vessels engaged in trade with Great Britain and France. The terms of treaty he was finally able to obtain from Great Britain made no reference to either impressment or indemnities for recent maritime seizures. Jefferson was so dissatisfied with the work of the American negotiators that he did not submit it to the Senate for ratification. Congress passed a nonimportation act, condemned French and British impressment and seizure actions, and threatened to cease trading with the two nations. However, the problem of harassment on the high seas persisted. Rationale for the first survey of the nation's coasts was twofold. Accurate charts of the entire coastline would help save the lives of seamen, benefit the interest of merchants, and increase revenue; and be useful in designating the maritime boundaries of the United States and discouraging belligerent searches and seizures. Passage of the survey of the coast marked the beginning of the first science agency of the federal government, now known as the National Oceanic and Atmospheric Administration (NOAA).

In the early 1800s, there was widespread counterfeiting. To counteract the problem, the Enforcement of Counterfeiting Prevention Act was approved in 1806. Although there was no law regarding counterfeiting coins prior to this act, it was assumed the penalty was death because of the statements printed on colonial currency.

Jefferson's 1806 proposal for legislation prohibiting the importation of African slaves was quickly heeded by Congress (the U.S. Constitution prohibited any interference with the slave trade for twenty years; that is, until 1808). The prohibition was laxly enforced, however, and the slave trade continued to flourish for decades.

Prior to the close of the Ninth Congress in March 1807, Jefferson signed legislation increasing the number of Supreme Court justices to seven. This marked the first time since the establishment of the federal judiciary, in 1789, that Congress had increased the number of justices on the Supreme Court. Authorizing for appointment of a seventh justice came in response to the geographic expansion of the nation and the increased caseload of the district courts in the West.

Major Acts

Cumberland Road (National Road) Act. Authorized a three-member commission to lay out a national road to run from Cumberland, Maryland, to Wheeling, Virginia (later West Virginia), along the Ohio River. The commissioners were to prepare a detailed report for the president on the proposed road, including detailed plans of the route proposed, the mileage between various points, estimated costs of construction, and a discussion of particularly troublesome topography. Construction of the Cumberland Road was placed under the direction of the president. Approved March 29, 1806 (2 Stat. 357–359).

Nonimportation Act. Prohibited the importation of a number of British goods including beer, leather goods, glass, and silverware after November 15, 1806. The act was not implemented until December 1807, while the Jefferson administration awaited the outcome of diplomatic negotiations with Great Britain. Approved April 18, 1806 (2 Stat. 379–381).

Office of Superintendent of Indian Trade Created. Authorized the president to establish trading houses where goods could be exchanged with the Indians on the frontiers, in Indian country, and on both sides of the Mississippi River. Established the office of superintendent of Indian trade to supervise government trading posts, and authorized appointment of an agent for each trading post. Approved April 21, 1806 (2 Stat. 402–404).

Enforcement of Counterfeiting Prevention Act. Enabled U.S. marshals and district attorneys to investigate and prosecute counterfeiters. Established the penalty for counterfeiting both foreign and domestic coins to be between three and ten years of hard labor, or no more than five years of hard labor and a $5,000 fine. Provided a penalty for importing counterfeit coins of from two to eight years hard labor, or two years of hard labor and a $4,000 fine. Approved April 21, 1806 (2 Stat. 404–405).

Survey of the Coasts of the United States Begun. Authorized the president to "cause a survey to be taken of coasts of the United States." Appropriated $50,000 to employ "proper and intelligent people," and "such public vessels" as would be needed to complete the survey. Approved February 10, 1807 (2 Stat. 413–414).

Judiciary Act of 1807. Increased the number of Supreme Court justices from six to seven. Established a seventh judicial circuit, consisting of Ohio, Kentucky, and Tennessee, and specified that the new justice be assigned to preside over the U.S. circuit courts within that circuit. Approved February 24, 1807 (2 Stat. 420–421).

Slave Trade Prohibition Act. Prohibited the African slave trade and importation of slaves into any place within the jurisdiction of the United States after January 1, 1808. Provided a penalty of forfeiture of vessels and cargo, with disposal of seized slaves to be left to the state in which the ship was condemned. Approved March 2, 1807 (2 Stat. 426–430).

Tenth Congress
March 4, 1807, to March 3, 1809

First session—October 26, 1807, to April 25, 1808
Second session—November 7, 1808, to March 3, 1809
(Second administration of Thomas Jefferson,
    1805–1809)

Historical Background

On June 22, 1807, the USS *Chesapeake,* a thirty-eight-gun frigate, was attacked by the British warship HMS *Leopard* off Norfolk, Virginia. After taking repeated broadsides and losing twenty-one of its crew (three were killed and eighteen wounded), the ship was forcibly boarded and four alleged British deserters were removed. Many felt the United States should declare war against the aggressor, but President Jefferson on July 2 instead ordered all British warships to leave American waters.

After the British announced in October that they would pursue the practice of impressment even more vigorously, Jefferson on December 18, 1807, asked Congress to establish an embargo on U.S. shipping to European ports. Three days later, Congress approved the Embargo Act of 1807. Just two weeks later, a Second Embargo Act expanded the prohibition to prevent coasting vessels and fishing and whaling boats from sailing to Canada or the West Indies, and added harsh penalties for violation of the embargo. In March 1808, a Third Embargo required even higher bonds, enlarged the penalties for violation, and extended the embargo beyond shipping to any exports carried by land or sea. Resistance to the embargoes was vigorous but only in certain regions. While the middle states followed the law, in New England, where the prohibition on shipping caused severe economic dislocation

and unemployment, protests were widespread and many shippers simply ignored the law.

Defiance of the law prompted President Jefferson to issue a proclamation in April 1808 that the existence of an "insurrection" along the northern border was "too powerful to be suppressed by the ordinary course of judicial proceedings." Six days after issuance of the proclamation, Jefferson signed the First Enforcement Act, prohibiting any vessel from departing for a port or district adjacent to foreign territory without the express permission of the president. Under this act, federal officials were given wide-ranging authority to ensure the embargo was not violated. The Jefferson administration attempted to regulate the movement of all goods within the United States, but resistance continued and smuggling grew. After the military was called out to enforce the laws, a stronger, Second Enforcement Act, was set in place in January 1809. Finally, outright defiance of the embargo increased to the point that representatives from New England and New York were able to successfully overturn the embargo just before Jefferson left office.

Although these measures were initially popular, their economic repercussions, together with the continuing British and French menace on the high seas, nearly destroyed the American shipping industry. They succeeded in curtailing American exports to Europe, but the economic effects of the embargo were disastrous for the commercial and navigating interests of New England and the middle states, and caused the South to suffer grievously because of lost markets. The Nonintercourse Act gave the president authority to proclaim a resumption of trade with either nation if it ceased violating the "neutral commerce of the United States."

James Madison, President Jefferson's handpicked successor, captured the White House in the 1808 election, with 122 electoral votes to 47 for Charles C. Pinckney. George Clinton was able to retain the vice presidency with a 113 to 47 electoral victory over Rufus King.

Major Acts

First Embargo Act (Embargo Act of 1807). Prohibited all American merchant vessels from leaving U.S. harbors and engaging in commercial intercourse with foreign countries. Foreign vessels were permitted to leave only with the cargo that was on board. Allowed shipping between points within the United States, but only if the owner of the ship posted a bond equivalent to double the value of the goods, and allowed the president to approve individual voyages abroad. Approved December 22, 1807 (2 Stat. 451–453).

Second Embargo Act. Expanded prohibition of the first Embargo Act to all coasting vessels as well as whalers, and fishing and river boats. Required vessels to post bonds guaranteeing that they would not sail to any foreign port. Added penalties that included forfeiture of a ship and its cargo, heavy fines, and denial of credit for use in custom duties. Imposed on a captain who failed to comply a heavy fine and forfeiture of the ability to swear an oath before any customs officer. Removed the warship exemption from applying to privateers or vessels with a letter of marque. Established a fine for foreign ships loading merchandise for export, and allowed for its seizure. Approved January 9, 1908 (2 Stat. 453–454).

Third Embargo Act. Prohibited, for the first time, the export of any goods by land or sea. Required much higher bonds than imposed in the first two embargo acts, enlarged the penalties for violation, and extended the embargo to include trade by land or inland waterway between the United States, Canada, and Florida. Granted the president broad discretionary authority to enforce, deny, or grant exceptions to the embargo. Authorized port authorities to seize cargoes without a warrant and to try any shipper or merchant who was thought to have merely contemplated violating the embargo. Approved March 12, 1808 (2 Stat. 473–475).

First Enforcement Act. Required all vessels of any size to receive clearance to sail, and to load cargo under the supervision of a federal Treasury official. Prohibited all ships with cargo to leave a port near a foreign territory, for any reason, without the express permission of the president. Authorized federal revenue cutters and naval vessels to stop, search, and bring back to port any American ship on mere suspicion that it might be attempting to evade the ban. Authorized federal officials to seize merchandise on shore in any area near foreign territory until the owner paid a bond guaranteeing their delivery within the United States. Approved April 25, 1808 (2 Stat. 499–502).

Second Enforcement Act. Authorized federal collectors to refuse permission to load cargo on a vessel if it was suspected the intent was to violate the embargo. Granted federal officials broader powers to detain vessels, and allowed them to seize cargoes from a ship, wagon, or other vehicle on suspicion they were heading abroad. Granted the president, for the first time, authority to call out the state militia and the military to enforce the embargo laws, rather than just to suppress insurrections. Approved January 9, 1809 (2 Stat. 506–511).

Illinois Territory. Divided the Indiana Territory, creating a new territory west of the Wabash River to be called Illinois. Provided for a territorial government for the Illinois Territory with Kaskaskia on the Mississippi River as the seat of the new government. Approved February 3, 1809 (2 Stat. 514–516).

Nonintercourse Act. Repealed the Embargo Act of 1807 effective March 15, 1809. Reopened trade with all nations except Great Britain and France. Authorized the president to begin trade with either of those nations if they agreed to stop violating the neutral rights of Americans on the high seas. Approved March 1, 1809 (2 Stat. 528–533).

Eleventh Congress
March 4, 1809, to March 3, 1811

First session—May 22, 1809, to June 28, 1809
Second session—November 27, 1809, to May 1, 1810
Third session—December 3, 1810, to March 3, 1811
Special session of the Senate—March 4, 1809, to
    March 7, 1809
(First administration of James Madison, 1809–1813)

Historical Background

On April 19, 1809, a little more than a month after his inauguration, James Madison issued a presidential proclamation renewing trade with Great Britain, as authorized by the Nonintercourse Act. Enthusiasm over Madison's action was short-lived, however, when London denounced the negotiations between the president and the British minister in Washington as unacceptable. As the year progressed, economic conditions continued to worsen and the president's posture toward England hardened. By 1810, the French and British had seized several hundred American ships and impressed some of the sailors aboard.

Continued aggressive action by the two nations prompted Congress in May 1810 to approve Macon's Bill No. 2, which declared that the United States would reopen trade with both Great Britain and France in return for their recognition of American neutrality on the high seas. The embargo restrictions were to be removed only if either or both countries made the appropriate concessions. Seizing on Macon's Bill as an opportunity to draw the United States into a war against Great Britain, French emperor Napoleon I announced a repeal of all decrees against the United States. President Madison, believing that Napoleon was sincere, responded by reopening trade with France. Several months passed before Madison realized that Napoleon had no intention of halting his actions against American shipping. Meanwhile, the likelihood of a British-American conflict loomed. When Great Britain continued its maritime harassment of American vessels, the president in 1811 issued a proclamation, backed by the Non-Importation Act of 1811, prohibiting British goods from being imported into the United States.

Madison took advantage of the interlude in commercial warfare to issue a proclamation on October 27, 1810, announcing that the United States had taken possession of West Florida, from the Mississippi to the Perdido Rivers. In 1811, Congress in a secret session conferred after-the-fact legitimacy to the president's action when it approved a resolution and act authorizing American rule over West Florida, if local authorities concurred or a foreign nation attempted occupation. The secret resolution declared that the United States could not see, "without serous inquietude," any part of Florida pass to "any foreign power." Diplomatic historian Alexander DeConde tells us that "[t]his 'no-transfer resolution' expressed an idea that was to become a fundamental principle of American foreign policy in the Western Hemisphere. From this time on United States policy clearly opposed the transfer of territory in the Americas to outside nations."[1] Congress also approved an enabling act authorizing representatives of the Territory of Louisiana (from the Sabine River to the Mississippi River and from the 33rd parallel to the Gulf of Mexico) to frame a constitution and state government in preparation for statehood.

Before adjourning, the Eleventh Congress approved the establishment of more federal Indian trading houses, amplified the duties of the superintendent of Indian trading, and appropriated additional funding for the Indian Trading Office.

Major Acts

Macon's Bill No. 2. Intended as a substitute for the unsuccessful Nonintercourse Act of 1809. Authorized restoration of all trade with Britain and France, if each recognized American neutrality. If they refused, trade with either or both would cease. Approved May 1, 1810 (2 Stat. 605–606). *(Nonintercourse Act, p. 36)*

No-Transfer Resolution of 1811. Resolved that "the United States, under the peculiar circumstances of the existing crisis, cannot, without serious inquietude, see any part of the said territory [Florida] pass into the hands of any foreign power." Approved January 11, 1811 (3 Stat. 471).

Extension of U.S. Rule over West Florida. Authorized the president to take possession of, and occupy, all or any part of the territory lying east of the Perdido River and south of the state of Georgia and the Mississippi Territory. Approved January 15, 1811 (3 Stat. 471–472).

Louisiana Enabling Act. Authorized the inhabitants of the Territory of Orleans (Louisiana), from the Sabine River to the Mississippi River, and from the 33rd parallel to the Gulf of Mexico, and of the Isle of Orleans to form a constitution and state government in preparation for statehood. Approved February 20, 1811 (2 Stat. 641–643).

Non-Importation Act of 1811. Prohibited British ships and goods from American ports. Approved March 2, 1811 (2 Stat. 651–652).

Indian Trading House Act of 1811. Reauthorized the president to appoint a superintendent of Indian trade to be responsible for all goods intended for trade with the Indians. Increased the duties of the superintendent to include the purchase and distribution of all goods needed for annuities and presents to the Indians as well as for treaty purposes. Authorized the president to open additional factories (trading houses) among the Indians, and appropriated additional funding for staff to support the new trading houses. Approved March 2, 1811 (2 Stat. 652–655).

Note

1. Alexander DeConde, *A History of American Foreign Policy*, 2d ed. (New York: Charles Scribner's Sons, 1971), 122.

Twelfth Congress
March 4, 1811, to March 3, 1813

First session—November 4, 1811, to July 6, 1812
Second session—November 2, 1812, to March 3, 1813
(First administration of James Madison, 1809–1813)

Historical Background

At the request of President James Madison, the Twelfth Congress convened a month early. It represented, in the words of historian Merrill D. Peterson, "a watershed in the history of the republic."[1] Although the seventy freshman members of Congress had not participated in the founding of the republic, they were intent on preserving it. President Madison, in his annual message of November 5, 1811, stressed that Great Britain and France had exhibited "hostile inflexibility in trampling on rights which no independent nation can relinquish," and he urged Congress to improve military preparedness.

Congressional sentiment in favor of war was heightened a few weeks later when reports of the Battle of Tippecanoe reached Washington. Attempting a preemptive expedition against Tecumseh, the charismatic leader of a confederation of northwestern Indian tribes, General William Henry Harrison, had fought a pitched battle and won a costly but indecisive victory when attacked by British-armed and -abetted Shawnee Indians at Tippecanoe in Indiana Territory. Congress approved a twenty-five thousand man increase in the army and a $1.9 million military supplies appropriation for the army and navy. Subsequently, the president was authorized to borrow $11 million to meet military expenses, call up an additional one hundred thousand militia, and survey six million acres that could be used as bounty for military service; and a 90-day embargo was adopted prohibiting all foreign trade by American shippers to permit American ships to make port before an actual declaration of war. These efforts were largely orchestrated by the War Hawks, a group of young, recently elected members of Congress, led by House Speaker Henry Clay of Kentucky, who sought war as a way of restoring the nation's honor.

Still, Madison hesitated to enter an armed conflict with either European power. Finally, he concluded that to restore morale, war with Great Britain, the most serious offender of American pride, was the most appropriate action. On June 1, 1812, Madison sent a message to Congress asking for a declaration of war. Madison condemned the British for denying American's normal trading relations; seizing American sailors, ships, and cargo; and inciting the Indians against American settlers. A three-day House debate produced a 79 to 49 vote favoring war. Federalist opposition in the Senate prompted a protracted discussion that ended on June 17 when the proponents of war prevailed 19 to 13. Ironically, on June 16, the British had suspended the Orders-in-Council that imposed the blockade restricting American ships from entering British ports. By then, however, it was too late.

On July 1, a higher tariff was placed on foreign imports and goods imported on foreign vessels as a means of raising money for the war. Five days later, another enactment sought to prohibit trade with America's enemies. Prior to the outbreak of war, British forces had purchased many supplies, particularly grain and flour, and naval stores from U.S. traders. In addition, there was considerable wagon trade across the Canadian border between the United States and Canada. The latter act was aimed at these transactions, but a considerable amount of illicit trade continued.

To counter British numerical superiority at sea, the United States licensed privateers—privately owned armed ships—to capture enemy vessels, and used an unprecedented act of Congress to authorize private citizens to destroy British vessels at any time and place. In both instances the attackers were rewarded with a bounty. The first War Department general staff was instituted to provide a management staff for the secretary of war. Because the staff consisted simply of a group of heads of administrative bureaus, it was not a general staff in the modern sense of the phrase. The General Staff Act of 1903 (32 Stat. 830) marks the beginning of the modern American military organization.

Amidst preparations for war, Congress admitted Louisiana to the Union, enlarged the Mississippi Territory, and created the Missouri Territory. It also approved the issuance of $5 million in Treasury notes to finance the war, doubled the duties on foreign goods, agreed to construct four additional ships for the navy, increased the army by twenty regiments, and authorized the president to retaliate against Indians aligned with the British.

While the War of 1812 was extremely popular in the West, Madison encountered continual opposition in New England. In the 1812 election, he carried the southern and western states as well as Vermont and Pennsylvania, garnering 128 electoral votes. DeWitt Clinton carried the rest of New England and the Middle Atlantic states, receiving 89 electoral votes. Democratic-Republican Elbridge Gerry won 131 electoral votes for the vice presidency against Federalist Jared Ingersoll, who got 86 electoral votes.

Major Acts

Army Increased. Provided for twenty-five thousand additional men to be enlisted in the army for five years, unless discharged sooner. Granted a noncommissioned officer or soldier "faithfully performing his duty" while serving his country an additional bounty of $16 and 160 acres of land upon completion of his enlistment. Approved January 11, 1812 (2 Stat. 671–674).

Military Supplies Appropriation. Appropriated $1.5 million for the purchase of arms, ordnance, and camp equipment for the army and $400,000 for powder, ordnance, and small arms for the navy. Approved January 14, 1812 (2 Stat. 674–675).

Military Expenses Loan. Authorized the president to borrow not more than $11 million at 6 percent interest to meet government military expenses. Approved March 14, 1812 (2 Stat. 694–695).

Embargo on American Shipping. Laid "an embargo on all [American] ships and vessels in the ports and harbors of the United States" for ninety days. Stipulated that the act did not apply to the departure of foreign ships and vessels. Approved April 4, 1812 (2 Stat. 700–701).

Additional Militia Authorized. Empowered the president to call up 100,000 militia from states and territories for six months of service. Appropriated $1 million to defray expenses incurred by the act. Approved April 10, 1812 (2 Stat. 705–707).

Louisiana Admitted to the Union. Declared that Louisiana (Orleans Territory) was one of the "United States of America, and admitted into the Union on an equal footing with the original States" effective April 30, 1812. Approved April 8, 1812 (2 Stat. 701–704). On April 14, 1812, Congress enlarged the state of Louisiana to include the Florida Parishes—that part of West Florida lying between the Mississippi and Pearl Rivers south of the 31st parallel. Approved April 14, 1812 (2 Stat. 708–709).

Bounty Lands for Military Service. Authorized the president to have six million acres surveyed and reserved to satisfy bounties to soldiers. Two million acres were to be surveyed in each of three territories—Michigan, Illinois, and Louisiana. Approved May 6, 1812 (2 Stat. 728–730).

Mississippi Territory Enlarged. Annexed the eastern part of West Florida, from the Pearl River to the Perdido River, south of the 31st parallel, to the Territory of Mississippi. Approved May 14, 1812 (2 Stat. 734).

Missouri Territory. Established the Territory of Missouri, consisting of the Louisiana Purchase north of the present-day boundary of Louisiana. Vested executive power of the territory in a governor appointed to a three-year term by the president; legislative power in a general assembly consisting of the governor, a nine-member legislative council appointed by the president, and a popularly elected house of representatives; and judicial power in a three-member superior court, inferior courts, and justices of the peace. Provided for an elected delegate to the U.S. Congress to represent the territory. Approved June 4, 1812 (2 Stat. 743–747).

Declaration of War with Great Britain and Ireland. Declared that war existed between the United Kingdom and its dependencies and the United States and its territories. Authorized the president to use the land and naval forces of the United States to carry out the war. Approved June 18, 1812 (2 Stat. 755).

Treasury Notes Issued to Finance the War of 1812. Authorized an issue of $5 million of Treasury notes to finance the War of 1812. Approved June 30, 1812 (2 Stat. 766–768).

Duties on Imports and Exports Increased. Doubled the duties on foreign goods, and increased duties on goods imported by foreign vessels by 10 percent. Approved July 1, 1812 (2 Stat. 768–769).

Trading with Enemies Prohibited. Banned American ships and vessels from departing from an American port to proceed or trade with enemies of the United States. Prohibited American citizens from transporting goods over land or by boat to any place in Upper or Lower Canada, Nova Scotia, or New Brunswick. Approved July 6, 1812 (2 Stat. 778–781).

Navy Enlarged. Authorized the construction of four ships carrying seventy-four guns each and six first-class frigates with forty-four guns each. Approved January 2, 1813 (2 Stat. 789).

Army Further Enlarged. Provided for the president to raise an additional twenty regiments to be enlisted for one year. Approved January 29, 1813 (2 Stat. 794–796).

Destruction of the Armed Vessels of the Enemy Encouraged. Declared that during the war with Great Britain it was "lawful for any person or persons to burn, sink, or destroy, any British armed vessel of war, except vessels coming as cartels or flags of truce." Offered a "bounty of one half the value of the armed vessel so burnt, sunk, or destroyed, and also one half the value of her guns, cargo, tackle, and apparel." Approved March 3, 1813 (2 Stat. 816).

General Staff within the War Department. Authorized the president to assign a "brigadier general to the principal army of the United States." Created the War Department general staff consisting of the departments of adjutant general, inspector general, and quartermaster general. Included within the three departments were the quartermasters, topographical engineers, adjutant general's corps, inspector general's corps, ordnance, hospital, physician and surgeon general, apothecary general, purchasing and pay departments, judge advocates, chaplains, U.S. military academy, and commanding generals of the military districts, and their logistical staff. Approved March 3, 1813 (2 Stat. 819–820).

Retaliation for Injustices by Indians. Authorized the president "to cause full and ample retaliation" for "any outrage or act of cruelty or barbarity" that "shall be or has been practiced by any Indian or Indians, in alliance with the British government." Approved March 3, 1813 (2 Stat. 829–830).

Note

1. Merrill D. Peterson, *The Great Triumvirate* (New York: Oxford University Press, 1987), 3.

Thirteenth Congress
March 4, 1813, to March 3, 1815

First session—May 24, 1813, to August 2, 1813
Second session—December 6, 1813, to April 18, 1814
Third session—September 19, 1814, to March 3, 1815
(Second administration of James Madison, 1813–1817)

Historical Background

The early months of the War of 1812 went poorly for the Americans. By 1813, the British had effectively blockaded the American coast. Near the end of December they captured Fort Niagara and burned Buffalo, New York. In 1814 exports and imports fell to less than 20 percent of prewar levels. Congress passed several financial measures that dramatically escalated the cost of the war, and a possible land-sea invasion became an increasing concern. After the British raided Washington and burned the Capitol, the White House, and all the executive departments except the Patent Office in August 1814, American resistance began to stiffen.

A month later, after the bombardment of Fort McHenry failed, a British assault on Baltimore, Maryland, was abandoned. At about the same time, several hundred miles to the north, American naval forces under the command of Captain Thomas MacDonough were victorious in the Battle of Lake Champlain. America's most decisive victory followed on January 8, 1815, with General Andrew Jackson's triumph at the Battle of New Orleans. On Christmas Eve 1814, unbeknown to most Americans, British and U.S. peacemakers concluded months of negotiations in Ghent, Belgium, with the signing of a peace treaty. Word of the Treaty of Ghent reached New York six weeks later, after the battle had been fought. Ratification was advised by the Senate on February 16, 1815.

Financing the war resulted in more than $63 million in debt. In 1813, a full year into the war, Congress approved a series of bills designed to increase the government's revenue. The initial measure, created collection districts with officials that were the original forerunners of tax collectors and internal revenue agents. Next, the office of commission of revenue was established to make sure taxes were collected. Subsequent bills levied taxes on refined sugar, carriages, distilled spirits, auction sales, retailers of liquor and imported goods, and bank notes and legal instruments. Congress explicitly designated these taxes as war measures, and provided for their automatic repeal within a year of the war's termination.

On three occasions during the conflict, the president was authorized to borrow a total of $35.5 million to defray the expenses the government was incurring. In an attempt to partially offset these loans, tax collection districts were created in each to collect taxes. As debate continued over how to raise sufficient funds to deal with the government's growing financial crisis, Congress in January 1815 approved four additional tax-related measures. These enactments levied a $6 million direct tax on states, a sales tax on goods manufactured within the United States, a sales tax on household furniture and watches, and strengthened the authority of tax collectors.

Earlier in the Thirteenth Congress, a means was provided for the distribution of congressional information on a regular basis to state and territorial executives, state legislatures, each state university and college, and state historical societies. This was the statutory antecedent to what was to become the Federal Depository Library Program. Following the burning of Washington in August 1814, Congress purchased nearly 6,500 volumes of Thomas Jefferson's personal library as the nucleus for a new congressional library and authorized $500,000 for rebuilding the Capitol, White House, and other federal buildings. Separate action increased the incentives of military service.

During the waning hours of the Thirteenth Congress, legislation was approved significantly reducing the naval establishment, limiting the strength of America's peacetime army, and authorizing a declaration of war against the Algerian regency for plundering American vessels in the Mediterranean. The war with Algiers was short-lived. In June 1815, an American squadron under the command of Captain Stephen Decatur had captured the Algerian flagship *Mashuda,* and demanded and secured a treaty that provided for an end to all tribute, reparations for U.S. vessels improperly seized, emancipation of all Christian slaves escaping to American men-of-war, and civilized treatment of prisoners of war. This marked the end of the piratical activities of the Barbary States.

Major Acts and Treaties

Creation of Collection Districts for the Purpose of Assessing and Collecting Direct Taxes and Internal Duties. Designated and established districts within each state for assessing and collecting direct taxes and internal duties. Direct taxes were to be assessed on all property including land, homes, improvements, and slaves. Approved July 22, 1813 (3 Stat. 22–34).

Office of Commissioner of Revenue. Established an officer in the Treasury Department to be known as the commissioner of revenue to be responsible for the "collection of the direct and internal taxes." Authorized appointment of district collectors and assessors to assist the commissioner. Approved July 22, 1813 (3 Stat. 39).

Revenue Acts of 1813. Levied a tax on refined sugar. Approved July 24, 1813 (3 Stat. 35–39). Imposed a tax on carriages. Approved July 24, 1813 (3 Stat. 40–41). Levied a tax on "distillers of spirituous liquors." Approved July 24, 1813 (3 Stat. 42–44). Levied a tax on auction sales of "merchandise and ships and vessels." Approved July 24, 1813 (3 Stat. 44–47).

Direct Property Tax on States and Counties. Imposed a direct tax of $3 million apportioned among the various states and counties of the United States. Approved August 2, 1813 (3 Stat. 53–72).

Duties on Retailers of Liquor and Imported Goods. Imposed a direct tax on "retailers of wines, spirituous liquors, and foreign merchandise." Approved August 2, 1813 (3 Stat. 72–73).

War Loans. Authorized the president to borrow $7.5 million to defray the expenses the government was incurring as the War of 1812 continued. Approved August 2, 1813 (3 Stat. 75–77). An additional loan of $25 million was authorized on March 24, 1814, and a $3 million loan was authorized on November 15, 1814 (3 Stat. 111–112; 3 Stat. 144–145).

Stamp Tax on Bank Notes and Legal Instruments. Imposed "duties on notes of banks, bankers, and certain companies; on notes, bonds, and obligations discounted by banks, bankers, and certain companies, and bills of exchange of certain descriptions." Approved August 2, 1813 (3 Stat. 77–81).

Legislation to Ensure Distribution of Congressional Documents. Authorized the distribution of the House and Senate journals and other congressional documents to the Library of the United States, executives of the several states and territories, to colleges and universities in each state, and to state historical societies. Approved December 27, 1813 (3 Stat. 140–141). In 1858, the principle of having depository libraries tied to congressional districts was established as Representatives were allowed to designate one depository library from their own district and each territorial Delegate to designate a depository from each territory. Approved March 20, 1858 (11 Stat. 368). In 1859, Congress provided for each Senator to designate a depository in their state. Approved February 5, 1859 (11 Stat. 379, Sec. 5).

Bounty Increased for Military Service. Increased the bounty for military service to $124 and 320 acres. Approved January 27, 1814 (3 Stat. 94–95).

Direct Tax of 1815. Imposed a $6 million direct tax on houses, lands, and slaves. Created a board of principal assessors that was given the duty of equalizing and proportioning valuations among the several counties or state districts. Approved January 9, 1815 (3 Stat. 164–180).

Sales Tax on Manufactured Goods. Imposed duties on "goods, wares, and merchandise manufactured within the United States." Specified items included pig iron, iron castings, rolled or slit iron, candles, hats and caps, umbrellas and parasols, paper, playing cards, saddles and bridles, paper, playing and visiting cards, boots and bootees, beer, ale and porter, tobacco products, and items made from leather. Approved January 18, 1815 (3 Stat. 180–186).

Sales Tax on Household Furniture and Watches. Imposed annual duties on "household furniture, and on gold and silver watches." Levied the duties on a valuation basis with the assistant and principal assessors responsible for determining the amount of tax. Approved January 18, 1815 (3 Stat. 186–192).

Purchase of the Library of Thomas Jefferson. Authorized the purchase of the library of Thomas Jefferson for the use of Congress at a sum of $23,950. Approved January 30, 1815 (3 Stat. 195).

Repair and Construction of Public Buildings in Washington. Authorized the president to borrow $500,000 to repair and rebuild the Capitol, the president's house, and other federal buildings. Approved February 13, 1815 (3 Stat. 205).

Treaty of Ghent. Provided for release of all prisoners taken in the War of 1812, restoration of all territory taken in that war (except West Florida), and appointment of an arbitration commission to settle the northeastern boundary between the United States and Canada. Concluded December 24, 1814 (8 Stat. 218–223). Ratification advised by the Senate February 16, 1815.[1]

Naval Reduction Act of 1815. Authorized the president to sell or lay up the barges and other vessels that made up the navy's gunboat flotilla and to remove the "armament, tackle and furniture" on all armed U.S. vessels on the Great Lakes before selling or laying them up, except those deemed "necessary to enforce the proper execution of revenue laws." Provided that monies arising from these sales be paid to the U.S. Treasury. Provided for the discharge and payment of commissioned and warrant officers and privates of the flotilla service. Approved February 27, 1815 (3 Stat. 217–218).

Army Reduction Act of 1815. Established a peacetime standing army of ten thousand men. Approved March 3, 1815 (3 Stat. 224–225).

Declaration of War with Algiers. Declared war with Algiers, which had been molesting American ships and insisting upon payment of tribute. Approved March 3, 1815 (3 Stat. 230).

Authority of Tax Collectors Strengthened. Strengthened the authority of collectors to bring suits without delay and to prosecute for breaches of revenue. Granted collectors authority to search and seize for violations of the tax laws. Specified that the collector had a duty to make an annual statement, listing in alphabetical order the names of all persons who paid to him or his deputies any tax, with an aggregate amount listed next to the name, to make one hundred copies of this list, and distribute it to the Commissioner, the town clerk, and others. Required that a copy of this list was to be posted at the local courthouse for public inspection. Approved March 3, 1815 (3 Stat. 239–244).

Note

1. *Journal of the Executive Proceedings of the Senate* (Washington, D.C.: Guff Green, 1828), 2:620.

Fourteenth Congress
March 4, 1815, to March 3, 1817

First session—December 4, 1815, to April 30, 1816
Second session—December 2, 1816, to March 3, 1817
(Second administration of James Madison, 1813–1817)

Historical Background

While the Capitol was under reconstruction, Congress met until December 1819 in the hastily built brick Capitol on the site of the current Supreme Court building. When the postwar Fourteenth Congress convened, it had to wrestle with a depleted federal Treasury and chaotic economic conditions. In his December 5, 1815, message to Congress, President Madison stressed the need for a protective tariff to increase "domestic wealth," enhance "external commerce," and help "enterprising citizens" whose interests would be threatened by foreign competition. He also spoke of needed reforms in banking, education, transportation, and national defense. Later that month, a peace treaty was signed with Algiers. The treaty ended the last major dispute with the Barbary Powers, although a naval presence was maintained in the Mediterranean until France annexed Algeria in 1830.

Congress approved Madison's request for the nation's first protective tariff and adopted an eight-year plan to expand the navy. When the War of 1812 ended, President Madison was faced with a flood of English goods and a substantial war debt. The tariff propelled protectionism to the forefront in an effort to protect war-born American manufacturing from the competition of revitalized Britishers. It was supported by both northern as well as southern members of Congress. The Naval Expansion Act of 1816, one historian has declared, "is one of the most important in the legislative history of the Navy as it committed the United States, for the first time to a policy of building up a fleet in peacetime which was comparable to those of European powers."[1]

To help stabilize the economy and restore the integrity of the nation's financial institutions, a charter was granted to the Second Bank of the United States. The second bank's charter was constructed much like the first bank's, including a 20 year time limit. One important difference was its capital of $35 million, three-and-a-half times that of its predecessor. The bank's capital represented over half of the total legal tender in circulation, thus making it the nation's dominant financial institution. In other action, Congress reduced the direct tax level, and prohibited foreigners from trading with the Indians residing in U.S. territory.

Another step toward national self-sufficiency was expressed in the Navigation Act of 1817. American shipowners benefited greatly when Madison signed this act, which prohibited ships owned by foreigners from carrying goods between American ports. With this protective umbrella, America's coastal trade flourished during the decades preceding the Civil War.

Among the most unpopular actions of the Fourteenth Congress was its decision to change congressional compensation from $6 a day to $1,500 a session. Public outrage over the change resulted in its repeal less than a year later. Passage of the compensation act, Richard Johnson of Kentucky told his House colleagues in December 1816, had "excited more discontent" than any other "measure of the Government, from its existence." Representative Johnson led the movement for both passage and repeal of the act.

Indiana was admitted to the Union as the nineteenth state on December 11, 1816. Three months later, Congress divided the Mississippi Territory into two smaller territories—the Mississippi Territory and the Alabama Territory. Congress also approved an enabling act that authorized representatives of the

Alabama Territory to frame a constitution and state government in preparation for statehood.

In his final annual message of December 3, 1816, President Madison recommended a constitutional amendment allowing Congress to enlarge its powers so that state funds could be used to construct a "comprehensive system of roads and canals, such as will have the effect of drawing more closely together every part of our country." Despite Madison's warning that the Constitution would have to be amended to effect such a change, Congress passed an internal improvements bill (Bonus Bill) that ignored his concerns. In his final act as president, Madison vetoed the Bonus Bill as unconstitutional.

In the 1816 election, the Democratic-Republicans endorsed James Monroe, who served in the Madison administration as secretary of state and secretary of war, for president and Daniel D. Tompkins, who was governor of New York, for vice president. The Federalists, meanwhile, were in disarray and failed to field candidates. Monroe received 183 electoral votes to 34 for Rufus King. Tompkins also received 183 electoral votes, with 22 votes going to John F. Howard.

Major Acts and Treaties

Treaty of Peace with Algiers. Terminated the Algerian War, and ended American subsidies to the governments of Algiers, Tunis, and Tripoli. Concluded June 30 and July 6, 1815 (8 Stat. 224–227). Ratification advised by the Senate December 21, 1815.[2]

Direct Tax Reduced. Reduced the amount of direct tax on the states and the District of Columbia to $3 million for 1816. Approved March 5, 1816 (3 Stat. 255–256).

Compensation Act of 1816. Provided that members of Congress receive an annual compensation of $1,500 instead of daily compensation and that the president pro tempore of the Senate and Speaker of the House receive $3,000 annually. Approved March 19, 1816 (3 Stat. 257–258). Repealed February 6, 1817 (3 Stat. 345).

Second Bank of the United States. Created the Second Bank of the United States for a term of 20 years, with an authorized capital of $35 million, of which the government was to supply one-fifth. The bank was to serve as a non-interest-paying depository for federal funds. In return for its charter privileges, the bank was to pay the government an annual bonus of $1.5 million. Approved April 10, 1816 (3 Stat. 266–277).

Indiana Enabling Act. Authorized the inhabitants of the Indiana Territory to form a constitution and state government in preparation for statehood. Approved April 19, 1816 (3 Stat. 289–291).

Tariff of 1816 (First Protective Tariff). Placed heavy duties on certain foreign manufactured goods, wares, and merchandise imported into the United States from any foreign port or place, as a means of protecting America's domestic manufacturers and eventually to lessen the need for foreign goods. Approved April 27, 1816 (3 Stat. 310–314).

Naval Expansion Act of 1816. Appropriated $1 million annually for eight years for the "gradual increase of the navy of the United States." Authorized the construction of nine ships of "not less than seventy-four guns each," twelve frigates of "not less than forty-four guns each," and "three steam batteries to be procured for harbour defense." Also authorized that the "block ship at New Orleans be completed." Approved April 29, 1816 (3 Stat. 321).

Indian Trading License Law of 1816. Provided that licenses to trade with Indians within the territorial limits of the United States would be granted only to citizens of the United States. Prohibited foreigners from either selling goods or purchasing articles from the Indians. Approved April 29, 1816 (3 Stat. 332–333).

Indiana Admitted to the Union. Accepted the constitution and state government formed by the people of the Indiana Territory on June 29, 1816, declared that Indiana was one of the "United States of America, and admitted into the union on an equal footing with the original States." Approved December 11, 1816 (3 Stat. 399–400).

Mississippi Enabling Act. Authorized the people of the western part of the Mississippi Territory to form a constitution and state government in preparation for statehood. Approved March 1, 1817 (3 Stat. 348–349).

Navigation Act of 1817. Prohibited the importation of "goods, wares, or merchandise" from any foreign port except in U.S. vessels or vessels of the country from which the goods were imported. Required that all cargo between one American port and another be carried in ships entirely owned by American citizens. Approved March 1, 1817 (3 Stat. 351–352).

Mississippi Territory Divided. Divided the Mississippi Territory into two smaller territories, the Mississippi Territory and the Alabama Territory, generally coterminous with the current boundaries of the states of Mississippi and Alabama. Approved March 3, 1817 (3 Stat. 371–373).

Notes

1. K. Jack Bauer, "Naval Shipbuilding Programs, 1794–1860," *Military Affairs,* v, 29 Spring 1965, 34.

2. *Journal of the Executive Proceedings of the Senate* (Washington, D.C.: Guff Green, 1828), 3:8–9.

Fifteenth Congress
March 4, 1817, to March 3, 1819

First session—December 1, 1817, to April 20, 1818
Second session—November 16, 1818, to March 3, 1819
Special session of the Senate—March 4, 1817, to March
    6, 1817
(First administration of James Monroe, 1817–1821)

Historical Background

The Federalist Party virtually passed from the national scene with the election of 1816. A number of Federalists, however, retained their partisan identity during James Monroe's two terms as president, and Federalists continued to control the state governments of Connecticut, Delaware, Massachusetts, and Maryland and had a significant representation in other states as well. Monroe, the last Revolutionary War officer to serve as president, occupied the White House during the Era of Good Feelings, which was characterized by the unchallenged dominance of the Democratic-Republicans. The disappearance of partisan conflict, Monroe biographer Harry Ammon has observed, forced the fifth president to rely on his personal contacts among members of Congress as well as those of his cabinet in securing the passage of legislation.

Neither Monroe nor the Fifteenth Congress, however, was prepared for the economic upheaval that culminated in the first peacetime depression in the nation's history. Immediately following the War of 1812, there was general prosperity, except for manufacturers, which faced stiff competition as a consequence of a dramatic influx of cheaper European imports. Several factors contributed to the subsequent Panic of 1819: extremely liberal credit policies by state banks, a speculative boom in western lands, widespread unemployment, and mismanagement of the Second Bank of the United States.

Monroe's first annual message had presented a glowing report on America's finances. The message also announced the Rush-Bagot Agreement, the first reciprocal naval disarmament agreement in the history of international relations. The Senate ratified the Anglo-American accord in April 1818. Among Madison's modest list of legislative proposals was a recommendation for a constitutional amendment authorizing federally sponsored internal improvements, a pension for Revolutionary War veterans, a response to British exclusion of American trade in several of its colonies, and a repeal of internal taxes approved during the war. Congress granted pensions to Revolutionary veterans and approved a measure imposing restrictions on British shipping, but it took no action on Monroe's other initiatives.

In other action, Congress established that the flag of the United States would have thirteen horizontal stripes, representing the thirteen original states, in alternate red and white, and a white star for each state on a background of blue. Senate ratification of the Adams-Onis (Transcontinental) Treaty allowed the United States to acquire Florida and settle Spanish claims to the Pacific Northwest. The Immigration Act of 1819 made possible for the first time the accurate compilation of statistics regarding those entering the United States. Mississippi and Illinois were admitted to the Union in 1817 and 1818, respectively. Also, an enabling act was approved for the Alabama Territory.

The waning hours of the Fifteenth Congress were the scene of the first major legislative battle on the slavery question since the Constitutional Convention of 1787. Rep. James Tallmadge Jr. of New York offered an amendment to the Missouri statehood bill prohibiting the further importation of slaves into Missouri and freeing slaves born in the state after its admission once they reached the age of twenty-five. Opinions regarding the amendment's propriety were espoused on Capitol Hill, in the nation's newspapers and pamphlets, in public by religious orators, and in private conversations of Americans throughout the country. A fierce debate followed with the House approving the amendment and the Senate defeating it.

Before adjourning, Congress left four important bills on President Monroe's desk as he prepared to return to private life. The first bill created the Arkansas Territory, established a temporary government for the new territory, and fixed its boundaries. Only after lengthy debate did Congress refuse to limit slavery in the new territory. The second authorized the president to employ the navy for the protection of American merchantmen and the suppression of piracy. This legislation resulted in the creation of the navy's first fighting force dedicated to combating piracy. The third authorized the president to formally take possession of East and West Florida, under the terms of the Adams-Onis Treaty, and to provide for a temporary government until a permanent one was established by Congress. The fourth formally placed responsibility for assigning names to the navy's ships in the hands of the secretary of the navy, a prerogative still exercised.

Major Acts and Treaties

Mississippi Admitted to the Union. Accepted the constitution and state government formed by a Mississippi Territory convention on August 15, 1817, and declared that Mississippi was one of the "United States of America, and admitted into the union on an equal footing with the original States." Approved December 10, 1817 (3 Stat. 472–473).

Military Pension Act of 1818. Authorized a life pension of $20 a month for officers and $8 for noncommissioned officers who served in the army or navy during the Revolutionary War. Approved March 18, 1818 (3 Stat. 410–411).

Flag Act of 1818. Provided that the United States flag was to retain thirteen stripes as a permanent part of its design, but a star would be added for each state at the time of admission to the Union. Approved April 4, 1818 (3 Stat. 415).

Rush-Bagot Agreement. Provided for mutual naval disarmament on the Great Lakes by Great Britain and the United States. Provided for the gradual demilitarization of land forces along the U.S.-Canadian border. Concluded April 28–29, 1817 (8 Stat. 231). Ratification advised by the Senate on April 16, 1818.[1]

Illinois Enabling Act. Authorized the inhabitants of the Illinois Territory to form a constitution and state government in preparation for statehood. Approved April 18, 1818 (3 Stat. 428–431).

Navigation Act of 1818. Closed the ports of the United States to "vessels owned by British subjects, arriving from a colony which, by the ordinary laws, [was] closed to vessels owned by citizens of the United States." Approved April 18, 1818 (3 Stat. 432–433).

Illinois Admitted to the Union. Accepted the constitution and state government formed by an Illinois Territory convention on August 26, 1818, and declared that Illinois was one of the "United States of America, and admitted into the Union on an equal footing with the original States." Approved December 3, 1818 (3 Stat. 536).

Adams-Onis (Transcontinental) Treaty. Provided for the acquisition of Florida from Spain and defined the western boundary of the Louisiana Territory. In exchange the United States renounced claims to Texas, and claims of American citizens amounting to $5 million were assumed by the U.S. government. Concluded February 22, 1819 (8 Stat. 252–273). Ratification advised by the Senate February 24, 1819.[2] Approval again advised by the Senate February 19, 1821.[3]

Steerage Act of 1819. Established rules and procedures for passenger ships bringing immigrants to the United States, most important of which was numerical registry of immigration. This made it possible for the first time to compile accurate statistics on immigration. Approved March 2, 1819 (3 Stat. 488–489).

Alabama Enabling Act. Authorized the inhabitants of the Alabama Territory to form a constitution and state government in preparation for statehood. Approved March 2, 1819 (3 Stat. 489–492).

Arkansas Territory Established. Provided for the establishment of a separate territory in the southern part of the Missouri Territory to be called the Arkansaw Territory (not officially spelled Arkansas until later). Authorized the establishment of a temporary government for the new territory, with the seat of government being the post of Arkansaw, on the Arkansaw River. (Consisted of present-day Arkansas as well as part of Oklahoma.) Approved March 2, 1819 (3 Stat. 493–496).

1819 Act to Protect the Commerce of the United States and Punish the Crime of Piracy. Authorized the president to employ as many armed navy vessels as necessary to protect the merchant vessels of the United States. Provided that any person committing piracy, upon conviction was to be punished with death. Approved March 3, 1819 (3 Stat. 510–514).

President Authorized to Take Possession of East and West Florida. Authorized the president to take possession of the territories of East and West Florida, and remove the Spanish officers and soldiers there and transport them to Havana in accord with the Adams-Onis Treaty of 1819. Authorized the president to employ the militia of any state or territory to maintain order, and to appoint officers and prescribe the management of the territories until Congress provided a governmental structure for the territories. Extended to the inhabitants of the territories U.S. revenue laws and laws concerning the slave trade. Approved March 3, 1819 (3 Stat. 523–524).

Declaration of the Manner in Which Naval Ships Shall Be Named. Declared that all ships of the U.S. Navy be named by the secretary of the navy, under the direction of the president of the United States, according to the following rule: first class shall be called after the states of this Union; those of the second class after the rivers; and those of the third class after the principal cities and towns. Stipulated that no two navy vessels bear the same name. Approved March 3, 1819 (3 Stat. 538).

Notes

1. *Journal of the Executive Proceedings of the Senate* (Washington, D.C.: Guff Green, 1828), 3:134.

2. *Journal of the Executive Proceedings of the Senate* (Washington, D.C.: Guff Green, 1828), 3:177–178.

3. *Journal of the Executive Proceedings of the Senate,* 3:244.

Sixteenth Congress
March 4, 1819, to March 3, 1821

First session—December 6, 1819, to May 15, 1820
Second session—November 13, 1820, to March 3, 1821
(First administration of James Monroe, 1817–1821)

Historical Background

Throughout 1819, the issue of slavery remained at the forefront of American consciousness. The debate between proslavery and antislavery factions in Congress over the admission of Missouri to the Union thrust the nation into the first sustained discussion of the issue. The Missouri Compromise of March 1820 provided for the admission of Maine as a free state, authorized Missouri to form a constitution with no restriction on slavery, and barred slavery from the rest of the Louisiana Territory north of 36° 30' latitude. The compromise, as historians have noted, ended the debate over the extension of slavery "for almost a generation. The South obtained its immediate objective, with the prospect of Arkansas and Florida entering as slave states in the near future; the North secured the greater expanse of unsettled territory and maintained the principle of 1787, that Congress could keep slavery out of the Territories if it would."[1]

When the Missouri constitution was completed in July 1820, it contained a clause barring "free Negroes and mulattoes" from entering the state. This clause prompted a bitter debate, with northerners arguing that it violated Article IV, Section 2 of the U.S. Constitution, which declared that "the citizens of each State shall be entitled to the privileges and immunities of the citizens of the several States." Because blacks were already citizens in several states, northern members of Congress threatened to exclude Missouri from the Union until the clause was eliminated. Finally, early in 1821, Henry Clay

offered a resolution requiring the Missouri legislature to make a "solemn" promise that it would not enact any law excluding any citizen "from the enjoyment of any of the privileges and immunities" to which they were entitled under the Constitution. Missouri was formally admitted as a state on August 10, 1821. Alabama had been admitted to the Union in December 1819.

A less animated, yet sharp, debate during the Sixteenth Congress focused on the terms under which western lands should be sold. Easy credit for purchasers, coupled with the Panic of 1819, made Congress anxious to end a land policy that had left the federal government holding $21 million in land debt. Although the Public Land Act of 1820 allowed settlers to purchase smaller parcels and reduced the minimum price per acre by 37.5 percent, the requirement that all future land sales be made in cash made acquisition of public land more difficult for most settlers. Passage of the Relief Act of 1821, following twelve weeks of debate, afforded debtors a variety of generous financial terms for paying off earlier public land purchases.

"The most significant event of Monroe's administration," it has been argued, "was passage of the Tenure of Office Act of 1820, which opened the door to the spoils system." This act fixed the term of a significant number of federal officials at four years. Although the intent of the law was to constrain presidential power, in practice it allowed presidents to use their appointment and removal power liberally upon entering office. Monroe, as well as his immediate predecessor, Thomas Jefferson, foresaw the disastrous consequences of the act and "warned against intrigue and corruption that would result from this legislation, which changed the earlier Federal practice of permitting administrative and executive officials, except Cabinet officers, to serve during good behavior, as distinct from elective officers who served fixed terms."[2]

Despite the animosity surrounding debate over the admission of Missouri, and rumors that a new political party might be on the horizon, President Monroe was renominated and nearly unanimously elected to a second term. Monroe received 231 electoral votes to 1 for Secretary of State John Quincy Adams. Vice President Daniel D. Tompkins was reelected with 218 votes.

Major Acts

Alabama Admitted to the Union. Accepted the constitution and state government formed by an Alabama Territory convention on August 2, 1819, and declared that the state of Alabama was one of the "United States of America, and admitted into the Union on an equal footing with the original States." Approved December 14, 1819 (3 Stat. 608).

Maine Admitted to the Union. Accepted the action of the state of Massachusetts in separating the "district of Maine from Massachusetts proper, and forming the same into a separate and independent state," and the action of Maine in forming "themselves into an independent state" and "establishing a constitution." Declared that the state of Maine was one of the "United States of America, and admitted into the Union on an equal footing with the original states" effective March 15, 1820. Approved March 3, 1820 (3 Stat. 544).

Missouri Compromise of 1820. Authorized the inhabitants of Missouri to "form a constitution and state government," and stipulated that slavery was "forever prohibited" in the remainder of the Louisiana Territory north of 36° 30' north latitude, except in the state of Missouri. Approved March 6, 1820 (3 Stat. 545–548). Certain provisions of the Missouri Compromise were subsequently held unconstitutional in *Scott v. Sandford,* 19 How. (60 U.S. 393 [1857]). *(Kansas-Nebraska Act, p. 92)*

Public Land Act of 1820. Stipulated that all public land purchases would have to be paid for in cash after July 1, 1820; reduced the minimum price per acre from $2.00 to $1.25; and provided for the sale of a minimum tract of 80 acres instead of 160. Approved April 24, 1820 (3 Stat. 566–567).

Tenure of Office Act of 1820 (Four Years' Law). Limited the term of office of "all district attorneys, collectors of customs, naval officers and surveyors of the customs, navy agents, receivers of public moneys for lands, registers of the land offices, paymasters in the army, the apothecary general, the assistant apothecaries general, and the commissary general of purchases," to a four-year term. Approved May 15, 1820 (3 Stat. 582).

Land Act of 1821 (Relief Act). Provided that a public land debtor could give up part of his land to complete payment on the rest. Extended the credit of public land debtors for four, six, or eight years, depending on the amount of purchase money the debtor had initially paid—the smaller the payment, the longer the credit terms. Debtors who completed payment of their land in cash prior to September 21, 1821, were given a 37.5 percent discount—which equaled the difference between the old minimum cost of $2.00 per acre and the new cost of $1.25. Approved March 2, 1821 (3 Stat. 612–614).

Second Missouri Compromise; Missouri Admitted to the Union. Declared that the state of Missouri would not become one of the "United States of America, and admitted into the Union on an equal footing with the original States," until it agreed that nothing in its constitution could be interpreted as abridging the "privileges and immunities" to which any citizen was entitled under the Constitution of the United States. Approved March 2, 1821 (3 Stat. 645). On August 10, 1821, President Monroe issued a proclamation announcing that the state of Missouri had "assented to the condition prescribed by Congress" and had been admitted to the Union (3 Stat. 797, Appendix II).

Notes

1. Samuel Eliot Morison, Henry Steele Commager, and William E. Leuchtenburg, *The Growth of the American Republic,* 7th ed. (New York: Oxford University Press, 1980), 1:398.

2. *Biography of an Ideal: A History of the Federal Civil Service* (Washington, D.C.: U.S. Office of Personnel Management, U.S. Civil Service Commission, 2003), 181.

Seventeenth Congress
March 4, 1821, to March 3, 1823

First session—December 3, 1821, to May 8, 1822
Second session—December 2, 1822, to March 3, 1823
(Second administration of James Monroe, 1821–1825)

Historical Background

Partisan politics reemerged in the Seventeenth Congress. During the election of 1820, James Monroe had run virtually unopposed. By December 1821, John Quincy Adams, Henry Clay, John C. Calhoun, William H. Crawford, and Andrew Jackson had all announced their candidacies to succeed Monroe three years hence. The Monroe administration, and particularly Secretary of State Adams and Secretary of War Calhoun, came under increasing criticism from supporters of Clay, Crawford, and Jackson. When it subsequently became apparent that President Monroe would not support the candidacy of Treasury Secretary Crawford, Crawford also ceased to lend his support to administration policies on Capitol Hill. Amidst this political unrest, the Era of Good Feelings began to wane.

After American acquisition of Florida under the Adams-Onis (Transcontinental) Treaty in February 1821, Congress approved a territorial government for Florida. Ratification of the treaty also removed a major obstacle to formal recognition of several Latin American states that had recently gained independence. On March 8, 1822, President Monroe sent a special message recommending that Congress and the executive branch work together in extending recognition to five new Latin American states. Two months later, Congress responded with a $100,000 appropriation for diplomatic missions to each.

A protracted lobbying effort by private fur traders and fur companies, as well as legislators from frontier states, culminated in May 1822 in the abolition of the trading house system, which had been established at the request of President George Washington in 1795. Washington saw the system as a way to exclude the Spanish and English from Indian trade by offering cheaper and better goods.

The first significant federal land grant for roads was made in 1823, when Congress gave Ohio a 120-foot right-of-way for a public road from Maumee to the Western Reserve. To defray the costs of construction, the act allowed for much of the adjacent 60,000 acres to be sold to the public.

Major Acts

Establishment of Territorial Government for Florida. Created the Florida Territory and established a territorial government consisting of a territorial governor appointed for three years and a territorial secretary appointed for four years who would act as governor in the case of the death, removal, resignation, or absence of the governor. Vested legislative power in the governor and a thirteen-member legislative council appointed annually by the president and judicial power in two superior courts, inferior courts, and justices of the peace. Prohibited importation of slaves into the territory. Provided that citizens of the territory were to be represented by one delegate to Congress. Approved March 30, 1822 (3 Stat. 654–659). A year later, this act was rewritten with three major additions: (1) bills approved by the legislative council were made subject to approval or veto by the governor, (2) two attorneys would represent East and West Florida, respectively, and a marshal was to be appointed for each of the territory's two superior courts, and (3) revenue laws of the United States were to have effect in the territory. Approved March 3, 1823 (3 Stat. 750–754).

Latin American Republics Act. Appropriated $100,000 for diplomatic missions to certain Latin American republics (Argentina, Chile, Colombia, Mexico, and Peru) recently rendered independent of their former domination by European powers. Approved May 4, 1822 (3 Stat. 678).

Indian Trading Houses Abolished. Authorized and required the president to close Indian trading houses and settle the accounts of the superintendent of Indian trade. Approved May 6, 1822 (3 Stat. 679–680).

Maumee Road Act. Authorized the state of Ohio "to lay out, open and construct a road from the Lower Rapids of the Miami of Lake Erie, to the western boundary of the Connecticut Western Reserve." Granted to the state all public lands for one mile on each side of the road to finance construction of the road. Required that the land not be sold for less than $1.25 an acre. (Originally the land had been ceded to the United States by the Chippewa, Ottawa, and other tribes in the Treaty of Brownstown of November 25, 1808). Approved February 28, 1823 (3 Stat. 727–728).

Eighteenth Congress
March 4, 1823, to March 3, 1825

First session—December 1, 1823, to May 27, 1824
Second session—December 6, 1824, to March 3, 1825
(Second administration of James Monroe, 1821–1825)

Historical Background

As the possibility of European intervention in Latin America and Russian expansion into the Oregon Territory grew stronger in 1823, President James Monroe consulted with former presidents Thomas Jefferson and James Madison, as well as his cabinet, on an appropriate American response. Ultimately, Monroe chose to issue a policy statement that was included in his annual message of December 2. The Monroe Doctrine declared that (1) the American continents should "henceforth not be considered as subjects for future colonization by any European power," (2) any attempt on the part of these powers to interfere in the affairs of the Western Hemisphere would be regarded "as dangerous to our peace and safety," and (3) the United States had not and would not interfere in the affairs of European nations.[1] Although Monroe did not know it at the time, British opposition to intervention had already largely forestalled such intentions by other European countries. Monroe's pronouncement was favorably received by the American press, but it aroused little sustained attention abroad. In time, however, it would become a fundamental tenet of American foreign policy. With the threat of war behind them, the members of the Eighteenth Congress turned to domestic concerns.

On March 30–31, 1824, House Speaker Henry Clay proposed the adoption of a "genuine American system" that would expand American markets and lessen the nation's dependence upon foreign goods.[2] Protective tariffs and a government-sponsored system of internal improvements were seen as the foundation of the "American system." Clay worked with unrestrained enthusiasm to convince Congress of the need for both initiatives.

The Supreme Court's ruling in *Gibbons v. Ogden* (22 U.S. 1 [1824] vastly expanded the powers of Congress through a single clause in the Constitution: the Commerce Clause of Article I, Section 8. The Court's landmark decision established the federal government's power to regulate any aspect of interstate commerce, including any mode of transportation, and that such regulation preempted conflicting regulation by the states. Since *Gibbons,* the Commerce Clause has provided the basis for sweeping congressional power over a multitude of national issues, including navigable rivers.

Within weeks of the Court's decision, two significant authorizations were passed that marked the real beginning of the federal navigation public works projects. The first authorized the president to make "the necessary surveys, plans, and estimates" of roads and canals deemed to be of national importance. The second authorization provided for the improvement of navigation on the Ohio and Mississippi Rivers. Since 1824, almost every Congress has passed at least one act to provide for the improvement of America's waterways. A stormy debate over whether Congress had constitutional authority to construct internal improvements preceded passage of the General Survey Act. President Monroe signed the survey act on the grounds that it called for the collection of information and not the construction of national internal improvements.

The Protective Tariff of 1824, the most critical ingredient of Clay's "American system," was depicted as the means for uniting the entire nation in a common purpose. No constitutional obstacles existed to a protective tariff, he passionately reminded his House colleagues, because the Constitution clearly granted the power to regulate interstate and foreign commerce. Following another lengthy debate, both the House and Senate, in close votes, concurred, as did President Monroe, who had recommended higher protective duties in his 1821, 1822, and 1823 annual messages.

Politics in 1824 was otherwise dominated by the four-candidate struggle to succeed Monroe. Because of the widespread fragmentation of the electoral vote, none of the three leading candidates—Andrew Jackson (ninety-nine votes), John Quincy Adams (eighty-four), and William H. Crawford (forty-one)—could claim a victory, even though Jackson had won a plurality of both popular and electoral votes. Under the Twelfth Amendment, the decision was made by the House of Representatives (choosing from the three candidates who received the most electoral votes) with each state having one vote. Although Clay, who had come in fourth (thirty-seven votes), was thus eliminated from House consideration, his decision to support Adams, coupled with his enormous influence in the House, was decisive. When the House voted on February 9, 1825, John Quincy Adams was chosen president on the first ballot with the votes of thirteen states. Jackson received the support of seven states and Crawford four. John C. Calhoun had been elected vice president with 182 electoral votes.

When Clay was selected as secretary of state shortly after the presidential election was settled, disappointed Jacksonians claimed the appointment was the result of a "Corrupt Bargain" and vowed to defeat Adams in four years. As the new president prepared to move to the White House, the birth of a two-party system had begun.

During the waning hours of the Eighteenth Congress, the Senate advised ratification of a treaty of peace with Russia. In the Russo-American Treaty, Russia accepted 54°40' north as the southern boundary of its territory in North America, and both countries agreed to a reciprocal right of trade along the entire northwest coast for 10 years.

Major Acts and Treaties

General Survey Act. Empowered the president to initiate the "necessary surveys, plans and estimates, to be made of the routes of such roads and canals as he may deem of national importance, in a commercial or military point of view, or necessary for the transportation of public mail." Approved April 30, 1824 (4 Stat. 22–23).

Tariff Act of 1824. Established, and thus raised, the rates on certain items, such as cotton goods, raw wool, and iron, at 37 percent. Approved May 22, 1824 (4 Stat. 25–30). *(Tariff Act of 1832, p. 64)*

First River and Harbors Act (1824). Appropriated $75,000 to improve navigation on the Ohio and Mississippi Rivers by removing sand bars, snags, and other obstacles. (This was the first inland river navigation bill enacted at the federal level, and the origin of the U.S. Army Corps of Engineers' responsibilities for navigation and water development programs.) Approved May 24, 1824 (4 Stat. 32–33).

Russo-American Treaty of 1824. Provided that the Pacific Ocean would be open to both countries for trade, fishing, and trade with the natives on those parts of the coast then unoccupied. Prohibited citizens from either country from proceeding to any place on the coast where there was a settlement of the other without consent of that government. Prohibited future American settlements north of 54°40', and Russian settlements south of 54°40'. Provided for a period of 10 years, ships of both countries would enjoy unrestricted fishing and trading with the natives along all parts of the northwest coast. Prohibited trade in arms and liquors. Concluded October 3, 1824 (8 Stat. 306–321). Ratification advised by the Senate March 3, 1825.[3]

Notes

1. *Annals of Congress,* 18th Cong., 1st sess., December 2, 1823 (Washington, D.C.: Printed by Gales and Seaton, 1856), 41:22.

2. *Annals of Congress,* 18th Cong., 1st sess., March 31, 1824 (Washington, D.C.: Printed by Gales and Seaton, 1856), 42:1978.

3. *Journal of the Executive Proceedings of the Senate* (Washington, D.C.: Printed by Duff Green, 1828), 8:424.

Nineteenth Congress
March 4, 1825, to March 3, 1827

First session—December 5, 1825, to May 22, 1826
Second session—December 4, 1826, to March 3, 1827
Special session of the Senate—March 4, 1825, to March
    9, 1825
(Administration of John Quincy Adams, 1825–1829)

Historical Background

Despite acknowledging in his inaugural address of March 4, 1825, that he was "less possessed of [public] confidence in advance than any of his predecessors," John Quincy Adams still felt that the "baneful weed of party strife" was a thing of the past. His optimistic annual message penned ten months later included proposals for a series of far-reaching measures. Adams called for significant internal improvements, a uniform system of weights and measures, establishment of a national university and an astronomical observatory, increased military preparedness, patent law reform, recognition of South American republics, a uniform bankruptcy law, funding for scientific explorations, surveys of natural resources, government support for the arts and sciences, and a new Department of the Interior. Unfortunately for Adams, his ideas did not enjoy broad support on Capitol Hill or elsewhere in the country. Twenty of the forty-six senators elected to the Nineteenth Congress opposed the Adams administration. In the House, the administration's party, the Democratic-Republicans, held only an eight-vote majority (105 to 97). Moreover, Vice President John C. Calhoun joined the opposition.

On December 26, 1825, Adams sent a special message to Congress stating his intention to send two delegates to the Panama Congress, called by Simón Bolívar,

to promote the unification of South America. Bolivar was the most charismatic leader to emerge during the Latin American struggle for independence from Spain. He led or directed successful military campaigns that liberated Venezuela, Colombia, Ecuador, Peru, and Bolivia. Adams's message immediately came under attack in the Senate, where a coalition led by Vice President Calhoun and Sen. Martin Van Buren of New York opposed the president's action on the grounds that the invitation had been accepted without consulting the Senate and that U.S. participation was not appropriate given the nation's tradition of remaining independent and neutral on such matters. A number of southern senators joined in opposition because slavery had been abolished in many Latin American countries and they feared an attack on U.S. slave interests by Latin American delegates. Ultimately, the Senate confirmed the nominations and approved the necessary appropriations for the two envoys to attend the conference, but neither diplomat participated in the proceedings. One American delegate died en route; the other arrived after the conference had adjourned.

Thanks to his earlier success as James Monroe's secretary of state for eight years, most of the foreign policy issues John Quincy Adams would have faced had been resolved by the time he became president. He had already secured the disarmament of the Great Lakes, fishing rights off the coast of Canada, a U.S.-Canadian boundary, the accession of Florida, and a U.S.-Spanish border west of the Mississippi River giving America strong claim to the Pacific Coast in the Northwest. These were all issues that previously had brought the nation into open conflict with Britain.

As president, John Quincy Adams devoted much of his attention to obtaining commercial agreements with other nations. During his four years in the White House,

Adams and his Secretary of State Henry Clay "concluded nine general commercial treaties, more than in any comparable period prior to the Civil War. Together, they preserved, against strong foreign dissatisfaction, earlier arrangements with Britain, France, and the Netherlands; and they initiated the successful negotiations with Austria, Turkey, and Mexico completed early" in the administration of his successor, Andrew Jackson.[1]

As historian Samuel Flagg Bemis observed, Congress paid little attention to Adams's other legislative initiatives. It was only willing to "pass small bills for particular projects here and there," to continue voting funds for the Cumberland Road, and to make "land grants to or subscribe unsystematically for stock in various canal companies." All of Adams's major proposals "remained unacted on in Congress and were the laughingstock of the opposition press."[2]

Major Act

Mission at Congress of Panama. Appropriated $18,000 for two envoys extraordinary and ministers plenipotentiary to attend the Panama Conference of 1826. Approved May 4, 1826 (4 Stat. 158).

Notes

1. Mary W. M. Hargreaves, *The Presidency of John Quincy Adams* (Lawrence, Kan.: University Press of Kansas, 1985), 89. See also Robert V. Remini, *John Quincy Adams* (New York: Times Books, 2002), 104.

2. Samuel Flagg Bemis, *John Quincy Adams and the Union* (New York: Alfred A. Knopf, 1956), 75–76.

Twentieth Congress
March 4, 1827, to March 3, 1829

First session—December 3, 1827, to May 26, 1828
Second session—December 1, 1828, to March 3, 1829
(Administration of John Quincy Adams, 1825–1829)

Historical Background

By the onset of the Twentieth Congress, anti-administration Jacksonians controlled both houses of Congress. Following the congressional elections of 1826, administration supporters were outnumbered in the Senate 28 to 20 and in the House 119 to 94. Jacksonian supporters embarked on a vigorous campaign to secure the popular vote of the critical states needed to ensure victory in the 1828 presidential election. Critical to this effort was the ability of Jacksonians in Congress to draft a tariff bill that would satisfy the manufacturers and farmers of the northern and Middle Atlantic states, who advocated higher protectionist tariffs, and southerners, who generally opposed all tariffs.

The bill that emerged from the House Committee on Manufactures on January 31, 1828, imposed exceedingly high tariffs on most imported raw materials as well as on imported manufactures that competed with similar goods produced domestically. Lower duties were placed on woolen goods that New England manufacturers felt needed greater protection. Jacksonians assumed that their "Tariff of Abominations" was too extreme to pass, but that the gesture would satisfy protectionist interests of the Middle Atlantic states and guarantee their electoral votes. Even the drafters of the bill were surprised when New Englanders, after gaining an increase in the duty on woolen imports, joined with Jacksonians of the western and Middle Atlantic states in approving the tariff. In signing the Tariff of Abominations in May 1828, John Quincy Adams provided a pivotal issue to the presidential campaign that would elevate Andrew Jackson to the White House a few months later. Jackson received 178 electoral votes; Adams, 83. John C. Calhoun was reelected vice president with 171 electoral votes.

At the beginning of his presidency, Adams in his first annual message to Congress presented an ambitious program for the creation of a national market that included roads, canals, a national university, a national astronomical observatory, and other initiatives. Even his supporters had trouble with his proposals, and critics challenged the supposed arrogance of a president who had been narrowly elected by the House and was not entitled to act as though he had received a national mandate for action. Despite Adams's obvious political weakness, he was able to sign several dozen bills that provided funding for canal construction, river and harbor development, road improvements, and lighthouse preservation, which at least partially reflected his views on internal improvements. In addition, the Adams administration on its own was able to achieve considerable progress in support of harbor improvement and road and canal development by using military engineers for survey and construction operations, public land grants, and governmental subscription to corporate stock issues.

Major Act

Tariff of Abominations. Amended the tariff law by raising duties on imported goods in general to a rate of 41 percent, with special attention to cotton, woolens, iron, hemp, flax, wool, molasses, and sailcloth. Approved May 19, 1828 (4 Stat. 270–275).

Twenty-first Congress
March 4, 1829, to March 3, 1831

First session—December 7, 1829, to May 31, 1830
Second session—December 6, 1830, to March 3, 1831
Special session of the Senate—March 4, 1829, to March 17, 1829
(First administration of Andrew Jackson, 1829–1833)

Historical Background

Jacksonian Democrats captured the presidency and both houses of Congress in the 1828 elections, but their often conflicting state and sectional differences left it unclear as to how many members could be counted as firm supporters by the new administration. Toasts by President Andrew Jackson and Vice President John C. Calhoun at an April 1830 Jefferson Day dinner revealed their differing positions regarding Jackson's support for nationalism and Calhoun's devotion to states' rights. The breach, which ultimately resulted in a reorganization of the cabinet, was further exacerbated by the Eaton Affair, a society scandal that occupied much of Jackson's attention during his first two years in office. It stemmed from the refusal of the vice president's wife and the wives of three pro-Calhoun members of the cabinet to associate with Peggy Eaton, the wife of Secretary of War John H. Eaton. Prior to marrying the secretary of war, Mrs. Eaton, the daughter of a Georgetown tavern keeper and wife of a navy purser who was often at sea, had been the secretary's mistress. Reportedly distressed over the affair, the husband committed suicide while abroad, and the Eatons subsequently were married, at the urging of the president.

Few tangible insights regarding his intended policies were to be found in Jackson's inaugural address of March 4, 1829, the first to be delivered out of doors, at the Capitol, before a general audience. His first annual message nine months later was considerably more enlightening. On December 8, 1829, Jackson expressed a willingness to help American merchants, increase foreign trade, consider a reduction in the tariff, abolish the national debt, and approve a constitutional amendment allowing for the distribution of surplus revenues to the states once the debt was retired.

He also called attention to the government's "wholly incompatible" Indian policy. While "professing desire to civilize and settle them," the president declared, "we have at the same time lost no opportunity to purchase their lands and thrust them further into the wilderness." To resolve this contradiction, he proposed "an ample district west of the Mississippi" be provided to the Indian nations (tribes) in exchange for their holdings east of the Mississippi. Passage of the Indian Removal Act authorized the president to set aside western lands that might be used for the voluntary Indian emigration. Pressure for the removal of the Indians was strongest among land-hungry white settlers in the southeastern states.

Earlier in January 1830, one of Congress's most significant constitutional debates unfolded on the Senate floor. It began during consideration of a resolution offered by Sen. Samuel A. Foote of Connecticut to restrict temporarily the sale of public lands in the West, but it quickly became an emotional discussion on the nature of the Union. Sen. Thomas Hart Benton of Missouri denounced the Foote resolution as an attempt by northeastern interests to check the growth of the West. Sen. Robert Y. Hayne of South Carolina appealed to the West to revive its alliance with the South in denouncing the "selfish and unprincipled" attitude of the East, which favored federal intervention over states' rights.

Daniel Webster of Massachusetts responded in defense of the East, while condemning the senators who "habitually speak of the Union in terms of indifference, or even disparagement." As the debate continued, Hayne focused on a defense of state sovereignty and nullification. Webster emphasized that the people, not the states, created the Constitution, and the Supreme Court should be left to determine its meaning. Following the Webster-Hayne exchange, other senators periodically renewed the debate before the Foote resolution was finally tabled in late May 1830. Webster's remarks helped to momentarily forestall an alliance between southern and western legislators, but the issue of sectionalism later reemerged and grew increasingly troublesome.

Also in May 1830, a three member U.S. negotiating team appointed by President Andrew Jackson negotiated a navigation and commerce agreement between the United States and the Ottoman Empire, and signed the first treaty concluded by the United States with an Oriental state. The Senate advised ratification of the treaty in February 1831. That treaty, and a subsequent treaty signed in 1862, remained the basis of Ottoman-American relations until the First World War. In a separate action, the president was authorized to reopen trade between the United States and the British West Indies, which had been closed since 1826.

Near the end of the first session of the Twenty-first Congress, President Jackson vetoed a bill authorizing federal funds for the construction of a sixty-mile road between Maysville and Lexington, Kentucky. He argued that the measure was unconstitutional because it benefited a single state instead of the entire nation. Once again, Jackson emphasized in his May 1830 veto message that if Congress wanted to subsidize roads and canals, it should sanction them through a constitutional amendment.

Congress passed the Preemption Act of 1830 to protect settlers from the land speculators and claim jumpers, who had become an increasing menace in the West. By bowing to public pressure, Congress was able in essence to pardon pioneers who had settled on public lands before they could be surveyed and auctioned by the government. The act protected squatters by guaranteeing them both the right to claim land before it was surveyed, and to buy land upon which they had settled.

Extensive lobbying by Noah Webster, the American pioneer lexicographer and scholar, resulted in the first major revision of U.S. copyright law since 1790. The 1831 Copyright Act, doubling the length of time during which protection was afforded a copyright holder, allowed for a copyright to be extended by the family of an author who had died, and added music as one of the protected forms of art.

Major Acts and Treaties

Indian Removal Act. Called for the general resettlement of all Indians to lands west of the Mississippi River. Appropriated $500,000 to compensate the Indians and pay the costs of resettlement. Approved May 28, 1830 (4 Stat. 411–412).

Reciprocity Act of 1830. Authorized the president to open the ports of the United States when British colonial ports were opened to American vessels without discrimination. Approved May 29, 1830 (4 Stat. 419–420).

Preemption Act of 1830. Authorized settlers who occupied and cultivated public lands during 1829 to purchase up to 160 acres of that land at $1.25 per acre. Provided that in those instances when two settlers occupied the same quarter section, each would be able to purchase a half-quarter. Approved May 29, 1830 (4 Stat. 420–421).

Ottoman-American Treaty of Commerce and Navigation. Granted most favored nation treatment to merchants of each country with respect to duties, and other imposts." Assured American merchant vessels safe passage to and from Turkey. Allowed for each nation to open consulates. Accorded American citizens and Ottoman subjects with American passports personal immunity, and protected their property against the jurisdiction of the Ottoman courts. Allowed American missionaries to establish missions, schools, and hospitals in the Empire. Concluded May 7, 1830 (8 Stat. 408-409). Ratification advised by the Senate February 2, 1831.[1]

1831 Revision of the Copyright Act. Amended the Copyright Act of 1790 by doubling the term of a copyright from fourteen to twenty-eight years through a renewal process, and allowed copyright renewals by widows and children of deceased authors, inventors, designers, and engravers. Approved February 3, 1831 (4 Stat. 436–439). *(First Copyright Law, p. 13)*

Note

1. *Journal of the Executive Proceedings of the Senate* (Washington, D.C.: U.S. Government Printing Office, 1887), 4:149–150.

Twenty-second Congress
March 4, 1831, to March 3, 1833

First session—December 5, 1831, to July 16, 1832
Second session—December 3, 1832, to March 2, 1833
(First administration of Andrew Jackson, 1829–1833)

Historical Background

By the time the Twenty-second Congress convened, all of Andrew Jackson's original cabinet, with the exception of Postmaster General William T. Berry, had resigned or been replaced in the aftermath of the Eaton Affair. The Eaton Affair also cost the already politically isolated Vice President John C. Calhoun whatever chance he may have had of being anointed as Jackson's likely successor. That prize would ultimately go to Secretary of State Martin Van Buren, the lone member of the cabinet to socialize with the Eatons. Van Buren's solution to the Eaton Affair (asking for the resignation of the offending cabinet members and offering his own), and Calhoun's tie-breaking vote in the Senate rejecting Van Buren's subsequent nomination as minister to Great Britain, virtually assured his selection as Jackson's new running mate in 1832. Van Buren would win the vice presidency with 189 electoral votes.

Early in 1832, Congress began reconsidering two volatile political issues: a revision of the Tariff of Abominations (1828) and renewing the charter of the Bank of the United States. With the passage of the Tariff of 1832, President Jackson hoped for a short respite, but his July 10 veto of the bank rechartering bill led to a political firestorm.

Jackson's veto message, considered by many to be the most significant cast by any president, cited economic, political, social, and nationalist, as well as constitutional, arguments for rejecting the rechartering. "In effect," Jackson historian Robert V. Remini explains,

"it claimed for the President, the right to participate in the legislative process." With it, Jackson invaded what had been the "exclusive province of Congress."[1] Despite outraged responses by Henry Clay and Daniel Webster on the Senate floor, a July 13 attempt to override the veto failed. The issue of the bank, however, continued to remain at the forefront of public consciousness throughout the 1832 presidential election. Henry Clay unsuccessfully sought to use the veto as a principal reason for denying Jackson a second term. Although Jackson (with 219 electoral votes) would soundly defeat Clay (49), neither the president nor Congress had finished the debate over the bank.

Following Congress's summer recess, Jackson watched from his home in Tennessee as southern outrage over the Tariff of 1832 gained momentum. In November, a convention of South Carolina nullifiers meeting in Columbia passed an Ordinance of Nullification, which declared the tariff laws of 1828 and 1832 unconstitutional, null and void, and not binding on the state after February 1, 1833. The ordinance further asserted that if the federal government attempted to require the state to enforce payment of the duties, South Carolina would consider secession from the Union. During the next three months, the legislatures of Georgia, Mississippi, and Virginia also protested the tariff.

President Jackson was both conciliatory and firm. He called for a substantial reduction of tariff duties in his annual message of December 4, 1832, but he rejected nullification as well as secession in a December 10 proclamation to the people of South Carolina. Jackson's strongly worded proclamation declared that federal law was supreme and that any nullification of it by a state would be an act of rebellion. On January 16, 1833, Jackson asked Congress to pass the Force Bill, authorizing the president to use the military to enforce the revenue laws and put down any possible rebellion.

On March 1, the Force Bill was ready for the president's signature. The same day, a compromise tariff bill introduced by Sen. Henry Clay, which had been drafted in consultation with newly elected senator Calhoun of South Carolina (who had resigned as vice president the previous December), was also approved. With passage of these two acts the nullification debate concluded.

The first act of Congress to protect a natural resource was signed by President Andrew Jackson in April 1832. This enactment reserved four parcels of land with hot mineral springs in Arkansas Territory at Hot Springs for the public benefit. This protective act predated the establishment of Yellowstone National Park by four decades. Revisions to the patent law broadened the privilege to include two new categories of inventors in mid-1832: inventors who initially had inadvertently failed to comply with legal formalities of obtaining a patent, and alien inventors who had declared the intention to become a citizen.

On the diplomatic front, in July 1832 the Senate ratified a treaty that resolved many of the major diplomatic difficulties between the United States and France. It addressed both claims against the French government by U.S. citizens dating back to the Napoleonic Wars and French counterclaims based on alleged U.S. violations of a commercial clause in the Louisiana Purchase. A more than casual observer of these proceedings was former president John Quincy Adams, who in December 1831 had returned to Washington as a newly elected member of the House from the state of Massachusetts. He would serve for the next eight Congresses. Adams remains the only chief executive to serve in the House after being president.

Major Acts and Treaties

Tariff Act of 1832. Amended tariff law by lowering duties on many imported goods to a level slightly below that required by the Tariff Act of 1824. Approved July 14, 1832 (4 Stat. 583–594). *(Tariff Act of 1824, p. 56)*

Treaty Providing for the Final Settlement of Napoleonic Wars Spoliation Claims. Provided that France would pay 25 million francs and the United States 1.5 million francs for spoliations committed against the subjects of each nation during the Napoleonic wars. Concluded July 4, 1831 (8 Stat. 430–433). Ratification advised by the Senate January 27, 1832.[2]

First Protection for a Natural Resource. Set aside the thermal springs at Hot Springs, Arkansas, as a federal reservation "for the future disposal by the United States, and are not to be entered, pre-empted or appropriated for any other purpose whatever." Approved April 20, 1832 (4 Stat. 505).

Patent Acts of 1832. Provided the opportunity for a new patent to be issued in cases where a patent had become "invalid or inoperative" because an inventor had, "by inadvertence, accident, or mistake, and without any fraudulent or deceptive intention," not complied with the terms and conditions of patent law. Approved July 3, 1832 (4 Stat. 559). Expanded the category of potential patentees to cover all resident aliens who had declared an intention to become citizens of the United States, but required them "to introduce into public use in the United States the invention or improvement" within one year. Stipulated that patents granted to aliens would become void if the patentee failed to become a citizen of the United States as soon as they were entitled to under the law. Approved July 13, 1832 (4 Stat. 577).

Compromise Tariff of 1833. Amended tariff law by adding many imported items to the free list and provided for gradual reduction of duties above 20 percent until 1842 when all duties would be 20 percent. Approved March 2, 1833 (4 Stat. 629–631).

Force Bill. Authorized the president to use the army and the navy, if necessary, in the execution of revenue laws and in the collection of customs duties. Approved March 2, 1833 (4 Stat. 632–635).

Notes

1. Robert V. Remini, *The Life of Andrew Jackson* (New York: Harper and Row, 1988), 230.
2. *Journal of the Executive Proceedings of the Senate* (Washington, D.C.: U.S. Government Printing Office, 1887), 4:205.

Twenty-third Congress
March 4, 1833, to March 3, 1835

First session—December 2, 1833, to June 30, 1834
Second session—December 1, 1834, to March 3, 1835
(Second administration of Andrew Jackson, 1833–1837)

Historical Background

The ramifications of President Andrew Jackson's veto of the bill rechartering the Bank of the United States extended well beyond the 1832 presidential election. Jackson believed his resounding electoral victory provided him a popular mandate to sever the relationship between the federal government and the bank. In March 1833, the House unsuccessfully sought to temper the president's action by resolving that federal deposits might "be safely continued in the Bank of the United States," but to no avail. When two successive secretaries of the Treasury—Louis McLane and William J. Duane—refused to support the president's decision to transfer federal deposits to selected state banks, called "pet banks," Jackson appointed Attorney General Roger B. Taney as secretary of the Treasury. That autumn, Taney issued an order setting the president's plan in motion.

Financial panic quickly spread throughout the nation as the Bank of the United States retaliated by drastically curtailing its loans. The stage was set for a monumental political battle when the Twenty-third Congress convened. On December 11, 1833, the Senate, by a vote of 23 to 18, called upon President Jackson to submit a copy of a paper drafted by Taney that he had read to the cabinet listing the reasons that federal funds should be withdrawn from the bank. When Jackson refused the request on the grounds that it was an unconstitutional encroachment on the executive, Sen. Henry Clay of Kentucky introduced two censure resolutions. The first, which criticized the actions of Secretary Taney, was approved

on February 5, 1834. The second, adopted on March 28, 1834, charged the president with assuming "authority and powers not conferred by the Constitution and laws." (After repeated efforts, the Democrats finally were able to muster enough votes in January 1837 to expunge Jackson's censure from the record shortly before he left office.)

Within a week of Jackson's censure, the Democrat-controlled House registered its approval of the president's action. Jackson's own response was predictable: He sent a protest message to the Senate on April 15 and within a week also proposed a series of banking and currency reforms. The Coinage Act of 1834, the only one of his reform measures to be quickly adopted, was signed into law on June 28. It reduced the exchange rate of gold to silver to better reflect the intrinsic value of coins in circulation. The change, it was believed, would draw more gold back into circulation.

On June 30, 1834, a significant date in the history of Indian legislation and creation of Indian policy, two comprehensive statutes were signed into law that form the fabric of law on Indian affairs. The first was the final act, in a series of acts, "to regulate trade and commerce with the Indian Tribes." The second established an Office of Indian Affairs within the War Department to meet the changing conditions that the president had outlined in his 1833 annual message. A $25,000 appropriation was also approved that June to purchase George Washington's personal papers and books, an acquisition that would complete the government's records.

Major Acts

Coinage Act of 1834. Regulated and standardized the coinage of the United States and changed the ratio of silver and gold from 15 to 1 to 16 to 1. Approved June 28, 1834 (4 Stat. 699–700).

Purchase of the Books and Papers of George Washington. Appropriated $25,000 for the "Secretary of State to purchase the manuscript papers and a portion of the printed books of General George Washington" so that they might be deposited and preserved in the Department of State, under regulations prescribed by the secretary. Approved June 30, 1834 (4 Stat. 712).

Indian Trade and Intercourse Act of 1834. Defined Indian territory. Established specific requirements governing Indian trading licenses, bonding procedures, seizure of goods from persons violating the regulations, regulations governing sales and purchases from Indians (including alcohol), and guidelines for issuing passports to Indian country. Forbade the sale or conveyance of Indian land without prior approval from the Indian office. Restricted carrying and making communications to and from Indian country that would violate any treaty or other law of the United States, or arouse hostilities. Banned the sale of alcohol in the territory. Approved June 30, 1834 (4 Stat. 729–735).

1834 Indian Reorganization Act. Provided for the organization of an office of Indian affairs within the Department of War. Established a system of regional and local agents responsible for dealing with the Indian tribes, and systematic accounting procedures for the office in order to eliminate the confusion and embarrassment that had frequently arisen in financial matters relating to Indian affairs. Authorized the president to issue licenses to foreign traders. Authorized the War Department to take military measures to prevent wars between tribes. Approved June 30, 1834 (4 Stat. 735–738).

Twenty-fourth Congress
March 4, 1835, to March 3, 1837

First session—December 7, 1835, to July 4, 1836
Second session—December 5, 1836, to March 3, 1837
(Second administration of Andrew Jackson, 1833–1837)

Historical Background

At the outset of the Twenty-fourth Congress, the Whigs emerged for the first time as a formidable opposition in both houses of Congress. The Democrats held only a two seat (27–25) advantage in the Senate, while Whigs in the House held a sizable minority of 98 seats to the Democrats' 145. The Whig movement began in earnest with Kentucky senator Henry Clay's emergence as the leader of anti-Jackson forces in Congress. This new political coalition included National Republicans, champions of tariff protection, supporters of internal improvements, advocates of a national bank, nullifiers, states' righters, and those who saw Andrew Jackson as a dictator.

One of the several challenges facing this diverse political mixture was the need for a regulatory structure to monitor the state banks that had replaced the Bank of the United States as depositories of government funds. The Deposit Act, enacted in June 1836, required the secretary of the Treasury to designate at least one bank in each state and territory as a place of public deposit. In addition, beginning on January 1, 1837, all surplus government revenues over $5 million had to be distributed as loans among the states, in proportion to their representation in Congress.

As the summer of 1836 progressed, President Jackson became increasingly concerned about the dramatic increase in the sale of public lands that had brought on a land boom and threatened to destabilize the nation's banks. On July 11, Jackson ordered Treasury secretary Levi Woodbury to issue a Species Circular announcing that only gold or silver could be used to pay for public lands. In subsequent months, supporters of the president credited Jackson's action with having saved many western investors from bankruptcy. Some scholars claim that the circular caused the Panic of 1837, which lasted for several years after Jackson retired from the presidency. Others have attributed the panic to international economic forces.

A less controversial reform pushed by the Jackson administration was the Post Office Act of 1836. Postmaster General Amos Kendall worked closely with Congress in developing a department that could meet the growing needs of the nation. During the previous two decades, the number of local post offices had grown more than threefold from 3,200 in 1816 to 11,091 in 1836, while postal revenues more than tripled. The act also spelled out punishment for postmasters who deliberately detained the delivery of mail. This provision was a response to a controversy over the mailing and delivery of abolitionist tracts in slave states. Earlier in the session the Senate began the practice of immediately rejecting all petitions from northern antislavery groups, and the House adopted a gag rule to table all such petitions. The gag rule was rescinded in December 1844, after northern Democratic support dissipated.

On December 17, 1835, President Andrew Jackson, in a message to Congress, announced that an Englishman named James Smithson had bequeathed to the United States a substantial amount of money for the purpose of founding "at Washington an establishment under the name of the Smithsonian Institution for the increase and diffusion of knowledge among men." Six months later, the president signed legislation authorizing him to appoint an agent to prosecute the right of the United States to the Smithsonian legacy.

Also in 1836, a major review of the U.S. patent law was undertaken in response to complaints about patents being granted for things that were neither new nor original. Under the revised Patent Act of 1836, the Patent Office became a separate bureau in the State Department with a commissioner of patents in charge. Although frequently amended and revised, this act founded the American patent system and was an important step in bringing a semblance of order to the granting of patents.

Nearly a half century after enactment of the nation's first coinage act, the first major revisions in American coinage established a uniform fineness and weight for gold and silver coins. It also prescribed the mottoes and devices that should be placed upon the coins of the United States. This latter provision meant that the mint could make no changes without the enactment of additional legislation by the Congress.

The Twenty-fourth Congress increased the size of the Supreme Court from seven to nine justices to meet the demands of the expanding nation, an action every president since James Madison had urged. President Jackson recognized the independence of the Republic of Texas in March 1837. This action was preceded by House and Senate adoption of resolutions calling for the recognition of Texas. Two new states—Arkansas (June 15, 1836) and Michigan (January 26, 1837)—were admitted to the Union. Congress initially provided for the admission of Michigan in June 1836, but it insisted that an unsettled boundary dispute with Ohio must first be resolved. In December 1836, a Michigan convention agreed to the terms proposed by Congress and admission followed a month later.

The Whig Party emerged as a major challenger to the Democrats in the 1836 presidential election. Vice President Martin Van Buren, the Democratic candidate, was challenged by three Whig candidates—William Henry Harrison, his major opponent in the North and West; Hugh L. White, whose votes were in the South and the Southwest; and Daniel Webster, who attracted support in New England. The Whigs hoped that their multiple candidates would prevent Van Buren from obtaining a majority and that the election would then be decided by the House of Representatives. Van Buren, however, easily outdistanced all of the Whigs. (Van Buren received 170 electoral votes; Harrison, 73; White, 26; and Webster, 14.)

None of the four candidates for vice president received a majority of the electoral vote. Richard M. Johnson, the Democratic candidate, received 147 electoral votes, Whig candidates Francis Granger and John Tyler received 77 and 47 votes, respectively, and Independent Democrat William Smith received 23 votes. As a consequence, for the only time in American history, the election for vice president, as prescribed by the Constitution (Twelfth Amendment), was left to the U.S. Senate, which on February 8, 1837, chose Johnson (33 votes) over his leading rival, Granger (16 votes). In the congressional elections, the Whigs lost seven Senate seats, and the Democrats lost thirty-seven House seats although they retained a nominal majority. An additional twenty-four seats went to minor parties.

The 1836 elections marked a decisive turning point in the development of American politics. For the first time in the nation's history, "a truly national two-party system was inaugurated." This era lasted only "about twenty years, or until strong regional attitudes and the death of the Whig party restored an essentially sectional party system to the United States. At that point one-party states and sections would reemerge, but they would never again be as strong as before 1836."[1]

Major Acts

Clayton Act (Established Northern Boundary of Ohio). Declared that the northern boundary of Ohio be established at a "direct line from the southern extremity of Lake Michigan, to the most northerly cape of the Maumee (Miami) bay and that, after the line" is drawn, it shall intersect the eastern boundary line of the state of Indiana. Approved June 15, 1836 (5 Stat. 49–50).

Arkansas Admitted to the Union. Accepted the constitution and state government formed by an Arkansas Territory convention on January 30, 1836, and declared that the state of Arkansas was one of the "United States of America, and admitted into the Union on an equal footing with the original States." Approved June 15, 1836 (5 Stat. 50–52).

Deposit Act. Required the secretary of the Treasury to designate at least one bank in each state and territory as a place of public deposit of U.S. funds. Provided for the distribution of surplus revenue in excess of $5 million among the states, in proportion to their representation in the Senate and House of Representatives, as a loan subject to recall by the secretary of the Treasury. Approved June 23, 1836 (5 Stat. 52–56).

Congress Accepts Legacy Bequeathed by James Smithson. Authorized the president to appoint an agent or agents to pursue before the British courts "the right of the United States to the legacy bequeathed to them by the last will and testament of James Smithson," for the purpose of founding the Smithsonian Institution. Appropriated up to $10,000 to cover attendant expenses. Provided all funds received from the legacy be used to found and endow the Smithsonian Institution. Approved July 1, 1836 (5 Stat. 64). In December 1838, President Martin Van Buren reported to Congress that the bequest had been collected and deposited in the Treasury, and in August 1846, President James K. Polk signed the bill establishing the Smithsonian Institution according to the terms of the bequest. Approved August 10, 1846 (9 Stat. 102–106).

Post Office Act of 1836. Stipulated that postal revenues be paid into the Treasury and provided for the Post Office Department to receive appropriations from Congress. Specified the duties of the postmaster general. Created the positions of auditor and third assistant postmaster, and made provision for a number of additional clerks. Required that all proposals for transporting the mail be submitted in writing and that payment for such services would not be made until a contract was executed. Provided that appointment of all postmasters receiving an annual fee of more than $1,000 was subject to the "advice and consent" of the Senate. Specified penalties to be imposed on a postmaster who unlawfully detained "in his office any letter, package, pamphlet, or newspaper, with intent to prevent the arrival and delivery of the same." Approved July 2, 1836 (5 Stat. 80–90).

Patent Act of 1836. Established the U.S. Patent Office as a distinct and separate bureau in the Department of State, and authorized the appointment of a commissioner and examiners of patents. Required that applications for a patent include a drawing or model, be examined in the Patent Office, and be investigated before a patent was granted. When issued, a patent was good for 14 years, subject to an extension of 7 years. Appropriated $1,500 for the purchase of a library of scientific works and periodicals, both foreign and American. Approved July 4, 1836 (5 Stat. 117–125).

Coinage Act of 1837. Set forth the duties and increased the salaries of the officers of the United States Mint. Provided that "the standard for both gold and silver coins of the United States" was to be nine-tenths "pure medal" and one-tenth "alloy," and each coin minted should weigh a prescribed weight. Mandated that each coin struck at the United States Mint have on one side an impression emblematic of liberty with an inscription of the word "Liberty" and the year of the coinage, and that the reverse of gold and silver coins should have the representation of an eagle with the inscription "United States of America." Provided that the figure of the eagle be omitted from the reverse of the dime, half dime, cent, and half cent. Approved January 18, 1837 (5 Stat. 136–142).

Michigan Admitted to the Union. Acknowledged that a Michigan Territory convention on December 15, 1836, agreed to the northern boundary of the state of Ohio, and declared that the state of Michigan was one of the "United States of America, and admitted into the Union on an equal footing with the original States." Approved January 26, 1837 (5 Stat. 144).

Judiciary Act of 1837. Increased the number of Supreme Court justices from seven to nine and added two circuit courts. Approved March 3, 1837 (5 Stat. 176–178).

Note

1. Joel H. Silbey, "Election of 1836," in *History of American Political Elections 1789–1986*, ed. Arthur M. Schlesinger Jr. and Fred L. Israel (New York: Chelsea House Publishers, 1971), 1:599–600.

Twenty-fifth Congress
March 4, 1837, to March 3, 1839

First session—September 4, 1837, to October 16, 1837
Second session—December 4, 1837, to July 9, 1838
Third session—December 3, 1838, to March 3, 1839
Special session of the Senate—March 4, 1837, to March
    10, 1837
(Administration of Martin Van Buren, 1837–1841)

Historical Background

Soon after Martin Van Buren was inaugurated as president, New York banks suspended specie payments, which meant that an individual could no longer exchange paper money or bank notes for coin money. Nearly all of the nation's other banks quickly took similar action. The suspension action was precipitated in large part by a deepening commercial and financial panic that gripped the country. Bankruptcies were commonplace, unemployment was rising, farm prices were declining rapidly, and riots were breaking out among the poor. In response, President Van Buren issued a proclamation calling on the new Twenty-fifth Congress to meet in a special session on September 4, 1837, to consider the "great and weighty matters" that warranted their attention.[1] During the summer of 1837, Van Buren and his advisers had struggled to develop emergency measures that would both satisfy Democratic allies and quiet Whig critics.

Shortly after the special session convened, Van Buren sent Congress a message proposing that Treasury notes be issued to meet the immediate needs of the government, that a scheduled distribution of surplus state funds to state banks be postponed, that all government funds be withdrawn from the pet banks,

and that a federal subtreasury system be authorized to hold those funds. Congress agreed to the postponement of surplus fund distribution and authorized the issuance of $10 million in Treasury notes. A second issuance of Treasury notes totaling $5 million was subsequently approved. The Senate passed two different versions of an independent Treasury bill, in October 1837 and March 1838, but in each instance the House was unwilling to concur. Van Buren had to wait until July 1840 to see his request realized. By then it was too late to save his presidency.

By early 1838, signs of an improving economy emerged, and in April banks in New York announced resumption of specie payments. Other banks soon followed. In May, a bill sponsored by Whig senator Henry Clay repealing the Specie Circular (issued by the Jackson administration in 1836) was signed into law. Clay anticipated that the repeal would be of great symbolic importance as a rebuke to both the Jackson and Van Buren administrations. However, to his surprise, the resolution generated strong Democratic support.

Despite considerable southern opposition, Congress in 1838 created the Territory of Iowa. In 1839, in the aftermath of a tragic duel between Reps. William J. Graves of Kentucky and Jonathan Cilley of Maine that ended in the latter's death, the giving, delivering, or accepting of a challenge to a duel was banned in the District of Columbia. John Quincy Adams led the fight for passage in the House.

When the threat of war with Great Britain over the disputed northeastern boundary between Maine and New Brunswick arose early in 1839, Congress authorized a force of fifty thousand men and $10 million to protect American interests. Monies were also appropriated for a special minister to London to resolve the dispute. The bloodless Aroostock War was settled peacefully by General Winfield Scott who, at President Van Buren's direction, negotiated a truce between the governor of Maine and the lieutenant governor of New Brunswick. Great Britain and the United States permanently resolved the border issue three years later with ratification of the Webster-Ashburton Treaty. *(Webster-Ashburton Treaty, p. 75)*

In 1839, Congress, at the urging of commissioner of patents Henry L. Ellsworth, initiated a historically important agricultural program by authorizing the patent office to distribute seeds, and to collect and publish data of interest to farmers. The agricultural department that resulted was the predecessor of the Department of Agriculture, established in 1862. Subsequently, Ellsworth's annual reports dealt mostly with agriculture rather than with patents and called to attention the need for more knowledge about farming in the United States. Today Ellsworth is known as the "father of the United States Department of Agriculture."

The impetus for the first major expansion of the census came from Joseph Worcester, a compiler of dictionaries, atlases, and almanacs. Worcester suggested in his 1838 almanac that if statistics on population, manufacturers and agriculture, crime and pauperism, and education and religion "were collected regularly," it would "greatly increase the ability of the national and state governments," as well as society, to respond to the needs of the nation.[2] Worcester subsequently persuaded President Van Buren of the merit of his suggestion, and Congress embraced the idea a few months later.

Major Acts

Postponement of Fourth Installment of Deposits within States. Postponed the transfer of the fourth installment of deposits to be made directly to the states until January 1, 1839. Approved October 2, 1837 (5 Stat. 201).

Treasury Note Issue of 1837. Authorized $10 million in Treasury notes to relieve the national financial crisis caused by the Panic of 1837. Approved October 12, 1837 (5 Stat. 201–204).

Treasury Note Issue of 1838. Authorized additional Treasury notes to relieve the national financial crisis. Approved May 21, 1838 (5 Stat. 228).

Repeal of Specie Circular. Directed the secretary of the Treasury to receive the notes of specie-paying banks and to discriminate "as to the money or medium of payment" in which debts to the U.S. government were paid. Approved May 31, 1838 (5 Stat. 310).

Iowa Territory Established. Created the Territory of Iowa out of the western part of the Wisconsin Territory. Boundaries of the new territory were the Mississippi River on the east, the Missouri River on the west, Canada on the north, and Missouri on the south. Vested executive power in a governor appointed for three years by the president; legislative power in the governor and a legislative assembly (consisting of a popularly elected, thirteen-member council that would serve two years and a popularly elected, twenty-six-member House of Representatives that would serve one year); and judicial power in a supreme court, district courts, probate courts, and justices of the peace. Approved June 12, 1838 (5 Stat. 235–241).

Dueling Prohibited in District of Columbia. Prohibited any person in the District of Columbia from challenging another person to a duel or from harming an individual who refused to accept a challenge. Stipulated that individuals who violated the law would be subject to imprisonment and hard labor in a penitentiary. Approved February 20, 1839 (5 Stat. 318–319).

Census Act of 1840. Authorized the establishment of a centralized census office during each enumeration and provided for the collection of statistics pertaining to "the pursuits, industry, education, and resources of the country." Required new information on revolutionary war pensioners, schools and colleges, literacy, occupations, idiocy, and insanity, as well as commerce and manufacturing. Approved March 3, 1839 (5 Stat. 331–337). Amended February 26, 1840 (5 Stat. 368–369).

First Appropriation for the Promotion of Agriculture. Authorized the patent office to spend $1,000 for the collection and distribution of seeds, and the collection of agricultural statistics. Approved March 3, 1839 (5 Stat. 354, Sec. 9).

Defense of State of Maine. Authorized the president to resist any attempt by Great Britain "to enforce, by arms, her claim to exclusive jurisdiction over that part of the State of Maine which is in dispute between the United States and Great Britain." Provided that in the event Maine was invaded, the president was authorized to accept the services of up to fifty thousand volunteers and complete construction of the armed vessels previously authorized by law to repel those forces. Appropriated $10 million to carry out the military aspects of the act and $18,000 for a special minister to Great Britain. Approved March 3, 1839 (5 Stat. 355–356).

Notes

1. Officially, the first session of the Twenty-fifth Congress, held from September 4, 1837, to October 16, 1837, was a special session of Congress called by presidential proclamation. The official records—*Congressional Globe, Journal of the House of Representatives,* and *Journal of the Senate*—however, all identify this as the first session of the Twenty-fifth Congress. The special session of the Senate (from March 4, 1837, to March 10, 1837) convened to consider presidential nominations.

2. Joseph E. Worcester, *The American Almanac and Repository of Useful Knowledge* (Boston, Mass.: Charles Bowen, 1838), iii-iv.

Twenty-sixth Congress
March 4, 1839, to March 3, 1841

First session—December 2, 1839, to July 21, 1840
Second session—December 7, 1840, to March 3, 1841
(Administration of Martin Van Buren, 1837–1841)

Historical Background

Worsening economic conditions in late 1839 and early 1840 emphasized the significance of President Martin Van Buren's fervent appeal for an independent Treasury system in his third annual message. As the nation plunged quickly toward depression, the flow of British capital into the country virtually ceased, bank failures increased, and business activity declined. Banks once again began suspending specie payments. Finally on July 4, 1840, President Van Buren was able to sign the Independent Treasury Act he had requested for nearly three years. It passed the Senate on January 23, by a 24 to 18 margin. A 124 to 106 majority in the House supported the measure on June 30. Van Buren's enthusiasm was dampened, however, because little time remained to demonstrate the economic benefits of the legislation before the presidential election of 1840—just five months away. His inability to deal effectively with the economic distress experienced by most Americans, and the accession of the Whigs as a viable alternative to the Democrats, doomed his bid for a second term.

The 1840 presidential campaign, one of the first to employ rallies, dances, slogans, songs, parades, and campaign hats, captured the imagination of the nation. Van Buren ran on a platform that condemned the national bank, federally financed internal improvements, and congressional interference with slavery. The Whigs based their campaign on generalities and personalities. William Henry Harrison, the Whig standard-bearer, was portrayed as the hero of the Battle of Tippecanoe and a simple man of the people. Pictures were distributed of Harrison at the door of a log cabin, welcoming visitors to his humble home. John Tyler, his running mate, took little part in the campaign, but by election day his name was as well known as the Whig campaign song, "Tippecanoe and Tyler Too." The song's refrain, "Van, Van is a used up man," was being sung throughout the country. Voters were told that Harrison would return the government to the people. Van Buren conversely was depicted as an aristocrat living in luxury.

The excitement generated by the Whigs' "Log Cabin and Cider" campaign brought unprecedented number of citizens to the polls as Harrison and Tyler carried the election, 1,275,390 popular votes to 1,128,854 for Van Buren and Vice President Richard M. Johnson. Harrison's electoral vote plurality was 234, to 60 for Van Buren. Tyler received 234 electoral votes; Johnson, 48. The Whigs captured both houses of Congress for the first time.

Major Act

First Independent Treasury Act. Established federal depositories independent of state banks and private business, entrusted the government with the exclusive care of its own funds, and required progressive enforcement of the legal tender clause. Mandated that all government payments and disbursements be made in specie after June 30, 1843. Established subtreasuries at New York; Boston, Massachusetts; Philadelphia, Pennsylvania; St. Louis, Missouri; New Orleans, Louisiana; Washington, D.C.; and Charleston, South Carolina. Approved July 4, 1840 (5 Stat. 385–392). Repealed August 13, 1841 (5 Stat. 439–440). *(Repeal of the Independent Treasury Act, p. 75)*

Twenty-seventh Congress
March 4, 1841, to March 3, 1843

First session—May 31, 1841, to September 13, 1841

Second session—December 6, 1841, to August 31, 1842

Third session—December 5, 1842, to March 3, 1843

Special session of the Senate—March 4, 1841, to March 15, 1841

(Administrations of William Henry Harrison, 1841, and John Tyler, 1841–1845)

Historical Background

During the 1840 presidential campaign, the Whigs focused primarily on attacking the Independent Treasury Act and blaming the Van Buren administration for the ongoing depression. Shortly after delivering his March 4, 1841, inaugural address, William Henry Harrison issued a call for a special session of Congress to consider the "sundry important and weighty matters, principally growing out of the condition of the revenue and finances of the country."[1] Whig expectations for effecting change were short-lived. Within a month, Harrison succumbed to pneumonia, and John Tyler became the first vice president to succeed to the presidency. John Quincy Adams, who characterized Tyler as having been "never thought of" as president, expressed uncertainty and concern over Tyler's succession, as did many in the cabinet and on Capitol Hill. They felt he was not fully the president and his official title should be "Acting President." Even though he deemed himself qualified to exercise the duties and powers of the presidency, Tyler decided to take the presidential oath to dispel any uncertainty.

Although Tyler's status as a leading opponent of Andrew Jackson led him to affiliate with the Whigs in their attack on "executive despotism," he remained a Democrat. The Whigs placed him on their ticket because he was well known, a southerner, a states' righter, and a supporter of Whig senator Henry Clay. Clay mistakenly assumed, Oliver Chitwood writes, "that Tyler, a mild mannered Virginian with a soft exterior, would not have the temerity to strenuously oppose his politics."[2] Initially, Clay was able to push through a repeal of the Independent Treasury Act as well as new bankruptcy and preemption acts. The Bankruptcy Act of 1841 allowed debtors for the first time to voluntarily declare themselves insolvent. During the short period the act was in effect (August 19, 1841–March 3, 1843), more than thirty-three thousand debtors took advantage of it. The Preemption Act of 1841 brought together the political interests of the older states and new public land states. Under the act, settlement could be made only on public lands that had been surveyed and new states were granted 500,000 acres for internal improvements and 10 percent of the net proceeds from public land sales within the state. An amendment attached to the bill, however, provided that the distribution of public lands was to be suspended if the protective tariff rate rose above 20 percent, which it did within a year.

Whig hopes for cooperation with Tyler quickly faded. On September 9, 1841, for the second time in some thirty days, Tyler vetoed legislation designed by Clay to reestablish a Bank of the United States. As a result, the entire cabinet, with the exception of Secretary of State Daniel Webster, resigned in protest. A dispirited Henry Clay, who was suffering from ill health, retired from Congress on March 31, 1842. Soon afterward, however, he launched a campaign to win the White House in 1844.

Whig efforts to pass tariff legislation led to a standoff, when Tyler twice vetoed a Whig-favored bill in

74

1842. The subsequent enactment of legislation acceptable to the president provided much-needed revenue to the Treasury, which for several weeks had verged on bankruptcy. The Tariff Act of 1842 satisfied protectionists and ultimately created a budget surplus by the end of Tyler's presidency. Included in the tariff act was a relatively obscure provision designed to restrict the flow of obscenity by prohibiting the "importation of all indecent and obscene prints, paintings, lithographs, engravings and transparencies." Most historians credit this provision as prompting a domestic pornography industry in the United States. Prior to this enactment, almost all pornography was imported from Europe, but "as technologies of mass production appeared, [Americans] gradually capitalized on domestic production."[3]

Also, in August 1842, the Senate ratified the Webster-Ashburton Treaty between the United States and Great Britain, which provided for settlement of the long-disputed northeast boundary of the United States. In addition, legislation was approved that changed the beginning of the government's fiscal year from January to July, and amended the Judiciary Act so offenses committed under foreign authority and affecting foreign relations would be under the jurisdiction of state courts. A congressional reapportionment bill enacted in June 1842 mandated single-member districts in the House of Representatives to ensure that only one representative would represent a district in future Congresses.

Late in February 1843, Samuel F. B. Morse won the first battle in the struggle to give the nation a practicable electromagnetic telegraph line when Congress appropriated $30,000 for Morse to construct an experimental telegraph line. Soon thereafter construction began on a telegraph line from Baltimore to Washington. On May 24, 1844, Morse, before a crowd of dignitaries in the old Supreme Court chambers in the Capitol tapped out the historic first message,"What hath God wrought?" to his assistant in Baltimore, Alfred Vail.

Major Acts and Treaties

Repeal of the Independent Treasury Act. Ordered the removal of all government funds from the depositories created by order of the Independent Treasury Act of 1840. Approved August 13, 1841 (5 Stat. 439–440). *(Independent Treasury Act, p. 73)*

Bankruptcy Act of 1841. Established a uniform system of bankruptcy applicable to all persons owing debts that had "not been created in consequence of a defalcation as a public officer; or as an executor, administrator, guardian or trustee, or while acting in any other fiduciary capacity." Allowed merchants, bankers, brokers, underwriters, and marine insurers owing debts of more than $2,000 to petition their creditors and be declared bankrupt in certain cases. Approved August 19, 1841 (5 Stat. 440–449). Repealed on March 3, 1843 (5 Stat. 614).

Preemption Act of 1841. Provided a permanent authorization for settlers to stake claims on most surveyed lands and purchase a maximum of 160 acres at $1.25 an acre. Granted 500,000 acres of public land each to the states of Alabama, Arkansas, Illinois, Indiana, Louisiana, Michigan, Mississippi, Missouri, and Ohio; and established a similar grant for each new state admitted to the Union after the passage of the act. Stipulated that 10 percent of the proceeds from the sale of these lands would revert to the state where the land was located and the remaining 90 percent would be distributed among the other states based upon their representation in Congress. Distribution of funds was to cease whenever import duties exceeded 20 percent. Approved September 4, 1841 (5 Stat. 453–458). Distribution provisions were suspended on August 30, 1842 (5 Stat. 567).

1842 Apportionment Act. Required that Representatives "should be elected by districts composed of contiguous territory equal in number to the number of Representatives to which each said state shall be entitled, no one district electing more than one Representative." Approved June 25, 1942 (5 Stat. 491).

Webster-Ashburton Treaty. Established the present boundary between Maine and New Brunswick, defined the boundary line along the northern frontiers of New York and Vermont, and gave the United States navigational rights on the St. John River. Concluded August 9, 1842 (8 Stat. 572–577). Ratification advised by the Senate August 20, 1842.[4]

Defining and Establishing the Fiscal Year of the Treasury of the United States. Provided that after July 1, 1843, the fiscal year of the Treasury of the United States would commence on the first day of July in each year. Approved August 26, 1842 (5 Stat. 536–537).

Granting of Habeas Corpus Authorized. Empowered justices of the Supreme Court and district court judges to grant writs of habeas corpus when subjects of foreign countries were in the custody of the United States. Approved August 29, 1842 (5 Stat. 539–540).

Tariff Act of 1842. Restored duties to the levels effective in 1832, and simultaneously ended the distribution of the proceeds from public land sales to the states. Prohibited the "importation of all indecent and obscene prints, paintings, lithographs, engravings and transparencies." Approved August 30, 1842 (5 Stat. 548–567).

Appropriation for Construction of First Telegraph Line. Appropriated $30,000 "for testing the capacity and usefulness of the system of electro-magnetic telegraphs invented by Samuel F. B. Morse of New York for the use of the Government of the United States, by constructing a line of said electro-magnetic telegraphs, under the superintendence of Professor Samuel F. B. Morse." Approved March 3, 1843 (5 Stat. 618–619).

Notes

1. Officially, the first session of the Twenty-seventh Congress, held from May 31, 1841, to September 13, 1841, was a special session of Congress called by presidential proclamation. The official records—*Congressional Globe, Journal of the House of Representatives,* and *Journal of the Senate*—however, all identify this as the first session of the Twenty-seventh Congress. The special session of the Senate (March 4, 1841, to March 15, 1841) convened to consider presidential nominations.

2. Oliver Chitwood, *John Tyler: Champion of the Old South* (New York: American Biography Press, 1939), 210.

3. Joseph W. Slade, *Pornography in America: A Reference Handbook* (Santa Barbara, CA: ABC-CLIO, 2000), 16.

4. *Journal of the Executive Proceedings of the Senate* (Washington, D.C.: U.S. Government Printing Office, 1887), 6:129–132.

Twenty-eighth Congress
March 4, 1843, to March 3, 1845

First session—December 4, 1843, to June 17, 1844
Second session—December 2, 1844, to March 3, 1845
(Administration of John Tyler, 1841–1845)

Historical Background

With the Maine-New Brunswick boundary controversy resolved, the Tyler administration anxiously turned its attention to the question of Texas. Although Mexican president Antonio López de Santa Anna declared that any attempt by the United States to annex Texas would result in war, and President Sam Houston of Texas was initially less than enthusiastic about relinquishing independence, President John Tyler and several other administration officials favored annexation. Following considerable negotiation, Secretary of State John C. Calhoun concluded a treaty of annexation with the Republic of Texas on April 12, 1844. Under the terms agreed to, the public lands of Texas were ceded to the United States, the United States assumed up to a maximum of $10 million in Texas debt, and the citizens of Texas were extended "all the rights, privileges, and immunities, of citizens of the United States." While the treaty was under consideration, President Tyler promised to use U.S. naval and military forces to protect Texas against a possible attack by Mexico.

Ten days after the treaty was signed, Tyler submitted it to the Senate for ratification. His accompanying message reasoned that approval was in the interest of the entire nation, pointing out Texas would add a vast area of fertile lands, stimulate commerce, and enhance the security of the southern states. Former president Andrew Jackson as well as a number of proslavery politicians spoke out in favor of annexation, while former president Martin Van Buren and Henry Clay, among others, denounced the treaty. Many northerners saw the acquisition as a southern plot to spread slavery, a view strengthened by a note Secretary Calhoun sent to the British minister in Washington strongly defending the institution of slavery. After the Senate soundly rejected annexation by 35 to 16 on June 8, 1844, Tyler urged Congress to vote Texas into the Union by a simple majority, thereby obviating the necessity of a two-thirds Senate vote required for ratification.

When Congress adjourned on June 17, 1844, the debate over annexation shifted to the presidential campaign. James K. Polk, the Democratic candidate, ran on an expansionist platform that called for the acquisition of Texas and the "reoccupation of Oregon" (at the time jointly occupied with England). The Whig platform, upon which Henry Clay campaigned, made no reference to Texas. Clay personally equivocated about his opposition to annexation. Tyler, the first president to not run for reelection, withdrew as the nominee of the Tyler Democrats in August, when it became clear he could not win. While the margin of victory was less than 2 percent of the popular vote, Polk received 170 electoral votes to Clay's 105. Democrat George M. Dallas was elected vice president with 170 electoral votes; his Whig opponent, Theodore Frelinghuysen, received 105. The results of the 1844 congressional elections were equally satisfying to the Democrats, who regained the Senate from the Whigs and enhanced their control of the House.

The 1844 election was the last presidential contest to be held on the various dates set by each state. Soon after the returns had been counted, Congress approved a law establishing the first Tuesday after the first Monday in November as a uniform day on which presidential elections were to be held throughout the country.

In January 1845, the Senate approved the first treaty with China. The Treaty of Wang-Hsia (Wanghia), negotiated by Caleb Cushing, minister plenipotentiary, opened five Chinese ports to American merchants and ensured that Americans living in China would be subject only to U.S. laws and officials.

The paramount issue in the Twenty-eighth Congress remained the question of Texas. When the second session convened, Tyler used his annual message to once again urge the annexation of Texas. A joint resolution to achieve that end was approved by both houses of Congress in late February 1845. On March 1, three days before the presidential mantle passed to James K. Polk, Tyler signed the joint resolution into law. It marked the first time that a joint resolution was used to approve the acquisition or acceptance of a territory. During his final hours in office, Tyler achieved the distinction of being the first president to have a veto overridden, which requires a two-thirds majority vote in the House and Senate. The legislation prohibited the building of revenue cutters or steamers ordered by the president without prior congressional appropriations.

Before leaving office, Tyler affixed his signature to a bill admitting Florida into the Union. The Florida statehood bill also had provided for the admission of the state of Iowa; however, statehood was rejected by the voters of Iowa, who preferred to remain a territory rather than accept the western boundary suggested by Congress. This would have been forty miles west of the city of Des Moines rather than at the Missouri River. The present western boundary of Iowa (the Missouri River) was agreed upon by a second Iowa constitutional convention in May 1846.

Tyler also signed—on his last full day in the White House—two important postal service bills. The first bill proved to be one of the most significant pieces of postal reform legislation ever enacted. That enactment simplified and lowered the postal rates for letters, and set the parameters for a postal monopoly that essentially eliminated private mail delivery companies as competition. The second bill authorized the Post Office Department to contract with American ships for international transportation of mail and to establish rates for international mail.

Major Acts and Treaties

Treaty of Wang-Hsia (Wanghia). Provided for American consuls and trade in the Chinese ports of Amoy (Xiamen), Canton (Guangzhou), Foochow (Fuzhou), Ningpo (Ningbo), and Shanghai. Concluded July 3, 1844 (8 Stat. 592–605). Ratification advised by the Senate January 16, 1845.[1]

Establishment of a Uniform Time for Holding Elections for Electors of President and Vice President. Named the first Tuesday after the first Monday in November as election day for election of presidential and vice presidential electors. Approved January 23, 1845 (5 Stat. 721).

Texas Annexation Resolution. Declared the consent of Congress to the establishment of Texas as a state and for its admission to the Union. Approved March 1, 1845 (5 Stat. 797–798).

Postal Reform Act of 1845. Provided that the cost of mailing a letter would be based on the weight of a letter, not the number of sheets being mailed. Reformed postal contract procedures, established the star route system (roads where mail was carried under private contract), and placed the first restrictions on the franking privilege, which allowed members of Congress to send mail at taxpayers' expense. Also increased the penalties of private expresses operating in competition with the Post Office. Approved March 3, 1845 (5 Stat. 732–739).

Florida Admitted to the Union. Accepted the constitution and state government formed by a Florida Territory convention on January 11, 1839, and declared that the state of Florida was one of the "United States of America, and hereby admitted into the Union on an equal footing with the original States." Approved March 3, 1845 (5 Stat. 742–743).

Ocean Mail Contracts Authorized for Foreign Mail Delivery. Authorized the Postmaster General to award contracts for transporting mail to foreign countries to the lowest bidder. Required such contracts "be made with citizens of the United States, and the mail be transported in American vessels, by American citizens."

Established rates for between United States ports and England, France, "or any other foreign port not less than three thousand miles distant," and "any of the West India islands, or islands in the gulf of Mexico." Approved March 3, 1845 (5 Stat. 748–750).

Construction of Revenue Cutters and Steamers. Prohibited revenue cutters and steamers from being built or purchased unless an appropriation had been made for them. In the waning hours of the Twenty-eighth Congress the House joined the Senate to pass

Congress's first override of a presidential veto. The bill became law without the president's signature March 3, 1845 (5 Stat. 795–796).

Note

1. *Journal of the Executive Proceedings of the Senate* (Washington, D.C.: U.S. Government Printing Office, 1887), 6:385.

Twenty-ninth Congress
March 4, 1845, to March 3, 1847

First session—December 1, 1845, to August 10, 1846
Second session—December 7, 1846, to March 3, 1847
Special session of the Senate—March 4, 1845, to March
    20, 1845
(Administration of James K. Polk, 1845–1849)

Historical Background

Less than a month after the approval of the Texas annexation resolution, Mexico severed diplomatic relations with the United States. As tension over Texas continued to build, President James K. Polk sought a compromise solution to the question of a permanent boundary line between the United States and British Northwest Territory. By 1845, the deadlock over the Oregon Territory centered on whether the line should be drawn at the Columbia River, as Britain wanted, or further north at the 49th parallel, as proposed by the United States. The only area in dispute was a section of land west of the Rocky Mountains that now makes up the northwestern two-thirds of Washington State.

Major portions of Polk's first annual message to Congress in December 1845 addressed the Oregon question. The president declared that the United States was prepared to maintain its claim to Oregon and recommended that Great Britain be given one year to end joint occupation. He also evoked the Monroe Doctrine in opposing any European colonization of North America. In 1846 Congress completed action on legislation empowering the president to terminate the joint Anglo-American occupation of Oregon. In his first annual message Polk also called for tariff revision and an independent Treasury system. Within nine months, he was able to send the Senate a treaty establishing the

49th parallel from the Rockies to Puget Sound as the northern boundary of Oregon, sign the Walker Tariff Act lowering duties on imports, and approve legislation reestablishing government-run subtreasuries. Vice President George M. Dallas had the distinction of casting the tie-breaking vote in the Senate on the Walker Tariff Act, which lowered the tariff so it was primarily for revenue and only incidentally for protection.

A few weeks after passage of the Walker Tariff, Congress acted on a proposal by Treasury Secretary Robert Walker for the government to establish a bonded warehousing system based on the one employed by Britain. The Warehousing Act sought to stimulate commerce by exempting importers from paying customs duties on goods stored in a government warehouse while seeking the most profitable markets for sales. Previously, goods could not be landed at the port of delivery until the duties were paid except in special cases.

Resolving differences with Mexico, however, proved more elusive. On December 9, 1845, Polk sent a special message to Congress announcing that Texas had accepted the proposed terms for statehood, and on December 29 the Lone Star State was admitted to the Union. During the next several months, relations between Mexico and the United States continued to deteriorate. When news reached the White House on the evening of April 25, 1846, that Mexican troops had crossed the Rio Grande and killed or wounded sixteen American soldiers, the president and his cabinet were already discussing the propriety of drafting a war message. The message was sent to Congress on May 11. War was formally declared on Mexico two days later, and $10 million was appropriated to support the effort. The vote in favor of war was 174 to 14 in the House and 40 to 2 in the Senate. A number of factors contributed to the ultimate outbreak of hostilities: disagreement over the southwestern boundary of Texas, outstanding American claims against Mexico, Mexican outrage over the loss of Texas, and difficulties in negotiating with Mexico. An equally significant factor was the determination of President Polk to purchase the provinces of New Mexico and California or, if necessary, use force to obtain them.

U.S. military operations began when General Zachary Taylor led an expedition from Texas into northern Mexico on May 18, 1846. Taylor on September 28, 1846, captured the city of Monterey and in February 1847 crushed a counterattack led by Mexican president Santa Anna. Meanwhile, a second U.S. expedition, led by General Stephen W. Kearney, moved from Fort Leavenworth on July 3, 1846, captured Sante Fe, New Mexico, on August 18, and reached the Pacific at San Diego, California, on December 5. Kearney's forces joined the group of American settlers under John C. Fremont and marines and sailors landed by the U.S. Navy's Pacific squadron to complete the conquest early in 1847.

Gradually, as fighting continued, considerable opposition developed to "Jimmy Polk's War," especially among Whigs and antislavery Democrats, who suggested that it was intended to expand the boundaries of slavery. When Polk requested $2 million in August 1846 to facilitate peace negotiations, Rep. David Wilmot of Pennsylvania offered an amendment prohibiting slavery in any territory acquired from Mexico. Although the Wilmot Proviso was adopted by the House, a filibuster by southern senators prevented it from being voted on before the first session of the Twenty-ninth Congress adjourned on August 10. When the peace negotiations bill (which had grown to $3 million) was reconsidered in early 1847, the House again attached the proviso. This time the Senate refused to even consider the appropriation until the proviso was stricken. The debate over the proviso, however, had aroused the country, and during the presidential campaign it was a point of contention between the parties. Also in early 1847, the question of slavery in the Oregon Territory prompted spirited floor debate, with the House voting for exclusion, while the Senate tabled the bill.

Until 1846, the District of Columbia was a "10 Mile Square" diamond that spanned the Potomac River. During the previous six years, however, the residents of Alexandria, Virginia, had repeatedly petitioned Congress and the Virginia legislature to retrocede, or return, that portion of the District southwest of the Potomac River to Virginia. In February 1846, the Virginia General Assembly agreed to accept the retrocession of Alexandria County if Congress approved. That July, Congress approved the return of all the District's territory south of the Potomac River back to the Commonwealth of Virginia.

In other action, Iowa was admitted into the Union on December 28, 1846, an enabling act for the state of Wisconsin was approved, and the nation's first postage stamps were authorized in March 1847. An act providing for the admission of Wisconsin to the Union was also approved, but the constitution drafted by the first Wisconsin constitutional convention was rejected by people of the territory and further action was postponed until the next Congress.

Major Acts and Treaties

Texas Admitted to the Union. Declared that Texas was one of the "United States of America, and admitted into the Union on an equal footing with the original States." Approved December 29, 1845 (9 Stat. 108).

Declaration of War with Mexico. Declared that "by the act of the Republic of Mexico, a state of war exists between that Government and the United States." Authorized the president to employ up to fifty thousand volunteers to prosecute the war, and appropriated $10 million to carry out the provisions of the act. Approved May 13, 1846 (9 Stat. 9–10).

Oregon Treaty. Established the 49th parallel as the boundary line between U.S. and British possessions west of the Rocky Mountains and also guaranteed mutual access rights to certain waterways in the areas in question. Concluded June 15, 1846 (9 Stat. 869–870). Ratification advised by the Senate June 18, 1846.[1]

Retrocession of the County of Alexandria in the District of Columbia to the State of Virginia. Retroceded land within the District of Columbia south of the Potomac River back to Virginia. Justified the retrocession on the grounds that "no more territory ought to be held under the exclusive legislation given to Congress over the District which is the seat of the General Government than may be necessary and proper for the purposes of such a seat; and . . . experience hath shown that the portion of the District of Columbia ceded to the United States by the State of Virginia has not been, nor is ever likely to be, necessary for that purpose." Required the retrocession be accepted by a vote of the majority of the "people of the county and town of Alexandria." Approved July 9, 1846 (9 Stat. 35–36).

Walker Tariff Act. Reduced the duties on imports to levels comparable with those of the Compromise Tariff of 1833. Approved July 30, 1846 (9 Stat. 42–49).

Warehousing Act of 1846. Established a system of government warehouses where importers could place goods under government bond until such time as goods were sold. Allowed imported goods to also be transferred or re-exported through the distributional network of American ports without being subject to double taxation or excessive regulation. August 6, 1846 (9 Stat. 53–55).

Wisconsin Enabling Act. Authorized the inhabitants of the Wisconsin Territory to draft a constitution and form a state government in preparation for statehood. Approved August 6, 1846 (9 Stat. 56–58).

Independent Treasury Act of 1846. Established subtreasuries for the deposit of federal funds, and stipulated that all payments made to and by the U.S. government must be in gold, silver, or Treasury notes. Approved August 6, 1846 (9 Stat. 59–66).

Iowa Admitted to the Union. Accepted the constitution and state government formed by an Iowa Territory convention on May 18, 1846, and declared that Iowa was one of the "United States of America, and admitted to the Union on an equal footing with the original States." Approved December 28, 1846 (9 Stat. 117).

Appropriation to Secure Peace with Mexico. Appropriated $3 million "to enable the President to conclude a treaty of peace, limits, and boundaries with the Republic of Mexico." Approved March 3, 1847 (9 Stat. 174).

Postage Stamp Act. Authorized use of postage stamps in the United States for the first time. Approved March 3, 1847 (9 Stat. 201, Sec. 11).

Note

1. *Journal of the Executive Proceedings of the Senate* (Washington, D.C.: U.S. Government Printing Office, 1887), 7:93–95.

Thirtieth Congress
March 4, 1847, to March 3, 1849

First session—December 6, 1847, to August 14, 1848
Second session—December 4, 1848, to March 3, 1849
(Administration of James K. Polk, 1845–1849)

Historical Background

By the time the Twenty-ninth Congress adjourned on March 3, 1847, American military forces had taken possession of both New Mexico and California. During the next nine months before the Thirtieth Congress convened, U.S. military operations shifted to the Mexican heartland, when an expedition under General Winfield Scott captured the port of Vera Cruz (March 29) and then advanced to the Mexican capital, defeating the Mexicans at Contreras and at Churubusco. After a prolonged and bitter campaign, Scott occupied Mexico City on September 14 and raised the American flag over the National Palace. Soon afterward, Mexico surrendered and prolonged peace negotiations began. On February 2, 1848, less than two weeks after gold was discovered at Sutter's Mill, in California, U.S. commissioner Nicholas P. Trist and the Mexican commissioners signed a treaty in the village of Guadalupe Hidalgo, near Mexico City. Under the terms of the treaty, which officially ended the Mexican War, Mexico ceded California and New Mexico to the United States in return for $15 million and relinquished all claims to Texas north of the Rio Grande River. The United States also agreed to assume $3.25 million in claims against Mexico. The approximately 1.2 million square miles of newly acquired Mexican territory included the present states of Arizona, California, New Mexico, Nevada, Texas, and Utah, as well as parts of Colorado and Wyoming. The Senate ratified the treaty on March 10, 1848, by a vote

of 38 to 14. A motion to add the Wilmot Proviso was defeated by an almost identical 38 to 15 vote.

In June 1848, the Senate also ratified a treaty with New Granada (Colombia) granting the United States an exclusive right of transit across the Isthmus of Panama. The treaty was realized through the efforts of Benjamin A. Bidlack, the American chargé d'affaires in Bogotá, acting entirely on his own initiative. Bidlack's action was prompted by concern that Great Britain, France, or some other European power might seize the isthmus. The pact made possible the construction of the Panama Railroad, completed by American interests in 1855.

Following lively and extended debate in July and August, a bill organizing Oregon as a territory without slavery became law. Despite President Polk's support, repeated attempts in the Senate to secure passage of a bill that included a provision extending the Missouri Compromise line of 36°30' to the Pacific Ocean failed. In a special message accompanying his approval of the Oregon bill, Polk declared that if the legislation had prohibited slavery south of the Missouri Compromise line it would have been vetoed. Ironically, in signing the Oregon bill, Polk essentially nullified future attempts to extend slavery to the Pacific. Near the conclusion of the Thirtieth Congress, the Minnesota Territory was created from parts of the Iowa Territory and Wisconsin Territory.

Acting on the recommendation of Treasury Secretary Robert J. Walker, a congressional coalition of Whigs and public land Democrats secured passage of legislation creating a Department of the Interior in the waning hours of Polk's presidency. Although the idea of creating a cabinet-level department to oversee public lands was almost as old as the nation itself, the great territorial expansion resulting from the acquisition of the Oregon Territory (1846) and the Mexican Cession (1848) gave the proposal new impetus.

In November 1848, Polk's successor, Whig candidate Zachary Taylor of Mexican War fame, had handily defeated Democrat Lewis Cass and Free-Soiler Martin Van Buren in the presidential election. Taylor received 163 electoral votes; Cass, 127; Van Buren, none. In the race for vice president, Whig Millard Fillmore prevailed with 163 electoral votes over Democrat William Orlando, who received 127. In the congressional contests, the Democrats retained the majority in the Senate and assumed control in the House.

Major Acts and Treaties

Treaty of Guadalupe-Hidalgo. Terminated the state of war with Mexico, provided for Mexico to relinquish all claims to Texas north of the Rio Grande River, and ceded California and New Mexico to the United States. Provided that the United States would pay $15 million and assume responsibility for $3.25 million in adjusted claims by American citizens against the Mexican government. Concluded February 2, 1848 (9 Stat. 922–943). Ratification advised by the Senate, with amendments, March 10, 1848.[1]

Wisconsin Admitted to the Union. Accepted the constitution and state government formed by a Wisconsin Territory convention on February 1, 1848, and declared that Wisconsin was "one of the United States of America, and admitted into the Union on an equal footing with the original States." Approved May 29, 1848 (9 Stat. 233–235).

Treaty with New Granada (Bidlack Treaty). Granted the United States a right of way across the Isthmus of Panama. In return, the United States guaranteed the neutrality of the isthmus and the sovereignty of New Granada over it. Concluded December 12, 1846 (9 Stat. 881–901). Ratification advised by the Senate June 3, 1848.[2]

Oregon Bill. Established a territorial government for Oregon in which slavery was prohibited. Created what was officially the Territory of Oregon, encompassing all of what is today Oregon, Washington, and Idaho, and parts of what became Montana and Wyoming. Revised significantly the legislative branch of government by making the territorial legislature, known as the Legislative Assembly, a bicameral body. Provided for the popular election of legislators, and vacancies were filled by special election. Limited legislative sessions to sixty days. Prohibited the Legislative Assembly from passing laws interfering with land claims and with passing laws which taxed nonresidents at a higher rate than residents, from incorporating banks and financial institutions, and from acquiring debts in the name of the territory. Approved August 14, 1848 (9 Stat. 323–331).

Department of the Interior. Created the Department of the Interior with a presidentially appointed secretary of interior as its head. Consolidated in the new department responsibility for the office of commissioner of patents (formerly in the State Department); general land office (Treasury Department); "accounts of the marshals, clerks, and other officers of all the courts of the United States" (Treasury Department); mines in the United States (Treasury Department); commissioner of public buildings (Treasury Department); District of Columbia penitentiary (Treasury Department); commissioner of Indian affairs (War Department); commissioner of pensions (War and Navy Departments); "taking and returning the census of the United States" (State Department); and the patent office (Department of State). Approved March 3, 1849 (9 Stat. 395–397).

Minnesota Territory Organized. Created the Minnesota Territory from the unorganized federal territory west of the Mississippi River (formerly part of Iowa Territory) and de facto Wisconsin Territory (the part of Wisconsin Territory, between the Mississippi and St. Croix Rivers, not included in the state of Wisconsin when Wisconsin became a state on May 29, 1848). Included all of present Minnesota and parts of present North and South Dakota. Approved March 3, 1849 (9 Stat. 403–409).

Notes

1. *Journal of the Executive Proceedings of the Senate* (Washington, D.C.: U.S. Government Printing Office, 1887), 7:93–95.

2. *Journal of the Executive Proceedings of the Senate* (Washington, D.C.: U.S. Government Printing Office, 1887), 7:424.

Thirty-first Congress
March 4, 1849, to March 3, 1851

First session—December 3, 1849, to September 30, 1850
Second session—December 2, 1850, to March 3, 1851
Special session of the Senate—March 5, 1849, to March 23, 1849
(Administrations of Zachary Taylor, 1849–1850, and Millard Fillmore, 1850–1853)

Historical Background

The Mexican Cession further intensified sectional conflict in the United States. The North demanded that slavery be barred in America's new western holdings, while the South insisted on the right to expand the institution. Early in 1850, after returning to the Senate following a seven-year absence, Henry Clay introduced eight resolutions he hoped would permanently end sectional strife. He proposed admission of California as a free state; establishment of New Mexico and Utah as territories with no restrictions on slavery; resolution of the Texas–New Mexico boundary dispute; assumption by the U.S. government of Texas's pre-annexation debts; abolition of the slave trade in the District of Columbia; adoption of a policy of noninterference with slavery in the District; enactment of a more stringent fugitive slave law; and a formal declaration by Congress that it had no authority over the interstate slave trade.

What emerged in response to these resolutions was one of the most famous and eloquent debates in American history, which also was the final performance of the great triumvirate of Clay, John C. Calhoun, and Daniel Webster. Clay opened the debate on February 5, 1850, with a two-day defense of his measures. On March 4, Calhoun listened silently as his remarks in

opposition were read by a colleague. Three days later, Webster refuted Calhoun's charges against the North and framed a compromise in an attempt to make Clay's resolutions palatable to both the North and South.

On April 18 the proposals were referred to a special committee chaired by Clay. Early in May, the committee reported three pieces of legislation: an omnibus bill that dealt with California and the territorial issues; a stringent fugitive slave bill; and a bill prohibiting the slave trade in the District of Columbia. None of the three, however, was found acceptable. Also, the threat of a presidential veto of any compromise loomed. President Zachary Taylor's opposition stemmed from a belief that southerners in the Senate, through various amendments, were holding California hostage until they could garner support for Texas, a slave state, to acquire most of New Mexico, a free territory. On July 9, 1850, however, Taylor died. Calhoun had passed away on March 31, so his objections were silenced as well. Although Taylor's successor, Vice President Millard Fillmore, "did not support the omnibus principle or the sacrifice of New Mexico any more than Taylor did," Elbert B. Smith points out that Fillmore was helpful in developing an acceptable alternative.[1] Furthermore, Webster left the Senate and used his position as Fillmore's secretary of state to garner Whig support for the legislation.

During the final weeks of the floor battle, Sen. Stephen A. Douglas of Illinois replaced an exhausted Clay as leader of the compromise movement. By dividing the omnibus bill into separate measures, along with other parliamentary maneuvers, Douglas was able to fashion a different sectional majority in support of each bill that made passage possible. The legislation, collectively known as the Compromise of 1850, provided for the admission of California as a free state; resolution of the

Texas–New Mexico boundary dispute, together with the assumption of Texas's debt; establishment of territorial governments for New Mexico and Utah with a popular sovereignty clause; a stricter Fugitive Slave Act; and prohibition of the slave trade in the District of Columbia. Signed into law by Fillmore on September 18, the compromise included elements that were questioned by partisans of both North and South. In the final analysis, however, it was recognized as the best possible solution to nearly intractable issues and, as such, was greeted with great relief and hope. President Fillmore in his annual message of December 2 told Congress that he regarded the compromise measures as "a final settlement of the dangerous and exciting subjects which they embraced." Unfortunately, the sectional differences that threatened to disrupt the country in 1850 would reappear.

Before President Taylor's death, Secretary of State John M. Clayton and British Minister Sir Henry L. Bulwer signed a treaty in Washington on April 19, 1850, delineating the roles of the two countries in Central America. It provided that neither nation would exclusively control or fortify a Central American canal. That September, during the Fillmore administration, the first federal land grants were authorized. The original and sole purpose of the land grants was to aid in the construction of railroads. During the next two decades, these grants served as a modest model for subsequent grants received by railroad companies totaling more than 130 million acres.

Intense public pressure prompted Congress to reduce substantially letter postage rates in 1851. More importantly, the new postal act established the principle that the Post Office was a service to all the people and should be operated with that idea in mind rather than with undue concern about postal deficits. It specifically forbade the Postmaster General from reducing or curtailing postal service. The House Committee favorably reported the bill emphasized that the price of mail had "shut out from a great portion of our people the benefits intended to be conferred upon them by the establishment of the Post Office Department," and the committee proposed, "by the modifications which are recommended, to bring truth; intelligence, and useful knowledge to the door of every man in the Union, the richest and the poorest."[2]

Major Acts and Treaties

Clayton-Bulwer Treaty. Provided for a joint Anglo-American protectorate of the United States and Great Britain over a proposed canal to be built across Central America. Neither government was to obtain exclusive control of the canal or "occupy, or fortify, or colonize, or assume, or exercise any dominion" over any part of Central America. The canal was to be kept open to all nations. Concluded April 19, 1850 (9 Stat. 995–998). Ratification advised by the Senate May 22, 1850.[3]

Texas and New Mexico Act. Established the boundary between Texas and New Mexico. Authorized a payment of $10 million in compensation to Texas for relinquishing claims to New Mexico. Provided that New Mexico would be admitted to the Union with or without slavery, according to its constitution. Approved September 9, 1850 (9 Stat. 446–452).

California Admitted as a Free State. Provided for the admission of California to the Union as a free state. Approved September 9, 1850 (9 Stat. 452–453).

Utah Act. Established the territorial boundaries of Utah, and provided that it was to be a free or slave state according to the constitution it adopted upon admission to the Union. Approved September 9, 1850 (9 Stat. 453–458).

Fugitive Slave Act. Amended the 1793 Fugitive Slave Act by removing fugitive slave cases from state jurisdiction. Provided for the appointment of special federal commissioners to conduct hearings and issue warrants of arrest and certificates of return. Imposed a fine and imprisonment on any person harboring a fugitive slave or aiding his or her escape. Denied fugitive slaves the right of jury trial or the right to testify in their own behalf. Approved September 18, 1850 (9 Stat. 462–465). *(Fugitive Slave Act of 1793, p. 15)*

Railroad Land Grant Act of 1850. Authorized land grants to Alabama, Illinois, and Mississippi to aid in the construction of a railroad between Chicago and Mobile. Provided for a one-hundred-foot right-of-way and alternating sections not exceeding six miles in width on either side of the track. Approved September 20, 1850 (9 Stat. 466–467).

District of Columbia Slave Trade Act. Abolished the slave trade in the District of Columbia after January 1, 1851. Approved September 20, 1850 (9 Stat. 467–468).

Postal Act of 1851. Lowered the rate for a pre-paid half-ounce letter to three cents for any distance less than 3,000 miles. Doubled the price for letters transported more than 3,000 miles. Provided for free postage service for weekly newspapers transported within a single county, and a statutory assurance that "no post-office now in existence shall be discontinued, nor shall the mail service on any mail route . . . be discontinued or diminished, in consequence of any diminution of the revenue that may result from this act." Authorized establishment of postal routes within cities and towns, convenient places to deposit mail, and employment of mail carriers to receive and deposit mail. Approved March 3, 1851 (9 Stat. 587–591).

Notes

1. Elbert B. Smith, *The Presidencies of Zachary Taylor and Millard Fillmore* (Lawrence, Kan.: University Press of Kansas, 1988), 191.

2. U.S. Congress, House Committee on the Post Office and Post Roads, "Reduction of Rates of Postage," 31st Cong., 1st sess., H. Rept. 411 (Washington, D.C.: U.S. Government Printing Office, 1831), 2.

3. *Journal of the Executive Proceedings of the Senate* (Washington, D.C.: U.S. Government Printing Office, 1887), 8:186.

Thirty-second Congress
March 4, 1851, to March 3, 1853

First session—December 1, 1851, to August 31, 1852
Second session—December 6, 1852, to March 3, 1853
Special session of the Senate—March 4, 1851, to March
    13, 1851
(Administration of Millard Fillmore, 1850–1853)

Historical Background

Enactment of the Compromise of 1850 resulted in a momentary lull in debate over the slavery question. Both North and South hoped the debate would not erupt again, but it was far from forgotten. At the outset of the Thirty-second Congress, Stephen A. Douglas told his Senate colleagues that the compromise should be considered a "final settlement" of the slavery issue. It was time, he reasoned, to "cease agitating, stop debate, and drop the subject." Forty-four members of Congress went so far as to sign a pledge that they would not support a political candidate who was not totally committed to the compromise. When Sen. Charles Sumner of Massachusetts sought the repeal of the Fugitive Slave Act in August 1852, only three other senators were willing to support him. That November, Democrat Franklin Pierce captured the presidency by endorsing the compromise and pledging not to let slavery again become a political issue. Pierce won with 254 electoral votes; his Whig rival, General Winfield Scott, received 42 electoral votes. The tally was the same for Democratic vice presidential nominee William R. King and Whig nominee William A. Graham.

Despite the congressional compromise on slavery, the issue continued to intrude on the national consciousness. Harriet Beecher Stowe's celebrated novel *Uncle Tom's Cabin,* published in March 1852, helped convert thousands to the merits of the antislavery movement. Stowe's portrayal of the tragic aspects of slavery sold more than 300,000 copies in its first year alone. David M. Potter said that "history cannot evaluate with precision the influence of the novel upon public opinion, but the northern attitude toward slavery was never the same after *Uncle Tom's Cabin.* Men who had remained unmoved by real fugitives wept for Tom under the lash and cheered for Eliza with the bloodhounds on her track." Despite "a supreme effort to avert the dangers of the [Wilmot] Proviso and restore sectional harmony," the compromisers of 1850 had enacted in the Fugitive Slave Act "a firebrand vastly more inflammatory than the Proviso."[1]

Still, little sense existed of the impending crisis that would consume the nation in less than a decade.

For the Thirty-second Congress, the question of railroad subsidies was of greater importance. Federal aid to railroads would be a subject of considerable interest for much of the 1850s. In August 1852, Congress granted a one-hundred-foot right-of-way through public lands in the states to all railroads that were chartered at the time or might be chartered within the next ten years. If heavy cuts were made through hills, or earth fills across valleys or depressions were necessary, a maximum two-hundred-foot right-of-way was granted. Also, railroads were given the right to use earth, stone, and timber from adjacent public lands in constructing roadbeds, and they were granted sites for construction depots, watering places, and workshops. The provisions of the act were made applicable to public lands within the territories in 1855 and extended for another five years in 1862.

A second significant piece of railroad legislation signed into law in early March 1853 authorized the secretary of war to make explorations and surveys for determining the most practical and economic route for a railroad between the Mississippi River and the Pacific Ocean. This law, the first appropriation made toward the development of a rail route to the Pacific Coast, provided $150,000 for the survey. Its enactment resolved months of debate over possible routes such a venture might take. In February 1855, Secretary of War Jefferson Davis submitted the results of the surveys and explorations of five different routes across the West. Nothing could be agreed on, however, as northerners favored northern routes and southerners southern ones. Moreover, some in Congress continued to insist that the federal government had no right to make appropriations for internal improvements. Not until after the outbreak of the Civil War, and withdrawal of southern representation in Congress, was agreement finally reached on the construction of a railroad to the Pacific.

Two other transportation concerns, however, did capture immediate attention. During the eight months preceding passage of the Steamboat Act of 1852, seven boiler explosions aboard steamboats claimed nearly seven hundred lives. Congress responded to these maritime disasters by creating the Steamboat Inspection Service, one of the first federal agencies to regulate private industry. The act also established steamboat standards and a licensing system for all operators of passenger steamboats. Acting on frequent complaints about the quality of aids to navigation and management of the nation's lighthouses, Congress authorized a board of specialists to study the matter. The board found that lighthouses built during the previous few decades suffered from inadequate construction and design, and the entire lighthouse system needed to be revamped. With little delay, the board's recommendations were accepted and a U.S. Lighthouse Board was created to be responsible for lighthouse administration and construction. The new board moved quickly to apply new technology, upgrade equipment, and revise contracting procedures.

Soon after the discovery of gold in California, the government found it difficult to strike enough gold coins to meet the demand with just one mint. Also, it was not possible to transport all the gold to Philadelphia for coining as it was unsafe as well as time consuming. When President Millard Fillmore recommended that a branch of the United States Mint be established in California, Congress agreed and approved the construction of a second mint. Treasury Secretary Thomas Corwin chose San Francisco as the site for the new facility. With the Coinage Act of 1853, the United States moved closer to a single monetary standard based on gold, and one in which the value stamped on a coin was what the government said it was, not necessarily the value of the material from which that coin was made. Since the California gold rush, maintaining parity between the face value and the metal value of silver and gold coins had been difficult. While gold became more plentiful, silver supplies remained more-or-less constant. As a consequence, gold's value declined relative to silver and the price of silver rose, silver coinage did not circulate and, instead, was hoarded and eventually melted. Following passage of the act, silver coinage again began to circulate freely and steadily.

Near the conclusion of the Thirty-second Congress, the Washington Territory was created from the Oregon Territory. President Millard Fillmore signed an unusual piece of legislation authorizing William L. Sharkey, consul of the United States at Havana, to administer the oath of office to Vice President-elect King, who was in Cuba attempting to recover from tuberculosis. King was sworn in on March 24, 1853. A few days later, he left Cuba for his plantation in Alabama, where he died on April 18.

Major Acts

U.S. Mint Established in San Francisco. Provided for the establishment of a branch of the United States Mint in California. Stipulated that the branch would be under the direction of the director of the mint in Philadelphia, who would be responsible for prescribing such regulations as necessary to establishment of the branch. Approved July 3, 1852 (10 Stat. 11–13).

Right-of-Way Granted to All Railroads. Granted a right-of-way through public lands to all railroads chartered by any of the states within the next ten years. Also granted necessary sites not less than ten miles apart for depots, watering places, and workshops along the line or lines of the railroads. Approved August 4, 1852 (10 Stat. 28–29). The act was broadened to include public lands within the territories on March 3, 1855 (10 Stat. 683). On July 15, 1862, the provisions of the act, as amended, were extended for an additional five years (12 Stat. 577).

Steamboat Act of 1852. Created the steamboat inspection service under the control of the Treasury Department to establish stricter regulations and better oversight of vessels with steam propulsion. Required pilots and engineers of steamboats carrying passengers to be licensed. Stipulated that all steamboats be equipped with "suitable steam gauges." Called for annual inspections of steamboat boilers, and established standards for boiler construction. Provided for the appointment, of nine supervising inspectors who were experts in the construction and operation of commercial craft, and local inspectors, acting under the supervising inspectors. Approved August 30, 1852 (10 Stat. 61–75).

Lighthouse Board Created. Empowered a newly established nine-member U.S. lighthouse board, under the secretary of the Treasury, to "discharge all the administrative duties" relative to lighthouses and other aids to navigation. Designated the secretary of the Treasury as ex officio president of the board, which was authorized to elect a chairman and to divide the coast of the United States into no more than twelve lighthouse districts, to each of which the president was to assign an army or navy officer as lighthouse inspector. Approved August 31, 1852 (10 Stat. 119–121, Secs. 9–12).

Coinage Act of 1853. Reduced the amount of silver in coins of half-dollar and lower denominations to 93.1 percent of their previous weight. Restricted the legal tender status of silver coins to debts "not exceeding five dollars." Authorized the Treasury to purchase only limited amounts of silver to mint subsidiary coinage half dollars, quarters, dimes, and half dimes, an amount that would necessarily be less than holders of silver

would want to bring to the Treasury at overvalued prices. Approved February 21, 1853 (10 Stat. 160–161).

Washington Territory Established. Established the Washington Territory out of that portion of the Oregon Territory lying north of the Columbia River and the 46th parallel east to the summit of the Rocky Mountains. Provided for a territorial government, which included a governor, secretary of the territory, and a legislative assembly (consisting of a Council and House of Representatives). Vested judicial power in a supreme court, district courts, probate courts, and justices of the peace. Approved March 2, 1853 (10 Stat. 172–179).

Administration of the Oath of Office to Vice President-Elect William R. King. Authorized William L. Sharkey, consul of the United States at Havana, to administer the oath of office to William R. King, vice president-elect, at Havana or any other place on the island of Cuba. Also provided for the administration of the oath by any judge or magistrate in the United States. Approved March 2, 1853 (10 Stat. 180).

Transcontinental Railroad Survey. Authorized the secretary of war "to employ such portion of the corps of topographical engineers, and such other persons as he may deem necessary, to make such explorations and surveys as he may deem advisable, to ascertain the most practical and economical route for a railroad from the Mississippi River to the Pacific Ocean." Appropriated $150,000 to defray the expense of the explorations and surveys. Approved March 3, 1853 (10 Stat. 219, Sec. 10).

Note

1. David M. Potter, *The Impending Crisis, 1848–1861* (New York: Harper and Row, 1976), 130, 140.

Thirty-third Congress
March 4, 1853, to March 3, 1855

First session—December 5, 1853, to August 7, 1854

Second session—December 4, 1854, to March 3, 1855

Special session of the Senate—March 4, 1853, to April 11, 1853

(Administration of Franklin Pierce, 1853–1857)

Historical Background

In his inaugural address of March 4, 1853, President Franklin Pierce proclaimed that further territorial acquisition is "eminently important for our protection," the "preservation of the rights of commerce," and perhaps the "peace of the world." During the next two years, the actions of the Pierce administration confirmed his espoused intention of further expanding the boundaries of the United States.

When Pierce assumed the presidency, several transcontinental railroad routes were being actively debated. Most attractive to the new administration, favored by southern legislators, and championed by Secretary of War Jefferson Davis was one that ran through an area south of the Gila River in northern Mexico. Acting on Davis's suggestion, Pierce appointed James Gadsden, a southern railroad promoter, as U.S. minister to Mexico to purchase the land needed to make the southern route a reality. In the Gadsden Purchase, finalized on December 30, 1853, Mexico ceded to the United States a rectangular 29,640 square mile strip of desert land making up the southern part of present-day Arizona and New Mexico in return for a payment of $10 million. During Senate consideration of the Gadsden Purchase on April 25, 1854, twelve of twenty-two northerners opposed the treaty while all twenty-three western and southern senators supported it.

Other diplomatic endeavors during the Thirty-third Congress resulted in the approval of treaties expanding U.S. trade with Canada and Japan. Seeking to open commerce with Japan, which had not traded with Western countries for nearly three centuries, President Fillmore sent a four-ship naval squadron under Commodore Matthew C. Perry to the Far East. Perry successfully used both diplomacy and the veiled threat of force to secure limited American trading rights in Japan. In June 1854, the Senate approved the Treaty of Kanagawa opening the ports of Shimoda and Hakodate to American trade. A reciprocity treaty signed with Great Britain the same month expanded American fishing privileges in Canadian waters and allowed a lengthy list of raw materials to enter both the United States and Canadian provinces duty free.

President Pierce's attempt in 1854 to acquire Cuba from the Spanish proved to be far less successful. Cuba was particularly attractive to southern expansionists who harbored dreams of the Caribbean island becoming another slave state. Those aspirations were foiled when a confidential diplomatic dispatch prepared by three U.S. ministers meeting in Ostend, Belgium, recommending that Cuba be taken forcibly if Spain would not sell the island, became public in November. A shocked Pierce received the Ostend Manifesto amid another political disaster—the 1854 congressional elections that saw the Democrats lose an astonishing seventy-six House seats to Republicans, Whigs, and Know-Nothings.

The seeds of the Democratic electoral debacle had been planted six months earlier with enactment of the Kansas-Nebraska Act. While the Compromise of 1850 had supposedly settled the issue of slavery in the territories, construction of a transcontinental railroad to the Pacific through the center of the country forced

Congress to reconsider. In an effort to secure a central transcontinental rail route and resolve the question of slavery, Sen. Stephen A. Douglas of Illinois introduced legislation that left to their inhabitants the decision as to whether the territories of Kansas and Nebraska would enter the Union as slave states or free states. It also repealed the Missouri Compromise of 1820, which prohibited slavery north of the 36°30' line, further confirming the possibility that the two territories could enter as either slave or free states.

Passage of the Kansas-Nebraska Act prompted outraged antislavery sentiment in the North and Northwest, and it materially contributed to the final collapse of the second party system. The Whigs, whose fragile coalition of northern and southern elements had increasingly experienced internal dissension over the slavery question, began to fly apart. Grassroots elements representing disaffected Democrats, antislavery Whigs, Free Soilers, and nativist Know-Nothings began to coalesce as a new political force. These local groupings gradually emerged as a new political party, the Republicans.

Other enactments included the Graduation Act of 1854, which successfully brought together an emerging alliance of northerners and westerners who sought a reduction in the price of public lands. Supporters of the act, which had been promoted by Sen. Thomas Hart Benton of Missouri for three decades, argued that it would hasten the sale of less desirable tracts of land that had remained unsold for at least ten years by allowing settlers occupying the land a preemptive right of purchase. Using a graduated scale, the longer a section had been for sale the less it cost a settler. Before the act was repealed in 1862, an average of thirty million to forty million acres of public land a year were sold well below the earlier $1.25 per acre price. With the passage of the Citizenship Act of 1855, children of U.S. citizens born outside the jurisdictional limits of the United States were automatically granted citizenship. Furthermore, a federal court of claims was established with jurisdiction over lawsuits brought against the federal government.

The rapid influx of Irish, German, and Chinese immigrants into the United States after 1845 was accompanied by a series of steamship disasters and the prevalence of cholera, typhus, and smallpox among arriving immigrants. Enactment of the 1855 Passengers Act marked a genuine improvement in the quality of sea travel, which for the first time regulated the number of passengers allowed on a vessel, as well as the health and well-being of those on board.

Major Acts and Treaties

Gadsden Purchase Treaty. Arranged for the cession by Mexico of a strip of 29,640 square miles of desert land south of the Gila River in return for $10 million. Concluded December 30, 1853 (18 Stat. 503–506, part 2). Ratification advised by the Senate April 25, 1854.[1]

Treaty of Kanagawa. Opened the Japanese ports of Shimoda and Hakodate to U.S. trade, made provisions for U.S. ships and seamen shipwrecked in Japan, and allowed a U.S. agent to remain at Shimoda. Concluded March 31, 1854 (18 Stat. 446–449, part 2). Ratification advised by the Senate July 15, 1854.[2]

Kansas-Nebraska Act. Repealed the Missouri Compromise of 1820, so that the citizens in the territories of Kansas and Nebraska could determine whether the territories would enter the Union as slave or free states. All cases involving slavery could now be appealed to the territorial courts and the U.S. Supreme Court. Approved May 30, 1854 (10 Stat. 277–290). (*Missouri Compromise of 1820, p. 52*)

Canadian Reciprocity Treaty (Elgin-Marcy Treaty). Negotiated with the United Kingdom acting in behalf of Canada. Expanded American fishing rights along the coasts of Canada (then composed of only Ontario and Quebec) and the maritime provinces of New Brunswick, Nova Scotia, Prince Edward Island, and Newfoundland. Permitted Canadian fishing off the Atlantic Coast as far south as Norfolk, Virginia. Reciprocity provisions included a long list of commodities—chiefly agricultural products, which were to be admitted by the signatories duty-free. Concluded June 5, 1854 (18 Stat. 329–333, part 2). Ratification advised by the Senate August 2, 1854.[3] The treaty was abrogated on March 17, 1866 (18 Stat. 329, part 2).

Graduation Act. Reduced the price of public lands, on a graduated scale, that had been on the market for ten years or more. Lands on the market for ten to fifteen years were sold at $1.00 per acre, for fifteen to twenty years at 75 cents per acre, for twenty to twenty-five years at 50 cents per acre, for twenty-five to thirty years at 25 cents per acre, and for more than thirty years at 12 cents per acre. Applicable only to preemption lands. Approved August 4, 1854 (10 Stat. 574).

1855 Naturalization Act. Granted citizenship to women who married U.S. citizens, and to children born out of the limits and jurisdiction of the United States, whose fathers were citizens. Approved February 10, 1855 (10 Stat. 604).

Court of Claims Established. Established a federal court of claims consisting of three judges with authority to hear and decide claims brought against the United States that were based on the Constitution, federal law, regulations of the executive branch, or any express or implied contracts with the federal government. Approved February 24, 1855 (10 Stat. 612–614).

1855 Passenger Act. Limited the proportion of passengers to the tonnage on steam vessels—one passenger per two tons of vessel. Required ships to provide a specific amount of space for each passenger, sufficient food and water for each passenger, ventilators, healthy sanitary conditions, and a safe, clean privy for the exclusive use of every 100 passengers. Required ship captains to maintain good discipline among passengers. Required vessels to be inspected by the collector of customs. Provided fines for violation of the various regulations. Approved March 3, 1855 (10 Stat. 715–721).

Notes

1. *Journal of the Executive Proceedings of the Senate* (Washington, D.C.: U.S. Government Printing Office, 1887), 9:309–315.

2. *Journal of the Executive Proceedings of the Senate,* 9:357–358.

3. *Journal of the Executive Proceedings of the Senate,* 9:376.

Thirty-fourth Congress
March 4, 1855, to March 3, 1857

First session—December 3, 1855, to August 18, 1856
Second session—August 21, 1856, to August 30, 1856
Third session—December 1, 1856, to March 3, 1857
(Administration of Franklin Pierce, 1853–1857)

Historical Background

Six months after the Kansas-Nebraska Act was signed into law, the Nebraska Territory established a Free Soil government and convened its first legislature in an orderly fashion. The selection of a territorial assembly in Kansas a few weeks later, however, provoked a bitter struggle when hundreds of western Missourians flooded across the border to assure the election of a proslavery legislature. Conditions in Kansas grew more strained in July 1855 after the new legislature enacted severe penalties for antislavery activities and adopted a stringent slave code. Antislavery settlers responded by holding Free State conventions, first in Big Springs and then in Topeka, where they rejected the actions of the proslavery territorial legislature, drafted a constitution prohibiting slavery, and requested that Kansas be admitted to the Union as a free state. Voters in January 1856 elected an antislavery governor and state legislature.

Amidst the political chaos of two governors and two state legislatures—one chosen fraudulently, the other without legal sanction—President Franklin Pierce sent a special message to Congress on January 24, 1856, calling the Free State movement in Kansas an act of rebellion. Two weeks later, Pierce issued a proclamation formally committing his administration to the proslavery government. On Capitol Hill, Sen. Stephen A. Douglas of Illinois also denounced the Topeka Free State legislators

and introduced a bill authorizing Kansas to hold a constitutional convention and create a state government. Following heated debate, a three-member House investigative committee was established to review the elections in Kansas. The committee found that "every election" involving proslavery candidates had "been controlled, not by the actual settlers, but by citizens of Missouri; and, as a consequence, every officer in the Territory, from constable to legislators, except those appointed by the President, owe[d] their positions to non-resident voters."[1]

Tensions over Kansas were further exacerbated when Rep. Preston S. Brooks of South Carolina physically attacked Sen. Charles Sumner of Massachusetts on the Senate floor after Sumner delivered stinging remarks against proslavery actions in the territory. Brooks justified his actions by alleging that Sumner had defamed Brooks's cousin. (Sumner, who was severely injured, did not return to the Senate until December 1859.) Eventually, the Senate adopted an amendment to the Douglas bill that called for yet another constitutional convention in Kansas, while the House passed a bill to admit Kansas as a free state. Neither proposal was acted on by both houses. On August 1, 1856, the House refused to seat either the proslavery or Free State territorial delegates from Kansas. House Republicans in late August unsuccessfully sought to alter the administration's Kansas policy by attaching a rider to an army appropriations bill that prohibited federal troops from aiding the proslavery Kansas legislature. After a special session of Congress was called by President Pierce to reconsider the bill, the rider was dropped.

Throughout much of 1856, there was frequent civil strife between antislavery and proslavery settlers in Kansas. The most heavily publicized involved the murder in May of five proslavery settlers by radical abolitionist John Brown and six companions. In November and December alone, an estimated two hundred people from both factions were killed. When the Thirty-fourth Congress adjourned in March 1857, Kansas was still without a sanctioned government. "Bleeding Kansas" remained the dominant domestic issue as forces supporting slavery and those opposing its expansion continued to contend for an advantage.

Another issue of considerable importance to the president in 1856 was the propriety of federal involvement in internal improvements. On five occasions within a space of two months, Pierce rejected public works bills. In each instance, his veto was overridden by Congress—three times in July 1856 and twice in August 1856. The only other pre–Civil War president to have even one veto overturned was John Tyler. All five of Pierce's vetoes involved waterway improvement bills. They provided for removing obstructions at the mouth of the Mississippi River, deepening the channel over the flats of the St. Mary's River in Michigan, deepening the channel over the St. Clair Flats in Michigan, continuing improvement of the Des Moines Rapids in the Mississippi River, improving navigation in the Patapsco River, and rendering the port of Baltimore accessible to the U.S. war steamers. Pierce's veto message, in each case, emphasized his belief that Congress did not have the constitutional authority to authorize local internal improvements.

Franklin Pierce also suffered the indignity of not being chosen by his party to run for reelection. James Buchanan, selected on the seventeenth ballot by the delegates to the Democratic National Convention, went on in November 1856 to defeat John C. Fremont (Republican) and former president Millard Fillmore (Whig/Know-Nothing). Buchanan and his vice presidential running mate, John C. Breckinridge, received 174 electoral votes; Fremont and William L. Dayton, 114; and Fillmore and Andrew Jackson Donelson, 8. Results of the congressional elections also favored the Democrats, who retained control of the Senate and regained the House.

Before he left the White House, however, Franklin Pierce did affix his signature to several noteworthy pieces of legislation. In August 1856, Congress sanctioned the first official move by the United States toward the creation of an overseas empire, with the

Guano Islands Act. This enactment was prompted by the race to acquire guano (dried bird droppings), one of the most sought after fertilizers of the day. Previously, U.S. territorial acquisition had always been directed toward westward expansion across the North American continent with the intent of eventually elevating the new territories to statehood. That policy changed under the Guano Islands Act. For the first time, the United States was allowed to take possession of lands it had no intention of incorporating into the federal union. Over the next 30 years, U.S. sovereignty was claimed over some 30 islands, including Christmas Island and the Midway Islands. Also that August members of Congress doubled their compensation.

By 1857, the rapidly increasing population of California demanded faster and more frequent mail service to and from the East. The Overland California Mail Act allowed the Postmaster General to seek bids for an overland stagecoach service to carry passengers and mail between the Missouri River and San Francisco. A compromise between Northern and Southern congressmen left selection of the route the mail would travel up to the contractor.

Before the Thirty-fourth Congress adjourned, an enabling act that authorized the inhabitants of the Territory of Minnesota to frame a constitution and state government in preparation for statehood was approved. Treasury surpluses helped the Democrats obtain a legislative victory with the enactment of the Tariff of 1857, which reduced duties to the lowest level in several years. Achievement of an adequate supply of U.S. coins of all denominations allowed Congress to bar the further use of foreign coins as legal tender.

One of Franklin Pierce's final actions as president was signing a bill committing the U.S. government to match the support the British government had promised for the construction of a transatlantic telegraph cable proposed by Cyrus West Field. Some 18 months later, on August 15, 1858, Queen Victoria sent President James Buchanan her congratulations on the successful completion of the transatlantic cable. Before the cable was laid, communication between the two continents could travel no faster than the fastest steamships. "The government's backing of the cable was," one writer suggests, "analogous to the federal support of the transcontinental railroad in the 19th Century."[2]

Major Acts

Increase in Member Compensation. Increased the annual compensation of members of Congress from $1,500 to $3,000, and that of the president pro tempore of the Senate, Speaker of the House, and Vice President from $3,000 annually to $6,000. Made the increases retroactive to the beginning of the Thirty-fourth Congress. Provided that "voluntary absences by members from their public duties" would result in a deduction in the monthly payments of members. Approved August 16, 1856 (11 Stat. 48–49).

Guano Islands Act. Allowed American citizens to lay claim to any island in the world that met the following three criteria: (1) the island was uninhabited, (2) no other nation could effectively claim the island, and (3) the island had vast quantities of guano which the citizen claiming the island for the United States intended to mine. Stated that U.S. government can abandon all claims to any of these islands whenever it deemed necessary. Approved August 18, 1856 (11 Stat. 119–120).

Coinage Act of 1857. Barred the use of foreign coins as legal tender, and provided that when such coins were received they were to be recoined at the U.S. Mint. Authorized the secretary of the Treasury to prescribe such regulations as may be necessary to secure recoinage. Repealed acts making foreign coins legal tender. Approved February 21, 1857 (11 Stat. 163–164).

Minnesota Enabling Act. Authorized the inhabitants of the Territory of Minnesota to hold a constitutional convention, draft a constitution, and form a state government in preparation for admission as a state. Delineated the geographical boundaries of the state. Approved February 26, 1857 (11 Stat. 166–167).

Atlantic Cable Act of 1857. Authorized the secretary of state to "contract with a competent person, persons, or associations" to "lay down a submarine cable, to connect existing telegraphs between the coast of Newfoundland and the coast of Ireland, and for the use of such submarine communication" by the U.S. government once it was completed. Provided for a contract that would "give person, persons, or associations" who laid the cable a guaranteed source of income for 25 years. Stipulated that the government of Great Britain had to "enter into a like contract for this purpose with the same person, persons, or association, and upon terms of exact equality with those stipulated by the United States." Approved March 3, 1857 (11 Stat. 187–188).

Overland California Mail Act of 1857. Authorized the postmaster general to contract for the carriage of letters from somewhere on the Mississippi River to San Francisco for six years. Selection of the route to be traveled was the contractor's choice. Stipulated that the mail was to be carried using "good four-horse coaches or spring wagons, suitable for the conveyance of passengers." Approved March 3, 1857 (11 Stat. 190, Secs. 10–13).

Tariff of 1857. Modified the Walker Tariff Act of 1846, by reducing the duties on many imported goods to a general level of 20 percent. Expanded the free list, admitted most raw wool imports that were competitive with homegrown wool without a duty, and reduced duties on luxury items such as fine food, wine, spirits, and cigars. Approved March 3, 1857 (11 Stat. 192–195).

Notes

1. U.S. House Special Committee Appointed to Investigate the Troubles in the Territory of Kansas, *Kansas Affairs*, 34th Cong., lst sess., 1856, H. Rept. 200, 2.

2. Robert O. Woods, "A Cable to Shrink the Earth," *Mechanical Engineering*, v. 133, January 2011, 41.

Thirty-fifth Congress
March 4, 1857, to March 3, 1859

First session—December 7, 1857, to June 14, 1858
Second session—December 6, 1858, to March 3, 1859
Special sessions of the Senate—March 4, 1857, to March
    14, 1857; June 15, 1858, to June 16, 1858
(Administration of James Buchanan, 1857–1861)

Historical Background

On March 6, 1857, two days after President James Buchanan in his inaugural address condemned slavery agitation in Kansas, the U.S. Supreme Court handed down its decision in *Dred Scott v. Sandford.* The case stemmed from a suit brought by Dred Scott, a Missouri slave, who sought to gain his freedom. Scott claimed to be free by virtue of having lived for almost four years with his master in a free state (Illinois) and a free territory (Wisconsin). The Court disagreed, ruling that because Scott was a slave, he was a citizen of neither Missouri nor the United States and thus had no constitutional rights. A majority of the Court also held that Congress did not have the authority to abolish slavery in the territories and that, as a consequence, relevant provisions of the Compromise of 1850 were ruled unconstitutional. The Court's decision further inflamed the sectional differences within the country.

In early October 1857, Free Staters in Kansas captured a sizable majority of seats in the election for a new territorial legislature. Just two weeks later, a proslavery constitution was adopted by a convention held in the territorial capital of Lecompton. Only one article of the Lecompton Constitution, however, was put to a popular vote in December—whether to have a constitution "with slavery" or "without slavery." If voters chose to have a constitution without slavery, owning slaves already in the territory would still be legal. Free Staters, who by then were an overwhelming majority of the settlers in Kansas, refused to participate. The result was predictable; the constitution was adopted, 6,226 to 569 (with a large number of the yeas widely believed to be fraudulent).

A second vote on the entire Lecompton Constitution, called by the Free State–dominated Kansas legislature on January 4, 1858, resulted in its rejection by a 10,226 to 162 margin. Ignoring the advice of several friends, President Buchanan urged the admission of Kansas into the Union with the controversial Lecompton Constitution as its charter. An outraged Sen. Stephen A. Douglas of Illinois declared that the Lecompton Constitution made a mockery of popular sovereignty and urged Congress to reject it as a basis for admitting Kansas into the Union. The Senate voted to approve the admission of Kansas as a slave state over Douglas's opposition, while the House determined that another popular vote in the territory was necessary.

The impasse was resolved when Rep. William H. English of Indiana proposed a bill providing for another popular vote on the Lecompton Constitution. Under the English bill, if the constitution were approved and slavery accepted, Kansas would receive four million acres of public land and approximately 5 percent of the net proceeds from two million acres that were to be sold by the federal government in July. If it were rejected, statehood would be deferred until Kansas had a population of ninety thousand. On August 2, 1858, Kansans rejected the proslavery Lecompton Constitution by a vote of 11,812 to 1,926, deferring statehood for another two years.

Late in August 1858, the first of seven debates between Senator Douglas and his Republican challenger, Abraham Lincoln, was held in Ottawa, Illinois.

During their second, and most notable, debate, Douglas declared that despite the *Dred Scott* decision, slavery could be excluded from a territory if it were done through local legislation. Douglas's Freeport Doctrine, together with his opposition to the Lecompton Constitution, was widely criticized by southerners and would prove instrumental in the lack of southern support for his Democratic presidential nomination in 1860. As the two senatorial candidates continued their exchanges, Lincoln took a strong moral stand against slavery while Douglas evaded discussion of the moral aspects of the institution. Although Lincoln lost his bid to unseat Douglas, his eloquence and sound reasoning thrust him into the national spotlight. In the 1858 congressional elections, his fellow Republicans won control of the House. The Democrats retained the Senate.

Amidst the heated debate and controversy over slavery, Minnesota (May 11, 1858) and Oregon (February 14, 1859) were admitted to the Union. The Senate in June 1858 ratified the Tientsin Treaties, opening eleven new Chinese ports to American shipping, setting tariff and duty rates, and legalizing the opium trade.

Major Acts and Treaties

English Bill. Offered immediate admission of Kansas to the Union, plus a grant of four million acres of public land and 5 percent of the net proceeds from about two million acres to be sold by the federal government after Kansas's admission as a state, if the Lecompton Constitution were accepted by the voters. If rejected, the territory would not be admitted to the Union as a state until its population exceeded the "ratio of representation required for a member of the House of Representatives." Approved May 4, 1858 (11 Stat. 269–272).

Minnesota Admitted to the Union. Accepted the constitution and state government formed by a Minnesota Territory convention on August 29, 1857, and declared that Minnesota was "one of the United States of America, and admitted into the Union on an equal footing with the original States." Approved May 11, 1858 (11 Stat. 285).

Treaties of Tientsin. Opened eleven new Chinese ports to the United States, Great Britain, Russia, and France, and allowed navigation up the Yangtze River into the heart of China. Granted foreigners freedom to travel anywhere in the interior of China and permitted foreign diplomats to reside in Peking. Fixed the tariff on imports from China at 5 percent and legalized the opium trade. Concluded June 18, 1858 (12 Stat. 1023–1030). Ratified by the Senate on December 15, 1858.[1]

Oregon Admitted to the Union. Acknowledged that the "people of Oregon had framed, ratified, and adopted a constitution of State government which is republican in form, and in conformity with the Constitution of the United States," and declared that the state of Oregon had been "received into the Union on an equal footing with the other States." Approved February 14, 1859 (11 Stat. 383–384).

Note

1. *Journal of the Executive Proceedings of the Senate* (Washington, D.C.: U.S. Government Printing Office, 1887), 11:18–19.

Thirty-sixth Congress
March 4, 1859, to March 3, 1861

First session—December 5, 1859, to June 25, 1860
Second session—December 3, 1860, to March 3, 1861
Special sessions of the Senate—March 4, 1859, to March
     10, 1859; June 26, 1860, to June 28, 1860
(Administration of James Buchanan, 1857–1861)

Historical Background

Attention once again focused on Kansas during July 1859 when a convention met at Wyandotte for another try at constitution making. The Wyandotte Constitution, prohibiting slavery in the territory, was ratified on October 4, 1859, by a popular vote of 10,421 to 5,530. Less than two weeks later, halfway across the continent, radical abolitionist John Brown and eighteen other men seized the U.S. arsenal at Harpers Ferry, Virginia (now in West Virginia), in a failed attempt to secure arms for instigating a slave uprising. When Brown was hanged for treason on December 2, 1859, he became a martyr to many in the North. For southerners, the raid confirmed their worst fears—that abolitionists were willing to use force if necessary to destroy slavery. Echoing that theme, President James Buchanan warned in his third annual message to Congress that the "bloody occurrences at Harpers Ferry" symbolized "an incurable disease in the public mind, which may . . . terminate . . . in an open war by the North to abolish slavery in the South."

President Buchanan implored both North and South "to cultivate the feelings of mutual forbearance and good will toward each other." Instead, Congress erupted in a verbal battle over the implications of Brown's raid and the significance of *The Impending Crisis,* southerner Hilton R. Helper's passionate attack

on slavery. Early in February 1860, Sen. Jefferson Davis of Mississippi introduced seven resolutions in defense of states' rights, the institution of slavery, and the legality of recovering fugitive slaves. A month later, Rep. John Covode of Pennsylvania offered a resolution calling for the appointment of a special House committee to investigate the conduct of President Buchanan during consideration of the Lecompton Constitution. The committee would issue a report highly critical of the Buchanan administration.

By April 1860, when twenty-five hundred Democratic delegates gathered for their national convention in Charleston, South Carolina, the disruptive force of sectionalism was about to destroy the lone remaining political organization that represented the entire country. Most of the southern delegates arrived at the convention determined to adopt a platform providing for federal protection of slavery in the territories. When the convention instead approved language vaguely endorsing popular sovereignty and proposed that all questions involving slavery in the territories be left to the U.S. Supreme Court, delegates from eight southern states walked out, virtually assuring a Republican victory in November.

A second Democratic convention meeting at Baltimore in June selected Stephen A. Douglas as its presidential candidate, while southern delegates who had bolted the Charleston convention nominated Vice President John C. Breckinridge a few days later on a platform advocating slavery in the territories. A third presidential contender, John Bell, represented the Constitutional Unionist Party, which included remnants of the Whigs and Know-Nothings. Meanwhile, Abraham Lincoln embarked on his quest for the Republican nomination with a stirring speech at the Cooper Union in New York on February 27, 1860, followed by several successful addresses in New England. Lincoln condemned northern extremism as well as southern secessionist threats. Although he believed the institution of slavery was morally wrong and must be contained within its existing boundaries, Lincoln insisted that slavery should not be disturbed where it already existed. Lincoln believed that his compromise (guaranteeing slavery while simultaneously preventing its expansion) would settle the question. These views won him the Republican nomination at Chicago in May. The Republican Party platform appealed to both the North and the West. It called for a homestead law, a railroad to the Pacific, liberal immigration policies, and a protective tariff. Although Lincoln won only 40 percent of the popular vote in the 1860 election, Democratic fragmentation guaranteed him an Electoral College majority of 180 votes to 123 for Breckinridge, Bell, and Douglas combined. Lincoln's running mate was Hannibal Hamlin; Breckinridge's, Joseph Lane; Bell's, Edward Everett; and Douglas's, Herschel V. Johnson.

Anticipating the outcome of the presidential election of 1860, the South Carolina legislature remained in session until the results were known and then called a state convention. On December 20, the convention unanimously approved an ordinance of secession. In the minds of many southerners, a Republican president represented a mortal threat to the South's "peculiar institution." Abraham Lincoln, South Carolina declared in seceding from the Union, was a man whose "opinions and purposes [were] hostile to slavery." During the next six weeks, six additional southern states—Mississippi, Florida, Alabama, Georgia, Louisiana, and Texas—left the Union. On February 7, 1861, the seven seceding states adopted a constitution forming the Confederate States of America and elected Jefferson Davis as president. Even before the Confederate states officially joined together, they had begun seizures of U.S. federal government property.

Less than a month after the seven southern states left the Union, Congress approved a proposed constitutional amendment offered by Rep. Thomas Corwin of Ohio, which would have stopped Congress from "abolishing or interfering" with the "domestic institutions." After President Buchanan took the unusual step of signing the Corwin Amendment, which a president is not required to do by the Constitution, three states ratified it, but the onset of the Civil War stopped it from gaining any momentum. The time for reconciliation had passed.

The secession of southern states eliminated the major obstacle to the formation of free territories and made possible the creation of the Colorado, Dakota, and Nevada Territories. Several years of agitation for a transcontinental telegraph route also finally resulted in congressional support. Enactment of the National Telegraph Act in June 1860 was preceded by several weeks of intense legislative maneuvering in both the House and Senate. Revelations of fraud and mismanagement in government procurement prompted the inclusion of reform legislation in a Civil Sundry Appropriations Act that remained the primary law governing the procurement of supplies and nonpersonal services for the next 86 years.

By 1860, the reliance on newspapers and other printers for congressional and executive agency had become problematic. Twice within three years, scandals, fraud, and corruption were revealed by major congressional investigations, and ultimately provided the impetus for the bill creating the Government Printing Office. The Printing Act of 1860 broadened government publishing to not only include provided information, but for the first time disseminated and issued information directly as well. The official origin of the U.S. Army Signal Corps came in separate action with authorization for a signal office to the army staff in the War Department. With this appointment, "the United States Army became the first Army in the world to establish a separate communications branch."[1]

The Morrill Tariff of 1861, one of the last bills signed into law by President Buchanan, was precipitated by the panic of 1857, which had a drastic effect on federal revenues. It reversed the quasi-free trade policy established by the Walker Tariff of 1846 and began a trend toward protectionism that would increase with the outbreak of the Civil War. *(Walker Tariff Act, p. 82)*

Major Acts

Pacific Telegraph Act. Authorized the secretary of the Treasury to solicit sealed proposals for construction of a telegraph line between the western boundary of Missouri and San Francisco, California. Left the exact route of the line to the discretion of each bidder. As an incentive to the successful bidder, it provided a ten-year contract worth a maximum of $40,000 annually, a right-of-way through unoccupied public lands, and the right to establish repair stations at fifteen-mile intervals. Did not confer an exclusive right to construct a Pacific telegraph line. Established rates to be charged for each dispatch. Protected the telegraph contractors from excessive use by the government by authorizing additional payments when appropriate. Approved June 16, 1860 (12 Stat. 41–42).

Origin of the U.S. Army Signal Corps. Appropriated $2,000 for the "manufacture or purchase of apparatus and equipments for field signals," and added to the staff of the Army "one signal officer, with the rank, pay, and allowances of a major of cavalry, who shall have charge; under the direction of the Secretary of War, of all signal duty, and all books, papers, and apparatus connected therewith." Approved June 21, 1860 (12 Stat. 66).

Federal Procurement Act of 1860. Required all government purchases and contracts, except for personal services or when immediate delivery of an article was required, to be obtained from private industry through advertised procurement. Only when immediate delivery of an article or service was required could it be obtained by "open purchase or contract." Prohibited contracts or purchases when authorized by law or under an appropriation. Approved June 23, 1860 (12 Stat. 103–104, Sec. 3). See also Federal Procurement Act of 1861. Approved March 1, 1861 (12 Stat. 220, Sec. 10).

Printing Act of 1860. Established the Government Printing Office (GPO) and authorized the superintendent of public printing to construct a building, hire printing and binding staff, and carry out the printing needs of Congress as well as those of the executive and judicial branches of the government. Approved June 23, 1860 (12 Stat. 117–120).

Kansas Admitted to the Union. Accepted the constitution and state government formed by a Kansas Territory convention meeting in Wyandotte on July 29, 1859, and declared that the state of Kansas was one of

the "United States of America, and admitted into the Union on an equal footing with the original States." Approved January 29, 1861 (12 Stat. 126–128).

Colorado Territory Established. Created the Territory of Colorado. Provided that the executive power of the territory would be vested in a governor appointed by the president for four years and a secretary of the territory who was to act as governor "in case of the death, removal, resignation, or other necessary absence of the governor from the Territory." Vested legislative power in the governor and legislative assembly consisting of a council and house of representatives, and judicial power in a supreme court, district courts, probate courts, and justices of the peace. Approved February 28, 1861 (12 Stat. 172–176).

Morrill Tariff (Tariff Act of 1861). Substituted specific duties for ad valorem duties, raised duties generally from 15 percent to 28 percent, and greatly increased the rates on irons and woolens. Approved March 2, 1861 (12 Stat. 178–198). *(Tariff Act of 1862, p. 106; Morrill Tariff Amendments of 1864, p. 111; Tariff Act of 1875, p. 130)*

Nevada Territory Established. Created the Territory of Nevada from the western part of the Utah Territory. Provided that executive power would be vested in a governor appointed by the president for four years and a secretary of the territory who was to act as governor "in case of the death, removal, resignation, or other necessary absence of the governor from the Territory." Vested legislative power in the governor and legislative assembly consisting of a council and house of representatives, and judicial power in a supreme court, district courts, probate courts, and justices of the peace. Approved March 2, 1861 (12 Stat. 209–214).

Dakota Territory Established. Created the Territory of Dakota from the Minnesota Territory west of the present boundary of that state and the Nebraska Territory north of the 43rd parallel to the Missouri River. Provided that executive power would be vested in a governor appointed by the president for four years and a secretary of the territory who was to act as governor "in case of the death, removal, resignation, or other necessary absence of the governor from the Territory."

Vested legislative power in the governor and legislative assembly consisting of a council and house of representatives, and judicial power in a supreme court, district courts, probate courts, and justices of the peace. Approved March 2, 1861 (12 Stat. 239–244).

Corwin Amendment. Provided that the following article be proposed to the legislatures of the several states as an amendment to the Constitution of the United States, which, when ratified by two-thirds of the states, shall be part of the Constitution: "No amendment shall be made to the Constitution which will authorize or give to Congress the power to abolish or interfere, within any State, with the domestic institutions thereof, including that of persons held to labor or service by the laws of said State." Approved by President James Buchanan March 2, 1861 (12 Stat. 251).

Note

1. Rebecca Robbins Raines, *Getting the Message Through: A Branch History of the U.S. Army Signal Corps* (Washington, D.C.: Center of Military History, U.S. Army, 1996), 3.

Thirty-seventh Congress
March 4, 1861, to March 3, 1863

First session—July 4, 1861, to August 6, 1861
Second session—December 2, 1861, to July 17, 1862
Third session—December 1, 1862, to March 3, 1863
Special session of the Senate—March 4, 1861, to
　　　　March 28, 1861
(First administration of Abraham Lincoln, 1861–1865)

Historical Background

Compromises to avoid a civil war were proposed prior to Abraham Lincoln's March 4, 1861, inauguration. A February peace conference attended by delegates from twenty-one states failed, however, to achieve a solution to the crisis, when representatives from both northern and southern states refused to make substantive concessions. President Lincoln, in his inaugural address, sought to assure the South that there would be no invasion and that he did not intend "to interfere with the institution of slavery in the States where it exists." Lincoln did not believe he had the "lawful right to do so," and, furthermore, he had "no inclination to do so." But "we cannot separate," he maintained. The Union was "much older than the Constitution." The purpose for "establishing the Constitution was to 'form a more perfect Union,'" and "acts of violence within any State or States" to support secession were "insurrectionary or revolutionary." If it became necessary to use force to retain federal property and installations in the South, he would employ it. Confederate president Jefferson Davis held that the southern states, as sovereign states, had the right to self-determination. After South Carolina forces bombarded Fort Sumter on April 12–13, 1861, reconciliation was no longer possible.

By June 1861, eleven states—South Carolina, Mississippi, Florida, Alabama, Georgia, Louisiana, Texas, Virginia, Arkansas, North Carolina, and Tennessee—had seceded from the Union, ratified the Confederate Constitution, and joined the rebellion. During the first eight weeks of the Civil War, Lincoln proclaimed that a state of insurrection existed, blockaded southern ports, enlarged the army and navy, and drew funds from the federal Treasury to cover initial war expenses, all without congressional authorization.

Once Congress convened on July 4, 1861, it quickly moved to provide financial support for the measures Lincoln had already taken, The secretary of the Treasury was authorized to borrow $250 million during the next twelve months, the first federal income tax was approved, and tariff duties were increased. Additional revenues were generated through the Legal Tender Act of 1862 (authorizing the printing of large amounts of paper currency), Internal Revenue Act of 1862 (creating the Internal Revenue Bureau in the Treasury Department), Tariff Act of 1862 (dramatically raising tariff rates), and National Currency Act of 1863 (creating a National Banking System that replaced the chaotic state banking system in existence since Andrew Jackson's presidency). The latter was also designed to establish a uniform national currency that would eliminate the more than 10,000 types of paper money issued by individual banks, and guarantee that legal paper currency could be exchanged for gold or silver currency. The new currency was to be issued against federally backed bonds, as is modern money. The government financed the war by selling these bonds and the limited printing of the new "greenback" banknotes. In addition, the president was authorized to seize control of the railroads and telegraph for military use. Operation of the rail and telegraph lines was placed under the control of the military.

The First Confiscation Act of 1861 freed slaves being used by Confederates as either soldiers or laborers. An act embracing Lincoln's plan for compensated emancipation was enacted in April 1862, abolishing slavery in the District of Columbia. The Second Confiscation Act of 1862 freed slaves owned by traitors or supporters of rebellion, provided for seizure of rebel property, prohibited return of fugitive slaves, and authorized recruitment of blacks for the army.

Early in his presidency Lincoln may have considered emancipation to be unconstitutional and feared that adoption of antislavery measures might lead to the secession of loyal slave-holding border states. He ultimately changed his mind on the expediency and legality of emancipation, issuing a preliminary Emancipation Proclamation on September 22, 1862. The preliminary proclamation promised freedom to all "persons held as slaves" within areas still "in rebellion against the United States" after January 1, 1863. During the one-hundred-day interim before the end of the year, Lincoln entertained some editorial suggestions from his cabinet before he issued the final Emancipation Proclamation, following a New Year's Day 1863 reception at the White House. The document specifically designated those areas where the people were in rebellion and declared that all persons held as slaves in those areas "are, and henceforth shall be, free." In a largely successful effort to guarantee the continuing loyalty of Delaware, Kentucky, Maryland, and Missouri, the Emancipation Proclamation was limited in its coverage to slave states in rebellion.

Given the uncertain and shifting loyalties of the time, Congress was prompted to create the "iron-clad" oath, which required all individuals in civil, military or naval departments to make a declaration of both past and future loyalty to the Union. This oath is the earliest direct predecessor of the modern oath.

The president was authorized in March 1863 to suspend the writ of habeas corpus for the duration of the Civil War. For the first time, all able-bodied white males between the ages of twenty and forty-five were subject to conscription, and the president was authorized to present the Medal of Honor to members of the military in recognition of outstanding acts of heroism.

The Confederacy more than held its own on the battlefield during the war's first two years. In the east, federal armies struck into Virginia in four major offensives and numerous other actions, only to meet repeated defeats. Under a succession of commanders, the Army of the Potomac was bested, beginning with the historic first confrontation at Bull Run on July 21, 1861, and continuing with the Peninsular Campaign of April–July 1862 and the second Battle of Bull Run on August 24, 1862. Robert E. Lee, in command of the Confederate Army of Northern Virginia since June 1862, mounted a counterinvasion of Maryland in September. He was stopped by Union forces at the Battle of Antietam, whose twenty-three thousand casualties mark it as the bloodiest single day in U.S. military history. At year's end, the Army of the Potomac struck back and was repulsed with great loss at Fredericksburg on December 13.

In the West, constant skirmishes in the border states culminated in the bloody, but indecisive, Battle of Shiloh on April 6–7, 1862, while the first real federal victory was gained on May 1, when Commodore David Farragut's fleet captured New Orleans. The tide of battle surged back and forth over Tennessee and Kentucky for the balance of the year, but by the end of 1862 Ulysses S. Grant had begun a crucial campaign to seize Vicksburg, Mississippi, link up with federal forces in Louisiana, and divide the Confederacy.

Meanwhile, the U.S. Navy gradually tightened its blockade of southern ports, depriving the Confederacy of revenue from exported cotton and other commodities as well as the imports of munitions and war materiel it needed. One of the most significant battles in naval history occurred on March 9, 1862, when the Confederate ironclad *Virginia*, which had been converted from the abandoned steam frigate *Merrimack,* dueled with the *USS Monitor,* a revolutionary ironclad featuring such innovations as a revolving turret, at Hampton Roads, near the mouth of the Chesapeake Bay. Although the battle between the *Monitor* and the *Merrimack* had little effect on the outcome of the war, it changed the way ships were built. The United States Navy and navies in Europe abandoned the building of wooden ships and began building ironclads, ushering in a new era of iron warships.

On Capitol Hill, the war effort was paramount but not the only matter being considered. A two-decade effort to create a separate Department of Agriculture was realized. The new department, which would achieve cabinet rank in 1889, was to be headed by a commissioner responsible for dispensing information on subjects connected with agriculture. The department was to "procure, propagate, and distribute . . . new and valuable seeds and plants." Work was also completed on the Homestead Act, which provided 160 acres of free land in the West to all citizens and applicants for citizenship who occupied and improved the land for five years. The act was two decades in the making. Secession of the southern states also made possible the selection of a northern route for a railroad to the Pacific Coast. The Morrill Land Grant College Act provided public lands to loyal states to endow colleges focusing on agriculture and the mechanical arts.

President Lincoln on December 31, 1862, signed an act providing for the admission of West Virginia to the Union. A majority of the inhabitants of northwestern Virginia had opposed secession. After the Old Dominion joined the Confederacy, northwestern Virginians held two conventions at Wheeling and established a Reorganized Government of Virginia. President Lincoln on July 1, 1863, recognized the Reorganized Government, and after Union forces had gained control of most of the area, statehood subsequently was approved.

Early in 1863, the National Academy of Science was chartered to "investigate, examine, experiment, and report upon any subject of science or art" when requested to do so by the federal government. The Territory of Arizona was created from the western portion of the New Mexico Territory, and the Idaho Territory was formed from four existing territories—Dakota, Nebraska, Utah, and Washington.

The number of authorized seats on the Supreme Court reached its peak in March 1863 when Congress established a Tenth Circuit consisting of California and Oregon and created a new justiceship to serve that circuit. The disability and subsequent resignation of the judge of the California Circuit gave rise to proposals for incorporating the Pacific coast states within the regular circuit system, which it had not been previously.

Major Acts

National Loan. Authorized the secretary of the Treasury to borrow $250 million over twelve months for the Union effort in the Civil War. Approved July 17, 1861 (12 Stat. 259–261).

Revenue Act of 1861. Instituted a direct tax of $20 million on real estate, apportioned among the various states; imposed customs and duties on certain classes of imports; and inaugurated the first national income tax, which imposed a 3 percent tax on annual incomes in excess of $800. Approved August 5, 1861 (12 Stat. 292–313).

First Confiscation Act. Freed slaves employed as soldiers or laborers against the government of the United States. Approved August 6, 1861 (12 Stat. 319).

Railways and Telegraph Act of 1862. Authorized the president, when in his judgment the public safety should require it, to take possession of all railroad and telegraph lines within the United States, together with all their equipment and personnel, to prescribe rules and regulations for use of these lines, and to place them under military authority. Placed the "officers, agents, and employees belonging to the telegraph and railroad lines under military control . . . subject to all the restrictions imposed by the rules and articles of war." Approved January 31, 1862 (12 Stat. 334–335).

Legal Tender Act. Authorized the issuance of $150 million in paper currency known as "greenbacks" as legal tender for the payment of debts and the issuance of up to $500 million in 6 percent bonds. Approved February 25, 1862 (12 Stat. 345–348). Certain provisions of this act were subsequently held unconstitutional in *Hepburn v. Griswold*, 8 Wall. (75 U.S.) 603 (1870).

District of Columbia Emancipation Act. Abolished slavery in the District of Columbia. Appropriated $1 million to compensate owners of freed slaves, and set aside $100,000 to pay District slaves who wished to emigrate to Haiti, Liberia, or any other country outside the United States. Approved April 16, 1862 (12 Stat. 376–378).

Department of Agriculture. Established a separate Department of Agriculture "to acquire and diffuse among the people of the United States useful information on subjects connected with agriculture . . . and to procure, propagate, and distribute ... new and valuable seeds." Provided for the appointment of a commissioner of agriculture and specified his duties. Approved May 15, 1862 (12 Stat. 387–388). Department obtained cabinet status on February 9, 1889 (25 Stat. 659). (*Department of Agriculture Act, p. 151*)

Homestead Act. Provided a free grant of up to 160 acres of surveyed western public land to any citizen, or applicant for citizenship, over twenty-one years of age who occupied and improved it for five years. Allowed settlers to purchase the land for $1.25 an acre after six months of residence. Approved May 20, 1862 (12 Stat. 392–393).

Internal Revenue Act of 1862. Created an Internal Revenue Bureau in the Treasury Department, and established a graduated income tax and special taxes on luxuries, spirits, ales, beer, tobacco, iron, steel, glass manufactured products, coal, oil, paper, leather, silks, cotton, and woolens. Established licenses on trades and taxes on gross receipts of railroads, steamers, and express companies. Approved July 1, 1862 (12 Stat. 432–489).

Pacific Railroad Act. Authorized the Union Pacific Railroad and Central Pacific Railroad to build railroad and telegraph lines between Omaha, Nebraska, and San Francisco, California. Granted each railroad a four-hundred-foot-wide right-of-way, land for stations, buildings, and so on; and alternate sections of land within ten miles on each side of the track. Provided a government first mortgage loan to railroad companies of $10,000 in Treasury Department bonds for each mile of track built on the plains, $32,000 a mile in hilly terrain, and $48,000 in the mountains. Approved July 1, 1862 (12 Stat. 489–498).

Ironclad Oath. Required every individual elected or appointed to any federal office (civil or military), except for the president, to swear allegiance to the Constitution, and declare that they had never voluntarily borne arms against the United States or aided, recognized, or supported a rebellion hostile to the Constitution. (In 1864, the oath became mandatory for all members of Congress. After the war, Congress created an alternative vow for southerners as an act of

reconciliation. In 1884, the first section of the oath was repealed, leaving intact the oath used today.) Approved July 2, 1862 (12 Stat. 502–503).

Morrill Land Grant College Act. Granted states not in rebellion thirty thousand acres of public land for each senator and representative serving in Congress. Set a limit of one million acres per state. Established that proceeds from the sale of these lands were to be invested by the states in bonds used to endow at least one college having as its primary function the teaching of "agricultural and mechanical arts." Prohibited endowment monies from being used to erect buildings. Each land-grant college was to provide instruction in military tactics (subsequently Reserve Officers' Training Corps [ROTC] programs). Approved July 2, 1862 (12 Stat. 503–505).

Medal of Honor Act. Authorized the president to present "'medals of honor' ... in the name of Congress, to such non-commissioned officers and privates as shall most distinguish themselves by their gallantry in action, and other soldier-like qualities, during the current insurrection." Approved July 12, 1862 (12 Stat. 623–624).

Tariff Act of 1862. Increased the tariff rates of the Morrill Tariff (Tariff Act of 1861) by setting higher rates on commodities such as sugar, chocolate, and raw cotton, and by levying taxes on top of the old rates. Placed new duties on iron, alcoholic beverages, wool, clothing, china, and furs in addition to those set by the 1861 Tariff. Toughened enforcement by requiring that invoices be filed with custom officials. Approved July 14, 1862 (12 Stat. 543–561). (*Morrill Tariff [Tariff Act of 1861], p. 101; Morrill Tariff Amendments of 1864, p. 111; Tariff Act of 1875, p. 130*)

Second Confiscation Act. Authorized the federal government to free slaves in areas taken by Union forces, provided for the confiscation of rebel property through the courts, prohibited the return of fugitive slaves, and allowed the army to recruit blacks to engage in combat against the rebellion. Empowered the president to arrange for the colonization of freed slaves in a "tropical country" if they so desired. Approved July 17, 1862 (12 Stat. 589–592).

West Virginia Admitted to the Union. Declared that West Virginia was one of the "United States of America and admitted into the Union on an equal footing with the original States." Stipulated that the act would not take effect until after the president had issued a proclamation stating that "the people of West Virginia" had ratified a revised constitution providing for gradual emancipation. Provided that the act was to take effect sixty days after the issuance of the presidential proclamation. Approved December 31, 1862 (12 Stat. 633–634). President Abraham Lincoln issued a proclamation on April 20, 1863, stating that West Virginia had complied with the act of Congress approved on December 31, 1862, and declared and proclaimed that West Virginia would become a state in sixty days (13 Stat. 731–732). West Virginia was formally admitted into the Union on June 20, 1863.

Arizona Territory Established. Created the Territory of Arizona from the western portion of the New Mexico Territory. Vested executive power in a governor, legislative power in a council of nine members and a House of Representatives of eighteen members, and judicial power in a supreme court consisting of three judges and such inferior courts as the legislative council might by law prescribe. Provided a secretary, marshal, district attorney, and surveyor general for the territory. Provided that all officers of the territory be appointed by the president, subject to the advice and consent of the Senate. Prohibited slavery and involuntary servitude in the territory. Approved February 24, 1863 (12 Stat. 664–665).

National Currency Act of 1863 (National Banking Act). Established a National Banking System, created the position of comptroller of the currency, required member banks to invest one-third of their capital in U.S. securities, and authorized member banks to issue National Bank Notes up to 90 percent of their bond holdings. Approved February 25, 1863 (12 Stat. 665–682).

Conscription Act of 1863. Established a national system for drafting all able-bodied white males between the ages of twenty and forty-five for up to three years of military service. Exemptions were possible by providing a substitute or by paying a $300 fee. Approved March 3, 1863 (12 Stat. 731–737).

Habeas Corpus Act. Sanctioned actions taken by President Abraham Lincoln in April 1861, and authorized the president during the war to suspend the privilege of the writ of habeas corpus in any case necessary throughout the United States or any part thereof. Approved March 3, 1863 (12 Stat. 755–758). Certain provisions of this act were subsequently held unconstitutional in *The Justices v. Murray,* 9 Wall. (76 U.S.) 274 (1869).

Tenth Circuit Act of 1863. Repealed the California Circuit Act of 1855 and the circuit court jurisdiction of the United States District Court for the District of Oregon. Established a tenth judicial circuit consisting of circuit courts in Oregon, northern California, and southern California. Provided for the appointment of a tenth Supreme Court justice to serve the tenth circuit, and provided the new judge $1,000 a year for traveling expenses. (This act increased the size of the Supreme Court to its largest membership of 10 members. The size of the court was reduced back to nine members by the Judicial Circuits Act of 1866.) Approved March 3, 1863 (12 Stat. 794–795).

National Academy of Sciences Act. Incorporated the National Academy of Sciences and stipulated that the academy would receive no compensation from the federal government. Approved March 3, 1863 (12 Stat. 806–807).

Idaho Territory Established. Created the Territory of Idaho from parts of the Territories of Dakota, Nebraska, Utah, and Washington. Provided executive power vested in a governor appointed by the president for four years and a secretary of the territory who would act as governor "in case of the death, removal, resignation, or other necessary absence of the governor from the Territory." Vested legislative power in the governor and legislative assembly consisting of a council and house of representatives, and judicial power in a supreme court, district courts, probate courts, and justices of the peace. Approved March 3, 1863 (12 Stat. 808–814).

Thirty-eighth Congress
March 4, 1863, to March 3, 1865

First session—December 7, 1863, to July 4, 1864
Second session—December 5, 1864, to March 3, 1865
Special session of the Senate—March 4, 1863, to March
    14, 1863
(First administration of Abraham Lincoln, 1861–1865)

Historical Background

The years 1863 and 1864 saw the tide of battle slowly turn against the Confederacy, as the Union brought its overwhelming advantages in manpower and materiel to bear against southern armies and Lincoln finally found the right combination of military leadership: Ulysses S. Grant in the east and William Tecumseh Sherman in the west. In the east, Lee crushed another federal invasion at Chancellorsville, Virginia, in May 1863, and then exploited his advantage with an invasion of Pennsylvania that he hoped would bring the North to the bargaining table. Confederate hopes were dashed, however, with his defeat by the Army of the Potomac at Gettysburg in July, and for the balance of the year, the two eastern armies watched each other cautiously. In May 1864, Grant, now in overall command of the Union forces, launched the Army of the Potomac into Virginia. Lee parried his moves and inflicted great losses on the Union forces at the Wilderness, Spotsylvania, and Cold Harbor. But after each bloody engagement, Grant continued south, finally laying siege to Petersburg, Virginia, and the Confederate capital of Richmond in June. Both sides remained stalemated in their entrenchments for the rest of 1864.

Action in the west in 1863 was dominated by Grant's successful siege of Vicksburg, whose surrender on July 4, the day after Lee's repulse at Gettysburg, gave federal forces control of Mississippi. Later that year, fierce fighting continued in eastern Tennessee at the Battles of Chickamauga (September 19–20), Lookout Mountain (November 24), and Missionary Ridge (November 25) as Grant positioned the main Union army in the west to invade Georgia and attack the heart of the Confederacy. In May 1864, Sherman, in command in the west after Grant's promotion, drove into northern Georgia, where he was opposed by Confederate forces under Joseph E. Johnston in a series of delaying actions. As Sherman neared the outskirts of Atlanta in July, John Bell Hood, who had relieved Johnston, launched fierce attacks on the federal army (July 20–28), but was driven into entrenchments defending the city. After several unsuccessful attacks, Sherman bypassed Atlanta, forcing Confederate troops to withdraw to avoid entrapment, and the city fell on September 2. While Hood's army was destroyed in fruitless counterattacks into Tennessee later that year, Sherman began his famous march to the sea from Atlanta on November 16. Under orders to destroy all resources and property of military value, his army inflicted enormous destruction in a wide swath to Savannah, which fell on December 21.

At sea, the federal blockade continued to tighten its noose about the Confederacy, as most southern ports had been occupied or effectively closed to commerce. One of the last, Mobile, Alabama, was seized by Admiral David Farragut on August 5, 1864, after a fierce naval battle. Although Confederate commerce raiders such as the *Alabama* and *Shenandoah* sank hundreds of merchantmen and did lasting damage to the American merchant marine, they were unable to affect the outcome of the naval campaign.

On February 3, 1865, President Lincoln, Secretary of State William H. Seward, and three Confederate peace commissioners—Vice President Alexander H. Stephens, John A. Campbell, and Robert M. T. Hunter—discussed a possible end to the war during a four-hour secret meeting at Hampton Roads, Virginia, aboard the steamship *River Queen*. The Hampton Roads Conference ended without concrete agreement on peace terms. As the war played itself out, General Sherman took Columbia, South Carolina, and General John M. Scofield entered Wilmington, North Carolina. Meanwhile, Union-dominated conventions in Arkansas (March 1864), Louisiana (September 1864), and Tennessee (February 1865) adopted new state constitutions and abolished slavery. The loyal state of Maryland ended slavery in October 1864.

By 1864, the increased financial burden of the war had left the country with a debt of $1.8 billion. In response, higher tariffs were placed on foreign-produced commodities (such as coffee, sugar, and tea) that Americans would continue to use in large quantities. The last of the Morrill Tariff Acts, approved on June 30, resulted from a desire to offset the excise and income taxes being imposed on domestic producers, firmly established protectionism as a policy of the United States, and satisfied the financial necessities of the government.

Congress also made substantial amendments to the Currency Act of 1863 to speed up the conversion of the nation's banks to the newly created federally chartered system. Because bankers preferred to continue operating under less stringent state regulations, enticements were included in the Banking Act of 1864 to lure the remaining state-chartered banks to file for a federal charter and stop using private currency for daily transactions. Passage of the National Bank Act of 1864 signaled the start of the development of a uniform and stable national currency backed by U.S. government bonds. While there was a growing demand for a national currency, the overriding purpose of the act was to provide a reliable market for the government bonds sold by the new network of national banks to finance the Civil War.

An Internal Revenue Act was a subject of intense and bitter debate. It established a progressive income tax; increased the tax on distilled spirits, tobacco, interest, and dividends; imposed a tax on a variety of banking activities; and required that tax returns be filed by banks, insurance companies, and railroads.

An additional emergency income tax of 5 percent on 1863 incomes in excess of $600 was approved. This addendum arose out of concern that the Internal Revenue Act signed four days earlier would not provide the revenue needed to pay enlistment bounties, which had previously been authorized. Revenue collections for 1865 (when collections began under the new acts) exceeded those of 1864 by threefold.

Early in July 1864, the Northern Pacific Railroad was granted a four-hundred-foot right-of-way and alternating sections on either side of the track to construct a transcontinental rail line between Lake Superior and Puget Sound. The Northern Pacific thus was able to construct the twenty-one hundred miles of railroad between Ashland, Wisconsin, and Portland, Oregon, although the line was not completed until the mid-1880s. Continuing growth in the population of the northeastern part of the Idaho Territory led to the formation of the Montana Territory.

With enactment of the Immigration Act of 1864, the federal government for the first time attempted to encourage immigration to the United States. The act provided principally for enforcement of contracts in which immigrants pledged to use their wages to repay the expenses of emigration. The Immigration Act was repealed in 1868 because the commissioner of immigration was doing little else besides compiling statistics, and the transactions of the U.S. Emigrant Office in New York were largely being carried out by an immigrant aid society chartered by the state of Connecticut.

The emancipation of slaves came closer to fruition in 1864. On April 8, the Senate by a 38 to 6 vote approved a constitutional amendment abolishing slavery in the United States and declared that "Congress shall have the power to enforce this article by appropriate legislation." Although a substantial majority in the House also favored the amendment, when the joint resolution was voted on in June it fell far short of the two-thirds (93 yeas, 65 nays, 23 not voting) needed to forward it to the states. Intent on making the amendment part of the Constitution, the Republicans made it a plank in their party platform for the 1864 presidential election and Abraham Lincoln throughout the campaign urged its passage. The Democratic platform was silent on the issue.

Lincoln and his running mate, Andrew Johnson, each received 212 electoral votes. The presidential and vice presidential nominees on the Democratic ticket, George B. McClellan and George H. Pendleton, respectively, each got 21.

Lincoln's reelection and substantial Republican gains in the 1864 congressional elections indicated that if the Thirty-eighth Congress did not approve the Thirteenth Amendment, the next Congress clearly would. The measure, however, did not have to wait. When the constitutional amendment was reconsidered by the House in its second, or lame duck, session on January 31, 1865, it passed by a vote of 119 to 56. Lincoln signed the joint resolution the next day. Ratification by the requisite three-fourths of the states was achieved ten-and-a-half months later. *(Thirteenth Amendment, p. 111)*

The number of states in the United States continued to grow. Nevada became a state on October 31, 1864. Congress had approved the Nevada enabling act the previous March, and one for Nebraska in April.

Creation of the Freedmen's Bureau in March 1865 was intended to assist millions of destitute former slaves in making the transition to freedom and to administer abandoned farmlands in the war-devastated South. The bureau was to provide emergency food and shelter, as well as help freed slaves learn to provide for themselves. Within a year, Congress would strengthen the bureau's power after several southern states began to take repressive measures against blacks.

Although the Thirty-eighth Congress reached agreement on a Reconstruction plan to bring the South back into the Union, President Lincoln refused to sign the Wade-Davis bill and used a pocket veto to kill the proposal. He considered restoration of the Union to be a presidential prerogative. Sen. Benjamin F. Wade of Ohio and Rep. Henry W. Davis of Maryland, cosponsors of the plan, together with the other Radical Republicans, favored congressional control of Reconstruction. A critical clause in the Wade-Davis bill required that 50 percent (instead of 10 percent, as Lincoln favored) of those who cast votes in the 1860 elections take an oath of allegiance to the U.S. Constitution as well as the slavery-related laws and proclamations issued during the Civil War. In a July 4, 1864, proclamation, Lincoln had explained that he wanted "to declare a constitutional competency in Congress to abolish slavery in the States." Lincoln's veto angered Radical Republicans and foreshadowed President Andrew Johnson's disastrous confrontation with Congress.

Major Acts

Nevada Admitted to the Union. Authorized inhabitants of the Territory of Nevada to form a constitution and state government and when formed the state would be "admitted into the Union on an equal footing with the original States." Stipulated that the constitution should be submitted to a popular vote on the second Tuesday of October 1864, after which the president would issue a proclamation declaring the state admitted into the Union. Approved March 21, 1864 (13 Stat. 30–32). President Lincoln issued a proclamation admitting Nevada into the Union on October 31, 1864 (13 Stat. 749–750).

Nebraska Enabling Act. Authorized the inhabitants of the Territory of Nebraska to form a constitution and state government in preparation for statehood. Approved April 19, 1864 (13 Stat. 47–50).

Montana Territory Established. Created the Territory of Montana from the northeastern part of the Idaho Territory. Provided that executive power would be vested in a governor appointed by the president for a four-year term. Vested legislative power in the governor and a legislative assembly consisting of a seven-member Council and thirteen-member House of Representatives, and judicial power in a supreme court consisting of a chief judge and two associate judges, district courts, probate courts, and justices of the peace. Allocated another portion of the Idaho Territory to be part of the Dakota Territory. Approved May 26, 1864 (13 Stat. 85–92).

National Bank Act of 1864. Authorized the comptroller of the currency to hire a staff of bank examiners, to periodically examine banks, and to regulate lending and investment activities of national banks. Raised the tax on state-owned banknotes from 2 to 10 percent. Required national banks to have at least five board members, to have $50,000 to $200,000 in stable assets depending on the population of the city in which the bank was located, to deposit with the comptroller of the currency U.S. bonds equal to one-third of its capital, and to maintain a 25 percent reserve in lawful money against deposits. Limited total issue of national bank notes to $300 million. Allowed national banks to own real estate only if it were necessary for the transaction of business or had been required as a result of a foreclosure. Authorized the use of national banks as depositories for government funds other than customs duties. Approved June 3, 1864 (13 Stat. 99–118).

Morrill Tariff Amendments of 1864. Increased the average tariff rate from 37 percent to 47 percent. Established protective duties more extreme than any previously imposed. Generated additional taxes by including shipping and handling fees in the cost of an item. Imposed more rigid penalties on individuals who violated custom laws and charged a higher rate on items shipped on foreign vessels. Approved June 30, 1864 (13 Stat. 202–218). *(Morrill Tariff [Tariff Act of 1861], p. 101; Tariff Act of 1862, p. 106; Tariff Act of 1875, p. 130)*

Internal Revenue Act of 1864. Established a progressive tax of 5 percent on incomes between $600 and $5,000; 7.5 percent on incomes between $5,000 and $10,000; and 10 percent on incomes over $10,000. Provided for withholding of up to 3 percent on incomes up to $5,000 and on interest and dividends paid by banks, railroads, insurance companies, and so on. Raised the tax on distilled spirits from 60 cents to $1.50 a gallon; on smoking tobacco from 5 cents to 15 cents per pound; and on fine-cut chewing and plug tobacco from 15 cents to 35 cents per pound. Also raised the tax on dividends from 3 percent to 5 percent. Imposed a tax on the capital, circulation, and deposits of persons and corporations engaged in banking. Required that tax returns be filed by banks, insurance companies, and railroads. Approved June 30, 1864 (13 Stat. 223–306).

Northern Pacific Railroad Act. Authorized the Northern Pacific Railroad Company to build a railroad and telegraph line from Lake Superior to Portland, Oregon. Granted the railroad a four-hundred-foot right-of-way through public lands and alternating sections on either side of the track within twenty miles through states and forty miles through territories to aid in the construction of the railroad. Approved July 2, 1864 (13 Stat. 365–372).

Immigration Act. Authorized the president, by and with the advice and consent of the Senate, to appoint a commissioner of immigration within the State Department, who would hold the office for four years. Established a U.S. Emigrant Office in New York City to be run by a superintendent of immigration who, under the direction of the commissioner of immigration, would "make contracts with the different railroads and transportation companies of the United States for transportation tickets, to be furnished to such immigrants, and to be paid for by them," protecting "immigrants from imposition and fraud." Provided penalties for any immigration officer receiving any fee or reward for services performed beyond their salary. Approved July 4, 1864 (13 Stat. 385–387). Repealed March 30, 1868 (15 Stat. 58, Sec. 4).

Emergency Income Tax. Imposed an additional income tax of 5 percent on all incomes over $600 for the year ending December 31, 1863. The tax was to be collected by October 1, 1864. Approved July 4, 1864 (13 Stat. 417).

Freedmen's Bureau. Created the Bureau of Refugees, Freedmen, and Abandoned Lands to provide food, shelter, clothing, and fuel for "destitute and suffering refugees and freedmen" from "rebel States, or from any other district of the country within the Territory embraced in the operations of the army." Authorized the president, by and with the advice and consent of the Senate, to appoint a commissioner of the bureau and assistant commissioners for each state who had "authority to set apart, for the use of loyal refugees and freedman, such tracts of land within the insurrectionary states as shall have been abandoned." Approved March 3, 1865 (13 Stat. 507–509). *(New Freedmen's Bureau Act, p. 114; Freedmen's Bureau Discontinuance, p. 119; Freedmen's Bureau Discontinued, p. 127)*

Thirteenth Amendment. Abolished slavery and involuntary servitude, "except as a punishment for a crime whereof the party" had been duly convicted within the United States or any place subject to U.S. jurisdiction. Proposed by Congress January 31, 1865, and signed by President Lincoln February 1, 1865 (13 Stat. 567). Ratified by requisite number of states December 18, 1865 (13 Stat. 774–775).[1]

Note

1. U.S. Senate, *The Constitution of the United States: Analysis and Interpretation,* 108th Cong., 2d sess., 2004, S. Doc. 108-17, 30, n. 5.

Thirty-ninth Congress
March 4, 1865, to March 3, 1867

First session—December 4, 1865, to July 28, 1866
Second session—December 3, 1866, to March 3, 1867
Special session of the Senate—March 4, 1865, to March 11, 1865
(Second administration of Abraham Lincoln, 1865; administration of Andrew Johnson, 1865–1869)

Historical Background

Spring of 1865 brought both triumph and tragedy for the Union and the end of the great civil war. General William Tecumseh Sherman's western army drove north from Savannah, Georgia, deep into the heart of the Carolinas in pursuit of Joseph E. Johnston's Confederates. Further north, General Philip H. Sheridan, who had successfully completed a devastating campaign in the Shenandoah Valley, joined General Ulysses S. Grant's Army of the Potomac, which had been laying siege to Petersburg, Virginia, since June 1864. The long stalemate was broken when Grant and Sheridan's cavalry threatened to surround Petersburg and Richmond, Virginia. Failing in his efforts to turn back the federal armies, General Robert E. Lee ordered the abandonment of the Confederate capital and sought to escape, hoping to join his forces with those of Johnston in the Carolinas. Vigorously pursued and harried by Grant, Lee was forced to surrender at Appomattox Court House on April 9. Johnston would surrender his army, the last major Confederate force at large, on April 26.

On April 15, just six days after Lee's surrender, the North was plunged into mourning when President Abraham Lincoln died. He had been shot at Ford's Theatre in Washington, D.C., by actor and Confederate sympathizer John Wilkes Booth. Secretary of State William H. Seward was also assaulted in his home at the same time but survived his wounds. Lincoln's assassination and the subsequent discovery that Booth was part of a wider conspiracy intending also to murder Vice President Andrew Johnson and General Grant reinforced the determination of radical elements in the Republican Party to impose a harsh Reconstruction program on the defeated southern states.

With Lincoln's assassination, Vice President Johnson of Tennessee assumed the presidency. The principal question facing both the new president and Congress was how to restore the Union and reintegrate the defeated South. Conflict between the White House and Congress over Reconstruction had begun with President Lincoln's December 1863 Proclamation of Amnesty, which called for the creation of loyal state governments in which a minority of voters (at least 10 percent of those who had cast votes in the 1860 election) took an oath of allegiance to the Union and accepted emancipation. Radical Republicans in Congress faulted Lincoln's plan as being excessively lenient and pushed to require at least half the eligible voters to take an oath of allegiance. After the Thirty-eighth Congress refused to seat members from the states of Arkansas and Louisiana as they prepared for readmission under Lincoln's plan, there were hints of a more rigorous administration policy. Lincoln's assassination, however, left unanswered exactly what he had intended.

Although the Radical Republicans assumed they had an ally in Andrew Johnson, they quickly learned otherwise. When Johnson announced his Reconstruction plan, many Republicans were shocked. Johnson called for southerners who took an oath of allegiance to receive a pardon, amnesty, and restoration of their property, except for slaves. They were then to elect delegates to state conventions that would be required to proclaim that secession was illegal, repudiate state debts incurred during the rebellion, and ratify the Thirteenth Amendment, which abolished slavery. Former Confederate military and civil officers were barred from participating in this process, as were ex-Confederates with a taxable income of $20,000 or more. President Johnson's action in carrying out his plan quickly aroused criticism as he began to hand out pardons (more than thirteen thousand) to individuals who initially had been disqualified on the basis of wealth or position. At the same time, several southern states adopted "black codes" that placed legal as well as economic restrictions on former slaves and refused to ratify the Thirteenth Amendment or repudiate their Confederate debt.

When the Thirty-ninth Congress convened on December 4, 1865, it, too, refused to seat representatives from the seceded states and established a fifteen-member Joint Committee on Reconstruction. Early in 1866, moderate and Radical Republicans joined together to approve two proposals drafted by Senate Judiciary Committee chairman Lyman Trumbull of Illinois to invalidate the black codes. The first strengthened and extended the Freedmen's Bureau. The second made blacks U.S. citizens with the same civil rights as other citizens and conferred enforcement powers on the president and the federal judiciary.

The bills were sent to President Johnson for his signature in February and March, respectively, and were immediately vetoed. Johnson argued that the bureau was too expensive, unfairly favored blacks over whites, and discouraged former slaves from becoming self-reliant. Also, he asserted that its constitutionality was questionable given that the eleven states affected by the bill were not represented in Congress. Johnson viewed the second proposal, the Civil Rights Act, as an unconstitutional invasion of states' rights and suggested that blacks were not qualified to be citizens. The Senate, on February 19, 1866, attempted to override the Freedmen's Bureau veto but failed (30 to 18). Another attempt to extend the bureau was greeted with another veto, but this time Congress prevailed when it overrode the president's action in July. Johnson's veto of the 1866 Civil Rights Act was more easily overridden. The Senate vote of April 6 was 33 to 15, and the House vote three days later stood at 122 to 41.

Later in April 1866, the Joint Committee on Reconstruction reported a constitutional amendment declaring that all persons born or naturalized in the United States were U.S. citizens, as well as citizens of their respective states, and that any citizen's rights could not be abridged or denied without due process of law. Any state that enacted or enforced a law denying suffrage to any male citizen would be subject to proportional reductions in its representation in the House of Representatives. The amendment also excluded all former Confederate officials from holding federal or state office, repudiated the Confederate debt, and maintained the "validity of the United States public debt." The Senate approved the Fourteenth Amendment on June 8 (33 to 11), the House concurred on June 13 (120 to 32). It was then sent to the states for ratification.

More than two years elapsed before the Fourteenth Amendment became part of the Constitution. In the interim, abolitionists criticized it for not going far enough, southerners denounced its restrictions on ex-Confederates, and President Johnson questioned the right of Congress to adopt an amendment without the participation of southern senators and representatives. The Republicans were able, however, to turn the 1866 congressional elections into a highly successful referendum on the Fourteenth Amendment. They retained sizable majorities in both the House and Senate. In July 1866, Tennessee had become the first southern state to ratify the Fourteenth Amendment and the first to be readmitted to the Union.

Meanwhile, one of the fiercest political struggles in the nation's history played itself out over the next eighteen months. After a long, arduous debate, Congress in February 1867 approved a bill "to provide for the more efficient Government of the Rebel States." The First Reconstruction Act returned the South (with the exception of Tennessee, which had ratified the Fourteenth Amendment) to military rule until the ten states outside the Union established governments that guaranteed black suffrage. President Johnson's March 2 veto, which was not unexpected, condemned the bill as "utterly destructive" to the "principles of liberty." The veto was overridden hours later by a three-to-one margin in both houses.

Despite this impressive victory, congressional leaders feared that Johnson might use his authority as commander in chief to subvert their intentions. To further limit the president's power over Reconstruction, the Army Appropriations Act was amended to require the president and the secretary of war to issue all military orders through the general of the army—Ulysses S. Grant. Its enactment virtually deprived the president of command of the army and the power to obstruct Reconstruction. Johnson reluctantly signed the act after he decided that the army would be demoralized if it were deprived of funds.

In other March 1867 action, Congress overrode presidential vetoes of the Nebraska statehood bill and the Tenure of Office Act. Johnson opposed statehood for Nebraska on political grounds, believing its admission would further strengthen Republican control of Congress. His constitutional concerns centered on a clause that extended the elective franchise to blacks. The president asserted in his veto that Congress did not have the right to dictate suffrage requirements to a state. Congress felt otherwise. The Senate overrode the veto by a 31 to 9 vote; the House, 120 to 44. For the only time in American history, a statehood bill became law over a presidential veto. When Congress set aside the veto of the Tenure of Office Act, it became an impeachable offense for a president to remove appointed officeholders without first consulting the Senate. Radical Republicans saw this measure as a means of assuring that implementation of their Reconstruction plan was not undermined by unsympathetic Johnson appointees. Within a relatively short time, Johnson would test the constitutionality of the Tenure of Office Act. A Federal Bankruptcy Act was also enacted to deal with the financial stress brought on by the Civil War.

Major Acts

Civil Rights Act of 1866. Granted both federal and state citizenship to "all persons born or naturalized in the United States." Bestowed specified equal civil rights on all citizens (except Indians). Declared that no "state could deprive any person of life, liberty, or property without due process of law." Provided punishment for persons who prevented the free exercise of these rights and conferred enforcement powers on the president and the federal judiciary. Presidential veto overridden by Congress. Became law without the president's signature April 9, 1866 (14 Stat. 27–30).

Fourteenth Amendment. Declared that all persons born or naturalized in the United States were citizens and that any state withholding the vote of any male over twenty-one would be subject to proportional reductions in its representation in the House of Representatives. Disqualified former officeholders who aided the Confederacy from holding either federal or state office (except in those instances when this disability was removed by a two-thirds vote of both houses of Congress). Secured the validity of the Union debt, and repudiated rebel war debts as illegal and void. Empowered Congress to enforce the various provisions of the amendment through appropriate legislation. Proposed by Congress June 16, 1866 (14 Stat. 358–359). Ratified by requisite number of states July 9, 1868.[1]

New Freedmen's Bureau Act. Authorized continuation of the Freedmen's Bureau for two years and broadened the scope of its responsibilities and activities. Prohibited discrimination on account of "race or color or previous condition of slavery." Presidential veto overridden by Congress. Became law without the president's signature July 16, 1866 (14 Stat. 173–177). *(Freedmen's Bureau, p. 111; Freedmen's Bureau Discontinuance, p. 119; Freedmen's Bureau Discontinued, p. 127)*

Tennessee Readmitted to the Union. Acknowledged that the state of Tennessee had on February 18, 1865, by a large popular vote, adopted a state constitution abolishing slavery and had ratified the Fourteenth Amendment to the Constitution. Declared that the "State of Tennessee is hereby restored to her former proper, practical relations to the Union, and is again entitled to be represented by senators and representatives in Congress." Approved July 24, 1866 (14 Stat. 364).

Nebraska Admitted to the Union. "Accepted, ratified, and confirmed" the constitution and state government that the people of Nebraska had formed for themselves, and declared that the state of Nebraska was one of the "United States of America, and admitted into the Union on an equal footing with the original States." Stipulated that "within the State of Nebraska there shall be no abridgement or denial of the exercise of the elective franchise, or any other right, to any person by reason of race or color." Presidential veto overridden by Congress. Became law without president's signature February 9, 1867 (14 Stat. 391–392).

First Reconstruction Act. Divided the states of the former Confederacy (except for Tennessee) into five military districts, each commanded by a general authorized to use military courts and forces to maintain law and order. Provided that the ten rebel states were to be readmitted to the Union only after they had called constitutional conventions by both black and white eligible voters, established state governments guaranteeing black suffrage, and ratified the Fourteenth Amendment. Excluded persons disqualified under the proposed Fourteenth Amendment from participation in the state conventions. Declared that Congress reserved the right to determine whether a state had adhered to the provisions of the act. Approved March 2, 1867 (14 Stat. 428–430).

Tenure of Office Act. Prohibited the president from removing federal officials appointed with advice and consent of the Senate without first obtaining senatorial approval. Approved March 2, 1867 (14 Stat. 430–432). *(Tenure of Office Act Repealed, p. 149)*

Command of the Army Act. Required that the president and the secretary of war issue all military orders through the general of the army. Also disbanded the southern state militias. (Attached as an amendment to the Army Appropriations Act.) Approved March 2, 1867 (14 Stat. 486–487, Sec. 2).

Bankruptcy Act of 1867. Created U.S. district bankruptcy courts. Extended both voluntary and involuntary bankruptcy to monied and commercial institutions. Approved March 2, 1867 (14 Stat. 517–541). Repealed June 7, 1878 (20 Stat. 99).

Note

1. U.S. Senate, *The Constitution of the United States: Analysis and Interpretation,* 108th Cong., 2d sess., 2004, S. Doc. 108–17, 30, n. 6.

Fortieth Congress
March 4, 1867, to March 3, 1869

First session—March 4, 1867, to December 1, 1867

Second session—December 2, 1867, to November 10, 1868

Third session—December 7, 1868, to March 3, 1869

Special session of the Senate—April 1, 1867, to April 20, 1867

(Administration of Andrew Johnson, 1865–1869)

Historical Background

In an action unusual for the time, the Fortieth Congress convened moments after the Thirty-ninth Congress expired at noon on March 4, 1867. Radical Republicans controlling both houses of Congress immediately began working to further strengthen their position in the struggle with President Andrew Johnson over Reconstruction. The House adopted a resolution instructing the Judiciary Committee to continue its inquiry into certain charges against the president, which it had been investigating since early in the year. Within three weeks of convening, Congress overrode a presidential veto of the Second Reconstruction Act. The act required the army commanders in charge of the five military districts in the South to provide for registration of all qualified voters (excluding prominent Confederates), who would then elect delegates to state constitutional conventions. Ratification of new state constitutions drafted under the act required the approval of a majority of the qualified electors in the state.

Just before Congress adjourned on March 30 for a recess, Secretary of State William H. Seward and President Andrew Johnson visited Capitol Hill in hopes of having the Senate approve the treaty they had concluded at 4:00 a.m. that morning to purchase Alaska from Russia. When President Johnson realized that immediate consideration of the treaty would not be possible, he issued a proclamation calling the Senate into "an extraordinary session" to consider the treaty. By April 9, following an extensive lobbying effort by Secretary Seward and Sen. Charles Sumner of Massachusetts, chairman of the Foreign Relations Committee, thirty-seven of thirty-nine senators had been convinced of the value of Alaska's natural resources and the strategic gains the purchase afforded the United States in the Pacific and Arctic Oceans. The $7.2 million needed to pay for the acquisition was authorized fifteen months later, after a lengthy and critical debate in the House. Opposition stemmed principally from Secretary Seward's failure to consult Congress before concluding the treaty, a common presumption that Alaska was worthless, and a concern the purchase would establish a precedent for other indiscriminate annexations.

By early July 1867, the continuing conflict over who should control Reconstruction and the military commanders in the South prompted Congress's return to Washington to renew its battle with the president. The result was the Third Reconstruction Act, which empowered the five southern military commanders to remove and appoint state officials at their discretion and to determine the eligibility of voters. Under the act, both military commanders as well as their subordinates were no longer bound in their actions "by any opinion of any civil officer of the United States." The president denounced the measure as unconstitutional, but his veto was easily overridden the same day it was issued.

In August 1867, while Congress was in summer recess, Johnson renewed the struggle by suspending Secretary of War Edwin M. Stanton and naming General Ulysses S. Grant as his interim replacement. Soon after the Fortieth Congress reconvened in December, the president, in compliance with the Tenure of Office Act, sent the Senate his reasons for suspending Stanton, insisting that he was not covered by the act. In January 1868, the Senate refused to concur with Stanton's removal and he was reinstated by the president. Six weeks later, on February 21, Johnson fired Stanton. The Radical Republicans, who for much of the previous two years had sought plausible legal grounds for impeaching the president, now finally felt confident in taking such action. The House in December 1867 had rejected a Judiciary Committee recommendation to impeach Johnson, but Stanton's removal reopened the question. On February 24, 1868, by a 126 to 47 vote, the House adopted a resolution sponsored by Rep. John Covode of Pennsylvania to impeach the president for "high crimes and misdemeanors in office." Next, Rep. Thaddeus Stevens of Pennsylvania, chairman of the House Committee on Reconstruction, offered, and the House approved, resolutions calling for the appointment of two special committees. The first was to prepare specific articles of impeachment against the president, and the second was to present and argue the charges before the Senate.

On March 2 and 3, 1868, the House adopted eleven articles of impeachment—eight involving the president's alleged violation of the Tenure of Office Act by removing Secretary of War Stanton, a ninth contending that he had violated provisions of the Command of the Army Act, a tenth charging him with making "intemperate, inflammatory, and scandalous harangues" against Congress in speeches, and an omnibus article covering a variety of charges. The House appointed seven managers to argue the charges before the Senate. The second longest impeachment trial in the nation's history followed in the Senate, extending from March 13 to May 26. With thirty-five senators voting "guilty" and nineteen "not guilty" on May 16 and by an identical vote on May 26 on three separate impeachment articles, Johnson escaped conviction by a single vote (a two-thirds majority being necessary). The other articles were not voted on, and the

trial was ended when the Senate abruptly adopted a motion to adjourn.

Against the background of the impeachment struggle, Congress approved the Fourth Reconstruction Act, which became law without Johnson's signature on March 11. It declared that a new constitution in a state formally in rebellion could be approved by a majority of votes cast, instead of a majority of registered voters, as required in the Second Reconstruction Act. Congress also overrode the president's veto of a bill that repealed U.S. Supreme Court appellate jurisdiction over habeas corpus writs granted in 1867. The immediate intent of the bill was to forestall an adverse decision by the Supreme Court in *Ex Parte McCardle,* a case challenging the legality of the military courts in the South. "Passage of the Judiciary bill," Carlton Jackson argues in his extensive study of presidential vetoes, "meant that Congress now controlled not only the presidency, but the judicial branch as well."[1]

Following Johnson's acquittal by the Senate, seven states—Arkansas on June 22, 1868, and Alabama, Florida, Georgia, Louisiana, North Carolina, and South Carolina on June 25, 1868—satisfied the requirements of the Reconstruction Acts, including ratification of the Fourteenth Amendment, and were readmitted to the Union. Both admission bills overcame the president's contention that signing them would constitute an admission that the Reconstruction Acts were legal. Georgia, however, was returned to military rule when, after the withdrawal of federal troops, the state legislature expelled twenty-eight duly elected black members (twenty-five representatives and three senators) in September 1868. Not until July 1870, after the expelled legislators were reseated and the state legislature had again approved the Fourteenth Amendment and ratified the Fifteenth Amendment, was Georgia readmitted to the Union.

Two subsequent enactments provided for the discontinuance of the Freedmen's Bureau in those states that had reentered the Union and for the withdrawal of the bureau from the South by January 1, 1869. A veto, prompted by President Johnson's unwillingness to recognize the legality of the bureau, preceded final enactment of the latter legislation.

Earlier, on July 25, 1868, the Territory of Wyoming was created by partitioning off a 110,000 square mile rectangle at the southwestern edge of the huge Dakota Territory, together with some land taken out of Nebraska, Idaho, and Utah territories.

After the Civil War, labor turned its attention to winning an eight-hour workday. By 1868, six states and a number of cities had passed eight-hour day legislation, and after a national campaign collected several thousand signatures, Congress passed an eight-hour day law for all federal workers and employees of federal contractors. Inclusion of government contractors in the law was an innovation and it was seen as a step that would encourage the eight-hour day in other industries. While federal departments reduced employee hours, at the same time they reduced wages as well. It took four years before the law was enforced to labor's satisfaction. After Ulysses S. Grant became president in 1869, he issued a proclamation directing that there was to be no reduction in the wages paid government workers because their hours had been reduced. Three years later, after Grant's first proclamation continued to be flagrantly ignored, he issued a second.

Republican victory in the 1868 elections paved the way for the final piece of their Reconstruction program, which would result in universal suffrage throughout the country. The black southern vote proved decisive in Republican Ulysses S. Grant's victory (214 electoral votes) over Democrat Horatio Seymour (80) for the presidency. The electoral tally was the same for Republican nominee Schuyler Colfax and the Democratic nominee Francis P. Blair Jr. for the vice presidency.

Republicans placed the capstone on the Reconstruction era with the passage of the Fifteenth Amendment, forbidding any state from depriving a citizen of his vote "on account of race, color, or previous condition of servitude." Several scholars have argued that the primary objective of the Fifteenth Amendment was to enfranchise the northern and border state blacks. Others contend supporters were primarily motivated by a strong belief that it was the right thing to do. Despite these differing perspectives, general agreement exists that if the Republicans had not acted when they did, the opportunity to enact both the Fourteenth and Fifteenth Amendments might have been lost forever.

Major Acts and Treaties

Repeal of the Habeas Corpus Act of 1867. Repealed the grant of appellate jurisdiction to the U.S. Supreme Court under the Habeas Corpus Act of 1867. Approved March 27, 1868 (15 Stat. 44). The Habeas Corpus Act of 1867 had granted the Supreme Court appellate jurisdiction over "all cases where any person may be restrained of his or her liberty in violation of the Constitution or of any treaty or law of the United States" and sought their release through a writ of habeas corpus. Approved February 5, 1867 (14 Stat. 385–387).

Second Reconstruction Act. Required the army commanders in charge of the five military districts in the "rebel States" to provide for the registration of all male citizens twenty-one years of age qualified to vote for delegates to state conventions "for the purpose of establishing a constitution and civil government." Directed the commanders to set dates for holding election of delegates to the constitutional convention, and stipulated that the registered voters of each state should have an opportunity to vote for or against the constitution once it was drafted. Provided that once a constitution had been approved by the voters, it was to be submitted to Congress for its approval prior to the state being "declared entitled to representation" and that all elections were to be held by ballot. Presidential veto overridden by Congress. Became law without the president's signature March 23, 1867 (15 Stat. 2–5).

Alaska Purchase Treaty. Provided for the cession of the Russian possessions in North America. Stipulated that inhabitants of the ceded territory could return to Russia within three years or remain in the ceded territory (except for uncivilized native tribes) and be "admitted to the enjoyment of all the rights, advantages, and immunities of citizens of the United States." Subjected the uncivilized tribes "to such laws and regulations as the United States may, from time to time, adopt in regard to aboriginal tribes." Specified that the United States would pay $7.2 million for the ceded territory. Concluded March 30, 1867 (15 Stat. 539–544). Ratification advised by the Senate April 9, 1867.[2] President Andrew Johnson signed an appropriations bill that fulfilled the payment stipulated in the treaty on July 27, 1868 (15 Stat. 198).

Third Reconstruction Act. Empowered the commanders of each of the five military districts established in the former Confederate states (except Tennessee) with the authority, subject to the disapproval of the general of the army of the United States, to suspend or remove from office any civil or military official in his district. Provided each military commander with the power to determine the eligibility of voters. Stipulated that military commanders and their subordinates were not bound in their actions "by any opinion of any civil officer of the United States." Presidential veto overridden by Congress. Became law without the president's signature July 19, 1867 (15 Stat. 14–16).

Fourth Reconstruction Act. Provided that a majority of votes cast would decide adoption or rejection of the proposed new constitution in each of the former Confederate states, whereas the provisions of the Second Reconstruction Act required a majority of registered voters. Presidential veto overridden by Congress. Became law without the president's signature March 11, 1868 (15 Stat. 41).

Arkansas Readmitted to the Union. Acknowledged that Arkansas had "framed and adopted a constitution of state government which was republican" and had ratified the Fourteenth Amendment to the Constitution. Declared that the state was entitled to "representation in Congress as one of the states of the Union." Approved June 22, 1868 (15 Stat. 72–73).

Omnibus Act (Alabama, Florida, Georgia, Louisiana, North Carolina, and South Carolina Readmitted to the Union). Acknowledged that Alabama, Florida, Georgia, Louisiana, North Carolina, and South Carolina had "framed and adopted a constitution of state government which was republican" and had ratified the Fourteenth Amendment to the Constitution. Declared that the states were entitled to "representation in Congress as one of the states of the Union." Approved June 22, 1868 (15 Stat. 73–74). Georgia again lost the right to representation in Congress because its state legislature

expelled twenty-eight black members and alleged Ku Klux Klan activities kept blacks from voting in the 1868 presidential election. In response to an appeal from Governor Rufus Bullock, Georgia was again placed under military rule by virtue of the Georgia Act, which was approved on December 22, 1869 (16 Stat. 59–60).

Eight-Hour Day for Federal Workers. Stipulated that eight hours would "constitute a day's work for all laborers, workmen and mechanics now employed, or who may be hereafter employed, by or on behalf of the government of the United States." Approved June 25, 1868 (15 Stat. 77).

Wyoming Territory Established. Created the Territory of Wyoming from portions of the Dakota, Idaho, and Utah Territories. Provided that executive power would be vested in a governor appointed by the president for four years and a secretary of the territory who would act as governor "in case of death, removal, resignation, or other necessary absence of the governor from the Territory." Vested legislative power in the governor and legislative assembly consisting of a council and house of representatives, and judicial power in a supreme court, district courts, probate courts, and justices of the peace. Approved July 25, 1868 (15 Stat. 178–183).

Freedmen's Bureau Discontinuance. Authorized the secretary of war to discontinue the operations of the Freedmen's Bureau "in any State whenever such State shall be fully restored in its constitutional relations with the government of the United States." The bureau's education functions were not affected. Approved July 6, 1868 (15 Stat. 83). A second act, approved three weeks later, provided for the withdrawal of the Freedmen's Bureau on January 1, 1869, from all of the states where it had operated. The educational department of the bureau was to continue, as were the "collection and payment of moneys due the soldiers, sailors, and marines, or their heirs." Presidential veto overridden by Congress. Became law without the president's signature July 25, 1868 (15 Stat. 193–194). *(Freedmen's Bureau, p. 111; New Freedmen's Bureau Act, p. 114; Freedmen's Bureau Discontinued, p. 127)*

Fifteenth Amendment. Forbade any state in the Union to deprive a citizen of his vote because of race, color, or previous condition of servitude. Approved February 27, 1869 (15 Stat. 346). Ratified by requisite number of states February 3, 1870.[3] A subsequent act approved on April 10, 1869, required that the three southern states still outside the Union (Mississippi, Texas, and Virginia) ratify the Fifteenth Amendment as a condition for readmission into the Union (16 Stat. 40–41).

Notes

1. Carlton Jackson, *Presidential Vetoes, 1792–1945* (Athens, Ga.: University of Georgia Press, 1967), 124.

2. *Journal of the Executive Proceedings of the Senate* (Washington, D.C.: U.S. Government Printing Office, 1887), 15 (part 2), 675–676.

3. U.S. Senate, *The Constitution of the United States: Analysis and Interpretation,* 108th Cong., 2d sess., 2004, S. Doc. 208–17, 33, n. 7.

Forty-first Congress
March 4, 1869, to March 3, 1871

First session—March 4, 1869, to April 10, 1869
Second session—December 6, 1869, to July 15, 1870
Third session—December 5, 1870, to March 3, 1871
Special session of the Senate—April 12, 1869, to
     April 22, 1869
(First administration of Ulysses S. Grant, 1869–1873)

Historical Background

Soon after the Forty-first Congress convened in March 1869, a law was enacted "to strengthen the public credit" and "to remove any doubt as to the purpose of the government to discharge all just obligations to public creditors." The Public Credit Act further declared that all war bonds purchased during the Civil War would be redeemed in "coin or its equivalent." With this enactment, President Ulysses S. Grant was able to fulfill one of the key campaign pledges that had swept him into office.

Early in Grant's presidency, a judiciary act was enacted that increased the number of associate justices on the U.S. Supreme Court from seven to eight and, for the first time, provided retirement benefits for federal judges who had reached age seventy with at least ten years of service. The staff of the attorney general's office was severely tested by the enormous increase in litigation thrust on the federal courts as a consequence of the Civil War and its aftermath. In 1870, after four decades of proposals by several different presidents, legislation was enacted establishing a Justice Department with the attorney general as its head. Proponents successfully argued that creation of the new department would save the federal government a substantial amount in private legal fees and resolve a long-standing problem of different lawyers within the government issuing contradictory opinions.

Efforts to blunt the vigilante violence of the Ku Klux Klan and other white supremacy organizations in the South resulted in the enactment of two laws designed to protect the civil and political rights of African Americans. The first reaffirmed the political rights of blacks and authorized federal courts to use a variety of means of enforcement. The second placed federal, state, and local elections under U.S. government supervision. A third, related act recognized the need to extend naturalization laws to black immigrants. Other results of Reconstruction saw Hiram R. Revels of Mississippi, the first black senator, and Joseph H. Rainey of South Carolina, the first black member of the House of Representatives, sworn into office and assume their seats. Four states—Georgia, Mississippi, Texas, and Virginia—satisfied the conditions for reentering the Union and were granted congressional representation.

Responding to demands for tariff reform, Congress acted to reverse a decade-long trend toward higher duties with the passage of the Tariff Act of 1870. The primary focus of the bill was aimed at wartime tariffs put in place primarily to raise revenues. Protective tariffs were generally not affected. Other significant reform efforts included a revision of the patent and copyright law, establishment of a Civil Service Commission, and the end of treaty making with American Indians.

An effort to update patent and copyright law resulted in the transfer of copyright matters from the Patent Office to the Library of Congress, which continues to perform that responsibility today. In addition, the act consolidated more than two dozen existing patent acts and eight copyright laws. Agitation to establish a merit hiring system to replace the spoils system that had dominated federal service since the administration of Andrew Jackson slowly gained momentum after the Civil War. Shortly before President Grant's first inauguration, he spoke out in support of civil service reform, following up with a formal request for legislation in his second annual message to Congress. Acceding to the president's request, Congress created a Commission on Civil Service but failed to appropriate funds to continue its operations after 1873, as patronage remained an essential element of party politics.

Abandonment of the Indian treaty system came about as a result of a conflict between the House and Senate over the role each should have in making treaties. Except for appropriating funds, the House had no official voice on Indian matters, and the Senate remained steadfastly opposed to relinquishing any of its constitutional authority to approve treaties. Ultimately it was decided that the only way for both houses to have an equal voice on Indian legislation was for the treaty system to be abolished, a compromise the Senate was willing to agree to if existing treaties were not affected.

Acting on a suggestion of Spencer Fullerton Baird, assistant secretary of the Smithsonian Institution, Congress in 1871 authorized the president to appoint a commissioner of fish and fisheries to determine why the "most valuable food fishes of the coast and the lakes of the United States [were] rapidly diminishing in number." This act marked the first official government action involving conservation of renewable natural resources for future generations. That effort continues today under the U.S. Fish and Wildlife Service.

Early in 1871, a territorial government was created to meet mounting economic and political needs of the District of Columbia. The president would appoint a territorial governor, and a legislative assembly would be made up of an appointed eleven-member upper chamber and a popularly elected lower chamber. A presidentially appointed Board of Public Works was to be responsible for financing and carrying out public improvements. In 1874, following charges of corruption and excessive spending by the Board of Public Works, the District's territorial status was revoked.

Major Acts

Public Credit Act of 1869. Designed to "strengthen public credit" and "remove any doubt as to the purpose of the government to discharge all just obligations to the public creditors, and to settle conflicting questions

and interpretations of law." Declared "that the faith of the United States is solemnly pledged to the payment in coin or its equivalent of all obligations of the United States not bearing interest, known as United States notes, and of all the interest-bearing obligations of the United States, except in cases where the law authorizing the issue . . . has expressly provided that the same may be paid in lawful money or other currency than gold or silver." Approved March 18, 1869 (16 Stat. 1).

Judiciary Act of 1869. Enlarged the U.S. Supreme Court to "consist of the Chief Justice of the United States and eight associate justices, any six of whom shall constitute a quorum." Provided that "any judge of any court of the United States, who, having held his commission as such at least ten years, shall after having attained the age of seventy years, resign his office, shall thereafter, during the residue of his natural life, receive the same salary which was by law payable to him at the time of his resignation." Approved April 10, 1869 (16 Stat. 44–45).

Virginia Readmitted to the Union. Acknowledged that Virginia had "framed and adopted a constitution of state government which was republican" and had ratified the Fourteenth and Fifteenth Amendments to the Constitution. Declared that Virginia was entitled to "representation in Congress as one of the states of the Union." Required that before any member of the state legislature and any officer of the state entered upon their duties they shall take one of two oaths. The first oath provided an affirmation that they had not "taken an oath as a member of Congress, or as an officer of the United States, or as a member of any State legislature, or as an executive or judicial officer of any State, to support the Constitution of the United States, and afterward engaged in insurrection or rebellion against" the United States. The second oath affirmed that they had "by act of Congress, been relieved from the disabilities imposed upon [them] by the fourteenth amendment of the Constitution." Approved January 26, 1870 (16 Stat. 62–63).

Mississippi Readmitted to the Union. Acknowledged that Mississippi had "framed and adopted a constitution of State government which was republic" and "ratified the fourteenth and fifteenth amendments to the Constitution of the United States." Declared that Mississippi was entitled to "representation in the Congress of the United States." Required that before members of the state legislature and officers of the state enter upon their duties they shall take one of two oaths. The first oath provided an affirmation that they had not "taken an oath as a member of Congress, or as an officer of the United States, or as a member of any State legislature, or as an executive or judicial officer of any State, to support the Constitution of the United States, and afterward engaged in insurrection or rebellion against" the United States. The second oath affirmed that they had "by act of Congress, been relieved from the disabilities imposed upon [them] by the fourteenth amendment of the Constitution." Approved February 23, 1870 (16 Stat. 67–68).

Texas Readmitted to the Union. Acknowledged that Texas had "framed and adopted a constitution of State government which was republic" and "ratified the fourteenth and fifteenth amendments to the Constitution of the United States." Declared that Texas was entitled to "representation in the Congress of the United States." Required that before members of the state legislature and officers of the state enter upon their duties they shall take one of two oaths. The first oath provided an affirmation that they had not "taken an oath as a member of Congress, or as an officer of the United States, or as a member of any State legislature, or as an executive or judicial officer of any State, to support the Constitution of the United States, and afterward engaged in insurrection or rebellion against" the United States. The second oath affirmed that they had "by act of Congress, been relieved from the disabilities imposed upon [them] by the fourteenth amendment of the Constitution." Approved March 30, 1870 (16 Stat. 80–81).

First Force Act (First Ku Klux Klan Act). Reaffirmed the right of citizens of the United States to vote at elections "without distinction of race, color, or previous condition or servitude." Provided penalties for infringement upon an individual's right to vote, subjected to heavy penalties those guilty of interfering with the civil or political rights of any person, and placed the enforcement of this law in the hands of the federal courts, which were authorized to employ U.S.

marshals and the regular army. Approved May 31, 1870 (16 Stat. 140–146). Certain provisions of this act were subsequently held unconstitutional in *United States v. Reese,* 92 U.S. 214 (1876); *James v. Bowman,* 190 U.S. 127 (1903); and *Hodges v. United States,* 203 U.S. 1 (1906). *(Federal Election Laws Repeal Act, p. 162)*

Establishment of the Justice Department. Created the Department of Justice as an executive department of the federal government with the attorney general as its head. Established the position of solicitor general, who, "in case of a vacancy in the office of Attorney-General, or in his absence or disability, shall have the power to exercise all the duties of that office." Provided for two "assistants of the Attorney-General, whose duties it shall be to assist the Attorney-General and solicitor-general in their performance of their duties." Transferred the law officers of the State, Treasury, and Navy Departments as well as the Bureau of Internal Revenue to the new department. Placed control over all criminal prosecutions and civil suits under the attorney general and the Justice Department. Provided that government cases tried before the U.S. Supreme Court could be presented either by the attorney general or the solicitor general. Approved June 22, 1870 (16 Stat. 162–165).

Patent and Copyright Act of 1870. Transferred responsibility for copyright matters from the Patent Office to the Library of Congress. Expanded copyright coverage to include paintings, statues, and other works of art. Consolidated more than two dozen patent acts and eight copyright laws. Authorized the commissioner of patents to promulgate rules and regulations. Approved July 8, 1870 (16 Stat. 198–217).

Naturalization Laws Extended to African Aliens. Extended naturalization laws to "aliens of African nativity and to persons of African descent." Approved July 14, 1870 (16 Stat. 256, Sec. 7).

Tariff Act of 1870. Placed some 130 articles, mainly raw materials, on the free list, and reduced rates on other commodities such as coffee, sugar, tea, and wines. Reduced the internal revenue tax, but continued protection of manufactured goods. Approved July 14, 1870 (16 Stat. 256–272).

Georgia Readmitted to the Union. Acknowledged that the state of Georgia had "complied with the reconstruction acts" and that "the fourteenth and fifteenth articles of amendment to the Constitution [had] been ratified in good faith by a legal legislature" of the state. Declared that the state of Georgia was entitled to "representation in the Congress of the United States." Approved July 15, 1870 (16 Stat. 363–364).

Office of Commissioner of Fish and Fisheries Created. Recognized a national interest in fisheries conservation by creating the independent office of commissioner of fish and fisheries. Authorized the president, with the advice and consent of the Senate, to appoint the commissioner "from among the civil officers or employees of the government" who had proven "scientific and practical acquaintance with the fishes of the coast." Directed the commissioner "to prosecute investigations and inquiries" on why there had been a decrease in "food fishes of the seacoasts and lakes of the United States," and to report to Congress on "what protective, prohibitory, or precautionary measures should be adopted." Approved February 9, 1871 (16 Stat. 593–594).

Territory of the District of Columbia. Created the Territory of the District of Columbia, which would have a presidentially appointed governor and secretary, both of whom would serve four-year terms. Vested legislative power in an assembly made up of an eleven-member upper chamber (Council) appointed by the president and a popularly elected lower chamber (House of Delegates), and vested judicial power in judicial courts already organized. Created a five-person presidentially appointed Board of Health "to declare what shall be deemed nuisances injurious to health," "to make and enforce regulations to prevent domestic animals from running at large," and to "prevent the sale of unwholesome food." Created a five-person presidentially appointed Board of Public Works to have "entire control of and make all regulations which they shall deem necessary for keeping in repair the streets, avenues, alleys, and sewers of the city, and all other works which may be intrusted to their charge by the legislative assembly or Congress." Approved February 21, 1871 (16 Stat. 419–429).

Second Force Act (Second Ku Klux Klan Act). Placed all elections in both the North and South under federal control, empowered federal judges to appoint elections superiors, and authorized U.S. marshals to employ sufficient deputies to preserve order at polling places. Approved February 28, 1871 (16 Stat. 433–440). (*Federal Election Laws Repeal Act, p. 162*)

Civil Service Commission. Authorized the president to prescribe rules and regulations that would best promote the efficiency of the civil service of the United States and to employ suitable persons to conduct interviews and establish regulations for those individuals who received civil service appointments. Approved March 3, 1871 (16 Stat. 514–515, Sec. 9).

Treaty Making with Indians Ended. Provided, as part of an Indian appropriations bill, that "no Indian nation or tribe within the territory of the United States shall be acknowledged or recognized as an independent nation, tribe, or power, with whom the United States may contract by treaty." Stipulated that existing treaties were not to be affected by this law. Approved March 3, 1871 (16 Stat. 566).

Forty-second Congress
March 4, 1871, to March 3, 1873

Historical Background

As the Ku Klux Klan continued its campaign of terror and intimidation in the South, the Third Reconstruction Force Act became law in April 1871. The act empowered the president to suspend the writ of habeas corpus and use federal troops to ensure that blacks were allowed to vote, hold office, and serve on juries. A year later, Sen. Matt W. Ransom of North Carolina and Rep. Sion H. Rogers of North Carolina took their oaths of office, giving the South full representation in Congress for the first time in a decade. Following the readmission to the Union of the last of the former Confederate states, the country gradually began to move beyond the Reconstruction era. In response to a recommendation by President Ulysses S. Grant, resolutions were introduced in both the House and the Senate to provide a general amnesty for individuals disfranchised under the Fourteenth Amendment. The Amnesty Act of 1872 restored the political rights of all ex-Confederate officials except for approximately five hundred to six hundred "Rebels," who had held a high federal office prior to the Civil War and violated their oaths to uphold the Constitution. Shortly thereafter, the Freedmen's Bureau was disbanded.

Attention in Washington, D.C., momentarily shifted to diplomacy during the spring of 1871, when Secretary of State Hamilton Fish and four other American commissioners negotiated an amicable claims treaty with five British commissioners. The Treaty of Washington included an expression of regret by the British for damage done by the *Alabama* and other Confederate ships built in England during the Civil War and established a five-nation arbitral commission to settle American claims for damages inflicted by the ships. The treaty also provided for arbitration on several other disputes between the two nations involving boundaries, fishing, and navigation. The Senate overwhelmingly approved the treaty by a vote of 50 to 12 less than three weeks after it was concluded. Ultimately, the United States was awarded $15.5 million in damages by the arbitral commission meeting in Geneva, Switzerland.

One of the most extensive personal lobbying efforts in the annals of Congress preceded the 1872 decision to set aside two million acres of public lands for the establishment of the nation's first national park near the headwaters of the Yellowstone River in Wyoming. Virtually every member of Congress was individually visited by supporters of the Yellowstone National Park bill, whose efforts were rewarded with nearly unanimous approval. Other public lands in 1873 were specifically designated for settlers who were interested in mining minerals or coal or were willing to plant trees in return for a larger homestead. President Grant's signature on the General Mining Act conveyed the right to file claims on "all valuable mineral deposits" in public lands. The Coal Lands Act permitted individuals, as well as associations of individuals, to acquire vacant and unreserved coal lands. Passage of the Timber Culture Act was designed to encourage settlers to plant and cultivate trees on the western prairies in return for the privilege of purchasing additional acreage.

Shifting to monetary matters, Congress approved a 10 percent reduction of duties with the Tariff Act of 1872 in an effort to reduce surplus revenue that had reached approximately $100 million. On February 12, 1873, coinage of the standard silver dollar was discontinued and gold was made the sole monetary standard for U.S. coins. Although passage of the Coinage Act aroused little interest on Capitol Hill or elsewhere at the time, soon afterward the decreased use of silver for monetary purposes and increased production of silver in the West caused the price of silver to decline significantly. Outraged leaders of the movement for the free coinage of silver charged that American and British financial interests had conspired to bring about the demonetization of silver and labeled the act the "Crime of 1873," even though silver had not been in circulation for several decades.

The first mail fraud legislation was adopted in 1872, as part of a general revision of the postal laws. Adoption of the Mail Fraud Act was an important turning point in the use of federal criminal sanctions, which previously had been reserved principally for conduct directly injurious to the federal government. This act, in contrast, extended federal jurisdiction to crimes clearly within the states' general jurisdiction and directly injurious only to private individuals, not to the central government.

President Grant in 1872 won an overwhelming reelection victory (3,598,235 to 2,834,761 popular votes) over Liberal Republican and Democratic challenger Horace Greeley, editor of the influential *New York Tribune*. Greeley died shortly after the election. As a result, electors pledged to Greeley split their votes among four candidates: Thomas Hendricks (42), Benjamin Gratz Brown (18), Charles J. Jenkins (2), and David Davis (1). Brown received 47 electoral votes in his race for the vice presidency on the ticket with Greeley. Grant and his running mate, Henry Wilson, each received 286 electoral votes.

Grant's electoral success, however, did little to dispel concerns that by early spring 1873 had begun to consume the administration. Republican success in

retaining control of both houses of Congress likewise proved a somewhat hollow victory. Stories of scandal and corruption involving members of the president's cabinet and his close friends became increasingly commonplace. An especially dark cloud hung over retiring vice president Schuyler Colfax and his successor, Henry Wilson, both of whom were among several government officials accused of being bribed by the Crédit Mobilier of America, a construction company owned by the Union Pacific Railroad. Grant's popularity was further eroded when, just before his second inaugural, he signed what was dubbed the Salary Grab Act, which doubled his salary from $25,000 to $50,000 annually and substantially increased the salaries of the vice president, Supreme Court justices, members of the cabinet, and members of Congress. The act also provided members of Congress with a retroactive bonus of $5,000. Public outrage over the "salary grab" and "back pay steal" forced the repeal of the act, except for the increases approved for the president and Supreme Court justices. Passing almost unnoticed among the various pieces of significant legislation enacted at the time was a law fixing the Tuesday after the first Monday in November as election day for representatives and delegates to Congress. This act brought House elections into conformity with the presidential election day, which had been set by Congress in 1845. (Popular election of senators would not be instituted until ratification of the Seventeenth Amendment in 1913.) (*Seventeenth Amendment, p. 194*)

Major Acts and Treaties

Third Force Act (Third Ku Klux Klan Act). Provided additional penalties for anyone who prevented blacks from registering, voting, holding an office, or serving on a jury. Barred members of white supremacy groups, such as the Ku Klux Klan, from serving on juries trying cases under the act. Empowered the president to use federal troops to enforce the act and to suspend the writ of habeas corpus in areas he declared to be in insurrection. Approved April 20, 1871 (17 Stat. 13–15). Certain provisions of this act were subsequently held unconstitutional in *United States v. Harris,* 106 U.S. 629 (1883). *(Federal Election Laws Repeal Act, p. 162)*

Treaty of Washington. Established an international commission in Geneva, Switzerland, to arbitrate claims by the United States against Great Britain for damages done to American shipping during the Civil War by British-built Confederate raiders. Concluded May 8, 1871 (17 Stat. 863–877). Ratification advised by the Senate May 24, 1871.[1]

Election Day Fixed. Established the Tuesday after the first Monday in November as the day for the election, in each state and territory, for representatives and delegates to Congress beginning in 1876. Approved February 2, 1872 (17 Stat. 28, Sec. 3).

Yellowstone National Park Act. Designated a two-million-acre tract of land "lying near the headwaters of the Yellowstone River . . . as a public park or pleasuring-ground for the benefit and enjoyment of the people." Placed the park under the exclusive control of the secretary of the interior. Barred commercial use of the park's "timber, minerals deposits, natural curiosities, and wonders." Approved March 1, 1872 (17 Stat. 32–33).

General Mining Act of 1872. Provided that "all valuable mineral deposits in the lands belong to the United States" and were "to be free and open to exploration and purchase . . . by the citizens of the United States." Required that not less than $100 worth of work be performed on each claim per year. Provided for patents to be issued for lands containing valuable deposits upon expenditures of $500 worth of work. Approved May 10, 1872 (17 Stat. 91–96).

Amnesty Act. Removed political and civil disabilities from all ex-Confederates except the five hundred to six hundred men who had served as "Senators and Representatives in the thirty-sixth and thirty-seventh Congresses, officers in the judicial, military, and naval service of the United States, heads of departments, and foreign ministers of the United States." Approved May 22, 1872 (17 Stat. 142).

Tariff Act of 1872. Made an across-the-board 10 percent reduction on tariffs for all manufactured products that were imported, including cotton, glass, iron, leather, paper, steel, and wool. Reduced duties on salt by 50 percent and on coal by 40 percent. Placed several raw materials on the free list. Approved June 6, 1872 (17 Stat. 230–258).

Mail Fraud Act of 1872. Made it a federal crime to defraud consumers through use of the mail. Prohibited any use of the federal mails—interstate or intrastate—in furtherance of "any scheme or artifice to defraud." Approved June 8, 1872 (17 Stat. 323, Sec. 301).

Freedmen's Bureau Discontinued. Provided that the Freedmen's Bureau would be discontinued after June 30, 1872, and "that all agents, clerks, and other employees then on duty shall be discharged, except such as may be retained by the Secretary of War." Approved June 10, 1872 (17 Stat. 366). *(Freedmen's Bureau, p. 111; New Freedmen's Bureau Act, p. 114; Freedmen's Bureau Discontinuance, p. 119)*

Coinage Act of 1873. Discontinued coinage of the standard silver dollar except for international trade, and made gold the sole monetary standard for the United States. Approved February 12, 1873 (17 Stat. 424–436).

Salary Grab Act. Increased the salary of the president from $25,000 to $50,000; that of the chief justice of the United States from $8,500 to $10,500; those of the vice president, cabinet members, and Supreme Court associate justices from $8,000 to $10,000; and those of senators and representatives from $5,000 to $7,500. Contained a retroactive provision to bestow on lame duck members of Congress a $5,000 bonus. Approved March 3, 1873 (17 Stat. 485–509). On January 20, 1874, the act was repealed, except for those provisions affecting the salaries of the president and justices of the Supreme Court (18 Stat. 4).

Timber Culture Act. Allowed any settler who planted and cultivated forty acres of trees for ten years to gain title to an additional quarter section of public land. Approved March 3, 1873 (17 Stat. 605–606). (*General Land Revision Act of 1891, p. 156*)

Coal Lands Act. Provided that a citizen, or anyone who had declared his or her intention to become a citizen, could make application for either vacant or unreserved coal lands of not more than 160 acres. Allowed an association of individuals to enter a 320-acre tract, and an association of four or more individuals to enter a 640-acre tract, if they expended at least $5,000 in work and improvements. Approved March 3, 1873 (17 Stat. 607–608).

Note

1. *Journal of the Executive Proceedings of the Senate* (Washington, D.C.: U.S. Government Printing Office, 1901), 18:105–109.

Forty-third Congress
March 4, 1873, to March 3, 1875

First session—December 1, 1873, to June 23, 1874
Second session—December 7, 1874, to March 3, 1875
Special session of the Senate—March 4, 1873, to March 26, 1873
(Second administration of Ulysses S. Grant, 1873–1877)

Historical Background

During the autumn of 1873, the boom of the post-war years and its accompanying rapid industrialization, economic expansion, and speculation ended abruptly. Several of the nation's leading financial firms, whose speculation had promoted a dramatic railroad boom, failed, and the New York Stock Exchange closed its doors for ten days. The Panic of 1873 triggered a depression that over the next five years saw three million workers lose their jobs, numerous banks close, businesses fail, farm prices drop dramatically, widespread mortgage foreclosures, and one in four railroads default on their bonds. As the depression deepened, pressure grew for legislation increasing the issuance amount of greenbacks (paper currency not backed by gold) in an effort to stimulate the economy. Congress responded with a currency bill that fixed the maximum amount of greenbacks in circulation at $382 million.

Even before the Panic of 1873, financial disaster had beset the territorial government of the District of Columbia because of financial mismanagement and overspending. An infusion of $3.5 million in federal funds proved insufficient for the District to avoid bankruptcy. The District's territorial government subsequently was abolished and replaced with a three-member commission appointed by the president, an arrangement that would continue to govern for more than ninety years, until 1967.

The nation's economic woes, coupled with continuing allegations of wrongdoing by members of the Grant administration, enabled the Democrats to regain control of the House of Representatives in the 1874 elections for the first time since before the Civil War. The Democrats also gained ten seats in the Senate but remained far short of a majority.

Following the election, lame duck Republicans of the Forty-third Congress addressed the financial concern that gripped the nation when it approved the Specie Resumption Act, which provided for the replacement, "as rapidly as practicable," of greenbacks with gold coin after January 1, 1879. Provision also was made for reducing the circulating greenback limit from $382 million to $300 million. (The resumption of specie payments was to be carried out under the administration of Rutherford B. Hayes.)

In response to protests from blacks, legislation guaranteeing all Americans equal access to public accommodations (inns, public conveyances, theaters, and so on) and the right to serve on juries was enacted, but no practical means for enforcement was provided. Also, in the waning hours of the second session, the 10 percent tariff reduction instituted in 1872 was set aside and duties were returned to prior levels, an action prompted by the need to generate increased revenue. President Grant's signature on an enabling act for the state of Colorado placed the territory's effort for statehood in reach within the next seventeen months.

Legislation approved during the waning hours of the Forty-third Congress made it possible for plaintiffs and defendants in cases before state courts to remove a case to a U.S. circuit court whenever the matter involved a question of federal law or if any members of the parties were from different states. Under the Judiciary Act of 1875, for the first time, all cases arising under the Constitution, federal laws, or treaties could be initiated in federal district courts. By establishing the full federal jurisdiction permitted by the Constitution, the act of 1875 fundamentally changed the role of the federal courts through the most sweeping extension of judicial power since the short-lived Judiciary Act of 1801. The chief significance of the act was its establishment of a generalized federal question jurisdiction—the jurisdiction that is seen today as an indispensable function of federal courts.

The Page Act was the first piece of American legislation to attempt to directly regulate immigration by prohibiting the entry of immigrants considered "undesirable." The act classified "undesirable" immigrants as any individual from Asia who was coming to America to be a contract laborer, any Asian woman who would engage in prostitution, and all people who were considered convicts in their own country. Tens of thousands of Chinese laborers had been brought to California and the American West as a result of the gold rush (1849) and the building of the transcontinental railroad (1860s). Although the Chinese were usually considered economic assets and good residents, their growing numbers alarmed many people living in the West. In December 1874, President Ulysses S. Grant called for curbs on two outgrowths of the Chinese immigration—forced "coolie" labor and prostitution. The Page Act became law the following March.

Major Acts

District of Columbia Government Reorganization. Abolished home rule in the District of Columbia, replacing it with a government of three commissioners appointed by the president. Levied a 3 percent tax on private real estate in the District, a 2.5 percent tax on real estate in Georgetown (an area within the District), and a 2 percent real estate tax on federal buildings and property within the District. Provided that the first and second comptroller of the Treasury were to audit and settle the financial accounts of the District. Approved June 20, 1874 (18 Stat. 116–121, part 3).

Currency Act of 1874. Limited the "amount of United States notes outstanding and to be used as a part of the circulating-medium" to not more than $382 million in any given month. Approved June 20, 1874 (18 Stat. 123–125).

Specie Resumption Act. Provided for the replacement, "as rapidly as practicable," of the Civil War fractional currency with silver coins. Reduced the limit on greenbacks in circulation from $382 million to $300 million. Directed the secretary of the Treasury to "redeem in coin" legal-tender notes presented for redemption on and after January 1, 1879. Approved January 14, 1875 (18 Stat. 296).

Civil Rights Act of 1875. Guaranteed equal rights to all citizens in public accommodations and on public conveyances. Prohibited exclusion of blacks from jury duty. Approved March 1, 1875 (18 Stat. 335–337). Certain provisions of this act were subsequently held unconstitutional in *Civil Rights Cases,* 109 U.S. 3 (1883).

Tariff Act of 1875. Reversed the trend of tariff reduction established by the Tariff Act of 1872, restoring duties to the levels previously established by the Morrill Tariff (Tariff Act of 1861) and the subsequent increases of 1862, 1864, 1867, and 1869. Approved March 3, 1875 (18 Stat. 469–470). *(Morrill Tariff [Tariff Act of 1861], 101; Tariff Act of 1862, p. 106; Morrill Tariff Amendments of 1864, p. 111)*

Jurisdiction and Removal Act of 1875 (Judiciary Act of 1875). Granted the U.S. circuit courts the jurisdiction to hear all cases arising under the Constitution and the laws of the United States, as long as the matter in dispute was worth more than $500. Expanded the right of removal, making it much easier for plaintiffs or defendants in cases filed in state courts to remove the case to the appropriate federal circuit court. Approved March 3, 1875 (18 Stat. 470–473).

Colorado Enabling Act. Authorized the inhabitants of the Territory of Colorado to form a constitution and state government. Declared that once the constitution had been submitted to the people of the territory for ratification, approved by a majority of the legal votes cast, and certified by the acting territorial governor, the president should issue a "proclamation declaring the State admitted into the Union on an equal footing with the original States, without any further action on the part of Congress." Approved March 3, 1875 (18 Stat. 474–476).

Page Act of 1875. Prohibited the importation of laborers from China, Japan, or any Asian country who did not voluntarily consent to come to work in America and Chinese women for the purposes of prostitution. Imposed a fine of up to $2,000 and maximum jail sentence of one year to anyone who tried to bring a person from China, Japan, or any Asian country to the United States with the intent to hold them to a term of service without their consent. Subjected ships to inspection if there was any suspicion of illegal immigrants on board or any one that was annoying or disturbing. Approved March 3, 1875 (18 Stat. 477–478).

Forty-fourth Congress
March 4, 1875, to March 3, 1877

First session—December 6, 1875, to August 15, 1876
Second session—December 4, 1876, to March 3, 1877
Special session of the Senate—March 5, 1875, to March
    24, 1875
(Second administration of Ulysses S. Grant, 1873–1877)

Historical Background

Before he died in July 1875, Andrew Johnson, the only former president to be elected senator, took part in a special Senate session called in March 1875 to act on a treaty with the Hawaiian Islands. Johnson joined with the majority who foresaw the political and strategic advantages in supporting the Hawaiian Reciprocity Treaty negotiated by Ulysses S. Grant's secretary of state, Hamilton Fish. The debate, however, quickly turned to the Grant administration's heavy-handed policies in occupied Louisiana, and Johnson used the occasion for a ringing denunciation of the president and his Reconstruction policies. Johnson's distaste for Grant's policies was shared by many on Capitol Hill. Although Grant announced on May 29 that he would not seek a third term, an overwhelming majority of the Democratic House still felt the need to repudiate the president. In December the House by a vote of 233 to 38 passed a resolution declaring that any departure from the "precedent established by [George] Washington and other Presidents of the United States, in retiring from the Presidential office after their second term . . . would be unwise, unpatriotic, and fraught with peril to our free institutions."

During the next few months President Grant suffered through the trial of his confidential secretary, Orville Babcock, who allegedly directed the Whiskey Ring scandal that saw the federal government being annually defrauded of millions of dollars in taxes through the sale of whiskey bearing forged revenue stamps. A few days after Babcock was acquitted, Secretary of War William H. Belknap, who was charged with accepting bribes for appointing and retaining an Indian post trader at Ft. Sill, Oklahoma, resigned following House adoption of a resolution calling for his impeachment. Belknap was ultimately acquitted when the Senate fell short of the two-thirds vote required. A more personal attack on Grant took the form of a bill to reduce the president's salary by 50 percent (from $50,000 to $25,000), which Grant promptly vetoed out of a "sense of duty" to his successors. He also pointed out that the current presidential salary was "one-fifth in value of what it was at the time of the adoption of the Constitution in supplying demands and wants."

Grant used his final annual message to Congress in December 1876 to review his eight years in the White House and apologize for his mistakes as president, especially in selecting assistants. "I have acted in every instance," he continued, "from a conscientious desire to do what was right, constitutional, within the law, and for the very best interests of the whole people." His failures were "errors of judgement, not of intent."

While financial instability and charges of corruption against the Grant administration continued to trouble the nation, the success of the Centennial Exposition of 1876 showcased the growing industrial and technological prowess of the United States. Opening in Philadelphia on May 10, the great fair commemorated a century of independence and attracted more than eight million paid admissions in its five-month run. Perhaps its most noteworthy highlight was Alexander Graham Bell's demonstration of his new invention, the telephone. The centennial summer was overshadowed, however, by the news that Lieutenant Colonel George Armstrong Custer's cavalry force had been wiped out on June 25 by Sioux and other Plains Indians at the Battle of Little Bighorn in the Dakota Territory.

That same summer, Congress revoked the legal tender status of the trade dollar, a special silver coin it had authorized three years earlier to facilitate trade between the United States and China, and to furnish a market demand for rising silver production. By 1876, however, silver mine owners in western states were dumping massive amounts of silver onto the market, the price of silver went into a tailspin, significantly reducing the intrinsic metal value of the trade dollar. Within a very short time, millions of discounted trade dollars returned to the United States, where they were spent at face value. To curb this abuse, Congress revoked the legal tender status of the trade dollar. This marked the first and only time the U.S. government revoked the legal tender status of any of our nation's coinage.

Early returns in the 1876 presidential contest indicated that Democratic candidate Samuel J. Tilden had been elected Grant's successor with a popular majority of more than a quarter of a million votes. The morning after the election, however, the votes of three pivotal states—Florida, Louisiana, and South Carolina—were still in doubt and would remain so for some time because of widespread threats to and intimidation of black voters and fraud by both parties. Ultimately, all three states sent two sets (Republican and Democratic) of Electoral College results to Congress, as did Oregon, where Republican nominee Rutherford B. Hayes had carried the state, but a dispute had arisen over the eligibility of an elector. With the Electoral College ballot stalled at 184 for Tilden (1 vote short of victory) and 165 votes for Hayes, the challenge of deciding which returns were authentic and which candidate had won fell to the Forty-fourth Congress.

Following a lengthy and bitter debate, the Republican-controlled Senate and the Democrat-controlled House agreed in January 1877 to create a special electoral commission, consisting of fifteen members drawn in equal numbers from the Senate, the House, and the U.S. Supreme Court, to settle the dispute. The commission's decision as to which votes in each of the four states would be counted was to be final, unless rejected by both houses of Congress. The House selected three Democrats and two Republicans; the Senate, three

Republicans and two Democrats. Two of the justices selected were Democrats; two were Republicans; and the fifth was to be chosen by the four already selected justices, with the tacit understanding that the justices would choose David Davis, who was identified with neither political party. Before the commission could meet, however, Davis, who had been elected a U.S. senator from Illinois, proclaimed himself ineligible and resigned from the Supreme Court. He was replaced by Justice Joseph P. Bradley, a moderate Republican. The commission deliberations, which lasted the better part of a month, ended with an 8 to 7 vote (Justice Bradley voting with the Republicans) in each case, to award all the disputed votes to Hayes. The Republican Senate upheld the commission's decision, while the Democrats in the House opposed it. After the House Democrats threatened to disrupt the formal vote count, Hayes agreed that as president he would withdraw federal troops from the South and, as a result, the vote continued. Shortly after 4 a.m. on March 2, 1877, the president of the Senate formally announced that Rutherford B. Hayes and William A. Wheeler had been elected president and vice president, respectively, with 185 electoral votes, and that challengers Samuel J. Tilden and his vice presidential running mate, Thomas A. Hendricks, had received 184 votes.

Before its final adjournment, Congress acted on the recommendations of President Grant, Secretary of the Interior Zachariah Chandler, and Commissioner of the General Land Office James A. Williamson for a Desert Land Act. This legislation was intended to make the acquisition of land in the arid West more attractive. Colorado's lengthy effort to be admitted to the Union was realized with President Grant's proclamation of August 1, 1876, confirming that the territory had adhered to the conditions set out in a March 1875 enabling act.

Major Acts and Treaties

Hawaiian Reciprocity Treaty. Permitted the free importation of "grades of sugar heretofore commonly imported from the Hawaiian Islands" as well as a number of lesser products. Allowed Americans to export freely to Hawaii a long list of products, most of which were commonly used in the islands. Provided that as long as the treaty was in force no other nation would have the "same privileges, relative to the admission of any articles free of duty," at Hawaiian ports. Concluded on January 30, 1875 (19 Stat. 625–627). Ratification advised by the Senate March 18, 1875.[1]

Legal Tender Status of the Trade Dollar Repealed. Revoked the legal tender status of the trade dollar and empowered the secretary of the Treasury "to limit, from time to time, the coinage thereof to such an amount as he might deem necessary to meet the export demand for the same." Approved July 22, 1876 (19 Stat. 215).

Colorado Admitted to the Union. President Ulysses S. Grant issued a proclamation on August 1, 1876, stating that the state of Colorado had complied with the act of Congress approved on March 3, 1875, and the "admission of the said State into the Union is now complete." Approved August 1, 1876 (19 Stat. 665–666).

Electoral Commission. Provided for an electoral commission of five senators, five representatives, and five U.S. Supreme Court justices, who were empowered to determine which set of presidential and vice presidential electoral returns would be accepted from the four states that had submitted duplicate and competing returns for the 1876 election. Approved January 29, 1877 (19 Stat. 227–229).

Desert Land Act. Enabled settlers in the states of California, Nevada, and Oregon and the territories of Arizona, Dakota, Idaho, Montana, New Mexico, Utah, Washington, and Wyoming to reclaim 640 acres of desert land that would not, without irrigation, produce agricultural crops. Required that those filing for desert lands to be citizens or to have filed a declaration to become citizens make a payment of 25 cents per acre at the time of filing, show proof of reclamation by irrigation within three years, and pay a balance of a dollar when proof of reclamation had been shown. Approved March 3, 1877 (19 Stat. 377). *(General Land Revision Act of 1891, p. 156)*

Note

1. *Journal of the Executive Proceedings of the Senate* (Washington, D.C.: U.S. Government Printing Office, 1901), 20:41–42.

Forty-fifth Congress
March 4, 1877, to March 3, 1879

First session—October 15, 1877, to December 3, 1877

Second session—December 3, 1877, to June 20, 1878

Third session—December 2, 1878, to March 3, 1879

Special session of the Senate—March 5, 1877, to March 17, 1877

(Administration of Rutherford B. Hayes, 1877–1881)

Historical Background

Almost immediately after the 1877 electoral commission report was accepted by Congress, and the disputed election of Rutherford B. Hayes as president was confirmed, accusations were levied that Samuel J. Tilden had been cheated out of the presidency. Rumors circulated that Hayes would never be permitted to take the oath of office, and *Harper's Weekly* reported "wild talk of an army of Democrats a thousand strong marching to Washington to do battle if necessary to prevent the infamy of a man not the choice of the people being made President by fraud." Anxiety was further intensified by the fact that inauguration day fell on a Sunday, and the formal ceremony at the Capitol would not be held until Monday, March 5, at noon. Several newspapers expressed the opinion that it was essential that Hayes take the oath privately on Sunday to assure that not one day pass without a president. Although Hayes did not entirely share these concerns, soon after he arrived in Washington, D.C., he discussed the question with the president pro tempore of the Senate, Thomas W. Ferry, who suggested that he consider taking the oath before Grant's term expired. Hayes secretly took the oath at the White House on Saturday evening in the presence of President Ulysses S. Grant and others

and then on Monday repeated the oath without incident on the East Front of the Capitol before an estimated crowd of thirty thousand.

Once in office, President Hayes brought twelve years of Reconstruction politics to an end by ordering the withdrawal of the last federal troops from the South. His action lent plausibility to rumors that Hayes had promised to withdraw the troops in return for acceptance of his administration's legitimacy by Southern Democrats. A year later, Congress approved a rider to an army appropriations bill that restricted the use of the army as a posse comitatus (part of a federal marshal's posse) in the execution of laws, except in such cases as were expressly authorized by law. With this act, the fundamental division between the military and civilian realms, which had often been blurred, was made more distinct. A well-organized lobby effort led by the *National Tribune* helped secure passage of the Arrears of Pension Act of 1879, resulting in millions of dollars of back payments to veterans.

Early in 1878, the passionate demand of Democrats for restoration of the silver dollar was realized. Although President Hayes and Secretary of the Treasury John Sherman fought to maintain the gold standard to assist business, the continuing effects of five years of economic distress had increased agitation among farmers, workers, and debtors for an inflated currency of silver as well as greenbacks. These forces had united to help the Democrats gain control of the House in the Forty-fourth Congress and prompted House passage in 1878 of a bill introduced by Rep. Richard P. Bland of Missouri for the free coinage of silver at a ratio of sixteen to one. That bill ultimately died in the Republican-controlled Senate.

The Democrats were not to be denied again. After the House again passed Bland's bill at the outset of the Forty-fifth Congress, Sen. William B. Allison of Iowa successfully attached a number of amendments that deprived the inflationists of their objective of "unlimited coinage" but did authorize the secretary of the Treasury to buy between $2 million and $4 million in silver each month to be coined into dollars. Allison's amendments also authorized the issuance of paper money backed by coin Treasury deposits. President Hayes's characterization of the Bland-Allison Act as a "grave breach of the public faith" had virtually no effect on Capitol Hill. His February 28, 1878, veto was overridden by both the Senate (46 to 19) and House (196 to 73) the same day it was issued. Hayes suffered further indignity in the November elections when the Republicans lost control of both houses of Congress.

In April 1878, the prevalence of major epidemic diseases such as smallpox, yellow fever, and cholera spurred Congress to enact the first federal quarantine act "to prevent the introduction of contagious and infectious diseases into the United States." The task of controlling epidemic diseases through quarantine and disinfection measures, as well as immunization programs, was vested in the surgeon general of the Marine Hospital Service. Passage of the act signaled the beginning of the shift of regulatory control of quarantine regulations from the states to the federal government. A year later, Congress established a National Board of Health to set rules for quarantines.

A permanent form of government was established that June for the District of Columbia, consisting of a three-member commission. Two of the presidentially appointed commissioners were to be civilians, and the third would be detailed from the Army Corps of Engineers. A National Board of Health was created, as a federal agency was needed to assume broad public health responsibilities. A plan for surveying and mapping the territories of the United States by the National Academy of Sciences, completed at Congress's request, prompted formation of the U.S. Geological Survey within the Department of the Interior. Attorney Belva Ann Lockwood's quest to be admitted to practice before the U.S. Supreme Court was realized when a bill that she drafted was enacted, authorizing all women who met certain qualifications to practice before the Court for the first time.

Major Acts

Bland-Allison Act. Provided for the secretary of the Treasury to make monthly purchases of between $2 million and $4 million worth of silver to be coined into silver dollars; made silver legal tender "except where otherwise" stipulated in contracts; and authorized the issuance of paper money backed by coin deposits in the Treasury. Authorized the president to invite European and Latin American countries to join the United States in an international "conference to adopt a common ratio between gold and silver, and to appoint, with the advice and consent of the Senate, three commissioners to attend the conference." Presidential veto overridden by Congress. Became law without the president's signature February 28, 1878 (20 Stat. 25–26). *(Sherman Silver Purchase Act, p. 156)*

National Quarantine Act. Authorized the Supervising Surgeon General of the Marine Hospital Service to make rules and regulations for detaining ships either having cases of contagious disease onboard or coming from foreign ports in which contagious disease were present. Required consular officers in foreign ports to report to the Surgeon General the existence of contagious diseases in foreign ports and the departure of ships from those ports bound for the United States, and to make weekly reports about sanitary conditions in those ports. Required the Surgeon General to notify U.S. ports of entry about inbound ships from such originating ports, and to make weekly reports to the medical officers of the Marine Hospital Service and local public health officials regarding information received from the consul officers. Approved April 29, 1878 (20 Stat. 37–38).

Permanent Government for the District of Columbia. Provided a permanent government for the District of Columbia under the direction of three commissioners, two appointed by the president, subject to the advice and consent of the Senate, and the third an officer of the Army Corps of Engineers of at least the rank of a captain, who would be detailed by the president to fulfill that responsibility. Required that the two civilian appointees to have lived in the district continuously for at least three years. Provided that Congress would appropriate monies for the District equal to 50 percent of the District's budget. Vested responsibility for all transactions relating to the District's sinking fund (a fund to which money is regularly added to redeem bonds when they reach maturity) in the treasurer of the United States. Approved June 11, 1878 (20 Stat. 102–108).

Posse Comitatus Act. Provided that it would be unlawful "to employ any part of the Army of the United States, as a posse comitatus, or otherwise, for the purpose of executing the laws, except in such cases and under such circumstances as such employment of said forces may be expressly authorized by the Constitution or by act of Congress." Approved June 18, 1878 (20 Stat. 152, Sec. 15).

Arrears of Pension Act. Established that all pensions paid to persons authorized to receive a military pension under previous laws, and granted in the future, were to commence from the date a pensioner was honorably discharged. When the pensioner had died as a consequence of wounds received in the service of the United States, the pension would be given to the pensioner's beneficiary from the date the pensioner had died. "Rate of pension for the intervening time for which arrears of pension are hereby granted shall be the same per month from which the pension was originally granted." Authorized the commissioner of pensions to adopt such rules and regulations for payments of arrears pensions as is necessary. Approved January 25, 1879 (20 Stat. 265).

Women Admitted to Practice before U.S. Supreme Court. Permitted any women who had "been a member of the bar of the highest court of any State or Territory or of the Supreme Court of the District of Columbia for the space of three years," maintained a good standing before that court, and was of good moral character to be admitted to practice before the Supreme Court of the United States. Approved February 15, 1879 (20 Stat. 292).

Creation of the U.S. Geological Survey. Established the U.S. Geological Survey as a bureau in the Interior Department with responsibility for "classification of the public lands, and examination of the geological structure, mineral resources and products of the national domain." Provided that the director of the survey would be appointed by the president, subject to the advice and consent of the Senate. Approved March 3, 1879 (20 Stat. 394–395).

National Board of Health. Established a National Board of Health composed of seven civilian members appointed by the president, subject to the advice and consent of the Senate, not more than one of whom resided in the same state; one navy medical officer; one medical officer of the Marine Hospital Service; and one officer of the Department of Justice. Specified that the duties of the board would "be to obtain information upon all matters affecting the public health, to advise the several departments of the government, the executives of the several states, and the Commissioners of the District of Columbia, on all questions submitted by them, or whenever in the opinion of the board such advice may tend to the preservation and improvement of the public health." Approved March 3, 1879 (20 Stat. 484–485).

Forty-sixth Congress
March 4, 1879, to March 3, 1881

First session—March 18, 1879, to July 1, 1879
Second session—December 1, 1879, to June 16, 1880
Third session—December 6, 1880, to March 3, 1881
(Administration of Rutherford B. Hayes, 1877–1881)

Historical Background

At the outset of the Forty-sixth Congress, Democrats sought to eliminate federal supervision of elections through repeal of the Force Acts. They viewed these enactments as an inappropriate intrusion of the Civil War and Reconstruction era. According to Ari Hoogenboom, they reasoned that repeal of the Force Acts would assure the selection of a Democrat as president in 1880.[1] President Rutherford B. Hayes, however, considered the laws critical in preventing fraud, intimidation, and violence in federal elections and in upholding voting rights granted under the Fourteenth and Fifteenth Amendments.

On seven occasions during the next two years, Hayes used presidential vetoes to thwart attempts to attach riders to appropriations bills that would have prevented the use of federal money, troops, and marshals from maintaining peace at the polls during national elections. The use of riders, he maintained, was an unprecedented attempt to "break down the functions of the Executive by coercion." Hayes labeled them as "radical, dangerous, and unconstitutional." In each case, money bills devoid of the riders were ultimately approved.

Congress's effort to provide for improved navigation on the Mississippi River was greeted far more enthusiastically by President Hayes. The need for such action was readily apparent. Following the Civil War, traffic on the nation's rivers had dwindled as railroads became increasingly convenient, more dependable, and faster. The establishment of the Mississippi River Commission in 1879 to draft plans for improvement of the river as a commercial waterway was intended to reverse this trend. As a result of the commission's efforts, several of the Mississippi's channels were deepened and widened, and the river's traffic increased significantly during the next several years.

Late in the Forty-sixth Congress, two very different pieces of legislation were approved. The first, the Foreign Gifts and Decorations Act of 1881, sought to address the question of how gifts and decorations conferred or presented to a civil, naval, or military officer of the United States by foreign governments should be lawfully handled. The solution agreed upon was to have such honors, if authorized by Congress, made through the Department of State and not be worn publicly by the recipient.

The second enactment was crafted in response to an earlier act being declared unconstitutional by the Supreme Court. In 1870, Congress passed the first trademark law in response to the rapid growth of trade that followed Reconstruction and the need of manufacturers for trade identity and better protection from infringement. Shortly after the act was amended in 1878, the Supreme Court struck down the act in *The Trade-Mark Cases,* 100 U.S. 82 (1879), for exceeding the powers granted by the patent and copyright clause of the Constitution. Congress responded with the Trademark Act of 1881. The new act, however, only provided for the registration of trademarks used in commerce with foreign countries and Indian tribes, and was based on the commerce clause of the Constitution. This law, however, was unable to accommodate the development of the American economy and underwent a major amendment in 1905.

Upon accepting the Republican nomination in 1876, Hayes pledged not to seek a second term, leading to considerable attention being focused during the final eighteen months of his presidency on the selection of his successor. With James A. Garfield's nomination on the thirty-sixth ballot as the Republican standard-bearer for the 1880 presidential campaign, Hayes passed his final months in the Oval Office resolving patronage disputes and assisting in the transition of his successor. In extremely close balloting, Garfield outpolled Democratic candidate Winfield S. Hancock by less than two thousand popular votes out of nine million cast. Garfield captured 19 states and 214 electoral votes. Hancock also carried 19 states but garnered only 155 electoral votes. The electoral vote tallies were the same in the race for vice president between Republican Chester A. Arthur and Democrat William H. English. For the first time in six years, the Republicans regained the House. The Senate was equally divided.

In his final annual message to Congress, Hayes again called for civil service reform, a theme that had dominated his entire presidency. He also urged Congress to reinforce the civil rights of blacks, recommended that the government of Utah be reorganized so the practice of polygamy could be abolished in the territory, and renewed his attack on greenbacks and silver dollars being minted under the Bland-Allison Act. Hayes called for codification of federal land laws, urged Congress to ease the country's judicial burden by creating additional circuit court judgeships, and asked for the U.S. Geological Survey to cover the entire nation. Much of what he sought would be realized, but not during his tenure.

Major Acts

Mississippi River Commission. Established the Mississippi River Commission, consisting of seven members appointed by the president, subject to the advice and consent of the Senate, including three commissioners drawn from the Army Corps of Engineers, one from the Coast and Geodetic Survey, and three civilians, two of whom were to be civil engineers. Authorized the commission to "direct and complete" surveys of the Mississippi River that might be deemed necessary to develop plans to "correct, permanently locate, and deepen the channel and protect the banks of the Mississippi River"; improve safety and ease of navigation; "prevent destructive floods"; and "promote, and facilitate commerce, trade, and postal service." Directed the commission to "report upon the practicability, feasibility, and probable cost of the various plans known as the jetty system, the levee system, and the outlet system, as well as upon such others as they may deem necessary." Approved June 28, 1879 (21 Stat. 37–38).

Foreign Gifts and Decorations Act. Required that gifts and decorations conferred or presented by a foreign government to any civil, naval, or military officer of the United States be tendered through the Department of State, and not to the individual person. Prohibited the delivery of such gifts and decorations unless so authorized by an act of Congress, and prohibited these decorations from being publicly worn by any officer of the United States. Approved January 31, 1881 (21 Stat. 604, Sec. 3).

Trade-Mark Act of 1881. Provided for the registration of trademarks used in commerce with foreign nations and the Indian tribes. Trademarks registered under the provisions of this act received protection for a period of thirty years, barring cases in which the trademark applied to another nation which set the "lifespan" of a trademark for a shorter period. Responsibility for overseeing the law was given to the Department of the Interior, with the commissioner of patents having responsibility for patents. Approved March 3, 1881 (21 Stat. 502–504).

Note

1. Ari Hoogenboom, *The Presidency of Rutherford B. Hayes* (Lawrence, Kan.: University of Kansas Press, 1988), 74.

Forty-seventh Congress
March 4, 1881, to March 3, 1883

First session—December 5, 1881, to August 8, 1882
Second session—December 4, 1882, to March 3, 1883
Special sessions of the Senate—March 4, 1881, to May
    20, 1881; October 10, 1881, to October 29, 1881
(Administrations of James A. Garfield, 1881, and Chester
    A. Arthur, 1881–1885)

Historical Background

Four months after his inauguration as the nation's twentieth president, on July 2, 1881, James A. Garfield was shot in the back while waiting for a train in Washington, D.C. His attacker, Charles J. Guiteau, a mentally unbalanced office-seeker, was subsequently convicted and executed. Garfield died from the wound on September 19, 1881. At 2:15 a.m. the following morning, Vice President Chester A. Arthur was sworn in as president by Justice John R. Brady of the New York Supreme Court.

Shock as well as revulsion over Garfield's assassination swept the nation as the dramatic reality of the spoils system dominated the headlines, and President Arthur pledged his support for civil service reform in his first and second annual messages to Congress. Public demand for civil service reform contributed to the Democratic Party's recapture of the House of Representatives in 1882. Not only did the GOP lose seats, the Democrats also profited from an expansion in the size of the House from 293 to 325 that was legislated following the 1880 census. The Democratic landslide in the 1882 House elections, however, finally prompted the lame duck Republican-controlled Forty-seventh Congress to act. Sensing that they might soon lose the White House as well, the GOP (Grand Old Party)

quickly seized upon Ohio senator George H. Pendleton's civil service reform act as an expedient means of regaining power. In January 1883, President Arthur signed the Pendleton Act, which created a three-member bipartisan Civil Service Commission to develop and administer competitive examinations for federal positions and established rules for a limited classified civil service. The act further provided for federal appointments to be apportioned among the states according to population, exempted federal employees from having to contribute to political campaigns or parties, and prohibited the removal of civil servants who refused to make political contributions.

Earlier Republican-supported initiatives firmly established the custom of providing pensions for the widows of presidents and imposed additional penalties on those who practiced polygamy, particularly in the Utah Territory. The latter act, which was sponsored by Sen. George F. Edmunds of Vermont, also barred polygamists from holding office or serving on juries and established a five-member "Utah commission" to supervise elections in the territory.

Racial prejudice and agitation over the effect on pay levels of poorly paid "coolie laborers" (Chinese) prompted demands by organized labor, especially on the West Coast, for a twenty-year restriction on Chinese immigration. In May 1881, the Senate ratified a treaty between the United States and China, concluded the previous November, which allowed the United States to prohibit Chinese immigration. Congress completed action on a bill to that effect on April 4, 1882. President Arthur vetoed the measure, declaring that the twenty-year suspension was "unreasonable." Failing to override the veto, Congress rewrote the bill, reducing the term of exclusion to ten years, and the Chinese Exclusion Act became law.

A second major piece of immigration legislation provided the first comprehensive attempt by the federal government to address the issue. Through the first century of American independence, immigration had been relatively open, with only occasional oversight and restrictions imposed by individual states. By the 1870s, however, increasing pressure was brought to bear against immigrants, especially Chinese laborers in California. While the Page Act of 1875 had reduced immigration of women from Asia, overall immigration continued to increase significantly. Growing concern both for the care of recently arrived immigrants, and the large financial burden that states were incurring as a consequence, prompted passage of the Immigration Act of 1882, which was designed to limit immigration.

As surplus revenues grew in excess of $100 million, calls were heard for significant tariff reform, but the only compromise that could be reached was a 5 percent reduction in the so-called Mongrel Tariff of 1883. Although more sweeping reductions were passed by both houses of Congress, members of the conference committee selected to resolve differences between the two versions were influenced by high-tariff supporters, who ignored many of proposals over which they were conferring. Also disregarded were the recommendations of the Tariff Commission, specifically set up by Congress to provide a more scientific basis for drafting tariff legislation, that duties be reduced by an average of 25 percent. It quickly acquired the name Mongrel Tariff for its motley mix of compromises that ultimately pleased no lobby group and had little effect on the economy. The act caused a flurry of political maneuvering in newspapers and magazines, and heightened the debate over tariffs and their use that would last for decades.

Instead of enacting major tariff reductions, Congress chose to spend the surplus on an unprecedented appropriation of nearly $19 million for river and harbor improvements. Although the bill covered several projects for large-scale improvements endorsed by the Mississippi River Commission and favored by President Arthur, it also contained significant appropriations for improvements designed to benefit only particular localities. Arthur argued that the total amount of the bill greatly exceeded the needs of the country and recommended that half of the amount called for in the bill be appropriated. The *New York*

Times called the bill "a monstrous swindle" that violated "every principle of economy and prudence." Several major newspapers, including the *Times,* accurately predicted a presidential veto. Arthur's recommendation that the appropriation be cut in half was widely supported, but his veto was overridden. Congress did, however, support the president's effort to use some of the surplus funds for naval construction, much neglected since the Civil War, with an initial appropriation of $1.3 million for four steel warships. These ships, the cruisers *Atlanta, Boston,* and *Chicago,* and the dispatch boat *Dolphin,* were the first major units built for the U.S. Navy since the Civil War. Their construction ended a long period of naval stagnation and betokened the growth of the modern steel navy.

Major Acts and Treaties

Immigration Treaty between United States and China. Gave the U.S. government the right to "regulate, limit, or suspend" the immigration of Chinese laborers into the United States, but "not absolutely prohibit" their entry. Provided that Chinese subjects "who were already in the United States" would "be allowed to go and come of their own free will and accord" and "be accorded all the rights, privileges, immunities, and exemptions which are accorded to citizens and subjects of the most favored nation." Concluded on November 17, 1880 (22 Stat. 826–827). Ratification advised by the Senate May 5, 1881.[1]

House Membership Increased. Provided that after March 3, 1883, the House of Representatives for the Forty-eighth Congress and each subsequent Congress would be composed of 325 members, and that whenever a new state was admitted to the "Union the Representative or Representatives assigned to it shall be in addition" to the 325. Approved February 25, 1882 (22 Stat. 5–6).

Presidential Widows Pensions. Granted former first lady and presidential widow Mary Todd Lincoln a pension of $15,000 in addition to any sum that might have accrued on her existing pension under the act of July 14, 1870, and an annual pension of $5,000 for the remainder of her natural life. Approved February 2, 1882 (22 Stat. 647). Granted a pension of $5,000 a year to former first ladies and presidential widows Lucretia R. Garfield, Sarah Childress Polk, and Julia Gardiner Tyler during the remainder of their natural lives. Approved March 31, 1882 (22 Stat. 652).

Edmunds Antipolygamy Act. Imposed penalties on the practice of polygamy and disqualified those who practiced or approved it from voting, holding public office, or serving on juries dealing with prosecutions for polygamy. Placed elections in Utah under the supervision of a board of five persons appointed by the president. Approved March 22, 1882 (22 Stat. 30–32).

Chinese Exclusion Act. Suspended the immigration of Chinese laborers to the United States for a period of ten years, and denied citizenship to all foreign-born Chinese. Approved May 6, 1882 (22 Stat. 58–61). *(Second Chinese Exclusion Act [Foran Act], p. 144; Geary Chinese Exclusion Act, p. 159)*

Creation of a Tariff Commission. Set up a nine-member Tariff Commission, to be appointed by the president from "civil life," to suggest reforms in view of the accumulating surplus in the Treasury. Approved May 15, 1882 (22 Stat. 64).

River and Harbor Appropriations. Appropriated nearly $19 million for more than four hundred river and harbor improvement projects in thirty-five states and four territories. Presidential veto overridden by Congress. Became law without the president's signature August 2, 1882 (22 Stat. 191–213).

Immigration Act of 1882. Prohibited all "undesirables," such as paupers, criminals, convicts, and the mentally insane, from entering the United States. Made an exception for foreigners convicted of political offenses, reflecting the traditional American belief that the United States is a haven for those persecuted by foreign tyrants. Gave the power over immigration enforcement to secretary of the Treasury, who was already responsible for overseeing customs in U.S. ports. Authorized the secretary of the Treasury to enter into contracts with individual states to administer immigration entry. Mandated that Treasury Department issue regulations for the orderly admission of immigrants and to collect a "head tax" of 50 cents for each arriving immigrant to defray administrative expenses. Approved August 3, 1882 (22 Stat. 214–215).

Pendleton Act. Established a bipartisan three-member Civil Service Commission to be appointed by the president, and instructed the commission to formulate and administer competitive examinations for determining the fitness of applicants for federal appointments. Further provided that no federal employee was under "any obligation to contribute to any political fund, or to render any public service, and that he will not be removed or otherwise prejudiced for refusing to do so." This act also made it a crime for any federal employee to solicit campaign funds from another federal employee. Approved January 16, 1883 (22 Stat. 403–407).

Navy Enlarged. Provided an appropriation of $1.3 million for the construction of one steel cruiser of not more than forty-three hundred tons displacement, two steel cruisers of not more than twenty-five hundred tons displacement, and one dispatch boat, "as recommended by the Naval Advisory Board" in its report of December 20, 1882. Approved March 3, 1883 (22 Stat. 477–478).

Mongrel Tariff of 1883. Made the first general revision in tariffs since the Civil War. Expanded slightly the list of duty-free goods, raised tariff levels on most dutiable commodities, including textiles and iron and steel products. Lowered duties on finer grades of wool, cheaper grades of woolen and cotton goods, steel rails, copper, marble, nickel, and barley. Approved March 3, 1883 (22 Stat. 488–526).

Note

1. *Journal of the Executive Proceedings of the Senate* (Washington, D.C.: U.S. Government Printing Office, 1901), 23:66–67.

Forty-eighth Congress
March 4, 1883, to March 3, 1885

First session—December 3, 1883, to July 7, 1884
Second session—December 1, 1884, to March 3, 1885
(Administration of Chester A. Arthur, 1881–1885)

Historical Background

President Chester A. Arthur's December 1883 annual message to Congress included several important recommendations that would ultimately be enacted, such as federal aid to education, a presidential succession law, regulation of interstate commerce, and forest preservation. The Forty-eighth Congress, however, completed action on only one Arthur proposal when it ended military rule in Alaska by establishing a civil government there. Considerable uncertainty remained as to what form the government should take, so the First Alaska Organic Act included a curious collection of provisions. Alaska, in the act, was designated a "district" instead of a "territory." Provision was made for the appointment of a governor, a district court judge and clerk, a district attorney, a marshal, and four commissioners. Establishment of a legislative assembly or selection of a delegate to Congress was specifically prohibited. Although the civil laws of the state of Oregon and the mining laws of the United States were extended to the new territory, federal land laws were not.

Further restrictions were placed on foreign immigration, first by an amendment to the Chinese Exclusion Act, which provided harsher punishments for those violating the law, and then by enactment of the Foran Act, which prohibited immigrants from obtaining passage to the United States for services to be rendered at a later time. Craft unions were instrumental in assuring passage of the latter legislation, while organized labor continued its campaign against Chinese immigrants.

A Bureau of Animal Industry was created to overcome a rigid ban by Germany on the importation of virtually all American meat products because of concern over diseased pork. Strict inspection of meat products was also strongly advocated by the National Livestock Association. As the economy began to turn downward in 1883–1884, increased political activity on the part of trade and labor unions prompted the establishment of a Bureau of Labor within the Department of the Interior to provide the federal government with accurate statistics for making evaluations regarding the nation's labor force. Yielding to the repeated demands of President Arthur for legislation encouraging American shipbuilding, tariff duties on imported shipbuilding materials and supplies were eliminated, tonnage duties were reduced, consular fees were abolished, and restraints on the employment of seamen were eased.

A record wave of new immigrants arrived in America in the decade of the 1880s, and as many moved westward onto the Great Plains a confrontation between settlers and cattlemen began to emerge. Stockmen used homestead or preemption laws to acquire title to a few hundred acres near water and then attained control of thousands of additional acres by fencing lands to which they did not hold titles. Appeals by outraged settlers prompted an 1884 Senate-mandated investigation by special agents of the Land Office and 1885 legislation that authorized the Interior and Justice Departments to prosecute individuals illegally fencing public lands. Initially, the results of the act were dramatic, with fences being removed from more than a million acres, but later results proved far less spectacular.

By 1884, the enforcement of navigation regulations had become increasingly challenging. To address the complex issues relating to navigation, a bureau of navigation was added to the Treasury Department to administer navigation laws.

After Arthur was defeated for renomination at the Republican National Convention of 1884, his remaining few months in office were those of a lame duck. His governmental reform efforts, the party's poor showing in the 1882 midterm congressional elections, and the popularity of party stalwart and presidential nominee James G. Blaine proved to be insurmountable hurdles to his reelection hopes. Amidst one of the most sensational and bitter presidential campaigns in American history, candidates representing seven parties vied for the right to succeed Arthur as chief executive. Ultimately, the election came down to a contest between Democrat Grover Cleveland and Republican Blaine, with Cleveland emerging the victor with an Electoral College advantage of 37 (219 to 182), but a popular vote margin of less than thirty thousand votes. The vice presidential candidates, Democrat Thomas A. Hendricks and Republican John A. Logan shared the same electoral vote tally as their running mates. Cleveland's election placed a Democrat in the White House for the first time since before the Civil War. Control of the Forty-ninth Congress, however, remained divided, with the GOP holding the House, and the Democrats, the Senate.

Major Acts

Civil Government for Alaska. Created the District of Alaska. Vested executive power in a governor appointed for four years by the president. Vested judicial power in a district court, an appointed district judge, and four commissioners who would "exercise all the duties and powers, civil and criminal, now conferred on justices of the peace under the general laws of the State of Oregon." Prohibited the District of Alaska from having a legislative assembly or a delegate to Congress. Provided for an appointed marshal with the same authority and powers of the U.S. marshals of the states and territories. Made the general laws of Oregon and mining laws of the United States, but not U.S. general land laws, applicable to the District of Alaska. Designated Sitka as temporary seat of the district government. Approved May 17, 1884 (23 Stat. 24–28).

Bureau of Animal Industry. Directed the commissioner of agriculture to organize a Bureau of Animal Industry and appoint as a chief of the bureau a competent veterinary surgeon whose duty it would be to "investigate and report upon the condition of domestic animals of the United States." Charged the chief of the bureau with inquiring into and reporting on the "causes of contagious, infectious, and communicable diseases" among animals, determining means for preventing and curing these diseases, and collecting such information as would be valuable to the agricultural and commercial interests of the country. Authorized the commissioner of agriculture to appoint two competent agents to report on the best means for eliminating "pleuro-pneumonia and other contagious diseases among domestic animals." Prohibited the transportation of diseased livestock. Approved May 29, 1884 (23 Stat. 31–33).

American Shipbuilding Encouraged. Required that all officers of U.S. merchant vessels be citizens of the United States except "in cases where, on a foreign voyage or on a voyage from an Atlantic to a Pacific port of the United States," a vessel is deprived of the services of an officer below the grade of master. Stipulated specific wage payments when seamen were discharged under a variety of different conditions. Eliminated all tariff duties on all imported shipbuilding materials and supplies, reduced tonnage duties, eliminated consular fees, and lessened the restraints on the hiring and payment of seamen. Approved June 26, 1884 (23 Stat. 53–60).

Bureau of Labor. Established a Bureau of Labor in the Department of the Interior to "collect information upon the subject of labor in the United States, its relation to capital, the hours of labor, and the earnings of laboring men and women, and the means of promoting their material, social, intellectual, and moral prosperity." Approved June 27, 1884 (23 Stat. 60–61). *(Department of Labor Act, p. 151; Department of Commerce and Labor Established, p. 175; Department of Labor Established, p. 195)*

Second Chinese Exclusion Act (Foran Act). Amended the Chinese Exclusion Act of 1882 by placing stringent penalties on the master of any vessel attempting to land or permitting the landing of Chinese laborers. Exempted from the act those Chinese who were in the United States on or before November 17, 1880, or who were admitted on a certificate from the Chinese government, which had been endorsed by American diplomatic representatives abroad. Approved July 5, 1884 (23 Stat. 115–118). *(Chinese Exclusion Act, p. 142)*

Bureau of Navigation Created. Consolidated responsibility for administration of navigation laws in a new bureau of navigation within the Treasury Department under the "immediate charge" of a commissioner of navigation, appointed by the president with the advice and consent of the Senate. (Administration of laws relating to lighthouses, lifesaving, collection of revenue, and inspection of steam vessels remained outside the bureau's jurisdiction.) Approved July 5, 1884 (23 Stat. 118–119).

Prevention of Unauthorized Fencing of Public Lands. Prohibited the enclosure of federal lands unless a claim for the property had been filed with the proper land office. Declared that the assertion of right to exclusive use of any part of the public lands of the United States was unlawful, subject to a civil suit, a fine of not in excess of $1,000, and a maximum of one year in jail for each offense. Authorized the president to take such measures as were necessary to remove unlawful enclosures. Approved February 25, 1885 (23 Stat. 321–322).

Contract Labor Act. Prohibited the immigration of foreigners and aliens under contract or agreement to perform labor in the United States. Subjected the master of any vessel knowingly bringing such emigrant laborers into the United States to a fine of not more than $500 (for each alien laborer, mechanic, or artisan) and imprisonment of not more than six months. Exempted were "professional actors, artists, lecturers, or singers," "personal or domestic servants," and skilled workmen not otherwise obtainable for new industries. Approved February 26, 1885 (23 Stat. 332–333). *(Contract Labor Act Amended, p. 149)*

Forty-ninth Congress
March 4, 1885, to March 3, 1887

First session—December 7, 1885, to August 5, 1886
Second session—December 6, 1886, to March 3, 1887
Special session of the Senate—March 4, 1885, to
    April 2, 1885
(First administration of Grover Cleveland, 1885–1889)

Historical Background

When the presidential mantle passed to Democrat Grover Cleveland in 1885, hundreds of Republicans were entrenched in high-level federal positions. While the Pendleton of Act 1883 had brought a measure of civil service reform to the government, approximately 88 percent of all federal employees were still subject to removal by the president. As Cleveland began to exercise that prerogative, the Republican-controlled Senate sought to protect Republican appointees by challenging the president's authority to remove anyone without Senate approval. Cleveland immediately sent a special message to the Senate questioning the constitutionality of the 1867 Tenure of Office Act and insisted that the president alone had the power to remove or suspend officials. His message generated considerable support both in the media and among the American people. The Senate capitulated soon thereafter, and the Tenure of Office Act, which had been largely responsible for President Andrew Johnson's impeachment, was repealed.

Another source of considerable tension between the Cleveland White House and Congress was presidential vetoes. Although Cleveland had been in office for more than a year when he issued his first veto, he quickly established a record. His total of 202 vetoes for the Forty-ninth Congress was almost as much as the combined total of vetoes of all his predecessors. Most of Cleveland's rejections were private pension measures that previous presidents reviewed with only cursory interest. Although the Pension Office in many cases had already rejected the applications that reached Cleveland's desk, Congress during the post–Civil War years increasingly become a "rival pension court." Cleveland was determined, as Carlton Jackson observed, to arrest the growth of the pension roll, one-fourth of which, at the time, "it was generally agreed . . . was fraudulent."[1] Only twice during his first two years as president were Cleveland's vetoes overridden.

Following the November 1885 death of Vice President Thomas A. Hendricks, President Cleveland urged passage of a new Presidential Succession Act. The new law provided that in case of death, resignation, impeachment, or inability of both the president and vice president, the line of succession would then pass to the secretary of state and other cabinet officers in the order that their departments were created. Under the Presidential Succession Act of 1792, the president pro tempore of the Senate, followed by the Speaker of the House, was to "act as President" when both the presidency and vice presidency were vacant. When Hendricks died, the Forty-ninth Congress had not yet convened and there was neither a president pro tempore nor a Speaker to act as a successor if anything happened to President Cleveland. The potential complications of the situation prompted Cleveland's forceful request for a change in the law. While President James A. Garfield's lingering disability and subsequent death just five years earlier aroused considerable concern, it had not prompted congressional action.

In an effort to avoid another Hayes-Tilden type of election controversy, the timetable for counting electoral votes was modified by an 1887 law. The agreed-upon solution was to allow states more time to resolve any disputes that might arise over electors by shifting the date on which the electors met from the first Wednesday in December to the second Monday in January.

Legislation enacted in 1886 appropriated funds for a new building to house the Library of Congress. Eleven years later, the library moved from its cramped quarters in the Capitol to its own building across the street. The library's collections had grown tenfold (from a 100,000 items to one million) in four decades.

That summer, a provision contained in the constitution of several states prohibiting the passage of local or special laws was enacted to make the provision applicable to all of the Territories of the United States. In favorably reporting the measure, the House Committee on Territories contended that the "evils of special and local legislation have nowhere been more apparent and destructive of good government than in our Territories.... The corrupting and demoralizing influences of local and class legislation are now universally admitted.... The necessity of prohibiting such legislation is apparent to all who have given the subject serious consideration."

Prodded by the diligent lobbying effort of Secretary of the Interior Carl Schurz, and Helen Hunt Jackson's powerful criticism of U.S. Indian policy, *A Century of Dishonor*, Congress sought to dissolve the communal organization of Indian tribes of the West by offering individual ownership of reservation lands. The Dawes General Allotment (Severalty) Act, sponsored by Sen. Henry L. Dawes of Massachusetts, granted 160 acres to heads of households, 80 acres to single adults as well as orphans, and 40 acres to dependent children. Those Indians who gained title to their allotments were to be declared citizens. Supporters of governmental aid to agricultural research supported passage of the Hatch Experiment Station Act, which provided for federal-state cooperative experiment stations at land-grant colleges.

A decade of increasing public demands for federal regulation of the railroads led to the creation of the nation's first independent regulatory agency. Supporters of the Interstate Commerce Commission (ICC) Act hoped its enactment would signal the end of discriminatory practices of railroads that favored large corporations over small businessmen, farmers, and merchants. The act empowered the commission with broad investigative powers over the operational as well as the financial aspects of all railroads engaged in interstate commerce. Although the early efforts of the commission proved encouraging, within a decade activities by the railroads to circumvent the act and several U.S. Supreme Court reversals of commission decisions left the ICC virtually powerless. Other labor legislation tightened the prohibition on importation of contract laborers and legalized the incorporation of national trade unions.

In the latter part of January 1887, 39 years after the end of the Mexican War, a bill was finally enacted providing veterans of that conflict their first government pension. For more than a decade, Northern opponents had thwarted efforts by the National Association of Veterans of the Mexican War (NAVMW) to gain pensions for Mexican War veterans because of the presence of former confederates among the surviving veterans and denounced the pension bill as a "southern war claim." Only after Jefferson Davis renounced any personal benefit that might result from passage of a pension act did Congress finally relent.

From the early days of independence, many state governments barred or restricted nonresident foreign investment in real estate. Particularly strong feelings against foreign land ownership developed following the frenzy of land speculation by foreigners in the frontier areas in the 1880s. A reflection of these feelings are found in the Alien Property Act of 1887, which prevented future aliens from owning or leasing real estate in federal territories.

The Edmunds-Tucker Act, sponsored by Sen. George F. Edmunds of Vermont and Rep. John R. Tucker of Virginia, authorized the U.S. government to seize and administer the property of the Church of Jesus Christ of Latter-Day Saints (Mormons) in an attempt to eliminate polygamy. Not until 1896, when the Mormons renounced the practice of polygamy, was the property returned.

Major Acts

Presidential Succession Act of 1886. Provided that "in case of removal, death, resignation, or inability of both the President and the Vice President," the heads of the executive departments, in order of the creation of their offices (secretary of state, secretary of the Treasury, secretary of war, attorney general, postmaster general, secretary of the navy, and secretary of the interior), would succeed to the presidency. Approved January 19, 1886 (24 Stat. 1–2). (*Presidential Succession Act of 1947, p. 279*)

New Library of Congress Building. Appropriated $500,000 for the construction of a "fire-proof building" on East Capitol Street in Washington, D.C., "for the accommodation of the Library of Congress." Approved April 15, 1886 (24 Stat. 12–14).

Incorporation of National Trade Unions Legalized. Granted "National Trade Unions" the "power to make and establish such constitution, rules, and by-laws" as they "deemed proper to carry out [their] lawful objectives." Provided that an incorporated National Trade Union could define the duties and powers of its officers, prescribe their mode of election, and establish branches throughout the United States. Approved June 29, 1886 (24 Stat. 86).

Special Laws Prohibited in the Territories. Prohibited the passage of local and special laws in the Territories of the United States. Authorized territorial indebtedness to instances where the monies were used to suppress insurrections; provide for the public defense; or erect a penal institution, charitable institution, or education institution. Authorized municipal corporations in the Territories to issue bonds "for sanitary and health purposes, the construction of sewers, waterways, and improvement of streets," provided such projects were voted by the taxpayers of the municipality at an election called for the purpose. Approved July 30, 1886 (24 Stat.170–171).

Mexican War Service Pension Act. Granted pensions to the surviving soldiers and sailors of the Mexican War who served at least sixty days and were honorably discharged, and to the surviving widow of such officers and enlisted men providing they had not remarried. Stipulated that pension recipients must be 62 years of age or who was deemed disabled under the pension laws of the United States. Provided a pension of $8 a month to qualified recipients. Approved January 29, 1887 (24 Stat. 371–372).

Electoral Count Act. Fixed the "day for the meeting of electors of President and Vice President" as the "second Monday in January" following their appointment "at such place in each State as the legislature of each State shall direct." Delegated to each state the "final determination of any controversy or contest concerning the appointment of all or any" of its electors, and required that all disputes be settled at least six days prior to the meeting of electors. Specified that the Senate and House of Representatives should meet at 1:00 p.m. on the afternoon of the second Wednesday of February for the opening and reading of the electoral vote. Provided procedures for counting the electoral votes, handling objections and questions, and announcing a decision. Approved February 3, 1887 (24 Stat. 373–375).

Interstate Commerce Act. Created an Interstate Commerce Commission (ICC) composed of five presidentially appointed commissioners with "authority to inquire into the management of the business of all common carriers." Declared that all charges by interstate railroads must be "reasonable and just." Prohibited discriminatory rates, and outlawed the practice of charging more for a short haul than for a long haul over the same line. Required railroads to post their rates and forbade rate changes without ten days' public notice. Authorized the ICC to investigate railroad practices and to issue cease and desist orders. Required railroads to file annual reports with the ICC and adopt a uniform system of accounting. Approved February 4, 1887 (24 Stat. 379–387).

Dawes General Allotment (Severalty) Act. Authorized the individual allotment of Indian reservation lands to tribal members, and conveyed citizenship upon the allottee on termination of the trust status of the land or to any Indian who voluntarily established residence apart from his tribe and adopted the "habits of civilized life." Granted 160 acres of land "advantageous for agricultural and grazing purposes" to heads of families, 80 acres to single adults over eighteen and to orphan children under eighteen, and 40 acres to children under eighteen. Provided that no Indian could dispose of the land for at least twenty-five years and that the federal government would retain title to the land for that period, or longer if the president deemed an extension desirable. Conferred citizenship on all Indians who accepted the benefits of the act. Approved February 8, 1887 (24 Stat. 388–391).

Contract Labor Act Amended. Provided for the enforcement of the Contract Labor Act of 1885 by allowing the secretary of the Treasury to enter into contracts with state officials who could "take charge of local affairs of immigration." Authorized the secretary of the Treasury to prescribe regulations for the return of those individuals who entered the country illegally. Approved February 23, 1887 (24 Stat. 414–415). *(Contract Labor Act, p. 145)*

Hatch Agricultural Experiment Station Act. Appropriate $15,000 annually for the establishment and support of agricultural experiment stations administered by the land-grant colleges in each state for the purpose of "acquiring and diffusing among the people of the United States useful and practical information on subjects connected with agriculture, and to promote scientific investigation and experiment respecting the principles and applications of agricultural science." Stipulated that in those states or territories where two such colleges had been established, the appropriation made to the state would be equally divided between the two institutions "unless the legislature of the State or Territory shall otherwise direct." Approved March 2, 1887 (24 Stat. 440–442).

1887 Alien Land Act. Restricted the ownership of real estate in U.S. territories to American citizens and those who have lawfully declared their intentions to become citizens. Prohibited aliens or companies whose cooperative ownership was more than 20 percent alien from owning or leasing real estate in federal territories. Provided for the disposition of the lands already owned by nonresident aliens. Approved March 3, 1887 (24 Stat. 476–477).

Tenure of Office Act Repealed. Repealed the Tenure of Office Act of 1867. Approved March 3, 1887 (24 Stat. 500). *(Tenure of Office Act, p. 115)*

Edmunds-Tucker Antipolygamy Act. Dissolved the corporation known as the Church of Jesus Christ of Latter-Day Saints (Mormon) and authorized the attorney general of the United States to seize and administer the property and holdings of the church including "places of worship, and parsonages connected therewith, and burial grounds." Abolished election districts in the Utah Territory, and annulled militia laws of the Territory of Utah. Approved March 3, 1887 (24 Stat. 635–641).

Note

1. Carlton Jackson, *Presidential Vetoes, 1792–1945* (Athens, Ga.: University of Georgia Press, 1967), 149.

Fiftieth Congress
March 4, 1887, to March 3, 1889

First session—December 5, 1887, to October 20, 1888
Second session—December 3, 1888, to March 3, 1889
(First administration of Grover Cleveland, 1885–1889)

Historical Background

President Grover Cleveland continued his assault on pension bills in the Fiftieth Congress. He surpassed his own record for frustrating congressional desires with another 212 vetoes. Reaction to Cleveland's vetoes, however, was mild in comparison with the response to his December 1887 annual message, which was entirely devoted to a call for lower tariffs. Despite the fact that Treasury surpluses stood at more than $100 million, Cleveland's position on tariffs provided Benjamin Harrison and the Republicans the principal issue of the 1888 presidential campaign. Cleveland chose to leave most of the active campaigning to Democratic vice presidential candidate Allen G. Thurman. As a result, the campaign never got off the ground. Harrison's campaign, with running mate Levi P. Morton, was a model of efficiency. Although Cleveland won the popular count by ninety thousand votes, most of the margin came in southern states where a Republican had virtually no chance of winning. When the electoral ballots were counted, Harrison had 233 electoral votes to Cleveland's 168. Harrison carried both of the critical states—Indiana and New York—that had gone to Cleveland four years earlier. Harrison's coattails were also long enough for the Republicans to gain control over both houses of Congress.

Following the passage of the Chinese Exclusion Act of 1882, the Chinese government became increasingly frustrated with the growing violence against Chinese subjects living in America. Ultimately, the Chinese agreed to greater restrictions on immigration in exchange for the American government's promise to provide better security for the Chinese living in the United States. The resulting Bayard-Zhang Treaty, however, met massive opposition in China, mainly in provinces where most Chinese immigrants to America originated. Fearing the treaty would not be ratified, Congress passed the Scott Act in 1888. Under the new law, any Chinese laborers who had temporarily left the United States, or who chose to leave in the future, were prohibited from returning. The Scott Act canceled all previously issued "certificates of return," meaning that 20,000 Chinese laborers then overseas who held these certificates could not return to the United States.

When the Bureau of Labor was created in 1884, labor leaders were pleased but not fully satisfied. Four years later, a bill supported by the Knights of Labor, one of the most important American labor organizations of the 1880s, was introduced to raise the bureau's status to a cabinet-level department with a secretary as its chief officer. The American Federation of Labor was also a strong advocate of a Department of Labor. Sufficient support for the idea, however, did not exist on Capitol Hill. Instead, Congress chose to elevate the bureau to the status of an independent, but not cabinet-level, department. Even without cabinet status, the Department of Labor continued to increase in size and prestige during the next twenty-five years, prior to the establishment of the cabinet-level Department of Commerce and Labor.

The first law providing for federal arbitration of labor disputes involving railroads and other common carriers and their employees was enacted in the fall of 1888. Growing concern over railroad labor-management disputes prompted an investigation and hearings by the Senate Committee on Education and Labor in 1882–1883. A bill was reported by the House Committee on Labor in 1886, but no final action was taken on it. When a bloody strike broke out against the Chicago, Burlington, and Quincy Railroad, Congress finally acted. The Arbitration Act of 1888 provided for adjustment of labor disputes between common carriers through voluntary arbitration conducted by a three-member "wholly impartial and disinterested" board. Under the act, the president was authorized to appoint a second three-member commission to investigate the cause of labor disputes. The initiative for the second commission could originate with the president, the parties in dispute, or a governor. Six years after the law's enactment, President Cleveland, in 1894, during his second administration, invoked the investigatory provision of the act during the Pullman strike that threatened to halt the nation's rail traffic.

Agricultural groups meanwhile were pushing cabinet-level status for the Commission on Agriculture, which had been established as an independent agency in 1862. The first bill to achieve this end was introduced in 1874 and was reintroduced regularly thereafter. Supporters argued that "agriculture was the bedrock of the nation's wealth" and "should be duly protected and encouraged." Opponents considered the proposal to be "special interest legislation and that the post of Secretary of Agriculture would be merely a political plum."[1] Near the close of President Cleveland's first administration, opposition to creation of a Department of Agriculture subsided and cabinet status was achieved. Its establishment was the culmination of a decade-and-a-half popular movement by the National Grange, farmers' alliances, and other farm groups for an executive department in Washington, D.C., representing their interests, clothed with the same dignity and power as other departments. Also in February 1889, an omnibus bill became law that provided for the division of the Dakota Territory into the states of North Dakota and South Dakota and included enabling provisions for Montana and Washington.

Major Acts

Department of Labor Act. Transformed the Bureau of Labor (created in 1884 as part of the Department of the Interior) into an independent department, but without cabinet rank. Provided that the department would be under the direction of a presidentially appointed commissioner of labor. Approved June 13, 1888 (25 Stat. 182–184). (*Bureau of Labor, p. 144; Department of Commerce and Labor Established, p. 175; Department of Labor Established, p. 195*)

Scott Act (Chinese Exclusion Act of 1888). Excluded the immigration of "all persons of the Chinese race," excepting "Chinese officials, teachers, students, merchants, or travelers for pleasure or curiosity." Permitted Chinese laborers who had come to the United States prior to 1882 to leave and return only if he had "a lawful wife, child, or parent in the United States, or property therein of the value of one thousand dollars, or debts of like amount due him and pending settlement." Required all Chinese who qualified for entry, excepting "diplomatic or consular officers and their attendants," to obtain certificates of clearance in advance from U.S. representatives in China. Approved September 13, 1888 (25 Stat. 477–479).

Railroad Arbitration Act of 1888. Provided a means for common carrier labor conflicts to be settled through voluntary arbitration by a three-member "impartial and disinterested" arbitration board, and empowered the president to name a three-member investigatory committee with power to act as a board of conciliation. Approved October 1, 1888 (25 Stat. 501–504).

Department of Agriculture Act. Raised the Department of Agriculture to cabinet level under the supervision and control of a secretary of agriculture, who was to be appointed by the president and confirmed by the Senate. Approved February 9, 1889 (25 Stat. 659). (*Department of Agriculture Established, p. 105*)

North Dakota, South Dakota, Montana, and Washington Enabling Act. Provided for the division of the Territory of Dakota into two states, and authorized the inhabitants of Montana, North Dakota, South Dakota, and Washington each to form a constitution and state government in preparation for statehood. Declared that once the constitution had been submitted to the people of each territory for their ratification, approved by a majority of the legal votes cast, and certified by the acting governor of the territory, the president should issue a "proclamation announcing the result of the election of each, and thereupon the proposed States which have adopted constitutions and formed State governments as herein provided shall be deemed admitted by Congress into the Union . . . on an equal footing with the original States." Approved February 22, 1889 (25 Stat. 676–684).

Note

1. Wayne D. Rasmussen and Gladys L. Baker, *The Department of Agriculture* (New York: Praeger, 1972), 11.

Fifty-first Congress
March 4, 1889, to March 3, 1891

First session—December 2, 1889, to October 1, 1890
Second session—December 1, 1890, to March 3, 1891
Special session of the Senate—March 4, 1889, to April 2, 1889
(Administration of Benjamin Harrison, 1889–1893)

Historical Background

During the Fifty-first Congress, the Republicans held the presidency as well as a majority in both houses of Congress for the first time since 1881. Their numbers swelled even further with the addition of congressional delegations from five new states—North Dakota, South Dakota, Washington, Idaho, and Wyoming—admitted to the Union between November 1889 and July 1890. (The enabling acts for North Dakota, South Dakota, Washington, and Idaho were approved by the Fiftieth Congress. These states were admitted upon issuance of a presidential proclamation declaring that conditions imposed by Congress had been met. The citizens of Idaho and Wyoming had already held constitutional conventions prior to approval of their statehood acts.)

The legislative agenda of the Fifty-first Congress, which has been characterized as the most ambitious of the late nineteenth century, included expanded military pensions, appropriations for the expansion of naval reconstruction begun in 1881, an antitrust measure, a silver purchase act, tariff legislation, creation of a federal court of appeals, a new immigration law, and expanded copyright coverage. In addition, with the Oklahoma Organic Act of 1890, a formal territorial government was established for homesteaders who just a year earlier had participated in one of the wildest land rushes in American history.

In his March 4, 1889, inaugural address, President Benjamin Harrison expressed a desire to see the United States become a world naval power and called for the "construction of a sufficient number of modern war ships" to attain this goal. Following considerable administration lobbying, Congress approved construction of three coastal defense battleships and a large cruiser. "By the time Harrison left the White House" in 1893, the nation "was well on its way toward naval stature in world affairs."[1]

Passage of the Dependent and Disability Pension Act of 1890 expanded pension rolls by recognizing the claims of virtually everyone connected with the Civil War, including the disabled, minors, and dependent parents. The Sherman Antitrust Act, the nation's first such statute, was enacted in response to public pressure for strong federal action against monopolies. It declared illegal every "contract, combination in the form of trust or otherwise, or conspiracy, in restraint of trade or commerce among the several states, or with foreign nations." The loosely worded act, sponsored by Sen. John Sherman of Ohio, authorized the attorney general to file criminal as well as civil suits in enforcing the law, but few successful prosecutions resulted initially.

Attention then shifted to appeasement of the pro-silver forces in Congress, whose support was needed to fulfill Republican pledges for a higher protective tariff. While the Sherman Silver Purchase Act, also sponsored by John Sherman, was not totally satisfactory to westerners, it did commit the secretary of the Treasury to purchase 4.5 million ounces of silver bullion per month. Although it represented a compromise for advocates of silver currency, fears that President Harrison would veto any bill providing for free coinage made it palatable.

153

Among the most controversial achievements of Republicans proved to be the highly sought-after McKinley Tariff Act. During the 1888 presidential election, Democrats had urged a reduction in the tariff, while Republicans argued for an increase. When the Republicans captured Congress as well as the White House, they viewed their victory as a popular mandate for protectionism. Philosophical differences, however, among House Republicans, Senate Republicans, and the administration resulted in a protracted Senate debate that produced nearly five hundred amendments to the bill crafted by Rep. William McKinley of Ohio, chairman of the House Ways and Means Committee. The most important Senate amendment satisfied the administration's desire for reciprocal tariff agreements, which enabled the president to suspend free trade on certain agricultural imports without awaiting congressional approval. The McKinley Tariff Act increased customs duties an average of 49.5 percent.

Following 12 failed efforts, Senator Justin Morrill saw Congress finally pass the Second Morrill Land Grant College Act, 28 years after passage of the first in 1862. The new act stipulated that no money would go to states whose land-grant colleges based admissions on race—unless those states provided institutions for both white and African American students and "equitably divided" the federal funds it received. This latter provision inspired the creation of the nation's historically black land-grant colleges, also known as "1890 institutions." Within three years after the passage of the Second Morrill Act, each of the 17 states which maintained a dual system of schools had officially accepted the provisions of the act.

In November 1890, Republicans lost control of the House in the midterm elections and in two years would lose the White House to the Democrats. They were, however, able to complete work on five long-standing issues before the Fifty-first Congress adjourned—the U.S. Supreme Court's excessive backlog, federal land reform, international copyright protection, immigration reform, and a European boycott of American pork.

The Circuit Court of Appeals Act of 1891, drafted to deal with the increasing backlog of cases pending before the U.S. Supreme Court, shifted appellate burdens to newly created circuit courts of appeal. The General Land Revision Act of 1891 repealed the Preemption Act (1841), Timber Culture Act (1873), and Timber Cutting Act (1878); amended the Desert Land Act (1877) and the homestead acts; and eliminated the auctioning of public lands. Passage of the revision act culminated years of agitation for public land reform. During debate on the revision act, conferees added a one-sentence provision that authorized the president to set aside forest reserves (national forests) from public domain land to protect western watersheds from erosion and flooding, and preserve the nation's timber supply from over-exploitation. Over time, this inconspicuous clause shifted federal priorities in the West from selling public land to managing public resources, and from land development to land conservation. In 1905, the Forest Reserves went from USDI (Interior) to the USDA (Agriculture) and became the U.S. Forest Service. Passage of the Forest Reserve Act of 1891 followed two decades of congressional debate of public land policy. The debate addressed homesteading policy and its abuses such as the blatant fraud in granting title to public lands, as well as the general theft of public natural resources.

An increasing concern over the federal government's ability to deal adequately with the dramatic increase in immigrants during the 1880s led to enactment of the Immigration Act of 1891. The act broadened the alien classes denied entry into the United States, limited the assistance individuals or companies might provide immigrants, and established an Office of Superintendent of Immigration. The Immigration Act also provided for an inspection of arriving immigrants, medical examinations for new immigrants, and deportation of illegal aliens.

More than a half century of discussions preceded enactment of the International Copyright Act of 1891, which extended copyright protection to foreign authors, inventors, designers, map makers, chart makers, composers, and artists whose "state or nation" provided the same privilege to American citizens or was a party to an international agreement providing for reciprocity in copyright.

One of the principal stated objections of Germany and several other European nations regarding the importation of American pork was satisfied by the Meat Inspection Act of 1891, which made microscopic inspection of meat compulsory. Other factors contributing to the abandonment of the decade-old embargo were German chancellor Otto von Bismarck's retirement and a provision of the McKinley Tariff Act that allowed the president to exclude products from any nation that discriminated against American exports.

By the time it concluded, the Fifty-first Congress proved to be one of the most productive of the nineteenth century. It passed 611 bills, among which was legislation admitting five new states, creating a new territory, and record appropriations for internal improvements, pensions, expanded copyright coverage, a new immigration law, new naval construction, and a second land-grant college act that totaled more than $1 billion. The overgenerous spending of the first "Billion-Dollar Congress," however, left many Americans shocked and bitter. Their displeasure was evident in the congressional election of November 1890. When the votes were counted, House Republicans had lost 93 seats—being reduced from a 179 to 152 majority to a 238 to 86 minority.

Major Acts

North Dakota, South Dakota, Montana, and Washington Admitted to the Union. President Benjamin Harrison issued two proclamations on November 2, 1889, stating that North Dakota and South Dakota had each complied with the enabling act approved on February 22, 1889, and proclaimed "that the admission of the said [states] into the Union is now complete." President Harrison issued similar proclamations on November 8 and November 11, 1889, stating that Montana and Washington, respectively, had complied with the enabling act and proclaimed that they also were admitted into the Union. Approved November 2, 1889, November 8, 1889, and November 11, 1889 (26 Stat. 1548–1553).

Territory of Oklahoma. Created the Oklahoma Territory out of the western half of the unorganized Indian Territory (included primarily that area not reserved for the Five Civilized Tribes), plus a strip of land west of the 100th meridian, which had been acquired from Texas in 1850. Provided for a temporary government for the territory. Approved May 2, 1890 (26 Stat. 81–100).

Dependent and Disability Pension Act. Granted pensions to veterans of the Union forces who had served at least ninety days during the Civil War, been honorably discharged, and suffered from a physical or mental disability that rendered them unable to earn a livelihood. Provided pensions to minor children, dependent parents, and widows who had married veterans before passage of the act and had to work for a living. Approved June 27, 1890 (26 Stat. 182–183).

Battleship Act of 1890 (Fiscal 1891 Naval Appropriations). Authorized construction of "three seagoing coast-line battle ships designed to carry the heaviest armor and most powerful ordnance," "one protected cruiser," and "one torpedo boat." Approved June 30, 1890 (26 Stat. 205–206).

Sherman Antitrust Act. Empowered the federal government to prosecute any corporation or person entering into contracts in restraint of interstate trade or commerce with foreign countries. Provided fines of $5,000 and jail terms of up to one year for persons found guilty of monopolizing or attempting to monopolize commerce. Gave any private individual "injured in his business or property" by monopolistic practices the right to sue for triple damages. Assigned jurisdiction over such cases to the federal circuit courts. Approved July 2, 1890 (26 Stat. 209–210).

Idaho Admitted to the Union. Accepted the constitution formed by an Idaho Territory convention on July 4, 1889, and subsequently ratified and adopted by the people of the Idaho Territory on November 1, 1889. Declared that Idaho was one of the "United States of America" and "admitted into the Union on an equal footing with the original States." Approved July 3, 1890 (26 Stat. 215–219).

Wyoming Admitted to the Union. Accepted the constitution formed by a Wyoming Territory convention on September 30, 1889, and subsequently ratified and adopted by the people of the Wyoming Territory on November 1, 1889. Declared that Wyoming was one of the "United States of America" and "admitted into the Union on an equal footing with the original States." Approved July 10, 1890 (26 Stat. 222–226).

Sherman Silver Purchase Act. Required the U.S. Treasury to purchase 4.5 million ounces of silver bullion each month at the prevailing market price and to issue legal tender Treasury notes redeemable in gold or silver at the option of the federal government. Repealed the Bland-Allison Act of 1878. Approved July 14, 1890 (26 Stat. 289–290). *(Bland-Allison Act, p. 136; Repeal of Sherman Silver Purchase Act, p. 162)*

Second Morrill Land Grant College Act. Required that federal funds should be "equitably divided" between white and black colleges, and that no money shall be paid out under the act to any state or territory for the support and maintenance of a college where a distinction of race or color was made in the admission of students. Stated that if a state established and maintained separate colleges for white and African American students they would be held in compliance with provisions of the act, if the funds received were equitably divided among the institutions. Approved August 30, 1890 (26 Stat. 417–419).

McKinley Tariff Act. Raised duties to an average of 45.5 percent. Provided for the first comprehensive protective duties on agricultural products. Raised the duties on all foreign articles that under previous tariff laws could compete with similar articles of domestic production. Authorized the president to enter into limited reciprocity treaties with countries "producing and exporting sugars, molasses, coffee, tea, and hides." Approved October 1, 1890 (26 Stat. 567–625).

Courts of Appeals Act (Evarts Act). Established a court of appeals in each of the nine federal judicial circuits, but maintained the circuit courts to operate as trial courts alongside the district courts. Established an additional judgeship for each circuit and authorized the circuit justice, the circuit judges, or district judges to preside over each three-person court of appeals. Provided that in diversity suits and in several categories of cases before the courts of appeals, there was no right of appeal to the Supreme Court, although those courts could certify cases for a decision from the high court. Allowed Supreme Court justices to grant a writ of certiorari to hear individual appeals. Approved March 3, 1891 (26 Stat. 826–830).

Immigration Act of 1891. Extended the alien classes denied entry into the United States to include "idiots, insane persons, paupers or persons likely to become a public charge, persons suffering from a loathsome or a dangerous disease, persons who have been convicted of a felony or other infamous crime or misdemeanor involving moral turpitude, polygamists, and also any person whose ticket or passage is paid for with the money of another or who is assisted by others to come" unless they clearly do not belong to an excluded class. Excluded from the provisions of the act were persons convicted of political offenses. Prohibited transportation companies from soliciting immigration. Prescribed penalties for persons aiding illegal aliens. Created an Office of Superintendent of Immigration. Required that arriving immigrants be inspected and undergo a medical examination. Prescribed penalties for violation of the act and procedures for deportation. Approved March 3, 1891 (26 Stat. 1084–1086).

Meat Inspection Act of 1891. Required the secretary of agriculture to appoint inspectors to assure that "all cattle intended for export to foreign countries" be "free from disease." Prohibited all vessels carrying cattle for exportation to a foreign country unless the owner or shipper had an "official certificate attesting to the sound and wholesome condition" of the cattle from an appointed inspector. Authorized the secretary of agriculture to cause the inspection of "all cattle, sheep, and hogs which are subjects of interstate commerce and which are about to be slaughtered at slaughter-houses, canning, salting, packing, or rendering establishments." Excluded animals slaughtered by farmers for personal use. Approved March 3, 1891 (26 Stat. 1089–1091).

General Land Revision Act of 1891. Repealed the Preemption Act of 1841, Timber Culture Act of 1873, and Timber Cutting Act of 1878; amended the Desert Land Act of 1877 and homestead acts; and eliminated the auctioning of public lands. Authorized the president to set aside and reserve forest lands (subsequently called national forests). Approved March 3, 1891 (26 Stat. 1095–1103). *(Preemption Act of 1841, p. 75; Timber Culture Act, p. 127; Desert Land Act, p. 134)*

Forest Reserve Act of 1891. Empowered the president by proclamation to create "forest reserves" (later known as national forests) by withdrawing land from the public domain. Laid the legislative foundation for what became the National Forest system. Approved March 3, 1891 (26 Stat. 1103, Sec. 24).

International Copyright Act. Extended copyright protection to foreign authors, inventors, designers, map and chart makers, composers, and artists whose "state or nation" permitted American authors the benefit of copyright protection on substantially the same basis as it did its own citizens. Granted protection also to individuals whose governments were party to an international agreement providing for reciprocity in copyright. Approved March 3, 1891 (26 Stat. 1110, Sec. 13).

Note

1. Homer E. Socolofsky and Allan B. Spetter, *The Presidency of Benjamin Harrison* (Lawrence, Kan.: University of Kansas Press, 1987), 96–97.

Fifty-second Congress
March 4, 1891, to March 3, 1893

First session—December 7, 1891, to August 5, 1892
Second session—December 5, 1892, to March 3, 1893
(Administration of Benjamin Harrison, 1889–1893)

Historical Background

Benjamin Harrison's final two years as president were marked by repeated but generally unsuccessful efforts by the Democratic-dominated House of Representatives to repeal much of the domestic legislation passed by the Republican Fifty-first Congress. Although Democrats held a commanding majority in the House, Harrison obtained support for legislation that addressed one of his most serious concerns—the need to improve the safety conditions of railroad employees. All four of his annual messages contained an urgent plea that special consideration be given to the plight of yardmen and brakemen, thousands of whom were either maimed or killed each year. The Safety Appliance Act of 1893 for the first time required that all railroads engaged in interstate commerce use cars equipped with automatic couplers, safety handholds, and power or train brakes on a certain number of freight cars, by January 1898. Locomotives were to have driving-wheel brakes. The Interstate Commerce Commission was assigned responsibility for assuring that railroads complied with the new safety standards.

President Harrison signed the Geary Act, extending the suspension of Chinese immigration for another ten years, just hours before the Chinese Exclusion Act of 1882 was to expire. Without the extension, Congress was fearful that nothing would "prevent the Chinese hordes from invading our country in numbers so vast, as soon to outnumber the present population of our flourishing States on the Pacific slopes." Chinese laborers already within the United States were required to obtain certificates of residence either through documents or by "at least one creditable white witness" authenticating their right to residence.[1]

Agitation of an even longer duration preceded enactment of the eight-hour workday for federal blue-collar workers. Congress had first established an eight-hour federal workday in 1868, but that law did not produce the desired results and most of private industry failed to follow suit. The wages of federal workers were reduced by 20 percent after the shorter workday was put into effect, and private contractors engaged in government work were not covered by the law. With the Panic of 1873 and the six-year depression that followed, even the eight-hour workday that had been achieved through strikes was swept away. During the 1880s, the movement for a shorter workday was revived, but not until after the turn of the century did the ten-, nine-, and eight-hour workday finally begin to become a reality for a broad segment of American blue-collar workers. In August 1892, Congress again enacted an eight-hour workday for all laborers and mechanics employed by the federal government as well as any contractor or subcontractor of a public works project. This act, like its predecessor, however, suffered from a lack of enforcement.

The Compulsory Testimony Act of 1893 was crafted in response to a Supreme Court ruling (*Counselman v. Hitchcock,* 142 U.S. 547 [1892]) that an immunity statute must provide absolute immunity against future prosecution concerning matters about which the witness had testified. The act granted immunity from prosecution to witnesses who were compelled to testify before the Interstate Commerce Commission. The 1893 act became the "basic form for numerous federal immunity statutes until 1970."[2]

A rider attached to the 1893 legislation providing diplomatic and consular appropriations authorized the appointment of America's first ambassadors. Although the Constitution had always provided for the appointment of "Ambassadors, other public Ministers and Consuls," Congress had stubbornly opposed approving any appointment higher than that of minister. Debate over diplomatic rank had raged since George Washington's first term as president, but it took on added importance in the 1890s as U.S. envoys abroad were regularly being accorded a lower precedence than representatives of other nations who bore the senior title of ambassador.

The presidential election of 1892 pitted Republican incumbent Benjamin Harrison against his Democratic predecessor, Grover Cleveland. The overwhelming midterm Democratic House candidates' victory of 1890 as well as prominent Democratic victories at the state level proved a harbinger of the future electoral defeat of Harrison and congressional Republicans. Cleveland and his vice presidential running mate, Adlai E. Stevenson, won with an electoral vote margin of 277 votes to 145 votes for Harrison and his running mate, Whitelaw Reid. Displeasure over the negative ramifications of the McKinley Tariff Act, a significant anti-Harrison sentiment throughout much of the country, and substantial support for Populist and Prohibitionist candidates worked together to assure the election of the only American president to serve nonconsecutive terms. Cleveland's coattails were sufficient to secure a Democratic majority in both houses of Congress as well.

Major Acts

Geary Chinese Exclusion Act. Extended the Chinese Exclusion Act of 1882 for ten years, and provided regulations for deportation of Chinese persons not lawfully entitled to remain in the United States. Required that all Chinese laborers entitled to remain in the United States obtain certificates of residence from district collectors of internal revenue. Approved May 5, 1892 (27 Stat. 25–26). Certain provisions of this act were subsequently held unconstitutional in *Wong Wing v. United States,* 163 U.S. 228 (1896). *(Chinese Exclusion Act, p. 142)*

Eight-Hour Workday. Limited laborers and mechanics "employed by the Government of the United States, by the District of Columbia, or by any contractor or subcontractor" of the public works of the United States or the District of Columbia to an eight-hour workday. Approved August 1, 1892 (27 Stat. 340).

Compulsory Testimony Act. Provided that "no person shall be excused from attending and testifying or from producing books, papers, tariffs, contracts, agreements, and documents before the Interstate Commerce Commission, or in obedience to the subpoena of the Commission. Provided that a witness could not be "prosecuted or subjected to any penalty or forfeiture for or on account of any transaction, matter or thing, concerning which he may testify or produce evidence, documentary or otherwise before said Commission, or in obedience to its subpoena." Provided, that "no person so testifying shall be exempt from prosecution and punishment for perjury committed in so testifying." Approved February 11, 1893 (27 Stat. 443–444). Repealed by the Organized Crime Control Act of 1970, October 15, 1970 (84 Stat. 931, Sec. 245).

Diplomatic Appropriations Act. Authorized the president at his discretion to designate U.S. diplomatic representatives as ambassadors in countries that sent ambassadors to the United States. Approved March 1, 1893 (27 Stat. 497).

Railway Safety Appliance Act of 1893. Required that all railroads engaged in interstate commerce have locomotives "equipped with a power driving-wheel brake and appliances for operating the train-brake system" and that a "sufficient number of cars" on each train be "equipped with power or train brakes so that the engineer on the locomotive drawing" a train "can control its speed without requiring brakemen to use the common hand brake for that purpose." Also required that all railroad cars used in moving interstate commerce be equipped with automatic couplers and safety handholds, or grab irons, on side ladders, rooftops, and ends of all freight cars after January 1, 1898. Delegated responsibility of assuring that the railroads adhered to the new safety standards to the Interstate Commerce Commission. Approved March 2, 1893 (27 Stat. 531–532).

Notes

1. U.S. House Committee on Immigration and Naturalization, *Chinese Immigration,* 52d Cong., lst sess., 1892. H. Rept. 255, 1.

2. Michael A. Petrillo, *Constitutional Police Procedure,* 2d ed. (Flushing, N.Y.: Looseleaf Law Publications, 158.

Fifty-third Congress
March 4, 1893, to March 3, 1895

First session—August 7, 1893, to November 3, 1893
Second session—December 4, 1893, to August 28, 1894
Third session—December 3, 1894, to March 3, 1895
Special session of the Senate—March 4, 1893, to
     April 15, 1893
(Second administration of Grover Cleveland, 1893–1897)

Historical Background

A national economic crisis occupied the nation's attention for the entire four years of Grover Cleveland's second administration. Signs of economic slowdown and deflation were evident for more than a year, leading to declining federal revenues and a growing deficit. Major railroads had grossly overextended themselves on miles of unprofitable track, and a persistent balance of payments deficit combined with redemption in gold of Treasury notes issued under the Sherman Silver Purchase Act to drive the nation's gold reserve close to the $100 million floor generally regarded as prudent. Ten days before Cleveland's inauguration, the ill-managed Philadelphia and Reading Railroad went into bankruptcy, leading to widespread unease in the financial markets and further redemption of Treasury notes. In April 1893 the $100 million gold reserve floor was breached, and on May 4 National Cordage declared bankruptcy, causing panic selling in Wall Street. Further collapses followed, especially among rail giants; banks called in loans and suspended payments on accounts; credit became impossible to obtain. By the end of the year, five hundred banks and more than fifteen thousand businesses had folded and 30 percent of the nation's rail system was insolvent. Although the fundamental causes of the Panic of 1893 were complex,

President Cleveland was convinced that the Sherman Silver Purchase Act of 1890 was the source of the depression and called a special session of Congress in August to urge its repeal. Only after an eighty-day filibuster by Senate silverites did Congress finally act on Cleveland's request. Repeal of the Silver Purchase Act, however, did little to halt the drain on the gold reserves or to alleviate the deepening depression.

Cleveland was further dismayed when his desire for a lower tariff met a less than enthusiastic response. "Nothing" more important than tariff reform, Cleveland emphatically told Congress in his 1893 annual message, "claims our attention." It "clearly presents itself as both an opportunity and a duty—an opportunity to deserve the gratitude of our fellow-citizens and a duty imposed upon us by . . . the emphatic mandate of the people." Because the Democrats controlled the White House as well as both houses of Congress for the first time since the Thirty-fifth Congress (1857–1859), when James Buchanan was president (and tariff reform had been a key plank in the Democratic platform in the 1892 election), Cleveland was optimistic. Once again the Senate proved to be a major hurdle, as more than six hundred amendments were made to the House-passed version of the legislation. Although Cleveland denounced Senate Democrats who had demanded changes that directly affected the economic interests of their states, the Senate version was ultimately accepted by the House. The Wilson-Gorman Tariff, which Cleveland allowed to become law without his signature, did little to fulfill the administration's promises of tariff reform, as duties were lowered only slightly (from 49 percent to 42 percent). The U.S. Supreme Court's subsequent 5 to 4 ruling in *Pollock v. Farmers' Loan & Trust Co.* that a 2 percent income tax provision within the act was unconstitutional further eroded the administration's popularity.

A decade-long movement for a holiday commemorating the contributions of American labor reached its climax in 1894. By that time, twenty-three states had recognized Labor Day as a legal holiday. Honoring labor with a federal holiday, Congress reasoned, was "important to the public weal" and "will in time naturally lead to an honorable emulation among the different crafts beneficial to them and to the whole public."[1]

A lengthy struggle also preceded passage of an enabling act in July 1894 that would result in statehood for the Mormon-dominated Utah Territory. Congress stipulated that the Constitution of the new state must provide for a "perfect toleration of religious sentiment," prohibit "polygamous or plural marriages," disclaim "all right and title to the unappropriated public lands" within the territory, declare that all Indian lands within the territory remain under Congress's jurisdiction, provide for assumption of all the territory's "debts and liabilities," and establish a school system open to all children.

Concerned over deteriorating relations with China prompted the Gresham-Yang Treaty, which the Senate advised ratification of in 1894. The treaty reinstated the right of Chinese laborers to return to the United States if they left for a visit providing they had wives, children, or parents living in America, or property or debts owed to them of at least $1,000. A decade later, China denounced the treaty and it expired. Not until 1943 when China became an American ally during World War II did Congress finally repeal the exclusion law, and the Chinese came under general immigration laws.

With the enactment of the Carey Desert Land Act, sponsored by Sen. Joseph M. Carey of Wyoming, the states would take the lead in reclaiming arid lands through irrigation. At the discretion of the secretary of the interior, each western state possessing desert lands could receive up to a million acres of public lands to be sold to settlers in 160-acre tracts. Twenty acres of tract had to be cultivated by each individual settler. Proceeds from the sale of the lands were to be used by the states to reclaim additional lands. Few potential settlers, however, had the capital to finance building of the irrigation systems needed to develop lands covered by the act.

Most of the provisions of the Force Acts of 1870–1871 were repealed in 1894. This action followed an unsuccessful attempt in 1890–1891 by President Harrison and Republican leaders in Congress to reinstate federal supervision of federal elections in the South where blacks were being systematically excluded from the polls in flagrant violation of the Fifteenth Amendment. Another three-quarters of a century would pass, however, before that goal would be realized with the Voting Rights Act of 1965. (*Voting Rights Act of 1965, p. 323*)

Congress passed the Printing Act of 1895, the first comprehensive government printing law, in an effort to centralize, as far as possible, all printing and binding at the Government Printing Office (GPO). The act created the federal depository library program as we know it by providing that "all government publications delivered to designated depositories or other libraries shall be for public use without charge."

Major Acts and Treaties

Repeal of Sherman Silver Purchase Act. Repealed the Sherman Silver Purchase Act of July 14, 1890, which in part provided for the secretary of the Treasury to purchase up to 4.5 million ounces of silver bullion per month. Approved November 1, 1893 (28 Stat. 4). (*Sherman Silver Purchase Act, p. 156*)

Federal Election Laws Repeal Act. Repealed the federal supervision of election clauses of the Force Bills of May 31, 1870, February 28, 1871, and April 20, 1871, and placed the responsibility for the conduct of elections entirely with the states. Approved February 8, 1894 (28 Stat. 36–37). (*First Force Act [First Ku Klux Klan Act], p. 123; Second Force Act [Second Ku Klux Klan Act], p. 124; Third Force Act [Third Ku Klux Klan Act], p. 126*)

Labor Day Holiday. Made the first Monday in September, "being the day celebrated and known as Labor's Holiday," a legal public holiday. Approved June 28, 1894 (28 Stat. 96).

Utah Enabling Act. Authorized the inhabitants of the Territory of Utah to form a constitution and state government. Required that the constitution "be republican in form, make no distinction in civil or political rights on account of race or color"—except for Indians—and not to be repugnant to the Constitution or the Declaration of Independence. Stipulated that it contain provisions (1) securing a "perfect toleration of religious sentiment," (2) prohibiting "polygamous or plural marriages," (3) disclaiming "all right and title to the unappropriated public lands lying within the boundaries" of the territory, (4) declaring all Indian lands within the territory "shall remain under the absolute jurisdiction of Congress," (5) providing for the state's assumption of all territorial "debts and liabilities," (6) and establishing a school system open to all children. Declared that once the constitution had been approved by a majority of the legal voters of the territory and certified by a board of commissioners known as the Utah Commission, the president should issue a proclamation "announcing the result of said election, and thereupon the proposed State of Utah be deemed admitted by Congress into the Union." Approved July 16, 1894 (28 Stat. 107–112).

Gresham-Yang Treaty. Repealed the Scott Act provision banning the return of Chinese laborers after visits to their homeland. Banned Chinese immigration to the United States. Allowed Chinese officials, teachers, students, merchants, and travelers to continue to come to the United States and reside there. Provided protection under U.S. laws to "Chinese laborers or Chinese of any other class, either permanently or temporarily residing in the United States." Concluded March 17, 1894 (28 Stat. 1210–1212). Ratification advised by the Senate August 13, 1894.[2]

Carey Desert Land Act. Authorized the secretary of the interior, with the approval of the president, to "donate, grant, and patent . . . free of cost" up to a million acres to each of the states possessing desert land for disposal to settlers. Limited each settler to 160 acres under the act, at least 20 of which had to be irrigated, cultivated, and reclaimed. Required that the states file maps showing their plans for irrigation and sources of water. Provided that the funds accruing to each state

from the sale of these lands were to be used to reclaim other lands within the state. Approved August 18, 1894 (28 Stat. 422–423, Sec. 4).

Wilson-Gorman Tariff Act. Reduced the average ad valorem tariff rate to approximately 42 percent, and permitted the federal government to levy a 2 percent income tax on personal incomes in excess of $4,000 per year as well as on corporate profits, gifts, and inheritances. Became law without the president's signature August 27, 1894 (28 Stat. 509–570). Certain provisions of the act were subsequently held unconstitutional in *Pollock v. Farmer's Loan & Trust Co.,* 157 U.S. 429 (1895). The legislation was sponsored by Rep. William L. Wilson of West Virginia and Sen. Arthur P. Gorman of Maryland.

Printing Act of 1895. Made the Government Printing Office (GPO) responsible for the printing of all three branches of the federal government, for the dissemination of government publications for sale, and for deposit in congressionally designated libraries nationwide. Required that an inventory of these documents be provided by way of monthly, annual, and biennial indexes, and prohibited the copyrighting of any government publication. Established the position of superintendent of documents within GPO, who, under the direction of the public printer, was responsible for the sale, distribution, and indexing of public documents. Approved January 12, 1895 (28 Stat. 601–624).

Notes

1. U.S. House Committee on Labor, *Labor Day a Legal Holiday,* 53d Cong., 2d sess., 1894. H. Rept. 902, 1.

2. *Journal of the Executive Proceedings of the Senate* (Washington, D.C.: U.S. Government Printing Office, 1906), 29, pt. 1, 774–775.

Fifty-fourth Congress
March 4, 1895, to March 3, 1897

First session—December 2, 1895, to June 11, 1896
Second session—December 7, 1896, to March 3, 1897
(Second administration of Grover Cleveland, 1893–1897)

Historical Background

Republicans regained control of Congress as a result of the 1894 midterm elections in one of the largest congressional realignments in history. Twenty-four states did not have a single Democratic member of Congress and six others states had only one, as the continuing depression and conflicting sectional differences left the Democratic Party in disarray. During President Grover Cleveland's final two years in office, even a sizable number of the Democratic minority felt little allegiance to his administration.

President Cleveland did, however, gain congressional support for resolving an eight-decades-old dispute between Great Britain and Venezuela over the boundaries of British Guiana (now Guyana) and the South American republic. During his second term, Cleveland gradually became convinced that if the British pursued their claims it would be in violation of the Monroe Doctrine and could lead to war. Initially, he sought to resolve the impasse through a diplomatic dispatch prepared by Secretary of State Richard Olney. Cleveland's July 1895 message to Britain repeated the offer the United States had made on several previous occasions to be an impartial arbitrator, but it also stated that American intervention was fully justified under the Monroe Doctrine. Several months later, Great Britain declared that the Monroe Doctrine was not recognized in international law and was not applicable in this instance. Cleveland immediately sent Congress a special message on December 17 declaring that the dispute represented a serious threat to the United States and requested an "adequate appropriation" for a presidential commission to study the matter, which was quickly approved. Ultimately, the British agreed to arbitration, and a treaty was signed that resolved the controversy just before Cleveland left office.

In January 1896, nearly a decade after the Edmunds-Tucker Act deprived Mormons of civil rights and the federal government took possession of most of the church's property, President Cleveland signed a proclamation admitting Utah to the Union. The president's signature followed an enabling act approved by Congress eighteen months earlier. In the spring of 1896, the Act of Oblivion, which removed the prohibition against individuals who had served as Confederate military officers or government officials during the Civil War from holding positions in the army or navy, became law. Passage of the act reflected the general sentiment on Capitol Hill that, three decades after the war, no reason existed to continue the prohibition. *(Edmunds-Tucker Antipolygamy Act, p. 149)*

Amid ongoing debate in the United States over what approach the nation should take regarding the Cuban War of Independence, Congress in April 1896, passed the Morgan-Cameron Resolution. The resolution, approved two years prior to the start of the Spanish-American War, recognized Cuban belligerency against Spain and called for Cuban Independence. Although the Morgan-Cameron Resolution did not carry the force of law, it did serve notice to President Grover Cleveland and Secretary of State Richard Olney of congressional sentiment in support of the Cuban rebels and against Spain.

Grover Cleveland and the Democrats, as the midterm elections of 1894 revealed, received much of the blame for the nation's hard times. Little had changed by 1896, as the American people waited with anticipation for a change in the White House. William Jennings Bryan electrified the Democratic National Convention and won his party's nomination with his "Cross of Gold" speech calling for free coinage of silver. He subsequently toured the nation in an eighteen-thousand-mile whistle-stop campaign. Republican standard-bearer William McKinley, by contrast, conducted a "front porch" campaign from his home in Canton, Ohio, leaving most details to his well-funded organization. A novel element in the 1896 presidential campaign was the emergence of the Populist Party, whose candidate, Thomas E. Watson, ran on a reform platform. After four years of hard times, McKinley's call for "the full dinner pail," a protective tariff, and a return to the gold standard captured the voters' imagination and resulted in a watershed election that sealed Republican political dominance for three decades. McKinley and vice presidential nominee Garret A. Hobart carried the day by each capturing 271 electoral votes to Bryan's 176. Bryan's running mate, Arthur Sewall, received 149 electoral votes, and Populist vice presidential candidate Thomas E. Watson received 27 votes. With this election, the Republicans, except for six of the eight years Woodrow Wilson served as president, would control both the White House and Congress until the New Deal.

During the waning hours of his second term, Cleveland vetoed a literacy bill that would have barred all immigrants over sixteen who could neither read nor write the English language or some other language. The provisions of the literacy bill, which represented the first of several efforts to impose a literacy test on immigrants, would ultimately become law in 1917 over President Woodrow Wilson's protests. Imposing a literacy test on immigrants, Cleveland proclaimed in his veto message, was a "radical departure" from the previous immigration policy, "unnecessarily harsh and oppressive," and a "misleading test" of "desirable citizenship." The House overrode the veto 195 to 37, but the Senate voted to refer the matter to the Committee on Immigration, where it died. (*Immigration Act of 1917, p. 205*)

Major Acts

Venezuela-British Guiana Boundary Commission. Appropriated $100,000 for the "expenses of a commission to be appointed by the President to investigate and report upon the true divisional line between the Republic of Venezuela and British Guiana." Approved December 21, 1895 (29 Stat. 1).

Utah Admitted to the Union. President Grover Cleveland issued a proclamation on January 4, 1896, stating that Utah had complied with the enabling act approved on July 16, 1894, and proclaimed that the admission of Utah "is now accomplished." Approved January 4, 1896 (29 Stat. 876–877).

Act of Oblivion. Repealed section 1218 of the Revised Statutes of the United States, as amended, that prohibited those individuals who held military or naval commissions or served in any official capacity in the civil government of the Confederate States from holding a position in the army or navy of the United States. Approved March 31, 1896 (29 Stat. 84).

Morgan-Cameron Resolution. Declared that "in the opinion of Congress, a condition of public war" existed between the Government of Spain and the people of Cuba, "and that the United States of America should maintain a strict neutrality between the contending powers." Resolved that "the friendly offices of the United States should be offered by the President to the Spanish Government for the recognition of the independence of Cuba." Approved April 6, 1896 (*Congressional Record*, v. 28, February 28, 1896, 2257–2258; March 2, 1896, 2342–2359; April 6, 1896, 3616, 3627–3628).

Fifty-fifth Congress
March 4, 1897, to March 3, 1899

First session—March 15, 1897, to July 24, 1897
Second session—December 6, 1897, to July 8, 1898
Third session—December 5, 1898, to March 3, 1899
Special session of the Senate—March 4, 1897, to March
    10, 1897
(First administration of William McKinley, 1897–1901)

Historical Background

In his first inaugural address, delivered March 4, 1897, President William McKinley called for higher tariffs to offset a Treasury deficit made worse by a deepening depression and the U.S. Supreme Court's decision to invalidate the income tax provisions of the Wilson-Gorman Tariff Act of 1894. Soon afterward, the president summoned a special session of Congress to enact legislation to increase revenues and provide more comprehensive protection for American industries. In response, the Republican-controlled Congress passed the Dingley Tariff, which imposed the highest average duty rates of the nineteenth century.

With the passage of the Dingley Tariff, American attention began to focus on the anti-Spanish rebellion in the Spanish colony of Cuba. This war for independence had begun in 1878, and after a temporary settlement in 1888, war reopened with renewed intensity in 1895. The Cuban struggle aroused considerable popular sympathy as reports of harsh Spanish treatment of Cuban civilians became widespread. On February 15, 1898, an explosion sank the American battleship USS *Maine,* which had been sent to Havana harbor to "show the flag" and protect American property and citizens. Two hundred sixty American sailors were killed in the blast. "Remember the Maine!" immediately became a

popular rallying cry as sentiment rapidly grew for a war against Spain. The administration assumed an antiwar stance until President McKinley on April 20, 1898, asked Congress for "forcible intervention" by the United States to secure peace in Cuba. Earlier action on Capitol Hill had provided the financial foundation for the effort with an emergency $50 million military appropriation. Recognition of Cuban independence, in legislation offered by Sen. Henry M. Teller of Colorado, and a formal declaration of war against Spain quickly passed following McKinley's war message. On June 13, Congress approved an extensive war revenue bill.

The war's initial engagement came on May 1, 1898, when Commodore George Dewey's U.S. Asiatic squadron annihilated a weaker Spanish fleet in Manila Bay, in the Philippines, at almost no cost in American lives. The city of Manila was subsequently seized by American forces. In the Caribbean, near the end of May, an American expeditionary force landed near Santiago de Cuba, where Spain's remaining fleet had taken refuge and was subsequently blockaded by the U.S. battle fleet. As American land forces tightened their grip, the Spanish fleet made a break for the open sea and was destroyed. The surrender of Santiago followed swiftly. In the war's final military action, American forces occupied Puerto Rico almost unopposed. Perhaps the most widely hailed hero of the war was McKinley's assistant secretary of navy, Theodore Roosevelt, who raised a regiment of volunteers (the Rough Riders) and led the capture of Spanish fortifications at San Juan Hill, one of the defenses of Santiago. With the Treaty of Paris signed on December 10, 1898, Cuba was established as an independent state. The treaty also provided for American acquisition of Puerto Rico, Guam, and the Philippines. The following March, an act was approved to reimburse the states and territories for the expenses they incurred in aiding the war effort.

Amidst the excitement of the American victories at Manila and Santiago, long-standing arguments against acquiring the Hawaiian Islands were swept aside as first the House and then the Senate adopted a joint resolution of annexation. On August 12, 1899, sovereignty over the islands formally transferred to the United States. The annexation movement was made easier as a consequence of an 1893 coup engineered by American residents of the islands that deposed the Hawaiian monarchy.

Meanwhile, on the domestic front, Congress sought a solution to continuing railroad labor disputes, which had been increasing in numbers and violence throughout the decade. In May 1898, legislation was approved that provided for mediation by the chairman of the Interstate Commerce Commission and the commissioner of the Bureau of Labor upon the request of either the railroads or their employees. If mediation failed, then a three-member commission was to be chosen to arbitrate the dispute. Amidst increasing concern over the growth of private monopolies, a nineteen-member nonpartisan Industrial Commission was authorized to investigate the "growing concentration of economic power" in the United States. It was also charged with investigating problems associated with immigration, agriculture, labor, and management. The commission's extensive findings, together with those of several subsequent studies, provided invaluable data upon which new legislative policies would be developed.

The Federal Bankruptcy Act, signed into law in the summer of 1898, capped an eight-year struggle for a permanent federal bankruptcy law. Prior to its enactment, only thirteen states had both voluntary and involuntary bankruptcy laws. The federal act would endure, without significant amendments, for nearly four decades. It provided for the liquidation and distribution of a debtor's assets as well as an agreement for reducing his or her debts. Dissolution of the Indian governments in the Indian Territory was rapidly advanced with the decisions, first, to have all civil and criminal cases involving Native Americans tried in U.S. courts (1897) and, second, to abolish tribal law and tribal courts (1898).

During the latter part of the nineteenth century, conservationists continued to promote the need for a national forestry system while bills to provide for effective administration and protection of the national forest reserves languished on Capitol Hill. Finally, after creating a National Forest Commission composed of leading scientists and conservationists to investigate the issue, Congress approved the Forest Management Act. The law provided the first national policy guidance for national forest use and management.

Although Democrats gained 50 House seats in the 1898 midterm elections, Republicans retained control of the lower house with a 185 to 163 majority. In the Senate, Republican dominance was further enhanced by six additional members.

Major Acts and Treaties

Forest Management Act (Forest Service Organic Act). Provided for the organization and management of the forest reserves. Reaffirmed the power of the president to create reserves and confirmed all reservations created prior to 1897, but limited the type of lands to be reserved in the future, stating: "No public forest reservation shall be established, except to improve and protect the forest within the reservation, or for the purpose of securing favorable conditions of water flows, and to furnish a continuous supply of timber for the use and necessities of citizens of the United States." Did not "authorize the inclusion therein of lands more valuable for the mineral therein, or for agricultural purposes, than for forest purposes." Approved June 4, 1897 (30 Stat. 11).

Jurisdiction of U.S. Courts Extended to Indian Territory. Provided that after January 1, 1898, the United States courts in the Indian Territory would have original and exclusive jurisdiction and authority to try and determine all civil and criminal cases therein. Approved June 7, 1897 (30 Stat. 83).

Dingley Tariff. Raised the average rate of customs duties to more than 50 percent for the first time in the nation's history. Permitted the president to negotiate reciprocal agreements with the approval of Congress. Approved July 24, 1897 (30 Stat. 151–213).

Emergency Military Appropriations. Provided $50 million in emergency military appropriations "to be expended at the discretion of the President" that would remain available until January 1, 1899. Approved March 9, 1898 (30 Stat. 274).

Recognition of Cuban Independence (Teller Amendment). Declared that the people of Cuba "are, and of right ought to be, free and independent." Demanded that the "Government of Spain at once relinquish its authority and government in the Island of Cuba." Declared that the United States had no intention "to exercise sovereignty, jurisdiction, or control" over the island of Cuba once its freedom had been obtained. Directed and empowered the president "to use the entire land and naval forces of the United States" in carrying out this resolution. Approved April 20, 1898 (30 Stat. 738–739).

Declaration of War with Spain. Declared that war existed and had existed between the United States and the Kingdom of Spain since April 21, 1898. Directed and empowered the president "to use the entire land and naval forces of the United States, and to call into actual service of the United States the militia of the several States, to such extent as may be necessary to carry this Act into effect." Approved April 25, 1898 (30 Stat. 364).

Erdman Act. Provided for mediation by the chairman of the Interstate Commerce Commission and the commissioner of labor in railroad disputes "upon the request of either party to the controversy." Declared that when disputes could "not be settled by mediation and conciliation" they were to be submitted to a three-member arbitration board consisting of a commissioner named by the employer, a commissioner named by the labor organization, and a third commissioner selected by the other two. Declared that it was unlawful for an employer who was a party to such arbitration to discharge the employees involved except for "inefficiency, violation of law, or neglect of duty." Declared that it was unlawful "for the organization representing such employees to order" or "for the employees to unite in, aid, or abet, strikes against said employer." Approved June 1, 1898 (30 Stat. 424–428). Certain provisions of this act were

subsequently held unconstitutional in *Adair v. United States,* 208 U.S. 161 (1908).

War Revenue Act. Authorized the imposition of a number of different taxes as a "means to meet war expenditures." Created special taxes on bankers, pawn brokers, commercial brokers, customhouse brokers, theaters, museums, concerts, circuses, public exhibitions, bowling alleys, and billiard rooms. Increased taxes on tobacco, cigars, cigarettes, and snuff. Imposed taxes on adhesive stamps, fermented liquors, seats and berths in parlor and sleeping cars, mixed flour, legacies, individual shares of personal property, and telephone service. Authorized the secretary of the Treasury to borrow sums not to exceed $100 million, and at rates not to exceed 3 percent, which might be necessary to meet public expenditures. Approved June 13, 1898 (30 Stat. 448–470). Certain provisions of this act were subsequently held unconstitutional in *Fairbank v. United States,* 181 U.S. 283 (1901), and *United States v. Hvoslef,* 237 U.S. 1 (1915).

U.S. Industrial Commission Created. Authorized the appointment of a nonpartisan Industrial Commission to be composed of five U.S. representatives appointed by the Speaker of the House, five U.S. senators appointed by the presiding officer of the Senate, and nine individuals appointed by the president from private industry and labor. Directed the commission to "investigate questions pertaining to immigration, to labor, to agriculture, to manufacturing, and to business, and to report to Congress and suggest such legislation as it may deem best upon these subjects." Granted the commission authority to hold hearings, call witnesses, and request pertinent papers. Approved June 18, 1898 (30 Stat. 476–477).

Curtis Act. Provided for the leasing of tribal lands in Indian Territory, incorporation of cities and towns, mineral leases in the territory, per capita payments directly to individuals instead of through tribal governments, abolition of Indian tribal laws and courts, and enlargement of the powers of the U.S. courts. Approved June 28, 1898 (30 Stat. 495–519).

Federal Bankruptcy Act. Established a uniform system of bankruptcy throughout the United States.

Created federal bankruptcy courts in the several states, the District of Columbia, the territories, the Indian Territory, and the District of Alaska. Provided for voluntary as well as involuntary bankruptcies. Extended bankruptcy coverage to traders and nontraders, and provided for creditor participation. Approved July 1, 1898 (30 Stat. 544–566).

Hawaiian Annexation. Provided for the annexation of the Republic of Hawaii as part of the United States, and provided that until such time as Congress provided for a government in the islands, all civil, judicial, and military powers would be vested in such persons as the president might appoint. Approved July 7, 1898 (30 Stat. 750–751).

Treaty of Paris (Peace Treaty between United States and Spain). Ended the Spanish-American War and secured from Spain a recognition of Cuba's independence and an agreement to assume the Cuban debt. Ceded Puerto Rico and Guam to the United States as a war indemnity, and ceded the Philippines to the United States in return for a payment of $20 million (30 Stat. 1754–1762). Concluded December 10, 1898. Ratification advised by the Senate February 6, 1899.[1]

Reimbursement to States and Territories for Expenses Incurred in Spanish-American War. Provided for reimbursement to the states and territories of expenses incurred in aiding the United States during the Spanish-American War. Required that all claims for reimbursement be presented in itemized form to the Treasury Department by January 1, 1902. Approved March 3, 1899 (30 Stat. 1356–1358).

Note

1. *Journal of the Executive Proceedings of the Senate* (Washington, D.C.: U.S. Government Printing Office, 1909), 31 (part 2), 1282–1284.

Fifty-sixth Congress
March 4, 1899, to March 3, 1901

First session—December 4, 1899, to June 7, 1900
Second session—December 3, 1900, to March 3, 1901
(First administration of William McKinley, 1897–1901)

Historical Background

Throughout much of his first term, President William McKinley avoided any action that would return the United States to the gold standard until the chronic shortage of gold had eased and silver sentiment waned. Finally, in his third annual message of December 5, 1899, he called for legislation, and the Gold Standard Act was signed into law on March 14, 1900. It signaled the end of two decades of debate involving one of American's greatest political controversies—the issue of silver's monetary role.

Following the Spanish-American War, concern arose that an immediate and complete withdrawal from Cuba would threaten the political stability of the island, as well as American financial and strategic interests there. As a consequence, Cuba remained under the U.S. Army control while policy makers determined what the future relationship between the United States and the island ought to be. After a Cuban constituent assembly failed to submit a satisfactory proposal, Secretary of War Elihu Root drafted, and Sen. Orville H. Platt of Connecticut introduced, an amendment to the Army Appropriations Bill of 1901 making Cuba a quasi-protectorate of the United States. The Platt Amendment limited the power of Cuba to make treaties, borrow money, or change certain policies established by American occupation forces. In addition, the United States reserved the right to intervene if necessary to preserve Cuban independence and either purchase or lease lands for naval bases there.

These articles were formalized in a 1903 treaty. Although this arrangement was never popular in Cuba, it remained in force until May 1934.

A second amendment to the Army Appropriations Bill, sponsored by Sen. John C. Spooner of Wisconsin, provided a temporary civil government for the Philippine Islands. The Spooner Amendment vested the president with all military, civil, and judicial powers necessary to govern the islands until Congress chose to take further action. Restrictions similar to those imposed on Cuba limited the power to grant franchises for mining and internal improvements. The formal transfer of power from military to civilian leaders took place on July 4, 1901. Filipino nationalists, who had already been in revolt against Spain in 1898, were angered when the United States moved to assume control of the archipelago. In February 1898, hostilities broke out between nationalist and U.S. troops. The American garrison was heavily reinforced, but it took three years of bitter guerrilla warfare to defeat the Filipino forces and exile their leaders to Guam. Subsequent legislation granted an increasing measure of self-government to the Philippines, leading to the Tydings-McDuffie Act of 1934, which provided for a ten-year transitional period that led to full independence on July 4, 1946.

No similar resistance was offered to the U.S. acquisition of Puerto Rico. The Foraker Act, sponsored by Sen. Joseph B. Foraker of Ohio, established a civil government in Puerto Rico, with a presidentially appointed governor and eleven-member executive council consisting of the heads of six administrative departments and five native Puerto Ricans. Legislative authority of the unorganized territory was vested in the executive council and an elected House of Delegates. A resident commissioner would represent Puerto Rico in Congress. Inhabitants of the island were considered "citizens of

Puerto Rico" until 1917, when they were granted American citizenship. Thirty years later, Puerto Ricans gained the right to elect their own governor and in 1951 were authorized to draft their own constitution.

A more modest effort for Alaska in 1900 produced a civil government with a presidentially appointed governor, surveyor general, judges, attorneys, and marshals; a new civil code; and a code of civil procedure. Efforts to secure an Alaskan delegate to Congress were realized six years later. Continuing differences among the tripartite protectorate over the Samoan Islands led to the Convention of 1900, which was ratified by the Senate in January 1900. The treaty settled the Samoan question and added Tutuila and all other islands of the Samoan group east of longitude 171° west to America's territorial holdings.

Congress took a different course with respect to Hawaii. The islands were made an incorporated territory of the United States (that is, they became an integral part of the United States with the implied promise of eventual statehood). Several factors influenced this distinction. For more than four decades, American missionaries, sugar planters, traders, whalers, expansionists, and the Navy Department had looked upon the islands with continuing interest. Their strategic value, commercial dependency on the United States, position as a natural gateway to Asian markets, and importance as a source of sugar, as well as anxiety over Japanese imperialist designs on Hawaii justified a more permanent status.

Establishment of the National Bureau of Standards within the Treasury Department (two years later it was transferred to the Department of Commerce) coincided with a rapid growth in American commerce and industry. In 1899 exports for the first time exceeded imports. The bureau, which had been the subject of discussion for nearly twenty years prior to its establishment, was intended to provide more accurate measurements and uniformity, precision, and control at all levels in the development of manufactured products. Passage of the Lacey Act, one of the most important federal wildlife preservation laws, drastically reduced, through strict regulation, the killing of wild animals and birds. The bill was sponsored by Rep. John F. Lacey of Iowa.

Featured once again in the election of 1900 were William Jennings Bryan and William McKinley, but the fervor of 1896 was lacking. With the return of prosperity, the Republicans' campaign slogan, "A Full Dinner Pail," captured the feeling of the nation. The election of 1900 cemented Republican dominance. McKinley, aided by the popularity of vice presidential nominee Theodore Roosevelt, widened his 1896 margin over Bryan. McKinley and Roosevelt received 292 electoral votes; Bryan and his running mate, Adlai E. Stevenson, 155. The Republicans retained control of both houses of Congress.

Major Acts and Treaties

Convention of 1900. Partitioned the Samoan Islands among the United States, Germany, and Great Britain. Allowed Great Britain to acquire the formerly German Tonga Islands and other concessions in West Africa, the United States to acquire the formerly English island of Tutuila and all the other islands of the Samoan group east of longitude 171° west, and Germany to acquire the formerly American islands of Upolu and Savaii and all other islands of the Samoan group west of longitude 171° west. Concluded December 2, 1899 (31 Stat. 1878–1880). Ratification advised by the Senate January 16, 1900.[1]

Gold Standard Act of 1900. Established the dollar consisting of 25.8 grains, nine-tenths fine, as the standard unit of monetary value, and placed all forms of U.S. currency on a parity of value with the dollar. Authorized a separate gold reserve of $150 million in the Treasury to maintain this parity. Provided for the reserve to be maintained by the sale of bonds and for the redemption of legal tender notes. Called for the retirement of 1890 Treasury notes, and liberalized laws governing national banks. Approved March 14, 1900 (31 Stat. 45–50).

Foraker Act. Provided for the establishment of civil government in Puerto Rico, to take effect May 1, 1900. Made the island an unorganized territory, with its residents made citizens of Puerto Rico (U.S. citizenship was granted in 1917). Empowered the president to appoint a governor and eleven-member executive council consisting of the heads of six administrative departments and five native Puerto Ricans. Vested legislative authority in the executive council and an elected thirty-five-member House of Delegates, and judicial authority in the "courts and tribunals of Puerto Rico" already established. Authorized qualified voters to elect a resident commissioner who was "entitled to official recognition as such by all Departments." Levied a reduced tariff of 15 percent ad valorem on all merchandise coming into the United States from Puerto Rico and all goods entering Puerto Rico from the United States. Declared that all native inhabitants were "citizens of Puerto Rico." Approved April 12, 1900 (31 Stat. 77–86).

Hawaiian Organic Act. Accorded Hawaii political status as an incorporated territory, and conferred American citizenship on all citizens of Hawaii at the time of annexation. Gave all laws of the United States, which were "not locally inapplicable," the same force and effect within the territory as elsewhere in the United States. Vested executive power in a presidentially appointed governor who would hold office for four years. Provided for a secretary of the territory who would act as governor in case of the death, removal, resignation, or disability of the governor; an attorney general; treasurer; commissioner of public works; commissioner of agriculture and forestry; superintendent of public works; superintendent of public instruction; auditor and deputy auditor; surveyor; and high sheriff. Vested legislative power in a territorial fifteen-member elected Senate and thirty-member elected House of Representatives, and judicial power in a "supreme court, circuit courts, and such inferior courts as the legislature may from time to time establish." Authorized the election of a delegate to Congress who would have a seat in the U.S. House of Representatives. Approved April 30, 1900 (31 Stat. 141–162).

Lacey Act. Made the interstate shipment of wildlife and birds killed in violation of state laws a federal offense. Prohibited the importation of foreign wildlife except under a special permit issued by the secretary of agriculture, and vested enforcement of the act with the secretary. Approved May 25, 1900 (31 Stat. 187–189).

Civil Government for Alaska. Provided for a presidentially appointed governor, surveyor general, judges, attorneys, and marshals for Alaska. Established a new civil code and a code of civil procedure. Approved June 6, 1900 (31 Stat. 321–552).

Platt Amendment. Prohibited Cuba from entering "into any treaty or other compact with any foreign power or powers which will impair or tend to impair the independence of Cuba," or assuming or contracting any public debt beyond the ability of its regular revenues to pay. Gave the United States the right to intervene in Cuban affairs to preserve independence and maintain law and order. Required Cuba to "sell or lease to the United States lands necessary for coaling or naval stations." Approved March 2, 1901 (31 Stat. 897–898).

Spooner Amendment. Authorized the president to establish a temporary civil government in the Philippine Islands "until otherwise provided by Congress." Restricted the president from granting or approving a franchise that was "not in his judgment clearly necessary for the immediate government of the islands and indispensable for the interest of the people thereof, and which [could] not, without great public mischief, be postponed until the establishment of permanent civil government." Approved March 2, 1901 (31 Stat. 910).

National Bureau of Standards Created. Established a National Bureau of Standards with responsibility for comparing the "standards used in scientific investigations, engineering, manufacturing, commerce, and educational institutions with the standards adopted or should be recognized by the Government." Authorized the bureau to construct standards necessary, test and calibrate standard measuring apparatus, solve problems that might arise in connection with standards, and determine the physical constants and properties of materials when such data were of importance to scientific and manufacturing interests and are not obtainable elsewhere. Approved March 3, 1901 (31 Stat. 1449–1450).

Note

1. *Journal of the Executive Proceedings of the Senate* (Washington, D.C.: U.S. Government Printing Office, 1909), 32:343.

Fifty-seventh Congress
March 4, 1901, to March 3, 1903

First session—December 2, 1901, to July 1, 1902
Second session—December 1, 1902, to March 3, 1903
Special session of the Senate—March 4, 1901, to
    March 9, 1901
(Second administration of William McKinley, 1901;
    first administration of Theodore Roosevelt,
    1901–1905)

Historical Background

On September 6, 1901, just six months into his second term, President William McKinley was shot by an anarchist at the Pan-American Exposition in Buffalo, New York. His death on September 14 thrust forty-three-year-old Theodore Roosevelt into the presidency on September 14, 1901. Three months later, the new administration signed, and the Senate ratified, the Hay-Pauncefote Treaty with Great Britain, which committed the United States to construct, control, and fortify an isthmian canal between the Caribbean Sea and the Pacific Ocean. This action was preceded by an earlier Hay-Pauncefote Treaty (1900) that, after being amended by the Senate, had been found unacceptable by the British.

A choice had to be made between a route through Nicaragua or one through Colombia. In January 1902, the Isthmian Canal Commission determined that the Colombian route would be the shortest as well as the cheapest. Congress concurred in June. The Spooner Act authorized construction of the canal through Panama, then a part of Colombia, at a cost not to exceed $40 million, providing that the United States could acquire the strip of land needed from Colombia. If these conditions were not met within a reasonable time, then the canal would be built in Nicaragua. The legislation was sponsored by Sen. John C. Spooner of Wisconsin.

In July 1902 President Roosevelt signed the Philippine Government Act, providing for a popularly elected assembly. The United States had acquired the Philippines through the Treaty of Paris of 1898, which ended the Spanish-American War.

Elevation of the Census Bureau from temporary to permanent status in March 1902 was the culmination of nearly seventy years of recommendations and efforts to establish a permanent census organization. Between 1790 and 1900, Congress had relied upon temporary organizations, and as a consequence was only able to compile the national decennial census. The new law allowed the bureau to begin performing a diversified program of censuses and surveys.

The Biologics Act of 1902 was passed after a contaminated smallpox vaccine caused an outbreak of tetanus and several children died from tetanus-contaminated diphtheria antitoxin. The act was the first premarket approval statute in history and gave the government the first control over the processes used to make biological products, or biologics, and the responsibility to ensure their safety for the American public. Passed four years prior to the first Pure Food and Drug Act, it remains the cornerstone of federal regulation of biologics.

At President Roosevelt's request, the Expedition Act was passed in February 1903 to expedite federal prosecution of antitrust suits. Creation of a combined Department of Commerce and Labor, with a Bureau of Corporations empowered to investigate and report upon the activities of corporations engaged in interstate commerce, further enhanced the president's campaign to curb the growth of trusts. Reinforcing the Interstate Commerce Act of 1887, the Elkins Act of 1903 attacked the practice of granting or receiving rebates on freight charges, a practice powerful shippers had long forced upon the railroads. The railroads supported the act, which was sponsored by Sen. Stephen B. Elkins of West Virginia, as a means of preventing a loss in revenues.

Recommendations by Secretary of War Elihu Root, as well as a presidential commission that found glaring defects in organization and administration of the War Department during the Spanish-American War, prompted two significant military reform enactments. The General Staff Act of 1903 established the office of chief of staff as a presidential adviser and focal control point for high level army activities, and provided the U.S. Army with a central planning body. The Militia Act of 1903, better known as the Dick Act, granted federal aid to the National Guard and authorized the War Department to establish procedures for a more direct and active role in organizing, training, and equipping the newly formed guard in line with the standards established for the regular Army.

Ardent conservationist Roosevelt also successfully sought passage of a measure embracing a national reclamation policy. Passage of the Newlands Act, which is frequently compared with the Homestead Act, ranks as one of the most significant measures in shaping the development of the West. It set aside most of the proceeds from the sale of arid and semi-arid western lands for the construction of dams and other reclamation projects, and it allowed for the establishment of the Reclamation Service.

The Immigration Act of 1903, the first comprehensive law for national control of immigration, established the Bureau of Immigration to administer all immigration laws (except the Chinese Exclusion Act). It expanded the federal government's power to regulate immigration, codified immigration law, refined the existing classes of inadmissible immigrants, and refined federal regulation of poor immigrants by amending contract labor and public charge provisions. The act also provided for the deportation of prostitutes, and made immigrants excludable on political grounds for the first time by adding anarchists to the list of inadmissible classes.

Major Acts and Treaties

Hay-Pauncefote Treaty. Abrogated the Clayton-Bulwer Treaty of 1850 with Great Britain, and gave the United States the right to build, operate, regulate, and fortify an interoceanic canal across the Isthmus of Panama. Declared that the canal would be open to ships of all nations "on terms of entire equality" and the charge of using it would be "just and equitable." Concluded November 18, 1901 (32 Stat. 1903–1905). Ratification advised by the Senate December 16, 1901.[1]

Permanent Census Bureau Act of 1902. Provided for a permanent Census Bureau headed by a director of the census appointed by the president, subject to Senate confirmation. Required the bureau to conduct a diverse program of censuses, including an annual compilation of vital statistics, a mid-decade collection of statistics on manufacturers, and compilations on defective, dependent, and delinquent classes of persons; crime and related matters; urban social conditions; religious bodies; and public indebtedness, valuation, taxation, and expenditures. Approved March 6, 1902 (32 Stat. 51–53).

Newlands Reclamation Act. Provided that 95 percent of all monies derived from the sale and disposal of public lands in sixteen arid or semi-arid western states was to be placed in a "reclamation fund," which would be used for the planning, construction, and maintenance of dams and other reclamation projects. Authorized the secretary of the interior to determine sites and construct irrigation works that could store, divert, and develop streams and rivers. Provided that, upon the recommendation of the director of the Geological Survey, an organization known as the Reclamation Service could be established to handle these activities. Approved June 17, 1902 (32 Stat. 388–390).

Spooner (Isthmus Canal) Act. Provided $40 million for the purchase of the rights, privileges, franchises, concessions, grants of land, right of way, unfinished work, plants, and other property owned by the New Panama Canal Company of France on the Isthmus of Panama. Authorized the president to purchase from the Republic of Colombia, under such terms as he might deem reasonable, perpetual control of a strip of land, not less than six miles wide, extending from the Caribbean Sea to the Pacific Ocean. Approved June 28, 1902 (32 Stat. 481–484).

Philippine Government Act. Declared the Philippine Islands to be an "unorganized" territory, and recognized the inhabitants of the islands as citizens of the Philippine Islands entitled to the protection of the United States. Confirmed the president's action in creating the Philippine Commission to govern the territory and provided for a Philippine Assembly consisting of not less than fifty or more than one hundred members to be elected by qualified voters for two-year terms, each member representing a constituency on the basis of population. Approved July 1, 1902 (32 Stat. 691–712).

Biologics Control Act (Virus-Toxin Law). Authorized the federal government, for the first time, to inspect manufacturing facilities, to monitor manufacturing processes, and to require standards for product quality and proper product labeling. Mandated the licensing of manufacturers and products, in addition to uniform labeling that included an identification of the item, the manufacturer's name and address, the expiration date and the license number. Created the hygienic laboratory of the U.S. Public Health Service, which eventually became part of the National Institutes of Health, to oversee manufacture of biological drugs. Approved July 1, 1902 (32 Stat. 728–729).

Dick Militia Act of 1903. Revised the obsolete Militia Act of 1792. Separated the militia into two classes—the organized militia, to be known as the National Guard, and the Reserve Militia. Called for each state or territory to have an adjutant general who would report annually to the secretary of war. Made funds available to Guard units and authorized the secretary of war to provide the same arms and equipment to the Guard as that issued to the regular Army. Required the Guard to attend 24 drills and a five-day encampment each year, and to be guided by Army rules and regulations while on active duty, which was limited to nine months. Approved January 21, 1903 (32 Stat. 775–780).

Expedition Act. Provided for the expedition of federal prosecution of federal antitrust suits when the attorney general requested that such proceedings be given precedence on circuit court dockets. Approved February 11, 1903 (32 Stat. 823).

Department of Commerce and Labor Established. Created the Department of Commerce and Labor as the ninth cabinet office headed by a secretary of commerce and labor appointed by the president, with the advice and consent of the Senate. Delegated to the new department the responsibility of fostering, promoting, and developing "the foreign and domestic commerce, the mining, manufacturing, shipping, and fishery industries, the labor interests, and the transportation facilities of the United States." Vested the department "with the jurisdiction and control of the departments, bureaus, offices, and branches of the public service" associated with those responsibilities. Approved February 14, 1903 (32 Stat. 825–830). (*Bureau of Labor, p. 144; Department of Labor Act, p. 151; Department of Labor Established, p. 195*)

General Staff Act of 1903. Established a General Staff Corps consisting of a chief of staff and 44 officers to prepare plans for the nation's defense and mobilization in the time of war, to investigate and report on the army's efficiency and its readiness to conduct military operations, and to provide assistance to the secretary of war, and general officers and other commanders. Authorized the chief of staff, as the principal military officer of the Army, deriving his powers from the president and secretary of war, to supervise all operations of the army through the general staff. Approved February 14, 1903 (32 Stat. 830–831).

Elkins Act. Defined what constituted unfair discrimination between shippers engaged in interstate commerce. Provided punishments for shippers, as well as railroad corporations, officials, and agents who gave or received rebates on the charges made for shipment of freight by rail. Approved February 19, 1903 (32 Stat. 847–849).

Immigration Act of 1903. Created the Bureau of Immigration under the Labor Department. Added to the admissible list individuals involved in prostitution, anarchists, and persons likely to become public charges including those suffering from contagious diseases, and persons convicted of certain crimes. Refined the federal regulation of poor immigrants by amending the contract labor and public charge provisions. Extended the time limit on deporting aliens in most inadmissible classes from one to three years. Provided for deportation within two years of arrival of "any alien who becomes a public charge by reason of lunacy, idiocy, or epilepsy," unless they could clearly demonstrate that the condition had begun after arrival. Reaffirmed all immigration and contract labor laws made after 1875. Approved March 3, 1903 (32 Stat. 1213–1222).

Note

1. *Journal of the Executive Proceedings of the Senate* (Washington, D.C.: U.S. Government Printing Office, 1931), 33:184–187.

Fifty-eighth Congress
March 4, 1903, to March 3, 1905

First session—November 9, 1903, to December 7, 1903
Second session—December 7, 1903, to April 28, 1904
Third session—December 5, 1904, to March 3, 1905
Special session of the Senate—March 5, 1903, to March 19, 1903
(First administration of Theodore Roosevelt, 1901–1905)

Historical Background

Less than six months after construction of an isthmian canal was approved by Congress, Secretary of State John M. Hay and Colombian minister Tomás Herrán reached an agreement providing for a route through Panama. Soon thereafter the Hay-Herrán Treaty was ratified by the Senate. The Colombian Senate, however, rejected the treaty, insisting on larger payments and greater sovereignty in the canal zone. After President Theodore Roosevelt made clear his unwillingness to concede to the demands of the Colombian government, local Panamanian leaders, fearful that the proposed canal might be built in Nicaragua if the impasse were not resolved, planned a revolt and declaration of independence to avoid losing the canal. Also at their request, a U.S. naval force was dispatched to prevent Colombian interference with the planned insurrection.

After Colombian forces were prevented from landing to suppress the rebellion, the United States immediately recognized the independence of the new Republic of Panama. Fifteen days after the uprising, Secretary of State John Hay and the new Panamanian minister to the United States, Philippe Jean Bunau-Varilla, signed a treaty giving the United States complete and permanent sovereignty over a ten-mile strip across the Isthmus of Panama. After the Senate approved the treaty on February 23, 1904, President Roosevelt named a seven-member Isthmian Canal Commission to supervise the construction of the canal, and the Panama Canal Zone was legally transferred to the United States in May. Prior to the transfer Congress appropriated $10 million to pay the Republic of Panama as called for in the treaty and authorized the president to take possession of the territory conveyed by the treaty for canal purposes, and established a temporary government of the Canal Zone at Panama.

A month after ratifying the Hay-Bunau-Varilla Treaty, the Senate ratified a treaty with Cuba that formalized the provisions of the Platt Amendment that had earlier been incorporated into the Cuban constitution of 1901. The Platt Amendment's conditions prohibited the Cuban government from entering into any international treaty that would compromise Cuban independence or allow foreign powers to use the island for military purposes. The United States also reserved the right to intervene in Cuban affairs in order to defend Cuban independence and to maintain "a government adequate for the protection of life, property, and individual liberty."

Elsewhere in Latin America, a number of Caribbean and Central American nations deeply in debt to various European nations faced the threat of intervention by their creditors. For the United States, the situation was problematic because of potential threats to the security of the proposed Panama Canal and the prospects for American economic hegemony in Latin America. To forestall such threats, Roosevelt asserted in his annual message of December 1904 that when a Latin American nation faced possible intervention by a European power, the Monroe Doctrine justified American involvement. The following January, he used this

Roosevelt Corollary to the Monroe Doctrine as the basis for entering into an agreement with the Dominican Republic easing the growing pressure placed on that nation by European creditors attempting to recover more than $32 million in debt. After Senate Democrats sharply criticized Roosevelt's action, the administration concluded a formal protocol with the Dominican government that was subsequently rejected by the Senate. Not to be deterred, the president used an executive order to achieve the same end. Although it was denounced as illegal, unconstitutional, and tyrannical, it lasted for twenty-eight months before a formal treaty was finally ratified by the Senate. (*Treaty with Santo Domingo [Dominican Republic], p. 183*)

Roosevelt also devoted considerable attention in his 1904 annual message to the importance of the nation's forest reserves. He requested that responsibility for their management be transferred from the Department of the Interior to the Department of Agriculture, where all forestry matters could be handled, a position supported by the secretaries of both departments. Legislation subsequently was enacted that provided for the Forest Service to place revenues raised from the reserves over the next five years in a special fund for forest protection, administration, improvement, and extension.

Because the Spanish-American War had caught the United States with inadequate shipping capabilities to meet the military requirements for invasion of Spanish colonies, the War Department had to buy or charter foreign-flagged ships. To avoid a repetition of the embarrassing unpreparedness in American shipping capability, the Military Cargo Preference Act of 1904 was enacted requiring 100 percent of military cargoes to be transported in U.S. flagged vessels. Passage of the act was a means for promoting the American merchant marine fleet, increasing American shipbuilders, ensuring the availability of American ships in an emergency, and offsetting foreign competition, which at the time, carried a high percentage of the nation's shipping trade.

Passage of the Trademark Act of 1905 allowed an individual to register a trademark and have it legally protected against imitation throughout the United States. Previously, trademarks had been only sporadically protected by state laws. Registration under the act constituted prima facie evidence of ownership.

Authority for federal legislation against injurious insects dates back to the Insect Pest Act of 1905, which prohibited the importation, shipping, or mailing of injurious insects except for scientific purposes. The act was adopted in an effort to bring national uniformity to a growing problem. Although several states had enacted legislation to address specific pest concerns in their respective states, the Insect Pest Act focused on the deliberate movement of pests for scientific purposes.

The results of the 1904 presidential campaign were predictable, given Roosevelt's considerable popular appeal and the ineffective front-porch approach of his opponent, conservative Democrat Alton B. Parker, a New York State appeals judge. During the campaign, one of the most apathetic in American history, the Democrats halfheartedly put forward Parker as a safe alternative to what they described as the president's radicalism and impetuosity. Last-minute charges of alleged Republican campaign fund improprieties were quickly rebutted by Roosevelt as his popularity reached its zenith. A Republican landslide left Roosevelt and his vice presidential running mate, Charles W. Fairbanks, with a popular plurality of more than 2.5 million votes. Roosevelt received the most electoral votes ever obtained by any candidate up to that point in U.S. history—336. Parker and Democratic vice presidential nominee Henry G. Davis won 140 electoral votes. On election night, even before the results were official, Roosevelt announced his intention not to seek reelection in 1908. As a result of the 1904 congressional elections, the Republicans increased their majority hold on the House and retained control of the Senate.

Major Acts and Treaties

Hay-Bunau-Varilla Treaty. Granted to the United States full and permanent sovereignty over a ten-mile-wide zone across the Isthmus of Panama and transferred to it all rights, properties, and concessions of the New Panama Canal Company and the Panama Railroad Company. Provided that the United States would pay the Republic of Panama $10 million and an annual fee of $250,000 starting nine years after the treaty took effect. Concluded November 18, 1903 (33 Stat. 2234–2241). Ratification advised by the Senate February 23, 1904.[1]

Treaty with Cuba. Prohibited Cuba from entering into any treaty with a foreign power that would impair its independence, and from acquiring foreign debt beyond its ability to pay from its own resources. Gave the United States the right to intervene to preserve Cuban independence or to preserve law and order. Provided that Cuba would "sell or lease to the United States lands necessary for coaling or naval stations." Concluded May 22, 1903 (33 Stat. 2248–2253). Ratification advised by the Senate March 22, 1904.[2]

Temporary Government for the Canal Zone at Panama. Authorized the president "to take possession of and occupy on behalf of the United States" the Panama Canal Zone. Vested powers of the temporary government of the zone in such person or persons as the president should direct. Authorized a payment of $10 million to the Republic of Panama as agreed to in the Hay-Bunau-Varilla Treaty. Approved April 28, 1904 (33 Stat. 429).

Military Cargo Preference Act (Military Transportation Act of 1904). Requiring that only "vessels of the United States, or belonging to the United States" be used to transport supplies to be used by the Army and Navy. Allowed for the president to contract with foreign flag carriers only when the charges of U.S. vessels were "excessive or unreasonable." Approved April 28, 1904 (33 Stat. 518–519).

Transfer Act of 1905. Transferred control of the nation's forest reserves from the Department of the Interior to the Department of Agriculture. Allowed the Forest Service to place all funds received for five years from timber cutting, grazing fees, or other uses of the reserves in a special Treasury fund administered by the secretary of agriculture. Authorized the secretary to use these funds "for the protection, administration, improvement, and extension of Federal forest reserves." Approved February 1, 1905 (33 Stat. 628).

Trademark Act of 1905. Authorized the registration of trademarks used in commerce with foreign nations, among the several states, and with Indian tribes. Required those desiring trademark protection to file an application in the U.S. Patent Office, pay a $10 registration fee, and prepare a written declaration verifying the right to ownership. Allowed citizens of other countries to file trademark applications if the trademark was already registered in a "foreign country which by treaty, convention, or law, affords similar privileges to citizens of the United States." Prohibited registration of any trademark that "consists of or comprises immoral or scandalous matter" or "consists of or comprises the flag or coat of arms or other insignia of the United States" of any state, a municipality, or a foreign nation. Approved February 20, 1905 (33 Stat. 724–731).

Insect Pest Act. Prohibited importation, interstate transportation, or mailing of any "insect in a live state which is notoriously injurious to cultivated crops, including vegetables, field crops, bush fruits, orchard trees, forest trees, or shade trees; or the eggs, pupae, or larvae of any" injurious insect. Excluded from the prohibition insects used for scientific purposes under rules and regulations prepared by the secretary of agriculture. Approved March 3, 1905 (33 Stat. 1269–1270).

Notes

1. *Journal of the Executive Proceedings of the Senate* (Washington, D.C.: U.S. Government Printing Office, 1931), 35:224–227.

2. *Journal of Executive Proceedings of the Senate,* 35: 260.

Fifty-ninth Congress
March 4, 1905, to March 3, 1907

First session—December 4, 1905, to June 30, 1906
Second session—December 3, 1906, to March 3, 1907
Special session of the Senate—March 4, 1905, to
    March 18, 1905
(Second administration of Theodore Roosevelt,
    1905–1909)

Historical Background

As a president elected in his own right, and armed with an overwhelming mandate, Theodore Roosevelt aggressively pursued more progressive policies following his 1905 inauguration. At President Roosevelt's urging, the first Employers' Liability Law was enacted, restricting use of common law defenses in compensation suits brought against railroads engaged in interstate and foreign commerce by employees injured while on the job. Eighteen months later, the U.S. Supreme Court declared the statute unconstitutional because it covered employees of interstate railroads who were injured in intrastate commerce. This defeat was later remedied with the passage of a second Employers' Liability Act by the Sixtieth Congress. Responding to widespread public demands for new and stricter legislation to curb railroad malpractices, and repeated requests by President Roosevelt, Congress broadened and strengthened the authority of the Interstate Commerce Commission (ICC). The Hepburn Act, sponsored by Rep. William P. Hepburn of Iowa, granted the ICC broad enforcement powers, including authority to set maximum railroad rates and to examine the financial reports of railroads. Railroads were required to adopt standardized bookkeeping procedures and restrict distribution of free passes.

A variety of concerns associated with the rapidly growing alien population in the United States prompted three separate pieces of immigration reform legislation. With the establishment of the Bureau of Immigration and Naturalization in June 1906, naturalization procedures were centralized and regularized. The Naturalization Act of 1906 implemented many of the recommendations of a presidential commission on naturalization which found that U.S. naturalization courts lacked uniformity, and there was little or no guidance on how courts were to apply or administer naturalization laws or administer the naturalization oath. The commission recommended classifying and summarizing naturalization laws into a code (re-codification), the creation of a federal agency to oversee naturalization procedures, and standard forms for all U.S. naturalizations. The act established the basic procedure for naturalization during the period 1906–1952.

Enactment of the Immigration Act of February 1907 occurred amid rising concerns over immigration that prompted President Theodore Roosevelt to call upon Congress to increase protection from unwanted immigration, especially in the nation's largest cities, and to codify earlier legislation. The act broadened the types of aliens denied admission into the United States, limited the number of contract laborers entering the country, and doubled the head tax on immigrant passengers. It also authorized the president to enter into international agreements to regulate immigration and created a Joint Commission on Immigration to investigate the immigration problem and to provide detailed reports to future Congresses regarding the need for refining immigration laws.

A third measure, approved in March 1907, established the basis for issuance of U.S. passports to non-Americans, specific requirements for the act of expatriation, and citizenship guidelines for marriages involving American citizens and foreign nationals. As U.S. businessmen, following the Spanish-American War, increasingly traveled abroad to investigate investment opportunities, pressure began to grow for higher quality consular officers leading to the first modern reform of the consular service.

The United States Court for China was created to serve the large number of Americans living and working in China. The court, "likely the strangest federal tribunal ever constituted by Congress,"[1] was given jurisdiction over matters as diverse as admiralty, contracts, probate, marriage and divorce, and activities of U.S. corporations in China. It was abolished in 1943.

Harvey W. Wiley, chief of the Bureau of Chemistry in the Department of Agriculture, was instrumental in organizing various pressure groups outraged over unsafe and falsely labeled foods, drugs, and medicine. Novelist Upton Sinclair's depiction in *The Jungle* (1906) of unsanitary conditions in the meat-packing industry further aroused the indignation of the American public. Amidst these developments, both a meat inspection bill and a food and drug bill were signed into law. The Meat Inspection Act required federal inspection of all meat involved in interstate or foreign commerce. The Pure Food and Drug Act prohibited misbranding and adulteration of food and medicines involved in such commerce.

Six years of lobbying by a broad range of organizations, including the Smithsonian Institution, made possible the first law to provide comprehensive protection for endangered archaeological and scientific sites on federal lands. The Antiquities Act was signed in June 1906.

Following the 1906 midterm elections, in which the Republicans retained a dominant position in both houses of Congress, campaign finance restrictions were adopted and the compensation given certain elected federal officials was significantly increased. During the 1904 presidential campaign, Democratic standard-bearer Alton B. Parker had claimed that several large corporations were supplying money for Theodore Roosevelt's reelection bid to obtain influence with the administration. Although the allegations aroused relatively little public interest at the time, subsequent investigations by public interest groups convinced Congress of the need to prohibit corporate campaign contributions. A lengthy debate preceded

adoption of a 50 percent increase in the annual compensation of the vice president, cabinet officers, senators, representatives, and the Speaker of the House. It marked the first time the salaries of these federal officials had been increased in more than three decades. To avoid the public indignation that forced the repeal of the Salary Grab Act of 1873, this compensation act did not become effective until after the next Congress had convened. *(Salary Grab Act, p. 127)*

With a continuing increase of the white population in both the Oklahoma Territory and the Indian Territory (governed by five separate Indian nations), pressure grew for statehood. For economic as well as political reasons, whites in the Indian Territory, most of whom were squatters, wanted joint statehood, while the Indian nations sought separate states. Congress resolved the issue in June 1906 by approving an enabling act for the admission of the twin territories as one state. Oklahoma was officially proclaimed a state seventeen months later. The act also included a statehood enabling provision for the Arizona and New Mexico Territories. Admission of Arizona and New Mexico was to be contingent upon approval by the inhabitants of both territories. In November 1906, New Mexicans accepted joint statehood, but Arizonans, fearful that the New Mexicans, who outnumbered them, would control the politics of the proposed state and impose higher taxes, rejected joint statehood.

During the waning hours of the Fifty-ninth Congress, the Senate approved a treaty with the Dominican Republic for an American customs receivership on the island. This action formalized an agreement President Roosevelt had effected through an executive order more than two years earlier.

Major Acts and Treaties

Consular Reorganization Act. Classified the consuls-general of the consular system of the United States into seven classes with annual salaries ranging from $3,000 to $8,000. Created a consular inspection corps of five officers with responsibility for inspecting each consular office at least every other year. Required that all consular clerks earning more than $1,000 be U.S. citizens. Prohibited consular officers receiving a salary of more than $1,000 a year from engaging in business activities or practicing law for compensation. Approved April 5, 1906 (34 Stat. 99–102).

American Antiquities Act of 1906. Authorized the president to designate by public proclamation objects or areas of historical or scientific interest as national monuments. Provided penalties for unauthorized excavation or destruction of a historic or prehistoric ruin. Limited the excavation of ruins to reputable scientific or educational institutions that placed any resulting collections in a public museum. Approved June 8, 1906 (34 Stat. 225).

Employers' Liability Act of 1906. Restricted the use of common law defenses in personal injury suits brought against railroads engaged in interstate and foreign commerce by employees injured on the job. Prohibited the use of insurance or other benefits as a defense against damage suits. Approved June 11, 1906 (34 Stat. 232–233). Certain provisions of this act were subsequently held unconstitutional in *Employers' Liability Cases,* 207 U.S. 463 (1908). *(Employers' Liability Act of 1908, p. 186)*

Arizona, New Mexico, and Oklahoma Enabling Act. Authorized the inhabitants of Oklahoma and the Indian Territory to draft a constitution and a state government, and the inhabitants of the Territories of Arizona and New Mexico to draft a constitution and state government. Declared that once the constitution had been submitted to the people of the proposed state of Oklahoma for their ratification, approved by a majority of the legal votes cast, and certified by the "governor of Oklahoma Territory and the judge senior in service of the United States court of appeals for the Indian Territory," the president would issue a proclamation announcing the results of the election and the "proposed State of Oklahoma shall be deemed admitted by Congress into the Union." Approved June 16, 1906 (34 Stat. 267–278).

Provided for a general election on November 6, 1906, in the Territories of Arizona and New Mexico

to determine if Arizona and New Mexico should "be united to form one State [Arizona]." If the inhabitants of both territories favored joint statehood, they were authorized to draft a constitution and form a state government. If the inhabitants of either territory voted against joint statehood, the other provisions of the act relating to joint statehood became null and void (34 Stat. 278–285). Arizona rejected the proposal for joint statehood by a vote of 16,265 to 3,141, while New Mexico accepted it 26,195 to 14,735.

Hepburn (Railway Rate Regulation) Act. Increased the membership of the Interstate Commerce Commission (ICC) from five to seven. Empowered the ICC to fix railroad rates, required that detailed annual reports be filed by all common carriers, and prescribed uniform accounting systems for railroad corporations. Expanded ICC jurisdiction to include express and sleeping-car companies, spurs, tracks, terminal facilities, pipelines (other than those used to transport oil and gas), ferries, and bridges. Curtailed the practice of granting free railroad passes. Prohibited railway corporations from carrying articles produced by themselves or by businesses in which they held an interest, except for timber and other materials necessary for railway operation. Declared that ICC orders were binding unless and until overridden by a court. Approved June 29, 1906 (34 Stat. 584–595).

Naturalization Act of 1906. Combined the immigration and naturalization functions of the federal government, and established the Bureau of Immigration and Naturalization in the Commerce Department in charge of "all matters concerning the naturalization of aliens." Established fundamental procedural safeguards regarding naturalization, such as fixed fees and uniform naturalization forms. Required an alien who wished to be naturalized speak English and that his or her legal immigration be verified. Required new citizens to swear "to defend the Constitution and laws of the United States of America against all enemies, foreign and domestic; and bear true faith and allegiance to the same." Approved June 29, 1906 (34 Stat. 596–607).

Meat Inspection Act. Authorized the secretary of agriculture to enforce sanitary regulations in packing establishments and to assume responsibility for federal inspection of companies slaughtering or preparing meats to be shipped across state lines. Approved June 30, 1906 (34 Stat. 674–679).

Pure Food and Drug Act. Prohibited the sale of adulterated and misbranded foods or drugs. Required that all foods and drugs be accurately labeled. Provided punishments for persons engaged in the manufacture, sale, or transportation of adulterated or mislabeled or poisonous or deleterious foods, drugs, medicines, and liquors, applicable to any of these items involved in interstate or foreign commerce. Approved June 30, 1906 (34 Stat. 768–772).

United States Court for China. Created a special court for the "District of China," the United States Court for China, which had extraterritorial jurisdiction over all American citizens within the district. Granted the court civil and criminal jurisdiction over American citizens within the District of China, which in turn was coincident with the Empire of China. Provided for appeals from the court to be taken to the Ninth Judicial Circuit in San Francisco, with further appeals to the United States Supreme Court, a judge appointed by the president for ten years, and a district attorney, marshal, and clerk whose terms were at the pleasure of the president. Approved June 30, 1906 (34 Stat. 814). Abolished when the United States relinquished all extraterritorial rights in China by a treaty of January 11, 1943 (57 Stat. 767).

Tillman Act. Prohibited nationally chartered banks and corporations from making monetary contribution to any political campaign, and prohibited other corporations from making political contributions to campaigns involving candidates for a federal office. Approved January 26, 1907 (34 Stat. 864–865).

Immigration Act of 1907. Authorized the president to enter into international agreements to regulate immigration. Created the U.S. immigration

commission (better known as the Dillingham Commission) to investigate immigration problems and their impact on the nation, further narrowed Asian immigration, limited Muslim immigration, broadened the excludable classes of immigrants, and expanded the definition of undesirable women immigrants. Required aliens to declare intention of permanent or temporary stay in the United States and officially classified arriving aliens as immigrants and nonimmigrants. Required ships to allow minimum amounts of deck space for each passenger and to provide manifests of their departing aliens. Contained the first statutory provision authorizing deportation based on criminal conduct within the United States. Approved February 20, 1907 (34 Stat. 898–911).

Treaty with Santo Domingo (Dominican Republic). Provided for the collection of customs by U.S. agents with the purpose of satisfying foreign and domestic creditors of the Dominican Republic. Formalized an agreement already in operation since 1905 under a presidential executive order. Concluded February 8, 1907 (35 Stat. 1880–1884). Ratification advised by the Senate February 25, 1907.[2]

Pay Increase for the Vice President, the Cabinet, and Members of Congress. Increased the compensation of the Speaker of the House of Representatives, vice president, and members of the cabinet to $12,000 a year. Increased the compensation of senators, representatives, delegates from territories, and the resident commissioner of Puerto Rico from $5,000 to $7,500 a year. Designated March 4, 1907, as the effective date of the act. Approved February 26, 1907 (34 Stat. 993–994, Sec. 4).

Citizenship and Expatriation Act. Established the basis upon which U.S. passports could be issued to persons who were not citizens of the United States. Detailed various methods of expatriation and forbade American citizens from expatriating while the country was at war. Provided that a foreign-born child shall be deemed a U.S. citizen by virtue of the naturalization of the parents. Stipulated that American women marrying aliens lost their American citizenship, and specified the means by which citizenship might be regained if an alien husband died or the marriage was terminated. Provided for citizenship to be granted to foreigners married to American citizens. Approved March 2, 1907 (34 Stat. 1228–1229).

Notes

1. Teemu Ruskola, "Colonialism without Colonies: On the Extraterritorial Jurisprudence of the U.S. Court for China," *Law & Contemporary Problems,* v. 71, Summer 2008, 219.

2. *Journal of the Executive Proceedings of the Senate* (Washington, D.C.: U.S. Government Printing Office, 1931), 37:205–206.

Sixtieth Congress
March 4, 1907, to March 3, 1909

First session—December 2, 1907, to May 30, 1908
Second session—December 7, 1908, to March 3, 1909
(Second administration of Theodore Roosevelt,
    1905–1909)

Historical Background

During the autumn of 1907, following a decade of prosperity in America, a brief but severe bankers panic occurred that threatened to bring about a complete collapse of the U.S. monetary system. The panic was prompted by an uncontrolled amount of speculative activity by commercial banks and trust companies. Catastrophe was averted through the joint efforts of Secretary of the Treasury George B. Cortelyou and investment banker J. P. Morgan. Cortelyou authorized large government deposits to be placed in several banks, while Morgan assembled a banking group that raised nearly $40 million in borrowed funds to help banks meet depositors' demands for withdrawals. In May 1908, Congress passed the Aldrich-Vreeland Act, sponsored by Sen. Nelson W. Aldrich of Rhode Island and Rep. Edward B. Vreeland of New York, providing for the issuance of emergency currency in the event of another panic. The act also established a National Monetary Commission to prepare a comprehensive plan for desirable and necessary banking reforms. The commission's proposals proved instrumental in development of the Federal Reserve Bank System Act approved five years later. *(Federal Reserve Act [Owen-Glass Act], p. 198)*

Early in January 1908, the U.S. Supreme Court declared the Employers' Liability Act of 1906 unconstitutional in the *Employers' Liability Cases* on the grounds that it covered instead employees not engaged in interstate commerce. The Court held that Congress

had exceeded its powers under the Commerce Clause in the Constitution. Three months later, Congress responded with a second version of the act. The Employers' Liability Act of 1908 remedied the defect of the first statute by limiting coverage to employees injured in interstate commerce. The new act was subsequently sustained by the Court in the *Second Employers' Liability Cases* (223 U.S. 1 [1912]). Amidst growing agitation by child labor reformers, a child labor law applicable to the District of Columbia was approved in May 1908. It was hoped that the District of Columbia Child Labor Law could serve as a model for state legislators to follow.

During the waning days of the Sixtieth Congress, notice was served to other nations that the United States was determined to rid itself of the evils of opium addiction by banning importation of the drug except for strictly medical purposes. This enactment, the first wholly antinarcotic legislation, was promoted by the State Department as a face-saving gesture aimed at proving U.S. credibility in calling the Shanghai Opium Conference, an attempt to monitor international traffic in opium.

Widespread demand by lawyers, as well as in the nation as a whole, provided an impetus for revision and codification of the U.S. Criminal Code in 1909. During the years since the Code's last revision in 1878, "more laws of a permanent nature had been passed" than in the preceding century. These laws, it was reported by the Special Joint Committee on the Revision of Laws, appointed by Congress to examine the problem, "were scattered throughout nearly twenty bulky volumes of the Statutes at Large." They were "commingled with a voluminous mass of temporary enactments, and [were] frequently found embodied in appropriation bills, the title and context of which would give no indication of their purport."[1]

Theodore Roosevelt, in one of his final actions as president, signed the criminal code provision into law.

The Enlarged Homestead Act of 1909 was passed to open up the arid lands of the West to those settlers willing to homestead them. It increased the acreage of homestead entries to 320 acres in seven western states and two territories. The act specified that one-fourth of the homestead be cultivated, and that irrigated, timber, and mineral lands were excepted. Favorable weather conditions temporarily enabled those taking advantage of the Enlarged Homestead Act to be successful, but in time spotty rainfall and a disregard for the scientific principles underlying dry farming tempered the early success of the act.

For several years prior to the Sixtieth Congress, people familiar with the nation's copyright laws stressed the need for a complete revision of copyright statutes. President Theodore Roosevelt used his December 1908 State of the Union message to join those calling for copyright reform. Three months after Roosevelt's appeal, Congress passed the Copyright Act of 1909, which would remain the framework of copyright protection until the Copyright Act of 1976. One of the principal goals of the act was to simplify and streamline the formalities required to obtain copyright protection.

Although his popularity remained unimpaired and his ambition undiminished, Roosevelt bowed to the two-term tradition and declined to run for president in 1908. Instead, he delivered the Republican nomination to Secretary of War William Howard Taft, his designated successor. Taft, as the Republican standard-bearer, captured a million more popular votes than William Jennings Bryan, who was making his third, and last, run for the presidency (7,676,258 to 6,406,801), and nearly double the Democratic opponent's electoral count (321 to 162). James S. Sherman was elected vice president by identical votes. Bryan and his running mate, John W. Kern, however, captured all 7 electoral votes of Oklahoma, which had been admitted as the forty-sixth state.

Major Acts

Oklahoma Admitted to the Union. President Theodore Roosevelt issued a proclamation on November 16, 1907, stating that the Territory of Oklahoma and the Indian Territory had complied with the act of Congress approved on June 16, 1906, and declared that the "state of Oklahoma is deemed admitted by Congress into the Union." Approved November 16, 1907 (35 Stat. 2160–2161).

Employers' Liability Act of 1908. Imposed liability on railroads engaged in interstate and foreign commerce for injuries negligently caused to any employee "while employed by such carrier in such commerce." Extended the statute of limitation on actions from one to two years. Approved April 22, 1908 (P.L. 100; 35 Stat. 65–66). *(Employers' Liability Act of 1906, p. 182)*

District of Columbia Child Labor Law. Provided for the regulation of child labor in the District of Columbia. Prohibited children under the age of fourteen from being employed or permitted to work in a District of Columbia "factory, workshop, mercantile establishment, store, business office, telegraph or telephone office, restaurant, hotel, apartment house, club, theater, bowling alley, laundry, boot-black stand, or in the distribution or transmission of merchandise or messages." Prohibited such children from being "employed in any work for wages or other compensation during school hours." Prohibited children under age sixteen from being permitted to work in such establishments unless the person for whom they worked kept records that were available to inspectors authorized by the act. Approved May 28, 1908 (P.L. 149; 35 Stat. 420–423).

Aldrich-Vreeland Emergency Currency Act. Provided that national banks with at least $5 million in capital and surplus could form "national currency associations" and in times of emergency could issue circulating notes based on commercial paper and state, county, and municipal bonds. Required national banks to pay interest on government deposits at a rate to be determined by the secretary of the Treasury. Established a National Monetary Commission consisting of nine senators and nine representatives to study the banking and currency systems of the United States and foreign countries. Established June 30, 1914, as termination date of the act. Approved May 30, 1908 (P.L. 169; 35 Stat. 546–553).

Opium Exclusion Act of 1909. Banned the importation of opium into the United States, except for medical purposes. Provided that individuals found in violation of the act could be subject to a fine not in excess of $5,000 and not more than two years in prison. Approved February 9, 1909 (P.L. 221; 35 Stat. 614).

Enlarged Homestead Act. Provided for enlarged homesteads of 320 acres on "nonmineral, nonirrigable, unreserved . . . public lands, which did not contain merchantable timber" in the states of Colorado, Montana, Nevada, Oregon, Utah, and Wyoming, and the territories of Arizona and New Mexico. Required five years of residence on the land and the continuous cultivation of crops other than native grasses. Approved February 19, 1909 (P.L. 245; 35 Stat. 639–640).

Copyright Act of 1909. Established that for an individual to own a copyright on a work, the individual must be the author of the work. Allowed originally published works to be copyrighted for 28 years and renewed for an additional 28 years. Accorded a copyright owner exclusive rights to print or otherwise copy, to make adaptations or versions, to sell, and to publicly perform their musical compositions. If an author allowed a musical composition to be recorded, other performers could record the work and pay a statutory royalty. Gave statutory recognition for the first time to employers as potential authors of their employees' work if the work was a "work made for hire." Required that all published works carry the "©" symbol or the word "Copyright," the year of first publication, and name of the author in order to receive copyright. Superseded by the Copyright Act of 1976. Approved March 4, 1909 (P.L. 349; 35 Stat. 1075–1088).

Criminal Code Revision of 1909. Codified all federal criminal and penal laws of the United States. Brought together all statutes and parts of statutes relating to the same subject. Eliminated redundant and obsolete enactments. Made appropriate alterations to reconcile contradictions, omissions, and imperfections in the original text. Embodied in the "revision such changes in substance of existing law . . . as were necessary and advisable." Approved March 4, 1909 (P.L. 350; 35 Stat. 1088–1159).

Note

1. U.S. Congress, Joint Committee on the Revision of Laws, *Revision and Codification of Laws, Etc.*, 60th Cong., 1st sess. (Washington, D.C.: Government Printing Office, 1908, S. Rept. 10, Part 1, 3.

Sixty-first Congress
March 4, 1909, to March 3, 1911

First session—March 15, 1909, to August 5, 1909
Second session—December 6, 1909, to June 25, 1910
Third session—December 5, 1910, to March 3, 1911
Special session of the Senate—March 4, 1909, to March
    6, 1909
(Administration of William Howard Taft, 1909–1913)

Historical Background

Within hours of his inauguration as the twenty-seventh U.S. president, William Howard Taft acted on one of his principal campaign themes and called Congress into special session (considered the first session) to make a "sizable reduction" in tariffs. The House quickly approved a tariff bill containing moderate rate reductions. When the debate shifted to the Senate, however, 847 amendments were appended (almost all calling for higher tariffs) before agreement was finally reached. Although the Payne-Aldrich Tariff as ultimately enacted did not include the drastic across-the-board reductions President Taft sought, it did impose a corporate income tax, which he had urged. It also granted discretionary authority to the president to add an additional 25 percent duty on all goods imported from nations "unduly" discriminating against U.S. exports. The legislation was sponsored by Rep. Sereno E. Payne of New York and Sen. Nelson W. Aldrich of Rhode Island.

As the Senate debated the tariff bill, a second Taft proposal, a constitutional amendment empowering Congress "to lay and collect taxes on incomes," was approved and proposed to the states for ratification. With the Sixteenth Amendment, Congress sought to overcome the constitutional limitation to levy direct taxes found in Article I. At the Constitutional Convention of 1787, the framers felt direct taxation should be undertaken only in extreme emergencies. The federal budget should instead be derived from duties, imports, and excise taxes, which under the Constitution had to be uniform throughout the country. Not until the Civil War did Congress approve the first income tax as a necessary emergency measure. Congress allowed that modest measure to expire in 1872. The income tax of 1894, declared unconstitutional a year later by the U.S. Supreme Court in *Pollock v. Framers Loan and Trust Company,* resulted from social pressures to levy some form of taxation on the wealthy generated by two prolonged postwar depressions.

Progressives repeatedly advocated reenactment of the income tax, but opponents successfully blocked such efforts until early 1909. When it appeared likely that a 3 percent tax on all incomes over $5,000 would be approved, Senate Majority Leader Nelson W. Aldrich of Rhode Island and other members of the Senate Finance Committee proposed a constitutional amendment granting Congress the power to levy an income tax. An amendment, they were confident, would delay enactment of an income tax because three-fourths of the states likely would be unwilling to ratify it. The maneuver proved unsuccessful, however, and the proposed constitutional amendment passed both houses of Congress by overwhelming majorities and was ratified three and a half years later.

The federal government's first attempt to regulate pesticide chemicals comprehensively occurred in 1910 with the passage of the Insecticide Act. It was passed in response to concerns expressed by chemical manufacturers, the Department of Agriculture (USDA), and farm groups about the sale of fraudulent or substandard pesticide products, which was common at the time. The intent was not to regulate the use of pesticides, but to ensure the effectiveness of such products and protect purchasers from deceptive labeling.

Following a decade in which the number of coal mine fatalities exceeded 2,000 annually, in 1910 the Bureau of Mines was established in the Department of the Interior. The bureau was to be a scientific, not a regulatory body, and it was intended to discover better tools and methods, and disseminate this knowledge about ways to improve mine safety. Technologies developed by the bureau helped to minimize mine accidents, primarily from methane and coal dust explosions. Many of these technologies were subsequently refined and marketed by the mining equipment industry.

After nearly four decades of debate, the postal savings system was created. Postmaster General John A. J. Creswell first recommended a postal savings bank for the United States in 1871. But it wasn't until the Panic of 1907, which shook the public's trust in private banks, that the concept really gathered widespread support. The Postal Savings Act authorized establishment of savings depositories in designated post offices around the country. The act was designed to entice hoarders to get their money out of hiding, to attract immigrants accustomed to saving at post offices in their native countries, to provide safe depositories for people who had lost confidence in banks, to furnish more convenient depositories for working people, to encourage thrift among the working class, and to pose no competition for banks. The postal savings system was officially ended on July 1, 1967.

With the enactment of the Mann-Elkins Act of 1910, sponsored by Rep. James R. Mann of Illinois and Sen. Stephen B. Elkins of West Virginia, the nation's transportation and communication systems for the first time came under the regulatory authority of the Interstate Commerce Commission (ICC). The act also strengthened the ICC's rate-setting powers.

President Taft signed legislation both he and his predecessor had recommended—the Publicity Act. It required that candidates for the U.S. House of Representatives and their campaign committees file itemized statements of all contributions and expenditures exceeding $10.

Progressive reformers achieved another victory with passage of the Mann Act (White Slave Traffic Act), making it a federal crime to transport women across a state line "for immoral purposes." For some time, sensationalized books, articles, and films had warned middle-class Americans that their daughters faced the threat of being kidnapped and forced into a life of prostitution in the nation's cities. Equally troublesome was the importation of foreign women to work in American brothels. Amidst considerable fanfare, the red-light districts of Chicago, New Orleans, and other cities were shut down or forced to operate more discreetly.

During the first decade of the twentieth century, rapid growth in conservation sentiment led to the approval of vast reservations of national forests in the West and increased pressure for legislation to protect the watersheds of major rivers in the East and South. Coupled with this effort was a recognition of the need to create and preserve national forests in the older states before they were logged over by the lumber industry. The Weeks Forest Purchase Act of 1911 authorized the Forest Service to acquire, manage, protect, and conserve the watersheds of navigable rivers east of the Mississippi River. It also provided matching funds to any state that established an acceptable program for protecting the forested watersheds. The bill was sponsored by Rep. John W. Weeks of Massachusetts.

Congress' first attempt at protecting military information was the Defense Secrets Act of 1911, which specifically criminalized the disclosure of government secrets. It was based in part on the British Official Secrets Act. Prior to the act, there were only two federal laws that generally dealt with espionage. One dealt with treason, and one with unlawful entry into military bases. The 1911 law was repealed in the Espionage Act of 1917, which still is in force.

The statehood process for the last remaining territories in the continental United States moved forward when an enabling act that authorized the qualified electors of Arizona and New Mexico to frame a state government and constitution became law in June 1910. The voters of the two territories acted in December 1910 and January 1911, respectively. It would be a year, however, before either territory was admitted to the Union.

Fifteen years of Republican dominance of the House of Representatives ended in 1910, when Democrats gained control for the first time since the Fifty-third Congress (1893–1895). Although the GOP retained a majority in the Senate, the presence of several insurgent Republicans in the upper chamber, combined with the new Democratic majority in the House, guaranteed that President Taft would face a more hostile Congress for the balance of his term.

Major Acts

Sixteenth Amendment. Authorized the imposition of "taxes on income, from whatever source derived, without apportionment among the several States, and without regard to census or enumeration." Approved July 12, 1909 (36 Stat. 184). Ratified by the requisite number of states February 25, 1913.[1]

Payne-Aldrich Tariff Act. Lowered duties to a general level of 38 percent while making sizable cuts in the duties on hides, iron ore, coal, oil, cotton, and footwear. Granted the president discretionary authority to add a 25 percent duty on all goods imported from nations "unduly" discriminating against U.S. exports, and established a Tariff Board to advise the president on such matters. Established a United States Court of Customs Appeals, and imposed a tax on interstate corporations. Approved August 5, 1909 (P.L. 5; 36 Stat. 11–118).

Insecticide Act of 1910. Established standards for the manufacture of Paris green, lead arsenate, insecticides, and fungicides, and provided for inspections, seizure of adulterated or misbranded products, and prosecution of violators. Required manufacturers to guarantee that these products met a certain percentage of concentration and were pure in nature prior to sale. Contained criminal sanctions and provisions for seizure of misbranded or adulterated items, but neither a registration requirement nor a safety oriented labeling requirement. Approved April 26, 1910 (P.L. 152; 36 Stat. 331–335).

United States Bureau of Mines Created. Established in the Department of the Interior a bureau of mining, metallurgy, and mineral technology, to be designated the United States Bureau of Mines. Charged the bureau with the responsibility of collecting data about mining and minerals and promoting the health and safety of mine workers. The bureau was abolished in 1995 and its functions were transferred to other agencies, primarily the U.S. Geological Survey. Approved May 16, 1910 (P.L. 179; 36 Stat. 369–370).

Mann-Elkins Act. Placed telegraph, telephone, cable, and wireless radio companies, as well as railroads, under the jurisdiction of the Interstate Commerce Commission (ICC). Empowered the ICC to suspend rate increases. Created a federal commerce court to enforce ICC orders, "to enjoin, set aside, annul, or suspend in whole or part any order" of the commission, to require an official to carry out their mandatory duty as it related to interstate commerce, and to bring suits against common carriers for passenger or freight fare discrimination. Authorized a special commission to investigate the need for a physical evaluation of railroads. Approved June 18, 1910 (P.L. 218; 36 Stat. 539–557).

Arizona and New Mexico Enabling Act. Authorized the qualified electors of Arizona and New Mexico to draft a constitution and framework for state government. Declared that once the constitution had been completed and submitted to the "qualified voters" of Arizona and New Mexico, a "certified copy of the same shall be submitted to the President and to Congress for approval." Stipulated that once the constitution was approved by Congress and the president, the governor should be notified of that action and within thirty days issue a "proclamation for the election of state and county officials, the members of the state legislature and Representatives in Congress, and all officers provided for in said constitution." Required the president to issue a proclamation announcing the results of the elections and the proposed state "shall be deemed admitted into the Union." Approved June 20, 1910 (P.L. 219; 36 Stat. 557–579).

Postal Savings Act. Created a board of trustees, consisting of the postmaster general, the secretary of the Treasury, and the attorney general, to be responsible for the control, supervision, and administration of specific post offices they were authorized to designate as postal savings depositories. Restricted deposits to a minimum of $1.00 and no more than $500, excluding interest. Provided for interest at 2 percent per annum to be paid on deposits. Required that 5 percent of the postal savings funds be deposited in the Treasury of the United States as a reserve, and the remainder deposited in national and state banks if secured by public obligations and if at least 2¼ percent interest is being paid. Approved June 25, 1910 (P.L. 268; 36 Stat. 814–819).

Publicity Act. Required that treasurers of political committees established in behalf of candidates for the U.S. House of Representatives to file reports with the clerk of the House, including an itemized statement of all receipts and expenditures in excess of $10 within thirty days of the election. Approved June 25, 1910 (P.L. 274; 36 Stat. 822–824).

Mann Act (White Slave Traffic Act). Prohibited transportation of women and girls across state lines for "immoral purposes." Approved June 25, 1910 (P.L. 277; 36 Stat. 825–827). The legislation was sponsored by Rep. James R. Mann of Illinois.

Weeks Forest Purchase Act. Authorized the U.S. Forest Service to acquire, manage, and protect the watersheds of navigable interstate rivers. Provided that each purchase of forest lands be approved by the legislature of the state in which the lands lie. Required that a National Forest Reservation Commission, composed of the secretaries of agriculture, interior, and war, as well as two members from each house of Congress, review such purchases. Provided that 5 percent of the proceeds derived from logging in national forests be given to the states where they were located, for schools and roads. Established federal-state cooperation in fire protection. Allowed states to enter into interstate compacts for conserving forests and water supplies. Approved March 1, 1911 (P.L. 435; 36 Stat. 961–963). *(Clarke-McNary Reforestation Act, p. 225)*

Defense Secrets Act of 1911. Imposed penalties on individuals who are not legally entitled to obtain information regarding national defense. Prohibited individuals from taking pictures or making sketches of ships or facilities connected with national defense without proper authority, and imposed penalties for communicating such information to unauthorized individuals or to a foreign government. Approved March 3, 1911 (P.L. 470; 36 Stat. 1084–1085).

Note

1. U.S. Senate, *The Constitution of the United States of America: Analysis and Interpretation,* 108th Cong., 2d sess., 2004, S. Doc. 108–17, 33–34, n. 8.

Sixty-second Congress
March 4, 1911, to March 3, 1913

First session—April 4, 1911, to August 22, 1911
Second session—December 4, 1911, to August 26, 1912
Third session—December 2, 1912, to March 3, 1913
(Administration of William Howard Taft, 1909–1913)

Historical Background

At the Constitutional Convention of 1787, the framers provided for the "Senate of the United States to be composed of two Senators from each State chosen by the Legislature thereof." As early as 1826, calls were made for the popular election of senators, but the movement did not begin to gain widespread support until after the Civil War. Between 1890 and 1912, nearly 150 proposed constitutional amendments were offered in Congress to establish the direct election of senators, and on five occasions the House overwhelmingly passed such initiatives. The Senate, however, continued to block these efforts until 1911, when senators feared that further obstruction could prompt another constitutional convention, one in which a wide range of other reforms or changes might also be proposed as amendments. In May 1912 Congress completed action on what would become the Seventeenth Amendment. Following the amendment's ratification by three-fourths of the states, reformers finally believed that democratization of the Senate would begin. They envisioned an end to a system many contended had filled the upper chamber of Congress with men who represented political machines and corporate interests instead of the people.

As the Panama Canal neared completion in 1912, Congress approved regulations governing the "opening, maintenance, protection, and operation" of the canal. The Panama Canal Act also provided a civil government for the Canal Zone. The most controversial clause in the legislation specifically exempted American coastwise shipping, such as between San Francisco and New York, from paying any tolls. Only after Great Britain exerted considerable diplomatic pressure, and President Woodrow Wilson made a dramatic appearance before Congress in March 1914 to urge repeal of the discriminatory clause, did the House and Senate repeal these provisions. The battle for repeal was particularly bitter in the Senate.

Responding to increased prohibitionist sentiment, Congress passed the Webb-Kenyon Act prohibiting the shipment of liquor into states where its sale or use was illegal. President Taft considered the act, sponsored by Sen. William R. Webb of Tennessee and Sen. William S. Kenyon of Iowa, to be an unconstitutional delegation of federal power to the states worthy of a veto. Both houses of Congress quickly overrode his veto by overwhelming majorities, an action subsequently upheld by the U.S. Supreme Court in *Clark Distilling Company v. Western Railway Company.* Much of the substance of the act was subsequently incorporated into the Twenty-first Amendment, which repealed Prohibition. *(Twenty-first Amendment, p. 239)*

In legislation further enlarging the federal regulatory role, the Interstate Commerce Commission (ICC) was given authority to use the physical valuation of railroads as a basis for rate making. Nearly a decade of opposition by the railroads had preceded approval of the Physical Valuation Act in March 1913. Only after the Supreme Court in 1911 sustained the ICC's refusal to approve an increase in rail rates, because of a failure on the part of the carriers to show the reasonableness of the increases sought, did the railroads finally acquiesce. In recommending passage of the bill, the House

Interstate and Foreign Commerce Committee emphasized that the "complaints of millions of shippers attest to the dissatisfaction of the people."

Legislation approved in June 1912 extended the forty-hour work week from regular salaried federal and District of Columbia employees to persons employed by private businesses engaged in federal contract work. Proponents correctly reasoned that the act would exert a gradual and beneficial influence on employment conditions in the private sector, leading to more widespread adoption of the forty-hour workweek.

Two months later, Congress approved the first protective legislation for whistleblowers after Presidents Theodore Roosevelt and William H. Taft issued executive orders that forbade federal employees from communicating directly with Congress without the permission of their supervisors. The Lloyd-La Follette Act began the process of protecting federal employees from unwarranted or abusive removal. It has acted as the foundation for the myriad of other whistleblower laws applying to federal employees, and served as a model for other whistleblower laws that protect private sector employees. Although the law was a response to adverse employment actions taken against those seeking improvements in wages and working conditions, the act has since functioned to protect federal employees from retaliation when exercising their First Amendment rights to criticize the agency which employs them.

The first law to regulate the importation and interstate shipment of plant products that might carry with them insects and diseases was enacted after the white pine blister rust, chestnut bright fungus, and citrus canker bacterium became established in the United States. The Plant Quarantine Act of 1912 allowed the Department of Agriculture (USDA) to impose plant quarantines and prevent the movement of quarantined plants. At this time, the United States was the only remaining major country without protection against the importation of infested plants.

In August 1911, for the first time in the nation's history, a proposed state constitution was rejected by a president. President Taft's veto of legislation admitting Arizona and New Mexico as states was based on his belief that the recall of judges provision in the proposed Arizona state constitution threatened the independence and integrity of the judiciary. Within a week,

Congress approved a second resolution calling for the repeal of the objectionable provision, and New Mexico and Arizona approved the new resolution and were admitted to the Union by presidential proclamation in January and February 1912, respectively. Legislation establishing a territorial government for Alaska became law in August 1912. The control and management of the territory's principal resources, as well as its judicial power, however, was retained by the federal government. Although the Alaskan Organic Act provided a constitution for the new territory, the Alaskan legislature was expressly forbidden to alter, amend, modify, or repeal any existing measures dealing with customs, internal revenue, disposition of lands, postal measures, or any general laws of the United States. Executive power continued to reside in a presidentially appointed governor.

During the Taft administration, the Department of Labor was separated from the Department of Commerce and Labor and given cabinet status, an effort that was the culmination of a half-century campaign by organized labor. In creating the new department, Congress gave it a clear mandate to represent actively the interests of the American worker. "The purpose of the Department," according to the act, was "to foster, promote, and develop the welfare of the wage earners of the United States, to improve working conditions, and to advance their opportunities for employment." President Taft signed the bill in one of his last official acts as president on March 4, 1913.

Democrats gained control of the White House for the first time in sixteen years with the election of Woodrow Wilson in 1912. During the campaign, incumbent William Howard Taft was challenged for the Republican nomination by both Sen. Robert M. LaFollette of Wisconsin and former president Theodore Roosevelt, who was increasingly opposed to Taft's foreign and domestic policies. After Taft was renominated by the Republican national convention in June, Roosevelt and his followers founded the Progressive (Bull Moose) Party, which nominated Roosevelt as president. The Democratic national convention, meanwhile, also proved contentious with Governor Woodrow Wilson of New Jersey securing the nomination after forty-six ballots.

Wilson won the election with 41.8 percent of the popular vote; Roosevelt came in second with 27.4 percent; and Taft trailed with 23.2 percent. Besides Wilson,

Roosevelt, and Taft, Eugene V. Debs, with running mate Emil Seidel, ran on the Socialist Party ticket. Debs received 6 percent of the popular vote, designating him as among the top vote-winning third-party candidates in U.S. electoral history. Wilson and Democratic vice presidential nominee Thomas R. Marshall received 435 electoral votes, to 88 for Roosevelt and Hiram W. Johnson, and 8 for Taft and James S. Sherman. Taft subsequently would become the chief justice of the United States, the only former president to serve on the Supreme Court.

Even though Wilson was elected as a minority president, the Democrats substantially increased their majority in the House. And when the Sixty-third Congress convened in March 1913, they would control the Senate for the first time since the Fifty-third Congress (1893–1895).

Major Acts

Arizona and New Mexico Admitted to the Union. On August 11, 1911, Congress approved a joint resolution providing for the admission of Arizona and New Mexico "into the Union upon an equal footing with the original States" in accordance with the terms of the enabling act of June 20, 1910. The resolution stipulated that the admission of the two states would take effect upon the issuance of a proclamation by the president.[1] On August 15, 1911, President William Howard Taft vetoed the joint resolution on the grounds that the recall of judges provision in the proposed Arizona state constitution threatened the independence and integrity of the judiciary.[2] The Senate on August 11 and the House on August 12, 1911, passed a second joint resolution calling for the exclusion of judges from the recall provision in the Arizona constitution, and on August 21, 1911, President Taft signed the measure (37 Stat. 39–43). On November 7, 1911, the voters of New Mexico approved the conditions laid out in the second joint resolution. On January 6, 1912, President Taft issued a proclamation stating that the Territory of New Mexico had complied with the enabling act of June 10, 1910, and declared that the state of New Mexico was admitted "into the Union on an equal footing with the original States" (37 Stat. 1723–1724). On December 12,

1911, the voters of Arizona approved the deletion of the recall of judges provision from their constitution, and on February 14, 1912, President Taft issued a proclamation stating that the Territory of Arizona had complied with the enabling act of June 20, 1910, and declared that the state of Arizona was admitted "into the Union on an equal footing with the original States" (37 Stat. 1728–1729).

Seventeenth Amendment. Provided that U.S. senators were to be elected by direct popular vote, and state legislatures could empower the chief executive of the state to fill vacancies pending a new election. Approved May 13, 1912 (37 Stat. 646). Ratified by the requisite number of states May 31, 1913 (38 Stat. 2049–2050).

Eight-Hour Workday for Federal Contractors. Limited the workday of laborers and mechanics employed by a contractor or subcontractor doing work for the federal government, a territory, or the District of Columbia to no more than eight hours. Provided a penalty for violations of the act. Approved June 19, 1912 (P.L. 199; 37 Stat. 137–138).

Plant Quarantine Act of 1912. Authorized the secretary of agriculture to promulgate and enforce quarantines and regulations needed to regulate the entry and interstate movement of known carriers of insect pests and plant diseases. Provided for the secretary to appoint a five member federal horticulture board in the Department of Agriculture made up of representatives of the bureaus of entomology, plant industry, and forest service to administer the act. Approved August 20, 1912 (P.L. 275; 37 Stat. 315–319). Repealed by the Plant Protection Act of 2000 (P.L. 106–224; 114 Stat. 454, Sec. 438).

Alaska Organic Act. Created the Territory of Alaska, and conferred legislative powers for the territory on an elected legislative assembly. Forbade the territorial legislature from altering, amending, modifying, or repealing any federal laws establishing the executive or judicial departments; laws relating to customs, internal revenue, licensing of business, trade, and postal matters; or laws relating to game, fish, fur seals, or fur-bearing animals. Provided that the Constitution and all the laws of the United States "not locally inapplicable" should "have the same force and effect within the territory as elsewhere in the United States." Designated the legal status of Alaska as that of an incorporated territory of the United States. Approved August 24, 1912 (P.L. 334; 37 Stat. 512–518).

Lloyd-LaFollette Act. Guaranteed the right of federal employees to furnish information to Congress, or to a member of Congress, without that right being interfered with or denied. Provided that "[n]o person in the classified civil service of the United States shall be removed or suspended without pay therefrom except for such cause as will promote the efficiency of such service." Granted federal employees certain statutorily defined rights in the event that their employing agencies sought to remove them from the civil service. Established procedures for the discharge of federal employees. Protected the right of federal employees to join unions. Approved August 24, 1912 (P.L. 366; 37 Stat. 555, Sec. 6).

Panama Canal Act. Provided regulations for the opening, maintenance, protection, and operation of the Panama Canal. Provided a civil government of the Canal Zone. Exempted U.S. ships engaged in coastwise trade from paying tolls. Prohibited any railroad from owning or controlling a shipping company with which it competed or might compete, unless the Interstate Commerce Commission determined that such an arrangement was in the public interest and competition was neither reduced nor eliminated. Approved August 24, 1912 (37 Stat. 560–569). The clause exempting U.S. ships from paying tolls was repealed on June 15, 1914 (P.L. 337; 38 Stat. 385–386).

Webb-Kenyon Act. Prohibited interstate shipping of intoxicating liquor into states where its sale was illegal. Empowered the states with the authority to control interstate liquor traffic as they deemed appropriate.

Presidential veto overridden by Congress. Became law without the president's signature March 1, 1913 (P.L. 398; 37 Stat. 699–700).

Physical Valuation Act. Empowered the Interstate Commerce Commission to make thorough investigations of all property owned or used by railroads and to establish cost and physical valuation as a basis for rate making and the fixing of a reasonable profit for the railroads. Approved March 1, 1913 (P.L. 400; 37 Stat. 701–703).

Department of Labor Established. Separated the Department of Commerce and Labor into two cabinet-level departments and established the U.S. Board of Mediation and Conciliation. Specified that the Department of Labor was "to foster, promote, and develop the welfare of the wage earners of the United States, to improve their working conditions and to advance their opportunities for profitable employment." Transferred the Children's Bureau, Bureau of Labor (to be called the Bureau of Labor Statistics), and the Bureau of Immigration and Naturalization (to be divided into two bureaus, the Bureau of Immigration and the Bureau of Naturalization) to the Department of Labor. Approved March 4, 1913 (P.L. 426; 37 Stat. 736–738). *(Bureau of Labor, p. 144; Department of Labor Act, p. 151; Department of Commerce and Labor Established, p. 175)*

Notes

1. *Congressional Record,* 62d Cong., 1st sess., 1911, 47:3829.

2. "Message of the President of the United States: Arizona and New Mexico," 62d Cong., 1st sess., *Congressional Record* (August 15, 1911), 47:3964–3966.

Sixty-third Congress
March 4, 1913, to March 3, 1915

First session—April 7, 1913, to December 1, 1913
Second session—December 1, 1913, to October 24, 1914
Third session—December 7, 1914, to March 3, 1915
Special session of the Senate—March 4, 1913, to March 17, 1913
(First administration of Woodrow Wilson, 1913–1917)

Historical Background

Riding the wave of his New Freedom campaign, Woodrow Wilson was able to gain congressional support for several pieces of legislation during his first twenty months as president. He dramatized his desire for tariff reform by calling a special session of Congress (first session) to deal with the question and then made a personal appearance to convey his views. His gesture of April 8, 1913, marked the first time a president had appeared before Congress since 1800. Despite a massive lobbying effort by conservatives, the Underwood Tariff Act that reached the president's desk for his signature was essentially what he had sought. It reduced duties on 958 articles and imposed the first personal income tax under the Sixteenth Amendment. The legislation was sponsored by Rep. Oscar W. Underwood of Alabama. *(Sixteenth Amendment, p. 190)*

Relying on disciplined Democratic majorities in the House and Senate, Wilson was also successful in winning approval for the Federal Reserve Act, the Federal Trade Commission Act, and the Clayton Antitrust Act. The Federal Reserve Act—also known as the Owen-Glass Act for its sponsors, Sen. Robert L. Owen of Oklahoma and Rep. Carter Glass of Virginia—created a government-controlled, decentralized banking system capable of assuring a more flexible currency and credit system. Passage of the Federal Trade Commission Act, the first significant modification of antitrust law in more than two decades, created a nonpartisan, five-member commission to prevent "persons, partnerships or corporations—from using unfair methods of competition." Its enactment was preceded by considerable debate among Taft Republicans, Roosevelt Progressives, and Wilsonian Democrats as to what should be the appropriate approach to antitrust reform. The Clayton Antitrust Act prohibited a number of specific business practices that would "substantially lessen competition or tend to create a monopoly." Although the intent of the Clayton Antitrust Act was to strengthen the Sherman Antitrust Act, Congress in the end produced a piece of legislation that satisfied few, and businesses found little difficulty in circumventing its restrictions. In signing the act on October 15, 1914, Wilson admitted that it was "so weak you cannot tell it from water."[1] *(Sherman Antitrust Act, p. 155)*

In recognition of the importance of mediation rather than arbitration in the settlement of labor disputes, amendments to the Erdman Act (1898) were adopted in 1913. The Newlands Act replaced the Erdman's voluntary arbitration with a permanent Board of Mediation and Conciliation for railway labor disputes vested with interventionist power. Its jurisdiction covered disputes over the negotiation of agreements and, in an important innovation, those arising out of the interpretation of agreements as well.

Heavy lobbying by the Association of Naval Militias finally prompted passage of the Naval Militia Act, which had failed at least four previous times to garner significant support for enactment. This measure defined the relationship that the state naval militias would have with the federal government, and made it possible for the president to call the naval militia when either national emergency or state of war existed.

The Cotton Futures Act of 1914, the first regulation of a commodities market, imposed a tax on cotton futures contracts that did not meet certain regulatory requirements, and authorized the secretary of agriculture to establish standards to be known as the "Official cotton standards of the United States." The intent of the act was to minimize speculative manipulation of the cotton market. Two years later, the act was rendered unconstitutional by a federal district court because it originated in the Senate. As a revenue act, it should have been drafted in the House. It was replaced by the Cotton Futures Act of 1916.

World War I began in Europe during the summer of 1914. Although the United States did not immediately enter the war, due in part to isolationist policies at the time, the War Risk Insurance Act was passed to insure American ships and their cargoes. It provided government insurance to American ships running the German submarine gauntlet to carry war supplies to Europe, and served as a supplement to commercial marine insurance.

Passage of the Smith-Lever Act of 1914, sponsored by Sen. Hoke Smith of Georgia and Rep. Asbury F. Lever of South Carolina, formalized agricultural extension work as a joint undertaking of the Department of Agriculture and the nation's land-grant colleges. The War Revenue Act of 1914 offset the tremendous decline in import duties brought on by the onset of World War I.

On June 28, 1914, the heir to the Austro-Hungarian throne and his wife were assassinated by Serbian nationalists in Sarajevo, the capital of Austria-controlled Bosnia. The murder led to an escalating series of threats and ultimatums between Austria and her German ally, and Serbia and its patron, Russia, and Russia's ally, France. Long-planned mobilizations and war programs were implemented, and by early August, conflict seemed almost inevitable. The European powers went to war in the summer of 1914, enjoying great public support and secure in their mistaken belief that the conflict would be short and decisive. The opposing nations were known as the Allies (Great Britain, France, Russia, and Belgium, later joined by Italy, Japan, and other European nations) and the Central Powers (Germany, Austria-Hungary, the Ottoman Empire, and Bulgaria).

In the west, Germany and France clashed at their common borders, but the main German thrust was into neutral Belgium, which outraged world opinion and drove Britain to enter the war on the side of France. The German army penetrated to within seventy miles of Paris before it was stopped by the combined Belgian, British, and French forces at the Battle of the Marne in September 1914. Both sides dug in, leading to four years of stalemated trench warfare, in which offensive followed offensive, with a few hundred yards of territory exchanging hands at the cost of casualties and human suffering. The widespread use of barbed wire and machine guns and the introduction of poison gas by the Germans in 1915 epitomized the emerging horrors of twentieth-century warfare.

On the eastern front, Germany and Austria repelled an initial Russian onslaught and gradually advanced into Russia's western provinces. By the end of 1916, the Russian economy was severely strained and the imperial regime was threatened by growing internal dissension. In 1915, Italy joined the Allies and undertook a fruitless and costly series of attempts to drive the Austrian army from its mountainous defenses. Here, too, a stalemate set in for more than two years. After an initial humiliation by the Serbs, Austria-Hungary was rescued by Germany, and their combined forces overwhelmed Serbia and Romania, which had joined the Allies, and occupied much of the Balkans by 1916. The growing conflict spread to the Ottoman Empire in the Middle East, Germany's colonies in Africa, and the borders of China, where Japan grabbed Germany's Asian outposts. It began to be known as the Great or World War.

Most Americans felt the United States would not be drawn into the war in Europe and the Far East. During August 1914, President Wilson issued a series of proclamations of neutrality in all of the conflicts involving the various belligerents and on August 18 told the American people that the "effect of the war upon the United States will depend upon what the American citizens say and do." He appealed to them to be "impartial in thought as well as action." In early September, Wilson told a joint session of Congress that the war in Europe had already begun to have an impact on the American economy and "affects us directly and palpably almost as if we were participants in the circumstances which gave rise to it." He concluded with what would prove to be a prophetic warning: "The occasion is not of our own making. We had no part in making it. But it is here. . . . We shall pay the bill, though we did not deliberately incur it." Eventually, the decision of the German government to use submarine warfare against the Allied forces would upset the neutral policy the United States sought to maintain.

Pressure from the Hague Opium Convention of 1912, which called upon signatories to enact restrictive domestic antinarcotics legislation, led to the enactment of the Harrison Narcotics Tax Act. This act, the first major use by Congress of its taxing power in the criminal justice field, was designed to eliminate the non-medical sale and use of opiates and cocaine, which were widespread, over-the-counter, and unregulated. It marked the beginning of America's war on drugs and established the foundation of future U.S. drug law. The nation's first major "anti-drug" law was adopted a full five years before National Alcohol Prohibition.

In January 1915, the U.S. Coast Guard was officially established through consolidation of the Revenue-Cutter Service and Life Saving Service in the Treasury Department. The decision to centralize marine search and rescue activities enjoyed bipartisan support on Capitol Hill. During the final hours of the Sixty-third Congress, passage of the La Follette Seamen's Act was seen as a means of improving the living and working conditions on board foreign as well as American vessels.

A lack of a government laboratory devoted to the science of flight prompted the creation of the national advisory committee for aeronautics, the predecessor organization for the National Aeronautics and Space Administration (NASA). The committee, which existed from 1915 until 1958, was founded just before the United States' entry into World War I, to bring competence to the backwardness of American aviation. The advisory committee's chartered mandate was "to supervise and direct the scientific study of the problems of flight, with a view of their practical solutions."

The nation sent a mixed message in the congressional elections of 1914. Although the Democrats retained control of both the House and Senate, they lost sixty-one House seats while increasing their Senate majority over the Republicans by nine. The 1914 congressional elections saw implementation of the Seventeenth Amendment, as U.S. senators were chosen for the first time by popular vote. (*Seventeenth Amendment, p. 194*)

Major Acts

Newlands Act of 1913. Established a full-time four-member board of mediation and conciliation to handle railway labor disputes, and definitively placed the main reliance for settlement of disputes upon mediation. Required the board, if disputes arose relative to the meaning or application of any agreement reached through mediation, to render an opinion when requested by either party to the dispute. Provided improved arbitration procedures were available when mediation failed. Permitted the mediation board to offer its services without first being invited into the dispute by either the labor unions or the carrier. Approved July 15, 1913 (38 Stat. 103–108).

Underwood Tariff Act. Reduced the average rates of duties from 38 percent under the Payne-Aldrich Tariff of 1909 to less than 30 percent. Reduced duties on 958 items including iron, steel, and woolens. Expanded the free list to include wool, sugar, iron ore, barbed wire, agricultural implements, hides, leather, footwear, hemp, wood, coal, and many foodstuffs. Empowered the president to negotiate reciprocal trade agreements, and provided for antidumping measures. Established a 1 percent tax on incomes above $2,000 with a $1,000 exemption for married men and a graduated 1 to 6 percent tax on incomes above $20,000. Approved October 3, 1913 (38 Stat. 114–202). (*Payne-Aldrich Tariff Act, p. 190*)

Federal Reserve Act (Owen-Glass Act). Authorized the secretary of the Treasury, the secretary of agriculture, and the comptroller of the currency, acting as the Federal Reserve Bank Organization Committee, to designate not fewer than eight or more than twelve cities to be known as Federal Reserve cities and divide the continental United States into districts containing one Federal Reserve city each. Provided that the districts thus created could be readjusted from time to time but could not exceed twelve. Created a Federal

Reserve Board of seven members (later enlarged to eight), including the secretary of the Treasury and the comptroller of the currency, with authority to raise or lower the rediscount rate prevailing in the several districts. Required that each Reserve Bank, barring an emergency, maintain a gold reserve amount equal to 40 percent of the notes it had issued. Approved December 23, 1913 (38 Stat. 251–275).

Naval Militia Act. Placed state naval militia organizations under the supervision of the Navy Department. Authorized the president to call state naval militias into federal service in the event of a national emergency or when a state of war existed. Authorized the Division of Naval Militia Affairs under the Bureau of Navigation to control all matters in connection with the naval militia. Stipulated that the naval militia and any future naval reserve must be called out first, before volunteers, in a time of emergency. Provided pay, transportation, and subsistence for members of the state naval militias while on training duty and when they were under orders from the Secretary of the Navy. Approved February 16, 1914 (38 Stat. 283–290).

Smith-Lever Act. Created the U.S. Department of Agriculture Extension Service to administer a system of agricultural agents throughout the nation to be supported by the cooperative efforts of the department and land-grant colleges. Provided that federal grants-in-aid were to be matched by state appropriations directed at bringing the latest agricultural research data directly to the nation's farmers. Approved May 8, 1914 (38 Stat. 372–375).

Cotton Futures Act. Imposed a tax of two cents per pound for cotton sold under a contract of sale for future delivery. Waived the tax if the contract specified the grade, type, sample, or description of the cotton involved in the contract, the price per pound at which the cotton was to be bought or sold, and the time when shipment or delivery of the cotton was to be made. Required that the cotton actually be transferred. Designated the Secretary of Agriculture as the referee of any disputes under such contracts. Authorized the Department of Agriculture to establish physical standards as a means of determining color-grade, staple length and strength, and other qualities and properties for cotton. (Subsequently, these standards were agreed upon and accepted by the leading European cotton associations and exchanges, and became known as the "Universal Standards for American Cotton.") Approved August 18, 1914 (38 Stat. 693–698).

War Risk Insurance Act. Established the Bureau of War Risk Insurance in the Treasury Department to administer an insurance program for U.S. merchant vessels and their cargoes. Approved September 2, 1914 (38 Stat. 711–712).

Federal Trade Commission Act. Established a five-member nonpartisan Federal Trade Commission (no more than three of whom could belong to the same political party) authorized to receive reports from corporations, investigate the activities of persons and corporations, and publish reports on its findings. Empowered the commission to issue orders to prevent unfair business practices, trade boycotts, mislabeling, adulteration of commodities, combinations, and false patent claims. Approved September 26, 1914 (38 Stat. 717–724).

Clayton Antitrust Act. Prohibited any discrimination in prices when the effect would "substantially lessen competition or tend to create a monopoly," and prohibited "tie-in" agreements that kept a buyer from purchasing or handling the products of the seller's competitors. Outlawed intercorporate stock holding and interlocking directorates among industrial corporations valued at $1 million or more. Authorized parties injured by monopolistic practices to seek relief through court injunctions, cease and desist orders from the Federal Trade Commission, and civil suits for threefold damages. Exempted labor and farm organizations from antitrust laws. Prohibited court injunctions in labor disputes unless necessary to prevent irreparable property damage. Declared strikes, peaceful picketing, and boycotts legal under federal law. Provided for a jury trial in contempt cases, except when the act of contempt took place in court. Approved October 15, 1914 (38 Stat. 730–740). The legislation was sponsored by Rep. Henry D. Clayton of Alabama.

Emergency War Revenue Act of 1914. Increased duties on fermented liquors; imposed license taxes on bankers, brokers, tobacco dealers, manufacturers, theaters, and other amusement enterprises; and imposed stamp taxes on promissory notes, insurance policies, bills of lading, steamer tickets, parlor car seats, sleeping-car berths, and telegraph and telephone messages. Approved October 22, 1914 (38 Stat. 745–764).

Harrison Narcotics Tax Act. Provided for the taxing and licensing of the producers, importers, manufacturers, and distributers who sold or dispensed opium, cocaine, or their derivatives. Required physicians, dentists, or veterinary surgeons prescribing narcotics to be licensed and keep records of drugs dispensed or prescribed. Exempted patent-medicine manufacturers from the act's licensing and tax provisions, providing they limited themselves to "preparations and remedies which do not contain more than two grains of opium, or more than one-fourth of a grain of morphine, or more than one-eighth of a grain of heroin in . . . one avoirdupois ounce." Approved December 14, 1914 (38 Stat. 785–790).

U.S. Coast Guard Created. Combined the Revenue-Cutter Service and Life-Saving Service into a new agency known as the U.S. Coast Guard. Stipulated that the Coast Guard was to "constitute a part of the military forces of the United States . . . under the Treasury Department in time of peace and [to] operate as a part of the Navy, subject to the orders of the Secretary of the Navy, in time of war or when the President shall so direct." Approved January 28, 1915 (38 Stat. 800–803).

National Advisory Committee for Aeronautics. Established the National Advisory Committee on Aeronautics to supervise and direct the scientific study of the problems of flight with a view to their practical solution, to determine problems which should be experimentally attacked, and to their investigation and application to practical questions of aeronautics. Authorized the committee to direct and conduct research and experimentation in aeronautics in such laboratory or laboratories, in whole or in part, as may be placed under its direction. Approved March 3, 1915 (38 Stat. 930).

Seamen's Act of 1915. Abolished the arrest and imprisonment of American seamen in the merchant marine of the United States as a penalty for desertion. Provided for the regulation of hours of work, size of crews, daily food provisions, payment of wages, and safety conditions. Required that 75 percent of the crewmen of each ship departing should understand the language spoken by the officers. Approved March 4, 1915 (38 Stat. 1164–1185).

Note

1. Arthur S. Link, ed., *The Papers of Woodrow Wilson* (Princeton, N.J.: Princeton University Press, 1979), 31:122.

Sixty-fourth Congress
March 4, 1915, to March 3, 1917

First session—December 6, 1915, to September 8, 1916
Second session—December 4, 1916, to March 3, 1917
(First administration of Woodrow Wilson, 1913–1917)

Historical Background

At the outset of World War I, President Woodrow Wilson sought to maintain a policy of neutrality toward all of the European belligerents. This position became increasingly difficult to maintain, however, as Allied demands for vital economic aid, food, and munitions continued to stimulate the American economy. Throughout the first three years of war, American industry and agriculture prospered greatly by filling huge orders for all sorts of manufactured goods and foodstuffs for the Allies, while the Central Powers were effectively cut off from trade by an increasingly stringent Allied blockade. Similarly, the Royal Navy kept the powerful German navy in port, except for a few raids and one major attack in 1916, which ended with the indecisive Battle of Jutland. Germany countered with submarine attacks against Allied shipping, which culminated with her 1915 announcement that her submarines would attack without warning any merchant ships entering a specified zone around the British Isles. On May 7, 1915, a German submarine sank the British liner *Lusitania* off the coast of Ireland, with the loss of 128 American lives. U.S. public opinion was outraged, and the Wilson administration sent a series of notes demanding that Germany pay reparations and disavow the sinking. The notes' severity led Secretary of State William Jennings Bryan to resign in protest, but Germany eventually agreed to compensate American losses and stop sinking passenger vessels on sight.

The sinking of the *Lusitania,* however, led to strained relations with Germany and the Central Powers.

Preparedness immediately became a political issue, and in December 1915 President Wilson recommended that Congress increase America's standing army by more than 50,000 and approved a federalized National Guard of 450,000. Following six months of intense political negotiations, the National Defense Act, which provided for an even larger army than Wilson had requested, was signed into law. Under this new authority, the president could direct the National Guard to serve under federal command. Since 1792, the president had the constitutional right to call the state militias into active service to enforce federal laws, suppress insurrection, and repel invasions. These troops, however, had retained state identities, and the respective state governors continued to appoint and promote officers. This new law granted the president the right to draft or order the National Guard into federal service upon declaration of war.

Increased demand and wartime losses led to a worsening shortage of shipping that adversely affected American trade. The U.S. Shipping Board was created both to remedy the situation and to ensure adequate shipping in the event of war. Its purpose was to promote, enhance, and regulate America's merchant fleet.

The outbreak of the First World War provided impetus for the Naval Expansion Act. "Never before," President Wilson said on signing the largest naval expansion bill in the nation's history up to that point, "by one single act of legislation, has so much been done for the creation of an adequate navy."[1] The act represented the culmination of 20 years of planning by the U.S. Navy's professional officers corps to build a fleet of top-rank status, and started the largest naval expansion in American history. The Army Appropriations Act of 1916 authorized the president to take control of the nation's transportation systems during wartime and created a Council of National Defense charged with determining how the economy might be best mobilized for war. In December 1917, eight months after the United States entered World War I, President Woodrow Wilson announced the nationalization of a majority of the nation's railroads under the Federal Possession and Control Act. At the time, the nation's major railroads were beset by numerous strikes. Although the role of the National Defense Council, which was disbanded in 1921, was limited to basically economic mobilization issues, did set a precedent for coordinative efforts that would be needed in World War II.

New taxes were levied by the Revenue Act of 1916 to finance the Shipping Act as well as other heavy expenditures approved by Congress during the previous two years. Progressively increasing opposition to free immigration, particularly directed at those arriving from southern and eastern Europe, led to the passage of a new immigration act. The most controversial provision of the Immigration Act of 1917 excluded aliens over sixteen who were unable to read. The legislation became law only after Congress overrode President Wilson's veto. During the previous two decades, several of Wilson's predecessors, including Grover Cleveland, Theodore Roosevelt, and William Howard Taft, had vetoed similar bills. Other significant provisions of the Immigration Act added further restrictions on Asian laborers seeking to enter the United States and made radical changes in deportation procedures.

Acting on the recommendations of a joint committee appointed to study the problem of federal aid for highway construction, Congress approved the Rural Post Roads Act of 1916. This established the basic pattern for a cooperative federal-state partnership in highway construction with a $75 million appropriation to be spent over a five-year period. With the signing of the Federal Farm Loan Act, President Wilson laid the cornerstone of a cooperative agricultural credit system that could extend long-term credit to farmers. It was similar to one established for commerce and industry through the Federal Reserve Act of 1913. The twelve land banks created under the Federal Farm Loan Act were authorized to pool the mortgages of individual farmers and issue bonds with the

mortgages as security. Lower mortgage rates were assured by making the bonds exempt from taxation. *(Federal Reserve Act [Owen-Glass Act], p. 198)*

Passage of the United States Grain Standards Act was the culmination of 25 years of investigation, public hearings, and debate. The rapid expansion of the U.S. grain industry created a need for a uniform system of grading in order to better facilitate trade. Independent attempts by local Chambers of Commerce, boards of trade, and major grain corporations to develop standards had resulted in inequalities among markets, emphasizing the need for federal legislation to reduce the confusion and corruption that characterized the trade. The objective of the Grain Standards Act, which led to creation of the first set of uniform grain standards, was to assure that wheat and other grains would be graded identically within human and experimental error at any point in the United States. For more than a decade prior to the dawn of the Twentieth Century, the Farmers' Alliance and other groups lobbied the federal government to license warehouses in which farmers could store crops until prices rose and to provide credit until crops could be sold. Legislation to achieve that end was finally enacted in the Warehouse Act of 1916 so farmers could be provided with the credit they needed to withhold their products from market temporarily. The act authorized the Secretary of Agriculture to license bonded warehousemen to issue warehouse receipts farmers could use as collateral for loans.

The Keating-Owen Child Labor Act of 1916 was the result of a lengthy effort by social workers, reformers, and unions to ban child labor on any manufactured product sold in interstate commerce. The legislation was sponsored by Rep. Edward Keating of Colorado and Sen. Robert L. Owen of Oklahoma. In 1918, the U.S. Supreme Court held the act unconstitutional by a five-to-four margin because it transcended the "authority delegated to Congress over commerce" and exerted a "power as to a local matter to which the Federal authority did not extend." Near the end of August 1916, President Wilson appeared before Congress to urge enactment of an eight-hour workday for railroad workers. His action was intended to deflect union threats for a nationwide railroad strike to achieve that goal. Enactment of the Adamson Act, sponsored by Rep. William C. Adamson of Georgia, paved the way for general acceptance of the eight-hour workday among other industries, a goal of organized labor since the 1880s. Legislation also was approved to provide compensation for all civilian federal employees for job-related injuries, disease, and death. The Federal Employees' Compensation Act of 1916 was molded in an effort to overcome the deficiencies of earlier acts that had covered only limited portions of the federal work force.

A landmark in vocational education was achieved with the Smith-Hughes Act of 1917, which created the Federal Board for Vocational Education and provided that federal grant-in-aid funds be matched by state and local contributions. The act was sponsored by Georgia senators Hoke Smith and Sen. Dudley M. Hughes. Also, the National Park Service was established in the Department of the Interior.

Under continual public and political pressure from the beleaguered states adjoining the lower Mississippi River that had suffered major floods in 1903, 1912, and 1913, the federal government was inexorably drawn into greater participation in flood control. The Flood Control Act of 1917 marked the first time that funds were openly and primarily appropriated for the purpose of flood prevention and control, and changed the federal government's activities on the nation's rivers from a single-purpose program (navigation improvement) to a limited dual-purpose program.

Enactment of the First and Second Jones Acts reaffirmed American intentions to eventually recognize the independence of the Philippines and made Puerto Rico a U.S. territory. Through the Jones Act of 1916, the Filipinos gained a popularly elected legislature and were able to assume control over most of their domestic affairs. Alterations to Puerto Rico's status in the Jones Act of 1917 were less sweeping. Although U.S. citizenship was extended to the island's inhabitants and an elected legislature was established, full self-government was deferred for three more decades. Amidst an increasing fear of German activity in the Caribbean, the Senate in 1917 approved a treaty with Denmark allowing the United States to purchase the Danish West Indies (Virgin Islands). Strategically, the Virgin Islands proved to be of great military importance as World War I progressed, especially in protecting the Panama Canal.

Woodrow Wilson's reelection bid in 1916 proved even more challenging than his campaign against

William Howard Taft and Theodore Roosevelt in 1912. In one of the closest elections in U.S. history, California was up for grabs. Wilson carried the state by fewer than four thousand votes. He and his vice president, Thomas R. Marshall, won with 277 electoral votes to 254 for Republican presidential nominee Supreme Court justice Charles Evans Hughes and vice presidential nominee Charles W. Fairbanks. The Democrats retained control of both houses of Congress, but with reduced majorities.

Major Acts

National Defense Act. Reorganized the armed forces of the United States into three distinct categories: the Regular Army, the Organized Reserves (including a training corps), and the National Guard. Authorized an increase in the strength of the Regular Army to 175,000 and a federalized National Guard to 450,000 within five years. Provided for a Reserve Officers' Training Corps at colleges and universities, construction of a plant for the production of nitrates and munitions, and creation of a signal corps. Approved June 3, 1916 (39 Stat. 166–217).

Federal-Aid Road Act of 1916 (Bankhead-Shackelford Act). Authorized $5 million in federal aid to the states for the construction of rural post roads (roads over which the United States mails were transported) for fiscal 1917, and provided for annual increases of $5 million per year for the four subsequent years, until the fifth year, when the amount available would be $25 million. Required that states match federal funds on a one-to-one ratio and create highway departments to administer the funds. Stipulated that the road construction would be done by the state highway departments subject to federal inspection. Established a system of highway classification. Approved July 11, 1916 (39 Stat. 355–359).

Federal Farm Loan Act. Established twelve regional Federal Land Bank districts, and established a Federal Land Bank in each with a minimum capital of $750,000 in which farm loan associations held membership. Created the five-member Federal Farm Loan Board, with the secretary of the Treasury as chairman, to administer the system. Provided that no loan could be less than $100 or more than $10,000 and could not exceed 50 percent of the appraised value of the land mortgaged or 20 percent of the value of permanent improvements. Limited interest on loans to 6 percent, amortized over a period of between five and forty years. Approved July 17, 1916 (39 Stat. 360–384).

United States Grain Standards Act. Authorized the secretary of agriculture to make investigations and to establish uniform federal grades and standards for quality and condition of all grain shipped in interstate and foreign commerce. Required that all existing state-level grain inspection systems be incorporated into a new federal system and the Department of Agriculture supervise all grain sales. Provided for a system for licensing and supervision of grain inspectors, and an appeals system for instances when it was thought grain had been graded incorrectly by the licensed inspector. Approved August 11, 1916 (39 Stat. 482–485, Part B).

Warehouse Act of 1916. Established a uniform regulatory system for storage of agricultural products, and required warehouse operators to accept products for storage without discrimination. Authorized the secretary of agriculture to license, audit, and inspect public warehouse operators in the business of storing agricultural products; and to license qualified persons to sample, inspect, weigh, and grade agricultural products. Permitted Federal Reserve member banks to issue loans to farmers based on the security of their staple crops, which were to be kept in federal storage units as collateral. Approved August 11, 1916 (39 Stat. 486–491, Part C).

Establishment of National Park Service. Created in the Department of the Interior the National Park Service to "promote and regulate the use of the Federal areas known as national parks, monuments, and reservations . . . by such means and measures as conform" to their "fundamental purpose." Stated that the fundamental purpose of the service was to "to conserve the scenery and the natural and historic objectives and the wild life therein and to provide for the enjoyment of the same in such manner and by such means as will leave them unimpaired for the

enjoyment of future generations." Approved August 25, 1916 (39 Stat. 535–536).

First Jones Act (Organic Act of the Philippine Islands). Declared that it was the purpose of the people of the United States to provide a more autonomous government for the Philippines. Granted a large measure of self-government to the islands, and promised independence "as soon as a stable government can be established." Provided for a popularly elected twenty-four-member Senate and ninety-member House of Representatives. Approved August 29, 1916 (39 Stat. 545–556).

Naval Act of 1916. Authorized almost $500 million for a three-year building program to produce 10 battleships, 6 battle cruisers, 10 scout cruisers, 50 destroyers, 9 fleet submarines, 58 costal submarines, and 16 auxiliary vessels. Established a naval reserve of officers and enlisted sailors to man the fleet during an emergency. Reformed the procedure for promoting naval officers. Increased the number of midshipmen admitted to the naval academy. Provided for the secretary of the navy to speed battleship construction through incentive contracts. Approved August 29, 1916 (P.L. 241; 39 Stat. 556–619).

Federal Possession and Control Act. Empowered the president, through the secretary of war, in time of war "to take possession and assume control of any system or systems of transportation, or any part thereof, and to utilize the same, to the exclusion as far as may be necessary of all other traffic thereon, for the transfer or transportation of troops, war material and equipment, and for other needful or for such other purposes connected with the emergency as may be useful or desirable." Approved August 29, 1916 (P.L. 242; 39 Stat. 645).

Council of National Defense. Established a council of national defense with the secretaries of war, navy, agriculture, commerce, labor, and interior as members with the secretary of war serving as chairman, "for the coordination of industries and resources for the national security and welfare." Directed the council to nominate for presidential appointment an advisory commission with individuals having special knowledge of the various industries to aid the council. Approved August 29, 1916 (P.L. 242; 39 Stat. 649–650).

Keating-Owen Child Labor Act. Prohibited the interstate shipment of goods manufactured by children. Fixed the minimum age and hours children could work in different industries: age fourteen for factories and age sixteen for mines and quarries. Approved September 1, 1916 (39 Stat. 675–676). Certain provisions of this act were subsequently held unconstitutional in *Hammer v. Dagenhart*, 247 U.S. 251 (1918).

Adamson Act. Established an eight-hour workday and time-and-a-half pay for overtime on interstate railroads. Approved September 3, 1916 (39 Stat. 721–722).

Shipping Act of 1916. Created a five-member U.S. Shipping Board as a permanent independent agency empowered to build, purchase, lease, or requisition vessels for commerce or military use. Authorized the board to operate or lease these vessels to American citizens and to establish strict controls over the transfer of privately owned U.S. ships to foreign registry or ownership. Provided for an Emergency Fleet Corporation capitalized at $50 million to purchase and construct merchant vessels. Stipulated that the board's authority to operate shipping lines would expire five years after World War I ended. Approved September 7, 1916 (39 Stat. 728–738).

Federal Employees' Compensation Act of 1916. Provided compensation for all civilian employees of the federal government injured or killed in performance of their duty, including traumatic injuries and occupational diseases. Stipulated that the compensation would be 66⅔ percent of monthly pay with a maximum of $66.67 per month and a minimum of $33.33 per month. Created a three-member Federal Employees' Compensation Commission to administer the program. Approved September 7, 1916 (39 Stat. 742–750).

Revenue Act of 1916. Increased the income tax rate for individuals and corporations from 1 percent to 2 percent, and raised graduated surtax rates on incomes over $80,000. Raised the surtax rate on incomes of $2 million and greater from 6 to 13 percent. Introduced a progressive income tax on inheritances ranging from 1 percent on amounts in excess of $50,000 to 10 percent on amounts in excess of $5 million. Established the U.S. Tariff Commission. Approved September 8, 1916

(39 Stat. 756–801).

Acquisition of the Danish West Indies. Provided for the purchase of the Virgin Islands in the West Indies from Denmark for $25 million. Concluded August 4, 1916. Approved September 7, 1916. Ratified by the Senate January 17, 1917 (39 Stat. 1706–1717).

Immigration Act of 1917. Required that prospective immigrants pass a literacy test as a condition of admission to the United States, but permitted immigration officials to exempt from the test foreigners who were fleeing religious persecution. Expanded inadmissible aliens to include parts of Afghanistan, Arabia, China, and Russia, most of the East Indian states and Polynesian Islands, and all of Burma, India, Siam, and the Malay states. Streamlined deportation procedures. Presidential veto overridden by Congress. Became law without the president's signature February 5, 1917 (39 Stat. 874–898).

Smith-Hughes Vocational Education Act. Created a Federal Board for Vocational Education charged with promoting vocational training in agriculture, trades, industries, commercial pursuits, and home economics in secondary schools. Provided federal grant-in-aid funds to be matched by state and local contributions to support the program. Approved February 23, 1917 (39 Stat. 929–936).

Flood Control Act of 1917. Established a congressional commitment to fund a long-range and comprehensive program of flood control for at least two flood-prone areas—the lower Mississippi and the Sacramento Rivers. Introduced the principle of including requirements that states and local interests make financial contributions for flood control. Authorized the Corps of Engineers to undertake examinations and surveys for flood control improvements, and to provide information regarding the relationship of flood control to navigation and water power. Approved March 1, 1917 (39 Stat. 948–951).

Second Jones Act (Organic Act for Puerto Rico). Made Puerto Rico a U.S. territory and extended U.S. citizenship to its inhabitants. Provided for a popularly elected legislature consisting of a nineteen-member

Senate and thirty-nine-member House of Representatives, with the U.S. Congress reserving the right to annul or amend any enactment of the legislature. Provided that four of the six heads of the executive departments (commissioners of agriculture and labor, health, and interior as well as the treasurer) be appointed by the presidentially appointed governor with the advice of the Puerto Rican Senate. Stipulated that the territory's attorney general and commissioner of education would be named by the president. Approved March 2, 1917 (39 Stat. 951–968).

Note

1. Arthur S. Link, ed., *The Papers of Woodrow Wilson,* v. 38 (Princeton, NJ: Princeton University Press, 1982).

Sixty-fifth Congress
March 4, 1917, to March 3, 1919

First session—April 2, 1917, to October 6, 1917

Second session—December 3, 1917, to November 21, 1918

Third session—December 2, 1918, to March 3, 1919

Special session of the Senate—March 5, 1917, to March 16, 1917

(Second administration of Woodrow Wilson, 1917–1921)

Historical Background

Shortly after his reelection as president, Woodrow Wilson made a final, unsuccessful, effort to win a negotiated peace between the Allies and the Central Powers. At the same time, he sought to preserve American neutrality. On January 22, 1917, Wilson used the setting of a packed Senate chamber to tell the world that a League of Nations should be organized to establish and maintain world peace. He bluntly told the embattled powers that only through "peace without victory" could permanent peace be realized. Soon thereafter, Germany announced that it would resume unrestricted submarine warfare against all belligerent and neutral ships. On February 4, Wilson made a dramatic appearance before Congress to announce the severance of diplomatic relations with Germany.

American opinion, previously divided, turned decisively against Germany in March 1917 with the publication of the Zimmermann Telegram, which had been intercepted and decoded by the British. The telegram revealed that Germany had secretly offered Mexico vast portions of the southwest United States if it supported the Central Powers in the event the United States entered the war on the side of the Allies. Disclosure of the telegram led to widespread agitation for U.S. entry into the conflict on the side of the Allies. On March 21, Wilson issued a call for a special session of Congress to convene April 2. A war resolution passed the Senate on April 4, by a vote of 82 to 6, and the House the following day, 373 to 50.

Following the declaration, Congress enacted measures that extended federal influence and control over all areas of national life. While pacifists, free speech advocates, and others opposed to the war for political reasons (for example, some German Americans) claimed these measures violated the Bill of Rights, most Americans supported such restrictions as necessary to the war effort.

To prosecute the war, Congress during the ensuing five months approved the Liberty Loan Act, to help finance American and Allied war needs; a Selective Service Act, to provide for the registration and classification of all men between the ages of twenty-one and thirty; the Lever Food and Fuel Control Act, to stimulate, conserve, and control the distribution of foods and fuels necessary for the war effort; and the War Revenue Act, to increase the tax revenues derived from corporations and individuals. The selective service act was amended 15 months later to expand the age of compulsory military service to cover those between the ages of 18 to 45, and provide training at institutions of higher learning.

After the United States officially entered World War I, the War Risk Insurance program was expanded to cover officers and crews of the Merchant Marines and armed forces members. Four months later, the Bureau of War Risk Insurance was expanded, once again, when Congress enacted revolutionary benefits for World War I veterans. Together the two amendments created the largest Government insurance system in the world and transformed the small Bureau of War Risk Insurance into a vast business enterprise.

Early in December 1917 the scope of American participation increased with a declaration of a state of war with Austria-Hungary. As hostilities continued, additional war measures were enacted that placed the nation's railroads under government control (Railroad Control Act), facilitated the extension of credit to vital war industries (War Finance Corporation Act), authorized exporters to organize trade associations without being subject to antitrust laws (Webb-Pomerene Export Trade Act, sponsored by Rep. Edwin Y. Webb of North Carolina and Sen. Atlee Pomerene of Ohio), and gave the president discretionary authority to reorganize executive agencies for the duration of the war (Overman Act, sponsored by Sen. Lee S. Overman of North Carolina). The U.S. Navy began immediate action against the German submarine menace and joined the British Royal Navy in joint operations, as a battleship squadron joined the British Grand fleet in European waters. At the same time, the time-consuming process of creating a large land army to assist in the great battle in France was begun with the passage of the Selective Service Act of May 10, 1917, which authorized compulsory military duty for all men between the ages of twenty-one and thirty (later expanded to cover those between eighteen and forty-five). In time, the U.S. Army grew to more than four million men, the U.S. Navy to 600,000, and the Marine Corps and Coast Guard to 79,000 and 9,000, respectively. Of these, more than four million were draftees.

When the United States declared war on Germany in 1917, more than a decade after the first flight of the Wright Brothers, military aviation was still practically nonexistent. America's involvement in World War I provided the impetus for expanding the aircraft industry and military aviation. The Aviation Act, passed three-and-a-half months after the United States entered the war, provided more than $600 million to build up the nation's aviation program. The appropriation was the largest for a single procurement program up to that point.

To protect the civil rights and legal interests of individuals in the armed services during World War I, legislation was enacted to ensure that they would not be distracted by legal obligations at home. Although the act did not prevent people from suing service members,

it did allow a court to suspend legal actions against them while they were on active duty. Some three months later, the first federal statute to mandate vocational rehabilitation programs for disabled veterans and the first to define legitimate disability was enacted. This legislation was the precursor to the Americans with Disabilities Act, as well as the precursor to the GI bill passed after World War II. The act was designed to help disabled veterans to overcome their disability and seek competitive employment. The Chamberlain-Kahn Act of 1918 was enacted as the United States entered World War I, to prevent U.S. soldiers from fraternizing with prostitutes and promiscuous women. Grants provided under the act constitute the first application of federal aid to states for health purposes. Although the act led to results long sought by reformers, passage was prompted less by moralizing than by the fact that at any given time typically one-third of active duty soldiers had sexually transmitted diseases.

World War I substantially increased the need for additional manpower to support the American military campaign in Europe. To address the shortage of available inductees, the Selective Service Act required that all males residing in the United States, including aliens, register for military service. To reward aliens who served in the military, the Alien Naturalization Act allowed any alien who had been a member of the Armed Forces for three or more years simply to file a petition for naturalization without a preliminary declaration of intention or proof of five years residence within the United States. Between May 9, 1918, and June 30, 1919, more than 192,000 aliens were naturalized at U.S. military bases or in courts nearby before being sent overseas to fight.

Legislation aimed at treasonable and disloyal activities was incorporated into the Espionage Act of 1917 and was subsequently supplemented with three other measures. The Trading with the Enemy Act prohibited commerce with enemy nations. The Sabotage Act provided for the punishment of persons guilty of disrupting activities related to national defense. The Sedition Act made it a felony to utter anything "disloyal, profane, scurrilous, or abusive" about the government, Constitution, flag, or armed forces. The Espionage Act was not the only form of legislation to discriminate against antiwar groups. Under the Alien Act of 1918, foreign residents of the United States suspected of disloyalty or even accused of membership in an organization that advocated violent overthrow of the government could be deported without a trial.

Adoption of daylight savings time, which appealed to many nations following the outbreak of World War I as an economy measure, lasted only seventeen months before rural Americans secured its repeal, over the veto of President Wilson. An even longer and more persistent campaign preceded the House and Senate votes to submit a proposed constitutional amendment to the states prohibiting the manufacture, sale, and transportation of alcoholic beverages in the United States. Within thirteen months, the Eighteenth Amendment was ratified by three-fourths of the state legislatures. A diverse group of advocates—the Anti-Saloon League, Women's Christian Temperance Union, and a broad range of religious as well as social reformers—prompted its adoption. There was also a widely held perception that prohibition was a patriotic as well as a moral issue.

The need for enabling legislation for a convention between the United States and Canada prompted passage of the Migratory Bird Treaty. Through the combined efforts of organized sportsmen, bird protectionist groups, and farm organizations, the federal government assumed a major responsibility for the protection of international migratory bird resources.

The first units of the American Expeditionary Force (AEF) arrived in France in May 1917, but more than a year passed before U.S. forces began to join the Allies at the front in large numbers. In the meantime, Germany, having concluded a treaty with the new Soviet government, was able to focus on a decisive offense on the western front. In May 1918, the Germans launched an all-out offensive intended to end four years of stalemated trench warfare. At America's insistence, the AEF served, with few exceptions, as a unified force, instead of being parceled out among other Allied armies. Under the command of General John J. Pershing, the AEF's growing numbers and skill materially aided the Allies in turning back the German offensive and beginning a counterdrive that brought about retreat and, finally, the collapse of the German army. Faced with defeat, Germany sued for a cessation of hostilities, and on November 11, 1918, the guns fell silent on the Western Front. The German surrender followed that of its Central Powers allies by a few weeks. The American contribution to victory was crucial. By November, more than one million American soldiers had joined the battle in Europe, and thousands of reinforcements arrived every week. By their numbers, enthusiasm, and growing skills, they were widely credited with tipping the balance in favor of the Allies and bringing the war to an end. At the outset of World War I, General John J. Pershing cabled a telegram to the War Department, urging appropriation for claims for injuries to persons and damages to property resulting from the acts or omissions of the United States military forces in Europe. The Indemnity Act of 1918 was drafted in response to General Pershing's request.

During the midterm congressional elections of 1918, President Wilson appealed to the American people for a Democratic Congress "for the sake of the nation itself." When the Republicans captured control of both the House and Senate, however, it was interpreted by many as a repudiation of Wilson's leadership.

Major Acts

Declaration of War with Germany. Declared that a state of war existed with Germany, and authorized the president "to employ the entire naval and military forces of the United States and the resources of the Government to carry on war against the Imperial German Government; and to bring the conflict to a successful termination all of the resources of the country are hereby pledged by the Congress of the United States." Approved April 6, 1917 (40 Stat. 1).

Liberty Loan Act. Authorized the issuance of $5 billion in long-term bonds to be sold at public subscription to be used for American war expenditures and loans to the Allies to purchase food and war supplies. (Five different bond issues were launched between May 1917 and April 1919, totaling nearly $21.5 billion.) Approved April 24, 1917 (40 Stat. 35–37).

Selective Service Act. Required that "all male citizens, or male persons not alien enemies who have declared their intention to become citizens," between the ages of twenty-one and thirty (subsequently broadened by the Manpower Act of August 31, 1918, to include all men between the ages of eighteen and forty-five) to register for military service. Provided for the classification of registrations according to their fitness for service, and established that the order of induction be determined by lottery. Prohibited the hiring of substitutes and the payment of bounties. Approved May 18, 1917 (40 Stat. 76–83).

War Risk Insurance Act Amendments. Provided insurance for the captains and crews of the merchant ships already insured under the 1914 Act against loss of life, personal injury, or capture by the enemy. Offered government-subsidized insurance policies to servicemen against death or total disability, established a compensation payment schedule, and allotments and survivor's benefits for family support. Provided free hospital, medical, and surgical services to disabled World War I servicemen, along with artificial limbs and trusses, dental care, and burial expenses. Established programs for rehabilitation and vocational training for veterans with dismemberment, sight, hearing, and other permanent disabilities. Approved June 12, 1917, and October 6, 1917 (40 Stat. 102–105, 398–411).

Espionage Act. Established fines up to $10,000 and twenty years imprisonment for persons found guilty of spying, sabotage, refusing military service, or obstructing recruitment. Empowered the postmaster general to withhold mailing privileges from all newspapers, periodicals, and other materials judged to be seditious. Approved June 15, 1917 (40 Stat. 217–231).

Aviation Act. Authorized the president to increase the size of the aviation section of the Army Signal Corps. Granted the president authority, through the War Department, to purchase, manufacture, maintain, repair, and operate airplanes; to establish and operate "aviation stations"; to train aviators; to pay for the research and development of aircraft and aeronautical factories; and to establish and maintain aviation courses at colleges. Appropriated $640 million to carry out the purposes of the act. Approved July 24, 1917 (40 Stat. 243–247).

Lever Food and Fuel Control Act. Authorized the president to fix prices and to place controls on output and consumption of food, feeds, fuel, fertilizer and fertilizer ingredients, tools, utensils, and implements and equipment required for the production of foods, feeds, and fuel. Prohibited the importation and manufacture of distilled spirits for the duration of the war. Approved August 10, 1917 (40 Stat. 276–287).

War Revenue Act of 1917. Enacted to "provide increased revenue to defray the expenses of the increased appropriations for the Army and Navy and the extensions of fortifications." Authorized a graduated personal income tax on incomes of more than $1,000; increased the corporate income tax, estate taxes, and excise and luxury taxes; raised postal rates; and established a graduated excise-profits tax on businesses. Approved October 3, 1917 (40 Stat. 300–338).

Trading with the Enemy Act. Prohibited commercial intercourse with nations at war with the United States. Authorized the president to place an embargo on imports and to establish censorship of any material passing between the United States and any foreign nation. Established an Office of Alien Property Custodian to take possession of property in the United States owned by persons residing in enemy countries, and set up a War Trade Board to license imports and exports to facilitate American trade and halt that of the enemy. Approved October 6, 1917 (40 Stat. 411–426).

Declaration of a State of War with Austria-Hungary. Declared that a state of war existed with Austria-Hungary, and authorized the president "to employ the entire naval and military forces of the United States and the resources of the Government to carry on war against the Imperial and Royal Austro-Hungarian Government; and to bring the conflict to a successful termination all of the resources of the country are hereby pledged by the Congress of the United States." Approved December 7, 1917 (40 Stat. 429).

Eighteenth Amendment. Prohibited the manufacture, sale, or transportation of intoxicating liquor within or into the United States. Approved December 19, 1917 (40 Stat. 1050). Ratified by the requisite number of states January 16, 1919 (41 Stat. 1941–1942). The Eighteenth Amendment was repealed in 1933 by the Twenty-first Amendment. (*Twenty-first Amendment, p. 239*)

Soldiers' and Sailors' Civil Relief Act of 1918. Authorized courts to suspend legal action against members of the armed forces during their time of service if the court determined that he was unable to defend himself in court because of active duty. Protect service members from such things as repossession of property, bankruptcy, foreclosure, or other such actions while they were in harm's way. Directed trial courts to take whatever action equity required when a service member's rights were involved in a controversy. Expired under its own provision six months after the cessation of hostilities. Approved March 8, 1918 (40 Stat. 440–449).

Daylight Standard Time Act. Established the standard time of the United States by dividing the continental United States into four time zones. Provided that clocks would be advanced ahead by one hour from the last Sunday in March to the last Sunday in October to conserve electric energy. Approved March 19, 1918 (40 Stat. 450–451). Repealed August 20, 1919 (41 Stat. 280–281).

Railroad Control Act. Placed the management of all railroads under federal control for the duration of the war and for up to twenty-one months following the war. Guaranteed the railway corporations an annual compensation for the use of their property equal to their average annual operating income for the three years ending June 30, 1917. Approved March 21, 1918 (40 Stat. 451–458).

War Finance Corporation Act. Created a War Finance Corporation with capital stock of $500 million and authority to issue $3 billion in bonds to underwrite financial institutions making loans to industries, individuals, and corporations engaged in business essential to the war effort. Approved April 5, 1918 (40 Stat. 506–515).

Webb-Pomerene Export Trade Act. Exempted exporters organized in associations from being subject to antitrust laws. Approved April 10, 1918 (40 Stat. 516–518).

Indemnity Act. Provided for indemnity for damages caused by American forces "abroad." Authorized resolution of claims made by inhabitants of France and other European countries that were not enemies of the United States. Prohibited "an enemy or an ally of an enemy" from filing claims against the United States. Approved April 18, 1918 (40 Stat. 532).

Sabotage Act. Provided for the punishment of persons guilty of disrupting or attempting to disrupt any activity related to national defense. Approved April 20, 1918 (40 Stat. 533–534).

Alien Naturalization Act. Allowed aliens serving in the U.S. military during World War I to file their petitions for naturalization without first filing a declaration of intention, and exempted them from the five-year requirement. Expanded the scope of the naturalization privilege to include Filipino Naval or Marine veterans and Puerto Rican veterans of any branch of the military who had honorably served for three years as well. Approved May 9, 1918 (40 Stat. 542).

Sedition Act. Amended the Espionage Act of 1917 by establishing severe penalties on anyone convicted of willfully making "false reports or false statements with intent to interfere with the operation or success of the military or naval forces of the United States"; promoting the "success of its enemies"; employing "disloyal, profane, scurrilous, or abusive language" about the government, the Constitution, the flag, or the military; urging the curtailment of the production of war materials; or advocating, teaching, defending, or suggesting such acts. Approved May 16, 1918 (40 Stat. 553–554). *(Espionage Act, p. 210)*

Overman Act. "Authorized the President to coordinate or consolidate existing executive bureaus, agencies, and offices . . . in the interest of economy and the more efficient concentration of the government" for the duration of the war. Authorized the president to create an executive agency for the jurisdiction and control over the production of airplanes, airplane engines, and airplane parts. Required that abolition of agencies be recommended to Congress for legislative action. Approved May 20, 1918 (40 Stat. 556–557).

Smith-Sears Veterans Rehabilitation Act (Soldier Rehabilitation Act). Established a federal vocational rehabilitation program designed to help discharged veterans with service-related disabilities return to civil employment. Expanded the role of the Federal Board of Vocational Education to provide services for vocational rehabilitation of veterans disabled during World War I. Established the first clear legal determination of what constitutes a legitimate war disability. Approved June 27, 1918 (40 Stat. 617–620).

Migratory Bird Treaty Act of 1918. Implemented the 1916 Convention between the United States and Great Britain (for Canada) for the Protection of Migratory Birds, and established responsibility for protection of international migratory bird resources. Restricted the hunting of migratory species. Approved July 3, 1918 (40 Stat. 755–757).

Chamberlain-Kahn Act (informally referred to as the American Plan). Directed the secretary of war and the secretary of the navy to adopt measures that would protect the military and naval forces from venereal diseases, and to administer a system of grants-in-aid to states to control the spread of venereal diseases. Established a division of venereal disease in the U.S. Public Health Service to study and investigate the cause, treatment, and prevention of venereal diseases. Approved July 9, 1918 (40 Stat. 886–887).

Manpower Act. Required that all men between the ages of 18 and 45 register for military service. Exempted individuals "engaged in industries, occupations, or employments including agriculture found to be necessary for the maintenance of the Military Establishment," "effective operation of military forces," or "maintenance of national interest during the emergency." Authorized the secretary of war to enter into contracts with public and private universities for special and technical training of soldiers. Approved August 31, 1918 (P.L. 209; 40 Stat. 955–957).

Alien Act 1918. Authorized the deportation of "aliens who are anarchists; aliens who believe in or advocate the overthrow by force or violence of the Government of the United States"; "who disbelieve in or are opposed to all organized government"; "who advocate or teach the assassination of public officials"; "unlawful destruction of property"; or "who, at any time after entering the United States, is found to have been at the time of entry, or to have become thereafter, a member of any" anarchist organization. Approved October 16, 1918 (P.L. 221; 40 Stat. 1012–1013).

Sixty-sixth Congress
March 4, 1919, to March 3, 1921

First session—May 19, 1919, to November 19, 1919
Second session—December 1, 1919, to June 5, 1920
Third session—December 6, 1920, to March 3, 1921
(Second administration of Woodrow Wilson,
        1917–1921)

Historical Background

The Allies dictated harsh peace terms to Germany and the other Central Powers at a series of conferences held at locations around Paris in the spring of 1919. Arriving in Europe to lead the American delegation, President Woodrow Wilson was hailed as a hero in London and Paris. Wilson sought unsuccessfully to soften the terms of the Treaty of Versailles, concluded between Germany and the Allies, arguing that the terms as drafted would lead to resentment and a desire for revenge. Although he failed in this effort, he secured support from the Allies for his visionary project of a League of Nations to guarantee peace and prevent future wars.

When President Wilson returned to the United States from the Paris Peace Conference of 1919, he found considerable opposition to his diplomatic efforts. In particular, members of the now Republican-controlled Senate resented Wilson's failure to consult with Congress on the peacemaking process or to invite a congressional delegation to accompany him to Paris. On March 4, Wilson's task grew even more formidable when Senator Henry Cabot Lodge of Massachusetts released a letter signed by more than one-third of the Senate opposing the Treaty of Versailles. (The number was significant because approval of a treaty requires a two-thirds vote of the Senate.)

Their goal was to defer consideration of the League of Nations covenants until after the treaty was completed. Although Wilson was unwilling to separate the league from the treaty, he agreed to several revisions, after which a revised treaty was submitted to the Senate for ratification on July 10. Following extensive Senate Foreign Relations Committee hearings, an exhausted and ailing Wilson set out on a tour of the United States seeking to mobilize support for the league. Wilson would cut short the tour and return to Washington, where he suffered a crippling stroke on October 2. On November 19, the treaty (with fourteen reservations offered by Senator Lodge) was rejected 39 to 55. A day later, a second vote on the treaty without the Lodge reservations produced an almost identical vote (38 to 53). A third vote on March 19, 1920, ended similarly (49 to 35).

Wilson's support for a proposed women's suffrage amendment was far more successful. The House on May 21, 1919, and the Senate on June 4 passed a proposed constitutional amendment granting women the right to vote. In August 1920, Tennessee became the thirty-sixth state to ratify the Nineteenth Amendment, and it was added to the Constitution. That November, seventy-two years after the first women's rights convention, at Seneca Falls, New York, in 1848, women across the country cast their first votes for federal elected officials as a matter of right under the Constitution. The active participation of women in the war effort as well as the growing influence of women's rights groups had turned the tide of public opinion.

At the urging of women's organizations, a Women's Bureau was established in the Labor Department to investigate matters pertaining to working women in industry, publish the results of its investigations, and formulate initiatives to improve their circumstances.

The bureau was born out of a time in which women worked long hours, received low wages relative to their male counterparts, and often worked in unhealthy or unsafe conditions. Today, the bureau is still the only federal agency mandated to represent the needs of wage-earning women in the public policy process.

Enactment of the Volstead Act in October 1919 provided the enforcement apparatus for the Eighteenth Amendment, which ushered in Prohibition. Final approval of the bill sponsored by Rep. Andrew J. Volstead of Minnesota was secured after Congress overrode a veto by President Wilson, who opposed the legal enforcement of certain moral values on the entire American people and felt the nation faced more pressing concerns.

By 1919, automobile vehicle thefts had become so numerous that the federal government intervened with passage of the National Motor Vehicle Theft Act (Dyer Act), which was designed to help states supplement their efforts to stem theft by making transportation of a stolen vehicle across state lines a federal offense. The act significantly expanded the policing powers of the Bureau of Investigations (the name was changed to Federal Bureau of Investigations in 1935).

With the end of World War I, Congress approved legislation terminating federal control of the nation's railroads and shipping industry. The Esch-Cummins Transportation Act of 1920 provided temporary financial assistance to the private railroad carriers during the first six months of the transition period. Named after sponsors Rep. John J. Esch of Wisconsin and Sen. Albert B. Cummins of Iowa, it also increased the authority of the Interstate Commerce Commission to regulate the railroads. The Jones Merchant Marine Act of 1920, sponsored by Sen. Wesley L. Jones of Washington, relegated the U.S. Shipping Board to a regulatory role similar to that of the Interstate Commerce Commission. Government ships were sold to private operators with the proceeds to be used for the construction of new vessels. The board was empowered to propose shipping routes, promote ship construction, and the improvement of port facilities.

Some 9,000 American Indian soldiers and sailors served in the armed services during the war. In 1919, those Indians who received an honorable discharge were afforded the opportunity to become citizens, five years before the Indian Citizenship Act granted citizenship to all American Indians. Subsequently, following months of careful consideration, work was completed on the National Defense Act of 1920, which provided for the postwar reorganization of the U.S. Army. This legislation marked the first time after a war that Congress debated at length the peacetime role of the army. Ultimately, it was decided to organize the army into tactical formations capable of a logically planned response to an emergency. The act acknowledged and authorized the historical practice of the United States having a standing peacetime army too small to be expanded to meet the needs of a large war and reliance on a new force of citizen-soldiers when large-scale mobilizations were necessary.

Also in 1920, the federal government was authorized to regulate hydroelectric power rates, control the recovery of valuable resources on public lands, and provide retirement annuities to federal employees. The Federal Power Commission was created to monitor the development of hydroelectric power on public lands and navigable streams and to set rates charged for such electricity. The U.S. Geological Survey was given the responsibility of overseeing exploration and leasing of federal lands where mineral, oil, and gas deposits existed. The Smith-Fess Vocational Rehabilitation Act of 1920 established the first broad-based federal program to provide vocational assistance to people whose disabilities were not the result of war. The fact that people born with disabilities, not just injured war veterans, were covered under the act, illustrated that Congress was beginning to have an appreciation for all people with disabilities.

During the first two decades of the twentieth century, pressure from federal employees and their representatives resulted in more than one hundred bills being introduced in Congress to provide a pension plan for federal civil servants. Finally on May 22, 1920, prompted by growing needs for an efficient and humane method of removing tenured employees whose most productive years were behind them and for reducing the federal bureaucracy to prewar levels, a civil service retirement bill cosponsored by the chairmen of the House and Senate Civil Service Committees became law. The first year after its enactment, approximately 330,000 federal employees became covered by the act. A second civil service reform act that July resulted in the first full-scale, enforced government hiring laws that gave a preference to nondisabled veterans, the widows of veterans, and the wives of injured soldiers. The initial enactment, a rider to the Census Act of 1919, only granted a veterans preference to those seeking employment in Washington, D.C. The second, a provision in a deficiency act extended the veterans preference to appointments anywhere in the classified service. Federal agencies were prohibited from using appropriated funds to lobby Congress following extensive use of telegrams by government agencies urging citizens to lobby members on legislation. The intent of the anti-lobbying statute was to protect the separation of powers by preventing executive agencies from pressuring legislators through the public.

Republican Warren G. Harding was elected president in 1920 on a platform of returning America to "normalcy." Harding's electoral vote margin over Democrat James M. Cox of Ohio was 404 to 127. The GOP vice presidential candidate was Calvin Coolidge; the Democrats,' Franklin D. Roosevelt. Republicans retained control of Congress, increasing their majorities in both houses.

Major Acts

Nineteenth Amendment. Amended the Constitution by extending the right of suffrage to women, stating that the "right of citizens of the United States to vote shall not be denied or abridged by the United States or by any State on account of sex." Approved June 5, 1919 (41 Stat. 362). Ratified by the requisite number of states August 26, 1920.[1]

Veterans Preference Act of 1919. Provided that preference "shall be given" in making appointments to clerical and other positions throughout the federal classified system "to honorably discharged soldiers, sailors, and marines, and widows of such and to the wives of injured soldiers, sailors and marines who themselves are not qualified, but whose wives are qualified to hold such positions." Approved July 11, 1919 (41 Stat. 37). The Census Act of March 3, 1919, contained a rider that granted preference in appointment in the classified service in Washington, D.C. to all honorably discharged soldiers, sailors, and marines and to their widows (40 Stat. 1293, Sec. 6).

Anti-Lobbying Act. Prohibited federal agencies, without express authorization from Congress, from using appropriated funds "directly or indirectly to pay for any personal service, advertisement, telegram, telephone, letter, printed or written matter, or other device, intended or designed to influence in any manner a Member of Congress to favor or oppose" legislation or appropriations. Allowed federal officers and employees to communicate with members only if requested to by a member who deemed it "necessary for the efficient conduct of public business." Approved July 11, 1919 (41 Stat. 68, Sec. 6).

National Prohibition Act (Volstead Act). Placed responsibility for enforcement of the Eighteenth Amendment with the Internal Revenue Bureau, and created the position of commissioner of Prohibition to administer the act. Defined intoxicating beverages as those containing more than one-half of 1 percent of alcohol, and specified penalties for the manufacturing, transportation, sale, and possession of liquor, except for industrial, medicinal, and sacramental religious purposes. Presidential veto overridden by Congress. Became law without the president's signature October 28, 1919 (41 Stat. 305–323). *(Eighteenth Amendment, p. 210)*

National Motor Vehicle Theft Act (Dyer Act). Made it a federal crime to drive a stolen vehicle across a state line or to deal in vehicles that had been driven across state lines. Imposed harsh sentences, up to ten years imprisonment plus fines. Approved October 29, 1919 (41 Stat. 324–325).

Citizenship for American Indian Veterans. Provided that any American Indian who received an honorable discharge from military service during World War I could, if he desired it, apply for citizenship and be granted it by a competent court without affecting rights to tribal or other Indian property. Approved November 6, 1919 (41 Stat. 350).

Mineral Leasing Act of 1920. Provided that deposits of coal, gas, oil, phosphate, shale, and sodium found on federal lands could be acquired through a leasing system, instead of by securing a patent, with royalties being paid to the United States as landowner.

Allocated 37.5 percent of the leasing royalties to the states in which the lands were located for education and roads, 52.5 percent for reclamation projects, and 10 percent to the federal Treasury. Approved February 25, 1920 (41 Stat. 437–451).

Transportation Act of 1920 (Esch-Cummins Act). Provided for the return of the railroads from federal to private control on March 1, 1920. Guaranteed that during the first six months of private operation railroads would receive earnings equal to the amount they would have received if federal control had continued. Allowed carriers ten years to pay for improvements made to their properties by the government, and established a loan fund to assist carriers in meeting maturing obligations, purchase new equipment, and improve operations. Directed the Interstate Commerce Commission (ICC) to fix rates that "under honest, efficient, and economical management" would allow the railroads a fair return on their investment. Authorized the Interstate Commerce Commission to recommend consolidation of competing railroad lines. Stipulated that carriers receiving a yearly net income in excess of 6 percent were to turn over one-half of their excess to the ICC to be held in a revolving loan fund for weaker railroads. Created a Railroad Labor Board to arbitrate labor disputes. Approved February 28, 1920 (41 Stat. 456–499). *(Railway Labor Act of 1926, p. 228)*

Civil Service Retirement Act of 1920. Provided pensions for permanent competitive employees in the executive branch and to regular employees of the District of Columbia government who had rendered at least fifteen years of service. Credit under the system was given for honorable active military service not used as a basis for a military retirement benefit under another law. Established three automatic retirement ages—sixty-two, sixty-five, and seventy. Provided retirement annuities based on the average of an employee's annual base salary for the last ten years of their career and length of service, up to thirty years. Required a 2.5 percent salary deduction from each covered employee's basic salary to be credited to a Civil Service Retirement Fund. Approved May 22, 1920 (41 Stat. 614–620).

Fess-Smith Civilian Vocational Rehabilitation Act. Served to extend the designation of disability legitimacy by providing federal funds at a 50 percent matching rate to state rehabilitation agencies for vocational training, job placement, and counseling by trained professionals to persons who, "by reason of a physical defect or infirmity, whether congenital or acquired by accident, injury, or disease [are], or may be expected to be, totally or partially incapacitated." Approved June 2, 1920 (41 Stat. 735–737).

National Defense Act of 1920. Provided for the restructuring of the land forces of the United States into three components: the Regular Army, the National Guard, and the Organized Reserves, which could be so regulated in peacetime that each could contribute its appropriate share of troops in a war emergency. Authorized a maximum Regular Army officer strength of 17,726 officers, and a maximum Regular Army enlisted strength of 280,000 men, a maximum National Guard of 435,000 men, and created three new branches—air service, chemical warfare service, and finance department. Charged the War Department with mobilization planning and preparation for the event of war. Approved June 4, 1920 (41 Stat. 759–812).

Women's Bureau Created. Established a Women's Bureau in the Department of Labor to "formulate standards and policies which shall promote the welfare of wage-earning women, improve their working conditions, increase their efficiency, and advance their opportunities for profitable employment." Authorized the bureau to investigate and report to the Department "upon all matters pertaining to the welfare of women in industry." Approved June 5, 1920 (41 Stat. 987).

Jones Merchant Marine Act. Declared that it was the policy of the "United States to do whatever was necessary to develop and encourage the maintenance" of a merchant marine "sufficient to carry the greater portion of its commerce and serve as a naval or military auxiliary in time of war or national emergency, ultimately to be owned and operated privately by the citizens of the United States." Directed the U.S. Shipping Board to determine as promptly as possible the shipping routes that should be established to promote foreign and coastwise trade and to sell or charter the vessels necessary to maintain these services. Provided that if no private citizen were willing to provide the service on terms satisfactory to the board, it would operate the vessels until the business could be sold at a satisfactory price. Reorganized the board and extended its life, and authorized the board to sell government-built ships to private operators, the proceeds up to $25 million to be used for loans to private owners for the construction of new craft. Delegated to the United States Shipping Board Emergency Fleet Corporation administration of the loans. Repealed emergency war legislation relating to U.S. shipping. Approved June 5, 1920 (41 Stat. 988–1008).

Federal Water Power Act. Created a Federal Power Commission, consisting of the secretaries of war, interior, and agriculture, to exercise administrative control over all hydroelectric power–generating facilities erected on federal lands and over navigable rivers. Authorized the commission to issue licenses for fifty years to concerns desiring to construct and operate such facilities, require uniform accounting systems, and regulate the rates of companies selling hydroelectric power across state lines. Approved June 10, 1920 (41 Stat. 1063–1077).

Note

1. U.S. Senate, *The Constitution of the United States: Analysis and Interpretation,* 108th Cong., 2d sess., 2004, S. Doc. 108–17, 36, n. 11.

Sixty-seventh Congress
March 4, 1921, to March 3, 1923

First session—April 11, 1921, to November 23, 1921

Second session—December 5, 1921, to September 22, 1922

Third session—November 20, 1922, to December 4, 1922

Fourth session—December 4, 1922, to March 3, 1923

Special session of the Senate—March 4, 1921, to March 15, 1921

(Administration of Warren G. Harding, 1921–1923)

Historical Background

Eight days after taking office, President Warren G. Harding appointed a citizens' committee headed by Charles G. Dawes to examine the needs of the hundreds of thousands of veterans returning from World War I. The Dawes Committee quickly concluded that veterans' care in the United States was in a "deplorable" condition and recommended the creation of an independent federal agency to attend to their needs. In response, Congress established the Veterans Bureau, the forerunner of the Department of Veterans Affairs. *(Department of Veterans Affairs Established, p. 394)*

The ravages of World War I left millions in Europe facing poverty, distress, hunger, and disease. As Europeans looked toward America, where the hope of a new life seemed to beckon, the postwar United States faced serious unemployment and housing problems as well as growing anti-immigration sentiment. Congress, in attempting to balance these pressures, approved the nation's first Immigration Quota Act, which permitted approximately 357,000 aliens to enter the United States each year. Most were from northern and western Europe. The act also effectively limited immigration from southern and eastern Europe. Recent large influxes

of immigration from those areas had been criticized on the grounds that the people were "too foreign" to be successfully assimilated and that they included "radicals" and communists. Throughout this period, public concern emerged over alleged acts of disloyalty, terror, and sabotage by various immigrant and leftist groups. With the enactment of the Cable Act, a married woman could be granted citizenship independent of her husband's status.

The National Budget and Accounting Act of 1921 marked the first step in the reform of the national budget process. It delegated to the president the responsibility for formulating an annual budget to be presented to Congress and established the Bureau of the Budget to "assemble, correlate, revise, reduce, or increase the estimates of the several [federal] departments or establishments." It also created the General Accounting Office to conduct an independent audit of government accounts. The lobbying efforts of a coalition of women's groups secured passage of the Sheppard-Towner Act of 1921, which allocated federal monies to the states for rural prenatal and baby care centers. The legislation was sponsored by Sen. Morris Sheppard of Texas and Rep. Horace M. Towner of Iowa. Also, in response to a request from Secretary of the Treasury Andrew W. Mellon for authority to deal with the problem of collecting the more than $10 billion the United States had loaned its allies during World War I, Congress created the World War Foreign Debt Commission. Passage of the first major tax bill following World War I marked the end of the extraordinary session of Congress called by President Harding to meet April 11, 1921, for the purpose of revising the federal revenue and tariff laws. Twice before, President Wilson had urged Congress to revise the Revenue Act of 1918, but his words fell upon the ears of a Congress dominated by a hostile party.

With the Republican landslide of November 1920, circumstances changed dramatically and soon after Harding's inauguration the extraordinary session convened. As passed, the 1921 revenue act pleased almost no one. Critics complained that it was a pastiche of unrelated, politically driven compromises. Republicans were disappointed in its modest rate reductions.

The Federal Aid Highway Act of 1921 established the basis for the federal aid highway program, which remained essentially unchanged until the Federal Highway Act of 1956. The act was the first to mandate that federal funds be used for roads that "were interstate in character," and launched the idea of a national highway system as well as a sustained period of highway construction that lasted until the United States entered World War II. This enactment laid the foundation for modern highway building in the United States, and "It remains the single most important piece of legislation in the creation of a national network—far more important than the later interstate highway bill, which would not have been possible, or necessary, without it. Prior to its passage, America had no grand plan for its roads, and the federal government had no legal interest in what the act termed 'an adequate connecting system of highways, interstate in character.' "[1]

Between 1921 and 1923, the farm bloc in Congress used the discontent of farmers in the South and Midwest, who were burdened with high interest rates and heavy property taxes, to achieve several significant legislative victories. President Harding's support in these efforts proved invaluable. The Packers and Stockyards Act authorized the secretary of agriculture to regulate and preserve competition among producers of livestock, poultry, and dairy products. The Grain Futures Act established government regulation of the commodity exchanges. The Capper-Volstead Act, sponsored by Sen. Arthur Capper of Kansas and Rep. Andrew J. Volstead of Minnesota, exempted farm cooperatives from antitrust laws. The Agricultural Credits Act provided short-term (six months to three years) loan assistance to farmers.

The outstanding diplomatic achievement of the Harding administration was the Conference on the Limitation of Armaments (Washington Armament Conference), which was held in Washington, D.C., from November 12, 1921, through February 6, 1922. The United States, Great Britain, France, Italy, and Japan as well as Belgium, China, Portugal, and the Netherlands were all represented at the proceedings. The delegates focused on resolving competing interests in the Pacific and Far East, and they reached agreement on a schedule of limitations and reductions on naval armaments. The conference produced seven treaties. The most important were the Four-Power Treaty, the Five-Power Naval Limitation Treaty, and the Nine-Power Treaty, all of which were ratified by the Senate in March 1922.

The Fordney-McCumber Tariff Act of 1922 established the highest tariff rates up to that time and gave the president, upon the recommendation of the Tariff Commission, power to raise or lower rates as much as 50 percent under certain conditions. The legislation was sponsored by Rep. Joseph W. Fordney of Michigan and Sen. Porter J. McCumber of North Dakota.

Responding to a backlog of cases in the federal courts, Congress in 1922 established a new form of court administration that advanced the institutionalization of an independent judiciary. Creation of the conference of senior circuit judges, later to be known as the Judicial Conference of the United States, was the culmination of more than a decade of public debate on the reform of judicial administration. The act, the first major reform of the federal judiciary since 1789, provided a formal mechanism by which members of the federal judiciary might develop national administrative policies, reassign judges temporarily, and recommend legislation. Increasingly vocal dissatisfaction over the lack of rigor in federal personnel classification policies prompted passage of the Classification Act of 1923, the first major legislation to provide for uniform job positions, salaries, and promotions in the federal government. Introduction of the principle of "equal compensation for equal work irrespective of sex" was a significant shift from past practice in both the public and private sectors. A personnel classification board was created to rationally group public positions into classes on the basis of comparable duties, responsibilities, and skills of each function.

Despite President Harding's considerable legislative success, the American electorate as a result of the 1922 midterm congressional elections reduced the Republican majorities in both the Senate and the House. Even many of the newly elected Republicans were disenchanted with the administration.

Major Acts and Treaties

Immigration Quota Act. Limited the number of persons of any nationality entering the United States each year to 3 percent of the foreign-born persons of that nationality listed in the 1910 census. Provided that no more than 20 percent of any nationality admissible during a year could be admitted in a single month. Set a total limit of approximately 357,000 immigrants per year. Approved May 19, 1921 (42 Stat. 5–7).

Budget and Accounting Act. Required the president to submit annual budget recommendations to Congress including estimates of expenditures and receipts for the following fiscal year as well as the current and previous fiscal years. Created the Bureau of the Budget (renamed the Office of Management and Budget in 1970), with a presidentially appointed director, to assist the president in carrying out his budgetary responsibilities. Established the General Accounting Office, under the comptroller general of the United States, for carrying out independent audits of the government's income and disbursements. Approved June 10, 1921 (42 Stat. 20–27).

Establishment of Veterans Bureau. Created the Veterans Bureau, an independent agency directly responsible to the president for administering all forms of veterans relief. Approved August 9, 1921 (42 Stat. 147–157).

Packers and Stockyards Act. Authorized the secretary of agriculture to regulate the operations of livestock dealers. Required operators of stockyards and facilities involved in producing poultry and dairy products to register with the department of agriculture and file a schedule of their charges. Prohibited any unfair, discriminatory, or manipulative practices that would result in a monopoly in the sale of such products. Approved August 15, 1921 (42 Stat. 159–169).

Federal Aid Highway Act of 1921. Provided $75 million in matching funds to the states for highway construction. Mandated that 7 percent of a state's total highway mileage be for federal-aid highways, divided into two categories: primary (interstate) routes; and secondary (intercounty rural) routes. Stipulated that primary routes received 60 percent of the money, while secondary routes received 40 percent. Required state highway departments to maintain all roads built with federal funds. Prohibited the use of federal funds for maintenance. Required states to coordinate their interstate sections so they did not suddenly end at a state's border. Approved November 9, 1921 (42 Stat. 212–219).

Sheppard-Towner Maternity and Infancy Act. Allocated federal aid to state programs that offered health care for mothers and children, particularly in rural areas. Authorized an annual appropriation of $1 million for a period of five years. Approved November 23, 1921 (42 Stat. 224–226).

Revenue Act of 1921. Reduced top marginal rate on individuals and repealed the excess-profits tax, the transportation taxes, and some luxury taxes. Reduced slightly the maximum surtaxes on individual incomes and increased the personal exemptions of heads of families and dependents. Permitted net losses of one year to be offset against net income of following years. Expanded the definition of tax exempt charitable organizations and permitted an estate tax deduction for charitable contributions. Introduced preferential treatment for capital gains at a rate of 12.5 percent. Approved November 23, 1921 (42 Stat. 227–321).

World War Foreign Debt Commission Created. Created a five-member World War Foreign Debt Commission consisting of the secretary of the Treasury and four members appointed by the president to work out a schedule for repayment of U.S. loans to foreign governments during World War I. Provided that refunding arrangements not extend beyond June 15, 1947 (twenty-five years), and that the interest rate be not less than 4.25 percent. Approved February 13, 1922 (42 Stat. 363). The act was amended in 1923 to provide for the repayment of Great Britain's debt over a sixty-two-year period at an average interest rate of 3.3 percent. Other adjustments followed. Approved February 28, 1923 (42 Stat. 1325–1327).

Cooperative Marketing Act (Capper-Volstead Act). Exempted agricultural cooperatives from the application of antitrust laws by allowing farmers to engage in cooperative buying and selling. Empowered the secretary of agriculture to prevent cooperatives from achieving and maintaining monopolies through hearings and court action. Approved February 18, 1922 (42 Stat. 388–389).

Four-Power Treaty. Abrogated the Anglo-Japanese Alliance of 1902 and provided that the United States, Great Britain, France, and Japan would respect each other's insular possessions in the Pacific Ocean. Concluded December 13, 1921. Ratification advised by the Senate March 24, 1922 (43 Stat. 1646–1651, Part 2).

Five-Power Naval Limitation Treaty. Provided that no new capital ships (defined as warships in excess of ten thousand tons with guns larger than eight inches) would be built by the signatories during the next ten years, and established a capital ship ratio of 5:5:3:1.75:1.75 for the United States, Great Britain, Japan, France, and Italy, respectively. Concluded February 6, 1922. Ratification advised by the Senate March 29, 1922 (43 Stat. 1655–1685, Part 2).

Nine-Power Treaty. Expressed agreement between the United States, Great Britain, France, Italy, Japan, Belgium, Holland, Portugal, and China to respect the "sovereignty, the independence, and the territorial and administrative integrity" of China and to maintain the principle of the open door. Concluded February 6, 1922. Ratification advised by the Senate March 30, 1922 (44 Stat. 2113–2121, Part 3).

Conference of Senior Circuit Judges Act. Established the conference of senior circuit judges consisting of the Chief Justice of the Supreme Court and the chief judge from each judicial circuit to advise Congress on the administrative needs of the judiciary. Required the chief judge in each district to prepare an annual report on the state of their district that the conference could use to suggest temporary transfers of judges, pending the approval of all courts involved. Authorized the conference to develop administrative policies and recommend legislation to Congress. Authorized 24 new district court judgeships. Approved September 14, 1922 (42 Stat. 837–840).

Fordney-McCumber Tariff Act. Raised rates on agricultural raw materials from 38 percent to 49 percent and on other commodities from 31 percent to 34 percent. Special protection was given to sugar and textile interests. Authorized the president to change individual tariff rates on the recommendation of the Tariff Commission (established in 1916), but such changes were limited to 50 percent of the congressional rates. Approved September 21, 1922 (42 Stat. 858–990).

Grain Futures Act. Established a federal licensing system that required grain commodity exchanges to be designated by the federal government as a "contract market." Authorized the secretary of agriculture to designate a board of trade as a contract market if it was located at the terminal of a market where grain sold was subject to futures contracts; allowed representatives of the Departments of Agriculture and Justice to inspect its books and records; prevented its members from disseminating false and misleading crop or market information; and provided established procedures to prevent manipulation of prices. Established a commission composed of the secretaries of agriculture and commerce and the attorney general to suspend or revoke the registration of an exchange as a contract market if it did not meet specific standards. Approved September 21, 1922 (42 Stat. 998–1003). Congress had enacted the Grain Futures Trading Act of 1921 (42 Stat. 187–191), which in part imposed a prohibitive tax of twenty cents per bushel on options and on grain futures contracts that were not traded on exchanges approved by the government. The U.S. Supreme Court in *Hill v. Wallace*, 259 U.S. 44 (1922) held that the 1921 act was an unconstitutional exercise of the congressional taxing power.

Cable Act. Granted a married woman U.S. citizenship independent of her husband's status. Provided that a woman would no longer lose her citizenship if she married an alien, nor would she automatically gain citizenship by marriage to an American citizen. Approved September 22, 1922 (42 Stat. 1021–1022).

Agricultural Credits Act. Authorized the creation of twelve Federal Intermediate Credit Banks, one for each Federal Land Bank district under the jurisdiction of the Federal Farm Loan Board. Capitalized each bank with $5 million subscribed by the government. Authorized the banks to make short-term loans (ranging from six months to three years) on land, crops, livestock, personal notes, and equipment. Authorized the creation of agricultural credit corporations by private interests. Approved March 4, 1923 (42 Stat. 1454–1482).

Classification Act of 1923. Provided for a standard classification of duties and responsibilities of federal personnel occupations and positions with salary levels assigned to the resulting positions. Divided work into five services—professional and scientific service; subprofessional service; clerical, administrative, and fiscal service; custodial service; and custodial-mechanical service. Applied only to the positions in Washington, D.C., and not to "the field" as government offices outside the Washington headquarters were known. Created a Personnel Classification Board to administer the act, and especially to "review" and "revise" allocations made by department officials. Approved March 4, 1923 (42 Stat. 1488–1499).

Note

1. Earl Swift, *The Big Roads: The Untold Story of the Engineers, Visionaries, and Trailblazers Who Created the American Superhighways* (Boston, Mass.: Houghton Mifflin Harcourt, 2011), 74.

Sixty-eighth Congress
March 4, 1923, to March 3, 1925

First session—December 3, 1923, to June 7, 1924
Second session—December 1, 1924, to March 3, 1925
(Administration of Warren G. Harding, 1921–1923; first administration of Calvin Coolidge, 1923–1925)

Historical Background

President Warren G. Harding died of a heart attack in San Francisco on August 2, 1923, while on a lengthy tour of the West Coast and Alaska. Calvin Coolidge, his vice president, was sworn in seven hours later, on August 3. Harding's death occurred as a wide range of scandals perpetrated by his political allies and cabinet members were being revealed. Although the president himself was never implicated in any wrongdoing, his administration was permanently and irreparably tarnished. In his first annual message of December 6, Coolidge called for reorganization and consolidation of the U.S. Foreign Service, revision of laws affecting the Veterans Bureau, and additional immigration limits on certain nationalities. Within less than a year, all three of the proposals had been enacted into law.

Soon after the end of the First World War, the American Legion had launched a movement to secure an additional bonus for former servicemen to compensate for the difference between their salary while in uniform and what they would have earned as civilians. Congress had approved the idea in 1922, but President Harding objected to the bill because no additional funds were provided to make the payments. Using similar reasoning, President Coolidge vetoed a second bonus bill in May 1924. This time, however, both houses of Congress overrode the veto, but actual payment was deferred until 1945. Although the Rogers Foreign Service Act

was not a radical departure from previous legislation, it was the culmination of a long struggle to remove the diplomatic and foreign service from the political arena. The Immigration Quota Act of 1924 changed the census basis for quotas from 1910 to 1890, reduced nationality quotas from 3 to 2 percent, and provided for establishment of permanent quotas based on national origin.

Surpluses in the federal Treasury prompted income tax cuts in 1924 that reduced both normal rates and surcharges. However, estate taxes were increased and a gift tax was created. Many of the tax cuts were made in response to recommendations by Secretary of the Treasury Andrew W. Mellon.

Through the Indian Citizenship Act, Congress granted citizenship to all noncitizen Indians born within the territorial limits of the United States. By this time, however, two-thirds of Native Americans were already citizens. Also in June 1924, a proposed constitutional amendment regulating child labor was submitted to the states for ratification. Congress crafted the amendment in frustration over twice seeing the U.S. Supreme Court strike down statutes abolishing child-made goods: one as an unlawful use of Congress's commerce power (*Hammer v. Dagenhart* [1918]) and the other as an improper use of its power to tax (*Bailey v. Drexel Furniture Company* [1922]). Supporters of the child labor amendment, however, were unable to gain the required three-fourths approval of the states needed for ratification. With passage of the Fair Labor Standards Act in 1938, which included restrictions on child labor, the issue became moot and a constitutional remedy was no longer necessary.

As a consequence of the Kelly Act, approved in 1925, commercial air carriers within four years assumed control over all U.S. Postal Service airmail routes previously operated by the government. The Air Mail Act, sponsored by Rep. Melville C. Kelly of Pennsylvania, also paved the way for federal regulation of the airline industry and provided the economic basis for development of commercial aviation in the United States.

Approval of the Clarke-McNary Reforestation Act helped satisfy appeals by the lumber industry for more adequate protection of its timberlands from fire, disease, and insects. The legislation, sponsored by Rep. John D. Clarke of New York and Sen. Charles L. McNary of Oregon, also allowed the federal government to purchase lands needed for lumber production, provided for federal-state cooperation in producing and distributing forest-tree seedlings, and created the impetus for establishment of state forestry agencies.

Rural sociology was established as a legitimate research discipline in the nation's agricultural experiment stations through the Purnell Act. This marked the first time research in the fields of rural economics, sociology, and home economics was emphasized as part of a program of the experiment stations. Ultimately, it proved to be the principal stimulus for the establishment of rural sociology programs in universities, and government rural sociological research. Only after a long and acrimonious debate was the "farm bloc" successful in securing passage of the Hoch-Smith Resolution of 1925. Passed as a direct result of the postwar difficulties experienced by the nation's farmers, it declared that Congress favored the adjustment of rail rates among the several industries, particularly agriculture, to promote their free interchange and commercial development. The act explicitly required the Interstate Commerce Commission (ICC) to give consideration to the relationship between agricultural freight rates and agricultural incomes.

Through the lobby efforts of Chief Justice William Howard Taft, the Supreme Court gained more control over its caseload with the passage of the Judiciary Act of 1925. The "judges' bill," drafted by three of the Court's justices—Willis Van Devanter, James C. McReynolds, and George Sutherland—afforded the Court greater discretion in its ability to select cases proposed for appeal. It was thus able to devote additional time and energy to constitutional issues and important federal legal questions. The basic purpose of the Federal Arbitration Act of 1925 was to address the needs of businesses frustrated by the unwillingness of courts to

enforce arbitration agreements, and to arbitrate and change the existing rules against arbitration. It provided the first federal legislation governing domestic and international arbitration agreements, put arbitration agreements on the same legal footing as other contracts, and required the judicial enforcement of arbitration agreements in any "contract evidencing a transaction involving commerce."

With passage of the Helium Act of 1925, the United States demonstrated early its commitment to this inert gas with many unique and useful properties. Need for a law requiring conservation was a foremost concern because it was estimated that 500 million cubic feet of helium was being wasted annually as a result of non-extraction of particular helium-rich natural gases. Prior to 1960 the federal government was the only domestic producer of helium.

President Coolidge signed the Federal Corrupt Practices Act, the basic campaign financing law that remained in effect until 1972, in February 1925. This law was drafted in the aftermath of *United States v. Newberry* (1921), a U.S. Supreme Court decision that limited the scope of federal election law. The new act required disclosure of receipts and expenditures by Senate and House candidates as well as groups that sought to influence federal elections in two or more states.

As a result of the 1924 presidential election, Calvin Coolidge won a full term in the White House over a deeply divided Democratic Party that had nominated John W. Davis as its standard-bearer after fourteen days of debate and 103 convention ballots. The Republican ticket of Coolidge and Charles G. Dawes received more popular and electoral votes than both the Democratic ticket of Davis and Charles W. Bryan and the Progressive ticket of Robert M. La Follette and Burton K. Wheeler combined. Democratic hopes for a continuation of the congressional gains of 1922 proved misplaced. The Republicans would remain the majority party in both houses of the Sixty-ninth Congress.

Major Acts

War Adjustment Compensation Act (Soldiers Bonus Act). Authorized a bonus of $1.25 for each day of overseas service and $1.00 for each day of domestic service for veterans of World War I who held the rank of captain and below. Provided a bonus in the form of a twenty-year endowment policy on which ex-servicemen might borrow from the government up to 25 percent of its full value. Presidential veto overridden by Congress. Became law without the president's signature May 19, 1924 (P.L. 120; 43 Stat. 121–131).

Rogers Foreign Service Act. Reorganized and consolidated U.S. diplomatic and consular services into the unified Foreign Service of the United States. Designated permanent officers below the rank of minister as foreign service officers and made them subject to diplomatic as well as consular assignments. Provided for initial appointment by open, competitive examination; subjected new hires to a period of probation; and made promotion strictly on merit. Established new salary and retirement plans. Approved May 24, 1924 (P.L. 135; 43 Stat. 140–146). The legislation was sponsored by Rep. John J. Rogers of Massachusetts.

Immigration Act of 1924 (Johnson-Reed Act). Lowered the annual immigration quota of each nationality to 2 percent for three years based on the 1890 census instead of the 1910 census. Established a complicated system beginning in 1927 apportioning immigration on the basis of "national origin." Completely excluded Japanese immigration. Provided that only 150,000 immigrants should be admitted in any one year. Approved May 26, 1924 (P.L. 139; 43 Stat. 153–169).

Indian Citizenship Act. Granted U.S. citizenship to "all noncitizen Indians born within the territorial limits of the United States." Approved June 2, 1924 (P.L. 175; 43 Stat. 253).

Revenue Act of 1924. Reduced income tax on incomes of less than $4,000 to 2 percent; on incomes from $4,000 to $8,000 to 4 percent; and above $8,000 to 6 percent. Lowered surtax to 1 percent on incomes between $10,000 and $14,000; to 40 percent on incomes in excess of $500,000. Repealed excise taxes on candy, yachts, motor boats, telephone and telegraph messages, and promissory notes. Exempted taxes on automobiles selling for less than $3,000. Increased estate tax rates and imposed a gift tax. Required that

the commissioner of internal revenue publish the tax payments of individuals with large incomes. Approved June 2, 1924 (P.L. 176; 43 Stat. 253–355).

Proposed Child Labor Amendment. Gave Congress the power "to limit, regulate and prohibit the labor of persons under 18 years of age." Sought to achieve uniformity of child labor standards throughout the nation. Approved June 4, 1924 (H. J. Res. 184; 43 Stat. 670). Has not been ratified by the requisite number of states.

World War Veterans Act of 1924. Provided for the decentralization of the activities of the Veterans Bureau by establishing regional offices. Consolidated, codified, revised, and reenacted the laws affecting the establishment of the Veterans Bureau and administration of the War Risk Insurance Act and the Vocational Rehabilitation Act. Approved June 7, 1924 (P.L. 242; 43 Stat. 607–630).

Clarke-McNary Reforestation Act. Expanded the Weeks Forest Purchase Act of 1911 by providing for the extension of national forests over lands already publicly owned, and broadened federal government power to acquire land for national forests within the watersheds of navigable streams. Provided for the federal government to match state (and private) funds to support forest protection, produce and distribute seedlings for reforestation, and aid farmers in using modern forestry practices to develop woodlands. Gave a strong impetus to the establishment of state forestry agencies. Approved June 7, 1924 (P.L. 270; 43 Stat. 653–655). *(Weeks Forest Purchase Act, p. 191)*

Hoch-Smith Resolution. Provided explicit guidance to the Interstate Commerce Commission "in adjusting freight rates that the conditions which at any time prevail in our several industries should be considered insofar as it is legally possible to do so, to the end that commodities may freely move." Specifically directed the commission, in view of the existing depression in agriculture, "to effect with the least practicable delay such lawful changes in the rate structure of the country as will promote the freedom of movement by common carriers of the products of agriculture affected by that depression, including livestock, at the lowest possible lawful rates compatible with the maintenance of adequate transportation service." Approved January 30, 1925 (Res. 46; 43 Stat. 801–802).

Kelly Act (Air Mail Act). Authorized the postmaster general to award contracts for airmail service to commercial air carriers on the basis of competitive bidding. Provided that contractors would receive up to 80 percent of revenue derived from the mail carried. Approved February 2, 1925 (P.L. 359; 43 Stat. 805–806).

Federal Arbitration Act of 1925. Declared that arbitration agreements are "valid, irrevocable, and enforceable except where revocation is permissible under law or equity." and federal courts must compel parties to arbitrate disputes covered by those agreements. Prescribed standards for the enforcement of arbitration agreements and awards. Approved February 12, 1925 (P.L. 401; 43 Stat. 883–886).

Judiciary Act of 1925 (Judges' Bill). Provided that most appeals from federal district courts would go directly to the court of appeals. Limited the right of appeal to those appeals court rulings that held a state law invalid under the Constitution, federal laws, or federal treaties; limited U.S. Supreme Court review of decisions in such cases to the federal question involved. Allowed Supreme Court review of appeals in all other cases only through the issuance of a writ of certiorari that could be granted or denied at the discretion of the Court. Approved February 13, 1925 (P.L. 415; 43 Stat. 936–942).

Purnell Act. Authorized for the first time annual appropriations for agricultural experiment stations to conduct investigations and experiments "bearing directly on the production, manufacture, preparation, use, distribution, and marketing of agricultural products," and "such economic and sociological investigations as have for their purpose the development and improvement of the rural home and rural life." Approved February 24, 1925 (P.L. 458; 43 Stat. 970–972).

Federal Corrupt Practices Act of 1925. Consolidated all federal laws relating to campaign funds except one (the solicitation of political contributions by senators and representatives). Set a limit on campaign expenditures (unless a state law prescribed a lower amount) at $10,000 for individuals seeking a U.S. Senate seat and $2,500 for a U.S. House of Representatives seat or an amount equal to three cents for each vote cast in the last general election for the office, up to $25,000 for the Senate and $5,000 for the House. Approved February 28, 1925 (P.L. 506, Title III; 43 Stat. 1070–1074).

Helium Act of 1925. Declared helium a critical war material, tightly controlled its production, and curtailed exports. Placed the helium program under government control. Made the U.S. Bureau of Mines responsible for all government helium production including the purchase, lease, or condemnation of land, conservation of helium gas, construction and operation of helium plants, conducting experimental work, and leasing of helium under certain conditions. Approved March 3, 1925 (P.L. 545; 43 Stat. 1111–1112).

Sixty-ninth Congress
March 4, 1925, to March 3, 1927

First session—December 7, 1925, to July 3, 1926
Second session—December 6, 1926, to March 3, 1927
Special session of the Senate—March 4, 1925, to
    March 18, 1925
(Second administration of Calvin Coolidge, 1925–1929)

Historical Background

As a consequence of the vast expansion of federal agencies during World War I, President Calvin Coolidge stressed in his December 9, 1925, budget message an urgent need for additional federal office buildings in the nation's capital. Less critical, but still a serious concern, was the lack of sufficient "Federal buildings at strategic locations throughout the country." This problem, according to Coolidge, needed to be addressed to assure the "efficient and economical administration" of the government. Six months later, Congress authorized an expenditure of $165 million for construction of new federal office buildings in the District of Columbia and throughout the country. The act provided the impetus for design and construction of the Federal Triangle, a coherent grouping of monumental public buildings lining the south side of Pennsylvania Avenue between the Capitol grounds and the Treasury Department. Coolidge's request came at a most opportune time—the federal Treasury surplus exceeded a billion dollars. Even after Congress lowered income tax rates, repealed the tax on corporation capital stock, and reduced estate taxes with the Revenue Act of 1926, the general prosperity of the nation (with the exception of many rural areas) still produced a $30 million surplus.

Also prominent among the lingering issues of the immediate postwar period was the need to eliminate governmental control over privately owned railroads. In 1920 the railroads had been returned to private operation after the owners gained guarantees that the advantages of unified operation, achieved under government control, would be retained. When the Railway Labor Board, established under the Transportation Act of 1920, proved ineffective as a mediating force in coping with the railway shopmen's strike of 1922, Congress replaced it through the Railway Labor Act of 1926, which substituted the principle of mediation for compulsory arbitration. Under the Railway Labor Act, a presidentially appointed board of mediation was established to deal with disputes through voluntary arbitration. For the first time, railroad workers were guaranteed the right to organize and bargain collectively through representatives, without interference from their employers.

Federal policy favorable to establishment of agricultural cooperatives was expressed in the Cooperative Marketing Act, which created the division of cooperative marketing within the Department of Agriculture to broaden the ability of farmers and their local, regional, and national cooperatives in gathering and sharing data on output, prices, and demand. It enabled federated cooperative systems and marketing agencies-in-common to effectively function as coordinated entities.

By 1925, commercial aviation was on the verge of moving into the mainstream of American transportation, but federal laws governing the development and regulation of the industry seemed unequal to the task. Enactment of the Air Commerce Act created the legal framework for that transition by placing responsibility for the development and regulation of civilian aviation under the jurisdiction of the secretary of commerce. President Coolidge's long-term goal of seeing the United States become a member of the permanent Court of International Justice seemed closer to realization when the Senate approved adherence by a 76 to 17 margin. The Senate, however, attached five reservations—one of which proved unacceptable to the court—and ultimately prevented the United States from joining.

President Coolidge used his December 7, 1926, annual message to issue a call for legislation to remedy a chaotic series of circumstances that threatened to destroy radio broadcasting in the United States. As a consequence of several court decisions, he told Congress, the authority of the Department of Commerce to regulate radio broadcasting had "broken down," resulting in the establishment of many more stations "than can be accommodated within the limited number of wave lengths available." Congress acted quickly, and on the following day, President Coolidge signed a joint resolution placing a freeze on the issuance of broadcasting licenses until specific legislation addressing the problem could be approved. Congress had been working on the radio legislation prior to the president's message and finished its work by February 1927. The Radio Act of 1927 provided for a Federal Radio Commission with the authority to oversee and regulate broadcasting in the United States.

Concern over large national banks driving small neighborhood state-chartered banks out of business prompted Congress to pass the McFadden Act. During the 1920s, many small banks failed, especially in agrarian and rural states—an average of two banks a day when the law was passed in 1927. The act severely restricted the ability of national banks to establish branches within a state and prohibited interstate branching. These restrictions remained in place until enactment of the Riegle-Neal Interstate Banking and Branching Efficiency Act in 1994.

The Republicans retained control of the Seventieth Congress (1927–1929) as a result of the November 1926 midterm elections, although they lost seven Senate seats and ten House seats.

Major Acts

Permanent Court of International Justice. Granted Senate approval to an agreement whereby the United States would join the Permanent Court of International Justice of the League of Nations (now the World Court).

Subjected the approval to five reservations aimed at safeguarding U.S. interests, one of which, relating to advisory opinions, proved unacceptable to the court. Because agreement could not be reached on this reservation, the United States did not join the court. Approved January 27, 1926.[1]

Revenue Act of 1926. Reduced personal income, inheritance, and corporation taxes; repealed the gift and capital-stock taxes; increased personal income tax exemptions and the corporate income tax rate; abolished a wide variety of excise taxes; and promoted greater uniformity in state inheritance taxation. Repealed the publicity clause relating to income tax returns. Approved February 26, 1926 (P.L. 20; 44 Stat. 9–131, Part 2). Certain provisions of this act were subsequently held unconstitutional in *Heiner v. Donnan*, 285 U.S. 312 (1932).

Air Commerce Act. Empowered the secretary of commerce to designate and establish civilian air routes; to establish, operate, and maintain all necessary air navigation facilities (runway lights for night flying, beacons, control towers, emergency fields, and radar equipment), except airports; arrange for research and development to improve such aids; and investigate accidents. Vested the Air Commerce Bureau with jurisdiction over the safety of civilian aviation, including the licensing of aircraft and pilots involved in interstate commerce. Approved May 20, 1926 (P.L. 254; 44 Stat. 568–576, Part 2). *(Federal Aviation Act, p. 304)*

Railway Labor Act of 1926. Abolished the Railroad Labor Board established under the Transportation Act of 1920, and replaced it with a five-member, presidentially appointed Board of Mediation to settle railroad labor disputes. Substituted the principle of mediation for compulsory arbitration in disputes between railroad employers and employees. Guaranteed rail workers the right to organize and bargain collectively through employee-chosen representatives, without interference from employers. Required railroads and their employees to exert every reasonable effort to voluntarily settle disputes. Provided for appointment of an emergency board by the president to investigate and report in cases of unadjusted disputes. Approved May 20, 1926 (P.L. 257; 44 Stat. 577–587, Part 2). *(Transportation Act of 1920 [Esch-Cummins Act], p. 216)*

Public Buildings Act. Authorized an expenditure of $165 million over a five-year period for construction of federal buildings, $50 million to be expended in the nation's capital and $115 million outside the District of Columbia. Delegated to the secretary of the Treasury the responsibility of "providing suitable accommodations in the District of Columbia for the executive departments, and independent establishments of the Government not under any executive department, and for courthouses, postoffices, immigration stations, customhouses, marine hospitals, quarantine stations, and other public buildings of the classes under the control of the Treasury Department in the States, Territories, and possessions of the United States." Required the secretary of the Treasury to submit annual estimates of monies expended under the authority of the act. Authorized the secretary of the Treasury to acquire a site for a building to house the Supreme Court of the United States. Approved May 25, 1926 (P.L. 281; 44 Stat. 630–635, Part 2).

Cooperative Marketing Act. Established the division of cooperative marketing in the Department of Agriculture to "promote the knowledge of cooperative principles and practices and cooperate in promoting such knowledge, with educational and marketing agencies, cooperative associations, and others." Authorized cooperative associations to "acquire, exchange, interpret, and disseminate past, present, and prospective crop, market, statistical, economic, and other similar information by direct exchange between such persons, and/or such associations or federations thereof, and/or by and through a common agent created or selected by them." Approved July 2, 1926 (P.L. 450; 44 Stat. 802–803).

Radio Control Act of 1927. Created a five-member presidentially appointed Federal Radio Commission (subsequently the Federal Communications Commission) to regulate radio communication according to "public convenience, interest, and necessity." Divided the United States into zones represented by individual commissioners. Empowered the commission with authority to issue and revoke licenses, "to hold hearings, summon witnesses, administer oaths, compel the production of books, documents, and papers and to make such investigations as may be necessary in the performance of its duties." Approved February 23, 1927 (P.L. 632; 44 Stat. 1162–1174, Part 2). *(Communications Act of 1934, p. 245)*

McFadden Banking Act. Permitted national banks and state chartered banks that were members of the Federal Reserve System to establish banks within their state only to the extent that state-chartered banks were authorized to do so. Prohibited banks from having branches in different states. Approved February 25, 1927 (P.L. 639; 44 Stat. 1224–1234).

Note

1. *Journal of the Executive Proceedings of the Senate* (Washington, D.C.: U.S. Government Printing Office, 1931), 64:547–558, part 1.

Seventieth Congress
March 4, 1927, to March 3, 1929

First session—December 5, 1927, to May 29, 1928
Second session—December 3, 1928, to March 3, 1929
(Second administration of Calvin Coolidge, 1925–1929)

Historical Background

During spring of 1927, a disastrous flood in the lower Mississippi Valley left 330 people dead, crops destroyed, and thousands homeless and destitute, and it resulted in damages totaling $300 million. Most of the region's roads, bridges, and railroads were unusable for weeks. The flooding vividly demonstrated the inability of local governments to maintain the levee system being used as the sole means of controlling the Mississippi River. The region turned to the federal government for help in protecting themselves from such disasters in the future, and Congress responded by authorizing $325 million for levees and diversion floodways over the next ten years. With the Flood Control Act of 1928, responsibility for the control of floods in the United States became a federal responsibility.

Further west, levees had also proved so ineffective in containing silt carried by the Colorado River that "in a year was equal to the amount of soil excavated in building the Panama Canal."[1] Construction of a dam in Boulder Canyon on the Arizona-Nevada border appeared to be the only solution to containing the floodwaters. Supporters of the project also stressed that it would generate an enormous amount of hydroelectric power and have the capability of storing irrigation as well as municipal water needed by the burgeoning communities in southern California and, eventually, by Arizona. The project got the go-ahead in

December 1928 and was completed eight years later. The dam was named Hoover Dam in 1930 by the secretary of the interior to honor President Herbert Hoover. After Hoover left office in 1933, the dam was designated Boulder Dam by the new secretary and continued to carry that designation until Congress officially renamed it Hoover Dam in 1947. The Boulder Canyon project marked the beginning of federal construction of large multipurpose water projects.

Efforts to expand the scientific research program of the Forest Service were realized in the McSweeney-McNary Act of 1928, which provided for a comprehensive ten-year timber conservation program. Key provisions of the legislation, sponsored by Rep. John McSweeney of Ohio and Sen. Charles L. McNary of Oregon, included funds for the first nationwide survey of the nation's forest reserves, establishment of forest experiment stations, and state forest fire prevention programs. Passage of the Migratory Bird Conservation Act of 1929, the most important game preservation legislation enacted up to that time, had been preceded by a decade of prolonged and bitter debate. Opponents had challenged earlier conservation proposals on the grounds that they were an unwarranted invasion of the rights of states and would necessitate creation of an unmanageable federal bureaucracy. Only after considerable compromise did a bona fide conservation bill emerge supported by sportsmen and conservationists alike. Among its most important provisions were comprehensive federal regulation of all migratory hunting and authorizations for the purchase of lands intended for use as bird refuges.

In enacting the Jones-White Merchant Marine Act of 1928, Congress sought to bolster America's share of oceanic shipping, which had been deteriorating since the end of World War I. The Jones-White Act increased mail subsidies to noncoastal shippers, appropriated $250 million for ship construction loans, and authorized the sale of remaining government-owned merchant vessels. It also permitted private companies to obtain first-class ships at about one-tenth of their original cost and underwrote the construction of sixty-eight new vessels. Enactment of the first naval construction bill was the culmination of two years of haggling over what the act should include. At the center of the controversy was a clause authorizing the president to suspend all warship construction in the event of a disarmament conference. The Naval Construction Act provided for the construction of fifteen light cruisers and an aircraft carrier over the next three years.

For a number of years prior to 1929, Congress has considered bills relating to the sale of prison-made goods. Extensive hearings were held on these measures relating to the problems attending the sale of such goods, in the open market, in competition with goods manufactured and produced by free labor. The Hawes-Cooper Act was the result of an unprecedented level of cooperation between organized labor and business, who collaborated in this instance against the sale, production, and distribution of "convict-made goods." The primary aim of the act was to "restrict the sale of prisoner-made products on the open market" and to "permit a state, if it so chose, to prohibit the sale of prisoner-made goods, whether made in other states or within its own borders."

Diplomatic discussions between the United States and France, prompted by the latter's desire to guarantee its security, ultimately led to the drafting of the Kellogg-Briand Pact, which was signed in Paris on August 27, 1928. Sixty-two nations eventually joined the treaty, which renounced aggression and outlawed war as "an instrument of national policy." Owing to overwhelming public support of the pact, and the fact that it in no way endangered U.S. sovereignty, the Senate approved it on January 15, 1929, by a vote of 85 to 1. Although it was the most thoroughgoing commitment to peace that the great powers had ever made, it had little tangible effect. In the 1930s, Japan, Italy, and Germany were all aggressors against other nations, and ultimately militarism would plunge the United States into another world war. America's own territorial holdings were officially enlarged in February 1929 when Congress formally accepted the seven Pacific islands comprising American Samoa, which had originally been ceded to the United States in 1900 and 1904 by Samoan high chiefs.

Both the 1928 presidential and congressional elections proved to be a great source of celebration for the Republicans. Herbert Hoover and his running mate Charles Curtis won a popular plurality of more than six million votes over Democrat Alfred E. Smith and his running mate Joseph T. Robinson. The Republican ticket won forty states and 444 electoral votes; the Democratic ticket, eight states and 87 electoral votes.

Major Acts and Treaties

Flood Control Act. Appropriated $325 million for flood control in the Mississippi Valley over a ten-year period. Approved May 15, 1928 (P.L. 391; 45 Stat. 534–539).

Jones-White Merchant Marine Act. Authorized the U.S. Shipping Board and the postmaster general to decide which shipping trade routes should receive mail subsidies and what types of ships should receive the aid. Stipulated that the act was only applicable to vessels that were built in American shipyards, remained under American registry during the entire ten-year term of the mail contracts, and employed crews at least 50 percent of whom were Americans. Established a $250 million ship construction loan fund from which private builders could borrow up to three-quarters of the cost of constructing, reconditioning, or remodeling a vessel. Permitted the sale of government-owned vessels at a low price. Approved May 22, 1928 (P.L. 463; 45 Stat. 689–698).

McSweeney-McNary Act. Authorized a comprehensive forest research program to "insure adequate supplies of timber and other forest products for the people of the United States[,] . . . promote the full use of forest lands in the United States," and "secure the correlation and the most economical conduct of forest research in the Department of Agriculture." Authorized the first comprehensive nationwide survey of forest reserves on all public as well as private lands. Provided for the establishment of regional forest experiment stations throughout the country. Approved May 22, 1928 (P.L. 466; 45 Stat. 699–702).

Boulder Canyon Project Act. Authorized a $165 million appropriation to "construct, operate, and maintain a dam and incidental works in the main stream of the Colorado River at Black Canyon or Boulder Canyon adequate to create a storage reservoir of a capacity of not less than twenty million acre-feet of water." Provided that the act would not take effect until the states of Arizona, California, Colorado, Nevada, New Mexico, Utah, and Wyoming ratified the Colorado River compact. Provided that the monies would be repaid from the proceeds of the sale of electric power and water. Approved December 21, 1928 (P.L. 642; 45 Stat. 1057–1066). Interior Secretary Ray L Wilbur named the Hoover Dam in 1930, an action that was subsequently confirmed in appropriation acts in 1931, 1932, and 1933. After President Herbert Hoover left office, Wilbur's successor, Harold L. Ickes, "in one of his first administrative acts as interior secretary," decreed that henceforth the dam would be called "Boulder Dam rather than Hoover Dam."[2] On April 30, 1947, the name Hoover Dam was restored in legislation signed into law by President Harry S. Truman (P.L. 43; 61 Stat. 56–57).

Kellogg-Briand Pact. Renounced war "as an instrument of national policy," and advocated arbitration as the appropriate means for settling international controversies. Concluded August 27, 1928. Ratification advised by the Senate January 15, 1929 (46 Stat. 2343–2348, Part 2).

Hawes-Cooper Act. Placed a restriction on the marketing of goods made by the "forced labor" prison of inmates. Made all prison-produced goods subject to the laws of the state to which they were shipped, irrespective of the place of origin. Allowed states to prohibit the sale of prison-made goods in their state, even if the goods were produced in another state. Approved January 19, 1929 (P.L. 669; 45 Stat. 1084).

Naval Construction Act of 1929. Authorized construction of fifteen light cruisers and one aircraft carrier within three years. Provided that in the event the United States became a signatory in an international agreement encouraging further naval reductions, the president was "authorized and empowered to suspend in whole or in part any of the naval construction authorized under the act." Approved February 13, 1929 (P.L. 726; 45 Stat. 1165).

Migratory Bird Conservation Act. Provided for comprehensive federal regulation of all migratory bird hunting, and required a federal bird license for migratory bird hunters. Authorized the creation of federal bird refuges. Approved February 18, 1929 (P.L. 770; 45 Stat. 1222–1226).

Administration of American Samoa. "Accepted, ratified, and confirmed" the cession of the six islands that comprise American Samoa as of the time they were ceded by Samoan high chiefs in 1900 and 1904. Declared that "until Congress shall provide for the government of such islands, all civil, judicial, and military powers shall be vested in such person or persons and shall be exercised in such a manner as the President of the United States shall direct." Approved February 20, 1929 (P. Res. 89; 45 Stat. 1253). A seventh island, Swains, a privately owned coral atoll, was made part of American Samoa by a joint resolution approved by Congress on March 4, 1925 (P. Res. 75; 43 Stat. 1357).

Notes

1. Paul W. Gates, *History of Public Land Law Development* (Washington, D.C.: U.S. Government Printing Office, 1968), 685.

2. Joseph E. Stevens, *Hoover Dam: An American Adventure* (Norman, Okla.: University of Oklahoma Press, 1988), 174. See also U.S. House Committee on Public Lands, "Restore the Name of Hoover Dam," 80th Cong., 1st sess., 1947, H. Rept. 87.

Seventy-first Congress
March 4, 1929, to March 3, 1931

First session—April 15, 1929, to November 22, 1929
Second session—December 2, 1929, to July 3, 1930
Third session—December 1, 1930, to March 3, 1931
Special sessions of the Senate—March 4, 1929, to March 5, 1929; July 7, 1930, to July 21, 1930
(Administration of Herbert Hoover, 1929–1933)

Historical Background

Between June 1924 and May 1928, a powerful agricultural alliance of western Republicans and southern Democrats labored on Capitol Hill to gain approval of a bill to create a Federal Farm Board that would purchase specific crop surpluses and hold them until market prices rose or sell them abroad for whatever price was attainable with the loss being underwritten through an equalization tax. President Calvin Coolidge twice vetoed the measure, arguing that it was special interest legislation involving unconstitutional price fixing. As Congress continued to wrestle with the problems associated with the depressed condition of American agriculture, the plight of the farmer had emerged as one of the dominant issues of the 1928 presidential election. Fulfilling a campaign pledge, President Herbert Hoover summoned a special session of Congress shortly after his inauguration.

On April 15, 1929, Congress approved the administration-sponsored Agricultural Marketing Act, which established a Federal Farm Board with power to oversee the purchase and sale of surplus farm commodities. The board was given a $500 million revolving fund for loans to farm cooperatives to help market crops effectively and control surpluses. The act did not include the plan sought by the congressional farm bloc to subsidize the sale of surplus commodities on the world market.

The chronic depression of the nation's agricultural sector prefigured greater troubles to come. Within months of Hoover's inauguration, the long prosperity of the 1920s came to an end, heralded by the greatest panic in Wall Street history. Throughout the decade, heated consumer spending had fueled industry profits, while dubious corporate mergers and expansions and speculation in stocks grew at a pace that troubled many economists. By mid-1929, the economy seemed first to have plateaued and then to have softened. Confidence collapsed in an unprecedented wave of panic selling on the nation's exchanges between October 24 and 29, 1929, marking the onset of the Great Depression.

Many theories have been offered as to its causes: saturation of the markets for consumer goods such as radios, refrigerators, and automobiles that had sustained much economic growth in the 1920s; widespread speculation in stocks, often bought on margin, with only a small percentage of the purchase price required, that led to wildly inflated values for popular shares; and a banking and financial markets regulatory infrastructure incapable of either restraining excesses or averting the effects of the collapses that resulted.

The market crash was followed by a growing surge of personal and corporate bankruptcies and bank failures, a self-reinforcing process that defeated Hoover's efforts to stimulate recovery and led to endemic unemployment, foreclosures, and widespread human suffering.

Most economic historians hold that the depression's gravity was exacerbated by passage of the Smoot-Hawley Tariff of 1930, sponsored by Sen. Reed Smoot of Utah and Rep. Willis Hawley of Oregon.

Originally intended to aid the agricultural sector by raising duties on imported foodstuffs, the act was transformed during its yearlong gestation period. Effective lobbying resulted in substantial increases in tariff rates on many classes of manufactured goods, on the theory that discouraging imports would stimulate the faltering U.S. economy. The bill in its final form troubled President Hoover and was strenuously criticized by the American Economic Association. Nevertheless, the president signed Smoot-Hawley into law in June. Instead of aiding the hard-pressed farmer, the act drove up prices of imported goods and provoked retaliatory tariff increases by other nations. International trade volume dropped dramatically, and the precipitous decline in prices and production in the United States continued.

Hoover achieved a major bureaucratic reform with the establishment of the Veterans Administration. For the sake of "efficiency, economy, and more uniform administration and better definition of national policies," he reasoned, consolidation of all government programs related to veterans under a single agency made good sense.

The winter of 1928–1929 found the United States in the grip of the worst outbreak of influenza since the 1918 pandemic and no progress was made on fighting the disease. Memories of this occurrence were fresh when the Ransdell Act created the beginning of the National Institutes of Health and affirming public funding of medical research.

A fixed 435-seat House of Representatives was essentially established in 1929 by the Permanent Apportionment Act, which ended the 19th century practice of increasing the House size after every census but one. There have been no permanent increases in the House size since that enactment. The proportional redivision of the House's 435 seats among the states has occurred automatically after every federal census since. The 1929 act "effectively froze the size of the House of Representatives, completing through a statute what arguably only a constitutional amendment can accomplish." It "placed the House's reapportionment on automatic pilot; and in so doing, provided an administrative answer to what previously had been considered a political question."[1]

In 1931, Congress passed the Federal Employment Stabilization Act to develop and implement public and private economic planning strategies, but interest within the federal government did not gain momentum until after the presidential election of Franklin D. Roosevelt, who vigorously pursued such strategies as part of the New Deal. The act was designed to make the timing of federal construction projects compatible with national economic needs. The history of federal legislation regulating compensation issues began in 1931, with the enactment of the Davis-Bacon Act. Adopted at the urging of the Hoover Administration, the act regarded as an emergency measure intended to stabilize the construction industry and ensure that workers involved in a public works project were paid the prevailing wage.

With the designation of Francis Scott Key's "The Star-Spangled Banner" as the national anthem of the United States, Congress officially recognized an emotional bond with the popular anthem that many Americans had long felt. The movement to gain congressional support for a national anthem largely fell on the shoulders of Captain Walter I. Joyce, national patriotic instructor of the Veterans of Foreign Wars. Opponents contended that the hymn was too militant and incited audiences with a warlike attitude. Joyce swayed Congress with petitions bearing the signatures of five million Americans, together with the endorsement of organizations representing fifteen million members.

The November 1930 midterm elections demonstrated that Republican dominance of national politics had played itself out. The Democrats won control of the House, and the Republicans barely hung on to their majority in the Senate.

Major Acts

Permanent Apportionment Act of 1929. Limited the membership of the House of Representatives to 435, a number established after the 1910 census. Created a procedure for automatically reapportioning state delegations in the House after every decennial census under a mathematical formula established by Congress based on shifts in population. Approved June 11, 1929 (P.L. 13; 46 Stat. 26–27, Sec. 22).

Agricultural Marketing Act. Established a Federal Farm Board (made up of eight members and the secretary of agriculture). Created a revolving fund of $500 million that the board could draw from to make low-interest loans to agricultural cooperatives to buy seasonal surpluses and support farm prices. Authorized the board to establish "stabilization corporations" to control and market agricultural surpluses, and to insure cooperatives and stabilization corporations against losses resulting from price fluctuations. Approved June 15, 1929 (P.L. 10; 46 Stat. 11–19).

Ransdell Act. Redesignated the Bureau of Public Health Service's Hygienic Laboratory as the National Institutes of Health, authorized $750,000 for the construction of two buildings, established fellowships for research into basic biological and medical problems, and authorized the acceptance of public donations "for use in ascertaining the cause, prevention and cure of diseases." Approved May 26, 1930 (P.L. 251; 46 Stat. 379–380).

Smoot-Hawley Tariff. Raised import duties on imported agricultural products from 38 percent to 45 percent, providing special protection for sugar, textile, citrus fruit, and cotton, and removed many items from the free list. Reorganized the U.S. Tariff Commission, outlined more specifically its powers, and detailed procedures for its advisory functions in conducting flexible tariffs, unfair trade practices, and foreign discrimination investigations, as well as in carrying out studies and preparing reports on all aspects of the international trade system. Approved June 17, 1930 (P.L. 361; 46 Stat. 590–763).

Veterans Administration Act. Authorized the president to consolidate and reorganize, by executive order, all existing federal programs for veterans (the Veterans Bureau, Pension Bureau, and National Homes for Disabled Soldiers) into a Veterans Administration. Approved July 3, 1930 (P.L. 536; 46 Stat. 1016–1018). On July 21, 1930, President Herbert Hoover established the Veterans Administration as an independent agency by Executive Order 5398.[2]

Federal Employment Stabilization Act of 1931. Established the Federal Employment Stabilization Board composed of the secretary of the Treasury, secretary of commerce, secretary of agriculture, and secretary of labor to advise the president of trends in employment and business activity and "of the existence or approach of periods of business depression and unemployment." Provided that if the president concurred, he was to ask Congress for emergency appropriations to be expended on authorized construction projects. Directed federal departments and agencies to prepare a six-year advance plan "for prompt commencement and carrying out of an expanded program at any time." Approved February 10, 1931 (P.L. 614; 46 Stat. 1084–1087).

Davis-Bacon Act. Required all contractors and subcontractors performing "construction, alteration and/or repair of any public buildings of the United States or the District of Columbia" in excess of $5,000 to pay laborers and mechanics no less than the local prevailing wage. Required that disputes over the prevailing rate be referred to the secretary of labor for a conclusive decision. Approved March 3, 1931 (P.L. 798; 46 Stat. 1494). The threshold for application of the Bacon-Davis Act was lowered to $2,000 in 1935 and has not been changed since.

Adoption of National Anthem. Declared that the "composition consisting of the words and music known as The Star-Spangled Banner is designated the national anthem of the United States of America." Approved March 3, 1931 (P.L. 823; 46 Stat. 1508).

Notes

1. Charles A. Kromkowski and John A. Kromkowski, "Why 435? A Question of Political Arithmetic," *Polity,* v. 24, Autumn 1991, 135.

2. *Public Papers of the Presidents of the United States: Herbert Hoover, 1930* (Washington, D.C.: U.S. Government Printing Office, 1976), 288–289.

Seventy-second Congress
March 4, 1931, to March 3, 1933

First session—December 7, 1931, to July 16, 1932
Second session—December 5, 1932, to March 3, 1933
(Administration of Herbert Hoover, 1929–1933)

Historical Background

As the Great Depression deepened, the nation's financial structure continued to disintegrate. Although President Herbert Hoover endorsed a series of measures that together constituted an unprecedented federal response to the crisis, his efforts to right the economy proved inadequate. The most important of Hoover's proposals was the Reconstruction Finance Corporation (RFC) Act, a prominent feature of his December 9, 1931, annual message. The RFC was authorized in January 1932 to make up to $2 billion in loans to such major economic institutions as banks, insurance companies, and railroads. In July 1932 its borrowing power was increased to $3.3 billion and its functions were enlarged. The RFC was also authorized to make loans to state and local governments for job-creating public works programs. During the first year and a half of its operation, the RFC pumped $3 billion into the economy. By the time President Dwight D. Eisenhower signed a bill ending the RFC in 1953, it had loaned $12 billion, of which only $800 million remained unpaid. Over the years, RFC funds were used to help finance such varied projects as the Golden Gate Bridge, back pay for Chicago schoolteachers, and the expansion of defense production in World War II.

As the European financial crisis worsened, Great Britain abandoned the gold standard in 1931 and speculators overseas began converting paper dollars into gold. Initially, President Hoover sought to have a provision included in the Reconstruction Finance Corporation Act to liberalize the discount rates on RFC bonds, but it was removed by House-Senate conferees. After the White House rejected the suggestion that the United States also leave the gold standard, Hoover successfully obtained legislation permitting member banks of the Federal Reserve System to borrow more freely. The Glass-Steagall Act of 1932, named for sponsors Sen. Carter Glass of Virginia and Rep. Henry B. Steagall of Alabama, authorized the use of government bonds and securities, as well as commercial paper, as collateral against Federal Reserve notes. As a consequence, the credit facilities of the reserve banks were significantly enlarged, increasing by more than $1 billion within three months.

In late 1931 Hoover called a national conference on housing and home ownership. At the conference, he announced his intention to recommend legislation creating a home loan discount bank system for building and loan associations. The purpose of the bill was to allow sound mortgage institutions time to recover, stimulate new home construction, increase employment, and promote home ownership. By 1932, conditions in the housing sector and the closely related savings and loan industry had grown dire. The Federal Home Loan Bank Act of 1932 created a series of banks providing discount facilities for homeowners similar to those made available to the commercial interests by the Federal Reserve Board. The act was designed to facilitate home ownership by providing low-cost funds to banks to use in mortgage and loan creation. It created a system of federally chartered home loan banks for the purpose of placing long-term funds in the hands of local institutions in order to alleviate the pressing need of homeowners for low-cost, long-term installment mortgages. The Federal

Home Loan Bank Board, which was to oversee the discount banks, was the first federal agency to oversee savings and loan institutions.

Under persistent pressure from labor unions, Congress enacted the Norris-LaGuardia Act, which recognized labor's right to organize, limited the power of the federal courts to issue injunctions in labor disputes, and outlawed "yellow dog" contracts, which required workers to promise not to join a union. The legislation was sponsored by Sen. George W. Norris of Nebraska and Rep. Fiorello H. LaGuardia of New York.

Faced with the largest deficit in American history, the Hoover Administration advocated a drastic increase in taxes. Congress responded by passing the Revenue Act of 1932, which imposed the largest peacetime percentage increase in taxes ever enacted. The attempt to balance the federal budget was also seen as a way to reduce the pressure on interest rates, and stimulate the economy. It was estimated at the time that the new law would raise roughly $1.1 billion in new revenue. Many economists since, however, "have blamed the further worsening of the Depression in 1932–33 on the new higher taxes." Others argue that the "greatest failing of Hoover's fiscal policies was in not spending enough, rather than taxing too much."[1]

In the summer of 1932, an estimated fifteen thousand to seventeen thousand unemployed World War I veterans marched on Washington, D.C., to demand immediate payment of adjusted compensation (bonus) certificates provided for in the Soldiers Bonus Act of 1924, but not payable until 1945. Although Congress had overridden President Hoover's veto of a bill in February 1932 authorizing a loan of 50 percent on the certificates, Democratic congressional leaders subsequently decided that the entire bonus should be paid in cash. The Bonus Marchers vowed to remain in Washington until Congress acted. After the Senate defeated the measure in mid-June, most veterans left the capital. Two thousand, however, refused to leave, and the initial attempt to remove them resulted in the deaths of two veterans and two police officers. Only after President Hoover then ordered federal troops to drive the veterans out with cavalry, infantry, and tanks did they finally vacate the various shacks and unused federal buildings that served as their homes during the standoff. Photographs and newsreels depicting American soldiers advancing on American veterans

with fixed bayonets shocked the nation and outraged some observers. *(Soldiers Bonus Act, p. 224)*

"A majority of both parties," the *Washington Post* editorialized in March 1933, had "joined in an effort to end the ridiculous system under which the Government undertook to encourage American industry to create jobs for workless Americans, and then purchased a considerable portion of its supplies from foreign countries."[2] The Buy American Act established a governmental policy to give preference to American products when purchased by the government for public use.

The Seventy-second Congress became the only Congress since 1789 to send more than one constitutional amendment to the states for ratification. With the completion of the ratification process in January and December of 1933, respectively, the Twentieth Amendment changed the beginning of presidential and congressional terms, while the Twenty-first Amendment repealed Prohibition.

On five occasions during the 1920s, the Senate had approved a Lame Duck Amendment, but final congressional action did not come until the Democrats captured the House as a result of the November 1930 elections. The beginning and ending of the presidential and vice presidential term was changed from March 4 to January 20, and future Congresses would assemble on January 3, unless otherwise stipulated by law. The terms of service of members of Congress had historically begun on March 4, and the Constitution had provided that a newly elected Congress would meet at least once a year in December, thirteen months after the elections. The Twentieth Amendment also clarified what happened when a vacancy occurred in the presidency or vice presidency prior to inauguration.

Prohibition, which had taken nearly a century to achieve, was undone in a little more than a decade by two forces. First, reapportionment of the House following the 1930 census had shifted power toward the urban areas that had always opposed Prohibition. Second, the high unemployment rolls of the Depression made the reopening of breweries and the attendant creation of jobs more appealing. After the Democrats gained ninety House seats and won a majority in the Senate as a result of the 1932 elections, it was clear that if the Seventy-second Congress did not act, its successor would.

Democrat Franklin D. Roosevelt on March 4, 1933, was sworn in as the nation's thirty-second president. His campaign promise of "a new deal" was about to unfold. Herbert Hoover's losing effort to win reelection had garnered him 15.8 million popular votes to 22.8 million for Roosevelt. The electoral vote margin was even more lopsided, 59 to 472. Roosevelt's vice presidential running mate was House Speaker John Nance Garner; Hoover's, incumbent vice president Charles Curtis.

Major Acts

Reconstruction Finance Corporation Act. Created a Reconstruction Finance Corporation (RFC) to make "fully and adequately secured" loans to agricultural and livestock credit associations, banks, building and loan associations, insurance companies, mortgage and loan companies, and railroads (with the approval of the Interstate Commerce Commission). Capitalized the RFC at $500 million, to be fully subscribed by the federal government, and authorized it to borrow an additional $1.5 billion by issuing tax-exempt bonds. Empowered the RFC to provide capital for government-owned corporations. Approved January 22, 1932 (P.L. 2; 47 Stat. 5–12).

Glass-Steagall Act of 1932. Authorized Federal Reserve banks to use government bonds and securities as well as commercial paper as collateral for Federal Reserve notes. Made $750 million worth of government gold reserves available for loans to private industry and businesses. Approved February 27, 1932 (P.L. 44; 47 Stat. 56–57).

Twentieth Amendment (Lame Duck Amendment). Declared that Congress would convene each year at noon on January 3 of the year following the elections, and the terms of president and vice president would end at noon on January 20. Specified that the vice president-elect would succeed to the presidency if the president-elect should die before being inaugurated. Provided that the effective date of the amendment would be the fifteenth day of October following its ratification (October 15, 1933). Approved March 2, 1932 (S. J. Res. 14; 47 Stat. 745). Ratified by requisite number of states January 23, 1933.[3] The Seventy-fourth Congress was the first to convene in January under the amendment's provisions, in 1935, and President Franklin D. Roosevelt's 1937 inauguration was the first to be held on January 20.

Norris-LaGuardia Anti-Injunction Act. Restricted the use of court injunctions in labor disputes to prevent strikes and boycotts. Provided for trial by jury for persons cited for violations of injunctions. Prohibited "yellow dog" contracts, by which employers, as a condition of employment, require their workers to promise not to join a union. Approved March 23, 1932 (P.L. 65; 47 Stat. 70–73).

Revenue Act of 1932. Raised personal and corporate income tax rates across the board. Increased income on the highest incomes from 25 to 63 percent, and corporate taxes by almost 15 percent. Doubled the estate tax, and cut personal tax exemptions in half. Imposed new taxes on gasoline, automobiles, trucks, tires, electricity, refrigerators; telephone, telegraph and radio messages; and many luxury and personal items. Approved June 6, 1932 (P.L.154; 47 Stat. 169–289).

Emergency Relief and Construction Act. Extended the scope and functions of the Reconstruction Finance Corporation (RFC), and authorized it to incur a total indebtedness of $3.3 billion. Authorized the RFC to provide $1.5 million in loans for construction by state and local governments of self-liquidating public works, to finance $322 million for public works not required to be self-liquidating, and to furnish $300 million in temporary loans to states unable to finance the relief efforts. Approved July 21, 1932 (P.L. 302; 47 Stat. 709–724).

Federal Home Loan Bank Act. Established a five-member Federal Home Loan Bank Board, whose role was to oversee a system of eight to twelve regional banks empowered to discount home mortgages and construction. Authorized the Federal Home Loan Banks, each of which was a separate corporation, privately owned by its members, to make advances to thrift institutions upon the security of home mortgages. Provided for an initial capitalization of $125 million. Provided that the aggregate outstanding advances made to any member bank could not exceed twelve times the amount paid in by the member for outstanding capital stock held by the bank. Required that member banks subscribe to stock in amounts equal to 1 percent of the subscriber's home mortgages. Empowered each Federal Home Loan Bank to issue bonds and debentures. Approved July 22, 1932 (P.L. 304; 47 Stat. 725–741).

Twenty-first Amendment. Provided for the repeal of the Eighteenth Amendment to the Constitution, thereby legalizing, once again, the manufacture, sale, and transportation of alcoholic liquors everywhere in the Union except in those states, counties, and municipalities where the act was forbidden by law. Approved February 20, 1933 (S. J. Res. 211; 47 Stat. 1625). Ratified by requisite number of states December 5, 1933.[4] *(Eighteenth Amendment, p. 210)*

1933 Buy American Act. Required that the government purchase all goods for public use (articles, materials, or supplies) from American firms, and only American-made materials could be used for construction of public works. Defined as American–made manufactured products which had at least 50 percent of its constituent parts and/or materials originated in the United States. Approved March 3, 1933 (P.L. 428; 47 Stat. 1520–1521, Title III).

Notes

1. Robert S. McElvaine, *The Great Depression: America 1929–1941* (New York: Times Books, 1993), 87–88.

2. "America First," *Washington Post,* February 5, 1933, 6.

3. U.S. Senate, *The Constitution of the United States: Analysis and Interpretation,* 108th Cong., 2d sess., 2004, S. Doc. 108–17, 36, n. 12.

4. *The Constitution of the United States,* 38, n. 13.

Seventy-third Congress
March 4, 1933, to January 3, 1935

First session—March 9, 1933, to June 15, 1933
Second session—January 3, 1934, to June 18, 1934
Special session of the Senate—March 4, 1933, to March
    6, 1933
(First administration of Franklin D. Roosevelt,
    1933–1937)

Historical Background

By inauguration day 1933, 25 percent of the nation's labor force was out of work, lengthy bread lines were common, and farm prices had fallen by more than 50 percent since the start of the Great Depression. During the previous three years, more than five thousand banks had failed, and currency hoarding was widespread. Millions of Americans gathered around their radios to listen to newly elected president Franklin D. Roosevelt's message of hope. "Let me assert my belief," Roosevelt reassured his anxious audience, "that the only thing we have to fear is fear itself." His promise of immediate action rallied the nation.

Within hours after taking office, President Roosevelt called a special session of Congress to address the economic crisis and issued a proclamation declaring a four-day bank holiday while officials at the Treasury Department worked round-the-clock to prepare an emergency banking bill. When Congress convened at noon on March 9, the bill was ready. By 7:30 that evening the bill had passed both houses of Congress, and a little more than an hour later it was signed into law by the president. The Emergency Banking Relief Act legalized the action the president had already taken, authorized the secretary of the Treasury to determine which banks were sound enough to be

reopened, prohibited the hoarding and exporting of gold, and authorized the Reconstruction Finance Corporation to provide funds to essentially solvent banks temporarily in need of funds.

On March 12, Roosevelt used a radio address to the nation, the first of his fireside chats, to "explain clearly" what the government had been doing during the banking holiday. Intermittently over the next twelve years, Roosevelt, speaking in a warm, intimate manner, used nationwide radio broadcasts to continually bolster the confidence and morale of the American people.

By the end of Roosevelt's first hundred days as president, Congress had approved fourteen major laws and helped him successfully launch the "New Deal for the American People" he promised in his campaign for the Oval Office. The Agricultural Adjustment Act brought relief to the American farmer with agricultural subsidies and production quotas designed to raise prices on agricultural commodities. The Economy Act empowered the president to reorganize as well as abolish federal agencies, reduce government salaries, and cut veterans pensions in an effort to lower expenditures. The National Industrial Recovery Act, which was subsequently declared unconstitutional, sought to restore the nation's economic prosperity through industrial fair practice codes and major public works projects. *(Twenty-first Amendment, p. 239)*

Creation of the Civilian Conservation Corps provided employment for 250,000 young men between the ages of eighteen and twenty-five. Passage of the Federal Emergency Relief Act made funds available to the states for the unemployed and hungry. The revival of an entire region was the goal in the creation of the Tennessee Valley Authority. The need for more adequate protection for bank depositors as well as investors prompted federal supervision of investment securities and a banking reform bill that established the Federal Deposit Insurance Corporation. Abandonment of the gold standard was promoted as a vehicle that would return the nation to solvency and lead it out of the Depression. Farms and homes were saved from foreclosure by the Home Owners' Loan Act and the Farm Credit Act. An Emergency Railroad Transportation Act aided the railroads in meeting emergency conditions (declining traffic, reduced earnings, and, in some instances, financial distress). Unprecedented unemployment made establishment of a national system of employment offices a priority.

During Roosevelt's second year in office, Congress was still generally willing to approve administration measures intended to help move the nation toward prosperity. In March 1934, however, the president was handed his first major defeat when his veto of a bill to restore the cuts made under the Economy Act was overridden. Other setbacks were administered by the U.S. Supreme Court, which would declare unconstitutional all or portions of eight major bills passed by the Seventy-third Congress.

Still, the legislative accomplishments of 1934 were far-reaching. Farmers benefited from legislation that authorized additional means for refinancing farms. The Taylor Grazing Act, sponsored by Rep. Edward T. Taylor of Colorado, prohibited further sale of western grazing lands held by the government and virtually closed the public domain to further settlement. At the urging of Secretary of State Cordell Hull and Secretary of Agriculture Henry A. Wallace, President Roosevelt proposed and gained approval of legislation that allowed him to negotiate bilateral trade agreements on a country-by-country basis. Although the Reciprocal Trade Agreements Act did little to lower tariffs during the Depression, it did, as the administration sought, transfer tariff-making policy from Capitol Hill to the White House.

An unprecedented decline in the price of silver prompted Congress to increase the use of the metal in the currency stock, as silver interests had urged since the beginning of the Depression.

Creation of the Federal Communications Commission and the Securities and Exchange Commission resulted from two distinct efforts to broaden federal regulation of American business. Long before his first year in office was completed, Roosevelt had awakened the nation to the potential impact of the radio through his fireside chats. Although Congress as early as 1929 had considered establishing a commission to regulate the emerging broadcasting industry, it did not act until after the president added his support to the proposal.

Despite strenuous opposition from the business and financial communities, Roosevelt was also able to convince Congress of the need to regulate stock markets so investors would be protected against unethical and fraudulent activities.

When the Rules Enabling Act was passed in 1934, the federal court system was overburdened and considered inefficient. Passage culminated of decades of activism for a single civil procedural system that could replace the hodgepodge of procedural rules being used by the federal judiciary. The origin of the Federal Rules of Civil Procedure can be traced to this act, which delegated comprehensive power to the U.S. Supreme Court to promulgate a single procedural system for federal district courts.

The Department of State and the Library of Congress were the principal repositories of records of the government prior to 1934, when a long campaign led by historian J. Franklin Jameson culminated in the establishment of the National Archives of the United States. The act stipulated that archives and records of the federal government be deposited in the National Archives, and that the records be placed under the charge of an Archivist of the United States.

The violent atmosphere of the Prohibition era and the attempted assassination of President-elect Franklin D. Roosevelt inspired legislation that imposed a heavy federal tax on the manufacture and distribution of machine guns, sawed-off shotguns, and other weapons thought to be favored by gangsters. The National Firearms Act of 1934 was the first attempt at federal gun-control legislation.

The National Housing Act of 1934, one of the most significant pieces of legislation in the history of home financing, created the Federal Housing Administration (FHA) to guarantee mortgage loans made by savings and loan institutions. This enactment opened the way for long-term mortgages that made home ownership for moderate-income Americans feasible for the first time.

With commercial banks and savings institutions seemingly reluctant to provide consumer credit, Congress approved the Federal Credit Union Act, which established a national system for chartering and supervising credit unions. Supporters contended that these cooperative depository institutions had the advantage of being established not for profit, but to serve their members.

The Roosevelt administration also effected changes in the nation's foreign policy. The president in his inaugural address had called for a "good neighbor" policy of nonintervention in U.S. relations with Latin America. His words were translated into action when the U.S. marine garrison occupying Haiti was withdrawn in 1934, and the Platt Amendment, permitting American military intervention in Cuba, was repealed. Concurrently, in Asia, the Philippines were granted commonwealth status, a large measure of internal self-government, and the promise of independence by 1946.

In the field of national defense, the Naval Parity Act mandated that the U.S. fleet be built to the full strength allowed under the Washington and London naval arms limitation agreements.

A series of new crime control laws were approved in an effort to curtail a widespread increase in racketeering, kidnapping, and other types of criminal wrongdoing.

Native American Indian tribes were allowed for the first time to organize tribal governments under the Indian Reorganization Act.

During and immediately after World War I, the European Allied nations, unable to sustain the huge costs of the war effort, had borrowed more than $11 billion from the United States. When a settlement could not be reached on how to address the debt issue, all of the countries except for Finland defaulted on their loans. Angered by the default, Congress passed legislation prohibiting new loans to any foreign country delinquent in its war obligations. None of the countries except Finland repaid their debts and the debts remained a source of U.S.-European tension until World War II.

Prompted by an activist, innovative president, and by its own awareness of the extreme gravity of the nation's condition, the Seventy-third Congress responded with a surge of vital legislation that places it among the great Congresses of American history. Many of its enactments influenced the course of national life throughout the twentieth century and beyond. Although the founders

had constructed a federal legislative system intended to forestall excessive concentrations of power and promote caution and compromise in lawmaking, the Seventy-third Congress demonstrated that the American model of checks and balances and separation of powers was capable of extraordinary achievements when spurred by extraordinary events.

The 1934 midterm congressional elections saw the Democrats increase their dominance of each house.

Major Acts

Emergency Banking Relief Act. Legalized the emergency actions taken by the president and secretary of the Treasury concerning national banks and Federal Reserve banks since the beginning of the Roosevelt administration on March 4, 1933. Accorded the president broad discretionary powers over transactions in credit, currency, gold, and silver, including foreign exchange. Required licensing of Federal Reserve banks by the Treasury Department and denied the right of operation to unlicensed Federal Reserve banks. Made it illegal to own or export gold, and authorized the secretary of the Treasury to call in all gold and gold certificates in the country. Enlarged the operations of Federal Reserve banks, and empowered the Reconstruction Finance Corporation to subscribe to the preferred stock of national banks and trust companies. Approved March 9, 1933 (P.L. 1; 48 Stat. 1–7).

Economy Act. Authorized a reduction in the salaries of federal employees by up to 15 percent and in veterans benefits by up to 10 percent. Authorized reorganization of government agencies with a view toward economy. Presidential veto overridden by Congress. Became law without the president's signature March 20, 1933 (P.L. 2; 48 Stat. 8–16). Certain provisions of this act were subsequently held unconstitutional in *Lynch v. United States*, 292 U.S. 571 (1934).

Civilian Conservation Corps. Authorized the president, "under such rules and regulations as he may prescribe and by utilizing such existing departments or agencies as he may designate," to provide employment of jobless male citizens in various projects aimed at conserving or improving the country's natural resources. Provided that this could include reforestation; prevention of forest fires, floods, and erosion; controlling plant pests and diseases; construction, maintenance, and repair of paths, trails, and fire roads in national parks and forests; or any other project the purpose of which was to restore the public domain. Approved March 31, 1933 (P.L. 5; 48 Stat. 22–23). With the authority granted to him by this act, President Franklin D. Roosevelt brought the Civilian Conservation Corps into existence on April 5, 1933, through Executive Order 6101.

Agricultural Adjustment Act. Created the Agricultural Adjustment Administration (AAA) to deal with problems of low farm prices by controlling surplus crops. Provided for farmers to be paid for limiting the production of seven basic commodities—wheat, cotton, corn, hogs, rice, tobacco, and dairy products. Provided refinancing of farm mortgages through the Federal Land Banks. Approved May 12, 1933 (P.L. 10; 48 Stat. 31–54). Certain provisions of this act were subsequently held unconstitutional in *United States v. Butler,* 297 U.S. 1 (1936).

Federal Emergency Relief Act of 1933. Created the Federal Emergency Relief Administration (FERA) to provide financial assistance to the nation's several million needy families. Authorized an appropriation of $500 million, half of which was allotted as direct payments to the states, with the balance being distributed on the basis of $1 of federal aid for every $3 of state and local funds spent on the poor and hungry. Approved May 12, 1933 (P.L. 15; 48 Stat. 55–58).

Tennessee Valley Authority Act of 1933. Established the Tennessee Valley Authority (TVA), an independent public corporation with a three-member board of directors, to maintain and operate properties owned by the government at Muscle Shoals, Alabama, "in the interest of national defense and for agricultural and industrial development," "to improve navigation in the Tennessee River," and "to control the destructive flood waters in the Tennessee River and Mississippi River Basin." Authorized the TVA to acquire real estate; build dams and reservoirs, power plants, and transmission lines; develop flood control, soil erosion, and reforestation programs; and manufacture nitrogen products for fertilizer and explosives. Approved May 18, 1933 (P.L. 17; 48 Stat. 58–72).

Securities Act of 1933. Required full disclosure to investors of new securities (notes, stocks, treasury stocks, bonds, and so on), with all new issues to be registered with the Federal Trade Commission. (In 1934 this function was transferred to the Securities and Exchange Commission.) Exempted federal, state, and municipal bonds; railroad securities; and securities of religious, charitable, and educational bodies. Approved May 27, 1933 (P.L. 22; 48 Stat. 74–95).

Gold Standard Repeal. Took the United States off the gold standard by canceling the gold clause in all federal and private obligations. Made contracts and debts payable in legal tender. Approved June 5, 1933 (P. Res. 10; 48 Stat. 112–113). Certain provisions of this resolution were subsequently held unconstitutional in *Perry v. United States,* 294 U.S. 330 (1935).

National Employment System Act. Established a national system of public employment offices to be maintained by the United States Employment Service (USES), within the Department of Labor. Transferred all the records, files, property, officers, and employees of the abolished employment service existing in the Department of Labor to the new bureau. Required each state to establish an agency vested with the powers necessary to coordinate USES activities and match federal appropriations for employment services. Approved June 6, 1933 (P.L. 30; 48 Stat. 113–117).

Home Owners' Loan Act of 1933. Created the Home Owners' Loan Corporation (HOLC) to refinance the home mortgage (first mortgage) indebtedness of all nonfarm homeowners. Authorized the corporation to have a capital stock not in excess of $200 million and an aggregate issue of not more than $2 billion in bonds. Empowered HOLC to furnish cash advances for taxes, repair, and maintenance up to 50 percent of appraised values on encumbered properties. Approved June 13, 1933 (P.L. 43; 48 Stat. 128–135).

Banking Act of 1933 (Glass-Steagall Act). Created the Federal Deposit Insurance Corporation for guaranteeing individual bank deposits up to $5,000. Extended the open-market activities of the Federal Reserve Board to enable it to prevent excessive speculation on credit. Permitted branch banking under certain conditions. Separated deposit and investment affiliates. Broadened the membership of the Federal Reserve System to include savings and industrial banks. Approved June 16, 1933 (P.L. 66; 48 Stat. 162–195). The legislation was sponsored by Sen. Carter Glass of Virginia and Rep. Henry B. Steagall of Alabama.

National Industrial Recovery Act. Created the National Industrial Recovery Administration (NIRA) to administer and enforce a system of industrial "fair practice codes" drafted by private trade and manufacturing associations and by the president for industries not having trade associations. The effect of these codes was to fix prices and establish production quotas for business and industry. Exempted businesses covered by the act from antitrust laws, and empowered the NIRA to seek court injunctions against code violators. Guaranteed the right of employees covered by the codes "to organize and bargain collectively through representatives of their own choosing." Created the Public Works Administration (PWA), under the secretary of the interior, to provide federal grants to states and cities for large public works projects such as airports, bridges, dams, hospitals, roads, sewage plants, and roads that required a substantial work force. Approved June 16, 1933 (P.L. 67; 48 Stat. 195–211). Certain provisions of this act were subsequently held unconstitutional in *Schechter Poultry Corp. v. United States*, 295 U.S. 495 (1935), and *Panama Refining Co. v. Ryan*, 193 U.S. 388 (1935).

Emergency Railroad Transportation Act. Created the position of federal coordinator of transportation to "foster and protect" interstate railroad transportation, to prevent and relieve obstructions as well as burdens "resulting from the present acute economic emergency," and to "safeguard and maintain an adequate system of transportation." Repealed the "recapture" clause of the Transportation Act of 1920. Placed railroad holding companies under the supervision of the Interstate Commerce Commission. Approved June 16, 1933 (P.L. 68; 48 Stat. 211–221). *(Transportation Act of 1920 [Esch-Cummins Act], p. 216)*

Farm Credit Act of 1933. Consolidated the government's various agricultural credit agencies into the Farm Credit Administration (FCA) to conform with an executive order that President Franklin D. Roosevelt issued on March 27, 1933. Established the Production Credit Corporation to supply funds for local farmer-owned production credit associations for short-term and intermediate-term loans to farmers. Established one central and twelve district banks to extend credit to farmer's cooperative associations. Approved June 16, 1933 (P.L. 75; 48 Stat. 257–273).

Gold Reserve Act of 1934. Authorized the president to set limits for devaluation of the dollar from fifty to sixty cents in relation to its gold content; to change the value within these limits from time to time, as deemed necessary; to impound in the Treasury the gold stocks held by the Federal Reserve banks; to assure to the government any profit that might accrue to the Treasury from an increase in the value of gold; and to use part of this profit to set up a fund (the Exchange Stabilization Fund) of $2 billion with which to stabilize the dollar. Approved January 30, 1934 (P.L. 87; 48 Stat. 337–344).

Federal Farm Mortgage Corporation Act. Established the Federal Farm Mortgage Corporation, and authorized an issue of $2 billion in bonds to further alleviate farm debt through favorable refinancing rates on farm mortgages. Approved January 31, 1934 (P.L. 88; 48 Stat. 344–349).

Tydings-McDuffie Philippines Independence Act. Provided for the complete independence of the Philippine Islands following a ten-year transitional period, contingent upon the adoption of a Philippine constitution and establishment of a republican form of government. Provided for the removal of all U.S. military bases. Left the status of U.S. naval bases in the Philippines for future discussions. Approved March 24, 1934 (P.L. 127; 48 Stat. 456–465). The legislation was sponsored by Sen. Millard F. Tydings of Maryland and Rep. John McDuffie of Alabama.

Naval Parity Act. Authorized construction of a full treaty strength U.S. Navy within the limits of the Five-Power Naval Limitation Treaty of 1922 and the London

Naval Limitation Treaty of 1930. Provided for the construction of more than one hundred naval vessels and more than one thousand aircraft. Approved March 27, 1934 (P.L. 135; 48 Stat. 503–505).

Independent Offices Appropriation Act. Restored the cuts made under the Economy Act of 1933. Increased salaries of government workers by $125 million and World War I veteran allowances by $228 million. Approved March 28, 1934 (P.L. 141; 48 Stat. 509–527).

Johnson Debt Default Act of 1934. Prohibited financial transactions (or loans) with any foreign government in default on its obligation to the United States. Declared that it would be a federal criminal offense for any person or corporation subject to the jurisdiction of the United States to engage in the sale of securities of any foreign government which is in default on the payment of its obligations to the U.S. government. Approved May 5, 1934 (P.L. 151; 48 Stat. 574).

Crime Control Acts. Empowered the federal government, through a series of six new laws, to punish persons who assaulted federal agents performing their law enforcement duties, crossed state lines to avoid prosecution or testifying, incited or participated in prison riots, robbed Federal Reserve banks, sent extortion or kidnap notes across state lines, and transported kidnap victims across state lines. Approved May 18, 1934 (P.L. 230–235; 48 Stat. 780–783).

Securities and Exchange Act of 1934. Created the Securities and Exchange Commission to license and regulate the operation of stock markets. Prohibited price manipulation. Empowered the Federal Reserve Board to regulate the use of credit in financing securities trading. Approved June 6, 1934 (P.L. 291; 48 Stat. 881–909).

Reciprocal Trade Agreements Act. Authorized the president to negotiate bilateral trade agreements on a country-by-country basis and reduce the rates of the Smoot-Hawley Tariff by as much as 50 percent. Stipulated that congressional approval was not necessary for the president to take such action. Approved June 12, 1934 (P.L. 316; 48 Stat. 943–945). (*Smoot-Hawley Tariff, p. 235*)

Indian Reorganization Act. Prohibiting further allotment of Indian lands, and permitted development of restricted tribal governments. Appropriated $2 million for the purchase of additional tribal lands. Directed the secretary of the interior to issue conservation regulations to prevent erosion, deforestation, and overgrazing on Indian lands. Provided an annual appropriation of $250,000 for loans to Indian students attending vocational and trade schools and preferential appointment of qualified Indians to positions in the Indian Office. Approved June 18, 1934 (P.L. 383; 48 Stat. 984–988).

Rules Enabling Act of 1934. Conferred upon the Supreme Court "the power to prescribe general rules for the district courts of the United States and for the courts of the District of Columbia, the forms of process, writs, pleadings, and motions, and the practice and procedure in civil actions." Stipulated that those rules "shall neither abridge, enlarge nor modify the substantive right of any litigant." Empowered the Supreme Court (subject to congressional approval) to also make the rules apply to equity cases. Approved June 19, 1934 (P.L. 415; 48 Stat. 1064).

Communications Act of 1934. Created the Federal Communications Commission (FCC) to regulate interstate and foreign telegraph, telephone, cable, and radio communications, which were previously the responsibility of the Interstate Commerce Commission and Federal Radio Commission. Approved June 19, 1934 (P.L. 416; 48 Stat. 1064–1105).

National Archives Act. Established the National Archives as the official depository for the records of the U.S. government, with a presidentially appointed archivist of the United States as its chief administrator with responsibility for making rules and regulations for preserving the documents. Established the national historical publications commission, which was to be responsible for recommending "historical works and collections of sources" that were "appropriate for publication and/or otherwise recording at public expense." Gave the National Archives authority to accept motion-picture films and sound recordings illustrative of historical activities of the United States. Approved June 19, 1934 (P.L. 432; 48 Stat. 1122–1124).

Silver Purchase Act of 1934. Authorized nationalization of domestic silver stocks and an increase in monetary value of the Treasury's silver holdings until they equaled one-third of the government's gold holdings. Imposed a 50 percent profits tax on certain transfers of silver to preclude a windfall for silver speculators. Approved June 19, 1934 (P.L. 438; 48 Stat. 1178–1181).

Federal Credit Union Act. Established a Federal Credit Union System to charter and supervise federal credit unions that could "make more available to people of small means credit for provident purposes through a national system of cooperative credit, thereby helping to stabilize the credit structure of the United States." Allowed credit unions to be chartered by their respective states or by the federal government. Approved June 26, 1934 (P.L. 467; 48 Stat. 1216–1222).

National Firearms Act of 1934. Imposed a tax on making and transferring machine guns, shotguns, or rifles having a barrel of less that 18 inches in length, and mufflers or silencers, as well as a tax on manufacturers, importers, and dealers of such weapons. Required that such firearms be registered with the Collector of Internal Revenue. Made unlicensed possession or transfer of such items a criminal offense. Approved June 26, 1934 (P.L. 474; 48 Stat. 1236–1240).

National Housing Act. Established the Federal Housing Administration (FHA) to insure banks, trust companies, mortgage companies, building and loan associations, and other private financial institutions against losses on mortgages on new construction as well as on repairs, alterations, and improvements of older properties. Created the Federal Savings and Loan Corporation to insure the deposits of member saving institutions. Increased the borrowing power of the Home Owners' Loan Corporation to $3 billion. Approved June 27, 1934 (P.L. 479; 48 Stat. 1246–1265).

Taylor Grazing Act. Prohibited further sales of some eighty million acres of public domain grasslands located in the western states. Authorized the Department of the Interior to regulate grazing on these lands through leases and restricted access. Approved June 28, 1934 (P.L. 482; 48 Stat. 1269–1275).

Seventy-fourth Congress
January 3, 1935, to January 3, 1937

First session—January 3, 1935, to August 26, 1935
Second session—January 3, 1936, to June 20, 1936
(First administration of Franklin D. Roosevelt, 1933–1937)

Historical Background

Despite two years of unprecedented federal spending, when the Seventy-fourth Congress convened in January 1935, 20 percent of the nation's work force remained unemployed. President Franklin D. Roosevelt told Congress in his annual message that together they could "eliminate many of the factors that cause economic Depression" and could "provide the means for mitigating their result." To achieve this goal, Roosevelt proposed a legislative program of social reform, much of which was embodied in the Social Security Act.

While differences between House and Senate versions of the Social Security Act were being resolved, work was completed on several other important measures devised to alleviate economic hardships. The Emergency Relief Appropriations Act, which provided for the establishment of the Works Progress Administration (WPA), appropriated $4.8 billion for federally financed construction projects aimed at reducing unemployment. A Soil Conservation Service was created to furnish financial and technical support needed to control and prevent massive soil erosion that had turned many areas in the Plains States into a dust bowl. A little more than a month after the U.S. Supreme Court held the National Industrial Recovery Act of 1933 unconstitutional in *Schechter v. United States* (1935), a mechanism for guaranteeing the rights of labor was set in place. The Wagner-Connery

National Labor Relations Act, sponsored by Sen. Robert F. Wagner of New York and Rep. Willliam P. Connery Jr. of Massachusetts, assured organized labor's right to collective bargaining. Interstate bus lines and trucking companies were placed under the application of Interstate Commerce Commission regulations with the enactment of the Motor Carrier Act, which was drafted to ensure that both industries established reasonable rates and uniform systems of accounting and that they did not discriminate between localities or persons. *(National Industrial Recovery Act, p. 244)*

The Social Security Act provided a system for meeting the basic needs of millions of elderly and unemployed Americans whose lives had been devastated by the Great Depression. Amidst a mountain of other proposals, six major laws were approved before the first session adjourned near the end of August 1935. These provided for (1) reorganization of the Federal Reserve Board, (2) elimination of large interstate utility monopolies, (3) mechanisms to stabilize the bituminous coal industry, (4) a neutrality act that authorized the president to embargo arms sales to combatants in the event of foreign conflicts, (5) a three-year farm mortgage moratorium for debt-ridden farmers (sponsored by Sen. Lynn J. Frazier of North Dakota and Rep. William Lemke of North Dakota), and (6) establishment of a railroad retirement system. The latter two measures were drafted to meet U.S. Supreme Court objections to the Farm Credit Act of 1933 and the Railroad Retirement Act of 1935.

In his January 3, 1935, budget message, President Franklin D. Roosevelt promised there would not be any new taxes. Just six months later, however, he shocked many when he sent a message to Congress recommending a broad revision of the existing tax code that included significant increases in surtaxes on large individual, inheritance, and gift taxes, corporation incomes, intercorporate dividends; and a constitutional amendment authorizing the general taxation of income from federal, state, and local securities. The Revenue Act of 1936, which embodied many of the president's proposals, became known as the "Wealth Tax Act," because it contained a provision to tax high-earning Americans, and closed loopholes that were allowing high earners to legally avoid paying tax.

Early in 1936, Congress responded to veterans' demands for an immediate payment on service (bonus) certificates not scheduled to mature for nearly a decade. *(Farm Credit Act of 1933, p. 244; Railroad Retirement Act of 1935, p. 249)*

After the Agricultural Adjustment Act (AAA) was declared unconstitutional on January 6, 1936, a different approach for limiting crop production was instituted. The new Soil Conservation and Domestic Allotment Act attempted to achieve the same goal as AAA by subsidizing farmers who agreed to plant soil-conserving crops instead of soil-depleting crops. An intended ancillary benefit was the reduction of soil erosion that had greatly contributed to the dust bowl. Under AAA, the government had contracted with the farmers to restrict their agricultural output. Creation of the Rural Electrification Administration made low-interest loans available to nonprofit farmer cooperatives for construction of power lines and electrical generating facilities in rural areas where 90 percent of the people still used gasoline engines to generate electricity and kerosene lanterns for light.

The Commodity Exchange Act of 1936 established much of the legal framework for regulation of the futures trading of agricultural commodities on organized exchanges in a manner similar to the Securities and Exchange Act passed two years earlier, which regulated stock exchanges. The act sought to facilitate honest and fair practices and to restrain fraud, excessive speculation, and manipulation in commodity exchanges. Other legislative initiatives sought to abolish monopolistic price discrimination, particularly by chain stores engaged in interstate commerce; assert federal responsibility for flood control in the nation's river basins; save the American merchant marine through more equitable subsidies; and provide a minimum wage and hour standard for contractors dealing with the federal government (bill sponsored by Sen.

David I. Walsh of Massachusetts and Rep. Arthur D. Healey of Massachusetts). Congress also established limited self-government for the Virgin Islands.

The Republicans nominated Governor Alfred M. Landon of Kansas and Frank Knox, a Chicago publisher, for president and vice president, respectively, in 1936. The GOP platform denounced the administration's New Deal policies as unconstitutional and economically unsound. President Roosevelt and Vice President James Nance Garner were renominated by the Democrats on a platform pledged to continue the New Deal. During the 1936 presidential campaign, Republicans outspent the Democrats by $5 million ($14 million to $9 million), but to no avail. Roosevelt and Garner carried all but two states (Maine and Vermont), earning 523 electoral votes, and captured 60.8 percent of the popular vote. Landon and Knox won 8 electoral votes and 36.5 percent of the popular vote. Roosevelt's popularity proved to have coattails, as the Democrats made gains in both the House and Senate, solidifying their already large majorities.

Major Acts

Emergency Relief Appropriation Act of 1935. Granted the president broad power to authorize $4.8 billion in "useful projects" to increase employment. (On May 6, 1935, using the authority granted him under the act, President Franklin D. Roosevelt established the Works Progress Administration [WPA], a large-scale national public works program designed to provide jobs for unemployed persons who were capable of working and could pass a means test.) Shifted the responsibility for the unemployable back to state and local governments. Approved April 8, 1935 (P. Res. 11; 49 Stat. 115–119).

Soil Conservation Act. Established the Soil Conservation Service within the Department of Agriculture to provide financial and technical support needed for control and prevention of soil erosion. Approved April 27, 1935 (P.L. 46; 49 Stat. 163–164).

Wagner-Connery National Labor Relations Act. Proclaimed that collective bargaining was an essential component of public policies addressing economic recovery. Created a presidentially appointed National Labor Relations Board (NLRB) empowered to hold elections for forming trade unions at the workers' request, certify that these trade unions, if approved, were recognized employee bargaining units, define unfair labor practices by employers, investigate such charges, and issue cease and desist orders as justified. Approved July 5, 1935 (P.L. 198; 49 Stat. 449–457). *(Taft-Hartley Labor-Management Relations Act, p. 279)*

Motor Carrier Act of 1935. Placed buses and trucks engaged in interstate commerce under the regulatory authority of the Interstate Commerce Commission (ICC), and required that applications for new routes be submitted to the ICC for approval. Approved August 9, 1935 (P.L. 255; 49 Stat. 543–567).

Social Security Act. Established a system of old-age and survivors' insurance and a cooperative federal-state program of unemployment compensation administered by a Social Security Board. Levied a payroll tax on all firms employing eight or more employees (with specified exceptions) for unemployment compensation and a tax on all eligible employers and employees for creation of a fund for payment of old-age and survivors' insurance. Authorized federal grants-in-aid to states for old-age assistance; relief of the destitute, blind, and homeless; dependent and delinquent children; and public health, vocational rehabilitation, and maternity and infant care. Approved August 14, 1935 (P.L. 271; 49 Stat. 620–648).

Banking Act of 1935. Provided for a reorganization of the Federal Reserve Board, changed the name of that body to the Board of Governors of the Federal Reserve System, and centralized the operations of regional Federal Reserve banks in the Board of Governors. Empowered the board to control reserve requirements, discount operations, interest rates, and open market operations (the purchase of government securities). Approved August 23, 1935 (P.L. 305; 49 Stat. 684–723).

Public Utility Holding Company Act of 1935. Granted authority to the Federal Power Commission and the Federal Trade Commission to regulate interstate transmission of electric power and gas. Delegated responsibility for supervising the financial practices of public utilities to the Securities and Exchange Commission. Provided for the regulation of the operations and corporate structure of such companies. Approved August 26, 1935 (P.L. 333; 49 Stat. 803–863).

Frazier-Lemke Farm Mortgage Moratorium Act. Allowed farmers a three-year moratorium against seizure of foreclosed property by paying a mortgagee a rental fixed by the courts. Approved August 28, 1935 (P.L. 384; 49 Stat. 942–945).

Railroad Retirement Act of 1935. Established a retirement system for all railroad employees, except those employed by street, interurban, or suburban electric railways. Provided that the system would be funded by a payroll tax paid in equal proportions by employees and employers. Created a three-member Railroad Retirement Board appointed by the president to administer the law. Approved August 29, 1935 (P.L. 399; 49 Stat. 967–974).

Bituminous Coal Conservation Act of 1935. Created a Bituminous Coal Labor Board and National Bituminous Coal Commission to administer regulations dealing with production quotas, price fixing, and labor. Levied a 15 percent tax on coal producers, 90 percent of which was remitted to producers who complied with the code set up to regulate soft coal prices. Approved August 30, 1935 (P.L. 402; 49 Stat. 991–1011). Certain provisions of this act were subsequently held unconstitutional in *Carter v. Carter Coal Co.*, 298 U.S. 238 (1936).

Revenue Act of 1935 (Wealth Tax Act). Increased the surtax rate on individual incomes over $50,000, the estate tax on individual estates over $40,000, and a progressive tax on individual incomes over $1 million until the rate reached 75 percent on incomes over $5 million. Lowered the tax rates on small corporations from 13 percent to 12.5 percent. Raised the tax rates on all corporation incomes above $50,000 to 15 percent. Levied additional graduated taxes on profits in excess of 10 percent. Approved August 30, 1935 (P.L. 407; 49 Stat. 1014–1028).

Neutrality Act of 1935. Authorized the president to prohibit the export of arms and other implements of war to belligerent countries, prohibit American vessels from carrying munitions to these countries, and restrict travel by American citizens on belligerent ships in wartime. Established a National Munitions Control Board to regulate licensing and registration of persons engaged in the business of manufacturing, exporting, or importing arms, ammunition, and implements of war. Approved August 31, 1935 (P. Res. 67; 49 Stat. 1081–1085).

Adjusted Compensation Payment Act of 1936. Authorized the issuance of nine-year interest-bearing bonds to World War I veterans convertible to cash at any time. Approved January 27, 1936 (P.L. 425; 49 Stat. 1099–1102).

Soil Conservation and Domestic Allotment Act. Provided subsidies for growers who agreed to plant a portion of their lands in soil-conserving crops such as alfalfa, instead of in soil-depleting ones such as wheat, corn, or cotton. Approved February 29, 1936 (P.L. 461; 49 Stat. 1148–1152). *(Agricultural Adjustment Act of 1938, p. 255)*

Rural Electrification Act of 1936. Provided statutory authorization for the Rural Electrification Administration (initially established by an executive order issued by President Franklin D. Roosevelt on May 11, 1935) empowered to make loans to electrical cooperatives and nonprofit organizations engaged in delivering electricity to rural areas. Approved May 20, 1936 (P.L. 605; 49 Stat. 1363–1367).

Commodity Exchange Act. Replaced the Grain Futures Act of 1922 and significantly expanded its coverage, by extended federal regulation, to a list of enumerated commodities that included cotton, rice, corn, barley, rye, flaxseed, grain, sorghum, mill feeds, butter, eggs, Irish potatoes, wool, wool taps, fats and oils (including lard, tallow, cottonseed oil, peanut oil, soybean oil, and other fats and oils), cottonseed meal, cottonseed, peanuts, soybeans, soybean meal, livestock, livestock products, and frozen concentrated orange juice. Changed the name of the Grain Futures Commission to Commodity Exchange Commission and provided the statutory framework under which the commission was to operate. Banned manipulation of commodity futures prices, and "futures commission merchants" to be registered with the federal government. Allowed futures and commodity options only to be traded on organized exchanges, prohibiting their sale in the over-the-counter market. Approved June 15, 1936 (P.L. 675; 49 Stat. 1491–1501).

Federal Antiprice Discrimination Act (Robinson-Patman Act). Prohibited price discrimination in the sale of goods between individuals and localities or when prices were so low as to destroy or eliminate competition. Empowered the Federal Trade Commission to abolish price discrimination that tended to promote monopoly or reduce competition. Approved June 19, 1936 (P.L. 692; 49 Stat. 1526–1528).

Flood Control Act of 1936. Declared that "flood control of navigable waters [and] their tributaries" was a "proper activity of the Federal Government in cooperation with" state and local governments. Authorized the Army Corps of Engineers to undertake major construction projects, such as the construction of dams and levees, and the Department of Agriculture to initiate work on watershed conservation. Approved June 22, 1936 (P.L. 738; 49 Stat. 1570–1597).

Virgin Islands Organic Act. Provided for limited self-government for the Virgin Islands through an elected legislative assembly composed of two municipal councils, one from the island of St. Croix and the other from the islands of St. John and St. Thomas. Vested executive power in a presidentially appointed governor whose veto could be overridden by a two-thirds vote of the assembly. Voting was restricted to those able to read and write the English language. Provided that the local government would retain the federal income taxes for local use, and the islands would receive direct appropriations annually from the federal government. Approved June 22, 1936 (P.L. 749; 49 Stat. 1807–1817).

Merchant Marine Act of 1936. Dissolved the U.S. Shipping Board Merchant Fleet Corporation. Established a new U.S. Maritime Commission, an independent regulatory agency empowered to develop the

American merchant marine through government aid. Directed the commission to determine the needs of the American merchant marine, investigate employment and wage conditions, and consider applications for construction subsidies. Eliminated subsidization of marine mail contracts, and substituted direct subsidies based on differentials between foreign and domestic operating and construction costs. Granted the commission authority to determine wages, minimum crews, and working conditions. Established a Maritime Labor Board to mediate labor disputes. Approved June 29, 1936 (P.L. 835; 49 Stat. 1985–2017).

Walsh-Healey Government Contracts Act. Provided prevailing minimum wage and maximum hours standards of an eight-hour workday and forty-hour workweek for all persons employed by contractors dealing with the U.S. government. Prohibited the use of child labor and convict labor in government contracts. Approved June 30, 1936 (P.L. 846; 49 Stat. 2036–2040).

Seventy-fifth Congress
January 3, 1937, to January 3, 1939

First session—January 5, 1937, to August 21, 1937
Second session—November 15, 1937, to December 21, 1937
Third session—January 3, 1938, to June 16, 1938
(Second administration of Franklin D. Roosevelt, 1937–1941)

Historical Background

Franklin D. Roosevelt embarked on his second term with one of the largest popular and electoral vote mandates in American history. Yet within days, he was being charged by many with trying to "subvert" the Constitution. Frustrated by the Supreme Court's action in declaring several major New Deal programs unconstitutional, Roosevelt on February 7, 1937, proposed that the president be allowed to appoint as many as six new Supreme Court justices and more than forty lower court judges. His declared objective was to ease the workload and increase the Court's efficiency. Roosevelt's court-packing plan was widely seen, however, as an attempt to tilt the Court in favor of administration policies, and it aroused widespread and bitter debate.

With a majority of Congress opposed to the plan, the president took his case directly to the people in a radio fireside chat. The ensuing confrontation led to a break among Democrats on domestic policy and enabled Republicans and conservative Democrats to block other administration-sponsored legislation. Congress, however, did approve portions of Roosevelt's proposal in the Supreme Court Retirement Act and Judicial Procedure Reform Act. The retirement act granted Supreme Court justices the same retirement other federal judges already received, while the judicial act reorganized the lower courts and reformed their procedures.

During April and May 1937, the Court, in a marked shift in attitude, upheld a number of New Deal measures, including the Wagner-Connery National Labor Relations Act, the Social Security Act, and the Frazier-Lemke Farm Mortgage Moratorium Act. In time, congressional opposition to administration proposals lessened as well.

Reenactment of the Bituminous Coal Conservation Act of 1935, except for the wages and hours provisions declared unconstitutional by the Supreme Court in *Carter v. Carter Coal Co.* (1936), provided for federal regulation of soft coal production. The Bankhead-Jones Farm Tenant Act established a Farm Security Administration to arrest the steady decline in farm ownership by helping renters became farm owners. Efforts to address the problem of low-cost housing and slum clearance led to the establishment of a U.S. Housing Authority authorized to make loans available to local governments for improving substandard housing. The housing legislation was sponsored by Sen. Robert F. Wagner of New York and Rep. Henry B. Steagall of Alabama. Congress for the first time provided federal aid to the states for the establishment of wildlife refuges.

Enactment of the Second Agricultural Adjustment Act signaled another effort to resolve the problem of farm surpluses. The first Agricultural Adjustment Act of 1933 had been declared unconstitutional, and the Soil Conservation and Domestic Allotment Act of 1936, designed to replace it, proved inadequate. The Second Agricultural Adjustment Act sought to sustain farm prices by limiting the volume of farm goods marketed by maintaining an "every-normal granary" in storing surplus crops until production declined and prices increased and by establishing a program of crop insurance for wheat growers. The storage provisions of the act were instrumental in preparing the nation for the ensuing war years. Marketing orders have been a fundamental component of U.S. agricultural policy since the 1937 Agricultural Marketing Agreement Act. By allowing the secretary of agriculture to fix minimum prices of certain products, the intent was to modify the conduct and performance of participants in selected agricultural commodity markets to achieve orderly marketing conditions, and prevent what was viewed as ruinous competition among farmers.

Although sentiment in the United States continued to be strongly isolationist, President Roosevelt was able to gain support for the $1 billion Naval Expansion Act. He was able to achieve this goal because of a perceived need to build a "two-ocean" navy capable of meeting the combined fleets of Germany, Italy, and Japan, which had already begun invasions of neighboring countries. The outbreak of the Spanish Civil War in 1936 and the rising tide of fascism in Europe increased support for extending and expanding the Neutrality Act of 1935. The 1937 act did contain one important concession to President Roosevelt—the so-called "cash-and-carry" principle—which allowed warring nations wishing to trade with the United States if they paid cash for their nonmilitary purchases and transported the goods themselves. The Foreign Agents Registration Act, the first attempt at major lobbying reform at the federal level, was enacted in 1938 to curtail the spreading of Fascist and Nazi propaganda. It was triggered by the rise of violent fascist regimes in Europe at the time of its passage.

Recognition by Congress that greater efforts should be made to combat the ever-increasing number of deaths from cancer in the United States prompted the National Cancer Institute Act. By 1937, cancer accounted for one out of every 10 deaths in the country. This act led to the creation of what has become the world's preeminent cancer research organization as well as the largest organization solely dedicated to cancer research. It established the precedent of separate institutes within the National Institutes of Health for research on particular diseases.

Although New Deal programs had done much to relieve suffering associated with the Great Depression and had established a system of regulatory structures

intended to forestall excesses in the business cycle, it was unclear whether they materially affected the course of the depression. The economy had begun to grow as early as March of 1933, but the recovery was hesitant and interrupted by occasional downturns. The worst downturn began in 1937, when the economy dipped into recession. Both corporate and capital gains taxes were reduced in 1938 to counter the slump, and as concessions to the business community. Subsequently, an Emergency Relief Appropriation Act was approved to further stimulate the economy.

The Civil Aeronautics Act of 1938 met the demand for new civil aviation legislation that had been building for five years. Uncertainties over airmail contracts and vigorous competition among various passenger carriers pointed to a compelling need for federal regulation of rates and routes. Equally important was an acknowledgment that the government's ability to develop the airways, promulgate safety regulations, and investigate accidents needed to be strengthened. Another five-year political struggle preceded final adoption of more stringent restrictions on food, drugs, and cosmetics. The resulting Federal Food, Drug, and Cosmetic Act represented the most significant and lasting contribution of the consumer movement in the New Deal era.

Proponents of federal regulation of hours and wages, as well as child labor, saw their efforts realized with the enactment of the Fair Labor Standards Act. It established maximum working hours and a minimum wage for all workers engaged in interstate commerce or the production of goods transported among states, and it prohibited any employment of minors under sixteen and hazardous work by minors under eighteen. Federal control over the natural gas industry was the result of extensive lobbying by industry representatives and conservationists. Passage and enactment of the Wagner-O'Day Act committed the federal government to support efforts to create and expand a stable market for products made by blind persons in sheltered workshops (nonprofit-making agencies). The primary goal of the act was to establish a mechanism by which goods produced by persons with visual disabilities would be purchased by government entities.

For nearly two decades prior to enactment of the Natural Gas Act of 1938, which placed regulation with the Federal Power Commission, states had used widely varied and often unenforced regulations to monitor the industry. In 1931, the Supreme Court held in *FTC v. Raladam* (283 U.S. 643 [1931]) that the Federal Trade Commission's prohibition of "unfair methods of competition" only included practices having a demonstrated adverse impact on competition. The Wheeler-Lea Act of 1938 eliminated this restriction by expanding the commission's jurisdiction to cover false or misleading advertising in addition to special powers to regulate advertising on food, drugs, cosmetics, and therapeutic devices.

The Republicans made gains in the congressional midterm elections of 1938, but the Democrats still enjoyed substantial majorities in both houses.

Major Acts

Supreme Court Retirement Act. Granted U.S. Supreme Court justices the same right to retire "from regular active service on the bench" and continue to receive their salary as was already the case for other federal judges. Approved March 1, 1937 (P.L. 10; 50 Stat. 24).

Bituminous Coal Act of 1937. Reenacted the principal provisions of the Bituminous Coal Conservation Act of 1935, with the exception of the wages and hours provisions that had been declared unconstitutional by the U.S. Supreme Court in *Carter v. Carter Coal Co.* (1936). Promulgated a code of fair competition for the bituminous coal industry. Placed bituminous coal production under federal control, levied a revenue tax of one cent per ton on bituminous coal, and imposed a penalty tax of 19.5 percent on sales by noncode producers. Approved April 26, 1937 (P.L. 48; 50 Stat. 72–94).

Neutrality Act of 1937. Authorized the president to invoke neutrality in a foreign war if the sale of war material to either side would endanger U.S. interests. Granted the president authority to bar belligerent ships from U.S. waters, and extended a 1935 embargo on exports of "implements of war" to include nations engaged in civil strife and undeclared wars. Introduced the "cash-and-carry" policy that permitted belligerent European nations to buy certain "nonwar" goods, designated by the president, if they paid cash for the goods and transported them on their own ships. Prohibited American citizens from traveling on ships of belligerent nations, and American merchant ships from transporting arms to belligerents even if those arms were produced outside of the United States. Barred private loans to nations at war. Approved May 1, 1937 (P. Res. 27; 50 Stat. 121–128).

Agricultural Marketing Agreement Act of 1937. Authorized the Secretary of Agriculture to fix the minimum prices of certain agricultural products, when the handling of such products occurs "in the current of interstate or foreign commerce or . . . directly burdens, obstructs or affects interstate or foreign commerce in such commodity or product thereof." Required regulation of imports into the United States of certain of these commodities whenever domestic shipments were subject to quality regulations under a marketing order. Reaffirmed the marketing agreements provisions of the Agricultural Adjustment Act of 1933 and redefined the process for establishing marketing orders. Approved June 3, 1937 (P.L. 137; 50 Stat. 246–249).

Bankhead-Jones Farm Tenant Act. Established a Farm Security Administration authorized to finance low-interest forty-year mortgages for renters who wanted to purchase their farms. Authorized loans for the purchase of farms, livestock, equipment, and supplies, and authorized rehabilitation loans for operating expenses and educational assistance. Approved July 22, 1937 (P.L. 210; 50 Stat. 522–533).

National Cancer Institute Act. Established the National Cancer Institute and made it the federal government's principal agency for conducting and fostering research and training on the causes, prevention, diagnosis, and treatment of cancer. Authorized the institute to collect, analyze, and disseminate the results of cancer research conducted in the United States and elsewhere. Called upon the institute to assist and promote similar research at other public and private institutions. Approved August 5, 1937 (P.L. 244; 50 Stat. 559–562).

Miller-Tydings Enabling Act. Provided that manufacturers and producers could establish a minimum resale price for their goods, and such retail prices did not constitute a restraint on trade or competition. Stated that any conclusion between competing enterprises to create a minimum resale price was illegal. Exempted fair-trade laws from the application of the Sherman Act and legalized resale-price-maintenance agreements between producers and retailers of products within those states where intrastate contracts had been legal. Approved August 17, 1937 (P.L. 314; 50 Stat. 693–694, Title VIII).

Judicial Procedures Reform Act. Provided that whenever any case arose in the federal courts involving the constitutionality of an act of Congress, the government might "intervene and become a party for the presentation of evidence." Provided also that whenever a lower federal court declared an act of Congress unconstitutional, "an appeal might be taken directly to the Supreme Court." Reformed certain procedural and organizational matters relating to the lower courts. Approved August 24, 1937 (P.L. 352; 50 Stat. 751–753).

United States Housing Act of 1937 (Wagner-Steagall Act). Created the U.S. Housing Authority as a public corporation under the Department of the Interior. Authorized the U.S. Housing Authority to make loans to local public housing agencies for low-rent housing or slum clearance projects; to provide capital grants to local public housing agencies not to exceed 25 percent of development and acquisition costs; and to grant subsidies for setting rents geared to income levels in areas where local agencies provided up to 25 percent of the federal grant. Authorized the U.S. Housing Authority to lend up to $5 million annually. Approved September 1, 1937 (P.L. 412; 50 Stat. 888–899).

Wildlife Restoration Act of 1937. Provided federal aid to states for the acquisition, restoration, and maintenance of wildlife habitat; management of wildlife areas and resources; and research into problems associated with wildlife management. Stipulated that no state was to receive these monies until it adopted laws "governing the conservation of wildlife," and prohibited hunting licensing fees from being used for anything except administration of fish and game departments. Approved September 2, 1937 (P.L. 415; 50 Stat. 917–919).

Agricultural Adjustment Act of 1938. Superseded the Soil Conservation and Domestic Allotment Act of 1936. Authorized the secretary of agriculture to limit the quantities of specific crops that could be marketed if overproduction threatened to reduce prices, and set acreage allotments for growers. Provided for an "every normal granary" by authorizing the Commodity Credit Corporation to lend money to farmers against surplus crops, and directed the government to store crops until production declined and prices rose. Established a Federal Crop Insurance Corporation to ensure wheat growers against natural disasters. Approved February 16, 1938 (P.L. 430; 52 Stat. 31–77). *(Soil Conservation and Domestic Allotment Act, p. 250)*

Wheeler-Lea Act (Advertising Act). Empowered the Federal Trade Commission (FTC) to protect consumers from "deceptive" advertising and other misleading "acts or practices." Gave the FTC jurisdiction over the advertising of foods, drugs, diagnostic and therapeutic devices and cosmetics, whenever such advertising is disseminated in interstate and foreign commerce by providing definitive and significant penalties for violation of orders to cease and desist from illegal practices. Approved March 21, 1938 (P.L. 447; 52 Stat. 111–117).

Naval Expansion Act. Authorized $1 billion to build a "two-ocean" navy over the ensuing ten years. Provided for a maximum increase of 135,000 tons in capital ships (battleships), 68,754 tons in cruisers, and 40,000 tons in aircraft carriers. Approved May 17, 1938 (P.L. 528; 52 Stat. 401–403).

Foreign Agents Registration Act. Required persons who acted as an agent for foreign principals in a political or quasi-political capacity to register and make periodic public disclosure of their relationship with the foreign principal, as well as activities, receipts, and disbursements in support of those activities. Approved June 8, 1938 (P.L. 583; 52 Stat. 631–633).

Work Relief and Public Works Appropriation Act of 1938. Provided loans and grants for work relief, Public Works Administration projects, construction of federal office buildings, and rural electrification projects; parity payments for producers of certain farm commodities; and funds for U.S. Housing Authority contracts. Approved June 21, 1938 (P. Res. 122; 52 Stat. 809–821).

Natural Gas Act. Granted the Federal Power Commission authority to regulate exportation and importation of natural gas; set rates for production, transportation, or sale of natural gas; ascertain value of property owned by natural gas companies; conduct hearings and investigations; and legally enforce the act. Required natural gas companies to preserve accounts, records, and memoranda. Approved June 21, 1938 (P.L. 688; 52 Stat. 821–833).

Chandler Act of 1938. Authorized the issuance of court orders to stay all creditors against a wage earner until a hearing could be held where the wage earner, creditors, and a judge determined what the wage earner could realistically pay creditors and still meet living expenses. Approved June 22, 1938 (P.L. 696; 52 Stat. 840–940). The legislation was sponsored by Rep. Walter Chandler of Tennessee.

Civil Aeronautics Act of 1938. Created a five-member Civil Aeronautics Authority to regulate and "promote the development and safety" of civil aviation. Established a three-member Air Safety Board within the authority to make rules and regulations governing aircraft accidents and conduct studies and investigations on measures to reduce and prevent future accidents. Approved June 23, 1938 (P.L. 706; 52 Stat. 973–1030). *(Federal Aviation Act, p. 304)*

Federal Food, Drug, and Cosmetic Act. Strengthened Federal Trade Commission control over food, drug, and cosmetic advertisements. Prohibited mislabeling of products, required manufacturers to list ingredients on product labels, and prohibited false and misleading advertising. Delegated enforcement of mislabeling provisions to the Food and Drug Administration and advertising provisions to the Federal Trade Commission. Approved June 25, 1938 (P.L. 717; 52 Stat. 1040–1059). Certain provisions of this act were subsequently held unconstitutional in *United States v. Cardiff*, 344 U.S. 174 (1952).

Federal Fair Labor Standards Act. Established a minimum wage of twenty-five cents an hour (to be gradually increased to forty cents an hour after seven years) and a maximum workweek of forty-four hours for the first year of employment, forty-two hours for the second year, and forty hours thereafter for employees of all firms engaged in interstate commerce. Prohibited child labor under the age of sixteen and hazardous work by those under eighteen. Exempted a number of occupations including farmers, domestics, and professionals. Approved June 25, 1938 (P.L. 718; 52 Stat. 1060–1069). *(Fair Labor Standards Act Amendments of 1949, p. 285; Fair Labor Standards Act Amendments of 1966, p. 325)*

Wagner-O'Day Act. Created the Committee on Purchases of Blind-Made Products, composed "of a private citizen conversant with the problems incident to the blind, and a representative from the Departments of the Navy, War, Treasury, Agriculture, Commerce, and Interior to determine the fair market price of all brooms, mops, and other commodities manufactured by the blind and offered for sale to the federal government by any non-profit agency for the blind." Mandated that any of these commodities procured by or for any federal department or agency "be procured from non-profit agencies for the blind." Approved June 25, 1938 (P.L. 739; 52 Stat. 1196).

Seventy-sixth Congress
January 3, 1939, to January 3, 1941

First session—January 3, 1939, to August 5, 1939
Second session—September 21, 1939, to November 3, 1939
Third session—January 3, 1940, to January 3, 1941
(Second administration of Franklin D. Roosevelt, 1937–1941)

Historical Background

Early in 1939, Congress granted the president limited authority to reorganize the executive branch in an effort to strengthen his control over the federal bureaucracy. Exercising this authority, President Franklin D. Roosevelt was able to create the Executive Office of the President and carry out additional reorganization proposals. The impetus for this action originated with the Brownlow Committee (formally known as the President's Committee on Administrative Management). The committee was headed by Louis J. Brownlow, a noted public administrator.

Following congressional investigations and a plea by the president, the Seventy-sixth Congress approved the Hatch Act, sponsored by Sen. Carl A. Hatch of New Mexico, which sought to eliminate partisanship within the federal government and restrict political activities by government employees. The constitutionality of the Hatch Act was confirmed by the U.S. Supreme Court in 1947 (*United Public Workers v. Mitchell)* and again in 1973 (*United States Civil Service Commission v. National Association of Letter Carriers).*

Relying heavily on improvements recommended by the Social Security Board, Congress amended the original Social Security Act and raised the minimum standard of protection offered by it. Other changes advanced by two years the date benefits would begin to be paid, revised the benefit formula, extended coverage to new categories of recipients, and established monthly payments for survivors and dependents. The Federal Unemployment Tax Act of 1939 established a joint state-federal program for providing partial wage replacement payments to workers who involuntarily lost their jobs. The program was originally proposed as part of the Social Security Act of 1935.

As the year progressed it became obvious that Europe would soon be at war. Since March 1933, when German chancellor Adolf Hitler demanded that the Western powers rescind the military and political restrictions it had imposed on Germany through the Treaty of Versailles in 1919, the threat of another war loomed over Europeans. With the death of German president Paul von Hindenburg in 1934, Hitler assumed the presidency and adopted the title of führer. In October 1933 Hitler had abruptly withdrawn from the General Disarmament Conference in Geneva and from the League of Nations, and in March 1935 he announced that he would openly rearm, in defiance of the Treaty of Versailles. Hitler argued that Germany was released from its obligation by the failure of the Allies to honor their own pledges to reduce armaments. Late in 1935, Italian dictator Benito Mussolini's army seized Ethiopia. In March 1936 Hitler reoccupied the Rhineland in violation of the Treaty of Versailles. Two years later, in March 1938, he seized and annexed German-speaking Austria.

Hitler's next target was Czechoslovakia, which he threatened on grounds that its German minority was being discriminated against. After a prolonged crisis and threats of war, Britain, France, Germany, and Italy signed the Munich agreements in September 1938. The price of the year's peace gained by the Munich pact was the effective dismemberment of Czechoslovakia, a progressive democratic republic, and a growing conviction on Hitler's part that the West lacked the moral fiber to oppose his planned further aggressions.

In March 1939, Hitler ordered the occupation of what remained of Czechoslovakia and subsequently turned his attention to Poland, issuing demands that would have effectively eliminated the Polish corridor, leaving that nation cut off from access to the Baltic Sea. While France and Great Britain were eager to avoid conflict, both felt constrained to guarantee Poland's independence and territorial integrity.

Germany and the Union of Soviet Socialist Republics signed a nonaggression pact on August 27, 1939, protecting Hitler's eastern frontier in the event of war with the Western democracies and leaving him free to attack Poland. Germany launched an invasion of Poland on September 1, leading to declarations of war by Britain and France. Enjoying almost complete air superiority, Germany's mechanized armies crushed the ill-prepared Poles in four weeks, while Soviet troops occupied Poland's eastern provinces and, subsequently, the Baltic states of Lithuania, Latvia, and Estonia. As the year ended, Allied and German forces faced each other across the Franco-German border.

Earlier neutrality legislation had prohibited American companies from supplying war goods to belligerents, but when war broke out in Europe, President Roosevelt called a special session of Congress to revise the Neutrality Act of 1937. Several weeks of heated debate preceded passage of the Neutrality Act of 1939, which repealed the arms embargo established by the earlier act. Although the new act still proclaimed American neutrality, American companies were now allowed to sell arms, ammunition, and implements of war to the Allies on a "cash and carry basis" without becoming involved militarily. American ships, however, continued to be barred from carrying weapons and ammunition to Great Britain and France. The policy was replaced in March 1941 with the Lend Lease Act, which gave the Allies access to war materials without needing money. The Neutrality Acts as a whole failed a few months later when the United States was drawn into World War II by the Japanese attack on Pearl Harbor.

On April 9, 1940, Germany began its spring offensive with the surprise invasion of neutral Denmark and Norway. On May 10 a long-awaited assault was launched with, again, surprise attacks on neutral Belgium and the Netherlands. Bypassing France's Maginot line fortifications, the Germans broke through the French army at its weakest point and drove to the English Channel, trapping the entire British Expeditionary Force (BEF) and two French armies. After a fighting retreat, the entire BEF and more than 100,000 French troops were evacuated to Britain from the port of Dunkirk. Hitler then turned his forces to the south, crushing the remaining French armies and driving France from the war.

As American anxiety over German conquests in Western Europe increased, existing laws governing the admission and deportation of aliens were strengthened with enactment of the Alien Registration Act of 1940. The Smith Act, as it was frequently called, required all aliens living in the United States to be registered and fingerprinted, and it prohibited individuals or groups from advocating or teaching doctrines aimed at the overthrow of the U.S. government. The act was sponsored by Rep. Howard W. Smith of Virginia.

During the summer of 1940, while German forces assembled for the invasion of Britain, the German air force (Luftwaffe) battled Britain's Royal Air Force (RAF) for control of the skies over the United Kingdom. Aided by radar air warning stations and RAF fighter pilots, Britain resisted the German air assault, forcing Hitler to cancel the invasion and shift the Luftwaffe to indiscriminate night bombing of British cities. As 1940 ended, Hitler prepared to invade his erstwhile Soviet ally, while Britain defeated Italian armies in Libya and Ethiopia. (Italy had entered the war in June 1940.)

As the war in Europe continued to expand, tension between the United States and Japan increased dramatically during the final six months of 1940. After the Japanese occupied French Indochina in July 1940, President Roosevelt froze all Japanese assets in the United States and warned Japan that any additional attempts to extend Japanese military control in the Far East would prompt the United States to take immediate actions to protect its interests in the region. In September, when Japan entered into a military and economic alliance with Germany and Italy, the president imposed economic sanctions against Japan.

The hotly contested debate over the Selective Service Act of 1940, which consumed nearly eight hundred pages of the *Congressional Record,* incorporated all of the principal features recommended by the Army General Staff after more than a decade of study. In his budget message of January 3, 1940, President Roosevelt had requested that Congress impose sufficient taxes to cover emergency defense expenditures, while avoiding taxes that would "decrease consumer buying power." Twice during the next nine months Roosevelt was able to sign revenue bills designed to produce the funds needed to sustain the expanding defense program. The first tax measure primarily affected individuals; the second was directed at corporations.

In November 1940 Roosevelt won an unprecedented third term as president. He and his running mate, Henry A. Wallace, received 449 electoral votes. Their opponents, Republican presidential candidate Wendell L. Willkie and vice presidential candidate Charles L. McNary, won 82 electoral votes. Democratic dominance on Capitol Hill remained virtually unchanged as a result of the congressional elections.

Major Acts

Administrative Reorganization Act of 1939. Authorized the president to investigate the organization of all federal agencies to determine what changes were necessary to reduce expenditures, increase efficiency, group agencies according to purpose, and eliminate duplication of effort. Prohibited the president from abolishing an executive department or creating a new one or from directing an agency to perform a function not specifically authorized by law. Exempted twenty-one agencies from reorganization. Provided that any reorganization plan submitted by the president had to sit before Congress for sixty days, during which time it could be disapproved (not amended) by a concurrent resolution of both houses. Amended the Budget and Accounting Act of 1921 to include any regulatory commission or board in the definition of "department and establishment." Authorized the president to appoint six administrative assistants at $10,000 per annum. Approved April 3, 1939 (P.L. 19; 53 Stat. 561–565).

Hatch Act. Prohibited "any person employed in any administrative position by the United States, or by any department, independent agency, or other agency of the United States[,] . . . to use his official authority for the purpose of interfering with, or affecting the election or the nomination of any candidate for the office of President, Vice President, Presidential elector, Member of the Senate, or Member of the House of Representatives, Delegates or Commissioners from the Territories and insular possessions." Prohibited federal employees from actively participating in political campaigns, soliciting or accepting contributions from work relief employees, and making use of official authority or favors to interfere with, or influence the outcome of, presidential or congressional elections. Approved August 2, 1939 (P.L. 252; 53 Stat. 1147–1149).

Social Security Amendments of 1939. Advanced payment of Social Security benefits from 1942 to 1940. Made average earnings, not total earnings, the basis for computing old-age benefits. Provided supplementary old-age benefits for elderly wives, and extended old-age insurance coverage to maritime workers, persons earning wages after they reached sixty-five, and employees of federal instrumentalities, such as member banks in the Federal Reserve System. Revised the benefit formula, extended coverage to new categories of recipients, and established monthly payments for survivors and dependents. Increased the maximum federal grant for the elderly and the blind, and increased the federal contribution toward state aid to dependent children. Approved August 10, 1939 (P.L. 379; 53 Stat. 1360–1402).

Federal Unemployment Tax Act. Required employers to contribute to the federal unemployment insurance fund as well as the state unemployment fund for each qualifying employee. Imposed (originally) a uniform federal tax on the payrolls of industrial and commercial employers that employed eight or more employees for at least 20 weeks per year. Provided that if a state has a state unemployment law that satisfied certain requirements, an employer could claim a 90 percent credit against the federal tax otherwise due for contributions to the state fund. Authorized the federal government to make grants to states for the administrative costs of any qualifying program. Allowed for each state to administer its own unemployment program, which would set the state tax rate, the taxable wage base, qualifications for receiving benefits, and the amount of such benefits. Approved August 10, 1939 (P.L. 379; 53 Stat. 1378–1379, Title III, 1381–1386, Title VI).

Neutrality Act of 1939. Ended the embargo on the sale and export of arms, ammunition, and war implements, and empowered the president to sanction cash-and-carry sales to belligerents. Prohibited U.S. citizens from traveling on the ships of belligerent nations, and from entering war zones. Banned U.S. ships from sailing to belligerent ports and war zones. Charged the National Munitions Control Board with issuing licenses for all arms imports and exports. Repealed the Neutrality Acts of 1935 and 1937. Approved November 4, 1939 (P. Res. 54; 54 Stat. 4–12). *(Repeal of Portions of the Neutrality Act of 1939, p. 263)*

Revenue Act of 1940. Added a 10 percent surcharge on incomes between $6,000 and $100,000. Lowered exemptions for married couples from $2,500 to $2,000 and for single people from $1,000 to $800. Increased the corporate tax to a maximum of 19 percent and excise taxes in most cases by 10 percent (tax on cigarettes was increased by 8 percent and on gasoline by 50 percent). Increased capital stock, gift, estate, and excess profits taxes by 10 percent. Approved June 25, 1940 (P.L. 656; 54 Stat. 516–527).

Alien Registration Act (Smith Act). Required all foreign nationals to register and be fingerprinted. Made it unlawful to advocate the forceful overthrow of the government, to teach such doctrine, or to organize or belong to any organization engaged in such activities. Approved June 28, 1940 (P.L. 670; 54 Stat. 670–676).

Investment Company Act of 1940. Provided the Securities and Exchange Commission with authority to regulate the activities of companies, including mutual funds, that engaged primarily in investing, reinvesting, and trading in securities and whose own securities were offered to the public. Required these companies to disclose their financial condition and investment policies to investors when stock was initially sold and, subsequently, on a regular basis. Approved August 22, 1940 (P.L. 768; 54, Title I Stat. 789–847).

Investment Advisers Act of 1940. Required that investment advisers and firms compensated for advising others directly, or through publications or writings about securities investments, register with the Securities and Exchange Commission and conform to regulations designed to protect investors. Prohibited advisory contracts that provided investment advisers a share of a client's capital gains or capital appreciation or that failed to provide notification of any change in assignment of the contract or a partnership advisory firm. Approved August 22, 1940 (P.L. 768, Title II; 54 Stat. 847–857).

Selective Training and Service Act of 1940. Instituted the first national peacetime draft in U.S. history. Provided for the registration of all males between twenty-one and thirty-five years of age for one year of active duty service and ten years in the reserves. Approved September 16, 1940 (P.L. 783; 54 Stat. 885–897). *(Selective Service Extension of 1941, p. 263)*

Second Revenue Act of 1940. Imposed an excess profits tax of 25 to 50 percent, and increased the normal corporation tax to 24 percent on incomes in excess of $25,000. Approved October 8, 1940 (P.L. 801; 54 Stat. 974–1018).

Seventy-seventh Congress
January 3, 1941, to January 3, 1943

First session—January 3, 1941, to January 2, 1942
Second session—January 5, 1942, to December 16, 1942
(Third administration of Franklin D. Roosevelt,
    1941–1945)

Historical Background

In his eighth State of the Union address, President Franklin D. Roosevelt asked Congress for the power to sell, exchange, lend, or lease war equipment to any nation whose defense he considered vital to the defense of the United States. He also emphasized the need for a rapid reorientation of America's industrial base toward armaments production. The ultimate defeat of the Axis nations, Roosevelt stressed, would constitute a victory for the Four Freedoms characterized as underlying the American political system—freedom of speech, freedom of religion, freedom from want, and freedom from fear. Despite bitter isolationist opposition, Congress approved the Lend-Lease Act, which gave the president broad discretionary powers to "sell, transfer title to, exchange, lease, lend or otherwise dispose of" articles to any country he decided was vital to U.S. security. During the next four years, Congress appropriated more than $50 billion in lend-lease aid.

Land warfare was renewed on the continent of Europe in April 1941, with Germany's swift conquest of Greece and Yugoslavia. On June 22, three million German troops launched a surprise invasion of the Soviet Union, catching Soviet leader Joseph Stalin's armies off guard. For five months the Germans drove relentlessly into Russia, inflicting defeat on the Soviet armies. Leningrad was surrounded and besieged, while the Wehrmacht (German army) drove nearly to the gates of Moscow. Unprepared for the Russian winter and surprised by a Soviet counteroffensive, the Germans were stopped just short of their goals and were forced to retreat by the end of the year. In North Africa, assistance in the form of elite Afrika Korps and General Erwin Rommel saved the Italians from defeat and led to bitter mobile warfare as Axis and British troops attacked and counterattacked across the desert.

During July and August 1941, the Roosevelt administration's request to extend the tour of duty of draftees from twelve to eighteen months generated a heated congressional debate. Without the extension, Roosevelt stressed, two-thirds of the strength of the army would be released from active duty and subject to recall in case of a national emergency. On August 18, he was able to sign the requested selective service extension, which had passed the House by a single vote (203 to 202). Two months later, the USS *Kearny*, which was one of several U.S. Navy ships escorting Allied merchant shipping near the U.S. coast, was torpedoed and damaged southwest of Iceland by a German submarine. Near the end of October, the American destroyer USS *Reuben Jones* was torpedoed and sunk off Iceland while engaged in convoy duty. Soon thereafter, Roosevelt successfully prevailed on Congress to repeal most of the neutrality restrictions of 1939, allowing U.S. merchant vessels to be armed and to carry cargoes bound for belligerent ports.

On December 7, 1941, Japan carried out a surprise attack on the U.S. fleet at Pearl Harbor in Hawaii. Despite warnings that conflict was imminent, U.S. military leadership discounted anything so daring as an attack on Hawaii. American forces were caught unprepared. In one devastating strike, the Japanese crippled the Pacific fleet, destroyed nearly two hundred planes, killed more than twenty-four hundred people, and ended the national debate over the United States' role in the world war. The following day, President Roosevelt told a joint session of Congress that December 7 was "a date which will live in infamy." Less than an hour after the president addressed a joint session of Congress on December 8, both houses passed a resolution declaring a state of war with the Empire of Japan. The lone dissenter was Rep. Jeannette Rankin of Montana, who in 1917 had also voted against going to war with Germany. On December 11, following German and Italian declarations of war on the United States, Congress adopted resolutions recognizing that a state of war existed with those countries as well. Six months later, the United States extended its declaration of war with Germany and Italy to include the fascist regimes in Bulgaria, Hungary, and Rumania, who had declared war against the United States.

With the nation at war, Congress had to consider an increasingly broad range of legislation dealing with reorganization of the executive branch, manpower needs, price controls, taxation, and wartime production. The First and Second War Powers Acts dramatically increased the president's authority to reorganize the executive branch and to enforce regulations relating to the establishment of allocation priorities for war materials and facilities. During the course of the war, twelve million American men would serve in the armed forces. Almost ten million joined as a result of the draft that Congress first expanded shortly after Pearl Harbor to include all males from ages twenty to forty-four and further expanded in November 1942 to include eighteen- and nineteen-year-old males. Also in 1942 women began to be employed by the armed forces in the newly established Women's Army Auxiliary Corps (WAAC) and Women Accepted for Voluntary Emergency Service (WAVES), which was part of the navy.

On the war front, the United States continued to sustain humiliating defeats. Guam and Wake Island were quickly seized by Japan, and most of the Philippines Islands were conquered with equal speed. Next the Japanese focused on the Bataan peninsula and Corregidor Island, where American forces subsequently lost as well. Simultaneous Japanese attacks throughout Southeast Asia swiftly crushed British and Dutch forces and led to the surrender of Singapore on February 15, 1942.

After regrouping, the Japanese navy launched its next offensive, designed to capture New Guinea and isolate Australia. Forewarned because the Japanese codes had been broken, the U.S. Navy forestalled the Japanese effort in the Battle of the Coral Sea. Japan's next thrust was launched at the Aleutian Islands and Midway, a tiny American island in the mid-Pacific. Once again, thanks to prior knowledge, the U.S. Navy was ready. In the Battle of Midway, U.S. aircraft carriers (absent at sea during the Pearl Harbor attack) sank four Japanese carriers, the heart of their strike force, while losing only one of its own. The tide of the Japanese conquest had reached its high-water mark and began to recede. In August, U.S. Marines landed on Guadalcanal in the Solomon Islands. Although months of pitched land and naval battles for Guadalcanal lay ahead, the tide of the war on the Pacific front had turned.

Germany returned to the offensive in Russia in the summer of 1942, driving deep into Soviet territory, this time to the southwest, where Soviet armies made a stand at Stalingrad. After ferocious fighting, the Germans were surrounded and gradually destroyed. The Soviet Union drew increasing strength from its own vast resources and generous shipments of war materials from the United States and Britain.

Later in 1942, in North Africa, the British Eighth Army, reinforced by shipments of American equipment and the leadership of General Bernard Montgomery, defeated Rommel's Axis armies and drove west to the Tunisian border. Almost simultaneously, U.S. and British forces landed in Algeria and Morocco. Squeezing the Axis forces in Tunisia, the Allies compelled their surrender in May 1943.

The Revenue Act of 1941 was the largest tax law in U.S. history. The growing war effort, however, quickly saw it eclipsed by the Revenue Act of 1942. As a consequence of the 1941 adjustments, five million additional Americans were required to file tax returns. It was estimated that $3.5 billion in additional revenues would cover 60 percent of the expanding war expenditures. Following Pearl Harbor, however, the combination of war and inflation pointed to the need for increased taxes. Although the demands of war production put almost every American back to work, the cost of the war exceeded federal tax revenues. In May 1942, President Roosevelt expressed a need for immediate broad increases in taxation that prompted the Revenue Act of 1942. This measure established a national tax system that would continue into the twenty-first century. Roosevelt hailed the act as "the greatest tax bill in American history."[1] It increased taxes and vastly expanded the income tax system to the majority of the working population. In 1939, only 4 million Americans paid income tax. By 1943 this number rose to 43 million, and by the end of the war it was 50 million. The act raised surtaxes, corporation taxes, and inheritance taxes as well.

Seeking an effective means of controlling wartime inflation, Congress in 1942 gave the Office of Price Administration (OPA) statutory authority to control prices on all commodities except agricultural products and control rents in defense areas. An executive order issued nine months earlier had provided for the creation of OPA. By early spring 1942, most nonfarm prices had been frozen. Still, the inflationary spiral continued as farm prices increased.

The president in October 1942 was given the authority to fix farm prices, urban and rural rents, and wages and salaries. A new agency, the Office of Economic Stabilization, was created to enforce the new law and coordinate the activities of the different federal agencies dealing with prices and wages. Even this action, however, failed to halt the rise of consumer and wholesale price increases. Only after President Roosevelt took a series of administrative actions in April 1943 did prices finally stabilize for the remainder of the war.

Francis Bellamy's "Pledge of Allegiance to the Flag of the United States" received official recognition by Congress in an act signed into law on June 22, 1942. Republicans made substantial gains in both the House and Senate as a result of the 1942 elections, although the Democrats maintained their majority.

Major Acts

Lend-Lease Act. Empowered the president to authorize heads of government departments and agencies "to sell, transfer title to, exchange, lease, lend, or otherwise dispose of" any defense article to "the government of any country whose defense the President deems vital to the defense of the United States" without regard to the terms of any existing legislation. Provided for an initial appropriation of $7 billion and for the disposal of up to $1.3 billion of materials from existing government property. Approved March 11, 1941 (P.L. 11; 55 Stat. 31–33). The Lend-Lease Act was extended for an additional year in 1943. Approved March 11, 1943 (P.L. 9; 57 Stat. 20). In 1944 the Lend-Lease Act was again extended for an additional year. That Act included language prohibiting the president from assuming or incurring "any obligations on the part of the United States with respect to post-war economic policy or any post-war policy involving international relations except in accordance with established constitutional procedure." Approved May 17, 1944 (P.L. 304; 58 Stat. 222–223).

Selective Service Extension of 1941. Amended the Selective Training and Service Act of 1940 to increase the term of service for inductees from twelve to eighteen months. Approved August 18, 1941 (P.L. 213; 55 Stat. 626–628). *(Selective Training and Service Act of 1940, p. 260)*

Revenue Act of 1941. Raised excess profits tax, regular corporate tax, excise taxes, and surtaxes on individuals. Lowered exemptions for joint returns to $1,500 and single returns to $750. Approved September 20, 1941 (P.L. 250; 55 Stat. 687–728).

Repeal of Portions of the Neutrality Act of 1939. Repealed certain sections of the 1939 Neutrality Act by allowing U.S. merchant ships to be armed and carry cargoes to warring nations. Approved November 17, 1941 (P.L. 294; 55 Stat. 764–765). *(Neutrality Act of 1939, p. 260)*

Declaration of a State of War with Japan. Declared that a state of war existed between the United States and Japan. Authorized and directed the president "to deploy of the entire naval and military forces of the United States, and the resources of the Government to carry on the war against the Imperial Government of Japan; and to bring the conflict to a successful termination, all of the resources of the country are hereby pledged by the Congress of the United States." Approved December 8, 1941 (P.L. 328; 55 Stat. 795).

Declaration of a State of War with Germany. Declared that a state of war existed between the United States and Germany. Authorized and directed the president "to deploy of the entire naval and military forces of the United States, and the resources of the Government to carry on the war against the Government of Germany; and to bring the conflict to a successful termination, all of the resources of the country are hereby pledged by the Congress of the United States." Approved December 11, 1941 (P.L. 331; 55 Stat. 796).

Declaration of a State of War with Italy. Declared that a state of war existed between the United States and Italy. Authorized and directed the president "to deploy of the entire naval and military forces of the United States, and the resources of the Government to carry on the war against the Government of Italy; and to bring the conflict to a successful termination, all of the resources of the country are hereby pledged by the Congress of the United States." Approved December 11, 1941 (P.L. 332; 55 Stat. 797).

First War Powers Act. Authorized the president "to make such redistribution of functions among executive agencies as he may deem necessary, including any functions, duties, and powers hitherto by law conferred upon any executive department, commission, bureau, agency, governmental corporation, office, or officer." Authorized the president to also "utilize, coordinate, or consolidate any executive or administrative commissions, bureaus, agencies, governmental corporations, offices, or officers," to enter into contracts "without regard to the provisions of law, relating to the making, performance, amendment, or modification of contracts," and to "investigate, regulate, or prohibit any transitions in foreign exchange." Required that Congress approve recommendations to abolish statutory bureaus or functions. Approved December 18, 1941 (P.L. 354; 55 Stat. 838–841).

Selective Training and Service Act of 1940 Amendments. Provided that all men between the ages of eighteen and sixty-five must register, and all men from ages twenty to forty-five would be subject to training and service. Approved December 20, 1941 (P.L. 360; 55 Stat. 844–847).

Emergency Price Control Act of 1942. Established the Office of Price Administration with power to stabilize prices and "to prevent speculative, unwarranted, and abnormal increases in prices and rents." Exempted agricultural products from coverage of the act. Approved January 30, 1942 (P.L. 421; 56 Stat. 23–37).

Second War Powers Act. Authorized the president to allocate materials and facilities as necessary for the defense of the United States. Granted additional powers to several federal agencies, and covered a number of other items, including increasing penalties for priority violations and granting free postage for soldiers. Approved March 27, 1942 (P.L. 507; 56 Stat. 176–187).

Women's Army Auxiliary Corps Act. Created a Women's Army Auxiliary Corps (WAAC) of not more than 150,000 for noncombatant service with the Army of the United States. Approved May 14, 1942 (P.L. 554; 56 Stat. 278–282). *(Women's Army Corps Established, p. 268)*

Declaration of a State of War with Bulgaria. Declared that a state of war existed between the United States and Bulgaria. Authorized and directed the president "to employ the entire naval and military forces of the United States and the resources of the Government to carry on war against the Government of Bulgaria; and to bring the conflict to a successful termination, all of the resources of the country are hereby pledged by the Congress of the United States." Approved, June 5, 1942 (P.L. 563; 56 Stat. 307).

Declaration of a State of War with Hungary. Declared that a state of war existed between the United States and Hungary. Authorized and directed the president "to employ the entire naval and military forces of the United States and the resources of the Government to carry on war against the Government of Hungary; and to bring the conflict to a successful termination, all of the resources of the country are hereby pledged by the Congress of the United States." Approved, June 5, 1942 (P.L. 564; 56 Stat. 307).

Declaration of a State of War with Romania. Declared that a state of war existed between the United States and Romania. Authorized and directed the president "to employ the entire naval and military forces of the United States and the resources of the Government to carry on war against the Government of Romania; and to bring the conflict to a successful termination, all of the resources of the country are hereby pledged by the Congress of the United States." Approved, June 5, 1942 (P.L. 565; 56 Stat. 307).

Pledge of Allegiance Recognized. Declared that the Pledge of Allegiance to the Flag would be: "I pledge allegiance to the Flag of the United States of America, and to the Republic for which it stands, one Nation indivisible, with liberty and justice for all." Approved June 22, 1942 (P.L. 623; 56 Stat. 380, Sec. 7). In June of 1954, an amendment was made to add the words "under God" to the pledge of allegiance. Approved June 14, 1954 (P.L. 396; 68 Stat. 394).

Women Accepted for Voluntary Emergency Service Act. Authorized the establishment of Women Accepted for Voluntary Emergency Service (WAVES) as a unit of the U.S. Naval Reserves. Approved July 30, 1942 (P.L. 689; 56 Stat. 730–731).

Stabilization Act of 1942. Empowered the president to stabilize farm prices, nonfarm prices, rural rents, urban rents, salaries, and wages. Established the Office of Economic Stabilization to carry out the law and to coordinate the activities of the various federal agencies dealing with prices and wages. Placed a limit of $25,000 on annual salaries. Approved October 2, 1942 (P.L. 729; 56 Stat. 765–768).

Revenue Act of 1942 (Victory Tax of 1942). Increased individual income tax rates and corporate tax rates (top rate increased from 31 percent to 40 percent). Replaced 35–60 percent graduated rate schedule for excess profits tax with a flat 90 percent rate. Created a 5 percent Victory Tax on all individual income over $624, with postwar credit. Reduced personal exemption amount from $1,500 to $1,200 (married couples) and exemption amount for each dependent from $400 to $350. Substantially increased the estate and gift tax rates. Closed several loopholes, which for years had offered opportunities for avoiding taxes. Approved October 21, 1942 (P.L. 753; 56 Stat. 798–985).

Teenage Draft Act of 1942. Amended the Selective Training and Service Act of 1940 making eighteen- and nineteen-year-old males subject to the draft. Approved November 13, 1942 (P.L. 772; 56 Stat. 1018–1019).

Note

1. Steven A. Bank, Kirk J. Stark, and Joseph J. Thorndike, *War and Taxes* (Washington, D.C.: Urban Institute Press, 2008), 96.

Seventy-eighth Congress
January 3, 1943, to January 3, 1945

First session—January 6, 1943, to December 21, 1943
Second session—January 10, 1944, to December 19, 1944
(Third administration of Franklin D. Roosevelt,
        1941–1945)

Historical Background

By the time the Seventy-eighth Congress adjourned *sine die* on December 19, 1944, the end of the war was in sight. In Europe, after crushing Axis resistance in Tunisia, the Allies invaded and conquered Sicily in August 1943. The invasion of the Italian mainland at Salerno, near Naples, in September led to the surrender of the Italian government, which had deposed National Fascist Party Prime Minister Benito Mussolini. From there the Allies made slow progress up the Italian peninsula against German opposition.

On the Eastern Front, German attempts to return to the offensive in the summer of 1943 were defeated, and the Russian army's counterattacks threw the German forces back on a thousand miles of battlefront, following the siege of Leningrad. Russian strength grew as that of their German opponents declined, and continued Soviet attacks brought the Russians to the border of Germany by the end of 1944.

On June 6, 1944, the Allies landed on beaches along the Normandy coast of France. After tough fighting, the best German forces were trapped near Falaise, and the Allied armies broke out of Normandy, racing to the German frontier by September. They were joined in their victorious advance by Allied forces, which had landed on France's Mediterranean coast in August. Fighting on their own ground, the Germans stabilized the Western Front during the autumn, defeated an Allied airborne invasion of the Netherlands, and launched a dangerous, but ultimately unsuccessful, counterattack at the Battle of the Bulge.

In the Pacific, the U.S. naval strength was greatly increased as the full weight of American industrial capacity and manpower was brought to bear. Dual drives, one in the Solomon Islands and along the New Guinea coast and the other across the central Pacific, advanced against Japanese opposition. In July 1944 U.S. Army and Marine Corps forces invaded the Mariana Islands, a keystone of Japan's defensive perimeter. Japan's carrier fleet counterattacked, and in the Battle of the Philippine Sea, Japan's carrier air power was virtually destroyed. To the south, General Douglas MacArthur began the liberation of the Philippines when his army landed on the island of Leyte in October. Japan responded by attacking with its still-powerful surface fleet. In a series of fierce engagements, known collectively as the Battles of Leyte Gulf, the Japanese navy was destroyed as an effective opponent.

Early in World War II, Franklin D. Roosevelt's actions as president went largely unchallenged on Capitol Hill until a spirited struggle arose over how best to prevent strikes from threatening war-related industries. Although the labor unions had taken a no-strike pledge shortly after Pearl Harbor, the president's executive order freezing wages and prices in April 1943 prompted United Mine Workers president John L. Lewis to call an immediate strike. Congress reacted by authorizing the federal government to seize any industry producing war materials that faced a potential strike. Roosevelt vetoed the Smith-Connally Antistrike Act on the grounds that it would stimulate, not discourage, work stoppages, but his veto was overridden the same day.

As farm labor dwindled in the spring of 1943, Congress appropriated $26.1 million to help cover the costs of using migrant farm laborers from Central and South America. Also during the first five months of the year, two significant actions were taken to bring women volunteers into the mainstream of the American armed forces. The first bill provided a legal basis for licensed female physicians and surgeons to be granted commissions in the U.S. Army and Naval Reserves for the first time. The second established a Women's Army Corps within the U.S. Army. Within ninety days it had enlisted more than 75 percent of those who were serving in the Women's Army Auxiliary Corps, which would be phased out in September 1943.

A lengthy struggle surrounded efforts to repeal the various Chinese Exclusion Acts. Roosevelt told Congress that such action would "correct a historic mistake and silence distorted Japanese propaganda." The House Committee on Immigration and Naturalization in October 1943 favorably reported a repeal bill expressing the opinion of the American people that "freedom depends upon respect for the integrity of others and that their own freedom and security demand that they accord to others the respect that they ask for themselves." Near the end of the year, a repeal act providing for a quota of one hundred Chinese immigrants a year became law.

The Public Health Act of 1943 provided for long-sought organizational changes that would serve as the administrative basis for the Public Health Service (PHS) for the next two decades. As a consequence, by the end of the war the PHS had developed a much higher profile in the United States and a well-earned international reputation. All of the laws affecting the functions of the Public Health Service were consolidated for the first time in the Public Health Service Act of 1944. The act "set the course for PHS policy making for decades to come," and its "provisions made PHS a vehicle for a new approach to public health in the United States, one organized around State-level planning, a commitment to a quasi-public system of health care financing, and the development of preventive measures through the subsidy of scientific research, health professions education, and facilities construction."[1]

Under the Current Tax Payment Act of 1943, the most far-reaching change made in the federal tax system during World War II, the pay-as-you-go system of withholding tax from individual paychecks on a weekly or biweekly basis was introduced. Other sources of income were also required to be reported, as were dividends paid to individual stockholders in corporations. When the administration sought to increase taxes by an additional $10.5 billion early in 1944, Congress responded with a modest tax increase of slightly more the $1 billion. President Roosevelt vetoed the revenue measure as "wholly ineffective and providing relief not for the needy, but for the greedy." It was the first presidential veto of a tax bill in American history. Congress promptly overrode the veto.

The return of the first wave of World War II veterans triggered passage in June 1944 of the GI Bill, which provided a broad array of education, employment, medical, and economic benefits and Veterans Administration-guaranteed loans for homes, farms, and businesses. It has been hailed as one of the most significant pieces of legislation ever produced by the federal government—one that impacted the United States socially, economically, and politically. But it almost did not come to pass as members of the House and Senate debated various provisions of the bill. Ultimately, despite their differences, all agreed something must be done to help veterans assimilate into civilian life.

Also that June, legislation was signed that established a veterans preference system for civil service employment. Subsequently, the GI Bill was extended in 1952 to veterans of the Korean War (Veterans Readjustment Benefits Act) and in 1966 to all veterans of military service (Readjustment Benefits Act), whether they had served during wartime or peacetime. *(Veterans Readjustment Assistance Act of 1952 [Korean GI Bill of Rights], p. 290; Veterans Readjustment Benefits Act [Cold War GI Bill], p. 324)*

Other postwar planning necessitated three weeks of consideration by a conference committee before agreement was reached on the disposal of surplus government property once hostilities ceased. Under the Surplus Property Act of 1944, a three-member Surplus Property Board was established to oversee the disposal of such property. Congress retained control over sales, and the proceeds were used to retire the national debt. President Roosevelt signed a bill centralizing responsibility for contract settlements, surplus disposal, and reemployment programs in the Office of War Mobilization and Reconversion.

Considerable attention was given to allowing soldiers to cast absentee ballots in the 1944 presidential and congressional elections. The central issue was whether there should be a federal ballot or state ballots. The federal ballot made it easier to vote for a presidential candidate, while ballots regulated by the states would allow state officials to be chosen. Ultimately, Congress approved a limited federal ballot and recommended that the states immediately enact legislation to allow for absentee voting. Members of the armed forces accounted for 5.6 percent of the total popular vote for president in 1944.

Franklin Roosevelt garnered a fourth term with 53.4 percent of the popular vote, while Republican Thomas E. Dewey captured 45.9 percent. Roosevelt and his vice presidential running mate, Harry S. Truman, won 432 electoral votes; Dewey and John W. Bricker, 99. The Democrats retained solid majorities in both houses of Congress.

Major Acts

Army and Navy Female Physicians and Surgeons Act. Provided for the inclusion of licensed female physicians and surgeons in the Medical Departments of the Army and Navy for the remainder of the war and six months thereafter as the secretaries of war and the navy might consider necessary. Stipulated that those appointed under this act would be commissioned in the U.S. Army or Naval Reserve and "receive the same pay and allowances and be entitled to the same rights, privileges, and benefits as a member of the Officers' Reserve Corps of the Army and the Naval Reserve of the Navy with the same grade and length of service." Approved April 16, 1943 (P.L. 38; 57 Stat. 65).

Farm Labor Supply Act. Appropriated $26.1 million for the administrator of food production and distribution to assist "in providing an adequate supply of workers for the production and harvesting of agricultural commodities essential to the prosecution of the war." Stipulated that these funds could be used to recruit workers; provide transportation, supervision, shelter, protection, and health care for such workers and their families; lease, repair, alter, and operate labor supply centers; pay personnel and administrative expenses; and pay or reimburse public or private agencies or individuals for furnishing services and facilities. Exempted workers from North and South America who desired to perform agricultural labor in the United States from paying the head tax required by Section 2 of the Immigration Act of 1917. Approved April 29, 1943 (P.L. 45; 57 Stat. 70–73). (*Immigration Act of 1917, p. 205*)

Current Tax Payment Act. Instituted the pay-as-you-go system of withholding taxes from individual paychecks on a weekly or biweekly basis. Required employers to withhold 20 percent of wages and salaries beyond exemptions, taxpayers to report other income quarterly, and corporations to report all dividends paid to stockholders. Approved June 9, 1943 (P.L. 68; 57 Stat. 126–150).

Smith-Connally Antistrike Act. Authorized the president to take possession of any industry producing materials necessary to the war effort. Prohibited promotion of strikes, lockouts, or other interruptions in production after the government had taken control of an industry. Required unions in plants not essential to the war effort to observe a thirty-day cooling-off period before striking. Prohibited unions from making monetary contributions to political campaigns or candidates. Presidential veto overridden by Congress. Became law without the president's signature June 25, 1943 (P.L. 89; 57 Stat. 163–169).

Women's Army Corps Established. Established a Women's Army Corps (WAC) in the Army of the United States "for the period of the present war and for six months thereafter." Limited enlistment to women between the ages of twenty and fifty. Provided that the commander of the WAC could not be promoted above the rank of colonel and its other officers above lieutenant colonel. Provided for the repeal of most of the Women's Army Auxiliary Corps

Act of 1942. Approved July 1, 1943 (P.L. 110; 57 Stat. 371–372). *(Women's Army Auxiliary Corps Act, p. 264)*

Public Health Service Act of 1943. Provided that the Federal Health Service would consist of the Office of the Surgeon General, the National Institutes of Health (NIH), the Bureau of Medical Services, and the Bureau of Health Services. Authorized the surgeon general to assign functions to the Office of Surgeon General, NIH, and the two bureaus. Authorized the surgeon general to establish, transfer, and consolidate such divisions, sections, and units within each organization as necessary for the efficiency of the service. Approved November 11, 1943 (P.L. 184; 57 Stat. 587–589).

Magnuson Act (Repeal of Chinese Exclusion Acts of 1943). Repealed the Chinese Exclusion Acts of 1882, 1884, 1888, 1892, 1893, and 1898. Approved December 17, 1943 (P.L. 199; 57 Stat. 600–601).

Revenue Act of 1943. Increased income, corporate, and excise taxes slightly. Repealed the victory tax, and lowered individual income tax exemptions to $1,000 for married couples and $500 for unmarried persons. Made no changes in estate, gift, and corporation taxes. Liberalized allowances for depletion in extractive industries. Presidential veto overridden by Congress. Became law without the president's signature. The first tax bill to become law by virtue of Congress overriding a presidential veto. Approved February 25, 1944 (P.L. 235; 58 Stat. 21–94).

Soldier Vote Act. Authorized absentee voting in time of war by "members of the land and naval forces, members of the merchant marine, and others absent from the place of their residence." Established a U.S. War Ballot Commission to administer the act. Prohibited the commission from subverting any state voting laws applicable to the voters involved. Approved April 1, 1944 (P.L. 277; 58 Stat. 136–149).

GI Bill (Servicemen's Readjustment Act of 1944). Provided veterans of World War II with an array of benefits including occupational guidance; tuition and expenses for education; preference in hiring for many jobs; assistance in obtaining loans for homes, farms, and businesses; and unemployment and hospitalization benefits. Approved June 22, 1944 (P.L. 346; 58 Stat. 284–301).

Veterans Preference Act of 1944. Established a system that gave "honorably discharged veterans, their widows, and the wives of disabled veterans, who themselves are not qualified," preference in being appointed, reinstated, reappointed, or retained in civilian positions in "all establishments, agencies, bureaus, administrations, projects, and departments of the Government." Approved June 27, 1944 (P.L. 359; 58 Stat. 387–391).

Public Health Service Act of 1944. Consolidated and revised substantially all existing legislation relating to programs and activities of the Public Health Service. Authorized the service to make grants-in-aid for research to public and private institutions for investigations in any field related to the public health. Authorized the service to work with and support the efforts of State health departments in general public health work. Established a national tuberculosis program in the service that could exercise responsibility for leadership and assistance to the states. Strengthened the Commissioned Corps of the service, moving it to a broader base, with the commissioning of nurses, sanitarians, and specialists in other specific fields related to public health. Expanded the Office of Surgeon General. Authorized the National Institutes of Health to conduct clinical research. Confirmed the service's broad power and duties with respect to foreign and inter-state quarantine, research into the causes and prevention of disease, medical and hospital care of merchant seaman, and medical service to the Coast Guard. Approved July 1, 1944 (P.L. 410; 58 Stat. 682–720).

Surplus Property Act of 1944. Established a three-member board to supervise the disposal of surplus government property through transfer or sale at fair market value. Assigned preferences in acquiring such property to other federal agencies, state and local governments, nonprofit educational institutions, veterans, and small businesses. Approved October 3, 1944 (P.L. 457; 58 Stat. 765–784).

War Mobilization and Reconversion Act of 1944. Created the Office of War Mobilization and Reconversion (OWMR) to act as the primary coordinator for resolving problems "arising out of the transition from war to peace." Empowered the OWMR to promote and assist "in the development of demobilization and reconversion plans by the executive agencies" and "settle controversies between executive agencies in the development and administration of such plans." Provided the director of the OWMR with general supervision over the Contract Settlements Act and the Surplus Property Act of 1944. Approved October 3, 1944 (P.L. 458; 58 Stat. 785–792).

Note

1. Lynne Page Snyder, *Public Health Reports,* v. 109, July-August 1994, 471.

Seventy-ninth Congress
January 3, 1945, to January 3, 1947

First session—January 3, 1945, to December 21, 1945
Second session—January 14, 1946, to August 2, 1946
(Fourth administration of Franklin D. Roosevelt, 1945;
first administration of Harry S. Truman,
1945–1949)

Historical Background

The war in Europe moved to its climax in early 1945. From west and east, Allied and Soviet forces drove into the heart of Adolf Hitler's Germany. Less than three months after his fourth inauguration, President Franklin D. Roosevelt died of a cerebral hemorrhage on April 12, 1945, in Warm Springs, Georgia. Vice President Harry S. Truman assumed the presidency the same day. As Roosevelt was laid to rest, Soviet armies launched the final drive to Berlin. On April 25, American and Russian troops met at Torgau, on the Elbe River. Five days later, Hitler committed suicide in Berlin as Soviet troops approached his underground headquarters. On May 7, the German high command surrendered at Reims, France, and the following day, President Truman and British prime minister Winston Churchill declared the war in Europe over.

Truman had been president for less than two weeks when delegates from fifty nations gathered in San Francisco to begin writing the United Nations (UN) Charter. A preliminary draft of the charter had been prepared at the Dumbarton Oaks Conference in the fall of 1944 by representatives of the United States, Great Britain, the Soviet Union, and China. President Roosevelt, who died shortly before the United Nations Conference convened, avoided President Woodrow Wilson's mistake of failing to include members of

Congress in drafting the League of Nations Covenant after World War I, by appointing two senators and two representatives to the delegation. Unlike the League Covenant, the UN Charter approved on June 26, 1945, focused not on terms of peace but on a new world organization that allowed small powers an unprecedented large voice, promoted freedom of debate and recommendation by all of its members, and afforded the opportunity to mobilize the potent force of world opinion against aggression. Late in July, following a week of hearings and a week of debate, the Senate approved the charter. At the time of its creation, many Americans viewed the United Nations as the world's leading peacekeeping organization. Late in July, the Senate, following a week of hearings and a week of debate, approved the charter and near the end of the year provided for the appointment of representatives to the United Nations.

U.S. forces had seized the Pacific island of Iwo Jima at great cost in early 1945. On April 1, U.S. Marine Corps and Army forces invaded Okinawa, just 360 miles southwest of Japan. Japanese resistance resulted in heavy American casualties, prompting fears that an Allied invasion of Japan would be costly to the armed forces of both sides and to Japanese civilians. On August 6, 1945, the United States dropped an atomic bomb on the Japanese city of Hiroshima, killing between 70,000 and 140,000 of its inhabitants. On August 8, the Soviet Union, previously neutral in the Pacific conflict, declared war on Japan, and on August 9, a second atomic bomb devastated the city of Nagasaki, where between 35,000 and 70,000 lost their lives. The bombs were developed in secret under the code name Manhattan Project, directed by Brigadier General Leslie R. Groves. At its height, the project employed more than 129,000 people, most of whom had no idea of its purpose, at several different locations around the country, without any public knowledge of its activities. The total expenditures for the project exceeded $2 billion dollars in congressionally appropriated funds designated to be used by the president for secret purposes. The Japanese government sued for peace, accepting Allied terms on August 14. The instrument of surrender was signed on September 2, 1945, aboard the USS *Missouri* in Tokyo Bay.

President Truman sent a special message to Congress in October 1945, urging the creation of an atomic energy commission "to control all sources of atomic energy and all activities connected with its development and use in the United States." Only after intensive debate on Capitol Hill, as well as in the scientific community, did the Atomic Energy Act become law. It established a presidentially appointed five-member civilian Atomic Energy Commission and a Joint Committee on Atomic Energy in Congress.

During World War II, more than 200,000 Filipinos fought in defense of the United States against the Japanese in the Pacific theater of military operations. They shared the fate of their American counterparts on the battlefield, in prisoner of war camps, and throughout the countryside as part of the guerrilla resistance. Following World War II, however, Congress passed the Rescission Act of 1946, which declared that the Filipino veterans in the Philippine Commonwealth Army were ineligible for veterans benefits because the United States had given the Army of the Philippines $200 million after the war.

The War Brides Act was the first of several related measures to allow United States soldiers to bring their alien brides and families into the United States following World War II. It was enacted to expedite the admission of alien spouses and minor children of U.S. Armed Forces into the United States by providing them nonquota immigrant status. Initially, Asian women could not take advantage of the War Brides Act because the 1924 Immigration Act categorized them as racially ineligible for both immigration and naturalization. A 1947 amendment to the War Brides Act allowed Asian wives of U.S. servicemen to immigrate. As soldiers went back to farming following World War II, the availability of credit became a significant issue. Passage of the Farmers Home Administration Act reflected the consensus that a restructuring of the Farm Security

Administration (FSA) was necessary to meet the growing credit needs of the postwar period. The FSA concentrated on helping individual farmers acquire their own farms, just as the Federal Housing Authority helped people own their own homes.

The Export-Import Bank of the United States, first created by executive order in 1934 to "assist in financing U.S. trade with the Soviet Union," was established as an independent organization by the Export-Import Bank Act of 1945. Within a decade after its creation, the mission of the bank expanded to include the provision of loans and grants to U.S. companies seeking to export their products.

By approving American participation in the International Monetary Fund and the International Bank for Reconstruction and Development (subsequently to be known as the World Bank), Congress helped to stabilize international currencies and eliminate restrictions on foreign exchange transactions. The bank was specifically designed to guarantee loans or to make direct loans to war-torn and economically backward areas. Memories of the Great Depression of the 1930s prompted enactment of the Employment Act of 1946, which committed the federal government to developing policies to achieve full employment.

The Council of Economic Advisers was established to assist the president in the preparation of an annual report analyzing the nation's economic conditions and offering a program to achieve the purpose of the act. The act also created a Joint Economic Committee in Congress to evaluate the report and make its own recommendations. In response to a U.S. Supreme Court ruling in *United States v. South-Eastern Underwriters Association* (1944) that insurance was interstate commerce and, thus, subject to federal antitrust laws and regulation by Congress, the McCarran-Ferguson Act was approved. This enactment, sponsored by Sen. Patrick A. McCarran of Nevada and Sen. Homer Ferguson of Michigan, delegated primary authority in regulating the insurance industry to the states.

Early in 1946, President Truman triggered a six-month foreign aid debate with a request for a multibillion-dollar loan to Great Britain. Not until July was the president able to sign a fifty-year $3.75 billion loan to assist Britain in removing trade and currency restrictions that hampered postwar programs for economic reconstruction and trade liberalization. Congress later approved the Fulbright Scholars Act, an international educational and cultural exchange program designed to promote better understanding between the peoples of the United States and other nations. The act was sponsored by Sen. James W. Fulbright, of Arkansas.

Several months before the end of World War II, the Roosevelt administration had begun developing plans to stimulate postwar domestic aviation. Enactment of the Federal Airport Act of 1946, which included $500 million for construction of airports, provided a major commitment toward fulfilling that goal. Later in the year, a $375 million authorization was made for grants to states and nonprofit groups to help compensate for the lack of new hospital construction during the Depression and World War II.

The Hobbs Anti-Racketeering Act of 1946 was designed to battle organized crime, particularly to combat racketeering in labor management disputes. Federal trademark law as it now exists in the United States is based on the Lanham Trademark Act of 1946. Congress, in passing the act, attempted to modernize, simplify, and unify existing federal trademark law. Although there had been several earlier federal trademark laws, there was a recognized need for a national and uniform protection of trademarks. The Lanham Act was the first measure to combine a system of trademark registration with a set of federally enforceable substantive rights.

Following nine months of study by Congress, the Justice Department, and various bar organizations, President Truman in May 1946 signed the Administrative Procedures Act. It established principles and procedures for a broad range of government activities, including rule making, agency adjudication, and judicial review of administrative decisions. With the Legislative Reorganization Act of 1946, Congress reformed its own internal structure by reducing the number of standing committees, strengthening its professional staff and information resources, establishing lobbying registration requirements, and providing for an annual legislative budget to complement the president's budget.

The Federal Regulation of Lobbying Act, which was passed as part of the reorganization act, was the first federal lobbyist registration law. It did not directly restrict the activities of those lobbying Congress, but it

did require that they register and report their related expenses. The act stood as the primary federal lobbying disclosure law for nearly a half century, until it was significantly modified with the enactment of the Lobbying Disclosure Act of 1995. The application of the law was narrowed by the U.S. Supreme Court in 1954, in *United States v. Harris,* and frequent criticisms were made that the act was weak and ineffective.

Federal aid to school lunch programs, which had begun a decade earlier under the auspices of the Department of Agriculture, was put on an entirely new basis with the passage of the National School Lunch Act of 1946. For the first time, regular federal appropriations were authorized to provide states cash grants for public and private school lunch programs.

Since its enactment in 1946, the Federal Tort Claims Act has been the legal mechanism by which individuals injured by the wrongful or negligent acts or omissions of federal employees may seek and receive compensation from the federal government through an administrative process and, if necessary, through the federal courts. Prior to the act, it was very difficult to recover damages for government wrongdoing because of the doctrine of sovereign immunity, which provided that the government could not be sued without its consent.

A reorganization initiative designed to develop professional opportunities to attract foreign service officers and to train them to become a "disciplined corps" of civil servants prompted the Foreign Service Act of 1946. Previously, there had been little control over the selection of diplomatic and consular personnel representing the United States.

With the establishment of the Indian Claims Commission, Congress attempted to address unresolved claims by Indians regarding land transactions with the federal government. It was perceived to be a necessary step in preparing Indian tribes to manage their own affairs. Near the end of the Seventy-ninth Congress, the Coordination Act, a landmark conservation measure, established a government-wide policy for protecting existing fish and wildlife during the construction of new water projects.

In November 1946, for the first time since the Seventy-first Congress (1929–1931), the Republicans captured the majority in both the Senate and the House.

Major Acts

McCarran-Ferguson Act. Declared "that the continued regulation and taxation by the several States of the business of insurance is in the public interest, and the silence on the part of the Congress shall not be constituted to impose any barrier to the regulation or taxation of such business by the several States." Assigned regulation of the insurance industry to the states, with an exception for acts of Congress that specifically related to insurance. Reasserted the applicability of the antitrust laws against agreements or acts of boycott, coercion, or intimidation by insurance companies. Approved March 9, 1945 (P.L. 15; 59 Stat. 33–34).

U.S. Participation in the United Nations. Provided for United States membership in the United Nations, which consisted of six chief organs: General Assembly, Security Council, Economic and Social Council, International Court of Justice, Trusteeship Council, and Secretariat. Concluded June 26, 1945. Ratified by the Senate July 28, 1945 (59 Stat. 1031). In December 1945, Congress provided for appointment of representatives of the United States in the organs and agencies of the United Nations. Approved December 20, 1945 (P.L. 264; 59 Stat. 619–621).

Bretton Woods Agreements Act. Authorized the United States to join the International Monetary Fund and the International Bank for Reconstruction and Development. Approved July 31, 1945 (P.L. 171; 59 Stat. 512–517).

Export-Import Bank Act of 1945. Made the Export-Import Bank an independent agency of the federal government operating under a renewable charter. Authorized the bank to finance and facilitate exports and imports and the exchange of commodities and services between the United States and foreign countries. Approved July 31, 1945 (P.L. 173; 59 Stat. 526–529).

War Brides Act. Allowed non-Asian honorably discharged military personnel to bring alien spouses and alien minor children to the United States if they apply for admission within three years. Approved December 28, 1945 (P.L. 271; 59 Stat. 659). The Alien Fiancée Law of 1946 permitted American military personnel to bring a foreign fiancée to the United States providing they officially married them within three months of arrival. Approved June 29, 1946 (P.L. 471; 60 Stat. 339–340). In 1947, the War Brides Act was amended to eliminate race as a determining factor in allowing alien spouses and children of military personnel to enter the country. Approved July 22, 1947 (P.L. 213; 61 Stat. 401). An act passed on August 19, 1950, extended the War Brides Act again to cover all military spouses and minor children, with a form of expiration established by the restriction that the marriage had to occur before March 19, 1952. Approved August 19, 1950 (P.L. 717; 64 Stat. 464–465).

Filipino Rescission Act of 1946. Stated that the service of Filipino soldiers during World War II "shall not be deemed to be or to have been . . . in the military or national forces of the United States or any component thereof for the purposes of any law of the United States conferring rights, privileges or benefits upon any person by reason of the service of such person or the service of any other person in the military or naval forces of the United States." Approved February 18, 1946 (P.L. 301; 60 Stat. 14). The 1990 Immigration and Naturalization Act allowed for the naturalization of natives of the Philippines who performed "active-duty service under United State command during World War II." Approved November 29, 1990 (P.L. 109–649; 104 Stat. 5048–5049, Title IV, Sec. 408f). In 2003, Congress granted limited war-related veterans disability benefits, as well as veterans health benefits, to Filipino veterans living in the United States; Filipino veterans living outside the United States were not covered by this legislation. Approved December 6, 2003 (117 Stat. 2044, Title I, Sec. 103). In 2009, President Barack Obama signed the American Recovery and Reinvestment Act of 2009, which contained a provision that allowed for the release of previously appropriated funds providing one-time payments of $15,000 to Filipino World War II veterans who are U.S. citizens, and $9,000 to Filipino World War II veterans who are non-citizens. Approved February 17, 2009 (P.L. 111–5; 123 Stat. 200–202, Title X, Sec. 1002). The $198 million appropriation for payments to eligible Filipino World War II veterans was contained in the 2009 Continuing Resolution. Approved September 30, 2008 (P.L. 110–329; 122 Stat. 3583, Div. A, Sec. 160).

Employment Act of 1946. Declared it to be the policy and responsibility of the federal government to use all practical means to assist industry, agriculture, labor, and state and local governments in promoting maximum employment, production, and purchasing power. Required the president to submit an annual economic report to Congress outlining programs and policies to achieve this end, and established a three-member Council of Economic Advisers to assist the president in developing economic policy. Established a Joint Economic Committee in Congress to study the matters addressed in the report, analyze means of furthering the policy of full employment, and prepare recommendations as well as findings for the Senate and House regarding the president's economic report. Approved February 20, 1946 (P.L. 304; 60 Stat. 23–26).

Federal Airport Act. Authorized a seven-year, $500 million program of matching federal grants to cities and states for construction of airports in the continental United States and $20 million for Alaska and Hawaii. Authorized the administrator of the Civil Aeronautics Administration and the War and Navy Departments to prepare a national plan for the development of public airports. Approved May 13, 1946 (P.L. 377; 60 Stat. 170–180).

National School Lunch Act of 1946. Authorized regular federal cash grants to the states for nonprofit school lunch programs in public and private schools. Stipulated that at least 75 percent of funds be reserved for cash grants to the states for local purchases, while the remaining 25 percent could be used by the Department of Agriculture to assist the program. Approved June 4, 1946 (P.L. 396; 60 Stat. 230–234).

Administrative Procedures Act. Required federal agencies to give notice of proposed rules, receive and consider written comments on such proposals, and publish final rules in the *Federal Register*. Prescribed standards and procedures for agency adjudications, and set out hearing procedures. Provided judicial review for individuals claiming legal injury because of any agency action. Codified existing doctrines defining judicial review of administrative action. Approved June 11, 1946 (P.L. 404; 60 Stat. 237–244).

Hobbs Anti-Racketeering Act. Made it a federal crime to interfere with interstate commerce by extortion, robbery, or physical violence. Proscribed heavy penalties for those who used extortion, robbery, or other criminal means to disrupt interstate commerce. Approved July 3, 1946 (P.L. 486; 60 Stat. 420–421).

Lanham Act (Trademark Act of 1946). Provided for a national system of trademark registration and protection for the owner of a federally registered trademark against the use of similar trademarks if such use was likely to result in consumer confusion. Stated when owners of trademarks may be entitled to federal judicial protection against infringement, and established other guidelines and remedies for trademark owners. Approved July 5, 1946 (P.L. 489; 60 Stat. 427–446).

British Loan Act. Authorized a loan of $3.75 billion to Great Britain and a grant of $650 million in settlement of lend-lease, provided that Britain eliminated emergency foreign exchange controls and discriminatory import restrictions. Approved July 15, 1946 (P.L. 509; 60 Stat. 535).

Fulbright Scholars Act. Amended the Surplus Property Act of 1944 to authorize the secretary of state to enter into executive agreements with foreign countries to use currencies acquired from the sale of surplus property abroad for educational purposes. Established an international educational and cultural exchange program under the direction of the secretary of state for American citizens to attend schools or institutions of higher learning abroad and for citizens of foreign countries to attend American schools or institutions of higher learning. Provided for the selection of exchange students and payments for transportation, tuition, maintenance, and other expenses incidental to scholastic activities. Approved August 1, 1946 (P.L. 584; 60 Stat. 754–755). *(Surplus Property Act of 1944, p. 269; Mutual Educational and Cultural Exchange Act, p. 312)*

Atomic Energy Act. Transferred control over all aspects of atomic energy research and development from the War Department to a five-member civilian Atomic Energy Commission (AEC) appointed by the president. Created a Military Liaison Committee to provide coordination between the AEC and the Department of Justice, a General Advisory Committee of nine scientists, and a Joint Committee on Atomic Energy to be composed of nine senators and nine representatives with oversight responsibility over the AEC. Approved August 1, 1946 (P.L. 585; 60 Stat. 755–775).

Legislative Reorganization Act of 1946. Reduced the number of standing House committees from forty-eight to nineteen and standing Senate committees from thirty-three to fifteen. Provided for preparation of an annual legislative budget to complement the president's budget. Raised the salaries of senators and representatives from $10,000 to $12,500. Provided for professional committee staffs, and strengthened the Legislative Reference Service. Banned certain types of private bills. Approved August 2, 1946 (P.L. 601, Titles I and II; 60 Stat. 812–839).

Federal Regulation of Lobbying Act. Required lobbyists to register with the secretary of the Senate and clerk of the House and file quarterly financial reports on their activities. Required organizations soliciting or receiving money for the principal purposing of lobbying Congress to also file quarterly reports with the clerk of the House. Approved August 2, 1946 (P.L. 601, Title II; 60 Stat. 839–842).

Federal Tort Claims Act. Waived the government's immunity from tort liability by permitting the suits against them for money damages, loss of property, personal injury, or death provided circumstances fit within the strict limits of the act. Permitted recovery of money damages because of a negligent or wrongful act or omission by the federal government or an employee of the federal government while the employee was acting within his/her scope of employment or office. Approved August 2, 1946 (P.L. 901; 60 Stat. 842–847, Title IV).

Foreign Service Act of 1946. Declares that the objective of the act is "to improve, strengthen, and expand the Foreign Service of the United States" and revise the laws relating to its administration. Created the position of Director General of the Foreign Service with responsibility for administering the service. Created a Board of Foreign Service to make recommendations to the Secretary of State regarding personnel management of the service. Provided for increases in the salaries and allowances of ambassadors, ministers, and foreign service officers. Introduced the merit system for promotions to all but appointive positions. Established the Foreign Service Institute to furnish in-service training. Approved August 13, 1946 (P.L. 724; 60 Stat. 999–1040).

Hill-Burton Hospital Survey and Construction Act. Authorized a five-year, $375 million program of federal grants to states for hospital construction based on state assessments of local needs. Required that states provide $2 for each federal $1. Provided $3 million for surveys of state hospital needs. Approved August 13, 1946 (P.L. 725; 60 Stat. 1040–1049).

Indian Claims Commission Act. Established a three-member Indian Claims Commission to consider all outstanding claims by Indian tribes of unfair treatment in land transactions with the federal government. Provided that judgments favorable to the Indians were to result in compensatory monetary awards. Approved August 13, 1946 (P.L. 726; 60 Stat. 1049–1056).

Farmers Home Administration Act of 1946. Authorized the Secretary of Agriculture to make production and subsistence loans, in lieu of the emergency and rural rehabilitation loans previously made, to farmers who could not secure credit elsewhere, and to insure farm mortgages. Consolidated the Farm Security Administration with the Emergency Crop and Feed Loan Division of the Farm Credit Administration so "eligible farmers" could "obtain their agricultural credit and services at one central point." Stated that the main purpose of the act was "to simplify and improve credit services to farmers and promote farm ownership by . . . authorizing Government insurance of loans to farmers." Approved August 14, 1946 (P.L. 731; 60 Stat. 1062–1080).

Fish and Wildlife Coordination Act of 1946. Required federal agencies, as well as other public and private agencies using federal permits or licenses for water projects, to first consult the Fish and Wildlife Service to determine what measures were necessary to prevent or reduce harm to existing fish and wildlife. Stipulated that water projects include conservation features for fish and wildlife, and established procedures for the Fish and Wildlife Service to automatically review each proposed water project to determine its possible effect on fish, birds, and wildlife. Empowered the Fish and Wildlife Service with authority to cooperate in a broad range of activities with the various states and other federal agencies. Approved August 14, 1946 (P.L. 732; 60 Stat. 1080–1082).

Eightieth Congress
January 3, 1947, to January 3, 1949

First session—January 3, 1947, to December 19, 1947
Second session—January 6, 1948, to December 31, 1948
(First administration of Harry S. Truman, 1945–1949)

Historical Background

During the first seven months of 1947, Congress completed two significant actions relating to the presidency. First, a top GOP priority after assuming control of the Eightieth Congress was ratification of a proposed constitutional amendment limiting the tenure of all future presidents to two terms. The Twenty-second Amendment became effective on February 27, 1951. Second, President Harry S. Truman completed a two-year effort to resolve a deep concern regarding the inadequacies of the Presidential Succession Act of 1886. The new act placed the Speaker of the House and the president pro tempore of the Senate, both of whom had been popularly elected, next in the line of succession to the presidency after the vice president. Under the earlier act, the order of succession had been the vice president and then the presidentially appointed secretary of state and other members of the cabinet in the order that their respective departments were established.

Much other work of the Eightieth Congress focused on the foreign policy challenges that confronted the United States in the aftermath of the Second World War, and none occupied more attention than managing relations with the Soviet Union. Even before the war ended, the uneasy alliance between the United States and the Soviet Union had begun to unravel, and by 1947 the former allies were adversaries in a global geopolitical ideological struggle. While neither at war or peace, the two hostile superpowers were, as Bernard M. Baruch observed, involved in a "cold war," which would last for half a century. When Soviet pressure against the West began to build at the outset of the cold war, President Truman thwarted the extension of communism across the eastern Mediterranean by asking Congress to make a commitment to support Greece, where a Soviet-supported communist insurgency had come close to toppling the government, and Turkey, where widespread fear existed of a Russian invasion. On March 12, 1947, Truman appeared before a joint session of Congress to urge adoption of what was to become known as the Truman Doctrine. "I believe," he declared, that "it must be the policy of the United States to support free peoples who are resisting attempted subjugation by armed minorities or by outside pressures" wherever such conditions exist. To resolve the most immediate threat, he requested $400 million for military and economic assistance to Greece and Turkey. Congress passed the Greek-Turkish Aid Act. Another $350 million in economic aid was approved for Austria, Greece, Hungary, Italy, Poland, China, and Trieste.

"To a significant degree," one author has suggested, "contemporary U.S. public diplomacy has been dictated by legislation, The initial law legitimizing public diplomacy, so to speak, was the United States Information and Education Exchange Act of 1948."[1] The Smith-Mundt Act, as it is known, made culture, education, and information an integral part of American foreign policy by recognizing the importance of educational and cultural exchanges.

On June 5, 1947, Secretary of State George C. Marshall, in a celebrated Harvard University commencement address, suggested that even more massive American economic aid was needed to assure the postwar recovery of Europe. Marshall's proposal was endorsed by President Truman, as well as the War Department, and subsequently was embraced by the sixteen-nation Committee of European Economic Cooperation. Following long and sometimes bitter debates on Capitol Hill, Congress in April 1948 approved the Marshall Plan (Foreign Assistance Act). During the next four years, Congress authorized more that $13 billion in economic aid to countries in Western Europe.

When the lengthening shadow of communist aggression threatened to spread to the Western Hemisphere, representatives from the United States and eighteen Latin American nations met in Rio de Janeiro to sign the Inter-American Treaty of Reciprocal Assistance. The Rio Treaty provided that an attack on any of the signatories would be considered an attack on all and would be met with collective economic, political, and military sanctions. It was ratified by the Senate 72 to 1 in December 1947. The Displaced Persons Act allowed 200,000 European refugees to enter the United States.

A two-year struggle to unify the armed services of the United States concluded with the passage of the National Security Act. The army, navy, and air force were placed under the civilian authority of a newly created position of secretary of defense, and three new agencies were created to coordinate national security policy, intelligence activities, and economic mobilization—the National Security Council, Central Intelligence Agency, and National Security Resources Board, respectively. Ten months after the Department of the Air Force was created in the National Security Act of 1947, Congress designated the Civil Air Patrol as the civilian auxiliary of the Air Force. A war claims commission was created in July 1948, to adjudicate claims and pay out compensation to American prisoners of war and civilian internees of World War II.

Also in July 1948, Congress approved an agreement placing two thousand small islands in the western Pacific that been acquired during the war under the trustee system of the United Nations, with the United States as the administering authority of the Trust Territory of the Pacific Islands.

The most significant piece of domestic legislation approved by the Republican-dominated Eightieth Congress was the Taft-Hartley Act, enacted over President Truman's veto on June 23, 1947. Republican congressional candidates had promised to address the public's frustration with the millions of workers who had struck various industries following the war. Taft-Hartley, which was bitterly opposed by organized labor, outlawed the closed shop, jurisdictional strikes, and secondary boycotts. The legislation was sponsored by Sen. Robert A. Taft of Ohio and Rep. Fred A. Hartley Jr. of New Jersey.

"The Commodity Credit Corporation Act of 1948," according to agricultural historian Oscar C. Stine, "was important because it achieved three purposes. It stabilized, supported, and protected farm incomes and prices; it assisted in maintaining adequate supplies, and facilitated an orderly distribution of commodities."[2] Anticipating growing farm problems as demand shifted to prewar levels, the act provided postwar adjustment policies and programs including provision for export promotion programs as one way of supporting farm income and stabilizing commodity supplies at a time of uncertainty.

After a half-century of debate, Congress adopted the Federal Water Pollution Control Act of 1948, which provided the first comprehensive statement of federal interest in clean water programs in the twentieth century. At the time, because water pollution was considered a state and local problem the act only provided technical assistance funds to those entities. It contained no federal regulatory authority or required goals, objectives, limits, or even guidelines.

On July 24, 1948, cold war tensions increased dramatically when the Soviet Union blockaded rail, water, and highway routes to West Berlin. The United States, Great Britain, and France responded with an airlift of vital supplies that continued until September 1949 (several months after the Soviets had lifted the blockade on May 12, 1949).

The last months of 1948 were dominated by the presidential election campaign. New York governor Thomas E. Dewey, the Republican nominee, was widely favored to oust President Truman. Two third-party candidates, those of Progressive Party nominee and former vice president Henry A. Wallace and States' Rights Democrat Party nominee and South Carolina governor Strom Thurmond, added to the election's complexity. During his whistle-stop campaign between Labor Day and election day, Truman traveled more than twenty thousand miles across the country by train and made 250 speeches. As he moved toward his surprising victory, the president used his veto of Taft-Hartley to rally support among American labor and ridiculed the Republican-controlled Eightieth Congress as antilabor and antifarmer and as a "do-nothing" Congress unwilling to pass the domestic legislation both parties had promised in their platforms. The Truman and Alben W. Barkley ticket received 303 electoral votes; Dewey and Earl Warren, 198; and Thurmond and Fielding L. Wright, 39. The Democrats regained control of both houses of Congress.

Major Acts and Treaties

Twenty-second Amendment. Provided that "no person shall be elected to the office of President more than twice." Prohibited any person who had served more than two years of a predecessor's term, either because of death, resignation, or disability, from being elected President more than once. Approved March 21, 1947. Ratified by requisite number of states February 27, 1951 (61 Stat. 959).

Greek-Turkish Aid Act. Provided $400 million in economic and military aid to the governments of Greece and Turkey, both of which were engaged in defending against Soviet encroachment. Approved May 22, 1947 (P.L. 75; 61 Stat. 103–105).

Foreign Relief Act. Provided $350 million in American economic assistance to several countries damaged by the effects of World War II and the severe winter of 1946–1947. Stipulated that not more than $15 million of the funds authorized were to be available to countries or territories other than Austria, China, Greece, Hungary, Italy, Poland, and Trieste. Approved May 31, 1947 (P.L. 84; 61 Stat. 125–128).

Taft-Hartley Labor-Management Relations Act. Amended the Wagner-Connery National Labor Relations Act of 1935. Expanded the membership of the National Labor Relations Board, and separated the agency's investigative and judicial functions. Outlawed closed shop agreements and secondary strikes. Made unions liable for breach of contract or damages resulting from jurisdictional disputes. Required a sixty-day cooling-off period for termination of a contract. Authorized the president to obtain an eighty-day injunction against strikes that might endanger national health or safety. Required that union finances be made public, prohibited unions from contributing to political campaigns, and prohibited Communists from holding union offices. Allowed states to impose additional restraints on union activity by passing right-to-work laws. Presidential veto overridden by Congress. Became law without the president's signature June 23, 1947 (P.L. 101; 61 Stat. 136–162). *(Wagner-Connery National Labor Relations Act, p. 248)*

Presidential Succession Act of 1947. Changed the order of succession in the event of the death of the president of the United States, making the Speaker of the House of Representatives and then the president pro tempore of the Senate next in the line of succession to the presidency after the vice president. Approved July 18, 1947 (P.L. 199; 61 Stat. 380–381). *(Presidential Succession Act of 1886, p. 147)*

Trusteeship Agreement for the Trust Territory of the Pacific Islands. Authorized a trusteeship agreement between the United States and the United Nations Security Council for the area in the Pacific known as Micronesia. Gave the United States full administrative, legislative, and jurisdictional power as well as authority to apply U.S. laws to the Trust Territory of the Pacific Islands. Made the United States responsible for the political, economic, social, and educational advancement of the inhabitants of the trust territory. Authorized the United States to establish military bases in the territory and to close all or part of the area for security reasons. Required that the United States submit an annual report to the United Nations on its administration of the trust territory. Approved July 18, 1947 (P.L. 204; 61 Stat. 397).

National Security Act. Replaced the War and Navy Departments with the National Military Establishment headed by a secretary of defense and consisting of separately administered Departments of the Army, Navy, and Air Force under the "general direction, authority, and control" of the secretary. Designated the Joint Chiefs of Staff, which consisted of the uniformed heads of the three services, as the "principal military advisers" to the president and the secretary. Created the National Security Council to coordinate national security policy, the Central Intelligence Agency to coordinate intelligence activities, and the National Security Resources Board to coordinate economic mobilization matters. Approved July 26, 1947 (P.L. 253; 61 Stat. 495–510).

Inter-American Treaty of Reciprocal Assistance (Rio Treaty). Pledged the signatories (the United States and eighteen Latin American countries) to aid any American nation that became the victim of attack in the Western Hemisphere with collective political and economic actions. Concluded September 2, 1947. Ratification advised by the Senate December 8, 1947 (62 Stat. 1681–1715).

United States Information and Educational Exchange Act (Smith–Mundt Act). Established an information service within the State Department "to promote a better understanding of the United States in other countries, and to increase mutual understanding between the people of the United States and the people of other countries." Provided for the exchange of books, publications, and other educational materials to and with other countries; and assistance to schools, libraries, and community centers overseas. Authorized the "preparation, and dissemination abroad, of information about the United States, its people, and policies through press publications, radio, motion pictures, and other informational media, and through information centers abroad." Authorized "interchanges on a reciprocal basis between the United States and other countries of students, trainees, teachers, guests, instructors, professors, and leaders in fields of specialized knowledge or skill." Approved January 27, 1948 (62 Stat. 6–14).

Foreign Assistance Act of 1948. Economic Cooperation Act of 1948 (Marshall Plan). Established the Economic Cooperation Administration, and authorized $5.3 billion for the first year of economic assistance to sixteen European countries. Provided $275 million for military aid to Greece and Turkey, $463 million for economic and military aid for China, and $60 million for a United Nations fund for children. Approved April 3, 1948 (P.L. 472; 62 Stat. 137–159).

Civil Air Patrol Act. Established the Civil Air Patrol as a volunteer civilian auxiliary of the new United States Air Force and "authorized the Secretary of the Air Force to extend aid to the Civil Air Patrol in the fulfillment of its objectives." Approved May 26, 1948 (P.L. 557; 62 Stat. 274–275). Two years earlier, in 1946, Congress had established the Civil Air Patrol as a federally chartered corporation, the purpose of which was "to encourage and aid American citizens in the contribution of their efforts, services, and resources in the development of aviation and in the maintenance of air supremacy," and to foster civil aviation in local communities. Approved July 1, 1946 (P.L. 476; 60 Stat. 346–347).

Displaced Persons Act of 1948. Authorized the admission of 200,000 European refugees displaced by World War II, 2,000 Czechoslovakians who fled their country following a Communist coup in February 1948, and 3,000 orphans under the age of sixteen. Approved June 25, 1948 (P.L. 774; 62 Stat. 1009–1014).

Commodity Credit Corporation Charter Act of 1948. Established the Commodity Credit Corporation (first created in 1933) as a federal corporation within the Department of Agriculture under a permanent federal charter. Gave the corporation wide-ranging authority to carry out agricultural price and income support activities. Authorized the sale of agricultural commodities to other government agencies and foreign governments, and food donations to domestic, foreign, or international relief organizations. Approved June 28, 1948 (P.L. 806; 62 Stat. 1070–1075).

Federal Water Pollution Control Act of 1948. Authorized federal support for research on water pollution problems, loans to help finance construction of wastewater treatment plants, and financial grants for state and local governments for water pollution control programs. Encouraged states to enact uniform laws and interstate compacts, and it explicitly recognized that water pollution control was primarily the responsibility of state and local governments. Allowed the federal government to initiate a public nuisance action for interstate pollution that endangered persons in a state other than the one in which the pollution originated under certain specified conditions. Approved June 30, 1948 (P.L. 845; 62 Stat. 1155–1161).

War Claims Act of 1948. Created a War Claims Commission with "jurisdiction to receive [and] adjudicate according to law," claims for compensating internees, prisoners of war, and religious organizations, who suffered personal injury or property damage at the hands of the Japanese and Germans during World War II. Provided for compensation payments to be drawn from a Treasury Department trust fund known as the War Claims Fund, which consisted of seized Japanese, German, and other Axis assets. Provided that owners of alien property seized during World War II would not be compensated, and did not offer compensation for civilian internees held by Germany. Approved July 3, 1948 (P.L. 896; 62 Stat. 1240–1247).

Notes

1. Hans N. Tuch, *Communicating with the World: U.S. Public Diplomacy Overseas* (New York: St. Martin's Press, 1990), 17.

2. Dennis S. Nordin and Roy V. Scott, *From Prairie Farmer to Entrepreneur: The Transformation of Midwestern Agriculture* (Bloomington: Indiana University Press, 2005), 185.

Eighty-first Congress
January 3, 1949, to January 3, 1951

First session—January 3, 1949, to October 19, 1949
Second session—January 3, 1950, to January 2, 1951
(Second administration of Harry S. Truman, 1949–1953)

Historical Background

On January 5, 1949, President Harry S. Truman appeared before Congress to deliver his fourth State of the Union address and urge a sweeping new Fair Deal program of social reform.

"With deep satisfaction," Truman signed the National Housing Act of 1949. During the previous four years, efforts to gain approval of the act had prompted more than nine thousand pages of hearings and feverish efforts by lobbyists. The final bill provided for a six-year federal low-rent housing program, a slum clearance program, and a farm improvement program. It established a national housing objective of "a decent home and suitable living environment for every American family."

Other important administration victories in 1949 were scored when the minimum wage was increased from forty to seventy-five cents an hour, 9.2 million additional workers were brought under the Social Security system, and Social Security benefits were increased by 70 percent. Although the minimum wage hike was bitterly contested by industry as well as farmers, proponents argued that increased purchasing power would produce a healthier economy. Passage of the Social Security Act of 1950 was the culmination of nearly two years of work by Congress to increase old-age and survivors insurance benefits and to broaden the coverage of unemployment insurance. President Truman hailed its passage as "an outstanding achievement" that would make "it possible for most families to obtain protection through the contributory insurance program."

Streamlining and reform of the federal government was another achievement of the Eighty-first Congress. The bipartisan Commission on the Organization of the Executive Branch of Government, established in 1946 and chaired by former president Herbert Hoover, studied government operations and recommended improvements. Acting on the commission's proposals, Congress early in 1949 approved the first presidential salary increase in forty years. Important steps toward streamlining the executive branch were made possible through the Reorganization Act of 1949, which was based largely on the commission's recommendations. Moreover, President Truman used this authority to submit forty-one reorganization plans to Congress during the next four years, twenty-nine of which were approved and another was superseded by legislation. These initiatives included such diverse efforts as consolidating all government job placement and unemployment compensation functions in the Labor Department (1949), establishing the Federal Maritime Board and the Maritime Administration (1950), and abolishing eighty government agencies in the District of Columbia government (1952).

Two other important legislative initiatives strongly influenced by the Hoover Commission recommendations were the Classification Act of 1949 and the Performance Rating Act of 1950, which addressed issues relating to personnel management in the federal government. The most fundamental commission's personnel recommendation called for the Civil Service Commission to "place primary emphasis on staff functions, rather than upon 'processing a multitude of personnel transactions.'" Both acts "recognized the Civil Service Commission as a standard-setting rather than an operating agency."[1]

The Agricultural Act of 1949 was the first statute to institute permanent federal price supports and distinguished basic from non-basic agricultural commodities. This enactment, along with the Agricultural Adjustment Act of 1938, makes up the major part of the permanent law that mandates commodity price and farm income support.

Foreign policy concerns increasingly focused on the actions of the Soviet Union. Early in April 1949, a Soviet coup that toppled the democratic government of Czechoslovakia brought the United States, Canada, and ten European nations together to draft the North Atlantic Treaty. Each agreed that "an armed attack against any one or more of them in Europe and North America [would] be considered an attack against all." It was hoped that the pact would contain Soviet expansionist ambitions, while at the same time preserve a territorial status quo on the European continent. In July 1949, the Senate approved the pact and provided for establishment of the North Atlantic Treaty Organization (NATO) to implement the treaty's provisions. Through the Foreign Economic Assistance Act of 1950, another $3.6 billion of aid was earmarked for a variety of additional commitments, including President Truman's Point Four program that provided technical aid and assistance for economically underdeveloped areas.

One of the most troubling developments occurred in China, where civil war had raged since late 1945 between Communist Party rebels under Mao Zedong and the Nationalist government of Chiang Kai-shek. By 1949, the corrupt and unpopular Nationalist regime had been defeated, and it retreated to the island of Taiwan. After some hesitation, the United States refused to recognize the Communist government, which led to more than two decades of hostility between the two nations.

The gravest international crisis since the Berlin airlift was precipitated when North Korean forces attacked their southern neighbors. A Japanese colony from 1905 to 1945, Korea had been partitioned after World War II into Soviet- (northern) and U.S.-dominated (southern) zones. The North Korean attack was a surprise, and southern forces were soon in precipitous retreat down the Korean peninsula. On June 27, 1950, in the absence of the Soviet delegation, the United Nations (UN) Security Council

asked UN members to provide troops to repel the invasion. This was the first international combat operation carried out under UN auspices. President Truman ordered U.S. forces into the struggle, but ill-prepared American troops were unable to stem the attack until most of South Korea was under Communist control.

Later that summer, Congress, acting on an administration proposal, amended the National Security Act of 1947 and enhanced the power of the secretary of defense by giving him "direction, authority, and control" over the army, navy, and air force. Although the Central Intelligence Agency (CIA) had been created by the National Security Act, it was not until 1949 that the agency was permitted to keep its budgets, staffing levels, salaries, and even job titles secret. The Central Intelligence Agency Act of 1949 provided the statutory authority that allows for the secrecy of the agency's budget.

As the demand for war goods began to build in 1950 with the expansion of the Korean War, President Truman asked Congress for authority to establish priorities for allocating scarce defense materials to prevent hoarding of those items most essential to the war effort. He also sought control over consumer credit, commodity speculation, and real estate credit. Enactment of the Defense Production Act gave him the power to establish the broad-ranging economic controls he sought.

Reinforced U.S. and South Korean troops launched a successful counterattack in September 1950, crushing Communist forces and pressing deep into North Korea. The military situation was once again reversed in November, when Chinese Communist forces joined the conflict and drove UN forces south. After desperate fighting, the line of battle was stabilized near the 38th parallel, the original dividing line of the two Koreas.

Growing concern about Soviet aggression in Eastern Europe and Southeast Asia, in addition to the knowledge that the Russians had successfully tested their own atomic bomb, prompted passage of the Federal Civil Defense Act in 1950. President Harry Truman in approving the legislation declared that the act was "designed to protect life and property in the United States in case of enemy assault," "to minimize the effects of an attack on our civilian population," and "to deal with the immediate emergency conditions which such an attack would create."[2]

With the signing of the Uniform Code of Military Justice Act, the modern military justice system was born. World War II demonstrated the need to modernize and revamp the nation's system of military justice. "It occurred because the old system had changed too slowly to meet the requirements of twentieth century America and its armed forces. The old system gave too much power to commanders and too little assurance of due process and fairness to America's sons and daughters in service to be acceptable.[3]

Pressure for legislation to curb or outlaw the Communist Party within the United States culminated in the enactment of the Internal Security Act, sponsored by Sen. Patrick A. McCarran of Nevada. The purpose of the legislation was to expose Communist-action and Communist-front organizations through a complex registration process. President Truman, in a lengthy veto message, argued that the act would require public identification of vital defense facilities and force the Department of Justice "to waste immense amounts of time and energy" in carrying out the provisions of the act and put the government "into the thought control business." Congress disagreed and overrode his veto by overwhelming majorities in both houses.

The Budget and Accounting Procedures Act of 1950, which President Truman called "the most important legislation enacted by Congress in the budget and accounting field since the Budget and Accounting Act 1921,"[4] improved and simplified the way government agencies processed financial information.

Five years of efforts to establish a National Science Foundation reached fruition in May 1950. Proponents of the foundation gained congressional approval only to have it thwarted by a presidential veto. Legislation also was enacted authorizing a 10 percent federal excise tax on fishing equipment, lures, and bait that could be used to assist states in fisheries research, management, and development. Another new law granted American citizenship to Guamanians and established limited self-government.

Although Democrats retained control of both houses of Congress in the 1950 midterm elections, charges that the administration was "soft on Communism" continued unabated as Republicans made significant gains at the federal and state levels.

Major Acts and Treaties

Compensation of President, Vice President, and Speaker of House. Increased the salary of the president from $75,000 to $100,000 annually; the vice president, from $20,000 to $30,000; and the Speaker of the House, from $20,000 to $30,000. Increased the president's expense account from $40,000 to $90,000, and authorized an expense account of $10,000 for the vice president. Approved January 19, 1949 (P.L. 2; 63 Stat. 4).

Executive Reorganization Act of 1949. Authorized the president to examine the organization of all executive branch agencies and determine what changes were needed to promote more effective management, reduce expenditures, increase efficiency, and eliminate duplication. Required that any reorganization plan had to be submitted to Congress by April 1, 1953. Provided that either house of Congress could disapprove any reorganization plan submitted by the president. Approved June 20, 1949 (P.L. 109; 63 Stat. 203–207).

Central Intelligence Agency Act of 1949. Provide for the administration of the Central Intelligence Agency (CIA), established pursuant to section 102, National Security Act of 1947. Permitted the CIA to use confidential fiscal and administrative procedures and exempted the CIA from many of the usual limitations on the expenditure of funds. Provided that CIA funds could be included in the budgets of other departments and then transferred to the agency without regard to the restrictions placed on the initial appropriation. Exempted the CIA from having to publish or disclose agency's "organization, functions, names, official titles, salaries, or number of personnel employed." Approved June 20, 1949 (P.L. 110; 63 Stat. 208–213).

Housing Act of 1949. Declared "that the general welfare and security of the Nation and the health and living standards of its people require housing production and related community development sufficient to remedy the serious housing shortage ... [and] the elimination of sub-standard and other inadequate housing through the clearance of slums and blighted areas." Established a national housing objective of "a decent home and suitable living environment for every American family." Authorized more than $1 billion in loans and $500 million in grants to assist in slum clearance, community development and redevelopment programs, low-income family housing, and farm housing and farm building programs. Provided for a decennial census of housing, and broadened the authority of the housing and home administrator to study housing needs, construction, and costs. Approved July 15, 1949 (P.L. 171; 63 Stat. 413–444).

North Atlantic Treaty. Specifically drawn "to promote stability and well-being in the North Atlantic area." Provided for a collective response to aggressive attacks on any of the twelve signatory nations (Belgium, Canada, Denmark, France, Great Britain, Iceland, Italy, Luxembourg, the Netherlands, Norway, Portugal, and the United States) of the North Atlantic Treaty. Stipulated that all actions undertaken within the framework of the United Nations Charter would be subject to review at any time after ten years. Established the North Atlantic Treaty Organization to implement the treaty provisions. Concluded April 4, 1949. Ratification advised by the Senate July 21, 1949.[5]

National Security Act Amendments of 1949. Renamed and converted the National Military Defense Establishment—the Departments of the Army, Navy, and Air Force—into an executive Department of Defense incorporating the three military departments "separately administered" by a secretary under the "direction, authority, and control" of the secretary of defense. Barred the secretary of defense from transferring, abolishing, or consolidating any of the services' combatant functions. Provided for a deputy secretary of defense and three assistant secretaries. Added a nonvoting chairman to the Joint Chiefs of Staff, and more than doubled the size of the joint staff from 100 to 210 officers. Dropped the three service secretaries as members of the National Security Council, and added the vice president. Approved August 10, 1949 (P.L. 63; Stat. 578–592).

Fair Labor Standards Act Amendments of 1949. Raised the minimum wage under the Federal Fair Labor Standards Act of 1938 from forty cents to seventy-five cents per hour. Extended coverage of the minimum wage to firms "affecting" interstate commerce and retail service firms making annual gross sales of more than $500,000 or having more than four outlets. Prohibited the use of child labor under certain circumstances. Directed the secretary of labor to administer the act's wage-hour provisions. Empowered the Labor Department to sue for back wages on behalf of employees at their request. Approved October 26, 1949 (P.L. 393; 63 Stat. 910–920). *(Federal Fair Labor Standards Act, p. 256)*

Classification Act of 1949. Established new and simplified schedules of grades and salaries for nearly half the civilian jobs of the Government in the executive branch (except those in the postal service and those paid on an hourly basis which were covered by other legislation). Provided for three new grade levels at the top of the classified structure ("supergrades" GS-16, 17, and 18). Authorized longevity step-increases above the maximum scheduled grade rate for employees with long, faithful, and efficient service. Delegated to each agency the authority to classify its own positions, below the three highest grades, in accordance with Civil Service Commission standards and subject to a review by the commission. Approved October 28, 1949 (68 Stat. 954–973).

Agricultural Act of 1949. Provided a comprehensive long-range federal price support program, which laid the foundation for the permanency of government price support policy by authorizing or requiring by law the price support of various commodities through loans, purchases, or payments. Added two items that had to be taken into account when calculating the parity index: (1) labor costs for items purchased by farmers in calculations of their buying power; and (2) payments to commodity producers of agreed upon commodity prices. Designated mandatory support for basic commodities and the following nonbasic commodities: wool and mohair, tung nuts, honey, Irish potatoes, and milk, butterfat, and their products. Approved October 31, 1949 (P.L. 439; 63 Stat. 1051–1062).

Uniform Code of Military Justice Act. Established a common criminal code for all military services. Ensured the protection of individual rights to the men and women who serve in our armed forces include the right to counsel; the privilege against self-incrimination; the right to a speedy trial; the right to compulsory process; and protection against double jeopardy. Introduced for the first time in the history of American military law the concept of a general court-martial fully staffed by legally trained counsel and presided over by the military counterpart of a United States judge. Created an independent civilian court, the Court of Military Appeals, to oversee the military justice system. Approved May 5, 1950 (P.L. 506; 64 Stat. 107–149).

National Science Foundation Act. Established a National Science Foundation to encourage a "national policy for the promotion of basic research and education in the sciences... [and] to initiate and support basic scientific research in the mathematical, physical, medical, biological, engineering, and other sciences" through grants and loans. Required the foundation, at the request of the secretary of defense, to support research activities associated with national defense matters, foster interchanges of information with scientists in the United States and foreign countries, and maintain a register of scientific and technical personnel. Authorized the foundation to evaluate data compiled by other federal agencies, establish special commissions as needed, and correlate private and public research projects. Authorized an appropriation of $500,000 to establish the foundation and annual appropriations of $15 million thereafter. Approved May 10, 1950 (P.L. 507; 64 Stat. 149–157).

Foreign Economic Assistance Act of 1950. Authorized $3,627,450,000 in appropriations for six foreign aid programs—the Marshall Program, economic aid to Korea, aid to the U.S.-recognized government of China, U.S. participation in the United Nations program to aid Palestine refugees, U.S. participation in UNICEF (United Nations International Children's Emergency Fund), and the Point Four program, which called for technical assistance and capital investment in economically undeveloped countries. Approved June 5, 1950 (P.L. 535; 64 Stat. 198–210).

Organic Act of Guam. Granted American citizenship to the inhabitants of Guam, and gave the island limited self-government. Provided for a unicameral legislature, an independent judiciary headed by a judge appointed by the president, and an appointed governor with veto power. Specified that the governor, in making appointments to executive agencies and other local posts, should give preference to Guamanians. Citizens of the island were required to pay U.S. federal income taxes, which were to be retained in Guam for use by the territorial government. Approved August 1, 1950 (P.L. 630; 64 Stat. 384–393).

Fish Restoration Act. Provided federal aid to states for management and restoration of fish having "material value in connection with sport or recreation in the marine or fresh waters of the United States." Approved August 9, 1950 (P.L. 681; 64 Stat. 430–434).

Social Security Amendments of 1950. Extended and improved the Federal Old-Age and Survivors Insurance System, and amended public assistance and child welfare provisions of the Social Security Act. Granted Social Security coverage for the first time to self-employed workers, domestics, and employees of state and local governments. Approved August 28, 1950 (P.L. 734; 64 Stat. 477–561). Certain provisions of this act were subsequently held unconstitutional in *Califano v. Goldfarb,* 430 U.S. 199 (1977).

Defense Production Act of 1950. Granted the president emergency authority to establish priorities, allocate materials and facilities, and requisition property for defense production; regulate consumer credit; make and guarantee loans to expand defense production; and establish a standby program for price and wage controls and consumer rationing. Provided guidelines for the settlement of labor disputes arising from the act. Approved September 8, 1950 (P.L. 774; 64 Stat. 798–822).

Budget and Accounting Procedures Act of 1950. Required the president to "transmit to Congress during the first fifteen days of each regular session, the Budget, which shall set forth his Budget message, summary data and text, and supporting detail." Called for the budget to be prepared on a performance basis, with financial information provided in terms of the functions and activities of the Government. Made the comptroller general responsible for setting the accounting principles and standards to be followed in preparing the budget, and agency heads responsible for following the new standards and maintaining accounting records and internal controls in conformity with the standards prescribed by the General Accounting Office (GAO). Approved September 12, 1950 (P.L. 784; 64 Stat. 832–845).

McCarran Internal Security Act of 1950. Established a five-member bipartisan Subversive Activities Control Board to, upon application of the attorney general, determine whether an organization was a Communist-action or -front group. Required that Communist organizations register with the Justice Department and submit information concerning their membership, finances, and activities. Provided for internment of Communists during national emergencies, and prohibited their employment in national defense work. Made it unlawful for government employees to give a Communist group member information affecting U.S. security or for Communist group members to receive such information. Presidential veto overridden by Congress. Became law without the president's signature September 23, 1950 (P.L. 831; 64 Stat. 987–1031). Certain provisions of this act were subsequently held unconstitutional in *Aptheker v. Secretary of State*, 378 U.S. 500 (1964); *Albertson v. Subversive Activities Control Board*, 382 U.S. 70 (1965); and *United States v. Robel*, 389 U.S. 258 (1967).

Performance Rating Act of 1950. Required the establishment of personnel appraisal systems within all agencies, with prior approval by the Civil Service Commission. Established three summary rating levels: Outstanding, Satisfactory, and Unsatisfactory. Provided a system for employees to appeal detrimental ratings to a board that consisted of a member of an agency, a member selected by the employees, and a chairperson from the Civil Service Commission. Required a 90-day written warning of an unsatisfactory rating and opportunity for employees to improve. Approved September 30, 1950 (64 Stat. 1098–1100).

Federal Civil Defense Act of 1950. Established the Federal Civil Defense Administration and directed it to develop a system to protect life and property from attack-related emergencies. Declared that it was "the policy and intent of Congress" that the "responsibility for Civil Defense shall be vested primarily in the several States and their political subdivisions." Authorized the administration to draw up plans and to provide the States and their political subdivisions with guidance, coordination and assistance, training, and matching grants on a fifty-fifty basis for the procurement of supplies and equipment. Approved January 12, 1951 (P.L. 920; 64 Stat. 1245–1257).

Notes

1. Harold H. Leich, "The Hoover Commission's Personnel Recommendations—A Progress Report," *The American Political Science Review*, v. 47, March, 1953, 101.

2. U.S. Presidents, Truman, *Public Papers of the Presidents of the United States: Harry S. Truman, 1951* (Washington, D.C.: U.S. Government Printing Office, 1965), 26.

3. John S. Cooke, "Introduction: Fiftieth Anniversary of the Uniform Code of Military Justice Symposium Edition," *Military Law Review*, v. 156, September 2000, 18.

4. U.S. Presidents, Truman, *Public Papers of the Presidents of the United States: Harry S. Truman, 1950*, 631.

5. *Journal of the Executive Proceedings of the Senate of the United States* (Washington, D.C.: U.S. Government Printing Office, 1950), 91:1302–1309; and 63 Stat. 2241–2253.

Eighty-second Congress
January 3, 1951, to January 3, 1953

First session—January 3, 1951, to October 20, 1951
Second session—January 8, 1952, to July 7, 1952
(Second administration of Harry S. Truman, 1949–1953)

Historical Background

The Chinese offensive launched in Korea in November 1950 pushed United Nations (UN) forces south, culminating in the fall of Seoul on January 4, 1951. After hard fighting, the situation was gradually reversed, and by March, UN troops reentered the capital. In July 1951, both sides began protracted negotiations. During 1952, both the war and truce talks remained at a stalemate.

Even though Democrats controlled both the House and Senate, President Harry S. Truman's relations with Congress in his final two years in office was largely unproductive. Congress ignored or rejected many of his initiatives, while subjecting the administration to increasing criticism on the grounds of alleged corruption, failure to contain threats to internal security, and its conduct of the Korean War. Truman was "defeated on most of his favorite domestic requests" and endured "endless wrangles on matters relating to the military and foreign aid." Truman biographer Donald R. McCoy attributes the president's problems on Capitol Hill to the "very conservative and, indeed, combative cast of the Congress that was elected in 1950." The fact that a majority of American's "consistently disapproved of his handling of the presidency during his last two years in office" made Truman's efforts even that much more difficult.[1]

On April 11, 1951, Truman dismissed General Douglas MacArthur, supreme UN commander in Korea and U.S. commander in Japan, for publicly differing with the president on war strategy. MacArthur, a hero of World War II, returned from Asia to a triumphant welcome, culminating in an address to a joint session of Congress on April 19.

Congress officially terminated the declaration of war with Germany in October 1951, and the Senate ratified the treaty of peace with Japan in March 1952. The treaty provided important recognition of Japanese nationalism, and made Japan a Cold War ally and strong friendly outpost in the western Pacific. The same day, Washington and Tokyo also signed a security treaty that permitted American armed forces to remain in Japan indefinitely after the peace treaty took effect and the Occupation ended.

Congressional approval of Truman's legislative proposals in 1951 and 1952 was 40.4 percent and 34.9 percent, respectively, substantially lower than his preceding four years, which had also exhibited a continuous decline. It took four months of bitter debate before Congress authorized the president to loan India $190 million to buy American grain needed to stave off an impending famine. Gaining support for this humanitarian measure was difficult because of India's expressed opposition to certain American diplomatic actions in the United Nations. Authorizations totaling nearly $14 billion were embodied in the Mutual Security Acts of 1951 and 1952, as the United States continued its policy of supporting rearmament of Europe through economic aid. Congress made substantial reductions in the president's foreign aid requests before approving them—by more than $1 million in 1951 and nearly $1.5 million in 1952. President Truman did, however, gain congressional support for the Mutual Defense Assistance Control Act that provided for the mandatory termination of aid to any nation supplying Russia or Soviet-dominated areas with arms or munitions.

The McCarran-Walter Immigration and Nationality Act, preserving the national origins quota system established by the Immigration Act of 1924, became law when Congress overrode the president's veto. The legislation was sponsored by Sen. Patrick A. McCarran of Nevada and Rep. Francis E. Walter of Pennsylvania.

President Truman signed a joint resolution approving a constitution drafted by Puerto Rico elevating the island to the status of a free commonwealth voluntarily associated with the United States. Under the act, Puerto Ricans were given the full rights of American citizens. They continued to elect a nonvoting delegate to Congress but did not vote in presidential elections.

A Korean GI Bill of Rights provided educational benefits, pay for certain service personnel, housing, business and home loan guarantees, unemployment insurance, and job placement and counseling services. Although many provisions of the Veterans Readjustment Act of 1952 were patterned after those in the Servicemen's Readjustment Act of 1944, several changes were made to prevent abuses encountered under the earlier statute. *(GI Bill [Servicemen's Readjustment Act of 1944], p. 269)*

Concern for the safety of the nation's coal miners became apparent, particularly following a disastrous coal mine explosion in West Frankfort, Illinois, in December 1951. Prominent among those who favored compulsory mine safety legislation were President Truman and United Mine Workers president John L. Lewis. The Coal Mine Safety Act Amendments of 1952 authorized the Federal Bureau of Mines to close mines in the case of imminent danger of fire, explosion, inundation, or mechanical disaster. In signing the bill, Truman characterized it as a "significant step" toward preventing mine accidents. He warned, however, that much remained to be done, as its provisions covered only problems that made up less than 10 percent of mine fatalities during the previous two decades.

By 1952, the rapid growth of interstate communications facilities, particularly those of radio and television, had given rise to a variety of fraudulent activities on the part of unscrupulous persons which were not within the reach of existing mail fraud law. The Wire Fraud Act of 1952 statute was enacted to address criminal conduct which was not within the reach of existing mail fraud laws.

On March 9, 1952, Truman, the last president not subject to the two-term limitation of the Twenty-second Amendment, announced that he would not run for reelection. That fall, he embarked on an eighty-five-hundred-mile campaign for Democratic standard-bearer and Illinois governor Adlai E. Stevenson II that covered twenty states and nearly one hundred cities. Despite the president's effort, Republican presidential nominee and retired general Dwight D. Eisenhower, who had served as supreme commander of Allied forces in Europe during World War II, handily defeated Stevenson. Eisenhower and running mate Richard M. Nixon won 55.1 percent of the popular vote and 442 electoral votes; Stevenson and running mate John J. Sparkman, 44.4 percent of the popular vote and 89 electoral votes. Eisenhower's triumph ended twenty years of Democratic control of the White House. The Republicans captured both the Senate and the House, as well as a majority of state governorships.

Major Acts and Treaties

India Emergency Food Aid Act. Authorized the president to loan $190 million to famine-stricken India for the purchase of American grain. Approved June 15, 1951 (P.L. 48; 65 Stat. 69–71).

Mutual Security Act of 1951. Authorized $7,483,400,000 for foreign military, economic, and technical aid; reauthorized an expenditure of $816.7 million in unexpended aid funds; and stipulated that at least 10 percent of the aid be in the form of loans. Abolished the Economic Cooperation Administration, and shifted its functions to the Mutual Security Agency. Approved October 10, 1951 (P.L. 165; 65 Stat. 373–387).

Termination of State of War with Germany. Proclaimed "[t]hat the state of war declared to exist between the United States and the Government of Germany by the joint resolution of Congress approved December 11, 1941, is hereby terminated." Provided that "notwithstanding this resolution and any proclamation issued by the President pursuant thereto, any property or interest which prior to January 1, 1947, was subject to vesting or seizure under the provisions of the Trading With the Enemy Act of October 6, 1917 (40 Stat. 411), as amended, or which has heretofore been vested or seized under that Act, including accruals to or proceeds of any such property or interest, shall continue to be subject to the provisions of that Act in the same manner and to the same extent as if this resolution had not been adopted and such proclamation had not been issued." Approved October 19, 1951 (P.L. 181; 65 Stat. 451).

Mutual Defense Assistance Control Act of 1951. Provided for mandatory termination of aid to any country supplying Russia and Soviet-dominated areas with arms or munitions. Stipulated that aid would also be terminated if strategic goods were supplied, unless the president determined that such shipments were not detrimental to national security. Approved October 26, 1951 (P.L. 213; 65 Stat. 644–647).

Treaty of Peace with Japan (Treaty of San Francisco). Recapitulated the terms outlined in the "document of surrender," including Japanese affirmation of its renunciation of rights to all territories surrendered by the armistice. Formally terminated war between the United States (as well as 46 Allied and Associated powers) and Japan. Provided for the withdrawal of occupation forces within ninety days and for restoration of full Japanese sovereignty in political and economic matters. Asked for and then excused reparations from Japan. Recognized Japan's right to maintain forces necessary for individual and collective self-defense. Required Japan to acknowledge the independence of Korea and renounce all claims to Formosa, the Pescadores, the Kuriles, Sakhalin, and the Pacific islands formally under Japan's mandate. Concluded September 8, 1951. Ratification advised by the Senate March 20, 1952.[2]

U.S.-Japan Security Treaty. Provided the basis for ending the Occupation of Japan. Granted the United States the right to indefinitely locate air, land, and sea forces in Japan in order "to contribute to the maintenance of international peace and security in the Far East and to the security of Japan against armed attack."

Stipulated that the Japanese, through rearmament would gradually and increasingly assume responsibility for their own defense. Approved September 8, 1951. Ratification advised by the Senate March 20, 1952.[3]

Mutual Security Act of 1952. Authorized $6,447,730,750 for foreign, military, economic, and technical aid to countries in Asia, Europe, Latin America, and the Near East. Permitted the transfer of up to 10 percent of the funds in any title from military to economic aid or from economic to military aid. Approved June 20, 1952 (P.L. 400; 66 Stat. 141–151).

McCarran-Walter Immigration and Nationality Act. Revised and codified immigration, naturalization, and nationality laws and regulations adopted since 1798. Continued the national origins quota system established by the Immigration Act of 1924, repealed the exclusion of Asian immigrants, placed a ceiling on immigrants from Asia-Pacific Islands, and repealed discrimination based on sex. Tightened provisions for the exclusion of aliens believed to be dangerous to the country, and facilitated the deportation of such immigrants. Established a Joint Committee on Immigration and Naturalization to "make a continuous study" of application of the law. Presidential veto overridden by Congress. Became law without the president's signature June 27, 1952 (P.L. 414; 66 Stat. 163–282). Certain provisions of this act were subsequently held unconstitutional in *Afroyim v. Rusk*, 387 U.S. 253 (1967), and *Schneider v. Rusk*, 377 U.S. 163 (1964).

Constitution of the Commonwealth of Puerto Rico. Provided approval of the new constitution drafted by Puerto Rico, and elevated the status of the island to a free commonwealth voluntarily associated with the United States. Granted the citizens of the commonwealth full rights of American citizenship, but did not provide for Puerto Rican representation in either house of Congress (except for a nonvoting resident commissioner) or participation in presidential elections. Approved July 3, 1952 (P.L. 447; 66 Stat. 327–328).

Veterans Readjustment Assistance Act of 1952 (Korean GI Bill of Rights). Provided benefits for individuals who served in the armed forces after June 27, 1950. Granted Korean War veterans who served more than ninety days to educational benefits equal to one and a half times the duration of their services, up to thirty-six months. Provided $100 to $300 mustering-out pay for veterans below the rank of major or lieutenant commander, business and housing loan guarantees similar to those granted World War II veterans, unemployment insurance, and counseling and job placement services. Approved July 16, 1952 (P.L. 550; 66 Stat. 663–691).

Federal Coal Mine Safety Act Amendments of 1952. Authorized the Bureau of Mines to order unsafe mines threatened with imminent disaster from fire, explosion, flooding, or cave-in to shut down until they were made safe. Applicable only to mines with fifteen or more employees. Approved July 16, 1952 (P.L. 552; 66 Stat. 692–710).

Wire Fraud Act of 1952. Extended the 1872 Mail Fraud Act provisions to cover the use of wire, radio, or television communications in interstate commerce to perpetrate a fraud. (Prosecutors have eagerly seized on this provision to go after consumer fraud, investment scams, the filing of false insurance claims, election fraud, bribery, and other forms of public corruption.) Approved July 16, 1952 (P.L. 554; 66 Stat. 722, Sec. 18).

Notes

1. Donald R. McCoy, *The Presidency of Harry S. Truman* (Lawrence, Kan.: University of Kansas Press, 1984), 296–297.

2. *Journal of the Executive Proceedings of the Senate of the United States* (Washington, D.C.: U.S. Government Printing Office, 1952), 94: 239–250; 3 UST 3169–3328. (UST refers to the State Department's multivolume series that began in 1950, entitled *United States Treaties and Other International Agreements*.)

3. *Journal of the Executive Proceedings of the Senate*, 94; 251–253; UST 3329–3340.

Eighty-third Congress
January 3, 1953, to January 3, 1955

First session—January 3, 1953, to August 3, 1953
Second session—January 6, 1954, to December 2, 1954
(First administration of Dwight D. Eisenhower, 1953–
    1957)

Historical Background

During his first year as president, Dwight D. Eisenhower presented ten executive branch reorganization plans to Congress. Eisenhower's first plan, calling for the creation of a Department of Health, Education, and Welfare, became effective early in April 1953, after both houses of Congress passed a joint resolution of approval. Each of his other plans went into effect after resolutions to disapprove the plans were defeated. Three plans reorganized executive departments or agencies (the Department of Agriculture, the Department of Defense, and the Export-Import Bank); three others established federal agencies (the Foreign Operations Administration, the U.S. Information Agency, and the Office of Defense Mobilization). Another three called for the deputy attorney general, not the solicitor general, to be acting attorney general in the absence of the department head, enhanced the power of the chairman of the Council of Economic Advisers, and transferred the payment of all airline subsidies that did not involve the transportation of mail to the Civil Aeronautics Board.

President Eisenhower was able to fulfill a campaign pledge when he signed the Submerged Lands Act of 1953. Until the late 1930s, it was generally assumed that the coastal states owned the oil-rich submerged lands within their historic boundaries. During the next decade this position was challenged by those who argued that the submerged lands belonged to the federal government, a position that was upheld by the U.S. Supreme Court in *United States v. California* (1947). Following several failed attempts to counteract the Court's decision, advocates of the position of the states succeeded in having Congress confirm states' ownership by law. In a separate action, the mineral-rich submerged lands beyond state boundaries on the outer continental shelf were placed under federal control.

Just six months after taking office, Eisenhower fulfilled another campaign pledge—to bring the Korean War, which had begun in June 1950, to an end. In a radio message on July 27, 1953, he described an armistice that called for a demilitarized zone near the 38th parallel.

The Small Business Administration (SBA) was created to make loans to small businesses unable to obtain private lenders. The purpose of the SBA was to "aid, counsel, assist, and protect insofar as possible the interests of small-business concerns in order to preserve free competitive enterprise." To "improve the foreign relations of the United States" and "promote the economic stability of American agriculture," Congress approved the sale and donation of $1 billion in surplus farm commodities to friendly foreign nations.

Eisenhower had declared in his first State of the Union message that the immigration policy of the United States was discriminatory and asked Congress to write new legislation to "guard our legitimate national interests and be faithful to our basic ideas of freedom and fairness to all." Although no immediate action was taken to revise immigration policy, Congress did authorize, in the Refugee Relief Act, the issuance of special nonquota visas to more than 200,000 refugees already in the United States.

The administration also encountered considerable resistance to its first comprehensive public housing proposal, offered in 1954. Eisenhower requested thirty-five thousand low-rent public housing units for each of the next four fiscal years but gained authorization for only one year when House Republicans by a three-to-one margin voted against the original proposal.

More than fifty years of discussion about constructing a deep-water navigation waterway between the Atlantic Ocean and the western shore of the Great Lakes reached a climax in 1954. In signing the St. Lawrence Seaway Act, sponsored by Sen. Alexander Wiley of Wisconsin and Rep. George A. Dondero of Michigan, President Eisenhower authorized an agreement between the American and Canadian governments to allow ships to travel twenty-three hundred miles inland to Duluth, Minnesota. The seaway was to be composed of a series of locks that made it possible for ocean-going ships to traverse the connections between the Great Lakes. Previously, rapids in the St. Lawrence and size restraints of existing waterways had restricted the lakes to specialized shipping.

Through the combined efforts of the Joint Committee on Internal Revenue Taxation, the House Committee on Ways and Means, and the Treasury Department, work was completed on the first comprehensive revision of the Internal Revenue Code since the ratification of the Sixteenth Amendment (1913).

The Communist Control Act of 1954 made it illegal for any Communist Party member to "hold office or employment with any labor organizations." In signing the bill, President Eisenhower expressed the belief that the act would strengthen the hand of the Justice Department in dealing with the communist menace.

Despite a bitter and lengthy debate in the Senate, Eisenhower's efforts to amend the Atomic Energy Act of 1946 proved successful. The Atomic Energy Act of 1954 permitted private industry for the first time to begin a program for developing peaceful uses for nuclear energy. It also authorized the president, with the approval of the Atomic Energy Commission, to enter into agreements for exchanging non-military atomic information and materials with friendly nations.

The Eighty-third Congress revised the Organic Act of the Virgin Islands in response to increasing political consciousness among its people. Congress also provided for a two-year review of possible revisions in tariff classifications.

The 1954 congressional elections were a disappointment to Republicans. After only two years of control over both houses of Congress, the Democrats regained slim majorities in the House and the Senate.

Major Acts

Department of Health, Education, and Welfare. Created the Department of Health, Education, and Welfare (HEW) to replace the Federal Security Agency (FSA). Transferred all agencies within the FSA to HEW. Placed the Social Security Administration, Office of Education, Food and Drug Administration, and Office of Vocational Rehabilitation within the new department. Approved April 1, 1953 (P.L. 13; 67 Stat. 18–19, 631–632).

Submerged Lands Act. Confirmed and established that the coastal states owned the submerged offshore lands and natural resources within their traditional boundaries. Confirmed the jurisdiction and control of the federal government over natural resources of the seabed of the continental shelf beyond the submerged lands. Approved May 22, 1953 (P.L. 31; 67 Stat. 29–33).

Small Business Administration Act. Created the Small Business Administration (SBA), and terminated the Reconstruction Finance Corporation's loan authority. Authorized $275 million for a revolving fund, $150 million of which was to be for loans to businesses unable to obtain credit at reasonable rates, $100 million to finance procurement contracts, and $25 million for disaster loans. Limited individual borrowers to ten-year loans for a maximum of up to $150,000. Provided for the termination of the SBA on July 30, 1955, unless extended by Congress. Approved July 30, 1953 (P.L. 163; 67 Stat. 230–240).

Refugee Relief Act of 1953. Authorized the admission to the United States of 209,000 refugees not provided for by regular quotas. Required, as did the

Displaced Persons Act of 1948, assurances from U.S. citizens that those being admitted had employment and housing. Stipulated that applicants must obtain certificates guaranteeing their readmittance to the countries issuing visas, if for some reason they were not allowed into the United States or were deported. Approved August 7, 1953 (P.L. 203; 67 Stat. 400–407). *(Displaced Persons Act of 1948, p. 280)*

Outer Continental Shelf Lands Act. Provided for exclusive federal control over the submerged lands of the outer continental shelf. Authorized the leasing of such lands by the secretary of the interior. Assigned 12.5 percent of oil and gas production and 5 percent of sulfur royalties in the outer shelf to the federal government. Approved August 7, 1953 (P.L. 212; 67 Stat. 462–471).

St. Lawrence Seaway Act of 1954 (Wiley-Dondero Act). Authorized the United States to cooperate with the Canadian government in constructing a deep-water navigation canal in the St. Lawrence River. Created a St. Lawrence Seaway Development Corporation to construct and operate the canal in cooperation with the Canadian Seaway Authority. Approved May 13, 1954 (P.L. 358; 68 Stat. 92–97).

Agricultural Trade Development and Assistance Act of 1954. Authorized the president to sell up to $700 million worth of surplus agricultural commodities to friendly foreign nations and to donate another $300 million in surplus commodities for "famine relief and other assistance." Approved July 10, 1954 (P.L. 480; 68 Stat. 454–459).

Revised Organic Act of the Virgin Islands. Provided for a governor appointed by the president with the consent of the Senate, a single-house "Legislature of the Virgin Islands," a central administration, and a judicial system headed by a presidentially appointed judge. Allowed the legislature to override a governor's veto by a two-thirds vote with the concurrence of the president. Authorized the territorial government to issue up to $10 million in revenue bonds, and required that federal excise taxes on all Virgin Islands products be paid to the territorial government. Approved July 22, 1954 (P.L. 517; 86 Stat. 497–510).

Housing Act of 1954. Authorized the construction of thirty-five thousand new public housing units in fiscal year 1955 for families displaced by government slum clearance programs. Granted the Federal Housing Administration (FHA) increased control over mortgages and loans it insured. Authorized $5 million in planning grants to state agencies of public works programs and a $50 million revolving fund for FHA loans to public agencies for public housing projects. Approved August 2, 1954 (P.L. 560; 68 Stat. 590–648).

Internal Revenue Code of 1954. Provided an estimated $1.4 billion in tax relief for fiscal year 1955. Reduced taxes on dividend income. Permitted retirees to claim an income credit of 20 percent, working widows and widowers an annual deduction of $600 for child care costs, and all taxpayers to deduct medical expenses exceeding 3 percent of gross income. Allowed deductions for dependents, charitable contributions, depreciation, nonoperating losses, and research costs. Approved August 16, 1954 (P.L. 591; 68A Stat. 1–928). Certain provisions of this act were subsequently held unconstitutional in *Marchetti v. United States,* 390 U.S. 39 (1968); *Grosso v. United States,* 390 U.S. 62 (1968); *Leary v. United States,* 395 U.S. 6 (1969); and *Haynes v. United States,* 390 U.S. 85 (1968).

Communist Control Act of 1954. Declared "that the Communist Party of the United States, although purportedly a political party, is in fact an instrumentality of a conspiracy to overthrow the Government of the United States" and, as a consequence, "should be outlawed." Deprived the party of the "rights, privileges, and immunities attendant upon legal bodies created under the jurisdiction of the laws of the United States, or any political subdivision thereof." Subjected the party to penalties under the Internal Security Act, and stripped Communist-infiltrated organizations of their rights under the National Labor Relations Act. Approved August 24, 1954 (P.L. 637; 68 Stat. 775–780). *(McCarran Internal Security Act of 1950, p. 287; Wagner-Connery National Labor Relations Act, p. 248)*

Atomic Energy Act of 1954. Amended the Atomic Energy Act of 1946 to encourage the development of commercial nuclear power. Authorized the president to enter into agreements with friendly nations for developing peaceful uses of atomic energy. Broadened the authority of the Atomic Energy Commission to license and regulate the private nuclear industry and to control the distribution of technical nuclear data to other nations. Approved August 30, 1954 (P.L. 703; 68 Stat. 919–961). *(Atomic Energy Act, p. 275)*

Custom Simplification Act of 1954. Directed the Tariff Commission to study revision of tariff classifications and, after holding adequate public hearings, report to Congress within two years. Transferred to the Tariff Commission responsibility for determining injury to domestic industry under the Antidumping Act of 1921. Approved September 1, 1954 (P.L. 768; 68 Stat. 1136–1141).

Eighty-fourth Congress
January 3, 1955, to January 3, 1957

First session—January 5, 1955, to August 2, 1955
Second session—January 3, 1956, to July 27, 1956
(First administration of Dwight D. Eisenhower,
        1953–1957)

Historical Background

The early days of the Eighty-fourth Congress were dominated by foreign policy concerns. Fearful of a military assault by mainland Chinese forces against Formosa and the Pescadores Islands, Congress on January 29, 1955, granted President Dwight D. Eisenhower his request for authority to use U.S. armed forces to ensure the security of the area. Within the next few weeks, the Senate approved a treaty establishing the Southeast Asia Treaty Organization (SEATO), to thwart the threat of Communist aggression in Southeast Asia. Protocols ending Allied occupation of West Germany and extending an invitation for the federal republic to become a member of the North Atlantic Treaty Organization were approved in April. On June 17, the Senate also ratified a treaty reestablishing Austria as a sovereign, independent, democratic state, as it was prior to German occupation in 1938. While the Reserve Forces Act that President Eisenhower signed into law in August 1955 fell "short of the program" he had sent to Congress the previous January, he nevertheless felt it contained "provisions that would definitely strengthen the [nation's] Reserve structure." Prominent among its features was an authorized increase of 1.4 million in Ready Reserve personnel (from 1.5 million to 2.9 million) and authority for the president to activate up to one million Ready Reserves in an emergency.

Twice in 1955, President Dwight D. Eisenhower sent messages to the Eighty-fourth Congress recommending air legislation to improve the air quality in the country. Twenty-four bills were introduced following Eisenhower's show of support for air-pollution legislation. In mid-July, the Air Pollution Control Act of 1955, the first federal legislation committed to investigating the issue was signed into law.

On April 12, 1955, Americans received the much-welcomed news that Dr. Jonas Salk had developed a vaccine against the frightening disease of polio. Four months later, the Poliomyelitis Vaccination Assistance Act, the first federal involvement in nationwide vaccination efforts, implemented a plan to have the vaccine distributed free of charge to children and expectant mothers throughout the country. The first federal legislation specifically designed to aid the construction of medical school research facilities was the Health Research Facilities Act of 1956. It provided matching grants equal to 50 percent of the cost of medical research facilities, and benefited practically all medical schools.

Although the motto "In God We Trust" was inscribed on certain U.S. coinage as early as 1864, not until 1955 was legislation approved calling for the placement of the inscription on paper currency as well. A year later, Congress designated "In God We Trust" as the official motto of the United States.

Early in 1956, Congress completed action on one of the largest and most important federal multipurpose water projects. Included in the $760 million Upper Colorado River project were four major dams and eleven smaller irrigation projects. Enactment of the project, which was strongly supported by the administration, was the culmination of a two-and-a-half-decade effort by Colorado, New Mexico, Utah, and Wyoming to secure much needed irrigation and drinking water, as well as power for their states. In gaining approval of the bill, proponents overcame the opposition of Californians fearful of a reduction in Colorado River water available to their own state and objections of those who considered the project too costly.

Eisenhower faced opposition from his own secretary of agriculture, Ezra Taft Benson, in gaining enactment of the Agricultural Act in 1956. The chief feature of Eisenhower's proposal, the soil bank program, would provide federal subsidies to farmers who took out of cultivation land that was being used to produce crops in greatest surplus. While Eisenhower's soil bank idea was received with considerably more enthusiasm on Capitol Hill than at the Agriculture Department, Congress's initial agricultural bill included rigid price supports of staple crops, prompting a presidential veto. Six weeks later, a more acceptable act was signed into law. Eisenhower reasoned that the soil bank would limit farm surpluses, improve the income of farmers, and produce long-term conservation benefits.

Among President Eisenhower's most significant legislative achievements was the Federal Aid Highway Act of 1956. The act, which consisted of the Highway Act (Title I) and the Highway Revenue Act of 1956 (Title II), authorized more that $31 billion over a thirteen-year period for what Eisenhower would later describe in his presidential memoirs as the "most gigantic federal undertaking in road-building" in the nation's history. "It was," he observed, the "biggest peacetime construction project of any description ever undertaken by the United States or any other country."[1] The act authorized completion of the entire forty-one-thousand-mile National System of Interstate and Defense Highways, provided for its financing, required that broad criteria be established for the interstate system, established a new method of apportioning interstate funds among the states, established a Highway Trust Fund, and authorized significant appropriations for forest, primary, and secondary roads.

A two-decade effort to regulate the activities of bank holding companies, check the growth of potential banking monopolies, and preserve the independent banking system in the United States culminated in passage of the Bank Holding Company Act of 1956. Under the act, the board of governors of the Federal Reserve was given responsibility for regulating holding companies controlling more than one bank, and the companies were required to divest themselves of most nonbanking business.

Congress extended the Water Pollution Control Act for five years, provided $15 million to assist the states with water pollution control programs, and earmarked $500 million in matching funds for local communities building sewage treatment facilities.

Legislation was signed into law that strengthened the government's ability to detect, arrest, and incarcerate drug users. The Narcotic Control Act of 1956 increased the penalties for narcotics violations and provided especially harsh penalties for drug trafficking, including the possibility of imposing the death penalty, for the first time, on adults who sold heroin to minors.

With great satisfaction, Eisenhower signed a bill establishing a new survivor benefit program for active duty as well as retired military personnel. An underlying goal of the act was to make a military career more attractive. In approving the act, the president declared that it would be a "measure of financial security" to military families that would "enable them to face the inherent hazards and uncertainties of military life with increased confidence." Over the president's objections, early retirement disability benefits were added to the Social Security program for those who could prove they were permanently "unable to engage in substantial gainful employment." Women also were made eligible to begin receiving benefits at age 62 instead of 65.

With passage of the Fish and Wildlife Act of 1956, a national policy for promoting both the protection and intelligent use of fish and wildlife resources was established.

Although the 1956 presidential election was a victory for the Republicans, with incumbent Eisenhower besting challenger Adlai E. Stevenson II even more soundly than he had four years earlier, the Democrats retained control of both the House and Senate. Eisenhower and Vice President Richard M. Nixon won 457 electoral votes; Stevenson and his running mate, Estes Kefauver, 73.

Major Acts and Treaties

Formosa and Pescadores Defense Act. Authorized the president "to employ the Armed Forces of the

United States for protecting the security of Formosa, the Pescadores, and related positions and territories of that area" against armed attack by mainland China. Provided that the president's authority would expire when he "determined that the peace and security of the area is reasonably assured." Approved January 29, 1955 (P.L. 4; 69 Stat. 7). The Formosa resolution was repealed on October 26, 1974 (P.L. 93–475; 88 Stat. 1439).

Southeast Asia Collective Defense Treaty and Protocol. Pledged the signatories (Australia, Great Britain, France, New Zealand, Pakistan, Thailand, the Philippines, and the United States) to resist armed attack against "the general area of Southeast Asia, and the Southwest Pacific" up to 21 degrees 30 minutes north latitude, a line that excluded Formosa. Concluded September 8, 1954. Ratification advised by the Senate February 1, 1955.[2]

Protocol on the Termination of the Occupation Regime in the Federal Republic of Germany. Provided for the termination of Allied (France, Great Britain, and the United States) occupation of the West German republic. Granted West Germany "full authority of a sovereign state over its internal and external affairs." Allowed the Allies to retain the right to station armed forces in that territory. Established a four-power commission to be responsible for disarmament and demilitarization in the republic. Concluded October 23, 1954. Ratified by the Senate April 1, 1955.[3]

Protocol to Admit West Germany to the North Atlantic Treaty Organization. Authorized the United States to extend an invitation to the Federal Republic of Germany to join the North Atlantic Treaty Organization. Concluded October 23, 1954. Ratification advised by the Senate April 1, 1955.[4]

Austrian State Treaty. Reestablished Austria as a sovereign, independent, and democratic state with its pre-1938 frontiers. Barred Austria from any economic or political union with Germany or from owning or making atomic weapons and guided missiles. Declared that Austria was "to join no military alliances and to permit no military bases on its territory." Provided for the withdrawal of occupation forces by the end of 1955, and stipulated that no reparations would be paid.

Granted Russia certain oil concessions and refineries. Signed by Austria, France, Great Britain, Russia, and the United States. Concluded May 15, 1955. Ratification advised by the Senate June 17, 1955.[5]

Motto "In God We Trust" Placed on Paper Currency. Required that the inscription "In God We Trust" appear on all paper and coin currency. Approved July 11, 1955 (P.L. 140; 69 Stat. 290).

Air Pollution Control Act of 1955. Stated that "in recognition of the dangers of . . . air pollution," it was "declared to be the policy of Congress to preserve and protect the primary responsibility and rights of the States and local governments in controlling air pollution, to support and aid technical research, to devise and develop methods of abating such pollution, and to provide Federal technical services and financial aid to State and local government air pollution control agencies." Approved July 14, 1955 (P.L. 159; 69 Stat. 322–323).

Reserve Forces Act of 1955. Permitted an increase in the Ready Reserve ceiling from 1.5 million personnel to 2.9 million personnel. Authorized an annual reserve enlistment of up to 250,000 men between the ages of seventeen and eighteen-and-a-half for the next four years. Provided that enlistees would serve from three to six months of active duty and remain draft-exempt if they attended forty-eight weekly drills and served seventeen days of active duty each year for the remainder of an eight-year obligation. Stipulated that those who failed to perform satisfactorily could be recalled to active duty for forty-five days or drafted for two years. Established a six-year military obligation for those who served two years of active duty, three years of Ready Reserve participation, and one year in the Standby Reserve. Approved August 9, 1955 (P.L. 305; 69 Stat. 598–605).

Poliomyelitis Vaccination Assistance Act of 1955. Provided $30 million in federal grant-in-aid to states for the purchase of the Salk polio vaccine, and for the costs of planning and conducting vaccination programs for children under 20 and expectant mothers. Allotted funds to the states according to the number of individuals in the age group noted above and pregnant women, less the number vaccinated in the program of the National Foundation for Infantile Paralysis, the per capita income of the state, and the cost of the vaccine. Approved August 12, 1955 (P.L. 377; 69 Stat. 704–707).

Upper Colorado River Project. Provided for the Bureau of Reclamation to construct four major dams—the Glen Canyon, Flaming Gorge, Navajo, and Cure-canti (all but the Navajo having major power features). Authorized eleven smaller irrigation projects—Central Utah, Emery, Florida, Hammond, La Barge, Lyman, Paonia, Pine River Extension, Seedskadee, Silt, and Smith Fork—with sizable electric generating units of their own. Authorized $750 million to finance the project. Approved April 11, 1956 (P.L. 485; 70 Stat. 105–111).

Bank Holding Company Act of 1956. Required bank holding companies that owned or controlled two or more banks to register with the board of governors of the Federal Reserve System, which was made responsible for regulation of such companies. Prohibited bank holding companies, with certain exceptions, from managing or controlling a company that had nonbanking interests. Approved May 9, 1956 (P.L. 511; 70 Stat. 133–146).

Soil Bank Act. Established the Soil Bank program as a major provision of the Agricultural Act of 1956 (Title I). Encouraged farmers to withdraw land from production that was being used to produce the crops in greatest surplus in exchange for federal subsidies. Provided $750 million per year for four years (1956–1959) to pay farmers for reducing crop acreage for corn, cotton, peanuts, rice, tobacco, and wheat. Approved May 28, 1956 (P.L. 540; 70 Stat. 188–198).

Federal Aid Highway Act of 1956. Authorized nearly $31 billion to be spent over thirteen years on the construction of the National System of Interstate and Defense Highways, forest roads, primary roads, and secondary roads. Prescribed that standards for the National System of Interstate and Defense Highways should be adopted by the secretary of commerce in cooperation with the state highway departments. Authorized the completion of the entire interstate system and provided for its financing. Approved June 29, 1956 (P.L. 627; 70 Stat. 374–387, Title I).

Highway Revenue Act of 1956. Established a Highway Trust Fund to help finance the interstate programs, and required that the trust fund never show a deficit. Amended the Internal Revenue Code of 1954 to earmark certain highway user fees and taxes, such as the taxes on motor vehicle fuel, tires, and trucks and buses, for the trust fund. Approved June 29, 1956 (P.L. 627; 70 Stat. 387–402, Title II).

Water Pollution Control Act Amendments of 1956. Authorized $50 million in annual matching grants to assist local communities in building sewage treatment facilities for fiscal years 1957–1966 and $3 million in matching funds to the states for fiscal years 1957–1961 for the development of water pollution control programs. Established a nine-member presidentially appointed Water Pollution Control Advisory Board. Authorized the surgeon general to study pollution problems and cooperate with other groups developing pollution control programs. Approved July 9, 1956 (P.L. 660; 70 Stat. 498–507).

Narcotics Control Act. Increased penalties for all illegal narcotics activities with the most severe judgments being placed on illegal trafficking offenses. Outlawed heroin, and provided juries with the option of the death penalty in those instances when adults sold heroin to minors. Granted enforcement officers of the Narcotics Bureau and Customs Bureau, as well as the attorney general, expanded authority in investigating narcotics cases. Approved July 18, 1956 (P.L. 728; 70 Stat. 567–576).

Health Research Facilities Act of 1956. Authorized a three-year, $90 million program of federal matching grants to public and nonprofit institutions for construction of facilities devoted to research in the "sciences related to health." Defined "sciences related to health" as including medicine, osteopathy, dentistry, and public health, and fundamental and applied sciences. Stipulated that the following items were not creditable for matching purposes: (1) costs for the acquisition of land or off-site improvements, and (2) obligations made prior to the award of the research facilities grant. Approved July 30, 1956 (P.L. 835; 70 Stat. 717–721).

"In God We Trust" Designated Official Motto. Resolved that the "national motto of the United States is hereby declared to be 'In God We Trust.'" Approved July 30, 1956 (P.L. 851; 70 Stat. 732).

Social Security Amendments of 1956. Created a disability benefit program for workers between the ages of fifty and sixty-four who suffered long-term disabilities. Required that recipients have at least twenty quarters of covered employment prior to the disability. Established a Federal Disability Insurance Trust Fund from which the payments were to be made. Provided that women, widows of deceased workers, and mothers of deceased workers who were eligible for full Social Security benefits could begin receiving them at age sixty-two. Stipulated that other women who retired at sixty-two would receive reduced benefits. Extended children's benefits beyond age eighteen if a total disability had been sustained prior to their eighteenth birthday. Approved August 1, 1956 (P.L. 880; 70 Stat. 807–856).

Servicemen's and Veterans' Survivor Benefits Act. Placed all servicemen under the Old-Age and Survivors Insurance System on a contributory basis. Established a monthly minimum payment to a widow at $112, plus 12 percent of a serviceman's basic pay at the time of his discharge or death, a fixed dollar rate for children of a deceased serviceman when there was no widow, and compensation based on need for dependent parents. Revised the six-month death gratuity paid to survivors to no less than $800 and no more than $3,000. Repealed the $10,000 free indemnity life insurance coverage provided for in service deaths since 1951. Approved August 1, 1956 (P.L. 881; 70 Stat. 857–887).

Fish and Wildlife Act of 1956. Granted the Secretary of the Interior broad authority to "take such steps as may be required for the development, advancement, management, conservation, and protection of fish and wildlife resources." Created the U.S. Fish and Wildlife Service within the Department of the Interior. Noted the importance of fish and wildlife to the "health, recreation, and well-being" of American citizens. Approved August 8, 1956 (P.L. 1024; 70 Stat. 1119–1124).

Notes

1. Dwight D. Eisenhower, *White House Years. Mandate for Change: 1953–1956* (Garden City, N.Y.: Doubleday and Company, 1963), I, 548.

2. *Journal of the Executive Proceedings of the Senate of the United States* (Washington, D.C.: U.S. Government Printing Office, 1955), 97:88–89; 6 UST 81–89.

3. *Journal of the Executive Proceedings of the Senate of the United States*, 97:377–379; 6 UST 4117–5687.

4. *Journal of the Executive Proceedings of the Senate of the United States*, 97:377–379; 6 UST 5707–5713.

5. *Journal of the Executive Proceedings of the Senate of the United States*, 97:669–670; 6 UST 2369–2535.

Eighty-fifth Congress
January 3, 1957, to January 3, 1959

First session—January 3, 1957, to August 30, 1957
Second session—January 7, 1958, to August 24, 1958
(Second administration of Dwight D. Eisenhower, 1957–1961)

Historical Background

On New Year's Day 1957, President Dwight D. Eisenhower held a four-hour conference with congressional leaders of both parties to solicit their support for a Mideast doctrine he would formally propose to a joint session of Congress later that week. Although the Eisenhower Doctrine aroused little enthusiasm on Capitol Hill, a modified version of the proposal was approved in early March. As enacted, it granted the president authority to extend economic and military aid to any Middle East nation threatened by armed Communist aggression. Later in the year, the president twice invoked the Eisenhower Doctrine to discourage Syrian attacks on Jordan.

Closer international cooperation on nuclear energy was achieved with the ratification by the Senate on June 18, 1957, of a treaty that provided for the establishment of an International Atomic Energy Agency composed of the United States and seventy-nine other nations. That fall, the Price-Anderson Nuclear Industries Indemnity Act was enacted to spur the development of the nuclear industry in the United States. It established a unique framework for handling potential liability claims that could arise in the event of a nuclear incident, which protected the public by assuring that funds were available to compensate victims for damages and injuries.

With enactment of the Civil Rights Act of 1957, the first federal civil rights bill since Reconstruction (1875),

Congress created a Commission on Civil Rights and empowered the attorney general to seek injunctions when individuals were denied the right to vote by state officials. Advocates of the legislation viewed the vote as the foundation of most subsequent civil rights legislation. Although a threatened southern filibuster of the bill never materialized, final passage was obtained only after Sen. Strom Thurmond of South Carolina spoke against it for twenty-four hours and eighteen minutes, which was the longest speech in Senate history.

On October 4, 1957, the Soviet government launched the first artificial earth satellite, *Sputnik*. A second Soviet satellite, with a dog aboard, was launched on November 3. These Russian achievements set off a space race that pitted the United States' prestige and scientific prowess against that of the Soviet Union. Creation of the Advanced Research Projects Agency (now known as Defense Advanced Research Projects Agency [DARPA]) can be directly attributed to the Soviet Union's launching of *Sputnik*, and to the realization that the Russians had developed the capacity to rapidly exploit military technology. President Dwight D. Eisenhower urged its establishment to maintain U.S. technological superiority over potential adversaries. It is perhaps best known for ARPANET, an early network of time-sharing computers that was the basis for the Internet.

In July 1958, Congress established a civilian-controlled National Aeronautics and Space Administration (NASA) to oversee all nonmilitary aeronautical and space activities. Permanent committees in both houses of Congress were set up to monitor the activities of NASA. The Russian advances in space technology also prompted the largest federal commitment to education in history. Passage of the massive National Defense Education Act of 1958 established a seven-year, $1 billion program of loans and grants designed to dramatically improve the teaching of science, mathematics, and foreign languages at all levels of American education.

Two important actions were taken in 1958 in an effort to improve the nation's various transportation systems. A $500 million program of guaranteed loans was authorized to aid the railroads in overcoming their increasing financial losses. In addition, the Federal Aviation Agency (FAA) was created to make and enforce air safety rules and to manage the country's airspace. The FAA assumed the functions of the Airways Modernization Board, which only a year earlier had been created to develop a "national system of navigation and traffic control facilities" for civilian and military aircraft.

Several major outdoor recreation initiatives stemmed from the studies of the Outdoor Recreational Resources Review Commission, which Congress created in June 1958. These included the Bureau of Outdoor Recreation (1963), Land and Water Conservation Fund (1964), National Trails System (1968), and National Wild and Scenic Rivers System (1968).

The admission of Alaska to the Union in July 1958 was the culmination of more than four decades of pressure to grant statehood to the territory. Alaska became the forty-ninth state.

President Eisenhower's plan to place an Office of Defense and Civilian Mobilization (subsequently renamed Office of Civil and Defense Mobilization) within the Executive Office of the President became effective in July 1958. Reorganization Plan No. 1 merged the functions of the Office of Defense Mobilization and Federal Civil Defense Administration into a single agency. Eisenhower, however, was frustrated in his efforts to centralize the administration of the army, navy, and air force in the office of the secretary of defense, and the three services continued to be administered by their respective secretaries. Congress did give the secretary of defense authority to assign new weapons systems and consolidate duplicate functions among the services. It retained the right to veto any plans for substantive changes in the functions of the army, navy, and air force.

A new law provided former presidents with an annual pension, office space, a staff allowance, and free mailing privileges. Widows of former chief executives were also authorized an annual pension. Congress sought to assure Harry S. Truman and other former presidents a dignified and financially secure retirement.

Another bill that became law appropriated $250 million to aid small business in obtaining long-term credit.

The 1958 midterm elections reflected both the nation's distress over the economic recession and its dissatisfaction with the administration's farm and foreign policies. The Democrats scored substantial gains in both the House and Senate, hanging on to their majority status.

Major Acts and Treaties

Middle East Resolution. Authorized the president "to cooperate with and assist" any Middle Eastern nation desiring assistance in developing economic and military strength to preserve their independence and protect themselves against armed Communist aggression. Authorized the use of $200 million in Mutual Security Act funds to carry out the program. Approved March 9, 1957 (P.L. 85–7; 71 Stat. 5–6).

International Atomic Energy Treaty. Established an International Atomic Energy Agency with a director and board of governors to work toward harnessing the atom for peaceful purposes on a worldwide scale. Signatories (the United States and the seventy-nine other member-nations) were authorized to make fissionable materials available at their discretion. Concluded October 23, 1956. Ratification advised by the Senate June 18, 1957.[1]

Airways Modernization Act of 1958. Established an Airways Modernization Board "to provide for the development and modernization of the national system of navigation and traffic control facilities to serve present and future needs of civil and military aviation." Approved August 14, 1957 (P.L. 85–133; 71 Stat. 349–351).

Price-Anderson Nuclear Industries Indemnity Act. Authorized the federal government to "indemnify and hold harmless the licensee and other persons indemnified . . . from public liability . . . which is in excess of the amount of insurance." Established a nuclear indemnity system that took into consideration the possibility of a nuclear power accident, which could result in destruction vastly greater than ever before experienced in an industrial context. Required commercial nuclear power plant licensees to obtain between $50 and $60 million in private insurance, and provided for the government to make $500 million available of compensation in case of a nuclear accident. Approved September 2, 1957 (P.L. 256; 71 Stat. 576–579).

Civil Rights Act of 1957. Established a six-member Commission on Civil Rights and a Civil Rights Division in the Department of Justice. Empowered the attorney general to seek court injunctions against obstruction and deprivation of voting rights by state officials. Approved September 9, 1957 (P.L. 85–315; 71 Stat. 634–638).

Advanced Research Projects Agency Created. Authorized the "Secretary of Defense to engage in such advanced projects essential to the Defense Department's responsibilities in the field of basic research and development which pertain to weapons systems and military requirements as the Secretary of Defense may determine after consultation with the Joint Chiefs of Staff." Approved February 12, 1958 (P.L. 85–325; 72 Stat. 13–14, Sec. 7). See also Department of Defense Directive 5105.15, February 7, 1958.

Outdoor Recreation Resources Review Act. Established a fifteen-member Outdoor Recreation Resources Review Commission consisting of members of Congress, presidential appointees, employees of federal agencies, and private citizens to conduct "a nationwide inventory and evaluation of outdoor recreation resources and opportunities" that would be required by 1976 and in 2000. Approved June 28, 1958 (P.L. 85–470; 72 Stat. 238–241).

Reorganization Plan No. 1 of 1958 (Creation of the Office of Civil and Defense Mobilization). Provided for the merger of the Office of Defense Mobilization and the Federal Civil Defense Administration into an Office of Defense and Civilian Mobilization within the Executive Office of the President. Effective July 1, 1958 (72 Stat. 1799–1801). On August 26, 1958, legislation was enacted changing the name of the new agency to the Office of Civil and Defense Mobilization (P.L. 85–763; 72 Stat. 861).

Alaska Admitted to the Union. Provided for the formal acceptance of the constitution of the state of Alaska, adopted on April 24, 1956. Granted the Alaskan government 102,550,000 acres of vacant, unappropriated, unreserved public land and an additional 800,000 acres of national forests and other lands. Set aside certain lands in Alaska for national defense establishments. Provided that Alaskans could elect two senators and one representative to the U.S. Congress, benefit from the extension of the federal judicial system and Federal Reserve System, and vote their approval of the conditions of statehood. Approved July 7, 1958 (P.L. 85–508; 72 Stat. 339–352).

National Aeronautics and Space Administration Act of 1958. Created the National Aeronautics and Space Administration (NASA) to coordinate and conduct all nonmilitary aspects of the nation's scientific activities relating to outer space. Authorized NASA to develop research facilities, build space vehicles, and hire scientists and engineers to further the space effort. Approved July 29, 1958 (P.L. 85–568; 72 Stat. 426–438).

Department of Defense Reorganization Act of 1958. Reaffirmed the control of the secretary of defense over the army, navy, and air force. Authorized the secretary to assign responsibility for the development and operation of new weapons systems and to consolidate common supply and service functions of the three separately organized military departments. Required the secretary to notify Congress of any plans to substantially change an established function of the three services, and granted to Congress the right to veto any such action. Increased the size of the Joint Chiefs of Staff from 210 to 400 officers. Approved August 6, 1958 (P.L. 85–599; 72 Stat. 514–522).

Transportation Act of 1958. Authorized the Interstate Commerce Commission (ICC) to operate a $500 million loan guarantee program to assist railroads in purchasing capital equipment and in maintaining property. Prohibited the payment of stock dividends by railroads having a federally guaranteed loan. Permitted the ICC to adjust interstate railroad rates and to permit railroads to discontinue interstate service when the service was deemed an "unjust and undue burden." Approved August 12, 1958 (P.L. 85–625; 72 Stat. 568–574).

Small Business Investment Act. Established a Small Business Investments Division within the Small Business Administration (SBA) to issue charters to small business investment companies. Authorized a $250 million increase in the SBA's revolving fund to finance such loans. Approved August 21, 1958 (P.L. 85–699; 72 Stat. 689–699).

Federal Aviation Act. Created a Federal Aviation Agency headed by a presidentially appointed civilian administrator empowered to regulate the use of the nation's airspace, develop air navigation facilities, make and enforce air safety rules, and conduct aviation-related research. Combined many of the functions of the Civil Aeronautics Administration and the Airways Mobilization Board. Provided that the Civil Aeronautics Board would retain its jurisdiction over investigation of accidents, airfares, and route allocations. Repealed the Air Commerce Act of 1926, the Civil Aeronautics Act of 1938, and the Airways Modernization Act of 1957. Approved August 23, 1958 (P.L. 85–726; 72 Stat. 731–811). *(Air Commerce Act, p. 228; Civil Aeronautics Act of 1938, p. 256)*

Former Presidents Act. Provided former presidents an annual pension of $25,000, an annual office staff allowance of $50,000, and free mailing privileges. Authorized the General Services Administration to provide suitable furnished office space for former chief executives, and granted an annual pension of $10,000 for their widows (in lieu of any other federal annuity or pension). Approved August 25, 1958 (P.L. 85–745; 72 Stat. 838–839).

National Defense Education Act of 1958. Established a seven-year, $1 billion program of loans and grants designed to improve the teaching of science, mathematics, and foreign languages. Authorized a program of loans for needy students; graduate fellowships for potential college instructors; grants to state educational agencies, colleges, and universities for guidance programs and foreign language institutes; grants and loans for educational television; and grants to the states to improve instructional facilities and vocational education. Approved September 2, 1958 (P.L. 85–864; 72 Stat. 1580–1605).

Note

1. *Journal of the Executive Proceedings of the Senate* (Washington, D.C.: U.S. Government Printing Office, 1959), 99:685–687; 8 UST 1093–1224.

Eighty-sixth Congress
January 3, 1959, to January 3, 1961

First session—January 7, 1959, to September 15, 1959
Second session—January 6, 1960, to September 1, 1960
(Second administration of Dwight D. Eisenhower,
    1957–1961)

Historical Background

During President Dwight D. Eisenhower's final two years in office, U.S.-Soviet relations ran the gamut from cordial to bitter. A six-month ultimatum set by Soviet premier Nikita Khrushchev for achieving a settlement on the occupation of Berlin passed by almost unnoticed in May 1959. Two months later, Vice President Richard M. Nixon received a friendly reception by Russian crowds on his thirteen-day tour of the Soviet Union. Then in September, at Eisenhower's invitation, Khrushchev visited the United States for consultations with the president and a transcontinental tour. After Khrushchev met with Eisenhower, it was announced that the president would visit the Soviet Union in 1960. This promising trend was reversed the following May when a U.S. U-2 high altitude reconnaissance plane piloted by Francis Gary Powers was shot down by Soviet missiles while in Soviet airspace. Khrushchev denounced the spy flight and withdrew the invitation to Eisenhower to visit Russia.

After more than four decades of legislative proposals, Congress voted in March 1959 to admit Hawaii into the Union as the fiftieth state. Alaska's earlier admission as a state added considerable pressure to the Hawaiian statehood movement.

A six-year inquiry into corruption and labor-management collusion by the Senate Permanent Subcommittee on Investigations, chaired by Sen. John L. McClellan of Arkansas, culminated in passage of the Landrum-Griffin Labor-Management Reporting and Disclosure Act of 1959. The legislation, sponsored by Reps. Phillip M. Landrum of Georgia and Robert P. Griffin of Michigan, provided a means for coping with misuse of union funds. It declared that Congress had found "a number of instances of breach of trust, corruption, disregard of the rights of individual employees" on the part of labor unions. With the intent of correcting these conditions, the act provided a "Bill of Rights" for labor union members, federal supervision of union elections, extensive reporting requirements for unions, and several major modifications of the Taft-Hartley Labor-Management Relations Act of 1947.

Of major significance to two million government workers and their families was the Federal Employees' Health Benefits Act of 1959, which authorized prepaid group health insurance for federal employees for the first time. At the time, prepaid health benefits were already available to 123 million other Americans, 75 percent of whom were enrolled in plans available to them through their employers. The estimated $214 million annual cost of the program was shared equally by the government and participating employees. In 1960, health care for the elderly prompted a lengthy debate in the Senate over two health care proposals endorsed by Vice President Richard M. Nixon and Sen. John F. Kennedy of Massachusetts, who would be Nixon's rival for the presidency that fall. Ultimately, both the Nixon- and Kennedy-backed plans were defeated on the floor of the Senate, while a modest federal-state matching grant program for the "medically needy" aged not receiving old-age assistance was approved.

A new pension system was approved for veterans with disabilities who served in World War I, World War II, or the Korean War using a sliding-scale formula based upon a veteran's income. Dependents' assets were also taken into consideration in determining survivor benefits. Another key provision extended benefits to veterans' widows of all three wars. Previously, only widows of World War I had been benefit recipients.

Perceived weaknesses in the Civil Rights Act of 1957 prompted amendments intended to strengthen the voting rights provisions. Federal judges were authorized to appoint referees to supervise voter registration in areas of apparent racial discrimination. Other provisions required federal election records to be retained and set criminal penalties for bombings, bomb threats, and mob action designed to obstruct court orders. Heightened interest in national forest management prompted a call for new legislation on the purpose of national forests. The Multiple Use Sustained Yield Act of 1960 gave legitimacy to the idea that national forests were to be used for multiple purposes, not just timber production, and sought to ensure that all possible uses and benefits of the national forests would be treated equally.

A 1960 law authorized the United States to participate in the International Development Association (IDA). Membership in IDA, it was hoped, would encourage other non-Communist nations to devote resources in underdeveloped countries in a multilateral effort that could help alleviate the drain on U.S. balance of payments.

The Senate approved a new ten-year security treaty with Japan, removing the remaining traces of the postwar occupation. The treaty with Japan committed the two nations to come to each other's defense in the event either was attacked "in the territories under the administration of Japan." It also affirmed U.S. rights to bases in Japan. Although the treaty affirmed Japan's independent status, it provoked massive demonstrations and widespread protest in Japan because of the recent revelation that three U.S. U-2s had been based there. Senate ratification of the Antarctic Treaty in August 1960, the earliest of the post–World War II arms limitation agreements, was significant both in itself and as a precedent. The treaty was the culmination of the work of a twelve-nation Washington conference on peaceful international scientific cooperation in Antarctica. The internationalization and demilitarization of Antarctica is cited as an example of nations exercising foresight and working in concert to prevent conflict before it develops.

The Twenty-third Amendment, granting the residents of the District of Columbia the right to vote in presidential elections, was sent to the states for ratification in June 1960. The amendment had received strong support from President Eisenhower.

In one of the most closely contested presidential elections of the twentieth century, the Democratic ticket of John F. Kennedy and Lyndon B. Johnson won the popular vote in 1960 by a margin of only 100,000 over the Republican ticket of Richard M. Nixon and Henry Cabot Lodge. A highlight of the campaign was a series of nationally televised debates between Kennedy and Nixon. Despite the close popular vote, the Electoral College margin was a comfortable 303 for Kennedy and Johnson to 219 for Nixon and Lodge. Fifteen electoral votes went to Virginia senator Harry F. Byrd for president; 14 electoral votes went to Strom Thurmond and 1 to Barry Goldwater for vice president. The Republicans in Congress recovered some ground after their disastrous 1958 losses, but the Democrats remained in the majority in both the House and Senate.

Major Acts and Treaties

Hawaii Admitted to the Union. Provided for formal ratification of the state constitution adopted by Hawaiian voters on November 7, 1950. Required approval of a referendum on statehood. Granted the state a trust of public lands, the proceeds from which could be used to support public schools, roads, and so on. Conveyed to the state all lands and property held by the territory as well as the United States at the time of admission, but allowed for Congress or the president, within five years after statehood, to reclaim any former U.S. lands. Allowed the state to elect two senators and one representative in the U.S. Congress. Approved March 18, 1959 (P.L. 86–3; 73 Stat. 4–13).

Veterans Pension Act of 1959. Revised the veterans pension system for those with disabilities who served in World War I, World War II, or the Korean War. Provided a sliding-scale formula for determining a veteran's benefits based on income and a widow's benefits based upon income and number of dependents.

Provided widows' benefits for the first time to those whose husbands had served in World War II and Korea. Approved August 29, 1959 (P.L. 86–211; 73 Stat. 432–436).

Landrum-Griffin Labor-Management Reporting and Disclosure Act of 1959. Declared that it was the continuing "responsibility of the Federal Government to protect employees' rights to organize, choose their own representatives, bargain collectively, and otherwise engage in concerted activities for their mutual aid or protection." Provided a "Bill of Rights" for union members guaranteeing them the right to nominate candidates, vote for union officials, and participate in union meetings. Required all unions to adopt constitutions and bylaws, prepare annual financial and organization reports, and submit semiannual reports on trusteeships to the secretary of labor. Required local unions to hold secret-ballot elections at least once every three years; intermediate bodies, every four years. Required national elections to be held every five years. Established requirements of fiduciary responsibility and bonding in officers, regulations governing boycotts and picketing, and outlawed "hot cargo" contracts under which an employer agreed not to do business with any other firm. Approved September 14, 1959 (P.L. 86–257; 73 Stat. 519–546). Certain provisions of this act were subsequently held unconstitutional in *United States v. Brown*, 381 U.S. 437 (1965).

Federal Employees Health Benefits Act of 1959. Provided federal employees with the unrestricted choice of enrolling in one of several group health insurance programs, with 50 percent of the cost to be paid by the government and employee contributions to be automatically deducted biweekly from payroll checks. Stipulated that a physical examination was not required either to enroll in the plan or for conversion to a private plan upon retirement. Delegated responsibility for the administration of the program to the Civil Service Commission through a newly created Bureau of Retirement and Insurance. Approved September 28, 1959 (P.L. 86–382; 73 Stat. 708–717).

Civil Rights Act of 1960. Authorized judges to appoint referees empowered to assist persons experiencing opposition in attempting to vote. Set criminal

penalties for persons obstructing a federal court order and transporting or possessing explosives, required that voting and registration records for federal elections be preserved for twenty-two months, and extended the Civil Rights Commission for two years. Approved May 6, 1960 (P.L. 86–449; 74 Stat. 86–92).

Multiple Use Sustained Yield Act of 1960. Declared "that the national forests are established and shall be administered for outdoor recreation, range, timber, watershed, and fish and wildlife purposes." Directs the Secretary of Agriculture "to develop and administer the renewable surface resources of the national forests for multiple use and sustained yield of several products and services obtained therefrom." Approved June 12, 1960 (P.L. 86–517; 74 Stat. 215).

Twenty-third Amendment. Permitted citizens of the District of Columbia to vote for president and vice president, and assigned three presidential electors to the federal district. Approved June 16, 1960 (74 Stat. 1057). Ratified by requisite number of states March 29, 1961.[1]

United States–Japan Security Treaty of 1960. Provided for the United States and Japan to come to each other's defense if either were attacked "in the territories under the administration of Japan." Granted the United States the right to maintain land, air, and naval bases in Japan. Stipulated that any major shifts in American forces, or the use of these bases for combat operations, were dependent upon "prior consultation" with Japan. Concluded January 19, 1960. Ratification advised by the Senate June 22, 1960.[2]

International Development Associations Act. Authorized U.S. membership in the International Development Association (IDA), and appropriated $320,290,000 as the U.S. subscription to the association, to be paid over five years. Required Congress to authorize all subscriptions or loans to IDA and amendments to the articles of agreement consented to under the act. Approved June 30, 1960 (P.L. 86–565; 74 Stat. 293–295).

Antarctic Treaty. Provided the legal framework for the region beyond 60° South latitude. Reserved the region for peace, promotes scientific investigations and international cooperation. Required an annual exchange of information about activities, and encourages environmental stewardship. Provided that Antarctica be used for peaceful purposes only. Prohibited the establishment of military bases, military maneuvers, weapons testing, or disposal of radioactive waste material in Antarctica. Concluded December 1, 1959. Ratification advised by the Senate August 10, 1960.[3]

Social Security Amendments of 1960. Increased federal matching grants to the states for medical care of the low-income elderly. Created a Medical Assistance to the Aged Program to reimburse the states for 50 to 80 percent of health care costs incurred in providing for "medically needy" persons sixty-five and older. Amended public assistance and maternal and child welfare provisions of the Social Security Act, and liberalized retirement earnings limitations for all beneficiaries. Approved September 13, 1960 (P.L. 86–778; 74 Stat. 924–997).

Notes

1. U.S. Senate, *The Constitution of the United States: Analysis and Interpretation,* 108th Cong., 2d sess., 2004, S. Doc. 108–70, n. 15; 75 Stat. 847–848.

2. *Journal of the Executive Proceedings of the Senate* (Washington, D.C.: U.S. Government Printing Office, 1960), 102:622–623; 11 UST 1632–1759.

3. *Journal of the Executive Proceedings of the Senate,* 102:689–690; 12 UST 794–829.

Eighty-seventh Congress
January 3, 1961, to January 3, 1963

First session—January 3, 1961, to September 27, 1961
Second session—January 10, 1962, to October 13, 1962
(Administration of John F. Kennedy, 1961–1963)

Historical Background

On January 20, 1961, John F. Kennedy took the oath of office as the thirty-fifth president of the United States. He was the youngest person ever elected chief executive. Kennedy declared in his inaugural address that the "torch had been passed to a new generation of Americans—born in this century, tempered by war, disciplined by a hard and bitter peace, proud of our heritage." He challenged Americans and free men everywhere "to bear the burden of a long twilight struggle . . . against the common enemies of man: tyranny, poverty, disease and war itself." Several of the programs enacted by Congress during the ensuing two years reflected the idealism Kennedy expressed.

Less than three months later, on April 12, 1961, Russian cosmonaut Yuri A. Gagarin became the first man to travel into space and orbit the earth on *Vostok I*. The Soviet success suggested that the United States was falling behind in the arms race and fueled new tensions between the two nations entwined in a bitter Cold War. It would be another 10 months before John Glenn became the first American to orbit the earth. Just six weeks after Gagarin's flight, however, President John F. Kennedy proposed before a joint session of Congress that "this nation should commit itself to achieving the goal, before this decade is out, of landing a man on the Moon and returning him safely to Earth." In July 1961, Congress responded to Kennedy's bold challenge by overwhelmingly approving the initial funding for NASA's Apollo lunar landing program.

Kennedy's first two years were also fraught with international tension, and in 1962, the United States came to the brink of nuclear war. In the Western Hemisphere, hostility between the United States and Cuba increased, as Cuban leader Fidel Castro implemented communism and aligned himself with the Union of Soviet Socialist Republics (USSR). The new Kennedy administration pressed forward in 1961 with an ill-conceived plan, inherited from the Eisenhower administration, to invade Cuba. Anti-Castro Cubans who landed at the Bay of Pigs on April 17, 1961, hoping to arouse a counterrevolution, were quickly isolated and captured—a humiliating blow to the United States.

On August 13, 1961, crisis erupted in Berlin, when the Soviet-dominated East German government closed border crossings, in violation of international agreements. Although the Western allies feared a new blockade or military action against Berlin, the USSR and East Germany contented themselves with constructing the Berlin Wall, which was to divide the historic capital of Germany for thirty-eight years. U.S.-USSR relations were further strained by Soviet resumption of atmospheric nuclear testing on September 1, 1961, terminating the mutual suspension in effect since 1959. The United States, Great Britain, and France, the newest nuclear power, followed suit.

Enacted at the request of President John F. Kennedy, the Foreign Assistance Act of 1961 has become the cornerstone of the United States' foreign assistance policies and programs. The act replaced the Mutual Security Act of 1951 as the fundamental law on American economic and military aid by scrapping a consolidated approach and separated, for the first time, military and humanitarian foreign assistance. It sought to take into account the new circumstances facing the United States during the Cold War in light of the dismantling of European colonial empires and the emergence of the Third World as an independent force in international politics.

The most dangerous superpower confrontation of the Cold War era was the Cuban Missile Crisis. In mid-October 1962, President Kennedy was given reconnaissance photos proving that the USSR was building missiles in Cuba that would threaten much of the United States. After considering a wide range of options and consulting with the congressional leadership, the president ordered a high-level military alert and announced a naval blockade to interdict shipment of military equipment to Cuba. He also announced that any attack launched against the United States from Cuba would be considered an attack by the USSR. Tensions remained high until Soviet leader Nikita Khrushchev agreed near the end of the month to remove the missiles; in return, the United States pledged not to invade Cuba.

The Area Redevelopment Act, endorsed by Kennedy in the 1960 presidential campaign, was a multimillion-dollar federal-aid program to assist in financing industrial and rural redevelopment and public facility loans. This act, which President Dwight D. Eisenhower had vetoed twice, was specifically aimed at those areas having the highest percentage of chronic unemployment and low-income families. Kennedy charged that the lack of adequate disarmament planning had been the Eisenhower administration's "most glaring omission in the field of national security and world peace." He promised to make disarmament a high priority. Kennedy asked Congress to create an independent disarmament agency, which it did within nine months of his taking office.

President Kennedy also gained congressional support for the Peace Corps, a cadre of young Americans who supplied needed skills and volunteer assistance in underdeveloped nations, including as English language teachers. Peace Corps volunteers had to learn the language of the region to which they were assigned; be "willing to serve under conditions of hardship, if necessary"; and be able to provide skilled assistance with agricultural, conservation, educational, economic, or rural development, or social needs. In September 1961, legislation was enacted revising and consolidating U.S. educational and cultural exchange programs that had been created during the previous fifteen years. Impetus for action originated with Sen. James W. Fulbright of Arkansas, the author of the original exchange program. (*Fulbright Scholars Act, p. 275*)

Enactment of the Housing Act of 1961 was, in Kennedy's opinion, the "most important and far-reaching Federal [housing] legislation" since 1949 and provided "an opportunity for a giant step toward better cities and improved housing." In addition, the act contained the first federal assistance to mass transportation.

Four new laws addressed the nation's special vocational needs. Employment-related provisions of the Area Redevelopment Act authorized special job training for workers in economically depressed areas. The Manpower Development and Training Act provided for the retraining of workers with obsolete skills and the development of a pool of workers for industries in which they were scarce. The Public Welfare Amendments sought to reduce the dependence of people receiving public assistance by providing special training to assist them in preparing to enter the work force. With the Trade Expansion Act, workers who had lost their jobs because of foreign competition received special training. Other provisions of this act, however, have attracted the greatest attention.

Congressional Quarterly proclaimed that passage of the Trade Expansion Act was President Kennedy's "most important legislative victory in the Eighty-seventh Congress." It gave him "virtually all of the basic authorities he had sought to cut tariffs and aid those injured by increased imports."[1] The president considered it the most important foreign economic policy initiative "since the passage of the Marshall Plan." His efforts to expand the foreign aid program were less successful. More than $1 billion was cut from the administration's 1962 foreign assistance budget before it gained approval. Aid was barred for communist nations or any other nations providing economic assistance to Cuba. In other action, Congress suspended Cuba's most-favored-nation trading status. The Tariff Classification Act also mandated the first complete revision of U.S. tariff schedules in more than three decades. By simplifying the tariff classifications, it was reasoned, businesses would become more interested in foreign trade.

Upon taking office in January 1961, President Kennedy faced a serious recession that within three months prompted him to ask Congress to design a tax incentive bill intended to help the nation's businesses and stimulate future economic growth. The Revenue Act of 1962, which was prepared by the House Ways and Means Committee, significantly altered many of the president's proposals. Still, the final bill contained an investment tax credit for businesses and was seen as "important" by the president and "a good start" in modernizing the nation's tax structure.

Self-employed individuals were given the same opportunity to defer a percentage of the taxes on their retirement fund contributions as individuals covered by corporate plans. The decade-long effort to secure passage of the act was successful in large part because Senate supporters made important modifications to the legislation that limited allowable tax deductions for retirement plan contributions and assured that most of the self-employed would have access to a (self-funded) pension plan.

The Senate approved a convention providing for the United States to join Canada and eighteen European nations as charter members in the Organization for Economic Cooperation and Development (OECD), a consultative body committed to the encouragement and expansion of economic growth, sound economic development, and world trade. Following the hijacking of three American airliners, two of which were flown to Cuba, hijacking was elevated to a federal offense, punishable by the death penalty.

Passage of Community Health Services and Facilities Act was encouraged by the 1961 White House Conference on Aging. The act expanded and improved community health services and facilities for the chronically ill and aged. "Effective public health measures and medical care depended," President John F. Kennedy emphasized, "in the last analysis, upon action at the community level" made possible by this enactment.[2]

Food and Drug Administration controls over the sale of manufactured drugs were strengthened in response to widespread concern over crippling birth defects caused by thalidomide, a tranquilizer used by pregnant women. Initially, use of thalidomide by pregnant women in Europe was identified as the probable cause of phocomelia—a condition producing seal-like flippers instead of limbs in their new-born children. Nearly four thousand American women also used the drug, with several instances of phocomelia resulting. The legislation was sponsored by Sen. Estes Kefauver of Tennessee and Rep. Oren Harris of Arkansas.

The effectiveness of the polio vaccine encouraged public health officers to think in broader terms, and resulted in the Vaccination Assistance Act of 1962. A federally coordinated program was established under the act that provided grants for intensive state and local childhood vaccine programs. Since its passage, polio, measles, mumps, and rubella have been eliminated and many other vaccine-preventable diseases are at record or near record lows.

At the president's behest, Congress established the quasi-public Communications Satellite Corporation to manage the satellite communications of the United States. A spirited and often contentious Senate debate over the merits of public ownership versus a strictly controlled private ownership preceded passage.

The first major effort to legislate ethical conduct of federal employees came with the adoption of the Bribery, Graft, and Conflicts of Interest Act of 1962. The covered employees were prohibited from "participating personally and substantially" on behalf of government in any "particular matter" in which the employee had a "financial interest." In August 1962, Congress enacted the most significant legislative revision of the depository library program since the passage of the Printing Act of 1895. This proved to be the last major revision of the program.

The Twenty-fourth Amendment, outlawing the use of poll taxes as a means of preventing citizens from voting in federal elections, was sent to the states for ratification in August 1962. Approval of the constitutional amendment, President Kennedy said, "culminates a legislative effort of many, many years to bring about the end of this artificial bar to the right to vote in some of our states."[3] The amendment went into effect on January 23, 1964.

In the November 1962 elections, the Democrats were able to maintain control of both houses of Congress.

Major Acts and Treaties

Organization for Economic Cooperation and Development Convention. Established the Organization for Economic Cooperation and Development (OECD), a consultative body consisting of the United States, Canada, and eighteen European nations. Provided that OECD would encourage economic growth, economic stability, and world trade among member as well as nonmember countries on a nondiscriminatory basis. Concluded December 14, 1960. Ratification advised by the Senate March 16, 1961.[4]

Area Redevelopment Act. Authorized the president to appoint an area redevelopment administrator under the secretary of commerce with authority to borrow $300 million from the Treasury to establish a revolving fund to finance industrial redevelopment loans, rural redevelopment loans, and public facility loans. Limited federal participation in redevelopment projects to a maximum of 65 percent of costs. Permitted 100 percent loans for public facilities. Appropriated other monies for technical assistance to redevelopment areas, vocational training for unemployed workers, and vocational retraining. Approved May 1, 1961 (P.L. 87–27; 75 Stat. 47–63).

Housing Act of 1961. Authorized $2 billion for urban renewal, $55 million for urban planning, special grants for the development of mass transit facilities and "open spaces" in cities, and 100,000 new public housing units. Expanded small community loans to be used to finance improvements in sewage, gas, and water services; and increased construction funds for elderly and farm housing. Approved June 30, 1961 (P.L. 87–70; 75 Stat. 149–192).

Initial Apollo Mission Funding. Authorized an initial $531 million to send a manned space vehicle to the moon and return it safely to the earth before the end of the 1960s. Approved July 21, 1961 (P.L. 87–98; 75 Stat. 216–218). Details of the authorization are found in "NASA Authorization," *Congressional Quarterly Weekly Report,* v. 19, July 7, 1961, 1205–1206; July 21, 1961, 1258. In August 1961, appropriators provided $549 million for the Apollo project. *Independent Offices Appropriation Bill, 1962,* 87th Cong., 1st sess., S. Rept. 620 (Washington, D.C.: U.S. Government Printing Office, 1961), 2; "Independent Offices Funds," *Congressional Quarterly Weekly Report,* v. 19, August 11, 1961, 1385; Independent Offices Appropriation Act, 1962. Approved August 17, 1961 (P.L. 87–141; 75 Stat. 355).

Foreign Assistance Act of 1961. Mandated the creation of an agency[5] to promote long-term assistance for economic and social development. Provided for

nonmilitary assistance intended "to strengthen the forces of freedom by aiding peoples of less developed friendly countries of the world, to develop their resources and improve their living standards, to realize their aspirations for justice, education, dignity, and respect as individual human beings, and to establish responsible governments." Provided for military assistance with the intention of "fostering an improved climate of political independence and individual liberty, improving the ability of friendly countries and international organizations to deter or, if necessary, defeat Communist or Communist-supported aggression, facilitating arrangement for individual and collective security, assisting friendly countries to maintain internal security, and creating an environment of security and stability in the developing friendly countries essential to their more rapid, social, economic, and political progress." Approved September 1, 1961 (P.L. 87–195; 7 Stat. 424–465).

Crimes in the Sky Act. Made the hijacking of an airplane in flight a federal offense, and provided for the enforcement of crimes committed aboard an aircraft while it was in flight. Approved September 5, 1961 (P.L. 87–197; 75 Stat. 466–468).

Mutual Educational and Cultural Exchange Act. Broadened the scope of the U.S. educational and cultural exchange programs. Amended immigration and tax laws affecting program participants. Approved September 21, 1961 (P.L. 87–256; 75 Stat. 527–538).

Peace Corps Act. Granted "permanent legislative authority" to the Peace Corps, established by Executive Order 10924 (March 1, 1961), to enlist "willing" young Americans to serve as technical instructors and in other roles in less developed countries to aid in meeting "their needs for trained manpower . . . and to help promote a better understanding of the American people" and "of other peoples on the part of the American people." Authorized $40 million for fiscal 1962 to carry out the purposes of the act. Approved September 22, 1961 (P.L. 87–293; 75 Stat. 612–627).

Arms Control and Disarmament Act. Established an independent U.S. Arms Control and Disarmament Agency to conduct research and develop studies, prepare recommendations, conduct negotiations, and draft inspection and disarmament control plans. Provided for a fifteen-member General Advisory Committee, and authorized a $10 million appropriation for the agency. Approved September 26, 1961 (P.L. 87–297; 75 Stat. 631–639).

Community Health Services and Facilities Act of 1961. Encouraging construction of facilities and development of services outside the inpatient acute care hospital model of healthcare delivery. Provided major federal grants were given to state governments for construction of nursing homes, creation of general public health services, planning for community health needs, and designing programs for outpatient services directed toward the aged and chronically ill. Extended and strengthened the 1946 Hill–Burton Hospital Survey and Construction Act. Approved October 5, 1961 (P.L. 87–395; 75 Stat. 824–827).

Manpower Development and Training Act of 1962. Authorized a new federal program to train workers to help alleviate unemployment and to provide skilled personnel in certain industries. Delegated to the secretary of labor the responsibility for determining manpower needs, developing training programs, selecting candidates for training, and placing trainees. Approved March 15, 1962 (P.L. 87–415; 76 Stat. 23–33).

Tariff Classification Act of 1962. Provided for the reclassification of the entire U.S. tariff schedule by directing the U.S. Tariff Commission to revise and consolidate the tariff laws of the United States in a more logical classification arrangement. Suspended Cuba's most-favored-nation trading status. Approved May 24, 1962 (P.L. 87–456; 76 Stat. 72–78).

Public Welfare Amendments of 1962. Broadened welfare aid to the most needy. Provided rehabilitation, training, and self-care in an effort to reduce recipients' dependency. Increased federal reimbursements to the states for rehabilitative services to public assistance clients from 50 to 75 percent. Authorized the secretary of health, education, and welfare to appoint a twelve-member Advisory Council on Public Welfare. Approved July 25, 1962 (P.L. 87–543; 76 Stat. 172–208).

Foreign Assistance Act of 1962. Amended the Foreign Assistance Act of 1961 to prohibit aid to Communist nations, countries providing items of strategic value to Cuba, and countries that permitted ships under their registry to carry economic aid to Cuba, unless the president determined otherwise. Approved August 1, 1962 (P.L. 87–565; 76 Stat. 255–263).

Depository Library Act of 1962. Established the current structure of Federal Depository Library Program. Placed the responsibility for administering the program in the Government Printing Office. Provided for the distribution of documents not printed by the Government Printing Office (GPO), thus greatly expanding the volume of publications available to depository libraries. Imposed a limit of two Representative designated libraries for each congressional district and two designations by each Senator. Provided for up to two regional depository libraries in each state and the Commonwealth of Puerto Rico. Added the highest appellate court of each state and the accredited law schools to the list of depositories. Approved August 9, 1962 (P.L. 87–579; 76 Stat. 352–356).

Twenty-fourth Amendment. Provided that no citizen would be denied the right to vote "by the United States or any State by reason of failure to pay any poll tax or other tax." Approved August 27, 1962 (76 Stat. 1259). Ratified by requisite number of states January 23, 1964.[6]

Communications Satellite Act of 1962. Authorized the president to name a group of incorporators to establish the Communications Satellite Corporation (COMSAT) as a quasi-public corporation charged with the managing of satellite communications for the United States. Provided for a fifteen-member board of directors—three selected by the president for a term of three years, six elected annually by public stockholders, and six elected annually by the communication carriers. Directed the president to aid COMSAT in the expeditious development of a satellite system, the National Aeronautics and Space Administration to provide satellite launching and other technical services on a reimbursable basis, and the Federal Communications Commission to regulate relations between COMSAT and its customers. Approved August 31, 1962 (P.L. 87–624; 76 Stat. 419–427).

Food, Drug, and Cosmetic Act Amendments of 1962 (Kefauver-Harris Amendments). Granted authority to the Food and Drug Administration to establish manufacturing standards to assure the proper production of drugs, require manufacturers to prove the effectiveness of a drug, and recall drugs considered unsafe. Approved October 10, 1962 (P.L. 87–781; 76 Stat. 780–796).

Self-Employed Individuals Tax Retirement Act of 1962. Permitted self-employed individuals owning an interest in a business, and considered an owner-employee, to contribute 10 percent of their annual net earnings up to $2,500 to a retirement fund. Required owners having less than a 10 percent interest to make contributions through a nondiscriminatory partnership. Required owners establishing a retirement fund to provide a pension fund for all employees with more than three years of service. Approved October 10, 1962 (P.L. 87–792; 76 Stat. 809–831).

Trade Expansion Act of 1962. Authorized the president to reduce tariffs by 50 percent through June 1967; eliminate duties on certain goods having a tariff of 5 percent or less; withdraw concessions to countries maintaining "unreasonable" restrictions on U.S. exports; impose import restrictions on countries placing burdensome restrictions on U.S. agricultural exports; restrict imports threatening national security; and raise tariffs on goods injurious to American workers and businesses. Approved October 11, 1962 (P.L. 87–794; 76 Stat. 872–903).

Revenue Act of 1962. Instituted a tax credit for businesses that modernized their production facilities and capacity by investing in new assets. Imposed taxes on the earnings of nonmanufacturing foreign subsidiaries of U.S. corporations that had previously been able to avoid taxes. Imposed new restrictions on the tax deductions businesspeople could claim for entertainment, travel, and similar expenses. Permitted businesses to deduct certain lobbying expenses. Increased taxes on earnings of thrift institutions, insurance companies, and cooperatives. Required institutions making interest and dividend income payments to report them. Approved October 16, 1962 (P.L. 87–834; 76 Stat. 960–1069).

Bribery, Graft, and Conflicts of Interest Act of 1962. Strengthened the criminal laws relating to bribery, graft, and conflict-of-interest laws governing federal employees. Relaxed some restrictions affecting part-time employees. Defined punishment for bribery of public officials and witnesses and for matters involving salaries of government officials. Exempted government employees who represented another, without compensation, in a disciplinary, loyalty or other personnel proceeding. Exempted government employees who, with a superior's approval, represented without compensation a parent, spouse, child, or person for whom the employee acted as a fiduciary. Approved October 23, 1962 (P.L. 87–849; 76 Stat. 1119–1126).

Vaccination Assistance Act of 1962. Authorized a three-year program of special project grants to states and, with state approval, to local communities to pay part of the cost for the immediate vaccination of children under five against four contagious diseases—polio, diphtheria, whooping cough, and tetanus. Provided for similar attacks on other diseases when vaccines were developed (measles added in 1965). Approved October 23, 1962 (P.L. 87–868; 76 Stat. 1155–1156).

Notes

1. *Congressional Quarterly Almanac,* 1962 (Washington, D.C.: Congressional Quarterly, 1962), 262.

2. U.S. Presidents (Kennedy), *Public Papers of the Presidents: John F. Kennedy, 1961* (Washington, D.C.: Government Printing Office), 1962, 645.

3. Anthony Lewis, "House Votes Poll Tax Ban; States' Ratification Needed," *New York Times,* August 28, 1962, 1.

4. *Journal of the Executive Proceedings of the Senate* (Washington, D.C.: U.S. Government Printing Office, 1961), 103:429–430; 12 UST 1728–1759.

5. The United States Agency for International Development created by Executive Order 10973 on November 3, 1961.

6. U.S. Senate, *The Constitution of the United States: Analysis and Interpretation,* 108th Cong., 2d sess., 2004, 41, n. 16; and 78 Stat. 1117–1118.

Eighty-eighth Congress
January 3, 1963, to January 3, 1965

First session—January 9, 1963, to December 30, 1963
Second session—January 7, 1964, to October 3, 1964
(Administration of John F. Kennedy, 1961–1963; first
   administration of Lyndon B. Johnson, 1963–1965)

Historical Background

John F. Kennedy's third and final year as president was distinguished by the first formal arms control agreement between the United States and the Soviet Union. Senate ratification of the Limited Nuclear Test Ban Treaty came eighteen years after the advent of nuclear weapons. On announcing the treaty, President Kennedy reminded the American people that frequently the two nations had "communicated suspicion and warnings to each other, but very rarely hope." Too often their discussions "produced only darkness, discord, or disillusion." The treaty offered "a shaft of light cut into the darkness."

Passage of the Equal Pay Act of 1963 required that employers engaged in interstate commerce pay men and women equal wages for doing the same work. Both Presidents Dwight D. Eisenhower and Kennedy, as well as a broad range of women's groups and labor unions, supported the act. Business organizations argued, however, that having the states pursue this goal would be more effective. Kennedy also enthusiastically backed legislation dealing with the challenges posed by mental health problems and mental retardation.

President Kennedy was assassinated in Dallas, Texas, on November 22, 1963, allegedly by Lee Harvey Oswald. A great outpouring of grief for the president's family, and sympathetic support for Vice President Lyndon B. Johnson as he assumed the presidency,

followed. Johnson, a formidable legislative strategist and tactician, successfully pressed and expanded Kennedy's legislative agenda.

In approving the most important vocational education legislation in nearly half a century, Congress authorized additional funds for existing programs and established a broad array of new programs. Although passage of the Clean Air Act of 1963 did not relieve state and local governments of primary responsibility for controlling air pollution, it did mandate a much more active and influential federal role in resolving the problem. The expense of combating the growing problem of air pollution in American's urban centers necessitated greater federal involvement, a position that had been advocated by President Kennedy.

President Kennedy's experience in personally having to cover sizable presidential transition expenses between election day and Inauguration Day prompted a proposal to appropriate official transition funds for both newly elected and retiring chief executives. Congress adopted a plan providing such funds after Kennedy's death.

The Higher Education Facilities Act of 1963 was the "first broad education bill enacted in the post-war period that did not have national defense overtones." During debate on the bill, "the national defense rationale of federal education receded, and the goal of equal educational opportunity began to emerge."[1] The act was passed in response to a strong nationwide demand for expansion of college and university facilities to meet the sharply rising number of young people demanding higher education.

The 1960s saw increasing tension as African Americans pushed for full civil rights and voting rights. Undeterred by legal barriers and intimidation, black organizations such as the National Association for the

Advancement of Colored People (NAACP), Southern Christian Leadership Conference, Congress on Racial Equality, and Urban League organized protests and demonstrations that culminated in the August 1963 March on Washington. The Rev. Dr. Martin Luther King Jr. electrified the crowd as well as the entire nation with a ringing call for racial justice and equality. Congress responded by approving the most sweeping civil rights legislation since Reconstruction. The Civil Rights Act of 1964 guaranteed the right of blacks to vote and have equal access to public accommodations, and it established enforcement procedures to prohibit discrimination in employment, education, and use of public facilities.

Sen. Mike Mansfield of Montana called the Urban Mass Transportation Act of 1964 a legislative miracle because it attracted enormous bipartisan support. In recognizing that the development of "efficient and coordinated mass transportation systems [was] essential" to solve the nation's urban problems, President Johnson declared that Congress had enacted "one of the most profoundly significant domestic measures" of the 1960s.

In 1964, President Johnson capitalized on the mood of the American people following the death of President Kennedy by proposing the furthest-reaching program of domestic legislation since the New Deal. The ten federal programs that made up the Economic Opportunity Act of 1964 were designed to wage what President Johnson called a War on Poverty, a coordinated attack on the multiple causes of poverty that had left one-fifth of the nation impoverished. They included training and educational opportunities for disadvantaged youth and adults, legal services for the poor, a public awareness program, and a domestic Peace Corps—VISTA, or Volunteers in Service to America.

Enactment of the Food Stamp Act of 1964 provided permanent authorization for a pilot program begun at the outset of the Kennedy administration to increase the food-buying power of low-income families.

Both Kennedy and Johnson pushed for enactment of an interest equalization tax on the purchase of certain foreign securities by American citizens.

Major natural resource measures provided for the incorporation of federally held wilderness areas into a National Wilderness Preservation System, and establishment of a Land and Water Conservation Fund.

Passage of the Wilderness Act, following more than a decade of discussion, assured that substantial wilderness areas would be preserved in their wild and unspoiled state, as conservationists had long sought. Supporters of the Land and Water Conservation Fund successfully argued the importance of accelerating the purchase of potential outdoor recreation sites before they fell prey to such powerful forces as urban and commercial development and new highway construction.

In 1963, the U.S. surgeon general's consultant group on nursing made several recommendations aimed at addressing an increasing shortage of nurses. Their recommendations prompted the Comprehensive Nurse Training Act of 1964, the first federal law to provide comprehensive funding for nursing education. On signing the act, President Lyndon B. Johnson said it was "the most significant nursing legislation in the history of our country."

The threat of communism in Southeast Asia remained at the forefront of American consciousness. Since the Eisenhower administration, the United States had provided military assistance to the government of South Vietnam, created as a part of the 1954 peace settlement that ended French control of its Asian colony, Indochina, after an eight-year war. In the early 1960s, communist North Vietnam and indigenous South Vietnamese communist and nationalist guerrillas (Vietcong) brought increased military pressure against the U.S.–supported government. Presidents Kennedy and Johnson responded with increased aid, but governmental instability after a U.S.–backed coup against President Ngo Dinh Diem contributed to a growing sense of demoralization in South Vietnam. Increasingly, the Vietcong guerrillas targeted U.S. personnel and installations in their attacks.

Events reached a crisis point on August 4, 1964, when American warships patrolling international waters off the coast of North Vietnam reported they were under attack by North Vietnamese gunboats. President Johnson responded by ordering retaliatory air strikes and sought congressional approval for his actions. Congress approved the Gulf of Tonkin Resolution declaring that the United States regarded the "maintenance of international peace and security in Southeast Asia . . . vital to its national interest and world peace." Although the resolution passed the House by a 414–0 vote and the Senate by an 88–2 vote, and Congress was put on record in support of the administration's Vietnam policy, several members later charged that the resolution had gained approval as a result of misrepresentation and deception on the part of the administration. Their concerns were based primarily on uncertainty surrounding the circumstances under which the Vietnamese gunboats attacked the American warships.

President Johnson scored one of the greatest popular-vote triumphs in American political history in winning the 1964 election. Johnson and his running mate, Hubert H. Humphrey, received 61.1 percent of the popular vote; Sen. Barry Goldwater of Arizona, the Republican presidential nominee, and his running mate, William E. Miller, received 38.5 percent. The electoral vote tally was a lopsided 486 for Johnson and Humphrey and 52 for Goldwater and Miller. In the congressional elections, the Democrats strengthened their hold in both the House and Senate.

Major Acts and Treaties

Equal Pay Act of 1963. Declared that no employer subject to the Fair Labor Standards Act could discriminate on the basis of sex in payment of wages to employees "at a rate less than the rate at which he pays wages to employees of the opposite sex ... on jobs the performance of which requires equal skill, effort, and responsibility, and which are performed under similar working conditions." Permitted differences in wages based on seniority, merit, and type of work, or other factors. Forbade employers from reducing the wage rate of any employee to comply with the act and unions from attempting to influence employers to discriminate against employees on the basis of sex. Approved June 10, 1963 (P.L. 88–38; 77 Stat. 56–57). *(Federal Fair Labor Standards Act, p. 256)*

Nuclear Test Ban Treaty. Bound the signatories (United States, Soviet Union, and Great Britain, and ultimately more than a hundred other nations) "to prohibit, to prevent, and not to carry out any nuclear weapon test explosion, or any other nuclear explosion at any place under its jurisdiction or control (a) in the atmosphere, beyond its limits, including outer space, or underwater, including territorial water or high seas, or (b) in any other environment if such explosion causes radioactive debris to be present outside the territorial units of the state under whose jurisdiction or control such explosion is conducted." Signatories also pledged to refrain from causing, encouraging, or in any way participating in any nuclear test anywhere else. Concluded August 5, 1963. Ratification advised by the Senate September 24, 1963.[2]

Mental Retardation Facilities and Community Mental Health Centers Construction Act of 1963. Provided federal grants to assist state and local governments' construction of community facilities for the mentally retarded and community mental health centers. Authorized expansion of programs training teachers of mentally retarded and deaf children, and authorized grants to states and college programs to improve the educational opportunity for handicapped children. Approved October 31, 1963 (P.L. 88–164; 77 Stat. 282–299).

Higher Education Facilities Act of 1963. Authorized $1.195 billion for the first three years of a planned five-year program to upgrade the nation's higher educational facilities. Provided grants and low-interest loans to public and nonprofit institutions of higher education (community colleges, colleges, and technical schools) to rehabilitate, or improve buildings to house the classrooms, libraries, laboratories and other facilities needed to expand enrollment. Stipulated the terms of eligibility for loans, provisions for loan agreements, and means for recoupment of improperly used grants. Approved December 16, 1963 (P.L. 88–204; 77 Stat. 363–379).

Clean Air Act of 1963. Declared that air pollution was the "primary responsibility" of state and local governments, and authorized matching federal grants to assist these jurisdictions as well as interstate agencies in developing programs to prevent and control air pollution. Directed the secretary of health, education, and welfare to establish a national air pollution research and development program, and authorized a committee to evaluate progress in improving automobile pollution. Authorized federal enforcement of state pollution laws at the request of governors. Approved

December 17, 1963 (P.L. 88–206; 77 Stat. 392–401). *(Clean Air Act Amendments of 1977, p. 362; Clean Air Act Amendments of 1990, p. 401)*

Vocational Education Act of 1963. Broadened and enhanced existing federal vocational education programs, and for the first time provided for training in industrial and technical skills. Placed special emphasis on involving out-of-school, out-of-work urban youth living in high-stress areas. Authorized permanent federal assistance for vocational training, to be allocated among the states on the basis of per capita income and population, and a twelve-member Advisory Council on Vocational Education to evaluate the programs. Approved December 18, 1963 (P.L. 88–210; 77 Stat. 403–419).

Revenue Act of 1964. Reduced personal income tax rates from 21 to 6 percent according to bracket and corporate tax by 4 percent, to 48 percent. Allowed a minimum tax deduction, added some itemized deductions, and tightened tax rules on stock option plans and sick pay exclusions. Provided stricter limits on tax deductions resulting from casualty and theft losses. Increased taxes on the sale of a building resulting from accelerated depreciation practices, and reduced capital gains on taxpayers sixty-five and older. Created a new deduction for moving expenses, liberalized child care deductions, broadened investment tax credits, and provided a minimum standard deduction. Approved February 26, 1964 (P.L. 88–272; 78 Stat. 19–146).

Presidential Transition Act of 1964. Authorized the "Administrator of the General Services to provide, upon request, to each President-elect and each Vice President-elect" suitable office space, compensation for office staff, services of detailed federal personnel, and funds for consultants. Covered travel expenses and subsistence allowances, communication services, printing and binding expenses, and postal expenses. Provided similar services for six months to former presidents after they retire. Authorized an appropriation of $900,000 for each presidential transition. Approved March 7, 1964 (P.L. 88–277; 78 Stat. 153–156).

Civil Rights Act of 1964. Expanded federal power to protect voting rights. Authorized the attorney general to institute lawsuits against state or local authorities who failed to desegregate public accommodations, public facilities, and public schools. Outlawed discrimination in federally funded projects and the denial of equal employment opportunities in businesses and unions with more than twenty-five members. Extended the Civil Rights Commission for four years. Required the Census Bureau to gather voting statistics by race. Created a Community Relations Service to help resolve civil rights disputes within communities and a five-member Equal Employment Opportunity Commission to end employment discrimination. Approved July 2, 1964 (P.L. 88–352; 78 Stat. 241–268)

Urban Mass Transportation Act of 1964. Authorized the "Housing and Home Finance Administrator to provide additional assistance for the development of comprehensive and coordinated mass transportation systems, both public and private, in metropolitan and other urban areas." Declared that this assistance be provided because the "predominant part of the Nation's population is located in" urban areas, "which generally cross the boundary lines of local jurisdictions and often extend into two or more States." Provided $375 million in loans and matching grants to assist states and localities in acquiring, constructing, and improving public mass transportation systems. Approved July 9, 1964 (P.L. 88–365; 78 Stat. 302–308).

Gulf of Tonkin Resolution. Declared support for "the determination of the President, as Commander-in-Chief, to take all necessary measures to repel any armed attack against the forces of the United States and to prevent further aggression in Vietnam." Affirmed U.S. determination to assist any signatory of the Southeast Asia Collective Defense Treaty that requested aid to defend its freedom. Approved August 10, 1964 (P.L. 88–408; 78 Stat. 384). *(Foreign Military Sales Act Amendments and Repeal of Gulf of Tonkin Resolution, p. 340)*

Economic Opportunity Act of 1964. Created an Office of Economic Opportunity to administer ten programs designed to address the multiple causes of poverty. Established programs for disadvantaged school dropouts (Job Corps), disadvantaged youths who remained in school (Neighborhood Youth Corps), talented disadvantaged students who sought a college education (Upward Bound), focusing public attention on the problems of poverty (Community Action Program), adult education, preschool education (Head Start), legal services to the poor, and volunteers to help combat poverty (Volunteers in Service to America). Approved August 20, 1964 (P.L. 88–452; 78 Stat. 508–534).

Food Stamp Act of 1964. Established a permanent food stamp program financed by the federal government in cooperation with state governments to "permit those households with low incomes to receive a greater share of the Nation's food abundance" and "to achieve a fuller and more effective use of food abundances." Authorized establishment of eligibility requirements for receiving food stamps. Approved August 31, 1964 (P.L. 88–525; 78 Stat. 703–709).

Wilderness Act of 1964. Established a National Wilderness Preservation System. Designated approximately 9.1 million acres of national forest lands, which by administrative action had previously been classified as "wilderness," "wild," or "canoe areas." Required congressional approval for additions to the system. Prohibited the use of airplanes, boats, commercial buildings, permanent roads, and so on and mining on lands constituting the system. Approved September 3, 1964 (P.L. 88–577; 78 Stat. 890–896).

Land and Water Conservation Fund Act of 1964. Created a Land and Water Conservation Fund administered by the secretary of the interior and empowered to receive revenues from various federal sources. Provided that monies from the fund could be used to make matching grants to states to acquire recreational lands, develop recreational facilities, and finance wilderness aspects of federal water projects. Authorized federal land acquisitions for national parks, wilderness areas, and national forests. Approved September 3, 1964 (P.L. 88–578; 78 Stat. 897–904).

Nurse Training Act of 1964. Provided for five years of support in four areas: construction grants for nursing schools, special project grants to increase the quality of nursing education, loans to nursing students and nursing schools, and expansion of advanced degree programs in nursing. Allotted $300 million dollars for nursing education, with $35 million of it specifically earmarked for collegiate training. Established loan and grant programs for those interested in becoming nurses. Approved September 4, 1964 (P.L. 88–581; 78 Stat. 908–919).

Notes

1. *Congressional Quarterly Almanac, 1963* (Washington, D.C. Congressional Quarterly Service, 1963), 194. Lawrence E. Gladieux and Thomas R. Wolanin, *Congress and the Colleges: The National Politics of Higher Education* (Lexington, Mass.: Lexington Books, 1976), 11.

2. *Journal of the Executive Proceedings of the Senate* (Washington, D.C.: U.S. Government Printing Office, 1964), 105 (part 1): 933–934; 14 UST 1313–1387.

Eighty-ninth Congress
January 3, 1965, to January 3, 1967

First session—January 4, 1965, to October 23, 1965
Second session—January 10, 1966, to October 22, 1966
(Second administration of Lyndon B. Johnson,
    1965–1969)

Historical Background

Lyndon B. Johnson moved quickly following his landslide election in November 1964 to create the Great Society that had been his presidential campaign theme. Supported by the largest party majority enjoyed by any president since Franklin D. Roosevelt, Johnson was able to push through a record volume of domestic legislation during the first session of the Eighty-ninth Congress.

High on the agenda were Medicare for the aged and Medicaid for the "medically needy" and poor, both proposed by President Harry S. Truman two decades earlier. Both programs were approved in late July 1965. As a tribute, Johnson signed the legislation at the Harry S. Truman Library in Independence, Missouri, with the former president at his side. The major elements of a national program drafted in 1964 by the President's Commission on Heart Disease, Cancer, and Stroke were enacted a month later. The intent of the act was to reduce the incidence of these illnesses—the nation's three major causes of death—by instituting cooperative regional arrangements to make the latest advances from biomedical research available to benefit the health of the American people. In November 1966, legislation was passed that emphasized comprehensive state health care planning, and introduced the concept that each person had the "right to health care."

Although a Johnson administration proposal to reshape the school lunch and milk programs was rejected, Congress did approve a pilot breakfast program for schools in poor areas and funds for equipment to improve the school lunch programs.

As a result of the Voting Rights Act of 1965, passed by bipartisan majorities in both houses of Congress, African Americans and other minority group citizens could register and vote, and run for political office under the guardianship of the federal government. On August 6, 1965, President Johnson told a nationwide television audience that the Voting Rights Act was a "triumph for freedom as huge as any victory that has ever been won on a battlefield." With this act, Johnson declared, "we strike away the last major shackle of those fierce and ancient bonds" African Americans had experienced since Jamestown. Earlier in the year, voting rights marchers in Selma, Alabama, were assaulted by the state police. Within a week, the president called upon Congress to "strike down restrictions to voting in all elections . . . which have been used to deny Negroes the right to vote." Other minorities benefited from elimination of the national origins immigration quota system, ending a struggle that began not long after its enactment in 1921.

The "keystones of the great fabulous first session of the 89th Congress," President Johnson felt, were education bills. Early in April 1965, he signed the Elementary and Secondary Education Act, the "most sweeping educational bill ever to come before Congress." Seven months later, a new law provided subsidies for middle-income undergraduates and scholarships for students of "exceptional financial need." It would, Johnson stressed, "swing open a new door for the young people of America . . . the door of education." The National Foundation on the Arts and the Humanities also was created in 1965.

Significant lobbying efforts by the president resulted in the creation of two new cabinet-level departments—the Department of Housing and Urban Development (HUD) in 1965 and the Department of Transportation (DOT) in 1966. The first, Johnson told Congress, will "give greater force and effectiveness to our efforts in the cities"; the second will "modernize and streamline" the federal government's transportation programs. Congress in creating HUD declared that the "welfare and security of the Nation and the health and living standards of our people require, as a matter of national purpose, sound development" of its communities and metropolitan areas. Establishment of DOT was necessary "to assure the coordinated, effective administration of the transportation programs of the Federal Government." Other important housing legislation included a four-year $7.8 billion appropriation for new and existing housing and urban development programs and a three-year $1.2 billion wide-ranging "demonstration cities" plan (later renamed "Model Cities") to revitalize America's decaying urban centers.

A decade of moderate congressional interest in traffic safety, increased public demands for safer automobiles and highways, and consumer advocate Ralph Nader's effective lobbying efforts brought about new laws establishing federal motor vehicle and tire standards, and traffic safety programs by the states. With his wife Lady Bird Johnson leading the effort to secure passage of the Highway Beautification Act of 1965, President Lyndon B. Johnson made passage of the Highway Beautification Act a priority. Although historians contend the act "did little to limit the spread of billboards along the highways," but it "is significant in the history of the American environmental movement for at least two reasons." The act significantly reduced the number of junkyards lining the highways, and "represented the first federal legislation to manage the aesthetic aspect of U.S. roadways."[1]

The passage of the Public Works and Economic Development Act of 1965 reflected a growing concern in the United States about areas not sharing in the overall economic prosperity of the nation. Many parts of the country were suffering from substantial and persistent unemployment and underemployment which caused unnecessary hardships and a waste of invaluable human resources.

To improve and expand federal programs for the elderly, an Administration on Aging was established within the Department of Health, Education, and Welfare. Grants totaling $17.5 million were authorized for fiscal years 1966–1967 to assist states as well as public and private nonprofit organizations in developing, establishing, expanding, and administering senior citizen programs. Veterans benefits were extended to those who had served in the armed forces since the expiration of the Korean War benefits.

For twelve months after President John F. Kennedy's death, the vice presidency was vacant, a condition that most observers considered unacceptable in an era of world tensions, instantaneous communications, and weapons of mass destruction. In July 1965, Congress proposed a constitutional amendment to remedy the situation for the future. In the event of a vice presidential vacancy, the president was empowered to nominate a replacement who was subject to confirmation by a majority of both houses of Congress. In addition, the amendment established procedures for presidential disability. Ratification of the Twenty-fifth Amendment was completed in February 1967.

Americans today expect cigarette packaging and advertisements to include a health warning. The initial warning, however, dates from enactment of the Federal Cigarette Labeling and Advertising Act in 1965. At that time tobacco companies were only required to place a health warning on cigarette packages. Four years later, the requirement was extended to all print, television, and radio advertising with adoption of the Public Health Cigarette Smoking Act (P.L. 91–222; 84 Stat. 87–90).

Following several years of consideration and investigation, the Freedom of Information Act, which statutorily established the right of the American people to information about the government and its activities, was signed into law on Independence Day 1966. The act required federal agencies to publish rules and procedures in the *Federal Register* and make public final reports, opinions, and policy statements. The categories of information protected from disclosure were limited.

Both the president and organized labor were satisfied by the approval of a bill substantially increasing the minimum wage and extending coverage to an estimated 9.1 million additional workers. Consumer groups successfully lobbied for stronger controls on the packaging and labeling of household as well as personal goods, an achievement that had eluded the previous two Congresses. Crime legislation enacted in response to presidential requests strengthened and broadened federal control over depressant and stimulant drugs in an effort to reduce their illegal distribution, and it also provided for institutional treatment of drug addicts instead of prison time.

The Water Quality Act, which was endorsed by the administration, required states to establish and enforce water quality standards for all interstate waters within their boundaries. Another title was added to the Clean Air Act with the enactment of a bill to control the pollution caused by automobile exhaust. Passage of the National Historic Preservation Act in 1966 was a watershed event. It signaled America's commitment to preserving its heritage and marked a fundamental shift in how Americans and the federal government regarded the role of historic preservation in modern life. The act established the framework for national historic preservation that focused local, state, and national efforts on a common goal—preserving the historic fabric of our nation. Inspired by the plight of disappearing species, Congress responded with passage of the first federal law that attempted to deal with the issue comprehensively. Even though the 1966 act was limited in scope it reflected a significant concern with the plight of endangered species, and laid the foundation upon which later legislation was built.

By 1966, some 100 million Americans were observing daylight savings time based on their local laws and customs. Congress decided to step in and end the confusion, and to establish one pattern across the country. Several times since, Congress has made minor adjustments to daylight savings time observance in the United States.

The Vietnam War continued to escalate in scope and intensity. U.S. Army and Marine Corps forces were committed in large numbers to ground combat operations for the first time. U.S. Navy and Air Force warplanes undertook sustained bombing campaigns over South Vietnam and North Vietnam. Critics voiced their fear that the United States would be trapped in a land war against an elusive guerrilla army that could not be won, and they asserted that the conflict was "eroding" the Great Society. Others insisted the nation honor its commitment to contain communist aggression while seeking to build democratic government in South Vietnam. They maintained that defeat in Vietnam would stimulate communist guerrillas and lead to the domino-like collapse of other democratic governments in Southeast Asia.

By 1966 the escalating costs associated with the war in Vietnam and disenchantment over urban riots had begun to take its toll. Although the president was given sizable appropriations for the War on Poverty, he got far less than requested. His declining influence was also evident at the polls; the Republicans made notable gains in the midterm congressional elections.

Major Acts

Elementary and Secondary Education Act of 1965. Provided an estimated $1.4 billion in federal grants to the states for elementary and secondary schools. Stipulated that grants would be based on the average amount each state spent on its students and the number of children it had from low-income families (earning under $2,000 a year). Authorized grants for purchasing textbooks and library materials, supplementary communitywide educational centers, new research and training centers, and programs designed to strengthen state education departments. Approved April 11, 1965 (P.L. 89–10; 79 Stat. 27–58).

Twenty-fifth Amendment. Declared that whenever a vacancy in the office of the vice president occurred, the president shall nominate a person who would take office upon confirmation by a majority of both houses of Congress. Declared that the vice president shall become acting president if the president submits a written declaration to Congress that he is unable to perform his duties or if the vice president and a majority of the cabinet, or such other body as Congress by law may provide, declared the president to be incapacitated. Stipulated that in both instances the president was to inform Congress when his disability had ended. Allowed Congress twenty-one days to resolve any dispute over the president's disability. Proposed July 6, 1965 (79 Stat. 1327–1328). Ratified by requisite number of states February 23, 1967.[2]

Older Americans Act of 1965. Authorized a five-year federal grant program to develop and improve assistance to the elderly. Established an Administration on Aging within the Department of Health, Education, and Welfare (HEW) to administer the grants; provide technical assistance to state and local governments; assist the HEW secretary on matters concerning the aged; and conduct research, prepare materials, and collect statistics on the elderly. Authorized federal grants totaling $17.5 million for fiscal years 1966–1967 to states and public and private nonprofit organizations for developing programs for the elderly. Approved July 14, 1965 (P.L. 89–73; 79 Stat. 218–226).

Drug Abuse Control Amendments of 1965. Expanded and strengthened federal control over depressant and stimulant drugs. Required that manufacturers and distributors keep better records, strengthened the powers of federal inspectors and enforcement agents, and limited prescription refills. Approved July 15, 1965 (P.L. 89–74; 79 Stat. 226–236).

Federal Cigarette Labeling and Advertising Act. Required package warning label—"Caution: Cigarette Smoking May Be Hazardous to Your Health." Specified that no statement was required on cigarette advertisements. Required the Federal Trade Commission to report to Congress annually on the effectiveness of cigarette labeling, current cigarette advertising and promotion practices, and to make recommendations for legislation. Required Department of Health, Education, and Welfare to report annually to Congress on the health consequences of smoking. Approved July 27, 1965 (P.L. 89–92; 79 Stat. 282–284).

Social Security Amendments of 1965 (Medicare and Medicaid). Established a federally supported Medicare program for more than eighteen million Americans over sixty-five. Provided a basic insurance program covering hospital and posthospital services; a supplementary (voluntary) medical insurance program covering physician and surgeon payments, home health care, and other medical services; and a Medicaid program to assist needy and disabled persons not covered by Social Security. Approved July 30, 1965 (P.L. 89–97; 79 Stat. 286–353).

Voting Rights Act of 1965. Suspended the use of literacy tests and voter qualification devices for five years. Authorized appointment of federal examiners to supervise registration of voters in those states where tests had been used and less than one-half of the voting-age residents were registered or had voted. Directed the attorney general to institute proceedings against the use of poll taxes. Established criminal penalties for those individuals in violation of the act. Approved August 6, 1965 (P.L. 89–110; 79 Stat. 437–446). *(Voting Rights Act Amendments of 1970, p. 337; Voting Rights Act Amendments of 1975, p. 357; Voting Rights Act Amendments of 1982, p. 376)*

Certain provisions of this act were subsequently held unconstitutional in *Shelby County v. Holder,* 570 U.S. ___ (2013).

Housing and Urban Development Act of 1965. Established programs to provide rent supplements to low-income families; Federal Housing Administration (FHA) insurance on commercial loans; Veterans Administration mortgages; matching grants for construction of water and sewer facilities; grants for construction of community, health, and recreation centers; grants for urban beautification; and insured loans for rural housing and farm buildings. Extended funding for a variety of housing programs and FHA home mortgages. Established uniform land acquisition procedures, and increased authorization for student housing loans. Approved August 10, 1965 (P.L. 89–117; 79 Stat. 451–509).

Public Works and Economic Development Act of 1965. Superceded the Area Redevelopment Act of 1961. Established the Economic Development Administration (EDA) to generate jobs, help retain existing jobs, and stimulate industrial and commercial growth in economically troubled areas of the United States. Provided for EDA assistance to be available to rural and urban areas of the United States experiencing high unemployment, low income, or other severe economic distress. Approved August 26, 1965 (P.L. 89–136; 79 Stat. 552–576).

Department of Housing and Urban Development Act. Declared that establishment of a Department of Housing and Urban Development (HUD) was "desirable to achieve the best administration of the principal programs of the Federal Government which provided assistance for housing and the development of the Nation's communities." Transferred all powers, duties, and functions of the Federal Housing Administration,

Federal National Mortgage Association, Housing and Home Finance Agency, and Public Housing Administration to HUD. Approved September 9, 1965 (P.L. 89–174; 79 Stat. 667–671).

National Foundation on the Arts and the Humanities Act of 1965. Established a National Foundation on the Arts and the Humanities consisting of two autonomous subdivisions: a National Endowment for the Arts and a National Endowment for the Humanities. Provided for coordination of the foundation's operations through a Federal Council on the Arts and the Humanities, composed of nine federal officials (headed by the secretary of the Smithsonian Institution), who would advise the chairpersons of the two endowments. Authorized each endowment to make grants for a broad range of activities. Approved September 29, 1965 (P.L. 89–209; 79 Stat. 845–855).

Water Quality Act of 1965. Required each state to establish and enforce water quality standards for all interstate waters within their boundaries. Authorized the government to set federal standards if state standards proved too weak. Established a Federal Water Pollution Control Administration to administer the act. Authorized appropriations of $20 million a year in fiscal years 1966–1969 for matching grants to various jurisdictions for projects that helped prevent untreated sewage and wastes from being discharged into the nation's waters. Increased the existing federal grant program for construction of community sewage treatment plants by $50 million a year. Approved October 2, 1965 (P.L. 89–234; 79 Stat. 903–910).

Immigration and Nationality Act of 1965. Abolished the national origins quota system. Created a new system with a numerical ceiling of 170,000 non-Western Hemisphere immigrants per year with no more than 20,000 coming from the same country. Imposed a ceiling for the first time on immigrants (120,000) from the Western Hemisphere. Approved October 3, 1965 (P.L. 89–236; 79 Stat. 911–922).

Heart Disease, Cancer, and Stroke Amendments. Authorized the establishment and maintenance of regional medical programs designed to create "cooperative arrangements among medical schools, research institutions, and hospitals for research and training, including continuing education," and demonstration activities in patient care in treating heart disease, cancer, and strokes. Provided grants to public or nonprofit private universities, medical schools, research institutions, hospitals, and other public and nonprofit agencies, institutions, and associations to assist in constructing and equipping facilities involved in research, training, and treatment related to these three grave diseases. Approved October 6, 1965 (P.L. 89–239; 79 Stat. 926–931).

Motor Vehicle Air Pollution Control Act. Directed the secretary of health, education, and welfare to establish exhaust admission standards for new automobiles, and prohibited the sale of any vehicle not satisfying those standards. Approved October 20, 1965 (P.L. 89–272; 79 Stat. 992–1001).

Highway Beautification Act of 1965. Called for the control of outdoor advertising, including removal of certain types of signs, along the nation's growing interstate system and the existing federal-aid primary system. Required certain junkyards along interstate or primary highways to be removed or screened and encouraged scenic enhancement and roadside development. Encouraged "scenic enhancement" by funding local efforts to clean up and landscape the green spaces on either side of the roadways. Approved October 22, 1965 (P.L. 89–285; 79 Stat. 1028–1033).

Higher Education Act of 1965. Authorized $840 million for fiscal year 1966 to aid poor and middle-class undergraduates as well as graduate programs for public school teachers. Authorized a National Teachers Corps to improve elementary and secondary education in urban slums and impoverished rural areas; community service programs focusing on urban problems; grants to improve college libraries and to train librarians; a program to raise the academic quality of developing institutions; and grants to improve instruction in the sciences, humanities, arts, and education. Approved November 8, 1965 (P.L. 89–329; 79 Stat. 1219–1270).

Veterans Readjustment Benefits Act (Cold War GI Bill). Provided educational or vocational training and housing assistance to members of the armed services who served on active duty for more than 180 days between January 31, 1955, and July 1, 1967, and were honorably discharged. Waived the 180-day requirement for veterans who experienced service-connected disabilities. Authorized monthly veterans payments for education or vocational training based on length of service, marital status, number of dependents, and number of classes taken or type of training involved. Authorized the Veterans Administration to guarantee up to 60 percent of home loans up to $7,500; 50 percent of nonresidential real estate up to $4,000; and home loans up to $17,500 when private financing was not available. Approved March 3, 1966 (P.L. 89–358; 80 Stat. 12–28).

Uniform Time Act of 1966. Established a system of uniform (within each time zone) daylight savings time throughout the United States and its possessions, exempting only those states in which the legislatures voted to keep the entire state on standard time. Approved April 12, 1966 (P.L. 89–387; 80 Stat. 107–109).

Freedom of Information Act. Required the federal government and its agencies to make available to citizens, upon request, all documents and records except those included in exempt categories: documents relating to national security and foreign policy, internal personnel practices, information exempted by law, trade secrets, interagency and intra-agency memos, personnel and medical files, information relating to the regulation of financial institutions, law enforcement and investigatory information, and geological and geophysical information. Approved July 4, 1966 (P.L. 89–487; 80 Stat. 250–251). *(Freedom of Information Act Amendments of 1974, p. 353)*

National Traffic and Motor Vehicle Safety Act of 1966. Established a three-year traffic and motor vehicle safety program administered by the Department of Commerce (subsequently the Department of Transportation). Directed that federal motor vehicle standards be established for all new domestic and foreign automobiles, buses, motorcycles, trucks, and other motor vehicles by January 1, 1967, and for used cars within two years. Directed that federal motor vehicle tire standards be in place within two years, and a national register be maintained of drivers whose licenses were suspended or revoked. Approved September 9, 1966 (P.L. 89–563; 80 Stat. 718–730).

Highway Safety Act of 1966. Required each state to establish a highway safety program approved by the secretary of commerce that covered driver education, licensing, and pedestrian performance; vehicle registration and inspection; traffic control; highway design and maintenance; accident prevention, investigation, and record keeping; and emergency services. Stipulated that those states failing to implement an approved safety plan by December 31, 1968, would lose 10 percent of federal-aid highway funds to which they were entitled. Authorized $267 million in fiscal years 1967–1969 in matching grants to the states for highway safety programs. Approved September 9, 1966 (P.L. 89–564; 80 Stat. 731–737).

Fair Labor Standards Act Amendments of 1966. Broadened federal minimum wage and overtime pay protection, and increased the minimum wage from $1.25 to $1.60 per hour. Extended coverage to an estimated 9.1 million additional workers in retail stores, restaurants, hotels, and, for the first time, a third of the nation's agricultural workers. Approved September 23, 1966 (P.L. 89–601; 80 Stat. 830–845). Certain provisions of this act were subsequently held unconstitutional in *National League of Cities v. Usery,* 426 U.S. 833 (1976). *(Federal Fair Labor Standards Act, p. 256)*

Child Nutrition Act of 1966. Authorized a pilot breakfast program for schools in poor areas and funding to assist schools in purchasing equipment to be used in conjunction with the school breakfast and lunch programs. Approved October 11, 1966 (P.L. 89–642; 80 Stat. 885–890).

National Historic Preservation Act. Established preservation as a national policy and directed the Federal government to provide leadership in preserving, restoring, and maintaining the historic and cultural environment of the nation. Established the National Register of Historic Places that identifies districts, sites, buildings, structures, and objects significant in American history, architecture, archaeology, engineering, and culture. Created the Advisory Council on Historic Preservation charged with advising the president and the Congress on historic preservation matters and working with federal agencies to address historic resources in the fulfillment of their missions. Authorized matching grants, now called Historic Preservation Fund grants, to states. Approved October 15, 1966 (P.L. 89–665; 80 Stat. 915–919).

Endangered Species Preservation Act. Directed the Departments of Interior, Agriculture, and Defense to protect threatened species "insofar as practicable and consistent" with the primary purposes of the services, bureaus, and agencies within their departments. Required the Department of Interior to consult with and "encourage" all other federal agencies to conform to the purposes of the act "where practicable," and instructed the department to continue to compile lists of endangered species. Created the National Wildlife Refuge System, and authorized funds for the maintenance and expansion of the system. Approved October 15, 1966 (P.L. 89–669; 80 Stat. 926–930).

Department of Transportation Act. Established a Department of Transportation (DOT) "to assure coordinated, effective administration of the transportation programs of the Federal Government" and facilitate the "development and improvement of coordinated transportation service" by private enterprise as well as state and local governments. Established within DOT a Federal Highway Administration, Federal Railroad Administration, and Federal Aviation Administration. Transferred thirty-eight agencies or functions to DOT. Established a National Transportation Safety Board to investigate and determine the probable cause of transportation accidents. Excluded DOT from economic regulatory and rate-setting activities. Approved October 15, 1966 (P.L. 89–670; 80 Stat. 931–950).

Comprehensive Health Planning and Public Health Service Amendments of 1966. Committed the federal government to financially support a national plan for comprehensive health services on the state level through formula grants. Required each state to establish an agency to administer a health services planning program. Authorized exchange of health personnel between states and the Department of Health, Education, and Welfare to improve federal-state cooperation, and made grants to public health schools. Approved November 3, 1966 (P.L. 89–749; 80 Stat. 1180–1190).

Demonstration Cities and Metropolitan Development Act of 1966. Established a program to "rebuild slum and blighted areas" by "providing the public facilities and services necessary to improve the general welfare of the people living in those areas." Provided that participating demonstration cities (later named "Model Cities") be selected under strict federal standards and receive federal funds equal to as much as 80 percent of the contribution they were required to make (under existing law) as their share of federally assisted programs. Authorized federal grants of $24 million for planning projects in fiscal 1967 and fiscal 1968 and an additional $400 million in fiscal 1968 and $500 million in fiscal 1969 for carrying out the plans. Approved November 3, 1966 (P.L. 89–754; 80 Stat. 1255–1296).

Fair Packaging and Labeling Act. Required fair, nondeceptive packaging and labeling to assist consumers in making value comparisons between manufacturers. Exempted alcoholic beverages, certain drugs, meats, poultry, tobacco, and other products covered by earlier laws. Delegated responsibility for establishing labeling standards to the secretary of health, education, and welfare and the Federal Trade Commission and packaging standards to the secretary of commerce. Approved November 3, 1966 (P.L. 89–755; 80 Stat. 1296–1302).

Narcotic Addict Rehabilitation Act of 1966. Authorized the commitment of persons charged with narcotic offenses to mental institutions for long-term treatment and intensive follow-up care if the addict or a "related individual" requests such treatment. Provided that such commitments would be applicable to those accused of a nonviolent federal crime, those convicted of a federal crime, and those charged with any criminal offense. Authorized $30 million for fiscal years 1967–1968 to assist states and cities in developing narcotic treatment programs. Approved November 8, 1966 (P.L. 89–793; 80 Stat. 1438–1450).

Economic Opportunity Amendments of 1966. Provided authorizations for the Office of Economic Opportunity (OEO) through fiscal year 1970. Established a ceiling of forty-five thousand persons in the Job Corps, 23 percent of whom had to be women. Redefined the Community Action Program, set the federal share of the program at 80 percent, increased the ceiling on loans to low-income rural families, and established a statutory basis for the Head Start (preschool day care) program. Approved November 8, 1966 (P.L. 89–794; 80 Stat. 1451–1477).

Notes

1. Carol A. Zimring, "'Neon, Junk, and Ruined Landscape.' Competing Visions of America's Roadsides and the Highway Beautification Act of 1965," in *The World Beyond the Windshield: Roads and Landscapes in the United States and Europe* ed. Christ of Mauch and Thomas Zeller (Athens, Ohio: Ohio University Press; Stuttgart: Franz Steiner Verlag, 2008), 104–105.

2. U.S. Senate. *The Constitution of the United States of America: Analysis and Interpretation,* 108th Cong., 2d sess., 2004, S. Doc. 108–17, 41, n. 17.

Ninetieth Congress
January 3, 1967, to January 3, 1969

First session—January 10, 1967, to December 15, 1967
Second session—January 15, 1968, to October 14, 1968
(Second administration of Lyndon B. Johnson, 1965–1969)

Historical Background

The Vietnam War became an increasingly divisive issue, as U.S. military forces were unable to bring the conflict to a conclusion. President Lyndon B. Johnson was the target of bitter criticism, much of it leveled by senators and representatives of his own party. Throughout 1967, antiwar demonstrators called for U.S. withdrawal from Vietnam. Faced with an onslaught of mail from constituents angered by the burning of an American flag during a 1967 demonstration in New York's Central Park against the Vietnam War, Congress made it a crime to desecrate the flag. Two decades later, the act was declared unconstitutional by the Supreme Court in *Texas v. Johnson* (1989). In response, a modified version of the act was quickly passed, which was rejected by the Court in *United States v. Eichman* (1990).

A turning point in the war came in January 1968, when Vietcong and regular North Vietnamese army forces launched a dramatic, and initially successful, series of attacks. Although the assaults were eventually repelled, the effect on opinion elites in the United States was decisive. Many newspapers and influential television personalities concluded that the war was unwinnable and that they had been systematically deceived about its progress by their own government. A growing chorus from Congress, the media, youth, and academia called for the war's end.

President Johnson, who had conducted unsuccessful peace negotiations for some time, took dramatic steps to advance the process and simultaneously remove himself as a polarizing element in the national debate. On March 31, 1968, he announced a pause in the U.S. bombings of North Vietnam and his own withdrawal as a candidate for the Democratic presidential nomination. "With America's sons in fields [of battle] far away, with America's future under challenge right here at home, with our hopes and the world's hopes for peace in the balance every day," he declared, "I do not believe I should devote an hour or a day of my time to any personal partisan causes or to any duties other than the awesome duties of this office— the Presidency of your country."

President Johnson's 1967 State of the Union proposal to "develop educational television into a vital public resource to enrich our homes, educate our families, and to provide assistance in our classrooms"[1] was greeted with reservation on Capitol Hill. Congress did agree to establish a nonprofit Corporation for Public Broadcasting to assist educational television and radio financially, but permanent financing was not authorized ostensibly because of concerns over political pressures that might affect the corporation's activities.

Seeking to "promote employment of older persons based on their ability rather than age; to prohibit arbitrary age discrimination in employment;" and "to help employers find ways of meeting problems arising from the impact of age on employment," Congress in 1967 passed the Age Discrimination in Employment Act.

Senate approval in March 1967 of the USSR Consular Convention and Protocol, the first bilateral treaty between the United States and the Union of Soviet Socialist Republics, marked the first legislative endorsement of the Johnson administration's effort to "build bridges across the gulf" that divided the United States and Eastern Europe, "bridges of increased trade, of ideas, of visitors, and of humanitarian aid."[2] A second major agreement among the United States, Great Britain, the Soviet Union, and fifty-seven other nations was made a month later, when the Senate gave unanimous consent to a multilateral treaty governing the peaceful exploration of outer space.

Following a lengthy debate, Congress in 1968 approved the administration's request for the first tax increase in nearly two decades. The high cost of the Vietnam War, dwindling gold reserves, and a persistent balance-of-payment deficit were prominent factors that members took into consideration. Congress conditioned its approval on substantial reductions in fiscal year 1969 appropriations and the elimination of 250,000 federal civilian positions.

Congress gave the go-ahead to a two-year study of establishing national automobile emission standards and formally acknowledged that air pollution was a national problem warranting a larger federal role when states were not taking meaningful action.

Stronger federal meat inspection standards were set in place after the president appealed for legislation assuring the "wholesomeness of all meat products offered for sale." Consumer outrage over conditions revealed in the press and at congressional hearings led to even tougher standards than those sought by the administration. Stronger poultry inspection standards were also instituted. This enactment, which was similar to the Wholesome Meat Act, extended federal interstate poultry inspection standards to poultry sold within a state.

Congress also created a Quadrennial Commission to make recommendations to the president on pay rates for executive branch officials, federal judges, and members of Congress. A perceived need to close the pay "comparability gap" between government workers and those in the private sector deemed the measure essential.

In January 1968, the Elementary and Secondary Education Act specifically identified the education of "children of limited English-speaking ability" as "one of the most acute educational problems in the United States."[3] This was the first federal recognition of the needs of students with limited English-speaking ability and endorsement of federal funding for bilingual education.

After President Johnson outlined a comprehensive twenty-two-point anticrime program in February 1968, Congress spent the next four months shaping the most extensive crime bill ever enacted. Although the legislation contained several provisions that Johnson strongly opposed, it authorized more than $100 million in fiscal years 1968–1969 and an additional $300 million in fiscal 1970 for upgrading state and local police forces that the president had requested. The Omnibus Crime Control and Safe Streets Act, together with the Gun Control Act, put in place the most important gun control legislation in three decades. The crime act set restrictions on the interstate shipment of handguns. The gun act extended those restrictions to rifles and shotguns. Public support for more stringent control of guns dramatically increased following the assassinations of the Rev. Dr. Martin Luther King Jr. in April 1968 and Sen. Robert F. Kennedy of New York in June 1968. Kennedy, a younger brother of the late president John F. Kennedy, was seeking the Democratic presidential nomination.

The first open housing law that prohibited discrimination in the sale or rental of most housing was enacted in 1968. The Civil Rights Act of 1968 protected individuals exercising specific rights such as attending school, serving on a jury, working, and voting; provided criminal penalties for inciting or participating in a riot; and guaranteed the civil rights of American Indians. Low-interest subsidies were approved to assist more than 1.7 million low-income families seeking to purchase and rent decent housing. Other provisions of the Housing and Urban Development Act of 1968 provided funds for new urban development programs, urban planning grants, and development of entire new communities; authorized federal underwriting of insurance companies against property losses resulting from riots; and established a national flood insurance program.

After more than a decade of discussion at the committee level, Congress passed legislation enabling consumers to obtain accurate and complete credit information about themselves from creditors.

Amidst growing public opposition to the draft, Congress rejected the president's proposal to institute a selective service lottery. The House Armed Services Committee determined that the president's plan offered no discernable advantage to the random selection process already in place. The administration's most serious setback occurred when Congress reduced the president's fiscal 1968 foreign aid authorization request by nearly $787 million. The final authorization of $2,647,614,000 represented the smallest amount appropriated for the foreign aid program in its two decades of existence. Opposition stemmed both from discontent with Johnson's foreign policy initiatives and from concern over a growing budget deficit.

Noise became a major political and environmental issue in the 1960s with the widespread introduction of commercial jet aircraft. The Federal Aviation Administration estimates that areas affected by aviation noise increased sevenfold between 1960 and 1970. The initial step taken to confront what was coming to be recognized as not only an environmental issue, but also a health issue was the Aircraft Noise Abatement Act of 1968.

Conservationists were successful in gaining support for a bill creating a nationwide system of trails and a measure providing for the preservation of outstanding sections of America's wild and scenic rivers. A trails system was envisioned as providing the nation's expanding population greater opportunities to travel within, enjoy, and appreciate the "open-air, outdoor areas of the Nation." Only by establishing adequate controls over the country's most spectacular rivers, it was reasoned, could they be preserved for the "benefit and enjoyment of present and future generations." Authorization of the Central Arizona water diversion project and five reclamation projects in the Colorado River Basin was the culmination of more than two decades of bitter controversy, as well as intense lobbying by the Sierra Club and other conservation organizations. The projected cost of these projects was more than $1.3 billion, making them the largest reclamation program ever authorized in a single piece of legislation.

Sen. Eugene J. McCarthy of Minnesota, on an antiwar platform, made a strong showing in the New Hampshire Democratic presidential primary on March 12, 1968. He drew 42.2 percent of the vote to 49.5 for Johnson (who was a write-in candidate). Robert Kennedy, also a critic of the war, entered the race on March 16, 1968, and appeared to be on the road to clinching the nomination when he was shot and killed. At their party convention, the Democrats chose Vice President Hubert H. Humphrey as their standard-bearer on the first ballot. He did not participate in the primaries but had won the endorsement of state party organizations.

Humphrey and his running mate, Sen. Edmund S. Muskie of Maine, faced Republican challenger and former vice president Richard M. Nixon and his running mate, Maryland governor Spiro T. Agnew. A significant third-party candidate emerged in the form of former Alabama governor George C. Wallace of the American Independent Party. In one of the closest races in U.S. history, Nixon and Agnew received 43.4 percent of the vote; Humphrey and Muskie, 42.7 percent; and Wallace and Curtis E. LeMay, 13.5 percent. The Republican ticket's Electoral College victory was much more substantial—Nixon, 301; Humphrey, 191; and Wallace, 46. While their strength on Capitol Hill continued to erode, the Democrats remained in control of both chambers.

Major Acts and Treaties

U.S.-USSR Consular Convention and Protocol. Detailed the legal framework and procedure for operation of consulates in the United States and the Union of Soviet Socialist Republics (USSR), if and when any consulates were established. Extended immunity from criminal prosecution and civil lawsuits to consular officials and employees. Guaranteed quick access to consular officers by any of their citizens arrested within the borders of the other country. Concluded June 1, 1964. Ratification advised by the Senate March 16, 1967.[4]

Outer Space Treaty. Established general principles for the peaceful international exploration and use of outer space (including the Moon and other celestial bodies), and contained provisions for arms control in outer space, suspension of claims of national ownership or sovereignty, and the protection of astronauts. Obligated the signatories (the United States, Great Britain, the Soviet Union, and fifty-seven other nations) not to station in space or place into orbit any object carrying nuclear or other weapons of mass destruction (such as chemical or biological devices). Also prohibited weapons testing and military bases, fortifications, and maneuvers on celestial bodies. Concluded January 27, 1967. Ratification advised by the Senate April 25, 1967.[5]

Public Broadcasting Act of 1967. Authorized establishment of a nonprofit Corporation for Public Broadcasting to provide financial assistance for noncommercial educational television and radio stations. Prohibited the corporation from either owning or operating television and radio stations or related facilities. Extended federal grants for construction of educational television facilities for three years, and broadened their coverage to include educational radio facilities. Approved November 7, 1967 (P.L. 90–129; 81 Stat. 365–373).

Foreign Assistance Act of 1967. Reduced the fiscal year 1968 foreign aid authorization to the lowest level in its twenty-year history: $2,164,614,000 for economic aid and $787,691,000 for military assistance. Recommended that the president suspend foreign assistance to countries that had broken off diplomatic relations with the United States. Approved November 14, 1967 (P.L. 90–137; 81 Stat. 445–463).

Air Quality Control Act of 1967. Extended federal responsibility for combating air pollution if states did not take action to correct the problem. Expanded federal grants to states and local governments for developing and implementing air quality standards. Established a fifteen-member President's Air Quality Advisory Board headed by the secretary of health, education, and welfare. Authorized a two-year study of the impact of national emission standards and an expanded research and development program for controlling pollution. Approved November 21, 1967 (P.L. 90–148; 81 Stat. 485–507).

Wholesome Meat Act. Declared it "essential in the public interest that the health and welfare of the consumers be protected by assuring that meat and meat food products distributed to them are wholesome, not adulterated, and properly marked, labeled, and packaged." Required that animals be inspected before being slaughtered and that meat processors keep records of their transactions. Approved December 15, 1967 (P.L. 90–201; 81 Stat. 584–601).

Age Discrimination in Employment Act of 1967. Prohibited employers, employment agencies, and labor unions from discriminating against individuals between ages 40 and 65 with respect to any term, condition, or privilege of employment including hiring, firing, promotion, job assignment, layoffs, training, and fringe benefits. Declared it unlawful to harass a person because of his or her age, or to retaliate against an individual for opposing employment practices that discriminate based on age or for filing an age discrimination charge, testifying, or participating in any way in an investigation, proceeding, or litigation under the act. Applicable to employers with 20 or more employees, including state and local governments as well as the federal government. Approved December 15, 1967 (P.L. 90–202; 81 Stat. 602–608).

Quadrennial Pay Commission. Established a Quadrennial Commission to recommend pay rates to the president for executive branch officials, federal judges, and members of Congress. Provided that the president would subsequently make his own pay recommendations, which would take effect within thirty days unless Congress approved a different plan or vetoed the president's. Approved December 16, 1967 (P.L. 90–206, Title II, Sec. 225; 81 Stat. 642–645).

Bilingual Education Act. Provided federal grants to school districts for the development of bilingual educational programs; training designed to prepare individuals to participate in bilingual programs as teachers, teacher aides, and other ancillary education personnel; and acquisition of the teaching materials and equipment designed to meet the special needs of children with limited English-speaking ability. Approved January 2, 1968 (P.L. 90–247, Title VII; 81 Stat. 816–820).

Civil Rights Act of 1968. Prohibited discrimination in the sale or rental of about 80 percent of all housing. Provided criminal penalties for injuring or interfering with individuals exercising several specific rights and inciting or participating in riots. Prohibited Indian tribal governments as well as state governments from violating specific constitutional rights of American Indians. Approved April 11, 1968 (P.L. 90–284; 82 Stat. 73–92).

Consumer Credit Protection Act (Truth in Lending Act). Required that creditors disclose accurate and complete information to borrowers regarding the calculation of financial charges and total cost of credit being extended. Limited garnishments to 25 percent of a worker's take-home pay. Established a nine-member National Commission on Consumer Finance to study and make recommendations on the need for further regulation of the consumer finance industry. Approved May 29, 1968 (P.L. 90–321; 82 Stat. 146–167).

Omnibus Crime Control and Safe Streets Act of 1968. Authorized more than $100 million in fiscal years 1968–1969 and an additional $300 million in fiscal 1970 for state and local governments to upgrade their law enforcement. Granted police broad authority to conduct wiretaps, and sought to overturn three U.S. Supreme Court decisions that dealt with the rights of suspects during police interrogations. Established a Law Enforcement Assistance Administration within the Justice Department to administer law enforcement block grants contained in the act. Placed restrictions on interstate and foreign shipments of handguns and ammunition to individuals; banned interstate and foreign shipment of bombs, hand grenades, machine guns, and sawed-off shotguns; and prohibited the sale of handguns to persons under twenty-one. Approved June 19, 1968 (P.L. 90–351; 82 Stat. 197–239).

Revenue and Expenditures Control Act of 1968. Imposed a temporary 10 percent surcharge on personal and corporate income taxes to expire on July 1, 1969. Extended existing excise taxes on telephone service (10 percent) and automobiles (7 percent) through December 31, 1969. Required a $10 billion reduction in projected fiscal 1969 federal appropriations, a $6 billion reduction in fiscal 1969 spending, an $8 billion rescission in unspent appropriations from previous years, and a reduction in the federal civilian employee work force by 245,000. Approved June 28, 1968 (P.L. 90–364; 82 Stat. 251–274).

Flag Protection Act of 1968. Made it a federal crime, punishable by a $1,000 fine and/or a year in jail, to "knowingly" cast "contempt upon any flag of the United States by publicly mutilating, defacing, defiling, burning or trampling upon it." Define the term "flag of the United States" to include pictures or representations "which the average person . . . may believe . . . to represent the flag." Approved July 5, 1968 (P.L. 90–381; 82 Stat. 291). The act was declared unconstitutional in *Texas v. Johnson*, 491 U.S. 397 (1989). In response to *Johnson*, Congress passed the Flag Protection Act of 1989. Approved October 28, 1968 (P.L. 101–131; 103 Stat. 777). That act was declared unconstitutional in *United States v. Eichman*, 496 U.S. 310 (1990).

Aircraft Noise Abatement Act. Directed the Federal Aviation Administration to prescribe standards, through consultation with the secretary of transportation, for the measurement of aircraft noise and sonic boom, and to establish regulations to control and abate such noise. Limited this grant of authority to standards and regulations that were "consistent with the highest degree of safety," and "economically reasonable, technologically practicable, and appropriate for the particular type of aircraft, aircraft engine, appliance, or certificate to which it will apply." Approved July 21, 1968 (P.L. 90–411; 82 Stat. 395).

Housing and Urban Development Act of 1968. Stated that a national housing goal of "a decent home . . . for every American family" should be "substantially achieved" within ten years. Authorized a $5.3 billion, three-year housing program designed to provide more than 1.7 million units of new and rehabilitated housing for low-income families. Authorized federal underwriting of the insurance industry against riot losses, flood insurance for homeowners, and new urban renewal programs. Approved August 1, 1968 (P.L. 90–448; 82 Stat. 476–611).

Wholesome Poultry Products Act. Authorized the secretary of agriculture to work with state agencies to establish poultry inspection programs that were to be at least equal to federal standards. Established a criminal penalty provision for persons convicted of violating the act. Approved August 18, 1968 (P.L. 90–492; 82 Stat. 791–808).

Colorado River Basin Project Act. Authorized the construction, operation, and maintenance of public works projects on the Colorado River, including the Central Arizona Project to divert water to the Phoenix and Tucson areas, and five reclamation projects on the western slope of Colorado. Provided Arizona, California, and Nevada important water usage guarantees. Barred construction of dams on the portion of the Colorado River running through the Grand Canyon. Established a Lower Colorado River Basin Development Fund to fund and maintain the projects approved in the act. Prohibited the secretary of the interior for ten years from undertaking any reconnaissance studies of plans to import water into the Colorado River Basin from drainage basins lying outside the Colorado River Basin. Approved September 30, 1968 (P.L. 90–537; 82 Stat. 885–901).

National Wild and Scenic Rivers Act. Established a National Wild and Scenic Rivers System to preserve outstanding stretches of selected rivers throughout the country from incompatible development. Approved October 2, 1968 (P.L. 90–542; 82 Stat. 906–918).

National Trails System Act. Created a National Trails System composed of national scenic trails, national recreational trails, and connecting side trails. Designated two trails initially for inclusion in the system—the Appalachian Trail and the Pacific Crest Trail—and fourteen additional trails to be studied for possible inclusion. Approved October 2, 1968 (P.L. 90–543; 82 Stat. 919–926).

Gun Control Act of 1968. Banned most interstate shipments of rifles and shotguns to individuals, and generally prohibited individuals from buying guns except in their own states. Prohibited rifles, shotguns, or ammunition sales to persons under eighteen and handguns sales to persons under twenty-one. Provided new procedures and limitations for persons engaged in the firearms and ammunition business. Prohibited importation of foreign-made military surplus firearms and sale of firearms to convicted felons and fugitives from justice. Approved October 22, 1968 (P.L. 90–618; 82 Stat. 1213–1236).

Notes

1. Annual Message to Congress, January 10, 1967, *Public Papers of the Presidents of the United States: Lyndon B. Johnson* (Washington, D.C.: U.S. Government Printing Office, 1968), I, 6.

2. Remarks by Lyndon B. Johnson at Dedication of George C. Marshall Research Library, May 23, 1964. *Public Papers of the Presidents of the United States: Lyndon B. Johnson* (Washington, D.C.: U.S. Government Printing Office, 1965), I, 709.

3. U.S. Congress, Senate, *Elementary and Secondary Education Act Amendments of 1967,* 90th Cong., 1st sess., H. Rept. 726 (Washington, D.C.: U.S. Government Printing Office, 1967), 90.

4. *Journal of the Executive Proceedings of the Senate* (Washington, D.C.: U.S. Government Printing Office, 1967), 109:250–251; 19 UST 5018–5058.

5. *Journal of the Executive Proceedings of the Senate,* 109:464–466; 18 UST 2410–2498.

Ninety-first Congress
January 3, 1969, to January 3, 1971

First session—January 3, 1969, to December 23, 1969
Second session—January 19, 1970, to January 2, 1971
(First administration of Richard M. Nixon, 1969–1973)

Historical Background

Despite Lyndon B. Johnson's exit from the White House, the nation remained deeply conflicted over the Vietnam War. In the autumn of 1969, after a quarter-million antiwar demonstrators had descended upon Washington, D.C., President Richard M. Nixon announced a gradual withdrawal of American troops in Vietnam. Nixon, who had promised voters a "secret plan" to end the war, continued the Johnson policies of gradual reduction in U.S. troop levels and pursued peace negotiations with the Vietcong and North Vietnam. The centerpiece of his policy was "Vietnamization," a program to strengthen the armed forces of South Vietnam so that they would assume responsibility for military operations. At the same time, however, the president authorized military "incursions" against Vietcong "sanctuaries" in Cambodia and Laos. These operations led to further massive protests throughout the nation. On March 4, 1970, Ohio National Guardsmen killed four students protesting the war on the Kent State University campus.

During debates over U.S. military activities in Cambodia and expansion of the Vietnam War, the Senate twice voted to repeal the Gulf of Tonkin Resolution. The House eventually concurred. Efforts to ban funds for support of U.S. troops and advisers in Cambodia were, however, unsuccessful.

On a more positive note in the area of defense policy, the Senate in March 1969 had ratified the Nuclear Nonproliferation Treaty, which former president Johnson hailed at its signing as the "most important international agreement limiting nuclear arms since the nuclear age began." He called it a "triumph of sanity and of man's will to survive."

Comprehensive tax reform legislation removed an estimated 5.5 million lower-income taxpayers from the tax rolls. The bill coupled $9.1 billion in tax cuts with a 15 percent increase in basic Social Security benefits, to be initially financed by the Social Security Trust Fund. Tax liabilities were reduced for lower- and middle-income taxpayers primarily by higher exemptions and standard deductions, and they were increased for upper-income taxpayers through higher capital gains taxes and a minimum tax was imposed on some kinds of previously tax-free income.

Congress completed work on the National Environmental Policy Act, establishing a federal commitment to protect the environment, and a three-member Council on Environmental Quality was created to advise the president on environmental matters. The Water Quality Act, designed to clean up the waterways, made petroleum companies financially liable for oil spills in navigable waters of the United States and adjoining shorelines. More stringent controls were placed on sewage discharge in harbors and thermal pollution flowing into streams and rivers from nuclear power plants. Despite strenuous lobbying efforts by the automobile industry, the Clean Air Amendments represented the most stringent controls placed on automobile emissions. The Environmental Policy Act was amended to ensure that each federal department and agency conducting or supporting public works activities which affect the environment implement the policies established under existing law. To achieve this end the Environmental Quality

Improvement Act of 1970 vested additional responsibilities in the Council on Environmental Quality.

The Toy Safety Act, fashioned in large part in response to a National Commission on Product Safety report, sought more stringent controls on children's toys. In response to the death of 333 coal miners in 1967–1968, including a horrific 1968 Farmington, West Virginia, mine disaster that killed seventy-eight men, and a widespread miners' strike for compensation for blank lung, Congress passed the 1969 Federal Coal Mine Health and Safety Act. The Coal Act dramatically increased federal enforcement powers in coal mines, and was far more comprehensive than any previous federal legislation governing the mining industry. The lack of child-resistant containers that could protect children from swallowing toxic household substances contributed to enactment of the Poisoning Prevention Packaging Act. Congress cleared the first national occupational safety bill, following three years of tough negotiations between business and labor over what standards should be adopted and how they should be enforced.

The Economic Stabilization Act of 1970 provided a statutory basis for President Richard M. Nixon imposing a ninety-day freeze on prices, rents, wages, and salaries in August 1971. A second 60-day freeze followed in 1973 before controls were gradually phased out. Although the President's authority under this specific act subsequently lapsed on April 30, 1974, a precedent was set for future chief executives to exert power in budgetary matters. The act was held applicable to states and state officials in *Fry v. United States,* 421 U.S. 542 (1975).

The Ninety-first Congress also acted to extend the Voting Rights Act of 1965, reorganize the Post Office Department as the U.S. Postal Service, combat organized crime, and unify and revise federal drug laws. Growing support for lowering the voting age to eighteen was championed in Congress, which sought to make the change by statute. The U.S. Supreme Court, however, in 1970 *(Oregon v. Mitchell)* ruled that the law was applicable only to federal elections. Congress would respond by proposing a constitutional amendment. *(Twenty-sixth Amendment, p. 343)*

The Comprehensive Drug Abuse Prevention and Control Act significantly expanded rehabilitation, treatment, and drug abuse education programs. The District of Columbia Court Reorganization and Criminal Procedure Act modernized the D.C. court system, stiffened law enforcement measures, and eliminated jury trials for juveniles.

Other significant domestic initiatives were a three-year extension of the food stamp program and a $2.8 billion federal housing act. In reaction to a 1969 U.S. Supreme Court ruling, *Citizens Publishing Company v. United States,* Congress provided antitrust exemption to competing newspapers in the same city, enabling them to pool printing and business operations if one of them was "in probable danger of financial failure." The Family Planning Services and Population Research Act of 1970 was the first piece of federal legislation to exclusively provide funds as well as encouragement for family planning services and population research throughout the nation, and the only federal grant program dedicated solely to providing such family planning services. The act responded to President Richard M. Nixon's appeal to establish as a national goal "the provision of adequate family planning services to all who want them but cannot afford them."

Three critical transportation concerns—inadequate airports, deficient urban mass transit systems, and deteriorating passenger train service—were addressed through creation of an airport-airway development trust fund and a semiprivate corporation (AMTRAK) to operate a nationwide rail passenger service.

Responding to widespread complaints regarding problems associated with the explosion of credit cards in the late 1960s, Congress banned unsolicited mailings of credit cards and placed a $50 liability limit on the unauthorized use of cards. A nonprofit Securities Investor Protection Corporation was created to insure customers against losses that occurred when brokers became insolvent, and the Federal Reserve Board was given regulatory responsibility over one-bank holding companies. These holding companies had become an increasingly popular means for major banks to evade federal controls prohibiting them from expanding into nonbanking fields.

The Bank Secrecy Act of 1970 sought to curb the use of secret foreign bank accounts and financial transactions to avoid taxes and conduct illegal transactions. It authorized the secretary of the Treasury to prescribe regulations requiring banks and other financial institutions to maintain records of information thought to be useful in criminal, tax, and regulatory investigations and stipulated that individuals keep records of transactions through foreign financial institutions. Federal oversight of financial arrangements was extended to individual transactions when in the national interest.

The 1970 Legislative Reorganization Act called for the first major congressional reorganization in nearly a quarter of a century. The bill was designed to expedite House proceedings, remove much of the secrecy that had surrounded certain congressional proceedings, reduce the arbitrary power of committee chairpersons, provide Congress the tools it needed to more adequately evaluate federal budgetary and fiscal data, and expand the research and information sources available to members of Congress.

Although proponents of self-government for the District of Columbia continued to be thwarted in their efforts at gaining home rule, legislation providing for the election of the District's first nonvoting delegate to the House of Representatives in nearly a century was approved.

The 1970 congressional elections were strongly influenced by the continuing debate over the Vietnam War. President Nixon and Vice President Spiro T. Agnew campaigned vigorously for Republican candidates across the country, seeking support for their Indochina policies. The results were mixed, with Republican gains in the Senate and Democratic gains in the House. The Democrats, however, remained in the majority in both houses.

Major Acts and Treaties

Nuclear Nonproliferation Treaty. Banned the spread of nuclear weapons, established safeguard procedures, and encouraged peaceful uses of nuclear energy. Initial signatories included the United States, the Soviet Union, and sixty other nations. Concluded July 1, 1968. Ratification advised by the Senate March 13, 1969.[1]

Child Protection and Toy Safety Act of 1969. Provided for immediate exclusion from the marketplace of any toy or children's article deemed to be hazardous. Allowed the secretary of health, education, and welfare

to overrule such action if the item in question served a functional purpose and was properly labeled. Provided that any person adversely affected by such a determination could, within sixty days, seek review in a U.S. court of appeals. Required that manufacturers, distributors, or dealers repurchase banned items. Approved November 6, 1969 (P.L. 91–113; 83 Stat. 187–190).

Tax Reform Act of 1969. Increased personal income tax exemptions, lowered tax rates for single persons, provided a minimum standard deduction for low-income families, increased the standard deduction for taxpayers who did not itemize, repealed the 7 percent investment tax credit for machinery and equipment purchased, reduced the depreciation allowance on gas and oil, provided for the first time a minimum tax on "tax preference" (tax-free) income in excess of $30,000, raised the capital gains tax, tightened tax loopholes, and increased Social Security benefits by 15 percent. Approved December 30, 1969 (P.L. 91–172; 83 Stat. 487–742).

Federal Coal Mine Health and Safety Act of 1969 (Coal Act). Declared that the first priority and concern of all in the coal mining industry must be the health and safety of its most precious resource—the miner. Directed the secretaries of the Department of Health, Education and Welfare and the Department of the Interior to "improve and expand, in cooperation with the States and the coal mining industry, research and development and training programs aimed at preventing coal mine accidents and occupationally caused diseases in the industry." Mandated two annual inspections of surface coal mines and four at underground coal mines. Provided compensation for miners who were totally and permanently disabled by "black lung" disease. Approved December 30, 1969 (P.L. 91–173; 83 Stat. 742–804).

National Environmental Policy Act of 1969. Declared that it was the "policy of the Federal Government, in cooperation with State and local governments, and other concerned public and private organizations to use all practicable means and measures, including financial and technical assistance, in a manner calculated to foster and promote the general welfare, to create and maintain conditions under which man and nature can exist in productive harmony, and fulfill the social, economic, and other requirements of present and future generations of Americans." Established a three-member Council on Environmental Quality to advise the president on environmental matters. Directed all federal agencies to include environmental factors in their decision making. Approved January 1, 1970 (P.L. 91–190; 83 Stat. 852–856).

Water Quality Improvement Act of 1970. Authorized the federal government to clean up disastrous oil spills in navigable waters of the United States and adjoining shorelines, and made petroleum companies liable for up to $14 million of cleanup costs. Placed stringent restrictions on the flushing of raw sewage from boats and thermal pollution from nuclear power plants. Mandated that the secretary of the interior develop criteria covering the effect of pesticides in the water. Created an Office of Environmental Quality to act as a staff for the President's Council on Environmental Quality established by Congress in 1969. Approved April 3, 1970 (P.L. 91–224; 84 Stat. 91–115).

Environmental Quality Improvement Act of 1970. Strengthened the Council on Environmental Quality by establishing an Office of Environmental Quality in the Executive Office of the President to supplement council staff, to assist federal agencies in coordinating environmental quality programs, and to develop interrelated federal environmental quality criteria. Assigned to the council the additional responsibilities of: (1) reviewing the adequacy of existing environmental monitoring systems, (2) encouraging technological advancements, and (3) assisting federal agencies in developing environmental standards. Approved April 3, 1970 (P.L. 91–224, Title II; 84 Stat. 114–115).

Airport and Airway Development Act of 1970. Authorized $75 million in planning grants and $1.25 billion in construction grants over five years for construction and modernization of airports. Established user charge taxes on aviation fuel, airline passenger tickets, and air freight, to be placed in an Airport and Airway Trust Fund. Provided that tax revenues on aircraft tires and tubes be transferred from the Highway Trust Fund to the Airport and Airway Trust Fund. Approved May 21, 1970 (P.L. 91–258; 84 Stat. 219–253).

Voting Rights Act Amendments of 1970. Extended the Voting Rights Act of 1965 for five years (until August 1975), and lowered the voting age from twenty-one to eighteen for all federal, state, and local elections. Approved June 22, 1970 (P.L. 91–285; 84 Stat. 314–319). Subsequently, the U.S. Supreme Court on December 21, 1970, by a 5–4 decision, held that Congress had the power to lower the voting age to eighteen for federal but not state and local elections (*Oregon v. Mitchell,* 400 U.S. 112 [1970]). (*Voting Rights Act of 1965, p. 323*)

Newspaper Preservation Act. Declared it to be federal policy to preserve "a newspaper press editorially and reportorially independent and competitive" where a joint operation agreement had been or was entered into because of the economic distress of a newspaper. "Exempted from antitrust laws certain combinations and arrangements necessary for the survival of failing newspapers." Allowed competing newspapers in the same city to combine printing and business operations, but not editorial or reportorial staff, if one faced possible failure. Approved July 24, 1970 (P.L. 91–353; 84 Stat. 466–467).

District of Columbia Court Reform and Criminal Procedure Act of 1970. Provided for the modernization of the District of Columbia court system. Created a joint commission to supervise removal of judges for disability or misconduct. Lowered from sixteen to fifteen the age at which a juvenile could be prosecuted as an adult, and eliminated jury trials for juveniles. Provided that juveniles sixteen or older would be tried as adults if charged with murder, forcible rape, first-degree burglary, armed robbery, or assault. Provided for stiffer law enforcement measures. Approved July 29, 1970 (P.L. 91–358; 84 Stat. 473–668).

Postal Reorganization Act. Created an independent U.S. Postal Service to operate the nation's postal system. Granted an 8 percent pay increase, and retained civil service status for postal employees. Eliminated political influence over postal appointments and rates. Approved August 12, 1970 (P.L. 91–375; 84 Stat. 719–787).

Economic Stabilization Act of 1970. Empowered the president "to issue such orders and regulations as he may deem necessary to stabilize prices, rent, wages, and salaries at levels not less than those prevailing on May 25, 1970." Established standards to serve as a guide for determining levels of wages, prices, etc., which would allow for adjustments, exceptions, and variations to prevent inequities, taking into account changes in productivity. Approved August 15, 1970 (P.L. 91–379; 84 Stat. 799–780, Title II). The act was extended and amended on December 22, 1971 (P.L. 92–210; 85 Stat. 743–755); and on April 30, 1973 (P.L 93–28; 87 Stat. 27–29).

Nonvoting D.C. Delegate to the House of Representatives. Established a Commission on the Organization of the Government of the District of Columbia to "study and investigate organization and methods of operation of all departments, bureaus, agencies, boards, commissions, offices, independent establishments and instrumentalities of the government" of the District of Columbia. Provided for a nonvoting delegate to the House of Representatives to represent the District. Approved September 22, 1970 (P.L. 91–405; 84 Stat. 845–855).

Organized Crime Control Act of 1970. Authorized new legal guidelines relating to grand juries, witness immunity, perjury convictions, detention of recalcitrant witnesses, protection of witnesses, use of dispositions, and action used to obtain evidence. Declared that it was a federal crime to facilitate an "illegal gambling business" and to use income from organized crime to own or operate a business engaged in interstate commerce. Approved October 15, 1970 (P.L. 91–452; 84 Stat. 922–962).

Urban Mass Transportation Assistance Act of 1970. Expressed the findings of Congress that at least $10 billion in federal funds would be needed over the twelve-year period beginning in fiscal 1971 for urban mass transportation programs. Authorized $3.1 billion in grants and loans to state and local governments over six years for construction and improvement of mass transportation systems. Approved October 15, 1970 (P.L. 91–453; 84 Stat. 962–969).

Currency and Foreign Transactions Reporting Act (Bank Secrecy Act). Authorized the secretary of the Treasury to issue regulations requiring banks and other financial institutions to maintain records of account holders and persons with access to accounts, checks drawn and paid, checks received for deposit and collection, and foreign currency transactions. Required U.S. financial institutions and U.S. citizens, residents, and businesses engaged in foreign financial transactions or relationships to keep records of the identities and addresses of all parties involved, their legal capacities, and nature of the transactions or relationship, including amounts of money, credit, and property involved. Approved October 26, 1970 (P.L. 91–508, Title II; 84 Stat. 1118–1125).

Fair Credit Reporting Act. Prohibited issuance of unsolicited credit cards, and established a maximum liability of $50 for unauthorized use of a card. Placed financial liability for unauthorized use of a card on the issuer and merchant involved. Approved October 26, 1970 (P.L. 91–508, Title VI; 84 Stat. 1128–1136).

Legislative Reorganization Act of 1970. Revised committee rules and procedures in both the House of Representatives and the Senate, and required that all committee roll-call votes be made public. Established a standardized data processing system for federal budgetary and fiscal data. Increased the size of the permanent congressional staff. Expanded the staff, and redefined the responsibilities of the Congressional Research Service (formerly the Legislative Reference Service). Created a Joint Committee on Congressional Operations to study and recommend possible improvements in the operations and organization of Congress. Established an Office of House Legislative Counsel. Approved October 26, 1970 (P.L. 91–510; 84 Stat. 1140–1204).

Comprehensive Drug Abuse Prevention and Control Act of 1970. Expanded rehabilitation, treatment, and drug abuse education programs; unified and revised federal narcotics laws; revised the penalty structure for violations of these laws; and provided for the hiring of at least three hundred new enforcement staff. Approved October 27, 1970 (P.L. 91–513; 84 Stat. 1236–1296).

Rail Passenger Service Act of 1970. Created a semipublic National Railroad Passenger Corporation

(AMTRAK) governed by a fifteen-member board of directors, eight of whom were to be appointed by the president with the advice and consent of the Senate, to operate a nationwide rail system, beginning March 1, 1971. Authorized $40 million in federal grants and $100 million in guaranteed loans to establish the corporation. Authorized $200 million in loans for railroads to transfer their passenger operations to the corporation. Authorized the Interstate Commerce Commission to establish rail passenger regulations. Approved October 30, 1970 (P.L. 91–518; 84 Stat. 1327–1342).

Family Planning Services and Population Research Act of 1970. Provided federal funding for family planning services and research, and established the office of population affairs in the Department of Health, Education, and Welfare (now Department of Health and Human Services). Stated that the purpose of the act was "to assist in making voluntary family planning services readily available to all persons desiring such services," but stipulated priority was to be given "to persons from low-income families." Prohibited use of funds under the act "in programs where abortion is a method of family planning." Approved December 24, 1970 (P.L. 91–572; 84 Stat. 1504–1508).

Occupational Safety and Health Act of 1970. Authorized the secretary of labor to establish and enforce national safety standards, and created an Occupational Safety and Health Review Commission to carry out adjudicatory functions under the act. Authorized federal inspections and investigations of working conditions, research on occupational and health problems, occupational safety and health training programs, and research on job safety. Approved December 29, 1970 (P.L. 91–596; 84 Stat. 1590–1620). Certain provisions of this act were subsequently held unconstitutional in *Marshall v. Barlow's Inc.,* 436 U.S. 307 (1978).

Securities Investor Protection Act of 1970. Established a private nonprofit Securities Investor Protection Corporation to oversee the activities of registered brokers, dealers, and members of national securities exchanges. Created an insurance fund to protect investors against losses up to $50,000 occurring when

brokers become insolvent. Provided that the fund was to be financed through a combination of existing stock exchange trust funds, assessments, and lines of bank credit. Approved December 30, 1970 (P.L. 91–598; 84 Stat. 1636–1657).

Poisoning Prevention Packaging Act of 1970. Provided for special packing regulations for household goods that were potentially dangerous to children. Allowed manufacturers to prepare a conventional container for the elderly and handicapped providing it bore a special label stating that it was for "households without young children." Approved December 30, 1970 (P.L. 91–601; 84 Stat. 1670–1674).

Clean Air Amendments of 1970. Established specific deadlines for a 90 percent reduction of certain hazardous emissions from new automobiles. Authorized $350 million for new air quality research programs in fiscal years 1971–1973. Required each state to establish an air quality program. Authorized the Environmental Protection Agency (EPA) administrator to conduct tests, publish comparable test results, set warranty standards, prohibit sales of dangerous fuels, grant states money for vehicle inspection programs, formulate standards for aircraft admissions, and establish national air quality standards. Established an Office of Noise Abatement and Control within the EPA. Approved December 31, 1970 (P.L. 91–604; 84 Stat. 1676–1713).

Bank Holding Company Act Amendments of 1970. Placed holding companies that controlled a single bank under the regulatory authority of the Federal Reserve Board, and required that they divest themselves of most nonbanking business. Extended the Bank Holding Company Act of 1956, which provided for regulation of holding companies controlling more than one bank, to one-bank companies. Approved December 31, 1970 (P.L. 91–607; 84 Stat. 1760–1769).

Food Stamp Act of 1970. Established a nationwide standard for the food stamp program. Extended the food stamp program through fiscal 1973, provided free stamps for families with monthly incomes under $30, and required that recipients register for and accept employment as a condition of receiving stamps.

Approved January 11, 1971 (P.L. 91–671; 84 Stat. 2048–2052). Certain provisions of this act were subsequently held unconstitutional in *Department of Agriculture v. Moreno,* 413 U.S. 528 (1973), and *Department of Agriculture v. Murry,* 413 U.S. 508 (1973).

Foreign Military Sales Act Amendments and Repeal of Gulf of Tonkin Resolution. Authorized $250 million in fiscal 1970 and fiscal 1971 to finance credit sales of U.S. military materials to foreign countries. Placed restrictions on total credit sales, value of excess defense articles made available to foreign countries, and transfer of military equipment under assistance programs. Repealed the Gulf of Tonkin Resolution of August 10, 1964. Approved January 12, 1971 (P.L. 91–672; 84 Stat. 2053–2055). *(Gulf of Tonkin Resolution, p. 318)*

Note

1. *Journal of the Executive Proceedings of the Senate* (Washington, D.C.: U.S. Government Printing Office, 1969), 111:234–235; 21 UST 483–566.

Ninety-second Congress
January 3, 1971, to January 3, 1973

First session—January 21, 1971, to December 17, 1971
Second session—January 18, 1972, to October 18, 1972
(First administration of Richard M. Nixon, 1969–1973)

Historical Background

The state ratification process for the Twenty-sixth Amendment to the U.S. Constitution was completed in record time (one hundred days) in 1971. The amendment provided for the voting age to be lowered to eighteen for federal, state, and local elections. A proposed constitutional amendment guaranteeing women equal rights with men was sent to the states for ratification in 1972. Although thirty-five states had ratified the equal rights amendment (ERA) by January 1977, the process stalled in the face of growing criticism and concern over the amendment's potential consequences. Congress in 1978 extended by thirty-nine months the seven-year time limit it had set for states to approve the proposed amendment. Despite an extensive lobbying effort by ERA supporters, no other states ratified the proposed amendment during the extension period and it died on June 30, 1982, three short of the number of states needed for ratification. With the expiration of the extension, the action of the five states that had voted to rescind their ratification became moot.

Congress after nearly six months of protracted debate approved legislation authorizing a federal guarantee of $250 million in bank loans for the beleaguered Lockheed Aircraft Corporation at the administration's request. The main issue was whether the government should interfere with the free enterprise process by rescuing the nation's largest defense contractor from bankruptcy or let the serious unemployment problem grow worse.

Alaska Native land claims, which had remained unresolved for more than a century, were finally settled. Although the Alaska Purchase Treaty of 1867 had not confirmed these rights, they were acknowledged in the Alaskan Organic Act of 1884 as needing to be addressed in future legislation. *(Alaska Purchase Treaty, p. 118; Civil Government for Alaska, p. 172)*

The Revenue Act of 1971 cut federal tax liabilities by a projected $25.9 billion over three years in an attempt to stimulate the economy. The Joint Committee on Internal Revenue Taxation offered three reasons for the legislation—growth of the gross national product was too small, unemployment was too high, and capital goods expenditures were stagnant. Amidst a Nixon administration effort to stimulate the economy and bring the balance of payments under control, Congress extended the president's authority to impose controls on wages, salaries, prices, and rents for an additional four months. Executive authority to control interest rates and financial charges was expanded at the same time. The president had wielded these powers on August 15, 1971, when he ordered a comprehensive freeze on wages, prices, and rents and a 10 percent surtax on imports. He justified these interventionist actions on the grounds that inflation was out of control and threatened the nation's economic well-being. After ninety days, the freeze was replaced by wage and price controls that lasted through 1973.

On December 23, 1971, President Richard M. Nixon signed the National Cancer Act of 1971. The enactment of this legislation was hailed in the press as marking the beginning of a "war on cancer," evoking comparisons to the "war on polio" declared by Franklin D. Roosevelt which, after decades of research, culminated in the vaccine that practically obliterated that illness worldwide. Although a lot remains to be learned about the causes of cancer and its cures, there has been extraordinary progress in the understanding and treatment of cancer since 1971.

Revenue sharing, a program of federal payments to aid state and local governments, had been discussed for more than a decade, but it did not became a reality until the powerful House Ways and Means Committee chairman Wilbur D. Mills of Arkansas endorsed the idea. The revenue-sharing legislation provided $30.2 billion in federal assistance to state and local governments over a five-year period.

During the first week of 1972, President Richard M. Nixon announced his decision to "proceed at once with the development of an entirely new type of space transportation designed to transform the space frontier of the 1970s into familiar territory, easily accessible for human endeavor in the 1980s and 1990s." Supporters of the space shuttle program hailed the president's decision, while opponents portrayed it as wasteful. Both the House and Senate overwhelmingly agreed to go forward with the space shuttle project.

Spiraling increases in election campaign costs, particularly for radio and television time, prompted passage of the Federal Election Campaign Act. Pressure for placing a limit on the amount of money that candidates for president, vice president, and Congress could spend on political advertising had been building since at least the 1968 campaigns. Under the new act, candidates were required to fully disclose campaign contributions and expenditures.

An important milestone in women's history was reached with the signing of Title IX of the Higher Education Amendments of 1972. This one sentence, 37 word amendment, left an indelible mark on American education. It prohibited gender discrimination by federally funded institutions and became the primary tool for women's fuller participation in all aspects of education. Ironically, the act did not specifically mention women's participation in sports, although this is what it has become known for over the decades. The Special Supplemental Food Program for Women, Infants and Children Program (WIC) was also established in 1972 after the White House conference on food, nutrition, and health focused national attention on the problem of malnutrition and related health problems among low-income pregnant women and children. Since its establishment in 1972, WIC has become one of the central components of the nation's food and nutrition assistance system.

Congress provided for the election of nonvoting delegates to the House of Representatives from Guam and the U.S. Virgin Islands. Although the two jurisdictions previously had sent unofficial delegates to Congress, they essentially functioned as lobbyists, having no official status.

President Nixon's historic trips to Peking and Moscow in 1972 marked the first state visit by an American president to either communist country. His late February stay in mainland China ended more than two decades of official U.S. hostility toward the People's Republic of China. Following a week of private meetings, Nixon and Communist Party chief Mao Zedong issued a public communiqué agreeing on the need for increased contacts between the two nations. Two months later, in Moscow, the president signed seven agreements with the Soviet Union, including two arms accords limiting defensive antiballistic missile (ABM) sites and offensive missiles. The ABM treaty was ratified by the Senate on August 3, 1972. With this action the two superpowers were each limited to two antiballistic missile sites. The second accord, approved by Congress on September 30, 1972, authorized the president to accept a five-year interim agreement on offensive nuclear weapons between the United States and the Soviet Union.

The president's national security adviser, Henry A. Kissinger, continued to pursue negotiations to bring the Vietnam War to a conclusion. As American troop strength in Southeast Asia dwindled, it seemed that the president's "Vietnamization" strategy might be succeeding, especially when South Vietnamese forces repulsed a full-scale communist offensive in 1972. A peace agreement appeared near in late 1972 but faltered at the last moment. President Nixon responded by a massive bombing campaign of North Vietnam in the last days of the year, which prompted both sides to return to the bargaining table.

Congress responded to President Nixon's request for additional funds to deal with the growing problem of drug abuse in America by authorizing more than $1 billion over three years. The funds would be used to create a central office within the White House to coordinate and oversee the various federal antidrug programs, a National Institute on Drug Abuse, a National

Advisory Council on Drug Abuse, a National Drug Abuse Training Center, and formula grant programs to assist the states with drug abuse initiatives.

The Equal Employment Opportunity Commission (EEOC) was granted authority to take corrective action in employment discrimination cases. As a result, the EEOC could bring suit against employers and argue cases in federal court. The Supplemental Security Income Program for the Aged, Blind, and Disabled was historic in that it shifted responsibility from the states to the federal government for determining who among the aged, blind, and disabled would receive assistance and how much assistance they would receive. The program was "designed to provide a positive assurance that the nation's aged, blind, and disabled people would no longer have to subsist on below poverty level incomes."[1]

By overriding a presidential veto in mid-October 1972, Congress set in motion the most comprehensive and expensive environmental legislation yet enacted. President Nixon's characterization of the Federal Water Pollution Act as "laudable" but unacceptable because of its "budget-wrecking" price tag fell on deaf ears on Capitol Hill. The Water Pollution Act, which was strongly opposed by several major industries and a number of state and local officials, established the elimination of all pollution discharges in U.S. waters as a national goal to be achieved by 1985. To reach this goal, $24.7 billion in federal funds, including $18 billion in grants to the states for construction for waste treatment plants, was authorized.

Other major environmental measures resulted in the first major change in pesticide regulation in twenty-five years; imposed a permanent ban on the killing of most ocean mammals; and established a national program for the management, use, and protection of America's coastal zones and estuaries. These enactments were the culmination of a massive effort by environmental groups to sensitize the American people to growing evidence of serious damage being done to the nation's natural resources. In passing the Noise Control Act of 1972, Congress hoped, with the first legislation aimed solely at controlling noise pollution, to "promote an environment for all Americans free from noise that jeopardizes health or welfare." Although water and air pollution had been targets of corrective legislation for some time, not until this act was a significant step taken in the recognition and elimination of noise pollution.

The Federal Advisory Committee Act was a response to the proliferation of federal advisory committees, concerns about the duplication and ineffectiveness of such committees, and the lack of openness, accountability, reporting, and cost controls in the process. The act created an orderly procedure by which federal agencies could seek advice and assistance from citizens and experts.

Creation of the Consumer Product Safety Commission stemmed in large part from the work of the National Commission on Product Safety. The administration favored a consumer product safety agency established within the Department of Health, Education, and Welfare. Congress, however, accepted the commission's reasoning that only an independent agency with full authority to develop, establish, and ban products could fully protect consumers.

On June 17, 1972, political operatives of President Nixon's reelection committee broke in and were arrested at the offices of the Democratic National Committee at the Watergate complex in Washington, D.C. In their possession was sophisticated wiretapping equipment. Nixon dismissed the event as a "third-rate burglary" and disclaimed any knowledge of the incident. Revelations of what would become known as the Watergate scandal did not begin to have a public impact until 1973.

Nixon and Vice President Spiro T. Agnew swept to reelection victory over Democratic challenger George S. McGovern, U.S. senator from South Dakota, and his running mate, Sargent Shriver, by one of the greatest landslides in American history. The electoral vote tally was 520 for the Republican ticket and 17 for the Democratic. Nixon's coattails, however, were not long enough to prevent Democrats from retaining control of both houses of Congress.

Major Acts and Treaties

Twenty-sixth Amendment. Lowered the voting age to eighteen in all federal, state, and local elections. Approved March 23, 1971. Ratified by requisite number of states July 1, 1971 (85 Stat. 825–826).[2]

Emergency Loan Guarantee Act. Authorized a federal guarantee of up to $250 million in commercial bank loans for the Lockheed Aircraft Corporation, a major defense contractor, facing possible bankruptcy. Established an Emergency Loan Guarantee Board, consisting of the secretary of the Treasury, chairman of the Federal Reserve Board, and chairman of the Securities and Exchange Commission, to carry out the authority granted under the act. Approved August 9, 1971 (P.L. 92–70; 85 Stat. 178–182).

Revenue Act of 1971. Reduced individual and business taxes by a projected average of $8.6 billion over three years ($4.5 billion in 1971, $11.4 billion in 1972, and $10 billion in 1973). Accelerated scheduled increases in personal income tax exemptions and standard deductions; raised the minimum income levels at which taxpayers had to file tax returns; eliminated personal income tax for those with incomes below the poverty level; repealed a 7 percent excise tax on foreign and domestic automobiles; repealed a 10 percent excise tax on light trucks, light trailers, buses used for urban transportation, and domestic containers used to collect solid waste; reinstated a 7 percent tax credit for business investments that was eliminated by the Tax Reform Act of 1969; and created incentives for exports. Approved December 10, 1971 (P.L. 92–178; 85 Stat. 497–574). *(Tax Reform Act of 1969, p. 336)*

Alaska Native Claims Settlement Act. Provided that Alaska's Aleuts, Eskimos, and Indians would receive title to a total of forty million acres of Alaskan lands and, through native corporations established under the act, would retain mineral rights to these lands. Provided that the state's native population would share $462.5 million in federal grants and $500 million from state and federal mineral revenues. Approved December 18, 1971 (P.L. 92–203; 85 Stat. 688–716).

Economic Stabilization Act Amendments of 1971. Extended the president's authority to control wages, salaries, prices, and rents through April 30, 1973, and broadened his stabilization authority to include control of interest rates, finance charges, corporate dividends, and similar transfers. Approved December 22, 1971 (P.L. 92–210; 85 Stat. 743–755).

National Cancer Act of 1971. Mandated that a National Cancer Program be developed by the National Cancer Institute (NCI) director with the advice of the National Cancer Advisory Board (NCAB). Called for the annual budget of NCI to be submitted directly to the president. Authorized the director of NCI, in consultation with NCAB, to create new cancer centers and manpower training programs; appoint advisory committees; expand the physical location at NIH and other research facilities across the country; award contracts for research; collaborate with other federal, state, and local public agencies and private industry; conduct cancer control activities; establish an international cancer research data bank that collects, catalogues, stores, and disseminates results of cancer research; and award research grants. Approved December 23, 1971 (P.L. 92–218; 85 Stat. 778–786).

Federal Election Campaign Act of 1971. Placed a limit on the amount of money a candidate for president, vice president, or Congress could spend on political advertising. Required full disclosure of campaign contributions and expenditures. Restricted candidates to a maximum of ten cents per eligible voter or $50,000, whichever was greater, for all forms of media advertising. Approved February 7, 1972 (P.L. 92–225; 86 Stat. 3–20). Certain provisions of this act were subsequently held unconstitutional in *Buckley v. Valeo,* 424 U.S. 1 (1976).

Drug Abuse Office and Treatment Act of 1972. Established a Special Action Office for Drug Abuse Prevention in the Executive Office of the President headed by a "drug czar" to coordinate federal antidrug abuse activities. Required the president to develop a "comprehensive, coordinated, long-term federal strategy" to deal with drug abuse–related problems. Required the director of the Special Action Office to establish a National Drug Abuse Training Center to conduct programs to combat drug abuse. Established a National Institute on Drug Abuse in the National Institute of Mental Health to administer the drug abuse programs of the Department of Health, Education, and Welfare (HEW) and a National Advisory Council on Drug Abuse to advise the secretary of HEW on developing a national drug abuse strategy. Established formula grants to states for drug control programs. Approved March 21, 1972 (P.L. 92–255; 86 Stat. 65–85).

Proposed Equal Rights Amendment. Provided, if ratified by the requisite number of states, that "[e]quality of rights under the law shall not be denied or abridged by the United States on account of sex," and gave "Congress and the several States power within their respective Jurisdictions, to enforce the article by appropriate legislation." Stipulated that the proposed constitutional amendment be ratified by the legislatures of three-fourths of the states within seven years. Approved March 23, 1972 (86 Stat. 1523–1524). On October 20, 1978, President Jimmy Carter signed a joint resolution (even though his approval was not required) granting states an additional 39 months to ratify the proposed amendment (H. J. Res. 368; 92 Stat. 3799). On June 30, 1982, the amendment officially died three states short of the 38 needed for ratification.

Equal Employment Opportunity Act of 1972. Granted the Equal Employment Opportunity Commission authority to bring suit and argue cases in federal court against employers who it determined were engaging in discriminatory employment practices. Extended coverage of the act to businesses and labor unions with fifteen or more employees, state and local government agencies, appointed policy-making officials, and employees of educational institutions. Approved March 24, 1972 (P.L. 92–261; 86 Stat. 103–113).

Delegates to the House of Representatives from Guam and the U.S. Virgin Islands. Provided for the election of nonvoting delegates to the House of Representatives from Guam and the U.S. Virgin Islands. Approved April 10, 1972 (P.L. 92–271; 86 Stat. 118–119).

Space Shuttle Program. Authorized $3.4 billion for the National Aeronautics and Space Administration in fiscal 1973, $227.9 million of which was earmarked for the space shuttle program. Approved May 19, 1972 (P.L. 92–304; 86 Stat. 157–162).

Title IX Amendment of the Higher Education Act of 1972 (Patsy Mink Equal Opportunity in Education Act). Stated that: "No person in the United States shall, on the basis of sex, be excluded from participation in, be denied the benefits of, or be subjected to discrimination under any education program or activity receiving Federal financial assistance." Approved June 23, 1972 (P.L. 92–318; 86 Stat. 373–374, Title IX, Sec. 901). Renamed Patsy Mink Equal Opportunity in Education Act in 2002. Approved October 29, 2002 (P.L. 107–255; 116 Stat. 1734).

U.S.-USSR Antiballistic Missile Systems Treaty. Limited the United States and the Union of Soviet Socialist Republics (USSR) to two antiballistic missile (ABM) sites each—one protecting its national capital (Washington, D.C., and Moscow, respectively) and the other an offensive missile field. Concluded May 26, 1972. Ratification advised by the Senate August 3, 1972.[3]

Special Supplemental Food Program for Women, Infants and Children Program (WIC). Authorized a two-year federally funded pilot program under an amendment to the Child Nutrition Act of 1966 to assist states in safeguarding the health and nutritional well-being of low-income women, infants, and children during critical growth periods. Approved September 26, 1972 (P.L. 92–433; 86 Stat. 729–731, Sec. 17). Program was made permanent in 1975. Approved October 7, 1975 (P.L. 94–105; 89 Stat. 518–522, Sec. 17).

U.S.-USSR Strategic Arms Limitation Act. Authorized presidential acceptance of a U.S.-USSR five-year interim agreement limiting offensive nuclear weapons. Stipulated that the failure to negotiate an offensive arms treaty within five years would be grounds for repudiating the interim agreement with the Soviet Union. Approved September 30, 1972 (P.L. 92–448; 86 Stat. 746–747).

Federal Advisory Committee Act. Established a structured process for creating, operating, and terminating federal advisory committees that provide advice to the Executive Branch of government. Stipulated requirements for public notification about the creation and operation of federal advisory committees, public input, and data collection and reporting of federal advisory committee activities. Approved October 6, 1972 (P.L. 92–463; 86 Stat. 770–776).

Federal Water Pollution Control Act Amendments of 1972. Established a national goal of eliminating all pollutant discharges into U.S. waters by 1985 and an interim goal of making the waters safe for fish, shellfish, wildlife, and people by July 1, 1983. Placed strict limitations on what could be discharged into U.S. waterways. Authorized $24.7 billion in federal funds for comprehensive programs for water pollution control, interstate cooperation and uniform laws, grants for research and development of pollution control programs, and area-wide treatment management. Presidential veto overridden by Congress. Became law without the president's signature October 18, 1972 (P.L. 92–500; 86 Stat. 816–903). *(Water Quality Act of 1987, p. 392)*

Revenue Sharing. Established a five-year program of general revenue sharing—in the State and Local Fiscal Assistance Act of 1972—to distribute $30.2 billion in unrestricted federal funds to states and localities. Created a trust fund wherein the annual appropriations for federal-state revenue sharing would remain available without fiscal year limitations. Approved October 20, 1972 (P.L. 92–512; 86 Stat. 919–947).

Federal Environmental Pesticide Control Act of 1972. Broadened the government's authority to control pesticides and other pest killers. Required that all pesticides be registered with the Environmental Protection Agency, which would regulate their distribution and use. Approved October 21, 1972 (P.L. 92–516; 86 Stat. 973–999).

Marine Mammal Protection Act of 1972. Established a permanent moratorium on efforts to "harass, hunt, capture, or kill any marine mammal" or to import marine mammal products. Required that permits be granted for the killing and capturing of ocean mammals for scientific research or public display. Approved October 21, 1972 (P.L. 92–522; 86 Stat. 1027–1046).

Consumer Product Safety Act. Created an independent five-member Consumer Product Safety Commission to set standards for a wide variety of consumer products and to ban those products that presented an unreasonable risk of injury. Approved October 27, 1972 (P.L. 92–573; 80 Stat. 1207–1233).

Noise Control Act of 1972. Established a national policy to promote an environment for all Americans free of excessive noise that would be deleterious to public health and welfare. Charged the Environmental Protection Agency with the responsibility of coordinating federal efforts in noise control research, identifying noise sources, and the promulgation of noise criteria and control technology, establishing noise emission standards for commercial products, and developing low-noise emission products. Approved October 27, 1972 (P.L. 92–574; 86 Stat. 1234–1250).

Coastal Zone Management Act of 1972. Declared it national policy to effectively manage, protect, develop, and, when possible, restore the nation's coastal resources; and established a national program to achieve this goal. Authorized federal grants to the states for the development of coastal management programs under specific guidelines. Directed the secretary of commerce to consult and cooperate with other federal and state agencies in carrying out his responsibilities under the act. Approved October 27, 1972 (P.L. 92–583; 86 Stat. 1280–1289).

Supplemental Security Income Program for the Aged, Blind, and Disabled. Replaced a patchwork system of federal grants to states with a needs-based program for individuals 65 or older, blind, or disabled who have a limited income and resources. Established a uniform federal income limit with optional state programs supplementing that limit. Approved October 30, 1972 (P.L. 92–603, Title III; 86 Stat. 1465–1485).

Notes

1. U.S. Congress, Senate, Committee on Finance, *Social Security Amendments of 1972*, 92nd Cong., 2d sess., S. Rept. 92–1230, September 26, 1972 (Washington, D.C.: U.S. Government Printing Office, 1972), 384.

2. U.S. Senate, *The Constitution of the United States: Analysis and Interpretation*, 108th Cong., 2d sess., S. Doc. 108–117, 43, n. 18.

3. *Journal of the Executive Proceedings of the Senate* (Washington, D.C.: U.S. Government Printing Office, 1973), 114:462–466; 23 UST 3435–3461.

Ninety-third Congress
January 3, 1973, to January 3, 1975

First session—January 3, 1973, to December 22, 1973
Second session—January 21, 1974, to December 20, 1974
(Second administration of Richard M. Nixon,
    1973–1974; administration of Gerald R. Ford,
    1974–1977)

Historical Background

One of the country's biggest political scandals—Watergate—played out in 1973 and 1974 and led to the first resignation of a president in U.S. history.

The *Washington Post* reported in October 1972: "FBI agents [had] established that the Watergate bugging incident stemmed from a massive campaign of political spying and sabotage conducted on behalf of President Nixon's re-election."[1] Furthermore, a secret fund financed the operation. The televised hearings of the Senate Select Committee on Presidential Campaign Activities (Watergate Committee), held from May 17, 1973, to February 19, 1974, revealed a wide-ranging effort by the White House to conceal involvement by the Committee to Re-elect the President in the Watergate break-in. In June 1973, former White House counsel John Dean asserted that President Nixon and his closest aides had orchestrated the cover-up. Former White House aide Alexander P. Butterfield subsequently revealed to the committee the existence of a tape-recording system in the Oval Office and elsewhere in the White House.

On May 18, 1973, Attorney General Elliot L. Richardson named former solicitor general and Harvard law professor Archibald Cox as special prosecutor to investigate Watergate. Both the Watergate Committee and the special prosecutor's office went to court to get the White House tapes that were pertinent to their investigations. While the committee was stymied by a claim of violation of separation of powers, Cox essentially won the right to hear relevant tapes as a result of a ruling by Judge John J. Sirica, which was upheld on appeal October 12, 1973. In response, President Nixon unexpectedly announced that he would not pursue the case to the U.S. Supreme Court, saying he would provide the special prosecutor with written summaries of the tapes. He also directed Cox "to make no further attempts by judicial process to obtain tapes, notes, or memoranda of presidential conversations."

The events that subsequently unfolded came to be known as the "Saturday night massacre." After Cox rejected both the offer of summaries and the presidential directive, Nixon on Saturday, October 20, 1973, ordered Attorney General Richardson to dismiss the special prosecutor. Richardson refused, claiming such an action would jeopardize any future prosecutor's independence, and resigned. Deputy Attorney General William D. Ruckelshaus also refused to fire Cox and was dismissed. Solicitor General Robert H. Bork was elevated to acting attorney general and carried out the order to dismiss Cox. A firestorm of unfavorable public reaction led the president to reverse himself on October 23, when he announced he would deliver the tapes cited. On November 1, Texas trial lawyer Leon Jaworski was appointed the new special prosecutor.

In the aftermath of the Saturday night massacre, the House Judiciary Committee opened a full-scale impeachment inquiry. In the course of its investigation, the committee subpoenaed President Nixon for tapes and documents related to Watergate. On July 24, 1974, the U.S. Supreme Court unanimously rejected the president's claim of executive privilege for refusing to hand over subpoenaed material to Congress and the special prosecutor. On July 30, the House Judiciary Committee approved three articles of impeachment against President Nixon. The first, voted 27–11, charged that the president had obstructed justice by participating in the Watergate cover-up; the second, 28–10, that he had abused his presidential powers; and the third, 21–17, that he was in contempt of Congress for refusing to adequately comply with congressional subpoenas. The committee recommended to the full House that Richard M. Nixon be impeached—that is, removed as president.

On August 5, 1974, the White House released the transcripts of tapes that clearly showed President Nixon's participation in the Watergate cover-up. With impeachment and removal from office a certainty, Nixon, in a televised address to the nation August 8, said, "It has become evident to me that I no longer have a strong enough political base in Congress to justify continuing" the effort to stay in office. He officially resigned the next day.

In the midst of the Watergate inquiry, reports became public in August 1973 that Vice President Spiro T. Agnew was under investigation for alleged conspiracy, extortion, and bribery while executive of Baltimore County, governor of Maryland, and vice president of the United States. On October 10, 1973, Agnew avoided prison by pleading *nolo contendere* (no contest) to one charge of federal income tax evasion, becoming the second vice president in U.S. history to resign his office. (John C. Calhoun was the first, in 1832.) Setting in motion the first application of the Twenty-fifth Amendment, President Nixon on October 12 nominated House Minority Leader Gerald R. Ford of Michigan to be vice president. Both houses of Congress began consideration of the nomination, within the highly charged political atmosphere. Following committee hearings and floor debate, the nomination was approved and Gerald R. Ford was sworn in as Vice President on December 6.

Upon assuming the presidency on August 9, 1974, following Nixon's resignation, Ford asserted, "Our long national nightmare is over. Our Constitution works. Our great republic is a government of laws and not of men." In a controversial move, Ford on September 8 granted Nixon a "full, free and absolute pardon . . . for all offenses against the United States which he . . . has committed or may have committed" during his tenure as president.

When Ford ascended to the presidency, the vice presidency again was vacant. The lengthy confirmation of former New York governor Nelson Rockefeller, Ford's nominee to became the nation's second unelected vice president, was finally approved by the House and Senate on December 19, 1974. For the first and only time in U.S. history to date, neither the president nor the vice president was chosen by popular election.

American military involvement in the Vietnam War began to draw to a close with the Paris Peace Accords of January 1973, which provided that the twenty-five thousand American troops remaining in South Vietnam would be withdrawn in sixty days. (The "Vietnam era" would officially end on May 7, 1975, when President Gerald R. Ford closed the eligibility period for certain veterans benefits for those who had entered the military services since August 5, 1964.) More than forty-six thousand Americans died in combat in the Vietnam War, with another ten thousand succumbing to nonhostile causes. Approximately 300,000 Americans were wounded in the conflict.

In Cambodia, American planes continued their bombing until a legislative-executive agreement was reached that ended all military activity in Indochina on August 15, 1973. Congress formalized this position by banning the use of federal funds to support combat activities in the region.

Congress overrode Nixon's veto of the War Powers Resolution, which set a sixty-day limit on presidential commitment of U.S. troops to foreign hostilities or situations where hostilities appeared imminent, unless Congress consented to such action.

Early in October 1973, Syrian and Egyptian armed forces launched successful surprise attacks on Israeli forces holding occupied territory in the Golan Heights (Syria) and the Sinai Peninsula (Egypt). President Nixon ordered a massive airlift to resupply the struggling Israelis and a worldwide alert of U.S. armed forces when the possibility of Soviet intervention arose. After nearly three weeks of dangerously heightened international tensions, the Israelis turned back the attacks, and a temporary cease-fire was negotiated on October 24, followed by a more permanent arrangement on November 11.

Late in 1973, several Arab nations imposed an embargo on oil to the United States in retaliation for

American support of Israel, resulting in nationwide gasoline shortages. The oil crisis led directly to authorization of the long-delayed trans-Alaska pipeline. The 789-mile pipeline connecting the oil-rich North Slope and ice-free port of Valdez on the state's south-central coast was completed at a cost of approximately $8 billion in 1977. As the energy crisis deepened, President Nixon called for a Federal Energy Administration (FEA) that would give him broad authority to deal with the problems of energy shortages. A short-term FEA with limited powers was established instead. A second piece of President Nixon's energy plan was creation of the Energy Research and Development Administration.

The Agricultural and Consumer Protection Act of 1973 eliminated much of the farm subsidy program; farmers were to be reimbursed only if market prices dropped below those specified in the act. The Rehabilitation Act of 1973 was the first federal civil rights law to prohibit discrimination against people with disabilities. Late in 1973, Congress answered the president's call for a stronger endangered species law.

A $20 billion highway and mass transit bill for the first time allowed Highway Trust Fund monies to be used for urban mass transit projects. The financially troubled urban mass transit systems received an additional $11.9 billion in federal funds in 1974, to be spread out over six years. The Hazardous Materials Transportation Act of 1975 was passed "to protect the Nation adequately against risks to life and property which are inherent in the transportation of hazardous materials in commerce." It was enacted in response to public concerns over the fragmentation of the regulatory structure for transportation safety, lack of enforcement of existing regulations, and to harmonize conflicting state and local laws regarding the transportation of hazardous materials.

The imminent collapse of the bankrupt Penn Central, the nation's largest railroad, and six other lines prompted creation of an independent federal agency to design a new rail system for the Northeast and Midwest. The United States Railway Association was authorized to set up a for-profit Consolidated Rail Corporation within three hundred days to operate the system.

The Congressional Budget and Impoundment Control Act of 1974 provided for the establishment of House and Senate Budget Committees, advised by a staff of experts, to analyze the president's budget and recommend an overall fiscal policy for the government. The act also changed the starting date of the federal fiscal year from July 1 to October 1 and revamped the congressional budget process. The act was in large part a response to the administration's efforts to curb federal spending through presidential vetoes and impoundment of appropriated funds. An independent Legal Services Corporation was authorized to provide legal services to the poor in noncriminal cases. The legal services program had been part of the Office of Economic Opportunity.

The Housing and Community Development Act of 1974 represented a major adjustment in federal housing policy that authorized money to be spent for broad functional purposes, instead of specific activities allowable under block grants. It also initiated a new subsidy program providing rental assistance for low- and moderate-income families and an urban homesteading program. The Safe Water Drinking Act directed the Environmental Protection Agency to establish safe drinking water standards. The Employment Retirement Income Security Act offered the first federal effort to regulate private pension systems and safeguard the rights of the estimated twenty-three million employees that belonged to the plans.

A new campaign finance law established the first limits on political contributions and expenditures. Other significant provisions authorized the use of public funds to finance presidential election campaigns and stipulated disclosure and reporting dates. Congress overrode President Ford's veto of a major expansion of the Freedom of Information Act. The new amendments removed many of the bureaucratic obstacles that had previously thwarted citizens in efforts to obtain government information from federal agencies. President Ford opposed the act on the grounds that it gave federal judges the final say on classification decisions, narrowed the disclosure exemptions for investigatory law enforcement files, and established "unrealistic" deadlines for agency responses.

The Privacy Act was characterized by the bill's floor manager in the House as the first "comprehensive Federal privacy law since the adoption of the Fourth Amendment of the Constitution." For the first time, individuals were permitted to inspect information about themselves that was contained in federal agency files. One of the first federal privacy statutes passed by the Congress, the Family Educational Rights and Privacy Act of 1974, imposed nationwide standards of confidentiality for educational information about individual students.

Congress recognized the special needs of juveniles with the passage of the Juvenile Justice and Delinquency Prevention Act in 1974. This act, the single most important piece of federal legislation affecting youth in the juvenile justice systems across the country, established the principal program through which the federal government sets standards for juvenile justice systems at the state and local levels. Increased congestion and delays in the federal courts prompted passage of the Speedy Trial Act, which provided for the dismissal of charges against a person if he or she were not brought to trial within one hundred days. More than fifteen years of effort to draft a codified body of evidence law for the federal courts culminated in the passage of the Federal Rules of Evidence in 1975. The rules of evidence were proposed by the Supreme Court, with amendments made by Congress to promote truth, fairness, and efficiency.

As the United States edged ever deeper into its worst recession since the Great Depression of the 1930s, Congress enacted a compromise manpower and training act that provided state and local government block grants for training and public service jobs for the unemployed as well as underemployed. With the Disaster Relief Act of 1974, Congress began implementing standardized procedures for providing federal relief to citizens affected by natural disasters and instituted the concept of mitigation in disaster management. Previously more than 100 different federal agencies were collectively involved in disaster relief efforts. The act stressed a multi-hazard approach wherein government officials would prepare and respond to all types of disasters, rather than maintain separate capacities for different types of disasters.

The Trade Act of 1974 was approved after Congress and the administration resolved a lengthy controversy over congressional insistence that trade benefits for the Soviet Union be conditioned upon more liberal Soviet emigration policies.

Republican congressional candidates in November 1974 paid the price at the polls for the Watergate scandal and a weak economy. As a result, the Democrats in both houses strengthened their majority.

Major Acts

Prohibition on Funds for U.S. Combat Activities in Southeast Asia. Prohibited funds appropriated under the Second Supplemental Appropriation Act of 1973, or funds appropriated under any other act, from "being expended to support directly or indirectly combat activities in or over Cambodia, Laos, North Vietnam and South Vietnam by United States forces" after August 15, 1973. Approved July 1, 1973 (P.L. 93–50, Title III, Sec. 307; 87 Stat. 129).

Agriculture and Consumer Protection Act of 1973. Established a "target price" system under which the government paid farmers only if the market price was lower than the price specified in the act. Limited subsidies to $20,000 a year per farmer. Increased price supports for milk, and extended the Food for Peace and Food Stamp programs for four years. Provided the secretary of agriculture with authority to administer programs to resolve conservation and pollution problems, protect privately held forest lands, and encourage increased timber production. Approved August 10, 1973 (P.L. 93–86; 87 Stat. 221–250).

Federal-Aid Highway Act of 1973. Authorized $18.35 billion for the National System of Interstate and Defense Highways for fiscal years 1974–1979 from the Highway Trust Fund. Extended the completion date of the interstate system for one year (until June 30, 1979). Authorized a federal-aid urban highway system, and authorized the secretary of transportation to approve mass transit projects to draw upon Highway Trust Fund monies. Approved August 13, 1973 (P.L. 93–87; 87 Stat. 250–296).

Rehabilitation Act of 1973. Prohibited discrimination on the basis of disability in programs conducted by federal agencies, in federal employment, in the employment practices of federal contractors, and in programs receiving federal financial assistance, including state and local governments and private entities. Provided that the standards for determining employment discrimination under the act are the same as those used in Title I of the Americans with Disabilities Act. Approved September 26, 1973 (P.L. 93–112; 87 Stat. 355–394).

War Powers Resolution. Required the president "in every possible instance" to "consult with Congress before committing United States Armed Forces into hostilities or into situations where imminent involvement in hostilities is clearly indicated by the circumstances" and to regularly consult with Congress after making such a commitment. Required termination of such troop commitments within sixty days, unless Congress declared war, authorized continuation of the commitment, or was physically unable to convene as a result of an armed attack upon the United States. Authorized a thirty-day extension if the president determined and certified to Congress that unavoidable military necessity respecting the safety of the U.S. forces required their continued use to bring about a prompt disengagement. Presidential veto overridden by Congress. Became law without the president's signature November 7, 1973 (P.L. 93–148; 87 Stat. 555–560).

Trans-Alaska Pipeline Authorization Act. Directed the secretary of the interior to authorize the immediate construction of a trans-Alaska pipeline between Prudhoe Bay and the port of Valdez. Immunized the pipeline from further court challenges under the National Environmental Act of 1969, and restricted judicial review of the act to its constitutionality, actions violating constitutional rights, and actions not specifically granted by the act. Directed the president to ensure equitable allocation of Alaskan North Slope crude oil among the various regions of the country. Approved November 16, 1973 (P.L. 93–153, Title II; 87 Stat. 584–588).

Comprehensive Employment and Training Act of 1973. Authorized federal block grants to the states and local governments representing a population of more than 100,000 for job training and public service employment. Created a National Commission for Manpower Policy to identify the manpower needs and goals of the nation and to access how well the programs authorized by the act and other employment programs were meeting those goals. Consolidated the manpower programs authorized under the Manpower Development and Training Act of 1962, Economic Opportunity Act of 1964, and Emergency Employment Act of 1971. Approved December 28, 1973 (P.L. 93–203; 87 Stat. 839–883). *(Manpower Development and Training Act of 1962, p. 313; Economic Opportunity Act of 1964, p. 318)*

Endangered Species Act of 1973. Strengthened federal authority to protect endangered species of fish, plants, and wildlife "threatened" with extinction or those in immediate danger of becoming extinct. Made it a federal crime to buy, capture, hunt, sell, transport, import, and export endangered and threatened species or products made from them. Encouraged the establishment of state conservation and management programs to protect threatened and endangered species. Approved December 28, 1973 (P.L. 93–205; 87 Stat. 884–903).

Regional Rail Reorganization Act of 1973. Established the United States Railway Association, an independent federal agency, to plan the consolidation of seven bankrupt railroad lines in the Northeast and Midwest—the Ann Arbor, Boston & Maine, Central of New Jersey, Erie Lackawanna, Lehigh Valley, Penn Central, and Reading Railroads—into one corporation. Authorized the association to issue federally guaranteed loans up to $1.5 billion for the new corporation to take over selected routes of the seven railroads, repair track, and operate the new Consolidated Rail Corporation. Authorized $43.5 million to design the new system, $85 million to run the bankrupt railroads while the corporation was being developed, $250 million for benefit payments to those who lost jobs as a consequence of the reorganization, and $180 million in operating subsidies. Approved January 2, 1974 (P.L. 93–236; 87 Stat. 985–1023).

Federal Energy Administration Act of 1974. Reorganized and consolidated certain functions of the federal government in a temporary Federal Energy Administration (FEA) to manage short-term fuel shortages. Directed the president to report to Congress six months before the act's June 30, 1976, expiration date on recommendations for a permanent federal energy organization and what the future of the FEA should be. Authorized FEA appropriations of $75 million for fiscal year 1974 and $400 million for fiscal years 1975–1976. Approved May 7, 1974 (P.L. 93–275; 88 Stat. 96–115).

Disaster Relief Act of 1974. Created the first national program to provide direct assistance to individuals and households following a disaster. Stressed the concept of "multi-hazard" or integrated emergency management with federal, state, and local policies uniformly handling all types of hazards rather than deal with each disaster as a unique event. Instituted the family grant program, which supplied 75 percent of the funding for state-administered programs that provided money to purchase clothing, furniture, and essential needs following a disaster. Formalized efforts to mitigate disasters rather than merely responding to them. Firmly established the process of presidential disaster declarations. Approved May 22, 1974 (P.L. 93–288; 88 Stat. 143–164).

Congressional Budget and Impoundment Control Act of 1974. Established House and Senate Budget Committees to analyze the president's budget, recommend changes in fiscal policy, and set spending priorities. Created a Congressional Budget Office (CBO) to assist the Budget Committees as well as other committees and members of Congress in understanding issues relating to the budget information. Defined procedures that provided greater congressional control over the impoundment of funds by the executive branch. Revised congressional budget procedures, and moved the starting date of the federal fiscal year from July 1 to October 1. Approved July 12, 1974 (P.L. 93–344; 88 Stat. 297–339). *(Gramm-Rudman-Hollings Act [Balanced Budget and Emergency Deficit Control Act], p. 386)*

Legal Services Corporation Act of 1974. Established an independent Legal Services Corporation to provide legal assistance to the poor, a program previously in the Office of Economic Opportunity. Provided for an eleven-member board of directors appointed by the president and confirmed by the Senate. Stipulated that employees of the corporation were eligible for federal pensions and other benefits but were subject to laws and executive orders affecting federal agencies. Approved July 25, 1974 (P.L. 93–355; 88 Stat. 378–390).

Family Educational Rights and Privacy Act of 1974 (Buckley Amendment). Afforded parents the right to inspect, review, and amend all educational records pertaining to their children; and the right to have some control over the disclosure of personally identifiable information from education records. Transferred those rights to students, when they turn 18 years old or enter a postsecondary institution at any age. Applicable to every school, college, university, and other institutions of higher learning receiving federal financial assistance. Approved August 21, 1974 (P.L. 93–380; 88 Stat. 571–574, Sec. 513).

Housing and Community Development Act of 1974. Declared that the "future welfare of the Nation and the well-being of its citizens depend on the establishment and maintenance of viable urban communities as social, economic, and political entities." Merged ten urban development programs into a single block grant program. Authorized $8.4 billion in federal grants to local governments for community development activities over three years. Established a rental assistance program for low- and moderate-income families whose earnings did not exceed 80 percent of the median family income. Increased the size of mortgages guaranteed by the Federal Housing Administration. Required the Department of Housing and Urban Development (HUD) to establish safety and construction standards for mobile homes. Allowed HUD to sell federally owned inner-city properties in need of rehabilitation to families who agreed to make needed repairs and live in them. Banned sex discrimination in mortgage credit transactions. August 22, 1974 (P.L. 93–383; 88 Stat. 633–741).

Employee Retirement Income Security Act (ERISA). Established minimum federal funding standards for private pensions. Required firms that provided pension funds for their employees to adhere to federal rules. Established rules to be followed by pension fund trustees. Allowed individuals not covered by a pension plan to establish their own individual retirement accounts that qualified for special tax treatment. Approved September 2, 1974 (P.L. 93–406; 88 Stat. 829–1035).

Juvenile Justice and Delinquency Prevention Act of 1974. Provided states and localities with block grants for research, training, technical assistance, and evaluation for delinquency prevention programs, and greatly expanded protections for children who ended up in custody. Established the Office of Juvenile Justice and Delinquency Prevention in the Department of Justice to provide national leadership to federal, state, and local efforts to prevent delinquency, strengthen the juvenile justice system, and protect children. Approved September 7, 1974 (P.L. 93–415; 88 Stat. 1109–1143).

Energy Reorganization Act of 1974. Created a new Energy Research and Development Administration (ERDA) to direct federal research into the better use of existing fuels and the development of new sources of energy. ERDA took over most of the functions of the Atomic Energy Commission, which was abolished by the act, plus programs from the Department of the Interior, National Science Foundation, and Environmental Protection Agency. Approved October 11, 1974 (P.L. 93–438; 88 Stat. 1233–1254).

Federal Election Campaign Act Amendments of 1974. Established contribution and spending limits for individuals, political committees, and national and state political parties. Extended the limits to primary and general elections for the presidency, Senate, and House. Provided matching public funds of up to $5 million per presidential candidate. Stipulated specific disclosure and reporting requirements, and established a bipartisan Federal Election Commission to administer and enforce the campaign finance laws and public financing of presidential elections. Approved October 15, 1974 (P.L. 93–443; 88 Stat. 1263–1304). Certain provisions of this act were subsequently held unconstitutional in *Buckley v. Valeo*, 424 U.S. 1 (1976). *(Federal Election Campaign Act of 1971, p. 344)*

Equal Credit Opportunity Act. Prohibited any creditor from discriminating "against any applicant on the basis of sex or marital status with respect to any aspect of a credit transaction." Directed the Federal Reserve Board to issue regulations to implement the act within one year of date of enactment. Approved October 28, 1974 (P.L. 93–495, Titles V and VII; 88 Stat. 1521–1525). *(Equal Credit Opportunity Act Amendments of 1976, p. 357)*

Freedom of Information Act Amendments of 1974. Mandated deadlines for agency responses to

document requests, and required that agencies publish a uniform set of fees for such services. Required agencies to publish indices of their administrative activities or to furnish copies of the documents for the cost of duplication if indices were not published; to release unlisted documents even if their exact title was not known; and to prepare an annual report on all decisions to withhold information. Allowed federal judges to review government decisions to classify certain materials and to order payment of attorneys' fees and court costs for plaintiffs who won suits seeking information under the act. Presidential veto overridden by Congress. Became law without the president's signature November 21, 1974 (P.L. 93–502; 88 Stat. 1561–1565). *(Freedom of Information Act, p. 325)*

National Mass Transportation Assistance Act of 1974. Authorized an $11.9 billion, six-year program to assist urban mass transit systems in meeting operating and capital expenses. Provided $7.8 billion for capital grants and $4 billion for capital projects or operating costs. Approved November 26, 1974 (P.L. 93–503; 88 Stat. 1565–1575).

Safe Drinking Water Act. Directed the Environmental Protection Agency to establish national drinking water standards and regulations for state groundwater pollution control programs. Approved December 16, 1974 (P.L. 93–523; 88 Stat. 1660–1694). *(Safe Drinking Water Act Amendments of 1986, p. 387)*

Privacy Act of 1974. Provided "certain safeguards for an individual against an invasion of privacy by requiring Federal agencies" to allow information contained in federal agency files to be inspected and corrected or amended. Exempted records maintained by the Central Intelligence Agency, law enforcement agencies, and the Secret Service; statistical records; investigative material compiled for the purpose of determining suitability, eligibility, or qualifications for federal civilian employment, military service, federal contracts, or access to classified information; federal testing or examination materials; and military promotion evaluation materials. Approved December 31, 1974 (P.L. 93–579; 88 Stat. 1896–1910).

Federal Rules of Evidence Act. Established a comprehensive set of evidentiary rules (rules that govern the admission and exclusion of evidence) applicable in all civil and criminal cases in the U.S. courts of appeal, district courts, court of claims, and in proceedings before United States magistrates. Created special procedures for amending the evidence rules. (Although states are not bound by the Federal Rules of Evidence, most states use them as a model for their own rules.) Approved January 2, 1975 (P.L. 93–595; 88 Stat. 1926–1949).

Trade Act of 1974. Authorized the president to enter into trade agreements with other countries for the purpose of harmonizing, reducing, or eliminating tariff and nontariff trade barriers; eliminate tariffs on goods carrying duties of 5 percent and reduce higher tariffs by up to 60 percent; take corrective action whenever the United States had a large balance of payment surplus or deficit; and retaliate against unjustified or unreasonable foreign import restrictions. Established a congressional approval procedure for trade agreements, trade restrictions, and a number of different presidential trade decisions. Approved January 3, 1975 (P.L. 93–618; 88 Stat. 1978–2076).

Speedy Trial Act. Provided for the dismissal of charges against defendants accused of federal crimes if they were not brought to trial within one hundred days of their arrest. Approved January 3, 1975 (P.L. 93–619; 88 Stat. 2076–2089).

Hazardous Materials Transportation Act. Authorized the secretary of transportation to draw together previously fragmented enforcement and regulatory authority governing the movement of hazardous materials in commerce into one coordinated and consolidated body of law. Provided specific requirements for the safe transportation of hazardous materials by aircraft, rail car, marine vessels, and motor vehicles. Made provisions of the act applicable to all persons involved in the packaging, loading, and transportation of hazardous materials. Approved January 3, 1975 (P.L. 93–633; 88 Stat. 2156–2173).

Note

1. Carl Bernstein and Bob Woodward, "FBI Finds Nixon Aides Sabotaged Democrats," *Washington Post*, October 10, 1972, A1.

Ninety-fourth Congress
January 3, 1975, to January 3, 1977

First session—January 14, 1975, to December 19, 1975
Second session—January 19, 1976, to October 1, 1976
(Administration of Gerald R. Ford, 1974–1977)

Historical Background

Five months after assuming the presidency, Gerald R. Ford declared in his first annual message to Congress "that the state of the Union is not good." Millions of Americans were out of work, recession and inflation were eroding the economy, inflation continued to rise, plant capacity and productivity were stagnant, and the nation was too dependent on foreign oil. To stimulate the economy, President Ford recommended a one-year tax cut of $16 billion, three-quarters of which would go to individuals and one-quarter to promote business investments that would create jobs. Congress responded in March 1975 by approving the single largest tax cut in history to date.

Although the president felt the bill failed "to provide adequate relief to millions of middle-income taxpayers," he reluctantly signed the measure because the country needed the "stimulus and support of a tax cut." The $22.8 billion emergency tax reduction measure called for a $1.9 billion increase in federal spending, $18.1 billion in individual tax cuts, and $4.8 billion in business tax cuts. The Tax Reform Act of 1976 called for even greater reductions in taxes. Key provisions of that bill provided for curbs on investment tax shelters, increased taxes on the very wealthy, and important changes in estate and gift taxes. Also included in the act was the Earned Income Tax Credit (EITC), which offset Social Security taxes paid by low-income workers, to encourage them to seek gainful employment rather than welfare benefits, and to supplement wages. From a modest beginning, the EITC has grown to become one of the principal antipoverty programs in the federal budget.

While some were reluctant to enlarge federal involvement in energy policy, others distrusted the oil industry, which they believed had created the energy crisis. Strong regional and political differences among the committees dealing with the issue further complicated efforts to develop a national energy policy. Although the Energy Policy and Conservation Act of 1975 did not achieve all the goals its title implied, President Ford felt it set in "place the first elements of a comprehensive national energy policy" and provided a foundation upon which the country could "build a more comprehensive program."

Congress approved legislation assuring the right of the nation's more than eight million handicapped children to receive free and adequate public education. Another major legislative revision focused on federal statutes dealing with the authority of the Bureau of Land Management. The latter legislation consolidated and updated approximately three thousand public land laws. In addition, the Voting Rights Act of 1965 was reauthorized and its coverage extended.

Proponents of a more open government gained approval for the Government in the Sunshine Act, which required all multiheaded federal agencies to open their meetings to the public. Supporters of an effort to outlaw credit discrimination on the basis of age, race, color, religion, or national origin achieved their goal as well. Credit discrimination based on sex or marital status was banned in 1974. *(Equal Credit Opportunity Act, p. 353)*

At the president's urging, a new White House Office of Science and Technology Policy was established. The office would be headed by a presidential science adviser, a position that had been abolished three years earlier by a Nixon administration reorganization plan. A three-year Senate examination of presidential authority to declare "national emergencies" concluded with passage of the National Emergencies Act, which provided for congressional review of any future declarations. Fifteen years of legislative debate, involving discussions and negotiations with a number of interest groups, culminated in the first comprehensive revision of the nation's copyright laws since 1909.

The existing twelve-mile exclusive U.S. fishing zone off the nation's coasts was extended to two hundred nautical miles. Motivation for the action stemmed from a desire to protect the American fishing industry by assuring that foreign competitors did not deplete the dwindling supply of fish in the ocean areas adjacent to the coasts.

In the area of environmental policy, the Toxic Substances Control Act provided the first comprehensive law regulating toxic substances, and the Resource Conservation and Recovery Act offered a significant expansion of the federal solid waste and hazardous waste programs.

Passage of the National Forest Management Act of 1976, the primary statute governing the administration of national forests, was motivated by several different factors. These included the concerns of conservationists, growing interest in economic sustainability and renewability, increased attention given to recreational use of national forests, and court rulings that had curtailed certain types of logging and lumber industry practices.

One of the most heated legislative battles of 1975 involved efforts by New York City to secure federal loans needed to avoid bankruptcy. Supporters gained approval for the loan program only after New York State took steps to address the problem and President Ford abandoned his threat to veto any federal bailout.

Another intense, and sometimes bitter, struggle, between Secretary of Transportation William T. Coleman and Congress resulted in compromise legislation that authorized $6.4 billion for the modernization and revitalization of the railroads. The Railroad Revitalization Act, in President Ford's opinion, marked the "first significant reform of transportation regulation by any administration or Congress."

Vietcong and North Vietnamese regular forces opened a massive offensive early in 1975, violating the Paris Peace Accords. Deprived of U.S. military assistance and demoralized by their own unpopular and often corrupt government, the South Vietnamese armed forces collapsed in the face of the onslaught. The pro–U.S. forces of Cambodia and its military proved equally unable to resist their own communist opponents, the Khmer Rouge.

As the Vietcong and North Vietnamese stormed the capital of Saigon, the U.S. 7th Fleet deployed offshore to receive refugees. A flood of Vietnamese sought safety, leaving their homeland in an armada of boats and ships. As these events unfolded, Congress quickly considered and approved a measure containing $405 million for the resettlement of more than 131,000 Vietnamese and Cambodian refugees in the United States. Similar assistance was authorized in 1976 for resettlement of Laotian refugees. Legislation was also approved authorizing congressional review of commercial sales of major defense equipment to foreign nations.

A covenant granting U.S. commonwealth status to the Northern Mariana Islands in the Pacific provided self-government for their fourteen thousand residents. The United States, however, retained control over the defense and foreign affairs of the Northern Marianas. Placed under American administration after World War II, the people of the Northern Marianas sought continued association with the United States. Other island groups of the Trust Territory of the Pacific ultimately achieved their stated goal of full independence as well.

On July 4, 1976, Americans celebrated the nation's bicentennial, commemorating the two hundredth anniversary of the signing of the Declaration of Independence.

Democratic presidential candidate and former governor of Georgia Jimmy Carter and vice presidential candidate and Minnesota senator Walter F. Mondale triumphed at the polls on election day 1976. The frustrations accompanying the energy shortages of the 1970s, the revelations of the Watergate scandal, an ailing economy, and Ford's full and unconditional pardon of former president Richard M. Nixon all contributed to the defeat of Ford and his vice presidential running mate, Sen. Robert Dole of Kansas. The Carter-Mondale ticket received 297 electoral votes to 240 for Ford-Dole. As a result of the congressional races, Democrats increased their majorities in both houses.

Major Acts

Tax Reduction Act of 1975. Provided $22.8 billion in individual and business tax cuts, along with $1.9 billion in special countercyclical government spending. Increased the business tax credit, reduced oil and gas depletion allowances, and curbed foreign oil tax benefits. Approved March 29, 1975 (P.L. 94–12; 89 Stat. 26–67).

Earned Income Tax Credit. Provided financial assistance to low-income families in the form of a refundable tax credit to offset a taxpayer's income tax liability; if the credit exceeds tax liability, the additional amount is returned to the taxpayer as a refund. Approved March 29, 1975 (P.L. 94–12; 89 Stat. 30–32, Title II, Sec. 204). The Earned Income Tax Credit was initially enacted as a temporary measure. It was made permanent in the Revenue Act of 1978. Approved November 6, 1978 (P.L. 95–600; 92 Stat. 2771, Title I, Sec. 103).

Cambodian and Vietnamese Refugees. Appropriated $405 million for the relocation and resettlement of Cambodian and Vietnamese refugees in the United States. Stipulated that none of the funds could be used for military purposes. Approved May 23, 1975 (P.L. 94–24; 89 Stat. 89).

Voting Rights Act Amendments of 1975. Extended the Voting Rights Act of 1965 for an additional seven years. Broadened the act's coverage to included Spanish-speaking Americans, Native Americans, Asian Americans, and Alaska Natives. Mandated bilingual elections under certain conditions. Made permanent the nationwide ban on literacy tests. Approved August 6, 1975 (P.L. 94–73; 89 Stat. 400–406). *(Voting Rights Act of 1965, p. 323)*

Education for All Handicapped Children Act of 1975. Required each state by September 1, 1978, to provide a free and appropriate education for all handicapped children between the ages of three and twenty-one. Established priorities for the states to observe in determining which students should be covered and a new grant formula under which states would receive federal assistance in meeting the education needs of the handicapped. Provided additional special incentive grants to states for education of preschool handicapped children aged three to five. Approved November 29, 1975 (P.L. 94–142; 89 Stat. 773–796).

New York City Seasonal Financing Act of 1975. Authorized the secretary of the Treasury to make loans of up to $2.3 billion per year through mid-1978 to help New York City meet its seasonal cash needs. Required the city to repay the yearly loans at an interest rate of 1 percent above the prevailing Treasury rate by June 30 of each year. Stipulated that the authority to make the loans expired on June 30, 1978. Approved December 9, 1975 (P.L. 94–143; 89 Stat. 797–799).

Energy Policy and Conservation Act. Granted the president standby authority to deal with energy emergencies; provided for creation of strategic petroleum reserves; encouraged increased use of fossil fuels; encouraged conservation of energy supplies; encouraged improved energy efficiency in automobiles and other consumer products; reduced domestic energy consumption through voluntary and mandatory energy conservation programs; and provided a means for verifying energy data. Approved December 22, 1975 (P.L. 94–163; 89 Stat. 871–969).

Railroad Revitalization and Regulatory Reform Act of 1976. Authorized $2.1 billion in federal loans for the Consolidated Rail Corporation (ConRail) to acquire the Penn Central Railroad and other bankrupt lines. Authorized $3.945 billion in loans and grants to improve passenger service in the Northeast corridor, subsidize railroads that would otherwise cease to exist, and aid railroads outside the ConRail system. Authorized $125 million to assist local governments in providing subsidies for commuter rail services. Allowed railroads greater flexibility in setting freight rates. Established a finance committee composed of the secretaries of transportation and the Treasury and the chairman of the United States Rail Association to oversee the government's investment in ConRail. Approved February 5, 1976 (P.L. 94–210; 90 Stat. 31–150).

Equal Credit Opportunity Act Amendments of 1976. Amended the 1974 Equal Credit Opportunity Act by banning credit discrimination on the basis of age, race, color, religion, or national origin. Approved

March 23, 1976 (P.L. 94–239; 90 Stat. 251–255). *(Equal Credit Opportunity Act, p. 353)*

Commonwealth Status Granted to the Northern Mariana Islands. Granted approval of a covenant giving commonwealth status to the Northern Mariana Islands. Provided self-government for the islands, but allowed the United States to retain control over the islands' defense and foreign affairs. Authorized federal income taxes and other levies paid by the islanders to be returned to the commonwealth. Approved March 24, 1976 (P.L. 94–241; 90 Stat. 263–279).

Fishery Conservation and Management Act of 1976. Established "a zone contiguous to the territorial sea of the United States to be known as the fishery conservation zone" that extended the existing twelve-mile exclusive U.S. fishing zone off its coasts to two hundred miles. Approved April 13, 1976 (P.L. 94–265; 90 Stat. 331–361).

National Science and Technology Policy, Organization, and Priorities Act of 1976. Established an office of Science and Technology Policy in the Executive Office of the President. Authorized the president to appoint a director and four associate directors to advise him on "scientific, engineering, and technological aspects of issues that require attention at the highest level of the Government." Approved May 11, 1976 (P.L. 94–282; 90 Stat. 459–473).

Indochina Migration and Refugee Act Amendments. Amended the Indochina Migration and Refugee Act of 1975 to provide for the inclusion of refugees from Laos. Approved June 21, 1976 (P.L. 94–313; 90 Stat. 691).

International Security Assistance and Arms Export Control Act of 1976. Authorized congressional review of all commercial and government sales of major military defense equipment abroad valued at $7 million or more. Prohibited private companies from selling major defense equipment valued at $25 million or more to foreign countries. Approved June 30, 1976 (P.L. 94–329; 90 Stat. 729–769).

Government in the Sunshine Act. Required all U.S. government instrumentalities headed by two or more people to open their meetings to public scrutiny "where such deliberations determine or result in the joint conduct or disposition of official agency business." Allowed meetings to be closed for certain reasons. Provided procedures for court redress to open a meeting and provisions for regulating ex parte communications in any on-the-record agency proceeding. Approved September 13, 1976 (P.L. 94–409; 90 Stat. 1241–1248).

National Emergencies Act. Provided for a congressional review of national emergencies declared by the president. Established procedures for declaring and terminating national emergencies. Terminated four states of emergency dating back to 1933 that technically remained in effect. Approved September 14, 1976 (P.L. 94–412; 90 Stat. 1255–1259).

Tax Reform Act of 1976. Repealed and revised obsolete tax provisions in the U.S. tax code. Made significant changes in provisions dealing with tax shelter investments, minimum and maximum taxes, individual income taxes, alimony deductions, retirement income credits, child care expense credits, sick pay exclusions, moving expenses, use of homes and vacation homes for business purposes, foreign tax preferences, trusts, capital formation, estate and gift taxes, capital gains and losses, domestic international sales, tax-exempt organizations, corporate tax rates and surcharge exemptions, certain railroad and airline investment credits, and income earned abroad. Approved October 4, 1976 (P.L. 94–455; 90 Stat. 1520–1933).

Toxic Substances Control Act. Established as a national policy that manufacturers and processors should develop adequate data on the health and environmental effects of chemicals. Directed the Environmental Protection Agency to test chemicals that presented an "unreasonable risk of injury to health or environment"; establish standards for testing chemicals; ban and regulate the marketing, sale, distribution, or use of certain chemicals; keep records of all chemicals manufactured and processed in the United States; and monitor the effect of toxic substances regulations on employment. Prohibited the manufacture, sale, or distribution of polychlorinated biphenyls (PCBs) within two-and-one-half years. Approved October 11, 1976 (P.L. 94–469; 90 Stat. 2003–2051).

Copyright Law Revision of 1976. Provided for a general revision of federal copyright law (Title 17 of the United States Code). Defined the criteria for copyright protection as "original works of authorship fixed in any tangible medium of expression," including literary works; musical works; dramatic works; pantomimes and choreographic works; pictorial, graphic, and sculptural works; motion pictures and other audiovisual works; and sound recordings. Provided copyright protection to published and unpublished foreign works meeting specified criteria. Limited copying of protected works by schools and libraries. Imposed copyright liability on public broadcasters, cable television systems, and jukebox operators. Extending the duration of copyright protection to the lifetime of the author plus fifty years. Approved October 19, 1976 (P.L. 94–553; 90 Stat. 2541–2602).

Federal Land Policy and Management Act. Consolidated and updated approximately three thousand public land laws into a single statute that defined Bureau of Land Management (BLM) authority. Authorized the secretary of the interior to manage BLM lands and be responsible for developing comprehensive land-use plans for those properties. Approved October 21, 1976 (P.L. 94–579; 90 Stat. 2743–2794).

Resource Conservation and Recovery Act of 1976. Authorized a total of $365.9 million for solid waste programs through fiscal 1979. Directed the Environmental Protection Agency (EPA) to review solid waste regulations at least every three years, publish guidelines and establish a timetable for states to develop state or regional solid waste programs, and create expert panels to advise states and local governments on solid waste programs. Required the EPA to issue hazardous waste guidelines and regulations; identify specific wastes; establish waste safety standards; regulate waste treatment, storage, and disposal facilities; and assist states in establishing relevant waste programs. Directed the EPA to conduct several solid waste studies and demonstration projects. Approved October 21, 1976 (P.L. 94–580; 90 Stat. 2795–2841).

National Forest Management Act of 1976. Acknowledged that the "management of the Nation's renewable resources is highly complex," but declared that the public interest is served by the assessment of renewable resources and development of "a national renewable resources program, which is periodically reviewed and updated." Required the secretary of agriculture to assess forest lands, to develop a management program based on multiple-use, sustained-yield principles, and to implement a resource management plan for each unit of the national forest system. Provided detailed guidelines for the management of national forest lands, conduct of national forest planning and timber management practices, and participation of the public in national forest decision making. Approved October 22, 1976 (P.L. 94–588; 90 Stat. 2949–2963).

Ninety-fifth Congress
January 3, 1977, to January 3, 1979

First session—January 4, 1977, to December 15, 1977
Second session—January 19, 1978, to October 15, 1978
(Administration of Jimmy Carter, 1977–1981)

Historical Background

Little known outside of his native Georgia when he began campaigning for the presidency as a Washington outsider, Jimmy Carter entered office promising a "people's presidency" shorn of "imperial" trappings. He signaled this new style of leadership at his inauguration, when he and the first lady walked part of the way down Pennsylvania Avenue to the White House after his swearing in.

President Carter appeared before Congress to unveil an economic stimulus plan that blended individual and corporate tax cuts with increased federal spending. By the end of May 1977, after considerable reshaping on Capitol Hill, a three-year, $34.2 billion tax reduction package was sent to the White House for the president's signature. Taxes were cut an additional $18.7 billion in 1978, but this measure, in contrast to its predecessor, bore little resemblance to the administration proposal. Major provisions included reductions in capital gains and corporate income rates and a one-time capital gains exemption for profits earned by persons fifty-five and over on the sale of their home.

President Carter's request for a new cabinet-level Department of Energy that consolidated most federal energy programs into one agency was approved. The president's plans for encouraging Americans to dramatically curb energy consumption, however, faced a tougher test. Following a protracted and bitter debate, Congress opted for promoting conservation instead of penalizing waste. The new energy policy was intended to save between 1 million and 1.4 million barrels of imported oil a day. It provided tax incentives for efficient use of energy and penalties for inefficient use; established a variety of requirements and incentives for conserving energy; encouraged industries and utilities to begin using coal instead of gas or oil; and authorized the end of federal price controls on natural gas. The first major overhaul of offshore oil and gas leasing laws in a quarter century established guidelines for exploration and development of energy resources on the outer continental shelf.

The Clean Air Act Amendments of 1977 established a comprehensive program for meeting, as well as maintaining, air quality standards to protect the environment and permit, in President Carter's words, "economic growth in an environmentally sound manner." Passage of the Surface Mining Control and Reclamation Act was the culmination of a five-year effort by environmentalists that had twice previously won approval by Congress, only to then be vetoed by President Gerald R. Ford. In signing the bill, President Carter credited Congress with taking a "very courageous stand" for which the American people showed "favorable sentiment."

Congress enacted the Foreign Corrupt Practices Act of 1977 after revelations of widespread global corruption in the wake of the Watergate political scandal. The Securities and Exchange Commission discovered that more than 400 U.S. companies had paid hundreds of millions of dollars in bribes to foreign government officials to secure business overseas. Passage of the act was viewed as critical to stopping corporate bribery, which had tarnished the image of U.S. businesses, impaired public confidence in the financial integrity of U.S. companies, and hampered the efficient functioning of the markets.

Older workers also benefited as the permissible mandatory age for retirement for nonfederal workers was raised from sixty-five to seventy and was eliminated for most federal employees. Improved health care, supporters argued, allowed people to remain active much longer, and their right to work deserved to be protected. Opponents contended that raising mandatory retirement would add to the unemployment problems of younger Americans, protect inefficiency, and hinder efforts to vie with aggressive foreign competitors.

In 1978, Congress approved an enduring legislative monument to the late senator and vice president Hubert H. Humphrey in a bill sponsored by Rep. Augustus F. "Gus" Hawkins of California. Although many provisions of the Humphrey-Hawkins Full Employment Act were modified before final passage, it had a far-reaching emotional impact among African Americans and labor groups as a symbol of concern for the jobless. Another bill expanded the legal rights of working women by banning employment discrimination on the basis of pregnancy, childbirth, or related medical conditions.

Seeking to answer the credit needs of low- and moderate-income neighborhoods, Congress approved legislation designed to encourage federally regulated financial institutions to meet the lending needs of their entire community. A second banking measure, which responded to the rapid growth in foreign banks in the United States, provided for federal regulation of foreign bank operations in the United States.

A refinement of emergency law occurred in 1977 when action was completed on the International Emergency Economic Powers Act. The act allows the president, after consulting with Congress, to declare a national emergency in the event of a foreign threat to the United States, and to prohibit transactions with, or freeze assets of foreign powers. Although the act was designed to be more restrictive than the Trading with the Enemy Act of 1917, subsequent Supreme Court decisions have weakened Congress's role in the process.

Legislation was enacted to end most federal regulation of the commercial passenger airline industry. Airline deregulation, a top priority of the Carter administration, was designed to increase competition in air transit, resulting in substantially lower fares, new services, and new routes.

Civil service reform was characterized by President Carter as "absolutely vital" to an open, efficient, and respected government. Carter's plan to reorganize the civil service became effective in August 1978 after neither the House nor the Senate voted to block it. His reform proposals provided for the formal establishment of the Office of Personnel Management, Merit Systems Protection Board, and the Senior Executive Service.

President Carter's most significant foreign policy test of 1978 involved the Panama Canal. Thirty-eight days of Senate debate preceded ratification of two treaties Carter had negotiated calling for the United States to relinquish control over the Panama Canal by the year 2000. The first provided for the transfer to Panama, and the second guaranteed the United States the right to defend the canal following the transfer. Both treaties were ratified by the Senate by identical 68 to 32 votes, only one more than the two-thirds majority required.

Nearly three years of consideration preceded the March 1978 establishment of strict controls on the export of nuclear material to other nations. Legislation curtailed for the first time use of electronic surveillance in the name of national security. Revelations of widespread eavesdropping and disregard for the rights of U.S. citizens led to the restrictions.

On August 22, 1978, after more than a century of protracted efforts, a proposed constitutional amendment giving the District of Columbia full voting representation in Congress was approved and sent to the states for ratification. The proposed amendment died in 1985, when its statutory deadline for ratification expired with the approval of only sixteen of the necessary thirty-eight states. *(Proposed Constitutional Amendment Giving the District of Columbia Full Voting Participation in Congress, p. 363)*

American Samoa, a U.S. Pacific island possession, was granted a nonvoting delegate in 1978. With this act, Congress provided representation for all U.S. possessions and territories and the Commonwealth of Puerto Rico.

Congress created 152 new federal judgeships, the largest number created by a single act before or since, to relieve massive backlogs in federal court cases. The after-effects of the Watergate scandal were evident in three new laws. The Office of Inspector General was established in 1978, as an independent unit within executive branch departments and agencies to provide Congress as well as federal departments and agencies with objective and independent reviews of the efficiency and effectiveness of executive branch operations and activities.

The Ethics in Government Act required detailed public financial disclosure by top officials in all three branches of the federal government and placed new restrictions on postgovernment activities by former federal officials. The Presidential Records Act made most papers of retiring chief executives and vice presidents public property, beginning in 1981.

The nation's bankruptcy laws were revised for the first time in nearly four decades. An enormous increase in bankruptcies necessitated fundamental changes in that system as well as an upgrading of the status and character of federal bankruptcy judges.

As a result of the 1978 congressional elections, Democrats continued to control both chambers by comfortable majorities.

Major Acts and Treaties

Tax Reduction and Simplification Act of 1977. Set the standard deduction for single persons at $2,200 and for joint returns at $3,200 effective with the 1977 tax year. Adjusted tax tables and rates to reflect the change. Extended corporate tax cuts authorized in the Tax Reduction Act of 1975 through 1978. Provided employers a tax cut of $2,100 (50 percent of the first $4,200 of wages) in 1977 and 1978 for each new worker hired. Approved May 23, 1977 (P.L. 95–30; 91 Stat. 126–168). *(Tax Reduction Act of 1975, p. 357)*

Surface Mining Control and Reclamation Act of 1977. Established an Office of Surface Mining Reclamation and Enforcement within the Interior Department to administer the act's regulatory and reclamation programs, monitor state programs, and provide grants and technical assistance to the states. Established an Advisory Committee on Mining and Mineral Research and a self-supporting abandoned Mine Reclamation Fund to restore lands used in earlier mining operations. Set environmental protection standards for all major coal surface mining operations. Protected certain lands

regarded as unsuitable for surface mining. Authorized the administrator of the Energy Research and Development Administration to designate ten institutions of higher learning for establishing university coal research laboratories and to award up to one thousand graduate fellowships for study and research on the use of fuels and energy. Approved August 3, 1977 (P.L. 95–87; 91 Stat. 445–532).

Department of Energy Established. Established a cabinet-level Department of Energy, and consolidated most federal energy programs within the new department. Abolished the Federal Energy Administration, the Energy Research and Development Administration, and the Federal Power Commission, transferring functions of the three agencies to the Department of Energy. Approved August 4, 1977 (P.L. 95–91; 91 Stat. 565–613).

Clean Air Act Amendments of 1977. Extended existing automobile emission standards through the 1979 model year. Called for a tightening of emission standards beginning in 1980. Extended the deadline for cities to meet national clean air standards from 1977 until 1982, and allowed most industrial polluters an additional three years to comply. Established new air quality standards for national parks, wilderness areas, national monuments, and recreational areas. Directed the Environmental Protection Agency (EPA) to review the criteria for ambient air quality standards prior to 1981 and to conduct subsequent reviews every five years thereafter. Established a thirteen-member National Commission on Air Quality, and required the EPA and other federal agencies to conduct more than a dozen studies concerning air pollution. Approved August 7, 1977 (P.L. 95–95; 91 Stat. 685–796). *(Clean Air Act of 1963, p. 317)*

Community Reinvestment Act of 1977. Required federal financial supervisory agencies, "when examining financial institutions, to encourage such institutions to meet the credit needs of the local community in which they are chartered consistent with the safe and sound operation of such institutions;" to "access the institution's record of meeting the credit needs of its entire community, including low- and moderate-income neighborhoods, consistent with the safe and sound operations of such institution; and to "take such record into account in its evaluation of an application for a deposit facility by such institution." Approved October 12, 1977 (P.L. 95–128, Title VIII; 91 Stat. 1147–1148).

Foreign Corrupt Practices Act of 1977. Required issuers who must register their securities with the Securities and Exchange Commission (SEC) to keep detailed books, records, and accounts that accurately record corporate payments and transactions. Required SEC registered issuers to institute and maintain an internal accounting control system to assure management's control, authority, and responsibility over the firm's assets. Prohibited domestic corporations, whether or not registered with the SEC, from bribing a foreign official, a foreign political party, party official, or candidate, for the purpose of obtaining or maintaining business. Approved December 19, 1977 (P.L. 95–213; 91 Stat. 1494–1498, Title I).

International Emergency Economic Powers Act. Authorized the president, after consulting with Congress, to declare a national emergency in the event of "any unusual and extraordinary threat, which has its source in whole or in part outside the United States, to the national security, foreign policy or economy of the United States." Allowed the president to "investigate, regulate, or prohibit" a wide array of largely economic actions. Stipulated that once the emergency has gone into effect, the president must submit a detailed report to Congress explaining and justifying his actions. Approved December 28, 1977 (P.L. 95–223; 91 Stat. 1626–1629, Title II).

Nuclear Nonproliferation Act of 1978. Prohibited the U.S. government from exporting nuclear material unless assurances were received from the recipient nation that it was not to be used in weapons production. Required the same assurances before nuclear technology could be exported by the government. Stipulated a number of conditions under which exports of nuclear material would be banned, but provided that the president could continue such exports if he determined that a cutoff would harm national security or violate other nonproliferation agreements. Provided that Congress could override the president's decision by passing a

concurrent resolution within sixty days. Approved March 10, 1978 (P.L. 95–242; 92 Stat. 120–152).

Panama Canal Treaty. Granted the United States the right to regulate, manage, operate, maintain, improve, protect, and defend the Panama Canal until December 31, 1999, when Panama, whose role in canal activities would continue to increase, assumed complete control and responsibility for the canal. Established a Panama Canal Commission to operate and manage the waterway until it was turned over to Panama. Prohibited the United States from becoming involved in negotiations or construction of another canal in Panama or Latin America unless both countries agreed. Provided an annual payment to Panama of $10 million from canal revenues, and an additional amount of up to $10 million if revenues exceeded expenditures. Concluded September 7, 1977. Ratification advised by the Senate March 16, 1978.[1]

Age Discrimination in Employment Act Amendments of 1978. Raised the permissible mandatory retirement age for most nonfederal workers from sixty-five to seventy. Remove the age ceiling of seventy for most federal employees. Approved April 6, 1978 (P.L. 95–256; 92 Stat. 189–193).

Treaty Concerning the Permanent Neutrality and Operation of the Panama Canal. Declared that the Panama Canal would remain permanently neutral, secure, and open to peaceful transit by vessels from all nations on terms of equality in times of peace and war. Provided that after termination of the Panama Canal Treaty in 1999, only Panama would operate the canal and maintain military forces, defense sites, and military installations within its national territory. Provided that U.S. and Panamanian war vessels and auxiliary ships would be "entitled to transit the canal expeditiously." Concluded September 7, 1977. Ratification advised by the Senate April 18, 1978.[2]

Proposed Constitutional Amendment Giving the District of Columbia Full Voting Participation in Congress. Provided that the District of Columbia be treated as a state for purposes of congressional and Electoral College representation, participation in congressional elections, and ratification of proposed amendments to the Constitution. Required that the proposed constitutional amendment providing for D.C. representation in Congress be ratified by three-fourths of the states within seven years. Incorporated D.C.-related presidential election and Electoral College provisions of the Twenty-third Amendment, which it also repealed. Sent to the states for ratification on August 22, 1978 (92 Stat. 3795–3796). [The proposed amendment died in 1985, when its statutory deadline for ratification expired with the approval of only sixteen of the necessary thirty-eight states.]

International Banking Act of 1978. Subjected foreign banks operating in the United States to the federal bank regulatory system. Established special rules for foreign banks. Permitted foreign banks to establish interstate banks, but allowed them to accept deposits only from foreign sources or from international transactions. Empowered the Federal Reserve Board to set reserve requirements for foreign banks with $1 million or more in worldwide assets. Approved September 17, 1978 (P.L. 95–369; 92 Stat. 607–625).

Inspector General Act of 1978. Created Offices of Inspector General ("independent and objective units") within 12 federal departments and agencies. Delegated to each office responsible for supervising, conducting and providing policy for conducting audits and investigations on programs and operations of the agency; coordinating and recommending policies to promote the economy, efficiency, and effectiveness of the agency; preventing and detecting waste, fraud, and abuse in the agency; and keeping the agency head and Congress fully and currently informed about problems, deficiencies, and recommended corrective action. Approved October 12, 1978 (P.L. 95–452; 92 Stat. 1101–1109).

Civil Service Reform Act of 1978. Established an independent Office of Personnel Management (OPM) within the executive branch to administer and enforce civil service statutes and a three-member, presidentially appointed Merit Systems Protection Board (MSPB) to hear and adjudicate the appeals of employees or applicants for federal jobs. (Both OPM and MSPB were authorized as part of the Reorganization Plan No. 2 of 1978 [92 Stat. 3783–3787].) Created a Senior Executive Service of approximately eight thousand top managers and policy makers. Established merit pay for federal employees at the civil service levels GS-13 through GS-15, a Federal Labor Relations Authority to hear unfair labor practice complaints, and a ceiling on federal employees for fiscal years 1979–1981. Authorized increased management flexibility in firing incompetent employees and statutory labor rights for federal workers. Approved October 13, 1978 (P.L. 95–454; 92 Stat. 1111–1227).

Federal District and Circuit Judges Act of 1978. Created 152 new federal judgeships. Added 117 federal district court judgeships to the existing 398 and 35 federal circuit court of appeal judgeships to the existing 97. Approved October 20, 1978 (P.L. 95–486; 98 Stat. 1629–1634).

Airline Deregulation Act of 1978. Provided for the deregulation of commercial passenger air traffic and the phasing out of the Civil Aeronautics Board (CAB) by January 1, 1985. Facilitated new services and routes by airlines, and granted flexibility in raising and lowering fares. Permitted certified intrastate air carriers to automatically enter one new route a year until 1981 without seeking approval of CAB and to designate one route per year as ineligible for automatic entry. Provided assistance to airline employees adversely affected by deregulation, including up to six years' compensation for job loss, wage reduction, or forced relocation. Approved October 24, 1978 (P.L. 95–504; 92 Stat. 1705–1754).

Foreign Intelligence Surveillance Act. Established legal standards and procedures for obtaining electronic surveillance warrants for national security purposes. Required that all requests by the executive branch for electronic surveillance to obtain foreign intelligence information within the United States be heard by a special new court composed of seven federal district judges selected by the Chief Justice of the Supreme Court. Provided that appeals would be heard by three other district judges designated by the Chief Justice. Exempted certain National Security Agency surveillance from warrant requirements. Approved October 25, 1978 (P.L. 95–511; 92 Stat. 1783–1798).

Ethics in Government Act of 1978. Codified public financial disclosure provisions of the congressional ethics codes adopted by the House and the Senate in 1977. Applied the same disclosure requirements to members of Congress, the president, vice president, candidates for those offices, Supreme Court justices, and federal judges; executive, legislative, and judicial branch employees paid at the equivalent of a GS-16 salary or above; and military officers at the O-7 level or above. Established an Office of Government Ethics to develop rules and regulations pertaining to conflicts of interest in the executive branch. Barred former executive branch employees from representing anyone before their former agencies for one year after leaving office. Approved October 26, 1978 (P.L. 95–521; 92 Stat. 1824–1885).

Humphrey-Hawkins Full Employment and Balanced Growth Act of 1978. Declared that it was the policy of the U.S. government to promote full employment, increased real income, balanced growth, a balanced budget, growth in productivity, an improved balance of trade, and price stability. Provided for better coordination and integration of federal economic policy making to achieve the twin goals of reducing inflation and unemployment. Established procedures for congressional review of the president's annual economic report and biannual reports of the Federal Reserve Board. Prohibited discrimination on account of sex, race, age, religion, or national origin in any of the act's programs. Approved October 27, 1978 (P.L. 95–523; 92 Stat. 1887–1908).

Pregnancy, Sex Discrimination, Prohibition Act of 1978. Prohibited discrimination in every aspect of employment on the basis of pregnancy, childbirth, and related medical conditions. Required employers to carry disability and health insurance plans that covered pregnant workers. Allowed employers to exempt elective abortions or complications resulting from abortions from medical coverage. Required that employers, however, provide disability and sick leave for women recovering from an abortion. Approved October 31, 1978 (P.L. 95–555; 92 Stat. 2076–2077).

Delegate to the House of Representatives from American Samoa. Provided for the election of a nonvoting delegate to the House of Representatives from American Samoa. Approved October 31, 1978 (P.L. 556; 92 Stat. 2078–2079).

Presidential Records Act of 1978. Provided that beginning with the 1981 term, most of the records of presidents and vice presidents would become public property at the end of their tenure in office. Allowed the president and vice president to retain personal diaries, journals, and materials relating to private political matters, their election, or the election of any other official. Allowed presidents to restrict access to certain materials for up to twelve years if the documents were related to national defense, foreign policy, or trade secrets, or were confidential correspondence with advisers, personnel files, or presidential appointment files. Approved November 4, 1978 (P.L. 95–591; 92 Stat. 2523–2528).

Bankruptcy Reform Act of 1978. Authorized Congress to create permanent bankruptcy judgeships as it did other judgeships. Provided that persons would be appointed to these judgeships by the president with the advice and consent of the Senate. These judges would replace the bankruptcy "referees," who had been appointed by federal district judges in each judicial district. Made the term of bankruptcy judges fourteen years, at an annual salary of $50,000, and provided them with jurisdictional authority identical to that of a district judge in handling bankruptcy cases. Approved November 6, 1978 (P.L. 95–598; 92 Stat. 2549–2688).

Revenue Act of 1978. Provided for $18.7 billion in tax cuts, including generous capital gains reductions for 4.3 million taxpayers. Provided taxpayers over age fifty-five a once-only complete capital gains tax exclusion for up to $100,000 in profits from the sale of personal residences. Approved November 6, 1978 (P.L. 95–600; 92 Stat. 2763–2946).

Energy Tax Act of 1978. Provided homeowners tax credits for installing insulation (15 percent of the first $2,000 spent) and solar, wind, or geothermal energy equipment (up to 30 percent on the first $2,000 and 20 percent on the next $8,000). Established a 10 percent investment credit for businesses installing specific types of energy conservation equipment and tax incentives for companies producing synthetic fuels from coal or other resources. Imposed "gas guzzler" tax penalties on automobiles whose fuel economy averaged less than eighteen miles per gallon. Approved November 9, 1978 (P.L. 95–618; 92 Stat. 3174–3205).

National Energy Conservation Policy Act. Required utilities to inform consumers about energy conservation devices, such as insulation and storm windows. Mandated efficiency standards for major home appliances, provided grants for hospitals and schools to install energy saving equipment, and offered subsidies to low-income families for home conservation investments. Approved November 9, 1978 (P.L. 95–619; 92 Stat. 3206–3288).

Power Plant and Industrial Fuel Use Act of 1978. Required new industries and utilities to build plants that would use coal, and authorized the secretary of energy to order some industries, on a case-by-case basis, to switch fuels. Required existing utility plants using gas or oil to switch to coal or other fuels by 1990. Authorized the secretary of energy to exempt industries and utilities from these requirements

under certain conditions. Approved November 9, 1978 (P.L. 95–620; 92 Stat. 3289–3349).

National Gas Policy Act of 1978. Allowed for price controls on newly discovered natural gas that limited increases to approximately 10 percent a year until 1985. Established special pricing categories that made industrial users bear the major portion of higher prices until the cost reached a certain level, when residential users assumed more of the burden. Prohibited the installation of new decorative outdoor gaslights, and required that existing lights be eliminated in three years. Approved November 9, 1978 (P.L. 95–621; 92 Stat. 3351–3411). Certain provisions of this act were subsequently held unconstitutional in *Process Gas Consumers Group v. Consumer Energy Council*, 463 U.S. 1216 (1983).

Notes

1. *Journal of the Executive Proceedings of the Senate* (Washington, D.C.: U.S. Government Printing Office, 1978), 120:206–218; 33 UST 1–38).

2. *Journal of the Executive Proceedings of the Senate,* 120:346–369; 33 UST 39–140.

Ninety-sixth Congress
January 3, 1979, to January 3, 1981

First session—January 15, 1979, to January 3, 1980
Second session—January 3, 1980, to December 16, 1980
(Administration of Jimmy Carter, 1977–1981)

Historical Background

The United States faced growing domestic and international challenges, including runaway inflation, rising interest rates, economic stagnation, and increasing instability in the Middle East.

In January 1979, Shah Mohammad Reza Pahlavi of Iran, America's longtime ally, was deposed in a fundamentalist Islamic revolution. In November 1979, Iranian militants seized the U.S. Embassy in Tehran and took sixty-six American diplomatic personnel and visitors hostage, demanding that the shah, then in the United States for medical reasons, be returned to Iran to stand trial. In response, President Jimmy Carter banned all imports of Iranian oil, froze Iranian assets in the United States, ordered most Iranian diplomats to leave the country, and asked the United Nations Security Council to condemn the holding of the hostages. Thirteen of the American hostages (five women and eight black men) were released later in the month and one in July 1980. Despite a variety of efforts, diplomatic and military, fifty-two American hostages were not released until January 20, 1981, shortly after Ronald Reagan assumed the presidency.

President Jimmy Carter surprised many late in 1978 with his announcement that the United States would establish diplomatic relations with the People's Republic of China on January 1, 1979. A principal concession in the agreement with mainland China called for the United States to withdraw recognition of the nationalist Republic of China on Taiwan and terminate its mutual defense treaty with that nation. Breaking diplomatic relations with Taiwan presented Congress with several legal, economic, and strategic concerns regarding future relations between the two countries. Congress placed U.S. relations with Taiwan on an unofficial basis and pledged that the United States would continue to sell arms to Taiwan as was needed for it to "maintain a sufficient self-defense capability."

Four months after the March 26, 1979, signing of an Egyptian-Israeli peace treaty, Congress approved a special $4.8 billion economic and military aid package for the two countries. This action fulfilled a promise President Carter had made during thirteen days of negotiations with Egyptian president Anwar Sadat and Israeli prime minister Menachem Begin at Camp David, the presidential retreat in Maryland's Catoctin Mountains.

Substantial reductions in nontariff barriers were made to create new jobs and increase exports, and legislation implemented the Panama Canal treaties concluded in 1977.

Legislation was also approved that nearly tripled the number of refugees eligible for entry into the United States each year and that increased the number of legal immigrants allowed as well. The new quotas, supporters reasoned, ensured greater equality in the treatment of refugees and gave the force of law to the nation's commitment to human rights.

Growing concern over an increasing number of resignations of U.S. Foreign Service officers prompted the first reorganization of the service in more than two decades and establishment of a new Senior Foreign Service. This limited cadre of the service's best officers was modeled after the Senior Executive Service instituted for the civil service in 1978.

Oil production restrictions imposed by the Organization of Petroleum Exporting Countries (OPEC), the international petroleum producers' cartel, after the shah of Iran's fall disrupted the supply of imported oil to the United States, leading to wide-scale shortages of gasoline and home heating oil and steeply escalating prices. The cutbacks pointed out how ill-prepared the country was to deal with such situations. A United States Synthetic Fuels Corporation was created to stimulate commercial development of synthetic fuels with initial funding of $20 million.

A milestone in federal education legislation was reached with the consolidation of 152 education-related programs into a newly established Department of Education. The remainder of the Department of Health, Education, and Welfare was redesignated the Department of Health and Human Services. After nearly a decade of efforts, a new psychological counseling program for Vietnam War veterans was finally realized.

Congress authorized $3.5 billion in federal loan guarantees for the financially ailing Chrysler Corporation, the tenth largest business enterprise and the third largest automaker in the United States. A restructuring of the financial industry was approved in what Treasury Secretary G. William Miller characterized as the "most important legislation dealing with banking and finance in nearly half a century." The measure removed most of the distinctions between banks and savings and loan associations, and it offered customers as well as financial institutions much greater flexibility. The largest tax ever imposed on an American industry became law with the Crude Oil Windfall Profits Tax Act of 1980. Reports of record profits by oil companies coupled with unhappiness over recurring oil shortages and rising energy prices triggered passage. It was expected to provide the federal government with revenues of about $227 billion over the ensuing decade.

Congress acted to overturn the 1968 U.S. Supreme Court decision in *Zurcher v. The Stanford Daily,* which allowed surprise police searches of news organizations. The Privacy Protection Act placed stringent limits on such searches of organizations engaged in First Amendment protected activities. Congress also revised its oversight responsibilities of the Central Intelligence Agency (CIA) and other U.S. intelligence-gathering operations, and it required the president to give Congress

prior notification of covert actions. The burden of federally imposed paperwork was reduced with passage of the Paperwork Reduction Act of 1980. Procedures for disciplining federal judges for misconduct, without taking the drastic step of impeachment, were approved some thirty years after the issue first began to be discussed.

Companies desiring to mine the rich deposits of minerals on the ocean floor were allowed to begin exploration activities while an international agreement governing such activities was being negotiated. President Carter achieved a major victory with the signing of two transportation bills that sharply curtailed federal regulation of the trucking and railroad industries. These measures, coupled with the 1978 deregulation of commercial airlines, Carter characterized as the culmination of his four-year effort to "get the Federal Government off the backs of private industry by removing needless, burdensome regulation which benefits no one and harms us all." *(Airline Deregulation Act of 1978, p. 364)*

Congress also completed work on two significant environmental bills. The first, achieved after a nine-year, bitterly fought struggle, restricted the commercial development of more than one hundred million acres of Alaskan lands by placing them within national parks, forests, refuges, and wilderness areas. The second established a $1.6 billion "superfund" to be used to clean up toxic waste.

"Possibly the most inspired piece of legislation to be enacted in America over the past half-century was the Bayh-Dole act of 1980," according to *The Economist's Technology Quarterly* magazine. "More than anything, this single policy measure helped to reverse America's precipitous slide into industrial irrelevance."[1] Prior to this law, the federal government retained ownership of intellectual property developed by small business and nonprofit organizations, such as universities, using federal funds. With the passage of the Bayh-Dole Act, the federal government ceded its ownership rights to those entities.

Continuing economic uncertainties and concern over the Americans held hostage in Iran proved troublesome for Jimmy Carter in his bid for a second term. Republican Ronald Reagan and his vice presidential pick, George H.W. Bush, won the election with a popular vote majority of 50.7 to 41.0 percent for Carter and

Vice President Walter F. Mondale. Reagan and Bush won 489 electoral votes to 49 for Carter and Mondale. Reagan's coattails and discontent with the Democratically controlled Congress carried the Republican Party to its first Senate majority in nearly three decades. Although the Republicans made substantial gains in the House, the Democrats retained control.

Major Acts

Taiwan Relations Act. Declared it the policy of the United States "to preserve and promote extensive, close, and friendly commercial, cultural, and other relations between the people of the United States and the people on Taiwan." Specified that the United States would conduct its programs, transactions, and other relations through the American Institute in Taiwan, a nonprofit corporation. Pledged continued arms sales to the Taiwan government, and provided that the United States would take actions—which were not specified—in the event of an attack on Taiwan. Assured that all trade, transportation, and cultural links between the two countries remain in effect. Approved April 10, 1979 (P.L. 96–8; 93 Stat. 14–21).

Veterans Health Care Amendments of 1979. Authorized the Veterans Administration (VA) to provide outpatient counseling and mental health follow-up services for Vietnam War veterans and dental care for prisoners of war or totally disabled veterans. Established VA pilot programs for preventive health care and treatment and rehabilitation for veterans suffering from alcohol or drug problems. Prohibited construction or renovation appropriations for VA facilities costing more than $2 million or annual rentals of more than $500,000, unless approved by the House and Senate Veterans Affairs Committees. Approved June 13, 1979 (P.L. 96–22; 93 Stat. 47–67).

Special International Security Assistance Act of 1979. Authorized the president to provide Israel $2.2 billion in long-term arms sales loans to upgrade the Israeli Defense Forces and an $800 million military grant. Provided Egypt $1.5 billion in arms sales loans, $200 million in economic assistance, and a $100 million long-term low-interest loan. Fulfilled American pledges made as a result of the Camp David Peace Accords. Approved July 20, 1979 (P.L. 96–35; 93 Stat. 89 93).

Trade Agreements Act of 1979. Streamlined procedures for resolving complaints considered under U.S. countervailing duty law. Provided for speedy investigations and imposition of penalties under both the countervailing duty law and antidumping statutes, which barred imports at prices below home market prices. Established a new system of customs valuation using the price paid for merchandise when sold for export to the United States as the primary method of assessing customs value. Approved July 26, 1979 (P.L. 96–39; 93 Stat. 144–317).

Panama Canal Act of 1979. Established the Panama Canal Commission, an agency of the federal government, to operate and maintain the Panama Canal through 1999, when Panama would assume complete control of the waterway. Required that funds collected by the commission, including the canal tolls, were to be deposited in the U.S. Treasury and all commission expenditures be authorized and appropriated by Congress. Created a special civil service system for canal employees, procedures for setting tolls on the canal, and procedures to be adhered to during the transition period. Approved September 27, 1979 (P.L. 96–70; 93 Stat. 452–500).

Department of Education Established. Consolidated 152 education-related programs in a new cabinet-level Department of Education. Prohibited the department from increasing federal control over education. Stressed the need for the new department to strengthen the commitment to equal educational opportunities; assist public and private groups in improving education; encourage increased involvement in education; promote improvements in the quality and usefulness of education through federally supported research; and improve the coordination, efficiency, and accountability of federal education programs. Provided that all references to the Department of Health, Education, and Welfare "in any law, rule, regulation, certificate, directive, instruction, or other official paper in force . . . be deemed to refer and apply to the Department of Health and Human Services, respectively, except to the extent such reference is to a function transferred" to the secretary of education or Department of Education. Approved October 17, 1979 (P.L. 96–88; 93 Stat. 668–696).

Chrysler Corporation Loan Guarantee Act of 1979. Established a loan guarantee board consisting of the secretary of the Treasury, the comptroller general, and the chairman of the Federal Reserve Board, plus two ex-officio members—the secretaries of labor and transportation—to administer $1.5 billion in loan guarantees to the Chrysler Corporation. Required the Chrysler Corporation to obtain $487.5 million in wage concessions, $625 million in domestic and foreign loans, $250 million in state and local aid, and $180 million in aid or credit from dealers and suppliers; sell off $350 million in assets; develop an energy plan; and issue $162 million in common stock. Approved January 7, 1980 (P.L. 96–185; 93 Stat. 1324–1337).

Refugee Act of 1980. Established new procedures for admitting refugees and resettling them once they arrived in the United States. Created an Office of U.S. Coordinator for Refugee Affairs within the Department of Health and Human Services to administer all domestic refugee aid programs. Redefined the term *refugee* to include persons from all parts of the world, not just communist countries or the Middle East, as earlier law had permitted. Increased the number of refugees and immigrants that were allowed to enter the country. Approved March 17, 1980 (P.L. 96–212; 94 Stat. 102–118).

Depository Institutions Deregulation and Monetary Control Act of 1980. Contained as separate titles the Monetary Control Act of 1980, the Depository Institutions Deregulation Act of 1980, and the Consumer Checking Account Equity Act of 1980, as well as provisions relating to the powers of thrift institutions, state usury laws, truth in lending simplification, amendments to national banking laws, regulatory simplification, and foreign control of U.S. financial institutions. Removed most federal regulatory restrictions between commercial banks and savings and loan associations. Approved March 31, 1980 (P.L. 96–221; 94 Stat. 132–193).

Crude Oil Windfall Profits Tax Act of 1980. Levied a tax on the "windfall profits" American oil companies received as a result of President Jimmy Carter's April 1979 decision to gradually end controls on oil prices. Taxed the windfall at a rate between 30 and 70 percent depending on the type of oil, date well was tapped, method of its production, and its producer. Provided that 25 percent of net revenues derived from the windfall profits tax would be used to assist low-income families, 60 percent for income tax reductions, and 15 percent for energy and transportation programs. Authorized tax incentives to businesses and homeowners for conserving or producing energy. Approved April 2, 1980 (P.L. 96–223; 94 Stat. 229–308).

Deep Seabed Hard Mineral Resources Act. Authorized U.S. mining companies to explore the ocean floor for minerals until an international seabed treaty was negotiated. Prohibited commercial exploitation of the seabed minerals prior to January 1, 1988, so American mining companies could follow any rules that might be set down when the United Nations completed action on a Law of the Sea Treaty. Provided that if an international agreement were not reached by 1988, the act would govern ocean mining activities by U.S. companies. Approved June 28, 1980 (P.L. 96–283; 94 Stat. 553–586).

Energy Security Act. Established a national goal of synthetic fuel production capability equivalent to at least 500,000 barrels of crude oil a day by 1987 and at least two million by 1992. Established a Synthetic Fuels Corporation to provide loan guarantees, purchase guarantees, and price guarantees to encourage private industry to develop synthetic fuels. Directed the president to set targets for the nation's energy consumption and production. Provided $20 billion for the immediate development of synfuels and as much as $68 billion in the future. Approved June 30, 1980 (P.L. 96–294; 94 Stat. 611–779).

Motor Carrier Act of 1980. Set promotion of competitive and efficient trucking service as a national policy. Made it easier for trucking firms to obtain new operating authority from the Interstate Commerce Commission (ICC). Directed the ICC to eliminate certain restrictions regarding routes, broaden categories of commodities that could be hauled by a carrier, and study and present recommendations on motor carrier service to smaller communities. Eased restrictions on truckers carrying agricultural products, livestock, and cargo of corporate family members, and regulated exempt commodities on the same truck. Allowed trucking firms greater pricing flexibility. Set insurance minimums for interstate trucks. Approved July 1, 1980 (P.L. 96–296; 94 Stat. 793–826).

Privacy Protection Act of 1980. Prohibited federal, state, and local law enforcement officers from using warrants to search the offices of newspapers and other news organizations engaged in First Amendment–protected activities, except in specific circumstances. Required the attorney general to issue procedural guidelines for federal officers in searching for materials held by individuals not suspected of a crime and not working on First Amendment issues. Approved October 13, 1980 (P.L. 96–440; 94 Stat. 1879–1883).

Staggers Rail Act of 1980. Established a national policy aimed at minimizing regulation of the railroads and allowing competition as well as demand for services to determine reasonable railroad rates. Allowed the Interstate Commerce Commission to determine rate reasonableness when a railroad dominated a market or rates exceeded an established flexibility zone. Repealed antitrust immunity from collectively set rates. Eased restrictions on mergers and abandonment of lines. Approved October 14, 1980 (P.L. 96–448; 94 Stat. 1895–1966). Certain provisions of this act were subsequently held unconstitutional in *Railway Labor Executives' Assn. v. Gibbons,* 455 U.S. 457 (1982).

Intelligence Authorization Act for Fiscal Year 1981. Authorized fiscal 1981 appropriations for intelligence and intelligence-related activities of the U.S. government and the intelligence community staff and for the Central Intelligence Agency Retirement and Disability Fund. Reduced the number of congressional committees entitled to receive notification of covert activities from eight to two—the House and Senate Intelligence Committees. Required the president to "fully inform the intelligence committees in a timely fashion of intelligence activities in foreign countries, other than activities intended solely for obtaining intelligence information," and to provide a statement of reasons in cases where prior approval is not sought for an intelligence activity. Approved October 14, 1980 (P.L. 96–450; 94 Stat. 1975–1982).

Judicial Councils Reform and Judicial Conduct and Disability Act of 1980. Granted the chief judge and governing council of each federal judicial circuit the authority to investigate complaints against judges and magistrates in that circuit and impose sanctions short of impeachment. Allowed discipline decisions to be appealed to the U.S. Judicial Conference, which was authorized to create a standing committee to review such complaints. Approved October 15, 1980 (P.L. 96–458; 94 Stat. 2035–2041).

Foreign Service Act of 1980. Reorganized and consolidated the various components of the Foreign Service of the United States to create more uniform statutory terms and conditions of Foreign Service employment. Simplified the personnel categories in the Foreign Service, emphasized and reaffirmed the Foreign Service requirement of worldwide service availability, and established a new Senior Foreign Service with appointments to be made on the basis of merit, instead of seniority. Increased the mandatory retirement age of Foreign Service personnel from sixty to sixty-five. Approved October 17, 1980 (P.L. 96–465; 94 Stat. 2071–2170).

Alaska National Interest Lands Conservation Act. Provided for the placement of 104.3 million acres of Alaskan land into federal conservation units and for the federal government to retain control of an additional 124 million acres. Imposed varying degrees of restrictions on the exploration of oil, minerals, and timber on these lands. Finalized the conveyance of lands mandated by the Alaska Statehood Act, and completed transfer of some forty-four million acres of land due to Alaska Natives under the 1971 Alaska Native Claims Settlement Act. Approved December 2, 1980 (P.L. 96–487; 94 Stat. 2371–2551). *(Alaska Admitted to the Union, p. 303; Alaska Native Claims Settlement Act, p. 344)*

Comprehensive Environmental Response, Compensation, and Liability Act of 1980 ('Superfund'). Established a $1.6 billion emergency "superfund" to clean up toxic waste sites. Authorized the federal government to establish regulations for cleaning up such sites. Provided that the fund would be financed over five years from fees imposed on the chemical and oil industries (86 percent) and appropriations (14 percent). Imposed a liability limit for cleanup costs and damage to natural resources at $50 million. Authorized the president to order whatever emergency cleanup action was necessary to protect the public health, welfare, or environment from toxic pollutants. Approved December 11, 1980 (P.L. 96–510; 94 Stat. 2767–2811). (*"Superfund" Amendments and Reauthorization Act of 1986, p. 388*)

Paperwork Reduction Act of 1980. Proposed "to reduce paperwork and enhance the economy and efficiency of the Government and the private sector by improving Federal information policy making." Established an Office of Information and Regulatory Affairs in the Office of Management and Budget (OMB) with the responsibility for overall direction of federal information policy, statistical activity, records management, automatic data processing, and clearance of new paperwork requirements. Required that the OMB director review the paperwork requirements of existing laws and recommend legislation to reduce paperwork. Approved December 11, 1980 (P.L. 96–511; 94 Stat. 2812–2826).

Bayh–Dole Act (Patent Rights in Inventions Made with Federal Assistance). Created a uniform patent policy among the many federal agencies that fund research, enabling small businesses and nonprofit organizations, including universities, to retain title to inventions made under federally-funded research programs. Approved December 12, 1980 (P.L. 96–517, Chap. 38; 94 Stat. 3019–3025).

Note

1. "Innovation's Golden Goose," *The Economist Technology Quarterly*, December 14, 2002, 3. (Insert in *The Economist* v. 365, no. 8303, December 14, 2002 between pp. 48–49.)

Ninety-seventh Congress
January 3, 1981, to January 3, 1983

First session—January 5, 1981, to December 16, 1981
Second session—January 25, 1982, to December 23, 1982
(First administration of Ronald Reagan, 1981–1985)

Historical Background

Minutes after Ronald Reagan, the oldest person to be elected president of the United States, took the oath of office, Iran released the fifty-two U.S. hostages seized at the American Embassy in Tehran in 1979. In his first State of the Union message, Reagan, as he had done during the presidential campaign, called for substantial cuts in both federal spending ($41 billion) and taxes (10 percent over three years). He also requested a $5 billion increase in defense expenditures.

On March 30, 1981, as he was leaving a Washington, D.C., hotel, Reagan was shot by would-be assassin John W. Hinckley Jr. Reagan was the eighth president to be the victim of an assassination attempt and was the only one of the five who were wounded to survive. While Reagan underwent a two-hour operation to remove a bullet from his left lung and during his ensuing recovery, Vice President George H. W. Bush and the cabinet decided not to invoke the Twenty-fifth Amendment. *(Twenty-fifth Amendment, p. 322)*

The proposed tax cut was the linchpin of the supply-side economic theory endorsed by the Reagan administration. Tax reductions, the White House contended, would stimulate increases in savings, productivity, and economic growth that would more than compensate for the attendant loss of revenue. To achieve Reagan's economic program, the Economic Recovery Tax Act of 1981 called for $749 billion in

business and individual tax cuts for fiscal years 1982–1986. The Omnibus Reconciliation Act of 1981 cut $35.2 billion in projected fiscal 1982 federal spending. Together, these measures, according to Reagan, represented "an end to the excessive growth in government bureaucracy and government spending and government taxing." The record $199.7 billion in defense appropriations the president signed into law in December 1981 provided the financial support for the defense buildup Reagan had advocated during the 1980 presidential campaign.

Although the economy entered a period of sustained growth later in the first Reagan administration, the federal budget ran deficits throughout the Reagan presidency. (When Reagan entered office, the federal debt was less than $1 trillion. When he left, it was approximately $2.6 trillion.) Meanwhile, the nation edged into a recession, characterized by widespread business failures and rising unemployment.

By the end of 1981, Congress was less willing to go along with the president's economic proposals. At the same time, Congress and the president began to make greater use of omnibus legislation (in the form of continuing resolutions and reconciliation legislation) to accommodate conflicting budget priorities. Omnibus budget reconciliation acts have since become a key vehicle for changing entitlement programs and revenue policies, and omnibus appropriation acts have been used from time to time to wrap up congressional action on regular appropriation measures providing discretionary spending.

On September 24, 1981, President Reagan called for a second round of spending cuts as part of a $16 billion deficit reduction plan. Subsequent negotiations between the White House and Capitol Hill over the proposed spending cuts stalled, and action on most fiscal 1982 appropriations bills went on for several months. By the end of 1981, Congress was less willing to go along with the administration's economic proposals. The president suffered his first significant budget defeat in September 1982, when Congress overrode his veto of a $14.2 billion supplemental appropriations bill, which he characterized as a budget-buster. A sizable portion of the measure ($6.1 billion) was for federal salary raises scheduled to go into effect on October 1. Furthermore, the veto override kept thousands of federal employees from being furloughed.

In the autumn of 1982, President Reagan reevaluated his opposition to a tax increase as federal deficits continued to mount and the country remained in its worst recession in half a century. In September, he signed a $98.3 billion tax increase and a three-year $17.5 billion spending reduction package and a reconciliation bill that cut anticipated federal spending for fiscal years 1983–1985 by an additional $13.3 billion. Legislation calling for the first increase in the federal gasoline tax since 1959 also became law. The revenues derived from the five-cent-a-gallon increase were to be used to repair deteriorating highways and transit systems, complete the National System of Interstate and Defense Highways, and provide jobs for some of the twelve million unemployed, a post–World War II high.

When the Professional Air Traffic Controllers Organization (PATCO) struck in August 1981, President Reagan fired the union's more than eleven thousand members and revoked PATCO bargaining rights for violating the law prohibiting work stoppages by federal employees. The president's action spelled the end for PATCO. When twenty-six thousand members of the Brotherhood of Locomotive Engineers struck in September 1982, Congress, at the president's request, passed legislation ordering the engineers back to work after a four-day walkout.

President Reagan achieved only partial success in converting federal elementary and secondary education programs into block grants controlled by state and local authorities. The ongoing effort to return responsibility for certain functions to the states, and to provide them greater flexibility in their use of federal grants, had been an important element of the 1980 Republican platform. Retained over the president's objections were an annual $3.5 billion program of

compensatory education for economically disadvantaged children and an annual $1 billion program for education of the handicapped.

To avoid having the Old Age and Survivors Insurance (OASI) fund become insolvent, Congress allowed the OASI to temporarily borrow money from the fiscally healthier Hospital Insurance and Disability Insurance trust funds.

Veterans were assured of medical coverage for ailments attributed to the use of Agent Orange in the Vietnam War and nuclear weapons in World War II. A small business loan program also was established for disabled Vietnam veterans. The 1981 case *McCarty v. McCarty* brought the issue of whether or not a court could consider military retired pay as marital property and order a division of it, to the highest court in the land—the U.S. Supreme Court. The Court ruled that retired pay could not be divided as community property without congressional authorization. Shortly afterwards, in 1982, Congress provided that authority by enacting the Uniformed Services Former Spouses' Protection Act.

The Job Training Partnership Act of 1982 was designed to improve the employment status of disadvantaged young adults, dislocated workers, and individuals facing barriers to employment. It charged the state governments with substantial responsibilities for implementing its provisions. Until 1998, the act was the largest single source of federal funding for workforce development activities when it was replaced by the Workforce Investment Act (P.L. 105–220).

The Nuclear Waste Policy Act, four years in the making, required the president to select two permanent underground waste repository sites by 1987 and 1990, respectively, and the Department of Energy to develop temporary storage facilities.

Deregulation of the intercity bus industry in September 1982 faced virtually none of the opposition that had accompanied the enactment of regulatory reform laws affecting the airline (1978), railroad (1980), and trucking (1980) industries. A principal concern was whether smaller towns would suffer decreased service as a result of deregulation, an issue supporters contended was addressed in the act. An accelerated deregulation of financial institutions, in legislation sponsored by Sen. Edwin J. (Jake) Garn of Utah and Rep. Fernand J. St. Germain of Rhode Island, provided emergency assistance to remedy an emerging crisis in the savings and loan industry.

A U.S. Court of Appeals for the Federal Circuit was created to handle appeals in patent cases and decisions by the Merit Systems Protection Board.

With widespread bipartisan support in both houses of Congress, the Voting Rights Act was extended for an additional twenty-five years. A perceived need to stimulate technological innovation in the United States resulted in a measure requiring federal agencies with sizable research budgets to earmark a certain percentage of their funds for small businesses.

Patent fees were restructured to assist individual inventors, small firms, and nonprofit organizations in meeting the rising costs associated with the patent process. These smaller entities were required to pay 50 percent of the costs of approving and maintaining patents, while larger firms remained responsible for 100 percent of the costs.

Soon after President Reagan took office, he used his executive authority to provide military aid to the pro–American provisional government in El Salvador. Late in 1981, Congress approved the president's action by supporting El Salvador with increased aid, provided it met a number of conditions intended to promote the restoration of a democratic government.

In 1982, Rep. Edward P. Boland of Massachusetts, chairman of the House Permanent Select Committee on Intelligence, offered successful amendments to both the fiscal 1983 intelligence authorization and defense appropriations acts that limited the president's authority to covertly aid the contra rebels fighting the leftist Sandinista government in Nicaragua. A third, more restrictive, Boland Amendment was enacted in 1984 as part of an omnibus spending bill. It barred aid to contras by the Central Intelligence Agency (CIA), the Department of Defense, "or other agencies involved in intelligence activities."

Duties on more than two hundred imported articles were reduced in a miscellaneous tariff bill, which was considered important to small business.

President Reagan and the GOP urged voters in the 1982 midterm congressional elections to "stay the course," while Democrats claimed the administration's policy initiatives had produced and deepened the recession. As a result of the elections, the Republicans retained control of the Senate and the Democrats strengthened their majority in the House.

Major Acts

Economic Recovery Tax Act of 1981. Provided for individual and business tax rate cuts; accelerated depreciation of capital investments; and increased saving incentives and tax credits for rehabilitation of old buildings, research and development expenses, oil producers, estate and gift transfers, two-earner couples, charitable contributions, child care, sale of residences, and foreign-earned income. Indexed tax brackets to account for inflation, and raised child care credit. Approved August 13, 1981 (P.L. 97–34; 95 Stat. 172–356).

Omnibus Budget Reconciliation Act of 1981. Reduced projected fiscal 1982 federal spending by $35.2 billion, fiscal 1983 spending by $44 billion, and fiscal 1984 spending by $51.35 billion. Revised food stamp and public assistance eligibility requirements, eliminated minimum Social Security benefits, reduced funding for subsidized housing, reduced school lunch subsidies, reduced federal Medicare payments to the states, and consolidated a number of health and education programs into block grants. Approved August 13, 1981 (P.L. 97–35; 95 Stat. 357–933).

Education Consolidation and Improvement Act of 1981. Consolidated a variety of federal elementary and secondary educational programs into a single block grant to states. Divided the block grant programs into three parts: basic skills (reading, writing, computation skills), educational improvement (instructional equipment, libraries, guidance), and special projects (arts, gifted and talented programs, ethnic heritage studies). Simplified administration and reporting requirements for financial assistance used to meet the special education needs of disadvantaged children. Continued separate programs for economically disadvantaged and handicapped children. Approved August 13, 1981 (P.L. 97–35, Title V, Subtitle D, Sec. 551–596; 95 Stat. 463–482).

Veterans Health Care, Training, and Small Business Loan Act of 1981. Provided medical treatment for Vietnam veterans suffering ailments linked to exposure to Agent Orange or other toxic herbicides or defoliants and for World War II veterans exposed to nuclear radiation. Extended GI Bill eligibility for Vietnam veterans through December 31, 1983. Authorized the Veterans Administration to establish a small business loan program for disabled Vietnam veterans. Approved November 3, 1981 (P.L. 97–72; 95 Stat. 1047–1063).

Restrictions on Military Assistance and Sales to El Salvador. Required the military-civilian provisional government in El Salvador to meet certain conditions before it could receive U.S. aid: obtain substantial control over its military forces, demonstrate a good-faith effort to begin discussions with opposing factions, comply with internationally recognized human rights, and investigate the murders of six American citizens in El Salvador that took place in December 1980 and January 1981. Approved December 29, 1981 (P.L. 97–113, Title VII, Sec. 728; 95 Stat. 1555–1557).

Fiscal 1982 Department of Defense Appropriations. Appropriated $199.7 billion in defense appropriations for fiscal year 1982, including $1.913 billion to develop the MX missile, $2.093 billion for the B-1 bomber program, $1,348 billion for M-1 tanks, $2.909 billion for three cruisers, and $5.298 billion for tactical aircraft. Approved December 29, 1981 (P.L. 97–114; 95 Stat. 1565–1594).

Social Security Act Amendments of 1981. Allowed the Old Age and Survivors Insurance fund to borrow money from the Hospital Insurance and Disability Insurance trust funds through December 31, 1982. Restored the $122 minimum monthly benefit for Social Security recipients that had been eliminated by the Omnibus Budget Reconciliation Act of 1991. Approved December 29, 1981 (P.L. 97–123; 95 Stat. 1659–1665).

Federal Courts Improvement Act of 1982. Created a U.S. Court of Appeals for the Federal Circuit by consolidating the functions of the U.S. Court of Customs and Patent Appeals with the appellate division of the U.S. Court of Claims. Provided that the new court would have jurisdiction over all federal district courts in patent cases, appeals of decisions by the Merit Systems Protection Board, and certain other types of cases. Created a trial-level U.S. Claims Court to handle cases previously handled by the trial division of the U.S. Court of Claims. Approved April 2, 1982 (P.L. 97–164; 96 Stat. 25–58).

Voting Rights Act Amendments of 1982. Extended key provisions of the Voting Rights Act of 1965 for twenty-five years. Permitted jurisdictions affected by the law's central enforcement mechanism (a requirement that federal approval be given for any change in voting laws or practices) to avoid the preclearance requirement by proving that they had not engaged in voter discrimination for at least a decade. Allowed blind, disabled, or illiterate voters to receive aid in voting, and bilingual election materials to be provided in areas with large language minority populations. Approved June 29, 1982 (P.L. 97–205; 96 Stat. 131–135). *(Voting Rights Act of 1965, p. 323)*

Small Business Innovation Development Act. Required federal agencies having annual research and development budgets in excess of $100 million to set aside a certain percentage of their research budget for small businesses. Approved July 22, 1982 (P.L. 97–219; 96 Stat. 217–221).

Patent and Trademark Fee Restructuring. Authorized the restructuring of U.S. patent fees. Required large firms to pay 100 percent of the costs of patent user fees; smaller firms, individual inventors, and non-profit organizations, 50 percent. Authorized $76 million for the Patent Office in fiscal 1983. Approved August 27, 1982 (P.L. 97–247; 96 Stat. 317–323).

Tax Equity and Fiscal Responsibility Act of 1982. Provided for $98.3 billion in tax cuts and a projected $17.5 billion reduction in spending for fiscal years 1983–1985. Approved September 3, 1982 (P.L. 97–248; 96 Stat. 324–707).

Uniformed Services Former Spouses' Protection Act. Authorized (but did not require) state courts to treat disposable military retired pay as a marital asset or as community property in a divorce proceeding. Provided a mechanism for a former spouse to enforce a retired pay property award by direct payments by the uniformed services (Army, Navy, Marines Corps, Air Force, and Coast Guard) from the member's retirement pay. Approved September 8, 1982 (P.L. 97–252, Title X; 96 Stat. 730–738).

Fiscal 1983 Supplemental Appropriations Act. Provided $14.2 billion in new budget authority, including

$6.1 billion for federal salary increases, and $5 billion in increased borrowing authority for the Commodity Credit Corporation. Presidential veto overridden by Congress. Became law without the president's signature September 10, 1982 (P.L. 97–257; 96 Stat. 818–876).

Bus Regulatory Reform Act of 1982. Directed the Interstate Commerce Commission (ICC) to reduce its regulation of intercity buses, and removed a number of restrictions placed on the industry. Established a rule for determining reasonable rates, and allowed carriers greater flexibility in raising or lowering rates. Required the ICC to ensure that federal reform initiatives were not nullified by state actions. Approved September 20, 1982 (P.L. 97–261; 96 Stat. 1102–1129).

Railway Labor-Management Dispute Act. Ended a four-day railroad strike by ordering the twenty-six thousand members of the Brotherhood of Locomotive Engineers back to work. Imposed a settlement recommended by the "Presidential Emergency Board Numbered 194," and barred the union from striking again before June 30, 1984. Approved September 22, 1982 (P.L. 97–262; 96 Stat. 1130–1131).

Job Training Partnership Act of 1982. Established federal assistance for a nationwide system of job training programs, administered jointly by state and local governments and the private sector, to prepare youth and unskilled workers for entry into the labor force and provide job training to the economically disadvantaged. Directed the states to provide services to "those who can benefit from, and are most in need of, such opportunities," and required that the results "be measured by the increased employment and earnings of participants and the reduction in welfare dependency." Approved October 13, 1982 (P.L. 97–300; 96 Stat. 1322–1399). In 1998, the act was replaced by the Workforce Investment Act. Approved August 7, 1998 (P.L. 105–220, Title I; 112 Stat. 936–1059).

Garn-St. Germain Depository Institutions Act of 1982. Established a three-year program for ailing federally insured financial institutions that allowed them to receive Federal Deposit Insurance Corporation (FDIC) and Federal Savings and Loan Insurance Corporation (FSLIC) notes equal to a set percentage of

their loss during two previous quarters. Expanded the powers of both the FDIC and the FSLIC to arrange for mergers of failed banks and savings and loans (S&Ls). Required that rate differentials between banks and S&Ls be phased out. Increased the percentage of assets S&Ls could invest in nonresidential real estate, consumer lending, inventory loans, and personal property. Approved October 15, 1982 (P.L. 97–320; 96 Stat. 1469–1548).

Boland Amendments. Prohibited U.S. assistance to paramilitary groups "for the purpose of overthrowing the Government of Nicaragua or provoking a military exchange between Nicaragua and Honduras." Approved September 27, 1982 (P.L. 97–269; classified annex to the Intelligence Authorization Act for Fiscal Year 1983). Prohibited funds from being "used by the Central Intelligence Agency or the Department of Defense to furnish military equipment, military training or advice, or other support for military activities, to any group or individual, not part of a country's armed forces, for the purpose of overthrowing the Government of Nicaragua or provoking military exchange between Nicaragua and Honduras." Approved December 21, 1982 (P.L. 97–377, Title VII, Sec. 793; 96 Stat. 1865).

Surface Transportation Assistance Act of 1982. Authorized $53.6 billion for highway construction and repairs and $17.76 billion for mass transit systems in fiscal years 1983–1986. Raised the federal gasoline tax from five cents a gallon to nine cents a gallon and earmarked 1 percent of the increased tax for mass transit. Established a new block grant for mass transit, and substantially increased truck taxes. Approved January 6, 1983 (P.L. 97–424; 96 Stat. 2097–2200).

Nuclear Waste Policy Act of 1982. Directed the president to submit a recommendation for two sites as permanent federal repositories for nuclear waste by March 31, 1987, and March 31, 1990. Authorized the Department of Energy to temporarily store spent fuel rods from nuclear power plants, high-level radioactive wastes produced by reprocessing spent fuel to extract plutonium, and spent nuclear fuel from civilian reactors. Exempted nuclear waste produced by defense programs from most of the bill's provisions. Approved January 7, 1983 (P.L. 97–425; 96 Stat. 2201–2263).

Ninety-eighth Congress
January 3, 1983, to January 3, 1985

First session—January 3, 1983, to November 18, 1983
Second session—January 23, 1984, to October 12, 1984
(First administration of Ronald Reagan, 1981–1985)

Historical Background

President Ronald Reagan in 1983 faced foreign policy challenges in the Middle East, the Caribbean, and Central America.

In April 1983, a terrorist car bombing killed fifty-one persons, including seventeen Americans, at the U.S. Embassy in Beirut, and in August two marines were killed and fourteen others wounded in Beirut. Lengthy negotiations between Congress and the White House preceded adoption of a resolution authorizing the president to keep U.S. troops in Lebanon as part of multinational peacekeeping forces for another eighteen months. Support for U.S. involvement in Lebanon began to erode in October, when the U.S. Marine Corps barracks in Beirut was destroyed by a truck loaded with explosives. The driver and 241 American servicemen were killed.

American forces landed on the Caribbean island nation of Grenada in October 1983. Within a few days, U.S. troops freed American students held hostage at a local medical school and ousted the government. The president justified U.S. intervention on the grounds that Grenada's government had been infiltrated by Cuban Communist operatives and that plans had been made to station Cuban forces on the island. He further cited pleas for American action by neighboring island states and a chaotic political situation.

The administration continued to provide military aid to the government of El Salvador, which was struggling against a leftist insurgency allegedly supplied from Nicaragua. The administration also continued to supply arms, training, and other assistance to antigovernment guerrillas (contras) battling against the leftist Sandinista government of Nicaragua. The Sandinistas, who overthrew the long-time Nicaraguan military dictatorship in 1979, initially enjoyed wide popular support. However, the Sandinistas' increasingly close ties to Cuba and alleged support of leftist guerrillas in El Salvador alarmed the Reagan administration, which feared Cuban and Soviet penetration in Central America.

Congress limited covert aid for the rightist rebels fighting to overthrow the leftist government in Nicaragua to $24 million in fiscal 1984. The administration had requested $36 million. Congress provided $64.8 million in military aid for El Salvador in fiscal 1984, instead of $86.3 million that the administration requested. Two fiscal 1984 supplemental spending measures provided an additional $131.8 million in emergency military aid for the U.S.–backed government in El Salvador. Administration lobbying for further aid for the Nicaraguan rebels was rejected.

Although President Reagan's request for a 10 percent increase in the fiscal 1984 defense budget was trimmed by half, he won authorization and funding for the initial production of the controversial MX intercontinental ballistic missile. Inaugurating a new era in manned space exploration, the FY1985 authorization bill for the National Aeronautics and Space Administration authorized the agency to begin research and development on a permanent manned space station, which President Ronald Reagan had proposed in his State of the Union message of January 1984.

Proponents of educational benefits for new recruits into the all-volunteer military were successful in gaining support for a three-year trial program. Special health programs were created to treat veterans suffering from post-traumatic stress disorder and drug and alcohol abuse. A mechanism was established to review compensation claims by Vietnam veterans exposed to Agent Orange and by World War II veterans exposed to radiation during atmospheric atomic tests or the occupation of Hiroshima and Nagasaki.

Efforts to enact a trade bill providing greater protection to import-sensitive industries were not realized. Instead, a more modest measure was approved that granted limited import relief for the copper, steel, and wire industries; reduced barriers to foreign investments and high-tech products; and authorized free trade talks with Israel. The American international shipping industry's antitrust immunity was expanded, and federal regulation of the industry was revised.

Two economic emergencies loomed—record unemployment amid a deep recession and a Social Security system nearing insolvency. In April 1983, legislation extensively revamping Social Security was approved. Two-thirds of the relief funds were allocated for various public work projects, while the remaining third was to be used for health, humanitarian, and social service assistance. Congress followed through on a bipartisan study commission's recommendations to ensure the solvency of the Social Security system for the foreseeable future.

In October 1984, a more than three-year controversy over administration efforts to rid the Social Security disability rolls of ineligible recipients ended with the 3.8 million Americans covered by the plan being given greater protection against arbitrary action. The Voting Accessibility for the Elderly and Handicapped Act of 1984 was the first federal statute to focus exclusively on the voting problems experienced by older and disabled citizens and the need for accessible voting facilities and procedures for them.

President Reagan provided much of the impetus for the most comprehensive anticrime measure in nearly two decades. New sentencing guidelines, restrictions on insanity defenses, increased penalties for drug offenses, and new anticrime grants for states were among its most prominent provisions. In response to a dramatic increase in auto thefts, legislation was enacted requiring manufacturers to place identification numbers on major auto components of car lines having the highest theft rate.

In the face of rapidly rising medical costs, the Reagan administration put forth a plan in 1983, which was signed into law, revising formulas for Medicare reimbursements to hospitals for services rendered by calculating Medicare costs in advance through fixed payments. The 1984 "Baby Doe case," in which a Bloomington, Indiana, infant was born with Down Syndrome and other medical problems and was allowed to die, prompted legislation to ensure that severely handicapped infants were not denied appropriate medical care. Included in the act were additional aid for child abuse prevention programs and state grants for victims of domestic violence.

New warnings on cigarette packages and advertisements were mandated after the Federal Trade Commission reported that the existing warning had ceased to be effective. Tobacco industry officials reportedly withdrew their opposition to the new labels under growing pressure for a higher cigarette tax if an agreement was not reached. A study was also authorized to advise Congress on the feasibility of developing a fire-safe cigarette. Legislation to make inexpensive generic drugs available to consumers also became a reality in 1984, following two decades of debate. A national computerized network was established to match transplant donors and recipients, and a task force was created to study the ethical, financial, and legal issues associated with such surgery.

The U.S. Supreme Court had ruled in 1982 that the Bankruptcy Act of 1978 gave bankruptcy judges too much power and was unconstitutional. A 1984 law provided federal district courts with authority over bankruptcy matters and appointment of bankruptcy judges. To strengthen procedures for collecting delinquent child support payments, states were required to establish laws for withholding money from the paychecks of individuals delinquent in child support payments and to place liens on their personal property. To improve retirement benefits for women, people were allowed to leave the workplace temporarily without losing pension rights.

A national policy for cable television was adopted to balance the rights of the cable television industry and those of cities granting cable franchises. It replaced a hodgepodge of local regulations that the industry argued restricted its growth. Manufacturers of semiconductor chips were afforded copyright-style protection for the first time, because of growing concern that innovations in the field were becoming increasingly vulnerable to industrial piracy.

Growing pressure by Mothers Against Drunk Drivers (MADD) and in response to growing pressure to curb drunken driving by young people, legislation was cleared pressuring states to raise the minimum drinking age to twenty-one. Although the bill did not require states to adopt a minimum drinking age, it did call for a percentage of federal highway funds to be withheld from states not enacting such a law. States also were provided financial incentives for instituting minimum sentences for drunken drivers.

Originally opposing the legislation, President Reagan signed a bill creating a tenth federal holiday to honor civil rights leader Rev. Dr. Martin Luther King Jr. Opponents of the holiday balked at the cost of another federal holiday—an estimated $18 million, and questioned whether King was worthy of such recognition. Civil rights activists had pushed for the holiday since King's assassination in 1968.

President Reagan and Vice President George H. W. Bush won a landslide reelection victory in 1984. They got 525 electoral votes to 13 for their Democratic rivals. The Democratic presidential nominee, former vice president Walter F. Mondale, made history by choosing a woman, Rep. Geraldine A. Ferraro of New York, as his vice presidential running mate. Congressional elections left the balance of power on Capitol Hill as it was—with the Republicans in control of the Senate and the Democrats in the majority in the House.

Major Acts

Social Security Amendments of 1983. Raised retirement age of Social Security recipients from sixty-five to sixty-seven by 2027, delayed retirees' annual cost-of-living adjustments (COLAs) six months, made future annual COLAs payable in January, and increased payroll taxes for employees and employers. Required Social Security coverage of all new federal employees, members of Congress, the president, the vice president, federal judges, and legislative branch personnel who chose not to join the Civil Service Retirement System by December 31, 1983. Prohibited state and local

governments from withdrawing from the system, and required employees of nonprofit organizations to join the system. Provided for Medicare hospitalization costs to be determined in advance, according to rates established for specific medical conditions. Approved April 20, 1983 (P.L. 98–21; 97 Stat. 65–172).

MX Missile (Fiscal 1984 Department of Defense Authorization). Authorized $187.5 billion for most Defense Department activities except military construction, military pay, and pensions, including $6.2 billion for ten B-1 bombers, $2.1 billion for production of twenty-one MX missiles, and a classified amount to continue development of the stealth bomber. Approved September 24, 1983 (P.L. 98–94; 97 Stat. 614–707).

Multinational Force in Lebanon Resolution. Declared that the "removal of all foreign forces from Lebanon is an essential United States foreign policy objective in the Middle East," and that continued American participation "in the multinational peacekeeping force in Lebanon" was necessary "to obtain withdrawal of all foreign forces in from Lebanon." Invoked the 1973 War Powers Resolution as of August 29, 1983; authorized the president to keep U.S. forces in Lebanon for up to eighteen months; and required the president to report at least every three months on the status of U.S. forces in Lebanon. Approved October 12, 1983 (P.L. 98–119; 97 Stat. 805–808). *(War Powers Resolution, p. 351)*

Martin Luther King Jr. Holiday. Made the third Monday in January a legal public holiday honoring slain civil rights leader Rev. Dr. Martin Luther King Jr. Approved November 2, 1983 (P.L 98–144; 97 Stat. 917).

Aid to El Salvador and Nicaragua. Limited military aid for El Salvador to $64.8 million, and covert aid for antigovernment rebels in Nicaragua to $25 million, in a fiscal 1984 continuing resolution. Approved November 14, 1983 (P.L. 98–151; 97 Stat. 966). Limited covert aid for antigovernment rebels in Nicaragua to $24 million, in the fiscal 1984 defense appropriations bill. Approved December 8, 1983 (P.L. 98–212, Title VII, Sec. 775; 97 Stat. 1452). Limited covert aid for antigovernment rebels in Nicaragua to $24 million, in the fiscal 1984 intelligence authorization bill. Approved December 9,

1983 (P.L. 98–215, Title I, Sec. 108; 97 Stat. 1475). Appropriated $61.75 million in emergency aid for El Salvador, in a fiscal 1984 supplemental appropriations bill. Approved July 3, 1984 (P.L. 98–332; 98 Stat. 284–285). Appropriated $70 million in military aid for El Salvador, in a fiscal 1984 supplemental appropriations measure. Approved August 22, 1984 (P.L. 98–396, Title XII; 98 Stat. 1405).

Shipping Act of 1984. Broadened antitrust immunity of U.S. maritime industry for setting prices and dividing routes and cargoes. Provided expedited Federal Maritime Commission (FMC) procedures for approving such actions. Updated federal maritime regulations. Authorized the FMC to levy civil penalties for violating the act. Approved March 20, 1984 (P.L. 98–237; 98 Stat. 67–91).

Bankruptcy Amendments and Federal Judgeship Act of 1984. Authorized federal district courts to appoint a total of 232 bankruptcy judges and to refer all proceedings arising under or relating to federal bankruptcy law. Limited the authority of bankruptcy judges to hear and rule on cases under Title 11 of the U.S. Code. Authorized twenty-four new federal appeals court judgeships and sixty-one federal district court judgeships. Stipulated specific procedures for debtor employers in rejecting labor contracts. Approved July 10, 1984 (P.L. 98–353; 98 Stat. 333–392).

Initial Funding for Manned Space Station. Authorized the National Aeronautics and Space Administration to begin research and development on a permanent manned space station. Provided $150 million to begin work on the station and emphasized that the station "may only be used for peaceful purposes." Approved July 16, 1984 (P.L. 98–361, Title I, Sec. 101(a)(2), Sec. 107; 98 Stat. 422, 425).

Surface Transportation Assistance Act Amendments of 1984. Authorized $126.5 million in fiscal 1985 and $132 million in fiscal 1986 for federal highway safety fund grants to the states. Stipulated that 5 percent of a state's federal highway funds would be withheld in fiscal 1987 and 10 percent in fiscal 1988, if it did not have a minimum drinking age of twenty-one. Required states to spend at least 8 percent of their highway safety funds to promote use of automobile child safety restraints. Provided incentive grants for states to enact mandatory sentences for drunken drivers. Approved July 17, 1984 (P.L. 98–363; 98 Stat. 435–439).

National Minimum Drinking Age Act. Authorized the Secretary of Transportation to withhold 5 percent of their federal highway funds (not including highway safety funds) in fiscal 1978 and 10 percent in fiscal 1999 in those states "in which the purchase or public possession . . . of any alcoholic beverage by a person who is less that twenty-one years of age is lawful." Provided for the funds to be restored if a state subsequently raised its drinking age to 21. Encouraged states, through incentive grants programs, to pass mandatory sentencing laws to combat drunk driving. Approved July 17, 1984 (P.L. 98–36, Sec. 158; 98 Stat. 437–439).

Child Support Enforcement Amendments of 1984. Required each state to enact laws that allowed employers to withhold a portion of a paycheck if an individual was delinquent in child support payments, impose liens against real or personal property for overdue support, establish expedited court procedures to secure such payments, and make such information available to credit agencies if the arrearage exceeded $1,000. Provided that the federal government would pay a substantial portion of the administrative costs for child support enforcement in fiscal years 1984–1990. Approved August 16, 1984 (P.L. 98–378; 98 Stat. 1305–1330).

Retirement Equity Act of 1984. Required employers to permit employees to participate in private pension plans at age twenty-one instead of age twenty-five, as previously permitted. Allowed workers to temporarily leave a job and then return without losing pension rights unless the break in service exceeded specified limits. Required pension plans to provide survivor benefits for the spouse of a wage earner who died before reaching minimum retirement age. Approved August 23, 1984 (P.L. 98–397; 98 Stat. 1426–1455).

Drug Price Competition and Patent Term Restoration Act of 1984. Directed the Food and Drug

Administration (FDA) to use expedited approval procedures for generic drugs once the patent on a drug expired. Authorized an additional exclusive marketing right and a patent extension of up to five years on new drugs subject to FDA approval. Approved September 24, 1984 (P.L. 98–417; 98 Stat. 1585–1605).

Voting Accessibility for the Elderly and Handicapped Act. Contained provisions expressly intended to "promote the fundamental right to vote by improving access for handicapped and elderly individuals to registration facilities and polling places for Federal elections." Required, as of 1986, that polling places used in national elections across the United States be physically accessible to the elderly and handicapped. Declared that when accessible facilities were not available, such voters could be reassigned, upon request, to the nearest accessible polling place, or state election officials would have to provide alternate means of accommodating them. Required states without mail or door-to-door registration to provide a reasonable number of accessible registration sites. Approved September 28, 1984 (P.L. 98–435; 98 Stat. 1678–1680).

Child Abuse Amendments of 1984. Authorized $158.1 million in fiscal years 1984–1987 for child abuse prevention programs, $5 million annually in fiscal years 1984–1987 to encourage the adoption of handicapped and hard-to-place children, and $63 million in fiscal years 1985–1987 for matching grants to assist states in providing services for victims of domestic violence and programs to prevent such abuse. Required that states establish procedures for dealing with cases in which appropriate medical care was withheld from severely handicapped infants with life-threatening conditions to qualify for federal child abuse funds. Approved October 9, 1984 (P.L. 98–457, Title II, Sec. 201–Sec. 204; 98 Stat. 1755–1757).

Social Security Disability Benefits Reform Act of 1984. Established new review standards for termination of Social Security disability benefits, including a requirement that the combined effects of an individual's multiple impairments be taken into consideration in determining eligibility. Allowed the secretary of health and human services to terminate an individual's benefits if his or her medical condition improved,

ability to work was regained, impairment was not as serious as originally diagnosed, or personal behavior was suspect (were working, uncooperative, or could not be found). Approved October 9, 1984 (P.L. 98–460; 98 Stat. 1794–1813).

Comprehensive Crime Control Act of 1984. Established a seven-member, presidentially appointed commission to prepare uniform sentencing guidelines. Restricted use of insanity defense. Created a National Drug Enforcement Policy Board to coordinate federal drug enforcement activities, and increased the punishment for drug offenses. Created a block grant for state, local, and private nonprofit anticrime programs. Revised the witness protection program. Provided mandatory terms and fines for repeat state offenders as well as individuals guilty of credit card fraud, computer fraud, labor racketeering, terrorism, and trademark counterfeiting. Approved October 12, 1984 (P.L. 98–473, Title II; 98 Stat. 1976–2040).

Comprehensive Smoking Education Act. Required that four different labels be rotated periodically on cigarette packages and advertisements warning smokers that cigarette smoking causes cancer, heart disease, emphysema, and other health problems. Approved October 12, 1984 (P.L. 98–474; 98 Stat. 2200–2205).

National Organ Transplant Act. Authorized $2 million annually for a national computerized network to match organ donors and recipients and $25 million for fiscal years 1985–1987 for local and regional agencies to participate in the network. Established a Division of Organ Transplantation within the Department of Health and Human Services. Created a task force to study the ethical, financial, and legal issues associated with organ transplant surgery. Prohibited the sale or purchase of human organs for transplantation. Approved October 19, 1984 (P.L. 98–507; 98 Stat. 2339–2348).

Veterans Educational Assistance Act of 1984. Established a three-year test program under which new recruits entering military service between June 1985 and July 1988 could contribute $100 a month for their first year of service and be guaranteed at least $300 a month in education benefits for three years.

Established a separate program for enlistees in National Guard or reserve forces of $140 per month in education expenses for three years. Approved October 19, 1984 (P.L. 98–525, Title VII; 98 Stat. 2553–2572).

Veterans Health Care Act of 1984. Authorized the Veterans Administration to establish treatment programs for Vietnam veterans suffering from post-traumatic stress disorder and treatment guidelines for veterans suffering from drug and alcohol abuse and dependency. Approved October 19, 1984 (P.L. 98–528; 98 Stat. 2686–2696).

Veterans Dioxin and Radiation Exposure Compensation Standards Act. Required the Veterans Administration to establish a compensation review and payment system for Vietnam veterans who were exposed to dioxin (Agent Orange) between August 5, 1964, and May 7, 1975, and World War II veterans who were exposed to low-level ionizing radiation during atmospheric atomic weapons tests or who had served in occupied Hiroshima or Nagasaki, Japan, prior to July 1, 1946. Approved October 24, 1984 (P.L. 98–542; 98 Stat. 2725–2734).

Motor Vehicle Theft Law Enforcement Act of 1984. Required domestic and foreign automobile manufacturers to place identification numbers on fourteen parts of vehicle lines with high theft rates. Established penalties for trafficking in stolen auto parts and removing vehicle identification numbers. Approved October 25, 1984 (P.L. 98–547; 98 Stat. 2754–2773).

Cable Communications Policy Act of 1984. Limited the authority of cities to regulate basic cable television rates to two years, capped franchise fees a city could charge cable television companies, and prohibited cities from demanding that specific programs be shown. Permitted cities to grant and renew cable franchises, require that cable companies reserve channels for educational and public service uses, and ban programs judged obscene. Prohibited local television and telephone companies from owning local cable franchises unless permitted to do so by the Federal Communications Commission. Approved October 30, 1984 (P.L. 98–549; 98 Stat. 2779–2806).

Cigarette Safety Act of 1984. Created a fifteen-member group, four members of whom were to be from the Tobacco Institute, to advise Congress within two-and-a-half years on the possibility of producing a fire-safe cigarette that would be less likely to ignite household furnishing. Delegated the lead role in the study to the Consumer Product Safety Commission with prominent roles for the U.S. Fire Administration and the Department of Health and Human Services. Approved October 30, 1984 (P.L. 98–567; 98 Stat. 2925–2927).

Trade and Tariff Act of 1984. Permitted administration officials to begin discussions with Israel on the establishment of a free trade agreement between Israel and the United States. Granted the U.S. trade representative limited power to negotiate free trade agreements. Reduced barriers to American investment abroad, trade in high-technology items, and the U.S. wire trade. Authorized the president to negotiate voluntary copper import reductions and enforce voluntary restraints on steel imports. Approved October 30, 1984 (P.L. 98–573; 98 Stat. 2948–3050).

Semiconductor Chip Protection Act of 1984. Created a new section in the copyright title of the U.S. Code (Title 17) to protect manufacturers of semiconductor chips from unauthorized copying for ten years. Approved November 8, 1984 (P.L. 98–620, Title III; 98 Stat. 3347–3356).

Ninety-ninth Congress
January 3, 1985, to January 3, 1987

First session—January 3, 1985, to December 20, 1985
Second session—January 21, 1986, to October 18, 1986
(Second administration of Ronald Reagan, 1985–1989)

Historical Background

President Ronald Reagan's second inaugural address stressed the broad themes that dominated his first term—reducing the size and cost of the federal government and strengthening the defense forces—but generally touched only lightly or not at all on many of the issues that dominated the agenda of Congress over the next two years. "Major elements of the Congress' legacy" in 1985–1986, *Congressional Quarterly* observed, "did not become apparent until the end."

As members worked to seize the legislative initiative from the White House, the most intense confrontations in Congress repeatedly occurred over budget-related issues. In 1985 and 1986, a total of eight short-term stopgap funding bills were needed to keep the government running until long-term omnibus funding bills could be enacted.

On December 12, 1985, President Reagan signed the Gramm-Rudman-Hollings Act, an unprecedented effort to achieve a balanced budget within five years. The legislation, sponsored by Sens. Phil Gramm of Texas, Warren B. Rudman of New Hampshire, and Ernest F. Hollings of South Carolina, called for automatic spending cuts if each year's deficit ceiling was not achieved through the normal legislative process. Despite assertions by opponents that the measure was neither wise nor workable, anxiety over the political and economic consequences of continued deficit spending brought about quick adoption of the measure.

Many of the act's provisions were finalized in private by congressional leaders of both parties, without the benefit of committee hearings or markups. The United States in 1985 for the first time since World War I became a debtor nation, owing more to other countries than it was owed by foreign nations.

A $2 billion public stock offering of the government's 85 percent share of Conrail, the publicly owned freight railroad established in 1973, was provided in the Omnibus Budget Reconciliation Act of 1986. By selling Conrail, Congress was able to avoid spending cuts that might have been required under the Gramm-Rudman-Hollings Act.

Enactment of the Tax Reform Act of 1986, the first comprehensive reform of the Internal Revenue Code in more than three decades, capped more than two years of work by Congress, the Treasury Department, and the White House.

Congress enacted the most sweeping reorganization of the U.S. military establishment since the creation of the Department of Defense (DOD) in 1947. The plan, in legislation sponsored by Sen. Barry Goldwater of Arizona and Rep. William F. Nichols of Alabama, called for a shift in bureaucratic power within DOD from the separate armed services to senior officials—the Joint Chiefs of Staff (JCS) and the commanders in chief of combat forces in the field—who would coordinate the services. The JCS chairman was made the principal military adviser to the president and secretary of defense and was given responsibility for overall strategic planning, developing plans for military contingencies, and producing budget estimates that met JCS priorities. In separate action, absentee voting assistance for service personnel, their dependents, and U.S. citizens residing abroad was enhanced. Action also was completed on legislation to reduce the cost of the military retirement system by an estimated $3.2 billion annually. Under the new system, annuities for military personnel who left active duty with less than thirty years of service were reduced substantially. *(National Security Act, p. 279)*

While Congress did not provide humanitarian aid to UNITA (Union for Total Independence for Angola), a rebel group that was battling the leftist government of Angola, it did repeal the Clark Amendment, which barred U.S. intervention in that country. An additional $27 million in nonmilitary aid for anti-leftist contra rebels in Nicaragua was approved in 1985. The next year, President Reagan persuaded Congress to renew military aid to the contras. Congress in 1986 barred the Central Intelligence Agency from using secret contingency funds to aid the contras unless Congress specifically authorized it. In November 1986, after first denying it, Reagan admitted that his administration sold arms secretly to Iran, which the president had described as a terrorist nation, in hopes of freeing American hostages being held in the Middle East. Furthermore, some of the profits from the sales were illegally diverted to the Nicaraguan contras. Lawrence E. Walsh in December 1986 was named independent counsel to conduct an inquiry into the matter. A congressional investigation into the Iran-contra affair would begin in 1987.

President Reagan in April 1986 ordered air strikes against military installations in Libya, which he had charged with being the strongest supporter of terrorist attacks against Americans abroad. The bombardment renewed the debate over the role Congress should play in initiating armed conflicts, but no further action was taken on Capitol Hill.

Congress established a certification process for implementation of the first nonweapons-related nuclear cooperation agreement between the United States and a communist country. The U.S.-China nuclear cooperation agreement allowed the United States to sell nuclear fuel, equipment, and technology to China. Congress barred licensing or approval of nuclear transfers until thirty days after the president sent Congress a certification that China had met certain conditions. The required certifications were not issued until January 1998.

In February 1988 Congress added the United States to the many nations that imposed economic sanctions on the white minority government in South Africa for its failure to end apartheid. It overrode President Reagan's veto to enact the legislation. Congress rejected his assertion that the sanctions would "hurt the very people they are intended to help," arguing that he was not listening to broad public sentiment favoring such action. Immigration laws underwent their first comprehensive revision in more than three decades in response to widespread public concern of growing illegal immigration.

American agriculture in 1985 faced a financial crisis due to trade imbalances, rising interest rates, and declining land values. Legislators were confronted with the challenge of trying to address the plight of the American farmer while finding a way to reduce the rapidly increasing cost of federal farm programs. Congress reduced federal price support rates for major farm commodities, created new export incentives, and slightly reduced direct income subsidies.

Title X of the Consolidated Omnibus Budget Reconciliation Act of 1985, commonly referred to as COBRA, required employers to allow qualified workers who lost their health benefits the opportunity for a temporary extension of coverage under certain circumstances. Legislation barring most employers from setting a mandatory retirement age was applauded by senior citizen groups. Business groups claimed that it would disrupt turnover cycles and slow the advancement and hiring of younger workers. After three years and lengthy House-Senate conference negotiations, a new federal employee retirement plan was approved in June 1986. A key feature of the system was an optional thrift saving plan that allowed employees to contribute up to 10 percent of their annual income to tax-deferred investments and required the government to contribute up to an additional 5 percent.

An extensive overhaul of the Safe Drinking Water Act of 1974 significantly strengthened protection for the nation's drinking water. The five-year reauthorization established a timetable for limiting contaminants in water supplies, required that states use the "best available technology" to meet contaminant standards set by the Environmental Protection Agency, and mandated that states protect underground water supplies. President Reagan signed a $8.5 billion, five-year "superfund" hazardous waste cleanup bill after he was urged to do so by several of his advisers, as well as

Republican congressional leaders. Reagan had threatened to veto the fivefold increase in cleanup funds because it exceeded his proposal by more than $3 billion and imposed new taxes, some of which he believed were inappropriate.

Passage of the Water Resources Development Act of 1986, the first major water projects bill in a decade, signified a major change in water resource planning. Previously, the bulk of the construction costs of Army Corps of Engineers projects were borne by the federal government. The new direction called for non-federal interests (state, local, and private entities) to bear more of the financial burden through user financing and cost-sharing. The act initiated the sharing of construction costs on all types of civil works projects.

Extensive lobbying by the National Rifle Association (NRA) resulted in a revision of the federal gun control law that was enacted following the 1968 assassinations of the Rev. Dr. Martin Luther King Jr. and Senator Robert F. Kennedy of New York. The new act lifted the ban on the interstate sale of rifles and shotguns and barred the establishment of a national firearms registration plan. Comprehensive antidrug legislation was enacted against a background of growing national concern over illegal drug abuse. It provided increased penalties for drug-related offenses; additional drug enforcement, eradication, and interdiction activities; and new education, treatment, and rehabilitation programs. Emergence of a variety of new forms of communication technology necessitated a broadening of privacy protection to cover electronic mail, cellular phones, private satellite transmissions, and paging devices.

In the November 1986 midterm congressional elections, Democrats regained control of the Senate and retained the majority in the House.

Major Acts

Repeal of the Clark Amendment. Repealed "Section 118 of the International Security and Development Act of 1980 (prohibiting assistance for military or paramilitary operations in Angola)." Approved August 8, 1985 (P.L. 99–83, Title VIII, Sec. 811; 99 Stat. 264). The Clark Amendment was enacted in 1976 and was sponsored by Sen. Dick Clark of Iowa.

Aid to Nicaraguan Contras. Appropriated, in a fiscal 1985 supplemental appropriations measure, $27 million in nonmilitary aid for the contra rebels fighting the Nicaraguan government. Funds could be distributed by any U.S. agency except the Department of Defense and Central Intelligence Agency. Approved August 15, 1985 (P.L. 99–88, Title I, Chapter V; 99 Stat. 324–325). Barred, in the fiscal 1987 intelligence authorization bill, the Central Intelligence Agency (CIA) from using secret contingency funds to aid the contras unless Congress specifically authorized it or if money was reprogrammed or diverted from other CIA programs. Approved October 27, 1986 (P.L. 99–569, Title I, Sec. 106; 100 Stat. 3191). Provided, in fiscal 1987 continuing appropriations legislation, $70 million in military aid and $30 million in nonmilitary aid for contra guerrillas in Nicaragua. Approved October 30, 1986 (P.L. 99–591, Title II, Sec. 206, 208; 100 Stat. 3341-1–3341-300).

Gramm-Rudman-Hollings Act (Balanced Budget and Emergency Deficit Control Act). Amended the Congressional Budget and Impoundment Control Act of 1974. Required that the federal budget deficit not exceed $171.9 billion in fiscal 1986, $144 billion in fiscal 1987, $108 billion in fiscal 1988, $72 billion in fiscal 1989, $36 billion in fiscal 1990, and zero in fiscal 1991. Required the president to issue an emergency sequestration order setting in place automatic across-the-board spending cuts of a fixed percentage in nonexempt programs to achieve deficit targets if regular budget and appropriation actions failed to achieve deficit ceilings. Exempted from spending cuts were Social Security, interest on the national debt, and a number of programs for the poor and the elderly. Approved December 12, 1985 (P.L. 99–177, Title II; 99 Stat. 1038–1101). Certain provisions of the act were subsequently held unconstitutional in *Bowsher v. Synar,* 478 U.S. 714 (1986). *(Congressional Budget and Impoundment Control Act of 1974, p. 352)*

Nuclear Cooperation between the United States and China. Established a certification process for implementation of a nuclear cooperation agreement between the United States and the People's Republic of China signed July 23, 1985. Prohibited the United States from selling to China nuclear material, facilities, or components until thirty days after the president certified to Congress that arrangements had been made to assure the nuclear supplies provided were intended for solely "peaceful purposes"; China had provided "additional information concerning its nuclear nonproliferation policies" assuring it was not in violation of the Atomic Energy Act of 1954; and a report had been submitted to Congress "detailing the history and current developments" of China's "nonproliferation policies and practices." Approved December 16, 1985 (P.L. 99–183; 99 Stat. 1174–1175). *(Atomic Energy Act of 1954, p. 294)*

Food Security Act of 1985. Significantly reduced federal price supports and slightly reduced direct income subsidies to farmers for fiscal years 1986–1990. Authorized $169.2 billion for agricultural price supports, direct income subsidies, the Food for Peace program, food stamps, soil conservation programs, agricultural research, and federal farm credit agencies. Exempted certain Department of Agriculture export financing programs from requirements that half of specified cargoes be shipped on U.S.-flag vessels. Approved December 23, 1985 (P.L. 99–198; 99 Stat. 1354–1660).

Private Health Insurance Continuation Coverage under COBRA. Amended the Internal Revenue Code and Public Health Service Act to deny income tax deductions to employers for contributions to a group health plan unless such plan met certain continuing coverage requirements. Required employers with 20 or more employees who maintain group health insurance plans (including medical, dental, and vision coverage) to offer qualified employees, spouses, and dependent children the option of continuing coverage at their own expense for a limited period of time when an employee lost eligibility for company-provided benefits. Approved April 7, 1986 (P.L. 99–272, Title X; 100 Stat. 222–236).

Firearms Owners' Protection Act. Lifted ban on interstate sale of rifles and shotguns, allowed gun owners to transport firearms across state lines, barred establishment of a firearms registration plan, relieved gun dealers from having to record transactions involving their personal collections, and relaxed dealer licensing requirements. Restricted conditions under which federal officials could seize firearms or ammunition. Barred certain categories of people from transporting or owning firearms, and banned machine guns. Approved May 19, 1986 (P.L. 99–308; 100 Stat. 449–461). Subsequent revisions broadened the licensing and record-keeping requirements of gun dealers to include individuals engaged "in the regular and repetitive purchase and disposition of firearms for criminal purposes or terrorism" irrespective of whether it is done for profit; required gun dealers to keep records of transactions involving their personal collections; and narrowed the interstate transportation of a gun to those instances in which it is allowed by state law. Approved July 8, 1986 (P.L. 99–360; 100 Stat. 766–767).

Federal Employees' Retirement System Act of 1986. Created a new Federal Employees' Retirement System (FERS) to provide retirement benefits for all federal civilian employees including congressional staff and postal workers hired after December 31, 1983. Allowed employees covered by both the Civil Service Retirement System and Social Security to transfer to the new system. Allowed FERS employees to contribute up to 10 percent of their annual salary to an optional tax-deferred thrift savings plan, and required the government to contribute up to 5 percent of annual pay to the plan. Provided specified survivor benefits and disability benefits. Approved June 6, 1986 (P.L. 99–335; 100 Stat. 514–632).

Safe Drinking Water Act Amendments of 1986. Amended and reauthorized the Safe Drinking Water Act of 1974 for five years. Directed the Environmental Protection Agency to establish maximum contaminant level standards for water supplies and to assure that states use the "best available technology" to meet the standards. Established a schedule for regulating eighty-three toxic pollutants within three years. Required each state to develop a program for protecting underground water supplies. Authorized appropriations for technical assistance and grants. Established criminal penalties for tampering with water supplies. Approved June 19, 1986 (P.L. 99–339; 100 Stat. 642–667). *(Safe Drinking Water Act, p. 353)*

Military Retirement Reform Act of 1986. Reduced the annuity for military personnel who retired after twenty years of active duty from 50 percent to 40 percent of an individual's basic pay in their three highest-paid years. Provided for annuities to be increased annually by a percentage equal to the annual increase in the consumer price index minus 1 percentage point. Retained the formula for retirement after thirty years of active duty—75 percent of base pay averaged over the highest three years. Approved July 1, 1986 (P.L. 99–348; 100 Stat. 682–705).

Uniformed and Overseas Citizens Absentee Voting Act. Required states to allow military personnel, their dependents, and U.S. citizens living abroad "to use absentee registration procedures and to vote absentee ballot in general, special, primary, and runoff elections." Approved August 28, 1986 (P.L. 99–410; 100 Stat. 924–930).

Goldwater-Nichols Department of Defense Reorganization of 1986. Designated the chairman of the Joint Chiefs of Staff as chief military adviser to the president and secretary of defense. Made the chairman responsible for overall strategic planning, planning for certain military contingencies, and budget estimates for the armed services. Provided for a vice chairman of the Joint Chiefs of Staff to carry out duties assigned by the chairman. Consolidated a number of duplicative functions handled by parallel civilian and military officials in the army, navy, and air force. Approved October 1, 1986 (P.L. 99–433; 100 Stat. 992–1075b).

Comprehensive Anti-Apartheid Act of 1986. Imposed a series of economic sanctions against South Africa, including barring importation of that country's agricultural products, coal, steel, textiles, uranium, and uranium ore; barred U.S. loans to South African businesses; revoked the right of government-owned South African Airways to land in the United States; and prohibited American airlines from carrying passengers to and from South Africa. Encouraged the South African government to suspend the state of emergency imposed in July 1986, release African National Congress leader Nelson Mandela and other political prisoners, allow South African citizens to form political parties, establish a timetable for eliminating apartheid, and end military sanctions against neighboring countries. Presidential

veto overridden by Congress. Became law without the president's signature October 2, 1986 (P.L. 99–440; 100 Stat. 1086–1116).

"Superfund" Amendments and Reauthorization Act of 1986. Created a $8.5 billion fund for fiscal years 1987–1991 for cleanup of the most dangerous hazardous waste sites. Established a schedule for the Environmental Protection Agency to begin remedial cleanup actions on the 375 worst sites within five years. Called for the detoxicating of wastes whenever possible, instead of burying them in landfills. Authorized new programs to clean up leaking underground tanks used to store gasoline or chemicals. Required the governor of each state to develop plans for dealing with chemical spill disasters, and required industries to provide local communities with information on chemicals they handled and dumped. Established new taxes on petroleum, raw chemicals, and corporate income. Approved October 17, 1986 (P.L. 99–499; 100 Stat. 1613–1782).

Electronic Communications Privacy Act. Expanded privacy protection to cellular phones, computer transmissions, private satellite transmissions, paging devices, and electronic mail. Exempted radio communications available to the public, the radio portion of cordless telephone communication, communications between amateur radio operators, general mobile radio services, marine and aeronautical communications, public safety communications, and specified satellite transmissions. Approved October 21, 1986 (P.L. 99–508; 100 Stat. 1848–1873).

Conrail Privatization Act. Required the "Secretary of Transportation, in consultation with the Secretary of the Treasury and the Chairman of the Board of Directors" of Conrail to "retain the services of investment banking firms to serve jointly and be compensated equally as the co-lead managers" to coordinate and administer a public stock offering of the government's 85 percent share of Conrail. Called for Conrail to transfer $200 million to the secretary of the Treasury within thirty days of enactment of this act and up to an additional $100 million before sale of Conrail was finalized. Approved October 21, 1986 (P.L. 99–509, Title IV; 100 Stat. 1892–1911).

Tax Reform Act of 1986. Instituted a two-bracket tax system of 15 and 28 percent to replace the existing fourteen tax brackets (fifteen for single taxpayers), which ranged from 11 to 50 percent. Reduced the corporate rate on taxable income over $75,000 from 46 to 34 percent. Provided that corporate income up to $50,000 would be taxed at a rate of 15 percent, income from $50,000 to $75,000 at 25 percent, and above $335,000 at 34 percent. Reformed the tax code by curtailing or eliminating dozens of tax breaks. Increased personal exemptions for taxpayers, reinstated the standard deduction, eliminated the state sales tax deduction, required that medical costs exceed 7.5 percent of adjusted gross income before they could be deducted instead of 5 percent, taxed unemployment benefits as income, provided for phase out of deductions for consumer interest except for mortgages, and repealed income averaging. Approved October 22, 1986 (P.L. 99–514; 100 Stat. 2085–2963).

Anti-Drug Abuse Act of 1986. Provided stiffer penalties for drug-related offenses, created new offenses, and expanded enforcement efforts in the United States as well as in drug-producing countries. Authorized an additional $60 million for the Drug Enforcement Administration in fiscal 1987, $124 million for the federal prison system in fiscal 1987, and $230 million annually for state and local drug enforcement efforts in fiscal years 1987–1989. Created a Drug-Free Schools and Communities Program within the Department of Education and an Office of Substance Abuse Prevention within the Alcohol, Drug Abuse, and Mental Health Administration. Approved October 27, 1986 (P.L. 99–570; 100 Stat. 3207-1–3207-192).

Age Discrimination in Employment Amendments of 1986. Prohibited most employers from setting mandatory retirement ages. Exempted college faculty, firefighters, and police from the provisions of the act for seven years. Approved October 31, 1986 (P.L. 99–592; 100 Stat. 3342–3345).

Immigration Reform and Control Act of 1986. Made it unlawful for employers to knowingly recruit or hire illegal immigrants. Required that employers verify the status of an individual by examining either certificate of U.S. citizenship or naturalization, a passport, or resident alien card. Required that employees attest in writing that they are authorized to work in the United States. Established civil and criminal penalties for violating provisions of the act. Allowed temporary residence status to be given to illegal aliens who had resided continuously in the United States since before January 1, 1982, and aliens who had lived in the United States at least three years and had worked at least ninety days in American agriculture each year. Approved November 6, 1986 (P.L. 99–603; 100 Stat. 3359–3445).

Water Resources Development Act of 1986. Authorized $16 billion for 377 different water projects including dams, ports, waterways, flood control, and recreation projects, of which the federal government was to pay approximately $12 billion. Established new cost-sharing requirements for planning, construction, and operation and maintenance of projects for navigation, flood control, and other purposes, and also established user fees, guaranteeing that nonfederal interests played an important role in planning, financing, and maintaining water projects. Approved November 17, 1986 (P.L. 99–662; 100 Stat. 4082–4273).

One Hundredth Congress
January 6, 1987, to January 3, 1989

First session—January 6, 1987, to December 22, 1987
Second session—January 25, 1988, to October 22, 1988
(Second administration of Ronald Reagan, 1985–1989)

Historical Background

House and Senate select committees in 1987 investigated the Iran-contra affair, the covert administration operation that involved the sale of arms to Iran and the illegal diversion of the proceeds to the anti-Communist contras in Nicaragua. In a joint report released November 18, 1987, the committees concluded that President Ronald Reagan had permitted "a cabal of zealots" to conduct important aspects of the administration's foreign policy and criticized the White House for "secrecy, deception and disdain for the rule of law." However, the political impact of the committees' findings was blunted from the start because the congressional leaders had decided before the select committees began their investigations that impeachment of the president would not be considered an option. Independent counsel Lawrence E. Walsh secured the convictions of two key administration officials—former national security adviser John M. Poindexter and his deputy, Oliver L. North—for their role in the scandal. Both convictions subsequently were overturned on the grounds that their trials may have been tainted by the immunized testimony they gave before Congress. President George H. W. Bush, Reagan's successor, in 1992 pardoned former defense secretary Caspar W. Weinberger and five others involved in Iran-contra.

President Reagan in July 1987 nominated Robert H. Bork, a federal appeals court judge, to be an associate justice of the U.S. Supreme Court. Following a bitter three-month confirmation battle that highlighted Bork's conservative judicial philosophy, the Senate rejected the nomination by a 58 to 42 vote. Reagan's next nominee, federal appeals court judge Douglas H. Ginsburg, was forced to withdraw after he admitted to smoking marijuana while a law student and professor. Reagan's third nominee, federal appeals court judge Anthony M. Kennedy, was confirmed in February 1988.

Knowing it was going to be overridden, Reagan nevertheless issued a veto of the Clean Water Act of 1987 (Water Quality Act), which he called a "budget-buster" and said was "loaded with waste and larded with pork." The veto was soundly overridden and the $20.15 billion clean water bill became law without the president's signature.

Increased public concern about the strains being placed on the congested airports and aging air traffic control system prompted passage of a $21 billion, five-year airport renewal package. Included were provisions for five hundred additional air traffic controllers.

The U.S. Supreme Court in 1986 struck down the budget procedures provided for in the Gramm-Rudman-Hollings Act. A new automatic spending-cut procedure was adopted in 1987 to be used if Congress and the president failed to meet the act's deficit targets. The same bill extended the government's public debt limit, eased the act's deficit targets, and extended the balanced budget deadline for two years, to 1993.

The largest one-day stock market loss in Wall Street history—22.6 percent of its value, almost double the drop that precipitated the Great Depression—occurred on October 19, 1987. The market crash was a spur to the White House and Congress to reach agreement on a plan to reduce the federal budget deficit. A presidential task force in 1988 concluded that the largest institutional investors had relied too heavily on computerized trading programs and recommended tighter controls over the new kinds of stock market transactions.

Congress restored the broad coverage intended in four civil rights laws enacted in the 1960s and 1970s. The U.S. Supreme Court in 1984 had ruled in *Grove City College v. Bell* that only the "program or activity" of an entity receiving federal assistance, not the entire institution, was covered by antidiscrimination laws. The Civil Rights Restoration Act clarified that an entire institution was covered if any of its components received federal aid. Legislation offering a belated formal apology and providing $1.25 billion in reparations to Japanese Americans interned in relocation camps during World War II became law in 1988. Approximately half of the 120,000 Japanese American internees were still alive at the time, many in their seventies and eighties.

Extensive negotiations among members of both houses of Congress, civil rights lawyers, the administration, and the National Association of Realtors were needed to forge a compromise fair housing bill. The Fair Housing Act Amendments addressed the issues of race discrimination in the sale and rental of housing as well as discrimination against persons with disabilities and young families.

Faced with administration reluctance to deal with increasing trade deficits and currency imbalances, Congress produced a massive omnibus trade bill that reached far beyond the traditional trade issues. The Senate in 1988 approved the intermediate-range nuclear-force missiles treaty, the first U.S.-Soviet arms treaty to be ratified since 1972. The treaty banned intermediate-range nuclear missiles and called for the destruction of all existing missiles.

Buoyed by the success of an experimental GI Bill enacted in 1984 (the Veterans Educational Assistance Act of 1984) as an effective recruiting tool for the all-volunteer armed forces, Congress granted permanent status to more generous military educational benefits. Following a decade-long struggle, veterans in 1988 won the right to petition the courts when they felt they were treated unfairly by the federal government. A cabinet-level Department of Veterans Affairs was established in 1988, following President Reagan's surprise announcement in support of such action.

During the 1980s, an upsurge in the number of homeless people in the United States became a highly charged political issue. Notwithstanding partisan differences over the causes of and remedies for homelessness, a 1987 bill, named for the late representative Stewart B. McKinney of Connecticut and his work on behalf of the homeless, provided millions of dollars for emergency shelters and other types of aid for people living on the streets. The Family Support Act of 1988 called for stronger child support enforcement; state-run education, training, and work programs for welfare mothers; work requirements for some welfare mothers; and extended child care and medical benefits for those who left welfare and joined the work force.

A lengthy struggle to provide the thirty-two million elderly and disabled Medicare beneficiaries with protection against catastrophic medical expenses reached fruition in 1988. The measure also offered the program's first broad coverage of outpatient prescription drugs. The costs of the new benefits were passed on to recipients through substantially higher Medicare premiums. Under great pressure from senior citizens angry over the costs of the new benefits, Congress repealed much of the Medicare Catastrophic Coverage Act within eighteen months. An omnibus health bill containing the first significant federal funding to combat the acquired immune deficiency syndrome (AIDS) epidemic provided $670 million for AIDS education, anonymous testing, and health care for AIDS patients.

To give the U.S. Supreme Court more control over its caseload, Congress approved legislation allowing the High Court greater jurisdiction in deciding which cases to hear and eliminating its mandatory jurisdiction over certain cases. Although the special prosecutor law was struck down within a month as unconstitutional by the U.S. Court of Appeals for the District of Columbia, the U.S. Supreme Court reversed the decision in *Morrison v. Olson* (1988).

Three new laws answered Americans' concern about threats to their privacy. The Employee Polygraph Protection Act prohibited private sector use of lie detector tests for employment purposes. The Computer Matching and Privacy Protection Act provided safeguards on the federal government's use of computer cross-checking of an individual's records to detect abuse, fraud, and overpayments. The Video Protection Act barred video stores from releasing information regarding videotapes rented or purchased by their customers except under specifically defined circumstances.

After nearly one hundred years, Congress decided to have the United States join the Berne Convention for the Protection of Literary and Artistic Works, which provided international copyright protection for member nations. Proponents argued that such action was essential if American copyright holders were to be adequately protected abroad. Congress also adopted the recommendations of a two-and-a-half-year study by the U.S. Trademark Association that resulted in several changes in trademark law. These modifications placed American companies for the first time on equal footing with foreign competitors.

The Women's Business Ownership Act sought to identify and remove the discriminatory barriers encountered by women entrepreneurs. President Reagan allowed legislation requiring employers to give sixty days' advance notice of plant closings and large-scale layoffs to become law without his signature so as not to make the popular measure an issue in Vice President George H. W. Bush's quest to succeed him.

A comprehensive antidrug bill included a federal death penalty for major drug traffickers and provided for a cabinet-level "drug czar" to coordinate national efforts to reduce drug abuse and stem the flow of drugs into the United States.

In 1988, George H. W. Bush became the first sitting vice president to win election to the White House since Martin Van Buren in 1836. Bush and his running mate, Sen. Dan Quayle of Indiana, defeated the Democratic ticket of presidential nominee Michael S. Dukakis, governor of Massachusetts, and vice presidential nominee Sen. Lloyd Bentsen of Texas. Bush and Quayle garnered 426 electoral votes to Dukakis and Bentsen's 111 votes. In the congressional elections, Democrats retained the majority in both the House and Senate.

Major Acts and Treaties

Water Quality Act of 1987. Provided for a ten-year, $20.2 billion reauthorization of the Federal Water Pollution Control Act Amendments of 1972. Authorized $9.6 billion in fiscal years 1986–1990 for construction grants to state and local governments for sewage treatment facilities, $8.4 billion in fiscal years 1989–1994 for state-run revolving funds to be used for such construction, and more than $2 billion for other pollution control programs. Required that programs be established to protect the water and resources of the Chesapeake Bay and Great Lakes, protect the nation's estuaries (National Estuary Program), restore publicly owned lakes, and control discharge of industrial and municipal waste water. Presidential veto overridden by Congress. Became law without the president's signature February 4, 1987 (P.L. 100–4; 101 Stat. 7–90). *(Federal Water Pollution Control Act Amendments of 1972, p. 345)*

New GI Bill Continuation Act. Authorized for the first time a permanent educational benefits program (GI Bill) for veterans who began military service after June 30, 1985. Required participating recruits to complete three years of active duty with an honorable discharge to qualify for $300 a month and a maximum of $10,800 in educational benefits. Allowed individuals completing two years of active duty and four years of reserve service to qualify for $250 a month in benefits and a maximum of $9,000. Approved June 1, 1987 (P.L. 100–48; 101 Stat. 331–332).

Stewart B. McKinney Homeless Assistance Act. Authorized $443 million in fiscal 1987 and $616 million in fiscal 1988 for a broad range of assistance for homeless persons including housing, health care, food, alcohol and drug abuse counseling, mental health care, and job training. Established an Interagency Council on the Homeless to coordinate homeless assistance provided by fifteen federal agencies. Approved July 22, 1987 (P.L. 100–77; 101 Stat. 482–538).

Balanced Budget and Emergency Deficit Control Reaffirmation Act of 1987. Increased the public debt authority from $2.1 trillion to $2.8 trillion. Established new federal budget deficit targets for fiscal years 1988–1993, a new automatic spending-cut procedure, and a revised schedule for carrying out the procedure. Approved September 29, 1987 (P.L. 100–119; 101 Stat. 754–788). The original Gramm-Rudman-Hollings Act budget procedure was struck down in *Bowsher v. Synar, Senate v. Synar, O'Neill v. Synar* (478 U.S. 714 [1986]).

Airport and Airway Safety and Capacity Expansion Act of 1987. Authorized a $20.1 billion airport renewal package that included $8.7 billion in fiscal years 1988–1992 for Federal Aviation Administration (FAA) grants to airports for expansion projects and other improvements, $5.3 billion in fiscal years 1988–1990 for upgrading the air traffic control system, and $5.5 billion in fiscal years 1988–1990 to operate the air traffic control system. Required the FAA to have at least 15,900 air traffic controllers by September 30, 1988. Extended taxes and fees used to finance the Airport and Airway Trust Fund and the Department of Transportation's Essential Air Services Program, which was used to subsidize airline service to smaller communities. Approved December 30, 1987 (P.L. 100–223; 101 Stat. 1486–1535).

Civil Rights Restoration Act of 1987. Redefined the term *program or activity* in four civil rights laws, so any state or local government, educational institution, or corporation and other private entities receiving federal aid had to comply with antidiscrimination laws. Specified that this legislation was needed to address "certain aspects of recent decisions and opinions of the Supreme Court in *Grove City College v. Bell* (465 U.S. 555 [1984])," which had "unduly narrowed or cast doubt upon the broad application" of the four acts. (The four laws affected were Title IX of the Education Amendments of 1972, barring discrimination by race, color, or national origin; section 504 of the Rehabilitation Act of 1973, barring discrimination against the handicapped; the Age Discrimination Act of 1975, barring age discrimination; and Title IV of the Civil Rights Act of 1964, barring sex discrimination.) Approved March 22, 1988 (P.L. 100–259; 102 Stat. 28–32).

Intermediate-Range Nuclear Forces (INF) Treaty. Banned the signatories (the United States and the Soviet Union) from producing or testing intermediate-range nuclear-force missiles with a range of between three hundred and thirty-four hundred miles. Called for the destruction of 1,752 Soviet and 859 U.S. intermediate-range missiles. Concluded December 8, 1987. Ratification advised by the Senate May 27, 1988.[1]

Employee Polygraph Protection Act of 1988. Prohibited private sector employers from using lie detector devices to test employees or job applicants. Exempted federal, state, and local governments, consultants to national security agencies, and companies providing specified security services or manufacturing and distributing controlled drugs from the act's provisions. Approved June 27, 1988 (P.L. 100–347; 102 Stat. 646–653).

Administration of Justice Improvement Act of 1988. Allowed the U.S. Supreme Court greater discretion in deciding which cases it would hear by eliminating mandatory review of certain specified cases. Approved June 27, 1988 (P.L. 100–352; 102 Stat. 662–664).

Medicare Catastrophic Coverage Act of 1988. Placed a cap on the amount Medicare beneficiaries could be required to pay for hospital and physician bills after a patient had paid an annual deductible fee. Provided assistance for outpatient prescription drug costs after a deductible had been met by beneficiaries. Approved July 1, 1988 (P.L. 100–360; 102 Stat. 683–817). Repealed November 22, 1989 (P.L. 101–234; 103 Stat. 1979–1986).

Worker Adjustment and Retraining Notification Act. Required businesses with more than one hundred full-time employees to give sixty days' notice before closing a plant or laying off 33 percent or more employees for longer than six months. Exempted employers with fewer than one hundred full-time employees from the notice requirements. Became law without the president's signature August 4, 1988 (P.L. 100–379; 102 Stat. 890–895).

Civil Liberties Act of 1988 (Japanese Americans Reparations Act). Provided a payment of $20,000 to each surviving Japanese American who had been interned in a relocation camp in the United States during World War II. Aleuts evacuated in 1942 from the Aleutian and Pribilof Islands off Alaska received a $12,000 tax-free payment. Stipulated that heirs and decedents of a Japanese American internee could receive reparation only if the internee died after the date of enactment and specific conditions were met. Declared that Congress recognized "a grave injustice was done to both citizens and permanent resident aliens of Japanese ancestry by the evacuation, relocation and internment of civilians during World War II," and apologized "on behalf of the Nation" for this action. Approved August 10, 1988 (P.L. 100–383, Title I; 102 Stat. 903–911).

Omnibus Trade and Competitiveness Act of 1988. Established U.S. trade policy as a high priority of the president and as less subservient to foreign policy and domestic considerations. Focused on traditional trade issues of unfair foreign trade practices and relief for import-damaged domestic industries. Covered such considerations as currency exchange rates, third-world debt, patent protection, security-based restrictions on U.S. imports, and illegal business-related bribes by American firms abroad. Approved August 23, 1988 (P.L. 100–418; 102 Stat. 1107–1574).

Fair Housing Amendments Act of 1988. Authorized the Department of Housing and Urban Development to penalize those who discriminated in the sale or rental of housing. Barred discriminatory housing practices against the handicapped and families with young children. Approved September 13, 1988 (P.L. 100–430; 102 Stat. 1619–1636).

Family Support Act of 1988. Strengthened child support enforcement procedures. Established a Job Opportunities and Basic Skills Program for recipients of Aid to Families with Dependent Children to "assure that needy families with children obtained the education, training and employment that [would] help them avoid long-term welfare dependence." Guaranteed extended child care and medical benefits for twelve months to welfare families who became ineligible for assistance because of increased earnings. Authorized three demonstration projects that would examine how to reduce school dropouts, encourage skill development, and avoid future welfare dependence. Approved October 13, 1988 (P.L. 100–485; 102 Stat. 2343–2428).

Computer Matching and Privacy Protection Act of 1988. Required federal agencies to establish safeguards governing release of computer records for purposes of cross-checking an individual's records. Required "each agency conducting or participating in a matching program" to "establish a Data Integrity Board to oversee and coordinate" the agency's matching programs. Approved October 18, 1988 (P.L. 100–503; 102 Stat. 2507–2514).

Department of Veterans Affairs Established. Redesignated the Veterans Administration as the Department of Veterans Affairs, with cabinet-level status. Provided that the secretary of veterans affairs be appointed by the president, with the advice and consent of the Senate. Provided for eleven other top-level department officials also subject to confirmation and forty additional full-time inspectors general to complement those already employed by the Veterans Administration. Approved October 25, 1988 (P.L. 100–527; 102 Stat. 2635–2648).

Women's Business Ownership Act of 1988. Established a Small Business Administration (SBA) program guaranteeing commercial bank loans of up to $50,000 for small businesses, most of which were expected to be service-related firms owned by women. Authorized a $10 million SBA demonstration project for private organizations providing management and other types of assistance to firms owned by women. Established a National Women's Business Council to monitor federal, state, and local governments in assisting women-owned businesses. Approved October 25, 1988 (P.L. 100–533; 102 Stat. 2689–2698).

Berne Convention Implementation Act of 1988. Authorized the United States to participate in the Berne Convention for the Protection of Literary and Artistic Works. Made minor changes in U.S. copyright law necessary to conform with Berne Convention requirements. Approved October 31, 1988 (P.L. 100–568; 102 Stat. 2853–2861).

AIDS Amendments of 1988. Authorized $400 million for anonymous blood testing, counseling, and community- and home-based health services for acquired immune deficiency syndrome (AIDS) patients; $270 million for AIDS education over three years; and $2 million for a National Commission on AIDS. Approved November 4, 1988 (P.L. 100–607, Title II; 102 Stat. 3062–3111).

Video Privacy Act. Prohibited video stores from disclosing their customers' names, addresses, and information on the videotapes they rented or purchased, except in certain defined circumstances: when the customer had consented to the release of the information, law enforcement officials had obtained a warrant for such information, or a court order specified a "compelling need for release of the information." Approved November 5, 1988 (P.L. 100–618; 102 Stat. 3195–3197).

Trademark Law Revision Act of 1988. Allowed American companies to file a trademark application with the U.S. Patent and Trademark Office six months before a product was placed into commerce and to receive a six-month extension upon completion of a written request. Approved November 16, 1988 (P.L. 100–667; 102 Stat. 3935–3960).

Veterans' Judicial Review Act. Created a new judicial review procedure for veterans' claim cases. Established the Board of Veterans Appeals (BVA), in existence since 1933, as the first avenue of appeal instead of the last; created a U.S. Court of Veterans Appeals to review appeals of BVA decisions; and provided for the U.S. Court of Appeals to handle appeals challenging laws or regulations. Provided that the BVA chairman be appointed by the president with the advice and consent of the Senate for a term of six years; BVA board members, nine years. Permitted lawyers representing veterans to receive "reasonable rates" instead of the statutory $10 limit in existence since the Civil War. Approved November 18, 1988 (P.L. 100–687; 102 Stat. 4105–4138).

Anti-Drug Abuse Act of 1988. Established an Office of National Drug Control Policy in the Executive Office of the President with a director and two deputies as well as an associate director appointed by the president and confirmed by the Senate. Increased funds available for drug education, treatment, and prevention programs. Expanded federal drug interdiction programs. Stiffened penalties for convicted drug dealers, and allowed the death penalty for major drug dealers involved in an intentional killing. Denied certain federal assistance and other welfare benefits to repeat drug use offenders. Established new penalties for any individual who either bought or sold pornography, or facilitated the use of a child for portrayal of explicit sexual acts. Approved November 18, 1988 (P.L. 100–690; 102 Stat. 4181–4545).

Note

1. *Journal of Executive Proceedings of the Senate* (Washington, D.C.: U.S. Government Printing Office, 1989), 130:360–370.

One Hundred First Congress

January 3, 1989, to January 3, 1991

First session—January 3, 1989, to November 22, 1989
Second session—January 23, 1990, to October 28, 1990
(Administration of George H. W. Bush, 1989–1993)

Historical Background

In 1989, the Berlin Wall, once the symbol of a divided Europe, was torn down, as Soviet president Mikhail S. Gorbachev declared that the Cold War "epic" had ended and that the United States and the Soviet Union were at the beginning of a "long-lasting peaceful period." In 1990, East Germany and West Germany were reunited, and many lawmakers on Capitol Hill began to seek significant cuts in defense spending as the Cold War drew to a close. The growing crisis in the Persian Gulf, however, set the stage for a confrontation with Iraqi president Saddam Hussein and led to the postponement of further defense cuts.

Congress delegated to the Department of Defense the lead role in detecting and monitoring the shipment of drugs into the United States. Funds were provided both to help the new government of Panama rebuild its economy after U.S. intervention toppled leader Manuel Antonio Noriega and to assist the new government of Nicaragua headed by U.S.–backed democratic opposition leader Violeta Chamorro. A Bipartisan Accord on Central America, negotiated by Secretary of State James A. Baker III with congressional leaders, resulted in the approval of nonmilitary aid for U.S.–backed guerrillas (contras) in Nicaragua.

Acting on the recommendation of the select Iran-contra committee, which had spent ten months investigating the Reagan administration's secret arms sales to Iran and funding of the contra rebels in Nicaragua,

Congress established an office of inspector general in the Central Intelligence Agency. Following a Soviet-U.S. summit in Washington, D.C., the Senate approved two treaties in which the two nations agreed to end nuclear tests with an explosive force larger than 150 kilotons (150,000 tons of TNT). The two documents, originally signed in the mid-1970s, limited the power of underground nuclear weapons explosions and those for peaceful purposes. A variety of political obstacles had thwarted action on these agreements since they were negotiated by the administrations of Richard M. Nixon and Gerald R. Ford in 1974 and 1976, respectively. The Senate reacted quickly on the treaties after President George H. W. Bush and Soviet president Gorbachev signed protocols tightening verification procedures.

The most sweeping revision of immigration law in a quarter century led to a substantial increase in the number of immigrants allowed into the United States. A new trade agreement was also signed by President Bush and Soviet President Gorbachev, but Bush chose not to submit the pact to Congress until the Soviet parliament adopted more open emigration policies.

In August 1989, six months after President Bush proposed legislation be drafted to resolve a growing crisis in the savings and loan industry, he signed a measure that dramatically restructured regulation of thrift institutions. The Financial Institutions Reform, Recovery, and Enforcement Act addressed widespread savings and loans failures as well as management abuses that had plagued the industry. Bush's support for the savings and loan bailout represented a sharp departure from the position of the Reagan administration, which had insisted on letting the industry address problems without federal interference.

The $14.7 billion Omnibus Reconciliation Act of 1989 was the final product of eight months of confrontation over the fiscal 1990 budget agreement. It removed the U.S. Postal Service from the federal budget in an attempt to protect the quasi-private agency from possible cuts under the Gramm-Rudman-Hollings antideficit law. Lengthy budget talks in 1990 resulted in a second reconciliation bill intended to reduce the federal deficit by $28 billion in fiscal 1991 and by $236 billion over five years. The measure also incorporated significant procedural changes in the congressional budget process.

Late in 1989, revelations of political influence peddling, fraud, and mismanagement at the Department of Housing and Urban Development (HUD) during the Reagan administration led to adoption of a reform plan proposed by HUD secretary Jack Kemp. The Housing Reform Act subjected HUD to greater scrutiny, limited its discretion in distributing funds, imposed civil fines and jail time for program violators, and limited the ability of developers and investors to make large profits from HUD.

Rep. Jim Wright of Texas in 1989 became the first Speaker of the House to resign in midterm. He left Congress in the face of an ethics scandal that involved questionable financial dealings. The House Committee on Standards of Official Conduct identified sixty-nine alleged violations of House rules.

In the aftermath of Speaker Wright's resignation and a controversial, aborted attempt by Congress to raise its salary by 51 percent, the Ethics Reform Act of 1989 was enacted. The act banned honoraria for representatives, provided a process for reducing honoraria for senators, established automatic annual pay adjustment procedures for members of Congress, provided modest salary increases for members of Congress as well as top officials in the legislative and executive branches, and restricted their ability to lobby for a year after leaving government. In separate action, additional protections and procedural rights were offered to federal whistleblowers who reported waste, fraud, and abuse within their agencies. President Ronald Reagan had pocket-vetoed a similar bill, arguing it allowed the government to sue itself, which was unconstitutional.

The so-called Keating Five scandal came to light in 1989. The Senate Ethics Committee investigated allegations that five senators did favors for wealthy campaign contributor Charles H. Keating Jr., who headed a failed California savings and loan. The committee probe concluded in 1991.

In 1990, the Securities and Exchange Commission (SEC) was given broad new powers to crack down on securities violations in the United States. Other action broadened the SEC's regulatory oversight of U.S. securities markets and allowed it to supervise financial market participants more closely and monitor attempts to manipulate the securities market. The latter act significantly improved the ability of securities regulators to minimize stock market disruptions such as had occurred in October 1987, when more than a $1 trillion in paper wealth was wiped out in one week.

Appeals by consumer groups and health officials for policing of advertising claims about the health benefits of packaged foods resulted in the adoption of legislation mandating detailed nutritional labels on such products.

The Americans with Disabilities Act extended the same civil rights to the estimated forty-three million Americans with mental and physical disabilities already guaranteed to women and racial, religious, and ethnic minorities under the Civil Rights Act of 1964.

Spurred by the March 1989 Exxon Valdez oil spill and other large spills occurring within months of that catastrophe, the Oil Pollution Act of 1990 represented the culmination of almost 15 years of congressional efforts to reach a consensus on comprehensive federal oil spill legislation. The goal of the first comprehensive oil pollution statute was to restore natural resources that are injured and services that are lost as a result of oil spills, and reduce the occurrence of oil spills through preventive measures as well as increased preparedness. A major rewrite of the Clean Air Act established stricter federal controls on acid rain, automobile exhaust, gasoline, toxic air pollution, urban smog, and chemicals contributing to the depletion of the ozone layer

Legislation to lift wellhead price controls from natural gas for the first time since 1954 sailed through Congress in 1989 after ample gas supplies drove prices down. The measure ended 35 years of wrangling over price controls. Passage of legislation calling for new airline ticket fees and new guidelines on aviation noise was considered by Transportation Secretary Samuel K. Skinner to be the "most significant aviation legislation since deregulation."

In 1990, the Chief Financial Officers Act was heralded as the most comprehensive, far-reaching financial management legislation since the Budget and Accounting Act of 1950. The act sought to improve management through reliable, useful, and timely financial and performance information for day-to-day decision making and accountability. Prior to the passage of the act, "the seemingly never ending disclosures of fraud, waste, abuse, and mismanagement in federal programs painted a picture of a government unable to manage its programs, protect its assets, or provide taxpayers with the effective and economical services they expect."[1]

Securing enactment of the Native American Graves Protection and Repatriation Act was the culmination of decades of struggle by Native American tribal governments and their people to protect against grave desecration, to repatriate thousands of dead relatives or ancestors, and to retrieve stolen or improperly acquired religious and cultural property for Native owners. This is the primary federal law governing the rights of Native Americans and scientists to access and control Native American human remains. It represented fundamental changes in basic social attitudes toward Native peoples by the museum and scientific community and the public at large.

Although much of the existing framework of federal farm programs was retained in the 1990 omnibus farm bill, farm price and income supports were frozen as part of a plan to reduce subsidized crops by 15 percent.

The first increase in the federal judiciary since 1984 resulted in the creation of eighty-five new judgeships—seventy-four district court positions and eleven appellate court positions.

The first major test of the United Nations Security Council in the post–Cold War era to deal with an act of international aggression came in August 1990, when Iraq invaded its oil-rich neighbor Kuwait. President Bush and top officials in his administration initiated a diplomatic effort to convince the Security Council to approve a resolution authorizing the use of force against Iraq if it did not withdraw from Kuwait by a certain date. The Security Council on November 29 set January 15, 1991, as the deadline and permitted United Nations member states to use "all necessary force" to effect Iraq's withdrawal from Kuwait.

In the immediate aftermath of the invasion of Kuwait, President Bush issued an executive order prohibiting trade with Iraq and blocking Iraqi access to assets in the United States. Congress subsequently condemned Iraq's actions and authorized the president to cut off trade with countries supporting Iraq.

The 1990 midterm elections kept both houses of Congress in the Democrats' hands.

Major Acts and Treaties

Whistleblower Protection Act of 1989. Established an Office of Special Counsel as an independent federal agency with authority to investigate allegations of retribution against government employees exposing government waste or fraud; file complaints with the Merit System Protection Board; recommend disciplinary action; and review allegations of waste, fraud, and abuse within the federal government and forward them to the appropriate federal agency for further action. Approved April 10, 1989 (P.L. 101–12; 103 Stat. 16–35).

Implementation of Bipartisan Accord on Central America. Authorized the president to transfer to the Agency for International Development, from unobligated funds, up to "$49,750,000, to provide humanitarian assistance to the Nicaraguan Resistance, to remain available through February 28, 1990." Approved April 18, 1989 (P.L. 101–14; 103 Stat. 37–40).

Natural Gas Wellhead Decontrol Act of 1989. Provided for the elimination of federal controls on the wellhead price of natural gas, decontrolling gas as contracts expired or were renegotiated, or no later than January 1, 1993. Created a new subcategory of gas from "newly spudded [begun] wells" in gas fields subject to existing contracts that could be decontrolled after May 15, 1991. Approved July 26, 1989 (P.L. 101–60; 103 Stat. 157–161).

Financial Institutions Reform, Recovery, and Enforcement Act of 1989. Provided $50 billion over three years to close or sell approximately 250 insolvent savings and loan institutions. Created the Resolution

Trust Corporation to take over the failed thrifts and dispose of their assets. Abolished the Federal Home Loan Bank Board and Federal Savings and Loan Corporation, which had supervised the thrift industry and insured its deposits. Created an Office of Thrift Supervision within the Treasury Department to supervise thrifts, and delegated responsibility for insuring thrifts to the Federal Deposit Insurance Corporation. Established new net-worth requirements expected to affect an additional eight hundred savings and loan institutions. Approved August 9, 1989 (P.L. 101–73; 103 Stat. 183–553).

Department of Defense Designated as Lead Agency for Detecting and Monitoring Shipment of Illegal Drugs. Designated the Department of Defense as the "single lead agency of the Federal Government for the detection and monitoring of aerial and maritime transit of illegal drugs into the United States." Approved November 29, 1989 (P.L. 101–189, Div. A, Title XII, Sec. 1202a; 103 Stat. 1352–1690).

Ethics Reform Act of 1989. Established an annual automatic pay adjustment procedure for members of Congress based on private sector pay. Banned House members from receiving speaking fees or other honoraria beginning in 1991, and established a process for gradually reducing Senate honoraria levels. Eliminated a loophole in the Federal Election Campaign Act of 1979 (P.L. 96–187) that allowed House members who had been in office since the beginning of 1980 to convert campaign funds to personal use once they retired. Limited the amount of travel expenses a member could receive from private sources. Provided a pay raise for members of Congress, federal judges, and top legislative and executive branch officials. Established new restrictions on lobbying by government officials and members of Congress after leaving office. Approved November 30, 1989 (P.L. 101–194; 103 Stat. 1716–1783).

Department of Housing and Urban Development Reform Act of 1989. Required the Department of Housing and Urban Development (HUD) to distribute housing programs funds on a needs-based "fair-share" formula through open competition and to publicly announce such decisions. Required lobbyists, consultants, and lawyers who dealt with HUD, if they made more than $100,000 per year, to report their annual earnings. Authorized civil fines for violations of HUD mortgage programs or insured property improvement loans. Restricted use of the HUD secretary's discretionary funds. Approved December 15, 1989 (P.L. 101–235; 103 Stat. 1987–2059).

Omnibus Budget Reconciliation Act of 1989. Provided for a $14.7 billion deficit reduction. Removed the U.S. Postal Service from the federal budget and Gramm-Rudman-Hollings Act provisions. Approved December 19, 1989 (P.L. 101–239; 103 Stat. 2106–2491). *(Gramm-Rudman-Hollings Act [Balanced Budget and Emergency Deficit Control Act], p. 386)*

Fiscal 1990 Dire Emergency Supplemental Appropriations. Provided $4.3 billion in emergency appropriations for fiscal 1990, including $2.1 billion for mandatory spending programs and $1.4 billion in domestic discretionary spending. Added funds for food stamps, fighting forest fires, salaries and pensions for the Department of Veterans Affairs, and disaster assistance. Provided $462 million in emergency aid for Panama and $300 million in emergency aid for Nicaragua. Reduced defense spending for fiscal 1990 by $2 billion. Approved May 25, 1990 (P.L. 101–302; 104 Stat. 213–249).

Americans with Disabilities Act of 1990. Prohibited discrimination against the disabled in employment, public services, public accommodations, and services operated by private entities. Required that telecommunications be made available to those with speech and hearing impairments through special communications systems. Sought to establish "clear, strong, consistent, enforceable standards addressing discrimination against individuals with disabilities." Approved July 26, 1990 (P.L. 101–336; 104 Stat. 327–378).

Oil Pollution Act of 1990. Created a prevention, response, liability, and compensation regime to deal with vessel- and facility-caused oil pollution in U.S. navigable waters, adjoining shorelines, or the Exclusive Economic Zone (a territorial boundary extending out to 200 miles from the coastline). Provided greater environmental safeguards by setting new requirements for vessel construction and crew licensing and manning, mandating contingency planning, enhancing federal response capability, broadening enforcement authority, increasing potential liabilities, broadening financial responsibility requirements, and creating new research and development programs into spill response technologies. Approved August 18, 1990 (P.L. 101–380; 104 Stat. 484–575).

Threshold Test Ban Treaty (Limitation of Underground Nuclear Weapon Tests Treaty). Barred the United States and Soviet Union from underground tests of nuclear weapons with an explosive power greater than 150 kilotons (equivalent to 150,000 tons of TNT). Allowed the countries to use seismic measurements as well as a U.S.–backed method called CORTEX to measure the size of the explosions. Concluded July 3, 1974. Ratification advised by the Senate September 25, 1990.[2]

Peaceful Underground Nuclear Explosions Treaty. Barred the United States and Soviet Union from underground nuclear explosions for peaceful purposes, such as large-scale, earth-moving projects, with an explosive power of greater than 150 kilotons. Allowed the two countries to use seismic measurements as well as a U.S.–backed method called CORTEX to measure the size of the explosions. Concluded May 28, 1976. Ratification advised by the Senate September 25, 1990.[3]

Securities Market Reform Act of 1990. Provided the Securities and Exchange Commission with authority to close the nation's stock exchanges in an emergency, an action that had previously required presidential action; restrict program trading, a computer-driven trading technique; and track transactions by large traders to guard against market manipulation. Approved October 16, 1990 (P.L. 101–432; 104 Stat. 963–977).

Aviation Safety and Capacity Expansion Act of 1990. Authorized the secretary of transportation to "grant a public agency which controls a commercial service airport authority to impose a fee of $1.00, $2.00, or $3.00 for each paying passenger of an air carrier enplaned at such airport to finance airport related projects to be carried out in connection with such airport or any other airport which such agency controls."

Approved November 5, 1990 (P.L. 101–508, Title IX, Subtitle B; 104 Stat. 1388-353–1388-372).

Airport Noise and Capacity Act of 1990. Mandated the secretary of transportation to issue regulations establishing a national aviation noise policy and to submit to Congress recommendations on changes in state, local, and federal aircraft noise standards and procedures as well as standards and procedures for federal regulation of airspace. Approved November 5, 1990 (P.L. 101–508, Title IX, Subtitle D; 104 Stat. 1388-378–1388-384).

Revenue Reconciliation Act of 1990. Budget Enforcement Act of 1990. Called for reductions of $28 billion in fiscal 1991 and $236 billion over five years through tax increases, user fees, and savings in entitlement and other mandatory programs. Instituted significant modifications in the congressional budget process, including calendar changes; budget resolutions containing five-year projections in spending, revenues, and deficits; new automatic spending cuts, discretionary spending caps, and deficit targets; a requirement that mandatory spending increases or reduced revenues be deficit neutral; automatic sequestration if supplemental or emergency appropriations approved prior to July 1 exceeded spending caps; and cancellation of sequestration if the president requested supplemental or emergency funds or if a declaration of war had been made. Approved November 5, 1990 (P.L. 101–508, Title X; 104 Stat. 1388-400–1388-561). (P.L. 508, Title XIII; 104 Stat. 1388-573–1388-630).

Iraq Sanctions Act of 1990. Condemned Iraq's invasion of Kuwait on August 2, 1990, and declared support of the "actions taken by the President in response to that invasion." Granted the president authority to cut off trade with any foreign country not complying with the global embargo against Iraq. Approved November 5, 1990 (P.L. 101–513, Title V, Sec. 586; 104 Stat. 2047–2055).

Nutrition Labeling and Education Act. Required manufacturers of most packaged food items and some seafoods to display detailed nutritional information, including the amount of carbohydrates, cholesterol, dietary fiber, fat, saturated fat, protein, sodium, and sugar. Prohibited food manufacturers from making certain health and nutrition claims about products not fully tested or approved by the U.S. Food and Drug Administration. Charged the Department of Health and Human Services with defining nutritional terms such as *free, low, light* or *lite, reduced,* and *low fat.* Approved November 8, 1990 (P.L. 101–535; 104 Stat. 2353–2367).

Clean Air Act Amendments of 1990. Imposed stricter federal controls on smog and toxic emissions from industry and automobiles. Mandated development of cleaner automobiles and gasoline. Imposed limits on utility plant emissions that caused acid rain. Established a new deadline for urban areas failing to meet national air quality standards. Created deadlines for identifying and reducing industrial toxic air emissions, new limits on air pollutants causing acid precipitation and atmospheric ozone depletion. Authorized creation of a market for emissions trading between industrial air pollution sources. Approved November 15, 1990 (P.L. 100–549; 104 Stat. 2399–2712). *(Clean Act of 1963, p. 317)*

Chief Financial Officers Act of 1990. Established a Chief Financial Officer within 14 federal departments and 9 designated agencies to oversee all financial activities relating to the programs and operations of the agency; to develop and maintain an integrated agency accounting and financial system; to direct, manage, and provide policy guidance and oversight of agency financial management personnel, activities, and operations; and to prepare annually audited financial reports. Created a new position, the Deputy Director for Management in the Office of Management and Budget (OMB), to establish government-wide financial management policies for executive agencies. Created the Office of Federal Financial Management to coordinate the work of the agencies and to provide overall financial oversight to the executive branch. Approved November 15, 1990 (P.L. 101–576; 104 Stat. 2838–2855).

Native American Graves Protection and Repatriation Act. Required all federally funded institutions to inventory and identify Native American human remains and cultural items in their collections, and to consult with culturally affiliated Indian tribes, Alaska Native villages and corporations, and Native Hawaiian organizations regarding the return of these objects to descendants or culturally affiliated tribes and other organizations. Directed the secretary of interior to establish a Native American Graves Protection and Repatriation Review Committee to monitor the return of human remains and objects buried with them. Imposed penalties for disturbance of burial sites. Outlawed the sale of Native American human remains and burial artifacts. Authorized the secretary of the interior to award grants to assist in implementing provisions of the act. Approved November 16, 1990 (P.L. 101–601; 104 Stat. 3048–3058).

Food, Agriculture, Conservation, and Trade Act of 1990. Revised, extended, and froze federal farm price support and income support programs for five years. Established a triple-based acreage allotment plan under which farmers could plant a subsidized crop, leave the land idle, or grow a mixture of crops they selected for which a subsidy would not be paid. Reduced the amount of crop land eligible for income support payments by 15 percent. Approved November 28, 1990 (P.L. 101–624; 104 Stat. 3359–4078).

Cranston-Gonzalez National Affordable Housing Act. Reaffirmed the national housing goal that "every American family be able to afford a decent home in a suitable environment." Established HOME (Home Ownership Made Easy) Investment Partnerships to provide block grants to assist state and local governments in fulfilling housing needs; a National Home Ownership Trust program to provide financial aid to first-time home buyers; the HOPE (Home Ownership of Public and Indian Housing) program to promote home ownership of public and Indian housing by tenants; and supportive housing programs for the elderly, persons with disabilities, and the homeless. Authorized $27.5 billion in fiscal 1991 and $29.9 billion in fiscal 1992 to carry out the provisions of the act. Approved November 28, 1990 (P.L. 101–625; 104 Stat. 4079–4425).

Immigration Act of 1990. Increased immigrant quotas from 500,000 to 700,000 for the first three years of the act, and established a permanent level of 675,000 immigrants a year thereafter. Increased the number of immigrants admitted from dependent areas and the ratio of employment-based immigrants to family-sponsored immigrants. Authorized adjustments for Cubans and Haitians who had entered the United States without inspection prior to January 1, 1982. Granted forty thousand visas per year for fiscal years 1992–1994 to nationals from countries adversely affected by the 1965 Immigration and Nationality Act. Made it harder to exclude foreigners on the basis of their political beliefs and sexual orientation. Approved November 29, 1990 (P.L. 100–649; 104 Stat. 4978–5088). *(Immigration and Nationality Act of 1965, p. 324)*

Judicial Improvements Act of 1990. Created seventy-four federal district court judgeships and eleven federal circuit court of appeals judgeships. Mandated that federal judges adopt plans for expediting civil litigation. Approved December 1, 1990 (P.L. 101–650; 104 Stat. 5089–5137).

Notes

1. U.S. Government Accountability Office, *CFO Act 1990: Driving the Transformation of Federal Financial Management,* GAO-06–242T (Washington, D.C.: Government Accountability Office, Nov. 17, 2005), 2.

2. *Journal of the Executive Proceedings of the Senate* (Washington, D.C.: U.S. Government Printing Office, 1991), 132:629–631; 29 I.L.M., July 1990, 969–1024. (I.L.M. refers to *International Legal Materials* published by the American Association of International Law.)

3. *Journal of the Executive Proceedings of the Senate,* 132:629–631; 29 I.L.M., July 1990, 1025–1046.

One Hundred Second Congress

January 3, 1991, to January 3, 1993

First session—January 3, 1991, to January 3, 1992
Second session—January 3, 1992, to October 9, 1992
(Administration of George H. W. Bush, 1989–1993)

Historical Background

The One Hundred Second Congress convened against a backdrop of international crisis and the threat of war. By the end of 1990, nearly 500,000 American troops, along with military contingents from other nations, had assembled in Saudi Arabia in response to Iraqi president Saddam Hussein's invasion of Kuwait. On January 12, 1991, Congress approved a resolution condemning Iraq's actions and authorized the president to use military force if necessary to bring about Iraqi withdrawal from Kuwait. The historic vote was the first since World War II to send a large American force into combat.

In a televised address on January 16, 1991, President George H. W. Bush said that the United States and its allies would soon commence Operation Desert Storm, a military attack by coalition forces to remove the Iraqi troops in Kuwait. During the next six weeks, the superior allied forces engaged in thousands of air and missile strikes against Iraq and Iraqi-occupied Kuwait, followed by a ground invasion backed by air assaults. On February 25, Hussein agreed to withdraw his troops from Kuwait. Two days later President Bush announced a cease-fire and declared Kuwait to be liberated.

Congress provided a special benefits package for those who fought in the Persian Gulf War. It was fashioned so as not to violate the Omnibus Budget Reconciliation Act of 1990 (P.L. 101–508). Congress provided $42.6 billion to cover the costs of the war in a supplemental appropriation measure. Funds for the bill were to be drawn from money pledged by foreign governments. An additional $15 billion was provided to cover costs pending receipt of the foreign funds.

Congress also sent legislation to the White House providing treatment and compensation to Vietnam veterans suffering from illnesses caused by exposure to Agent Orange. Following the end of hostilities in the Persian Gulf, Congress removed the statutory ban on women flying combat missions.

Soviet leader Mikhail S. Gorbachev survived an attempted coup d'etat in August 1991. By this time, the Union of Soviet Socialist Republics (USSR) was beginning to fragment, and by year's end, it ceased to exist. Many of the former republics gained independence, while the remainder, under the leadership of Boris Yeltsin, emerged as the Russian Federation. To encourage and subsidize the change from communism to democracy, Congress passed the Freedom Support Act, which provided technical assistance and additional humanitarian aid for the former Soviet republics and earmarked funds for dismantling the republics' nuclear, biological, and chemical weapons.

The Strategic Arms Reduction Treaty (START), which was ratified by the Senate in October 1992, required the United States and the former Soviet Union to reduce their long-range missiles and bombers by approximately one-third. Although the Soviet Union had collapsed by the time the Senate acted, the four former Soviet republics that had assumed control of USSR nuclear forces stationed in their territory agreed to take on the obligations imposed by the treaty. In separate action, all underground nuclear test explosions were banned after September 30, 1996.

The Department of Energy was given the go-ahead to begin storing defense-related nuclear waste at the Waste Isolation Plant near Carlsbad, New Mexico.

Congress sought to enhance its oversight of intelligence activities by restricting covert activities that circumvented the Constitution or federal law.

A sweeping energy bill, forged in an effort to reduce the nation's dependence on foreign oil, restructured the electricity industry; mandated greater energy efficiency; encouraged conservation, renewable energy, and alternative fuels; and streamlined the licensing process for building nuclear power plants.

Twice in 1991, Congress had to appropriate funds for the Resolution Trust Corporation (RTC) to cover depositor losses in failed savings and loan associations as the cost of the thrift bailout continued to increase. Congress first provided $30 billion and then added $25 billion. A third effort, in 1992, to provide more funds to continue the savings and loan cleanup failed. A long-awaited overhaul of financial institutions was achieved through significant changes in the Federal Deposit Insurance Corporation and an infusion of $25 billion of borrowing authority into the insurance fund. Attached to the legislation were new savings account disclosure requirements.

Legislation reorganizing the government's efforts to fight mental illness and substance abuse was approved after a three-year controversy over the distribution to and state accountability for funds was resolved. Under the new structure, the three branches of the Alcohol, Drug Abuse, and Mental Health Administration were incorporated into the National Institutes of Health. Legislation was also passed making it a federal crime for parents living in another state to willfully avoid making child support payments.

A fundamental change in allocation formulas for federal highway and mass transit funds gave states additional flexibility in spending those monies. Much of the new funding was to come from tax revenues paid into the Federal Highway Trust Fund. The omnibus housing bill of 1992 raised Federal Housing Administration loan limits on single-family housing, established new subsidized housing rules for the elderly and disabled, and placed stricter controls on the Federal National Mortgage Association (Fannie Mae) and Federal Home Loan Mortgage Corporation (Freddie Mac).

Failing to transfer the Landsat Remote-Sensing Satellite Program to the private sector, Congress placed the program under the National Aeronautics and Space Administration and the Department of Defense. The Landsat program was developed to take pictures of Earth that could be used for environmental planning, oil and gas development, and military surveillance.

In 1991, legislation was enacted to overcome restrictions nine Supreme Court decisions had placed on antidiscrimination laws. The bill was signed by the president in the wake of Senate confirmation hearings of U.S. Supreme Court associate justice nominee Clarence Thomas, during which Anita F. Hill accused Thomas of sexual harassment when they had worked together, and a strong primary election showing in the Louisiana gubernatorial race by former Ku Klux Klansman David Duke. During the Thomas confirmation hearings, the Senate was forced to enter into a public and controversial discussion about sexual harassment as a result of an outcry by women across the country following Hill's allegations.

Legislation was enacted—over a presidential veto—that was designed to address complaints of price gouging, poor customer service, and discriminatory business practices by the cable television industry. President Bush had challenged the reasoning of the bill's sponsors that tighter regulations would result in lower cable rates.

The Twenty-seventh Amendment, a 203-year-old proposal to prohibit midterm congressional pay raises, was finally ratified by the requisite three-quarters of the states in May 1992.

Congress was beset by a series of controversies and ethics charges. The Senate Ethics Committee, in its 1989–1991 investigation of the Keating Five, found evidence that official actions taken by Sen. Alan Cranston of California were "substantially linked" to his fund-raising. The four other senators were criticized for using poor judgment, and two of them were also reproved for giving the appearance of acting improperly. Subsequently, revelations became public in 1991 that hundreds of sitting and former members had routinely overdrawn their House of Representatives bank accounts without penalty. The public saw the practice as further proof that members of Congress did not have to abide by the same rules as everyone else. An investigation, started in 1991, into allegations of embezzlement and drug dealing among the staff of the House Post Office would lead to findings that House members used the facility to convert campaign contributions and expense vouchers to cash. In response to the beating Congress was taking in its public approval ratings, members set up a Joint Committee on the Organization of Congress to study its structure and operation.

In 1992, a continuing mild recession, increasing voter dissatisfaction with solutions the two major political parties were offering to solve the nation's ills, and a widespread desire for change resulted in the most successful presidential campaign by an independent or third party candidate since 1912. Texas billionaire Ross Perot received 18.9 percent of the popular vote, but no electoral votes. The Democratic ticket of presidential candidate Bill Clinton, governor of Arkansas, and his running mate, Sen. Al Gore of Tennessee, defeated the Republican team of President George H. W. Bush and Vice President Dan Quayle, by 370 to 168 electoral votes. The Democrats retained their majority in both the House and Senate.

Major Acts and Treaties

Persian Gulf Resolution. Authorized the president to use U.S. armed forces pursuant to United Nations Security Council Resolution 678, which "authorized member states of the United Nations to use all necessary means, after January 15, 1991," to remove Iraqi forces from Kuwait. Required that the president, before exercising the authority granted in the resolution, make available to the Speaker of the House and president pro tempore of the Senate a determination that "the United States ha[d] used all appropriate diplomatic and other peaceful means to obtain compliance by Iraq." Approved January 14, 1991 (P.L. 102–1; 105 Stat. 3–4).

Agent Orange Act of 1991. Codified several decisions by the secretary of the veterans affairs to compensate Vietnam veterans suffering from diseases linked to dioxin (Agent Orange), used by the United States as a defoliant in that conflict. Established a review process to determine if other ailments were also caused by the defoliant. Required the National Academy of Sciences to analyze relevant existing studies and make recommendations to the secretary of veterans affairs. Approved February 6, 1991 (P.L. 102–4; 105 Stat. 11–20).

Resolution Trust Corporation Funding Act of 1991. Provided $30 billion for the Resolution Trust Corporation (RTC) to cover the losses of insured depositors at failed savings and loan associations. Directed the RTC to institute several management reforms and increase efforts to contract with companies headed by minorities and women. Approved March 23, 1991 (P.L. 102–18; 105 Stat. 58–66).

Persian Gulf War Veterans Benefits Act of 1991. Increased combat pay for military personnel serving in the Persian Gulf War from $110 to $150 a month. Increased the GI Bill educational benefit for enlisted personnel, reservists, and National Guard members from $300 to $350 a month. Doubled the death gratuity for families of those killed in the Persian Gulf from $3,000 to $6,000, and doubled the group life insurance benefit to $100,000. Authorized $15 billion in supplemental appropriations for the Persian Gulf conflict. Approved April 6, 1991 (P.L. 102–25; 105 Stat. 75–122).

Operation Desert Shield/Desert Storm Supplemental Appropriations Act. Appropriated $42.6 billion to cover the cost of the Persian Gulf War. Required that these appropriations be funded from an account composed of money pledged by foreign governments, insofar as possible. Provided an additional $15 billion in U.S. funds to be used as a bridge loan until foreign funds were collected. Stipulated that any unspent U.S. funds be returned to the U.S. Treasury. Provided $25 million for emergency loans to small businesses in communities adversely affected by the deployment of troops in the Persian Gulf. Approved April 10, 1991 (P.L. 102–28; 105 Stat. 161–168).

Fiscal 1991 Intelligence Authorization Act. Clarified and defined missions of the U.S. intelligence agencies. Required the president to report all covert activities to Congress. Stated that the "President may not authorize the conduct of a covert action" unless he "determines such action is necessary to support identifiable foreign policy objectives of the United States . . . and is important to the national security of the United States" and that such a determination be set forth in a written finding that meets certain conditions. Prohibited the president from authorizing covert acts that violated the

Constitution or U.S. laws. Authorized fiscal 1991 appropriations for the Central Intelligence Agency, Defense Intelligence Agency, National Security Agency, and other intelligence-related activities. Approve August 14, 1991 (P.L. 102–88; 105 Stat. 429–445).

Civil Rights Act of 1991. Reversed nine U.S. Supreme Court decisions from 1986 to 1991 that had made it more difficult for workers to win job discrimination lawsuits. Allowed plaintiffs to receive monetary damages in cases of intentional discrimination or harassment based on sex, religion, or disability. Approved November 21, 1991 (P.L. 102–166; 105 Stat. 1071–1100).

Emergency Unemployment Compensation Act Amendments of 1991. Provided up to seven additional weeks of unemployment benefits to individuals who lived in states that originally received six weeks of compensation, had not exhausted their state unemployment benefits as of March 1, 1991, and were still unemployed. Approved December 4, 1991 (P.L. 102–182, Sec. 3; 105 Stat. 1234).

Assignment of Women in the Armed Forces to Combat Aircraft. Repealed the "combat exclusion" law barring the assignment of women to combat aircraft in the U.S. Air Force, Navy, and Marine Corps. Established a fifteen-member Commission on the Assignment of Women in the Armed Forces to study the issue of assigning women to other combat roles. Approved December 5, 1991 (P.L. 102–190, Title V, Part D, Sec. 531, 541–550; 105 Stat. 1365–1370). (*Assignment of Women in the Armed Forces to Combat Ships, p. 412*)

Resolution Trust Corporation Refinancing, Restructuring, and Improvement Act of 1991. Provided $25 billion for the Resolution Trust Corporation (RTC) to cover the losses of insured depositors at failed savings and loan associations. Reorganized the management structure of the RTC by creating a presidentially appointed chief executive officer responsible for day-to-day corporation management in place of the Federal Deposit Insurance Corporation. Eliminated the RTC operating board of directors, and expanded membership and makeup of the RTC oversight board. Approved December 12, 1991 (P.L. 102–233; 105 Stat. 1761–1792).

Intermodal Surface Transportation Efficiency Act of 1991. Authorized $119.5 billion for highway programs and $31.5 billion for mass transit programs over six years (fiscal years 1992–1998). Allowed states considerable flexibility in determining how funds were spent. Specified that $6.2 billion of these amounts would be used for 539 priority projects identified by state highway departments and 57 new rail and bus systems. Created a National Highway System made up of the interstate highway network and primary arterial roads. Consolidated several federal highway programs into the Surface Transportation Program from which states could draw money for highway projects. Imposed new gasoline taxes. Required air bags on all passenger cars built after September 1, 1996. Approved December 18, 1991 (P.L. 102–240; 105 Stat. 1914–2207).

Federal Deposit Insurance Corporation Improvement Act of 1991. Increased the Federal Deposit Insurance Corporation (FDIC) borrowing limit from $5 billion to $30 billion to cover depositor losses in failed banks. Provided approximately $45 billion for the acquisition of the assets of failed banks that could be sold at a later date. Required that the two institutions establish a repayment schedule audited quarterly by the General Accounting Office. Granted FDIC the option of borrowing from banks as well as the Treasury in covering insurance fund losses. Required federal bank regulators to more closely monitor banks and thrifts and to seize or close those institutions not maintaining significant capital. Required banks, thrifts, and credit unions to disclose interest rates and conditions on savings accounts. Approved December 19, 1991 (P.L. 101–242; 105 Stat. 2236–2393).

Twenty-seventh Amendment. Provided that "[n]o law, varying the compensation for the services of the Senators and Representatives shall take effect, until an election of Senators and Representatives shall have intervened." Proposed by Virginia representative James Madison as one of the twelve original amendments to the Constitution, ten of which were ratified and became the Bill of Rights. Proposed September 25, 1789 (106 Stat. 5145–5146). Ratified by requisite number of states May 7, 1992.[1] Both the House and Senate recognized the validity of the proposed amendment as the Twenty-seventh Amendment to the Constitution on May 20, 1992.[2] *(Bill of Rights [First Ten Amendments], p. 12)*

Alcohol, Drug Abuse, and Mental Health Administration Reorganization Act. Disbanded the Alcohol, Drug Abuse, and Mental Health Administration (ADAMHA) and renamed its three research branches, placing them within the National Institutes of Health as the National Institute of Mental Health, the National Institute on Drug Abuse, and the National Institute on Alcohol Abuse and Alcoholism. Placed ADAMHA's remaining programs, which administered funds distributed to states for treatment and prevention services, in the Substance Abuse and Mental Health Services Administration. Approved July 10, 1992 (P.L. 102–321; 106 Stat. 323–442).

Strategic Arms Reduction Treaty (START). Provided for the United States and the four republics of the former Soviet Union (Russia, Ukraine, Belarus, and Kazakhstan) that had assumed control of the former Soviet nuclear arsenal to reduce their long-range missile arsenals and bombers by approximately one-third. Concluded July 31, 1991. Ratification advised by the Senate October 1, 1992. Entered into force on December 5, 1994.[3]

Nuclear Test Explosions Ban. Banned underground tests of nuclear weapons from October 1, 1992, to June 30, 1993. Allowed a limited number of underground tests between July 1, 1993, and December 31, 1996, if the president submitted an annual report containing specific information relating to the testing. Banned all underground explosive tests after September 30, 1996, unless another country conducted such tests. Approved October 2, 1992 (P.L. 102–377, Title V, Sec. 507; 106 Stat. 1343–1345).

Cable Television Consumer Protection and Competition Act of 1992. Required the Federal Communications Commission to establish customer service standards for cable operators, to ensure that basic cable television viewing rates as well as equipment rentals were reasonable, to develop safeguards prohibiting programmers from actions inhibiting competition, and to limit the access of children to indecent programs. Established rules that specified cable company obligations to commercial, educational, and lower-powered television stations. Presidential veto overridden by Congress. Became law without the president's signature October 2, 1992 (P.L. 102–385; 106 Stat. 1460–1504).

Energy Policy Act of 1992. Mandated greater energy efficiency for appliances, buildings, and plumbing equipment. Streamlined the licensing process for building nuclear power plants. Provided tax incentives for conservation and the use of renewable energy and alternative fuels. Required federal, state, and local governments to begin buying alternative fuel vehicles. Loosened restrictions on importing Canadian gas. Provided extensive funding for research and development projects within the Department of Energy. Provided funding for the development of clean coal technology, subsidies for operators of small mines, health benefits for retired workers, and a temporary ban on opening wilderness areas and park lands for mining. Approved October 24, 1992 (P.L. 102–486; 106 Stat. 2776–3133).

Freedom for Russia and Emerging Eurasian Democracies and Open Market Support Act of 1992 (FREEDOM Support Act). Authorized $410 million in bilateral assistance to the independent states of the former Soviet Union (Armenia, Azerbaijan, Belarus, Georgia, Kazakhstan, Kyrgyzstan, Moldova, Russia, Tajikistan, Turkmenistan, Ukraine, and Uzbekistan) in fiscal 1993. Allowed these monies to be used for a broad range of purposes. Stipulated that aid to a republic could be cut off for violations of human rights or international law or for failure to remove all blockades and troops from other independent states. Provided mechanisms for setting up democratic institutions and civil organizations, encouraging American business ventures, and establishing exchange programs, U.S. diplomatic posts, and other offices. Authorized use of previously appropriated defense and security assistance funds to dismantle nuclear, biological, and chemical weapons and to support their nonproliferation. Approved October 24, 1992 (P.L. 102–511; 106 Stat. 3320–3362).

Child Support Recovery Act of 1992. Imposed a federal criminal penalty on an individual who lived in another state and failed to fulfill child support obligations ordered by a court or administrative entity. Limited criminal liability to individuals who willfully avoided payments. Approved October 25, 1992 (P.L. 105–521; 106 Stat. 3403–3409).

Housing and Community Development Act of 1992. Provided a $66.5 billion two-year reauthorization of federal housing programs. Raised Federal Housing Administration mortgage loan limits on single-family housing. Allowed public housing authorities, with the approval of the Department of Housing and Urban Development, to designate separate housing for the elderly and disabled. Created rules to reduce and eliminate lead-based paint poisoning hazards in housing. Placed stricter controls on the Federal National Mortgage Association (Fannie Mae) and Federal Home Loan Mortgage Corporation (Freddie Mac). Established penalties for drug-related money laundering by financial institutions. Authorized federal bank regulators to revoke the charter or appoint a conservator for institutions convicted of money laundering. Approved October 28, 1992 (P.L. 102–550; 106 Stat. 3672–4097).

Land Remote Sensing Policy Act of 1992. Transferred management of the Landsat Remote-Sensing Satellite Program from the Department of Commerce to the National Aeronautics and Space Administration and the Department of Defense. Stipulated that government agencies and affiliated users be able to purchase Landsat images at cost. Approved October 28, 1992 (P.L. 102–555; 106 Stat. 4163–4180).

Defense Waste Disposal Act of 1992. Provided for the transfer of certain public lands near Carlsbad, New Mexico, to the Department of Energy, so it could begin storing for the first time certain defense-related nuclear waste at the Waste Isolation Pilot Plant there. Delegated site oversight responsibilities to the Environmental Protection Agency, which was to issue public safety standards ensuring that the waste had been disposed of safely. Authorized an annual $20 million payment to the state of New Mexico for associated costs. Approved October 30, 1992 (P.L. 102–579; 106 Stat. 4777–4796).

Notes

1. U.S. Senate, *The Constitution of the United States: Analysis and Interpretation,* 108th Cong., 2d sess., 2004, S. Doc. 108–17, 2004, 44, n. 19.

2. *Congressional Record,* 102d Cong., 2d sess., 1992, 138:11869–11870, 12051–12052.

3. *Journal of the Executive Proceedings of the Senate* (Washington, D.C.: U.S. Government Printing Office, 1993), 134:612–616.

One Hundred Third Congress

January 3, 1993, to January 3, 1995

First session—January 5, 1993, to November 26, 1993
Second session—January 25, 1994, to December 1, 1994
(First administration of Bill Clinton, 1993–1997)

Historical Background

With Bill Clinton's inauguration as president on January 20, 1993, the federal government's executive and legislative branches were controlled by the same party—in this case, the Democratic Party—for the first time in twelve years. Clinton and his vice president, Al Gore, represented a generational change, as they were both born after World War II. In his inaugural address, Clinton challenged Americans to help government solve the nation's problems by taking more responsibility for their communities and country. "Let us put aside our personal advantage," he declared, "so that we can feel the pain and see the promise of America." The president targeted a range of proposals for early action by Congress.

The first to bear fruit, the Family and Medical Leave Act, required employers with fifty or more employees to grant unpaid leave for family and personal medical emergencies. The act was almost identical to a bill President George H.W. Bush had vetoed in September 1992, objecting "to the Federal Government mandating leave policies for America's employers." Another early initiative supported by President Clinton, the National Voter Registration Act (more popularly known as the Motor Voter Act) was signed into law on May 20, 1993. Passage of the legislation, which authorized voter registration by mail and at state and local government offices, was the culmination of a five-year effort to boost voter participation by facilitating registration. Also set in law was Clinton's 1992 presidential campaign proposal for a national and community service program to provide educational awards for American youth aged seventeen and over who performed community service before, during, or after college or technical school. Broad-based bipartisan support accompanied enactment of the first national educational goals.

As part of his economic revival package, the president proposed tax increases on upper-income citizens to reduce the deficit. The bill, which incorporated spending cuts but did not include a domestic spending package initially championed by President Clinton, led to partisan strife in Congress. Confronted by a united Republican opposition, Vice President Al Gore's tie-breaking vote in the Senate was required to enact the Omnibus Budget Reconciliation Act of 1993. A key provision in the act overturned a long-standing policy of awarding radio spectrum licenses at no cost through lottery or merit review. Under the new policy, businesses were required to engage in competitive bidding to obtain a license. The administration estimated that auctioning the licenses would generate $7.2 billion in additional revenues.

Congress incorporated two important military policies and an important new program in the fiscal 1994 Defense Authorization Act. The first, the controversial "don't ask, don't tell" policy, continued the ban on homosexual conduct by military personnel but prohibited recruiters from asking prospective enlistees their sexual orientation. The second repealed the statutory ban on women serving on combat ships. A stockpile stewardship program was established under the direction of the secretary of energy to ensure the preservation of intellectual and technical competencies with respect to nuclear weapons.

In other action, Congress approved the final appropriation for the Resolution Trust Corporation, the agency created to resolve the savings and loan debacle of the 1980s, and called for its termination in two years.

Efforts to improve the management and accountability of government agencies resulted in the Government Performance and Results Act and the Federal Acquisitions Streamlining Act. The first of these two acts sought to shift the focus of management and decision making away from a preoccupation with activities that are undertaken, to a focus on the results, service quality, and customer satisfaction. The second simplified acquisition procedures for commercial items, initiated a computer-based acquisition system, and placed greater emphasis upon the use of past performance when selecting a contractor. It "launched a major transformation in the way that many federal employees thought about the jobs they did and how they should do them" by encouraging them "to think about the needs of the citizens for whom government programs had been created rather to focus on each's agency's self-interest."[1] Also, early in 1994, Congress adopted several key components of Vice President Gore's plan for "reinventing government," including a requirement calling for a federal employment reduction of more that 250,000 over six years and cash buyouts of up to $25,000 for federal employees who voluntarily retired or resigned. The Hatch Act was revamped, after two decades of calls for changes in the law limiting the political activities of civil servants. Under the new provisions, on-the-job restrictions were tightened while off-duty limits were eased.

Six years in the making, a six-year, $30.2 billion crime package became law in 1994. Most of the funds authorized in the legislation took the form of grants to state and local governments. A trust fund was created to pay for anticrime programs authorized by the act. The bill also increased punishment for a wide variety of offenses. The Brady Bill, the first major gun control legislation to come out of Congress in fifteen years, established a five-day waiting period for handgun purchases. The crusade for a new gun control law was led by former White House press secretary James S. Brady, for whom the bill was named, and his wife, Sarah. Brady was permanently disabled in the 1981 assassination attempt on President Ronald Reagan.

Additional limits were placed on the Food and Drug Administration's regulation of safety and labeling of dietary supplements. Manufacturers and consumers of vitamins, minerals, and herbal remedies had advocated the restrictions.

President Clinton's plan to overhaul the health care system, fashioned under the leadership of first lady Hillary Rodham Clinton, initially received favorable reviews when it was unveiled in 1993. Clinton's goal was to provide affordable health care to all Americans. Vigorous opposition to the proposal from the health insurance industry and Republicans, and widespread public concern about its sweeping and complicated nature prevented the legislation from coming to a vote.

Bankruptcy proceedings were made cheaper, faster, and fairer to both creditors and debtors. The new law also sought to encourage debtors to repay their obligations. In separate action, banks were allowed to establish branch offices nationwide, providing a long-sought victory for the largest financial institutions. Congress acted to reverse a controversial U.S. Supreme Court decision that allowed states and the federal government to restrict individual religious rights if it served a valid purpose.

The intent of the Community Development Banking and Financial Institutions Act was to promote economic revitalization and community development in distressed urban and rural communities across the nation. The goal was to improve the supply of capital, credit, private investment, and development services in those areas. With the Riegle-Neal Interstate Banking and Branching Efficiency Act, Congress eliminated most restrictions on interstate bank acquisitions and make interstate branching possible for the first time in seventy years.

Despite significant opposition from members of his own party, President Clinton was able to forge a majority in the House with Republican assistance to win approval of the North American Free Trade Agreement (NAFTA); Senate approval quickly followed. The tripartite treaty provided for the elimination of most tariff and trade barriers between the United States, Mexico, and Canada. The president argued that the agreement would create more high-paying, skilled jobs and prevent the loss of the lucrative Mexican market to foreign competitors. He agreed to several environmental and labor-related concessions in gaining its approval.

A rare, two-day, lame duck session opened on November 30, 1994, to consider legislation implementing the General Agreement on Tariffs and Trade (GATT).

The session became necessary after opponents of free trade policy used parliamentary procedures to stall action during the regular session. GATT, which President Clinton characterized as the "largest world trade agreement in history," was designed to reduce tariffs worldwide by approximately 40 percent. Eight years of protracted negotiations had preceded the signing of GATT in April 1994.

President Clinton requested $2.5 billion in economic and technical aid for the former Soviet republics. In exchange, the administration had to accept deep cuts in a number of other foreign assistance programs, including U.S. support for international financial institutions.

Fallout from the House Post Office scandal, which became public in 1991, continued. Among others, Dan Rostenkowski of Illinois, who had held the powerful position of chairman of the House Ways and Means Committee since 1981, was charged with criminal wrongdoing. He pled guilty to corruption charges in 1996 and was sentenced to jail.

The 1994 congressional elections were held amid allegations about President Clinton's personal life and questions concerning the involvement of the president and first lady with the Whitewater Development Company, a matter that had come under investigation by independent counsel Kenneth W. Starr. Furthermore, widespread dissatisfaction was evident with the Democratically led House and Senate, big government, career politicians, and a growing federal deficit. These issues, together with a well-coordinated GOP campaign in which the party emphasized national issues (midterm election normally focuses on local district contests) by offering a "Contract with America"—a list of ten Republican priorities—contributed to the conclusion of forty years of Democratic control of the House. When the ballots were counted, the Republicans gained fifty-four seats in the House. Not since the 1946 elections, when the Democrats lost fifty-five seats in the House, had the incumbent president's party lost more than fifty seats.

Major Acts

Family and Medical Leave Act of 1993. Required businesses with fifty or more employees to grant workers up to twelve weeks of unpaid leave during any twelve-month period to deal with the birth of a child, adoption of a child, or the placement of a foster child; care for a seriously ill child, spouse, or parent; or see to a serious health problem. Approved February 5, 1993 (P.L. 103–3; 107 Stat. 6–29).

National Voter Registration Act of 1993 (Motor Voter Act). Required states to provide all eligible citizens the opportunity to register to vote when applying for or renewing a driver's license, to register by mail, and to obtain registration forms at certain public assistance agencies. Approved May 20, 1993 (P.L. 103–31; 107 Stat. 77–89).

Government Performance and Results Act. Required federal agencies to (1) develop multi-year strategic plans that clarified their missions and describe methods for reaching them; (2) develop annual performance plans that the Office of Management and Budget could use to prepare a federal performance plan that would be submitted to Congress, along with the president's budget submission; (3) establish measurable goals for program activities and describe the methods for measuring performance toward those goals; and (4) prepare an annual report to Congress on how they performed against those goals. Approved August 3, 1993 (P.L. 103–62; 107 Stat. 285–295).

Omnibus Budget Reconciliation Act of 1993. Provided an estimated $504.8 billion reduction (according to the Office of Management and Budget) in the federal deficit over five years (fiscal years 1994–1998), $250.1 billion of which was to come from tax increases and $254.7 billion in spending cuts. Raised personal income tax rates on high-level earners to a maximum 39.6 percent. Provided for a 4.3 cents per gallon increase in the tax on transportation fuels and a $55.8 billion cut in Medicare. Set limits on discretionary spending for fiscal 1997 and 1998. Raised the public debt limit to $4.9 trillion. Approved August 10, 1993 (P.L. 103–66; 107 Stat. 312–685).

Communications Licensing and Spectrum Allocation Improvement Act. Required the Federal Communications Commission chairman and the assistant secretary of commerce for telecommunications to meet at least biannually to plan the management of radio spectrum licenses. Stipulated that the agenda of these meetings include auctioning spectrum licenses through competitive bidding and any other actions needed to promote efficient use of the spectrum. Required the secretary of commerce to identify which radio frequencies used by the government could be turned over to the private sector within eighteen months. Approved August 10, 1993 (P.L. 103–66, Title VI; 107 Stat. 379–401).

National and Community Service Trust Act of 1993. Created a Corporation for National and Community Service to administer a program of educational awards of up to $4,725 a year, for a maximum of two years, to individuals seventeen or older who performed community service before, during, or after their post-secondary education. Required recipients to be high school graduates or to agree to achieve general equivalency requirements. Authorized $300 million in fiscal 1994, $500 million in fiscal 1995, and $700 million in fiscal 1996 for the program. Required states to establish a commission on national service to apply for and allocate community service grants to state and private organizations operating such programs. Approved September 21, 1993 (P.L. 103–82; 107 Stat. 785–923).

Assistance for the New Independent States of the Former Soviet Union. Provided $2.5 billion in economic and technical aid to the newly independent states of the former Soviet Union ($1.6 billion of which was to be drawn from unexpended fiscal 1993 defense and foreign aid funds). Approved September 30, 1993 (P.L. 103–87, Title V, Sec. 560; 107 Stat. 966–967).

Hatch Act Reform Amendments of 1993. Revised and simplified the 1939 Hatch Act, which limited the political activities of federal employees. Barred federal employees from engaging in political activity while on the job, running for a partisan elective office, or soliciting contributions from the general public. Allowed federal employees to hold office in a political party, participate in political campaigns and rallies, publicly endorse candidates, and raise money within their agency's political action committee. Approved October 6, 1993 (P.L. 103–94; 107 Stat. 1001–1011). *(Hatch Act, p. 259)*

Religious Freedom Restoration Act of 1993. Reversed the 1990 U.S. Supreme Court decision in *Employment Division v. Smith,* holding that states could impose laws that incidentally limited religious freedom as long as they served a "valid" state purpose and were not aimed at inhibiting religion. Restored the stringent standard in church-state jurisprudence that allowed states to impose laws inhibiting religion only when they served a "compelling" government interest. Approved November 16, 1993 (P.L. 103–141; 107 Stat. 1488–1490).

Brady Handgun Violence Prevention Act. Required a would-be gun purchaser to wait five business days before buying a handgun, so local police could do a background check on the individual. Raised licensing fees for gun dealers and required them to notify the police of multiple gun purchases. Provided that the waiting period be replaced within five years by a "national instant criminal background check" system that could scan criminal records to screen out convicted felons and other ineligible buyers. Approved November 30, 1993 (P.L. 103–159; 107 Stat. 1536–1546).

Assignment of Women in the Armed Forces to Combat Ships. Repealed the "combat exclusion" law barring the assignment of women to combat ships. November 30, 1993 (P.L. 103–160, Div. A, Title V, Subtitle D, Sec. 541–543; 107 Stat. 1659–1661). *(Assignment of Women in the Armed Forces to Combat Aircraft, p. 406)*

Homosexuality in the Armed Forces. Declared that homosexual conduct would continue to be prohibited in the military, but prohibited recruiters from asking prospective enlistees if they were gay. Stipulated that investigations of suspected homosexuals could be initiated only by a senior officer acting on the basis of "credible information." Approved November 30, 1993 (P.L. 103–160, Div. A, Title V, Subtitle G, Sec. 571; 107 Stat. 1670–1673).

Stockpile Stewardship Program. Mandated that the secretary of energy establish a "stewardship program to ensure the preservation of the core intellectual and technical competencies of the United States in nuclear weapons, including weapons design, system integration, manufacturing, security, use control, reliability assessment, and certification." Approved November 30, 1993 (P.L. 103–160, Div. C, Title XXXI, Subtitle C, Sec. 3138; 107 Stat. 1946–1947).

North American Free Trade Agreement Implementation Act. Provided for the implementation of the North American Free Trade Agreement (NAFTA), which eliminated all tariffs and most other trade barriers between the United States, Mexico, and Canada within fifteen years. Provided for changes in existing federal laws governing trade and other matters to correspond with the tripartite agreement. Made changes in the 1988 U.S.-Canada Free Trade Agreement (P.L. 100–449). Approved December 8, 1993 (P.L. 103–182; 107 Stat. 2057–2225).

Resolution Trust Corporation Competition Act. Appropriated $18.3 billion for the Resolution Trust Corporation (RTC) to cover depositor losses of sixty-four failed savings and loan institutions under its control and for a limited number of future failures. Set December 31, 1995, as the termination date of RTC. Approved December 17, 1993 (P.L. 103–204; 107 Stat. 2369–2417).

Federal Work Force Restructuring Act of 1994. Required the federal government to reduce its work force by 252,000 positions over six years. Authorized federal agencies to offer cash buyouts of up to $25,000 to workers who voluntarily retired or resigned. Required employees who accepted cash buyouts and were rehired within five years to repay the full amount of the buyout. Approved March 30, 1994 (P.L. 103–226; 108 Stat. 111–124).

Goals 2000: Educate America Act. Established eight national education goals for elementary and secondary schools to be achieved by the year 2000. Prescribed that (1) children would start school ready to learn; (2) at least 90 percent of all high school students would graduate; (3) students advancing from grades four, eight, and twelve would demonstrate competence in particular subjects; (4) teachers would be afforded opportunities to enhance their skills; (5) the United States would become the first in the world in mathematics and science achievement; (6) every adult would become literate; (7) every school would be free of drugs and violence; and (8) schools would promote parent involvement. Created an eighteen member National Education Goals Board to oversee and report on progress in achieving the eight goals. Created a National Skill Standards Board to develop a national system of standards and testing to assure that students had the necessary skills to compete in the work force. Approved March 31, 1994 (P.L. 103–227; 108 Stat. 125–280).

Violent Crime Control and Law Enforcement Act of 1994. Authorized $30.2 billion over six years to fight crime in the United States; including $8.8 billion in grants to state and local governments for additional police, $7.9 billion for state prison construction, and $6.9 billion for crime prevention programs. Expanded the death penalty to several dozen new federal crimes, banned nineteen types of semiautomatic assault weapons, and mandated life imprisonment for three-time offenders. Created an anticrime trust fund to pay for the programs authorized in the bill. Approved September 13, 1994 (P.L. 103–322; 108 Stat. 1796–2151).

Community Development Banking and Financial Institutions Act. Established the Community Development Banking and Financial Institutions Fund (CDBFI) to assist communities in developing financial institutions (CDFI) in low-income areas and to provide coordinated development strategies across various sectors of the local economy that are designed to encourage small business, affordable housing, the availability of commercial real estate, and human development. Authorized the CDFI to provide matching grants, loans, equity capital, and technical assistance to community development banks, credit unions, and loan funds that made loans in inner cities and poor rural areas generally underserved by traditional banks. Approved September 23, 1994 (P.L. 103–325, Title I, Subtitle A; 108 Stat. 2163–2190).

Riegle-Neal Interstate Banking and Branching Efficiency Act of 1994. Allowed banks to establish branch offices nationwide and removed existing barriers to interstate bank ownership. Approved September 29, 1994 (P.L. 103–328; 108 Stat. 2338–2381).

Federal Acquisitions Streamlining Act. Repealed or substantially modified more than 225 federal acquisitions laws. Established a "preference" for commercial off-the-shelf products in meeting agency procurement needs rather than products specifically designed to meet burdensome government specifications. Established the Federal Acquisitions Network to reduce paperwork by providing a single electronic face to industry, and to increase interoperability between agencies. Mandated use of contractor past performance data in awarding contracts. Approved October 13, 1994 (P.L. 355; 108 Stat. 3243–3409).

Bankruptcy Reform Act of 1994. Revised the three main sections of the federal Bankruptcy Code—Chapters 7 and 11, which governed individual bankruptcies, and Chapter 13, which controlled business bankruptcies. Provided an expedited bankruptcy process, and sought to encourage debtors to work out repayment plans, instead of filing for bankruptcy. Made it more difficult for an individual to use bankruptcy as a means of not paying alimony and child support. Created a National Bankruptcy Review Commission to study and recommend changes in the Bankruptcy Code. Approved October 22, 1994 (P.L. 103–394; 108 Stat. 4106–4151).

Dietary Supplemental Health and Education Act of 1994. Allowed manufacturers of dietary supplements to make statements of nutritional support under certain conditions and to sell new products without Food and Drug Administration (FDA) approval, provided they submitted evidence of product safety to the FDA seventy-five days prior to marketing new products.

Allowed the FDA to block marketing of a new product if information provided did not assure that it was safe and to halt sales of products it could demonstrate caused a significant or unreasonable risk. Created a commission to recommend standards and procedures for settling labeling claims of supplements. Established an Office of Dietary Supplements within the National Institutes of Health to "promote scientific study of the benefits of dietary supplements in maintaining health and preventing chronic disease and other health-related conditions." Approved October 25, 1994 (P.L. 103–417; 108 Stat. 4325–4335).

General Agreement on Tariffs and Trade Implementation Act. Provided for the implementation of the General Agreement on Tariffs and Trade (GATT), predicted to reduce tariffs worldwide by nearly 40 percent. Made numerous changes to bring U.S. laws into conformance with the terms of GATT, which broadened the system of multilateral trade rules to cover such areas as agriculture, business accounting, computer services, intellectual property rights, and tourism. Provided financing to offset an expected $12 billion loss in tariff revenues during the first five years of the agreement. Approved December 8, 1994 (P.L. 103–465; 108 Stat. 4809–4993).

Note

1. Donald F. Kettl, *The Global Public Management Revolution*, 2d ed. (Washington, D.C.: Brookings Institution Press, 2005, 24–25.

One Hundred Fourth Congress

January 3, 1995, to January 3, 1997

First session—January 4, 1995, to January 3, 1996
Second session—January 3, 1996, to October 4, 1996
(First administration of Bill Clinton, 1993–1997)

Historical Background

The convening of the One Hundred Fourth Congress marked the first time since 1954 that Republicans held a majority in both the House and Senate. The House immediately began work on the ten broad proposals that constituted the Contract with America, which had been advanced as a national platform for many House Republican incumbents and challengers in the 1994 elections. In the first few weeks of 1995, the Republican majority in the House also made extensive changes in the chamber's structure and procedures, including eliminating several committees, changing committee jurisdictions, reducing committee staff, establishing term limits for congressional leaders and committee chairs, and reorganizing administrative services.

The first law produced by the new Congress satisfied the House Republicans' pledge to ensure that "all laws that apply to the rest of the country also apply equally to Congress." Passage of the Congressional Accountability Act extended protection under eleven federal labor and antidiscrimination laws to approximately thirty-four thousand congressional employees. The second piece of the Contract to become law restricted new unfunded federal mandates from being imposed on state and local governments without providing funds to pay for them. A third goal of the Contract, which was shared by the administration's "reinventing government" initiative, sought to reduce the federal paperwork burden placed on individuals, businesses, educational institutions, and state and local governments. It was achieved in May 1995.

Amidst a general atmosphere of rising partisan strife, agreement between Congress and the White House on fiscal matters proved difficult to achieve. Fourteen stopgap funding measures were required before the fiscal 1996 budget was complete. More significantly, the government shut down twice, and as a result the GOP congressional majority took a beating in public opinion polls.

A line-item veto measure, also advocated in the Contract with America and enacted into law, empowered the president to cancel items in spending bills if it could be shown that a cancellation would reduce the federal deficit, did not impair essential government functions, and did not harm the public interest. Congress provided for the use of a special "disapproval bill" in those instances when a president's action was considered inappropriate. The disapproval bill was subject to a presidential veto, with a two-thirds majority of each house needed to override. On June 25, 1998, the U.S. Supreme Court in *Clinton v. City of New York,* by a 6 to 3 ruling, held that the Line Item Veto Act violated Article I, Section 7 of the Constitution, which says, in part, that every bill "which shall have passed the House of Representatives and the Senate, shall, before it become a law, be presented to the President of the United States: If he approves he shall sign it, but if not he shall return it." The Line Item Veto Act, the majority of the Court held, was unconstitutional because it allowed the president to rewrite bills he had already signed into law.

Nearly two months of conference negotiations were needed to resolve House and Senate differences over riders attached to a bill that added more than 160,000 miles of heavily traveled regional roadways to the

National Highway System. Adoption of these controversial provisions further reduced federal mandates on states by allowing them to establish their own maximum speed limits, motorcycle helmet rules, and seat belt requirements. The 108-year-old Interstate Commerce Commission (ICC), the oldest federal regulatory agency, was officially abolished in December 1995, and its remaining functions were transferred to the newly created Surface Transportation Board within the Department of Transportation. This action completed the process that had been taking place over the preceding fifteen years, which had eliminated much of the authority of the ICC over surface transportation.

Congress also overhauled the telecommunications and information industry to promote competition and ease regulation. The key element of the bill allowed the seven regional Bell telephone companies, created under the 1982 court order that broke up the American Telephone & Telegraph Company, to begin offering long-distance service.

American farmers were given greater planting flexibility but declining federal subsidies, regardless of market conditions, in far-reaching agriculture legislation that replaced decades-old New Deal farm programs. Opponents argued that Congress, in moving agriculture toward a free market, would make it even more difficult for farmers to survive, as the safety net government had created for them was eliminated. Another dramatic shift in agricultural policy manifested itself in a sweeping overhaul of federal pesticide regulations. Although efforts to overhaul pesticide regulations had been made for nearly two decades, recent court decisions had interpreted pesticides so strictly that the Environmental Protection Agency had been prepared to cancel the use of certain common chemicals if Congress had not acted. The new standards, it was felt, represented an acceptable balance between consumers and the chemical industry.

The welfare program, which dated back to the 1930s, underwent major reform after lengthy negotiations between the president and congressional Republicans. In signing the legislation, President Clinton declared that its passage marked "an historic chance to make welfare what it was meant to be: a second chance, not a way of life." Under the new act, states were given broad authority in running their own welfare programs, and welfare recipients were generally limited to two years of assistance.

Renewal of the Safe Drinking Water Act of 1974 had the support of the White House, as well as members of Congress from both sides of the aisle. The measure streamlined federal regulation of drinking water and provided $7.6 billion for federal grants to states creating safe water revolving funds to help local water systems improve facilities. The 1976 Magnuson Fishery Conservation and Management Act (P.L. 94–265), which was sponsored by Sen. Warren G. Magnuson of Washington, was amended in 1996 to protect the fishing industry and assure that certain fishing areas were not depleted.

While the president's ambitious health care plan failed in 1994, bipartisan efforts closed gaps in existing programs. Among these was the Health Insurance Portability Act, guaranteeing that when individuals left a job, lost a job, or became self-employed, they could continue their health insurance coverage.

A perceived need to modernize regulation of the securities and mutual funds industry resulted in the elimination of duplicative state and federal regulation of the investment advisory industry, leaving that role to the Securities and Exchange Commission.

The imposition of new disclosure requirements on lobbyists was designed to close loopholes in the 1946 lobby law that enabled most lobbyists to avoid registering. The Lobbying Disclosure Act required any lobbyist who received more than $5,000 from a single client during a six-month period to register with the clerk of the House and the secretary of the Senate.

In response to Cuba's downing of two U.S. civilian planes in February 1995, Congress imposed sanctions against individuals and foreign companies that invested in properties claimed by U.S. citizens that had been confiscated by the communist government of Cuba.

Intense last-minute negotiations with the White House just before Congress adjourned led to the passage of legislation calling for increased funding to stem illegal immigration, enhance detention and deportation procedures, establish new penalties for alien smuggling and document fraud, set up programs to identify illegal aliens, and increase barriers to illegal aliens gaining access to federal benefits.

In November 1996, Bill Clinton became the first Democrat since Franklin D. Roosevelt in 1936 to be reelected to a second term. Clinton and Vice President Al Gore defeated former Senate Majority Leader

Bob Dole of Kansas and his running mate, Jack Kemp, secretary of housing and urban development during the Bush administration and former representative from New York. Clinton and Gore won the electoral vote by a 379 to 159 margin. Ross Perot, whose third-party candidacy failed to repeat its strong showing of 1992, received about 8.4 percent of the popular vote. In the congressional elections, the Republicans maintained their majority in both houses.

On December 21, 1996, House Speaker Newt Gingrich of Georgia, who was being investigated by the House Committee on Standards of Official Conduct, admitted that he had improperly managed the financing of his political activities and that he had lied to the committee in the course of its probe. Gingrich, who was largely responsible for engineering the Republican takeover of the House as a result of the 1994 elections, had repeatedly denied any wrongdoing. The One Hundred Fourth Congress closed with Gingrich's future uncertain.

Major Acts

Congressional Accountability Act of 1995. Required Congress to comply with eleven federal labor and anti-discrimination laws: Fair Labor Standards Act of 1938 (P.L. 101–157); Civil Rights Act of 1964 (P.L. 88–352); Age Discrimination in Employment Act of 1967 (P.L. 90–202); Occupational Safety and Health Act of 1970 (P.L. 91–596); Rehabilitation Act of 1973 (P.L. 93–112); Employee Polygraph Protection Act of 1988 (P.L. 100–347); Worker Adjustment and Retraining Notification Act of 1988 (P.L. 100–379); Americans with Disabilities Act of 1990 (P.L. 101–336); Family and Medical Leave Act of 1993 (P.L. 103–3); Veterans Reemployment Act of 1993 (P.L. 103–353); and the federal labor-management dispute procedures established in Title V (Chapter 71) of the U.S. Code. Allowed congressional employees to take claims to federal court following an initial mediation and counseling stage, and specified that the House and Senate ethics committees retained the power to discipline members, officers, and employees who violated rules on nondiscrimination in employment. Allowed members to discriminate in their hiring based on party affiliation and "political compatibility." Approved January 23, 1995 (P.L. 104–1; 109 Stat. 3–44).

Unfunded Mandates Reform Act of 1995. Restricted both Congress and executive agencies from imposing mandates on state and local governments, and subjected any intergovernmental mandate exceeding $50 million to a point of order in either the House or Senate. Required authorizing committees approving a bill or resolution containing a federal mandate to draw attention to the mandate in its report, explain how the costs of the mandate were to be borne, and submit the bill to the Congressional Budget Office for a cost estimate. Required federal agencies to notify authorizing committees if insufficient funds were available to carry out a mandate under their jurisdiction and to prepare cost-benefit analyses of intergovernmental mandates on private businesses exceeding $100 million annually. Approved March 22, 1995 (P.L. 104–4; 109 Stat. 48–71).

Paperwork Reduction Act of 1995. Established a goal of reducing the federal paperwork burden placed on individuals, educational institutions, and state and local government by 10 percent in fiscal years 1996–1997 and by 5 percent in fiscal years 1998–2001. Specified that all paperwork requirements, including those of a third party, were subject to review by the Office of Information and Regulatory Affairs (OIRA). Overturned the 1990 U.S. Supreme Court decision in *Dole v. United Steelworkers of America* stating that OIRA review did not extend to third parties such as the public or employees. Reauthorized OIRA, which was responsible for implementing the law for six years (fiscal 1996–2001), with an annual appropriation of $8 million. Approved May 22, 1995 (P.L. 104–13; 109 Stat. 163–185).

National Highway System Designation Act of 1995. Designated more than 160,000 miles of heavily traveled regional roadways to the National Highway System created by Congress in 1991 (P.L. 102–240). Eliminated federal maximum speed limits, and allowed state legislatures to adopt new limits. Eliminated penalties for states that did not mandate motorcycle helmets, and waived sanctions against states not requiring seat belts if seat belt use in those states increased. Required states to establish tougher policies toward drinking by drivers under the age of twenty-one. Barred the Environmental Protection Agency from requiring states to adopt a centralized approach to testing motor vehicle emissions. Approved November 28, 1995 (P.L. 104–59; 109 Stat. 568–634).

Lobbying Disclosure Act of 1995. Required lobbyists receiving more than $5,000 during a six-month period from a single client to register with the clerk of the House and secretary of the Senate. Required lobbyists to list the congressional chambers and federal agencies they contacted, issues discussed, and how much was spent. Applied similar requirements to organizations that used their own employees to lobby and spent more than $20,000 during a six-month period. Approved December 19, 1995 (P.L. 104–65; 109 Stat. 691–706).

Interstate Commerce Commission Termination Act of 1995. Provided for the official termination of the Interstate Commerce Commission (ICC). Transferred many responsibilities and functions of the ICC that had not been eliminated as a consequence of earlier laws deregulating railroad and truck lines to the Surface Transportation Board within the Department of Transportation. Modified federal labor law protection available to employees of railroads involved in mergers, and prevented rail carriers from shifting work from a carrier with a collective bargaining agreement to a carrier without an agreement. Approved December 29, 1995 (P.L. 104–88; 109 Stat. 803–959). Earlier legislation provided $13.4 million in closeout costs for the Interstate Commerce Commission. Approved November 15, 1995 (P.L. 104–50; 109 Stat. 452).

Telecommunications Act of 1996. Allowed the seven regional Bell telephone companies to enter into the long-distance market. Required the seven Bell companies and other phone companies to open networks to competition. Eased price controls on long-distance telephone companies, cable television companies, and broadcasters. Approved February 8, 1996 (P.L. 104–104; 110 Stat. 56–161). Certain provisions of the act were subsequently held unconstitutional in *Reno v. ACLU,* 521 U.S. 844 (1997), and *United States v. Playboy Entertainment Group Inc.,* 120 S.Ct. 1878 (2000).

Cuban Liberty and Democratic Solidarity (LIBERTAD) Act of 1996. Codified existing economic sanctions against Cuba, including the original embargo imposed by President John F. Kennedy in 1962, until a "democratic transition" was under way in Cuba. Permitted U.S. citizens whose properties had been confiscated by the Cuban government to sue persons, companies, or third countries that knowingly acquire or otherwise traffic in these properties. Required the State Department to deny entry into the United States to all persons who trafficked in expropriated properties in Cuba claimed by a U.S. citizen. Authorized U.S. assistance for democracy-building efforts in Cuba. Approved March 12, 1996 (P.L. 104–114; 110 Stat. 785–824).

Federal Agriculture Improvement and Reform Act of 1996 (Freedom to Farm Act). Replaced the existing federal farm policy of issuing subsidies when market prices dropped and requiring farmers to plant the same crop every year with a new seven-year system of fixed, declining federal payments regardless of market prices. Allowed farmers broad flexibility in choosing which crops to grow, and no longer required subsidized farmers to idle land to reduce production of certain crops. Phased out dairy price supports over four years, and scaled back peanut and sugar price-support programs. Reauthorized the food stamp program for two years. Provided $2.5 billion in conservation funding to help producers reduce soil erosion and manure runoff, and earmarked $300 million for a new rural development fund. Approved April 4, 1996 (P.L. 104–127; 110 Stat. 888–1197).

Line Item Veto Act. Gave the president the power to rescind, or cancel, individual spending items contained in appropriations bills or described in congressional reports unless both houses of Congress passed an identical special "disapproval bill" that would be subject to presidential veto. Enabled the president to rescind targeted tax breaks and new or increased entitlement spending. Declared that the president could cancel an item only if doing so would "reduce the Federal budget," "not impair any essential Government function," or "harm the national interest." Approved April 9, 1996 (P.L. 104–130; 110 Stat. 1200–1212). On June 25, 1998, the U.S. Supreme Court in *Clinton v. City of New York* (524 U.S. 417 [1998]) held that the Line Item Veto Act violated the Presentment Clause of the Constitution.

Food Quality Protection Act of 1996. Repealed provisions (the Delaney Clause) in existing law that prohibited even the most minute traces of cancer-causing pesticide residues in processed foods. Established a new safety standard that required a "reasonable certainty" that pesticide residues in both raw and processed foods would cause no harm. Required the Environmental Protection Agency (EPA) to consider special protections for infants and children when setting pesticide tolerance levels and to prepare information describing the risks of pesticides. Permitted the EPA to balance competing health risks when setting standards. Sought to expedite government approval of pesticides, especially those used on fruits and vegetables. Approved August 3, 1996 (P.L. 104–170; 110 Stat. 1489–1538).

Safe Drinking Water Act Amendments of 1996. Allowed the Environmental Protection Agency (EPA) greater flexibility in revising drinking water standards, and required the EPA to consider the risks and costs in setting new standards. Required water systems to notify customers within twenty-four hours of failure to comply with drinking water standards and to publish detailed reports including information on contaminants in system water. Permitted smaller water systems to obtain waivers from some expensive regulations. Authorized $7.6 billion through fiscal 2003 for federal grants to states that established drinking water revolving funds to help local water systems improve drinking water facilities. Approved August 6, 1996 (P.L. 104–182; 110 Stat. 1613–1693).

Health Insurance Portability and Accountability Act of 1996. Provided a health insurance "portability" guarantee for individuals who changed jobs, lost their jobs, or became self-employed, even with a preexisting medical condition. Established a four-year trial program for medical savings accounts, increased the deductibility of health insurance for the self-employed, and provided tax breaks to individuals receiving long-term care insurance benefits. Increased penalties for defrauding the government through federal health care programs. Approved August 21, 1996 (P.L. 104–191; 110 Stat. 1936–2103).

Personal Responsibility and Work Opportunity Reconciliation Act of 1996. Ended the federal guarantee of cash welfare benefits to all eligible low-income mothers and children. Created a block grant for Temporary Assistance for Needy Families to replace the Aid to Families with Dependent Children program and other related programs. Granted states broad authority in designing and running their own welfare programs. Required adult welfare recipients to begin working within two years of receiving aid, and capped benefits at a total of five years. Denied most illegal aliens and legal noncitizens, such as students and travelers, most federal benefits, and gave states discretion to deny Medicaid benefit to certain legal immigrants. Modified laws dealing with food stamps, immigration, supplemental security income benefits, child care programs, and child support enforcement. Approved August 22, 1996 (P.L. 104–193; 110 Stat. 2105–2355).

Economic Growth and Regulatory Paperwork Reduction Act of 1996. Made more than forty changes that eased regulation of the banking industry, simplified disclosure requirements under the Real Estate Settlement Procedures Act of 1974 and the Truth in Lending Act, strengthened the rights of consumers to correct errors in credit reports, facilitated businesses' use of credit information for marketing purposes and for prescreening credit offers, and allowed banks greater flexibility in removing and relocating automatic teller machines. Eased requirements on foreign banks seeking to open U.S. offices and branches. Relieved lenders of open-ended liability for environmental problems on foreclosed properties. Set in place a plan to fully capitalize the Savings Association Insurance Fund, which protected thrift deposits. Approved September 30, 1996 (P.L. 104–208, Title II; 110 Stat. 3009-394–3009-499). *(Consumer Credit Protection Act [Truth in Lending Act], p. 332)*

Illegal Immigration Reform and Immigrant Responsibility Act of 1996. Authorized an additional five thousand border patrol agents by fiscal 2001, an additional twelve hundred Immigration and Naturalization Service investigative agents, and $12 million for the second and third tiers of a triple fence along a fourteen-mile strip of the California-Mexico border. Streamlined detention and deportation proceedings. Increased penalties for alien smuggling and document fraud. Created three pilot programs to test the effectiveness of workplace verification systems. Made it more difficult for illegal immigrants to gain access to such benefit programs as housing assistance, Social Security, student aid, and welfare. Approved September 30, 1996 (P.L. 104–208, Div. C; 110 Stat. 3009-546–3009-724).

National Securities Markets Improvement Act of 1996. Limited state authority to regulate securities listed on national exchanges such as the New York Stock Exchange, American Stock Exchange, and National Association of Securities Dealers Automated Quotation (NASDAQ); mutual funds issued by registered investment firms; and a variety of other securities, transferring that role to the Securities and Exchange Commission. Allowed states to retain regulatory jurisdiction over smaller investment advisers (those managing assets of less than $25 million), to continue collecting fees on mutual fund offerings, and to prosecute for fraud. Allowed brokerage firms to borrow from financial institutions (insurance companies, pension funds, and other lenders) other than banks.

Provided for gradual reduction of Securities and Exchange Commission registration fees. Imposed a transaction fee on the NASDAQ over-the-counter exchange similar to fees accessed on the New York Stock Exchange. Approved October 11, 1996 (P.L. 104–290; 110 Stat. 3416–3451).

Sustainable Fisheries Act. Amended the 1976 Magnuson Fishery Conservation Act "to facilitate long-term protection of essential fish habitats." Delegated responsibility for developing management plans that were in the best economic and environmental interests of their local fisheries to eight regional fishery management councils. Required that the councils establish management plans to restore fish populations to "sustainable" levels. Imposed a moratorium on local councils approving or implementing new fishing quota programs prior to October 1, 2000, and required that the National Academy of Sciences submit a report on the programs by October 1, 1998. Approved October 11, 1996 (P.L. 104–297; 110 Stat. 3559–3621).

One Hundred Fifth Congress

January 3, 1997, to January 3, 1999

First session—January 7, 1997, to November 13, 1997
Second session—January 27, 1998, to December 19, 1998
(Second administration of Bill Clinton, 1997–2001)

Historical Background

For the first time since 1969, the federal government in 1998 had a budget surplus ($70 billion). The stage had been set a year earlier, when President Bill Clinton and Congress agreed in principle to balance the budget and followed through with the enactment of two measures: the Balanced Budget Act of 1997 and the Taxpayer Relief Act of 1997. The Balanced Budget Act of 1997 was estimated to produce a net $127 billion reduction in the federal deficit over five years. These savings would be achieved through Medicare and Medicaid changes, electromagnetic spectrum auctions, a cigarette tax increase, and other savings and taxes. The Taxpayer Relief Act of 1997 made the most dramatic tax cuts since 1981, an estimated $152 billion in net tax cuts over five years and $401 billion over ten years. Offsetting these tax cuts was $56 billion in tax increases over five years and $126 billion in tax increases over ten years. The tax relief package included a child tax credit for children under seventeen, reductions in capital gains and estate taxes, and tax credits for higher education. There were increases in the airline ticket tax, as well as on certain fuels and prepaid telephone calling cards to partially offset the loss of revenue.

The changes made in Medicare were the most extensive in more than two decades. Their primary intent was to restrain excessive growth of payments to doctors, hospitals, and other health care providers.

Approximately five million uninsured children would be covered over a five-year period by the new State Children's Health Insurance Program. The program was financed by a fifteen cents per pack increase in the federal cigarette tax.

The District of Columbia Revitalization Act dramatically changed the relationship between the federal government and the District of Columbia government. It called for the federal government to assume financial responsibility for the city's courts, prison system, and an underfunded pension system. In return, the District would gradually lose its annual federal grant. In addition, the act transferred control of nine of the city's departments to the Financial Control Board, which had been created by Congress in 1995 to oversee the city's finances.

Enactment of the Transportation Equity Act for the Twenty-first Century, the most expensive public works act passed by Congress, linked federal spending for highway programs to annual highway trust fund collections. It also guaranteed a predetermined level of core highway and mass transit programs by creating special categories within the discretionary portion of the federal budget for that purpose. To effect greater competition in ocean shipping, the Ocean Shipping Reform Act allowed confidential contracts between carriers and their customers for the first time.

A bipartisan effort to expedite Food and Drug Administration (FDA) procedures for regulating food, medical devices, and pharmaceuticals resulted in an agreement that allowed the FDA to use other federal agencies as well as private consultants to review certain new products. Similarly, bipartisan support cleared the way for an extensive overhaul of the Internal Revenue Service (IRS) that involved both a restructuring of the agency's management and new rights and protections for citizens dealing with the IRS.

Legislation designed to promote the adoption of abused and neglected children in foster care placed greater emphasis on protecting children's safety. To further expedite the process, states were given a financial incentive to find permanent adoptive parents for foster children. Both the House and Senate by overwhelming votes reauthorized and revised the Individuals with Disabilities Education Act, which had served since 1975 as the main federal education program for disabled students.

Following a U.S. Supreme Court ruling that credit unions had exceeded their charter restrictions by accepting members and groups that did not have a common bond (such as an occupation, association, or community), Congress passed the Credit Union Membership Access Act. The act allowed credit unions to be organized under three categories of membership—groups having a common bond, multiple common bonds, and community bonds—and concluded a debate that pitted the banking industry against the credit unions.

Responding to criticism that federal job training programs were antiquated and redundant, Congress approved the Workforce Investment Act, which consolidated more than sixty programs into block grants to be administered by the states. Under the act, individuals and states were allowed more flexibility in tailoring programs to their specific needs. Local public housing authorities were given greater latitude in using federal housing funds to develop programs through new block grants.

The Senate ratified the Chemical Weapons Convention signed by President George H. W. Bush in 1993, which banned the development, production, purchase, or stockpiling of chemical weapons for battlefield use. Ratification was achieved, however, only after the Clinton administration committed to a restructuring of the nation's foreign policy agencies and the president agreed to submit changes he had negotiated with Russia to the 1972 antiballistic missile treaty and the 1991 conventional forces in Europe treaty to the Senate as treaty amendments. Legislation implementing the Chemical Weapons Convention subsequently was signed into law. In separate action, the Senate extended North Atlantic Treaty Organization (NATO) membership to three former Soviet-bloc nations—Poland, Hungary, and the Czech Republic—an affirmation of the end of the Cold War.

Both the House and Senate engaged in lengthy debates over plans to reorganize foreign policy agencies outside the State Department before a compromise was signed into law as part of an omnibus appropriations measure. The Foreign Affairs Reform and Restructuring Act of 1998 granted the president authority to draft and submit a foreign affairs reorganization plan to Congress before the end of the year and mandated that the plan include the abolishing of three agencies and the reorganization of a fourth.

In October 1998, Congress by overwhelming bipartisan support passed the Iraq Liberation Act. The House supported it by a vote of 360 to 38 and the Senate did so unanimously. Support for efforts to remove the regime headed by Saddam Hussein from power in Iraq and to promote the emergence of a democratic government to replace that regime were spurred by Saddam Hussein himself when he decided to end Iraq's cooperation with UN weapons inspections. President Bill Clinton on signing the act issued a statement embracing the cause of freedom for all Iraqis, declaring he "categorically rejected arguments that this is unattainable due to Iraq's history or its ethnic or sectarian make-up. Iraqis deserve and desire freedom like everyone else." Four years later, Congress cited this act in its October 2002 resolution authorizing the use of force against Iraq.

More than $2 billion was authorized for increased efforts to find and eradicate drugs at their source in Central and South America and to reduce the flow of drugs from countries there. The significant increase in temporary visas issued to highly skilled foreign workers was approved in response to an expressed need of high-tech American companies for additional programmers and other workers with information technology skills.

To bring U.S. copyright law into conformity with that of many European countries, the United States extended the term of copyright protection. The Copyright Term Extension Act also was the result of a decade of lobbying on the part of Hollywood, the music publishing industry, and software and media corporations. Disney led the charge motivated by the fact that its copyright on the infinitely profitable Mickey Mouse was about to expire. The Digital Millennium Copyright Act was enacted in response to technological advances that facilitated large-scale reproduction and distribution of infringing content, and to implement two World Intellectual Property Organization Internet treaties. It made major changes to copyright laws and attempted to address copyrights in the digitally networked environment.

Two bills were passed to provide parents with protection against the detrimental aspects of the Internet. The Child Online Protection Act, prompted by growing concern about protecting children from unsuitable Internet content, prohibited distribution of material over the World Wide Web to children under seventeen considered "harmful to minors" and required Web operators to obtain proof that an individual was an adult before providing access to such materials. The Children's Online Privacy Protection Act of 1998 was crafted to protect the privacy of children and required operators of Web sites to obtain verifiable parental consent before collecting, using, or disseminating information about children younger than thirteen.

With the convening of the One Hundred Fifth Congress, the first order of business for the House of Representatives was to determine the fate of Newt Gingrich, who had acknowledged violating House rules the previous December. Although Gingrich was narrowly reelected as Speaker on January 7, 1997, he never assuaged the forces within the Republican conference that were discontented with his leadership. On January 21, Gingrich, on a 395 to 28 vote, became the first sitting Speaker to be reprimanded. Increasing unhappiness with Gingrich culminated in July, with an ill-conceived attempt to remove him as Speaker. Thereafter, although he devoted more attention to keeping in touch with House members and being more of a traditional Speaker, his future remained in doubt.

During the One Hundred Fifth Congress, several months of allegations about indiscreet conduct culminated in the House impeachment of Bill Clinton. It was the second such indictment of a president in American history, the other being Andrew Johnson in 1868. In January 1998, independent counsel Kenneth W. Starr, initially appointed to investigate the president's involvement in Whitewater, expanded his forty-one-month-old probe to include matters being pursued in a civil suit filed by former Arkansas state employee Paula Jones, who alleged that Clinton had sexually harassed

her while he was governor. Earlier, in May 1997, the U.S. Supreme Court had ruled that Jones could press her lawsuit against a sitting president.

Seeking to establish a pattern of behavior, Jones's lawyers questioned several women who had been linked to Clinton and, on January 17, 1998, questioned the president himself. In his testimony, Clinton, the first sitting president to testify as a civil defendant, denied having an affair with Monica S. Lewinsky, a former White House intern, who, in an earlier deposition, voiced a similar denial. Starr, however, had already acquired tape recordings from a former Lewinsky coworker, Linda R. Tripp, of telephone conversations in which Lewinsky described involvement with the president.

After the Lewinsky matter became public four days later, Clinton again denied having a "sexual relationship with that woman," and continued to do so for several months. Meanwhile, Starr had a grand jury impaneled and, on July 17, 1998, subpoenaed Clinton. The president subsequently agreed to testify before the grand jury via videotape, one day after Lewinsky was granted immunity for her testimony. Following his August 21 grand jury testimony, Clinton admitted publicly to having had an inappropriate relationship with Lewinsky. On September 9, Starr delivered a report (with thirty-six boxes of accompanying documents) to the House that outlined eleven possible grounds for impeachment. On September 11, the House voted 363 to 63 to release 445 pages of Starr's report. One week later, on September 18, the House Judiciary Committee voted to release Clinton's videotaped grand jury testimony and twenty-eight hundred pages of additional testimony. Three days thereafter, all four major televison networks broadcast Clinton's videotaped testimony.

On October 8, 1998, the House, by a 258–176 vote, approved a resolution launching an impeachment inquiry. Subsequently, the House Judiciary Committee approved four articles of impeachment, two of which were adopted on December 19 by the full House. The first of the two adopted articles, approved 228 to 206, charged Clinton with lying to a grand jury about the "nature and details of his relationship" with Lewinsky. The second, approved 221 to 212, accused Clinton of obstructing and impeding the administration of justice "personally and through his subordinates and agents, in a course of conduct or scheme designed to delay, impede, cover up, and conceal" his relationship with Lewinsky. Both votes were partisan, with Republicans voting almost unanimously to adopt the articles of impeachment and Democrats equally united in opposing them. While many Democrats condemned the president's conduct, they insisted that it did not rise to the level of "high crimes and misdemeanors" necessary for impeachment and removal from office. The Senate trial took place at the beginning of 1999.

Amidst the impeachment process, the congressional midterm elections were held. Although the Republicans kept their majority in the House, they had a disappointing showing and lost a number of seats. House Speaker Gingrich blamed himself for the GOP's electoral defeat and resigned from Congress shortly after the election. Rep. Robert L. Livingston of Louisiana emerged as Gingrich's likely successor, but Livingston, too, resigned from Congress, following revelations that he had had extramarital affairs. Rep. J. Dennis Hastert of Illinois subsequently was elected Speaker of the One Hundred Sixth Congress. As a result of the 1998 elections, the Republicans retained their advantage in the Senate.

Major Acts and Treaties

Chemical Weapons Convention. Banned the use of chemical weapons in combat even as a means of retaliation against chemical attack. Prohibited development, production, sale, use, or stockpiling of chemical weapons for battlefield use. Prohibited signatories from helping other nations engage in such activities or selling certain chemicals to nonsignatory nations. Required signatories to enact criminal penalties for attempts to thwart treaty aims. Established the Organization for the Prohibition of Chemical Weapons to monitor chemical weapons activities of signatory countries. Concluded January 13, 1993. Ratification advised by the Senate April 24, 1997.[1] In October 1988, Congress provided for implementation of the Chemical Weapons Convention. Established a legal framework for compliance inspections; procedures for the seizure, forfeiture, transfer, and possession of contraband chemical weapons; authority for fulfilling

convention record-keeping and reporting requirements; restrictions on certain chemicals; and a mechanism for protecting related confidential business information. Authorized the president to issue regulations applying treaty prohibitions to anyone in the United States and to U.S. citizens anywhere in the world. Approved October 21, 1998 (P.L. 105–277, Title XXVIII, Div. I; 112 Stat. 2681-856–2681-886).

Individuals with Disabilities Education Act Amendments of 1997. Revised and reauthorized the Education for All Handicapped Children Act of 1975. Broadened authority of school officials to discipline disruptive students for behavior not related to their disability, but required that suspended or expelled students continue to receive special education services. Created a new funding formula allowing states to reduce local spending for the program once federal appropriations reached $9 billion (the fiscal 1997 appropriation was $4 billion). Approved June 4, 1997 (P.L. 105–17; 111 Stat. 37–157). *(Education for All Handicapped Children Act of 1975, p. 357)*

Balanced Budget Act of 1997. Provided an estimated $263 billion in deficit reduction over five years, including $122 billion in entitlement program savings, most coming from Medicare ($115 billion) and Medicaid ($10.4 billion) and $140 billion from extending the limits on discretionary spending through 2002. Extended pay-as-you-go rules for entitlement and tax changes. Broadened Federal Communications Commission authority to auction electromagnetic spectrums carrying signals for cellular telephones, radio, and television. Restored an estimated $13 billion in welfare benefits cuts made in the Personal Responsibility and Work Opportunity Reconciliation Act of 1996 (P.L. 104–193), including certain benefits for legal immigrants and assistance for welfare recipients joining the work force. Approved August 5, 1997 (P.L. 105–33; 111 Stat. 251–787). *(Personal Responsibility and Work Opportunity Reconciliation Act of 1996, p. 419)*

Medicare Changes. Provided for a reduction in the growth of Medicare costs by reducing payments made to doctors, hospitals, and other health care providers. Established a Medicare+Choice program that broadened health care options available to Medicare beneficiaries beyond those previously available under health maintenance organizations, with out-of-pocket costs varying according to the plan selected. Created a pilot program to allow about 390,000 individuals to use tax-deductible medical service savings accounts instead of traditional Medicare to pay for health expenses. Approved August 5, 1997 (P.L. 105–33, Title IV, Subtitles A-G, Sec. 4000–4644; 111 Stat. 270–488).

State Children's Health Insurance Program (S-CHIP). Provided $20 billion in federal matching funds, which states were required to match to receive money for health care coverage for low-income children between fiscal years 1998 and 2002. Allowed states considerable flexibility in determining benefits packages. Based state funding allocations on a combination of a percentage of uninsured children and children living in families with incomes 200 percent below the federal poverty level. Offset costs of S-CHIP with a fifteen cents per pack increase in cigarette taxes. Approved August 5, 1997 (P.L. 105–33, Title IV, Subtitle J, Chap. 1–3, Sec. 2101–2110, 4911–4923; 111 Stat. 552–574).

National Capital Revitalization and Self-Government Improvement Act of 1997. Provided for the federal government to assume financial responsibility for District of Columbia prisons, courts, and a District employee pension system. Transferred control of nine District governmental departments—Administrative Services, Consumer and Regulatory Affairs, Corrections, Employment Services, Fire and Emergency Medical Services, Housing and Community Development, Human Services, Public Works, and Public Health—from the mayor and City Council to the Financial Control Board created by Congress in 1995 to oversee the city's finances. Required the board to establish management reforms with the assistance of consultants. Approved August 5, 1997 (P.L. 105–33, Title XI; 111 Stat. 712–787).

Taxpayer Relief Act of 1997. Provided an estimated $152 billion in tax cuts and $56 billion in offsetting tax increases over five years and $401 billion in tax cuts and $126 billion in offsetting tax increases over ten years. Provided for family and education tax cuts. Reduced capital gains, estate, and gift taxes, and

provided for expansion of individual retirement accounts. Increased deductibility of health insurance for the self-employed and certain home office expenses. Increased airline ticket tax; reinstated excise tax on gasoline, diesel fuel, special motor fuels, aviation fuels, and inland waterway fuels; consolidated excise tax on truck and truck tires; and clarified excise tax on prepaid phone cards and tax on kerosene. Approved August 5, 1997 (P.L. 105–34; 111 Stat. 788–1103).

Adoption and Safe Families Act of 1997. Provided states financial incentives and greater flexibility in finding permanent homes for foster children. Specified that states were not required to unite a family, as necessary under the 1980 Child Welfare Act (P.L. 96–272), if a court determined a child had been subjected to "aggravated circumstances," such as abandonment, torture, chronic abuse and sexual abuse, or a parent who killed or assaulted another child. Required states to expedite the process for making foster children available for adoption, run criminal record checks on prospective foster or adoptive parents, and provide insurance for adoptive children with special needs or disabilities. Approved November 19, 1997 (P.L. 105–89; 111 Stat. 2115–2136).

Food and Drug Administration Modernization Act of 1997. Required the Food and Drug Administration (FDA), when reviewing a medical device, to focus on the intended use listed on the manufacturer's label, to test for additional uses if it found the labeling false or misleading, and to require a warning against using the device in a way that was not intended. Allowed medical device manufacturers to contract with FDA-accredited consultants to review certain medical devices that manufacturers said were "substantially equivalent" to ones already on the market, but left the final decision to the FDA. Allowed food producers to use health and nutrient claims made by federal scientific agencies on packaging unless the FDA objected. Approved November 21, 1997 (P.L. 105–115; 111 Stat. 2296–2380).

Poland, Hungary, and the Czech Republic Join NATO. Provided U.S. approval for the admission of three former Warsaw Pact nations—Poland, Hungary, and the Czech Republic (formerly part of Czechoslovakia)—to the North Atlantic Treaty Organization (NATO). Ratified by the Senate April 30, 1998.[2]

Transportation Equity Act for the Twenty-first Century. Authorized $217.9 billion for surface transportation, including $174.6 billion for highways, $41 billion for mass transit programs, and $2 billion for safety programs, over six years. Guaranteed a 40 percent increase in federal funding for surface transportation by creating two new categories within the discretionary budget—a highway category providing funding for core highway programs at a level dictated by the annual revenue collections of the highway account in the highway trust fund, and a transit category providing funding for core mass transit programs at a statutory level not affected by an increase or decrease in trust fund receipts. Provided for additional funds through the annual appropriation process. Allowed states and local government more flexibility in using federal transportation funds. Approved June 9, 1998 (P.L. 105–178; 112 Stat. 107–509). Technical corrections to the act were incorporated in subsequent legislation. Approved July 22, 1998 (P.L. 105–206, Title IX; 112 Stat. 834–868).

Internal Revenue Service Restructuring and Reform Act of 1998. Directed the Internal Revenue Service (IRS) commissioner to develop and implement a plan to restructure management of the agency. Established a nine-member board to oversee IRS administration, management, conduct, execution, and application of the Internal Revenue Code. Granted taxpayers new rights and protections in dealings with the IRS. Approved July 22, 1998 (P.L. 105–206; 112 Stat. 685–833).

Credit Union Membership Access Act. Established membership standards for multigroup credit unions in response to the 1998 U.S. Supreme Court ruling in *National Credit Union Administration v. First National Bank and Trust* Co. that credit unions had exceeded legal authority by accepting members and groups without a common bond such as an occupation, association, or community. Allowed credit unions to continue to accept members from unrelated groups as long as

the number of potential members was more than three thousand. Required the National Credit Union Administration to issue guidelines and regulations to ensure credit union "safety or soundness." Approved August 7, 1998 (P.L. 105–219; 112 Stat. 913–935).

Workforce Investment Act of 1998. Repealed the Job Training Partnership Act of 1982 and the Adult Education Act of 1966, and amended the Wagner-Peyser Act of 1933 and the Rehabilitation Act of 1973. Consolidated more than sixty federal job training programs into block grants administered by the states. Made major changes in Job Corps residential education and training program for disadvantaged youth. Reauthorized vocational rehabilitation and adult literacy programs. Approved August 7, 1998 (P.L. 105–220; 112 Stat. 936–1247).

Ocean Shipping Reform Act of 1998. Allowed ocean ship carriers (primarily container ships) to sign confidential contracts with customers and not make the same terms available to all similarly situated customers. Allowed shore-side labor unions to obtain dock-movement information from contracts for use in monitoring collective bargaining agreements with ship operators. Required ship operators to make rates known to customers, but did not require that rates be filed with the Federal Maritime Commission. Approved October 14, 1998 (P.L. 105–258; 112 Stat. 1902–1917).

Quality Housing and Work Responsibility Act of 1998. Replaced existing federal public housing and low-income rental assistance programs with block grants to local housing authorities for capital improvements, Section 8 rental assistance certificates and vouchers, and operating costs. Granted local housing authorities greater latitude in setting rents, selecting tenants, and choosing and evicting residents. Required that a minimum rent up to $50 be established for public housing and rental vouchers. Required adult residents of public and assisted housing to either contribute eight hours of public service within their communities or participate in financially self-sufficient programs for eight hours a month. Approved October 21, 1998 (P.L. 105–276, Title V; 112 Stat. 2518–2680).

American Competitiveness and Workforce Improvement Act of 1998. Increased the number of temporary visas issued to highly skilled foreign workers (H-1B nonimmigrant aliens) from 65,000 to 115,000 in both fiscal 1999 and fiscal 2000, and 107,500 in fiscal 2001. Required H-1B dependent companies (companies sponsoring a certain percentage of H-1B immigrants or hiring workers who do not have masters degrees and would earn less than $60,000 a year) to show that they had made good-faith efforts to find American workers and to promise not to lay off existing workers with similar skills. Approved October 21, 1998 (P.L. 105–277, Div. C, Title IV; 112 Stat. 2681-641-2681-658).

Children's Online Privacy Protection Act of 1998. Required operators of World Wide Web sites to obtain verifiable parental consent before collecting, using, or disseminating information about children under thirteen, and allowed parents to "opt out" of dissemination of information already collected about children. Required operators of Web sites collecting information to disclose usage plans. Approved October 21, 1998 (P.L. 105–277, Div. C, Title XIII; 112 Stat. 2681-728-2681-735).

Child Online Protection Act. Prohibited commercial distribution of material considered "harmful to minors" over the World Wide Web to children under seventeen. Required operators of Web sites to ask for proof that Web surfers are adults before providing access to such materials. Established a nineteen-member Commission on Online Child Protection to conduct a study of technologies and methods to help reduce access by children to material on the Web harmful to minors. Approved October 21, 1998 (P.L. 105–277, Div. C, Title XIV; 112 Stat. 2681-736-2681-741).

Foreign Affairs Reform and Restructuring Act of 1998. Granted the president authority to draft and submit a foreign affairs reorganization plan to Congress by December 20, 1998. Mandated that the presidential plan include abolishment of the Arms Control and Disarmament Agency, U.S. Information Agency, and International Development Cooperation Agency, merging the functions and personnel of these agencies into the Department of State. Required that the U.S. Agency for International Development be reorganized and stipulated that the agency's administrator report to, and be under the direct authority of, the secretary of state. Approved October 21, 1998 (P.L. 105–277, Div. G, Title IV; 112 Stat. 2681-761–2681-854).

Sonny Bono Copyright Extension Act of 1998 (commonly referred to as the "Mickey Mouse Protection Act"). Extended copyright protection for works created on or after January 1, 1978, from the life of the author plus 50 years, to the life of the author plus 70 years. Extended the copyright for corporate, anonymous or pseudonymous works to 95 years from the year of first publication, or 120 years from the year of creation, whichever expires first. Extended copyright coverage of those works in existence prior to January 1, 1978, and which were still in their first term on January 1, 1978, an additional 20 years. Extended copyrights in their renewal term at the time of the effective date of this act to 95 years from the date the copyright was originally secured. Approved October 27, 1998 (P.L. 105–298; 112 Stat. 2827- 2828). In 2003, the U.S. Supreme Court upheld the constitutionality of the act (*Eldred v. Ashcroft,* 537 U.S. 186 [2003]).

Digital Millennium Copyright Act. Implemented two World Intellectual Property Organization (WIPO) treaties—the WIPO Copyright Treaty and the WIPO Performances and Phonograms Treaty (Title I). Established limitations on the copyright liability for online service and access providers (Title II, "Online Copyright Infringement Liability Limitation Act"). Exempted computer maintenance and repair companies from copyright liability for the reproduction of computer programs that occurred by mere activation of a computer for purposes of maintenance or repair (Title III, "Computer Maintenance Competition Assurance Act"). Contained provisions relating to the functions of the Copyright Office, distance education, the exceptions in the Copyright Act for libraries and for making ephemeral recordings, "webcasting" of sound recordings on the Internet, and the applicability of collective bargaining agreement obligations in the case of transfers of rights in motion pictures (Title IV). Created federal design protection for vessel hulls (Title V, "Vessel Hull Design Protection Act"). Approved October 28, 1998 (P.L. 105–304; 112 Stat. 2860–2918).

Iraq Liberation Act. Expressed the sense of Congress that: "It should be the policy of the United States to support efforts to remove the regime headed by Saddam Hussein from power in Iraq and to promote the emergence of a democratic government to replace that regime." Authorized the president to provide "Iraq democratic opposition organizations" grant assistance for radio and television broadcasting; defense articles from the stocks of the Department of Defense, defense services of the Department,

and military education and training for such organizations; and humanitarian assistance to individuals living in areas of Iraq controlled by such organizations. Approved October 31, 1998 (P.L. 105–338; 112 Stat. 3178–3181).

Notes

1. *Journal of the Executive Proceedings of the Senate* (Washington, D.C.: U.S. Government Printing Office, 1998), 139:180–198.

2. *Journal of the Executive Proceedings of the Senate* (Washington, D.C.: U.S. Government Printing Office, 1998), 140:199–211.

One Hundred Sixth Congress
January 3, 1999, to January 3, 2001

First session—January 6, 1999, to November 22, 1999
Second session—January 24, 2000, to December 15, 2000
(Second administration of Bill Clinton, 1997–2001)

Historical Background

On February 12, 1999, at the end of a twenty-day trial presided over by Chief Justice William H. Rehnquist, the Senate acquitted President Bill Clinton on the two charges on which the House had impeached him in December 1998. Article One charged the president with providing "perjurious, false, and misleading testimony" about the nature of his relationship with White House intern Monica S. Lewinsky before a federal grand jury. It was rejected by a 55–45 vote, 12 short of the two-thirds (67) majority required by the Constitution. Article Two charged the president with directing a "scheme designed to delay, impede, cover up and conceal" his affair with Lewinsky and other evidence unfavorable to him in a sexual harassment lawsuit filed by Paula Jones, a former Arkansas state employee. It was rejected by a 50–50 vote. An attempt to gain a vote on a bipartisan resolution censuring the president for "shameful, reckless and indefensible" conduct was subsequently rejected on a procedural vote.

In April 2000, U.S. District Judge Susan Webber Wright issued the first contempt citation against a sitting president for Clinton's testimony in the Jones case and fined him $90,686. He did not contest the finding.

One of the most significant legislative accomplishments of the One Hundred Sixth Congress was a historic, bipartisan rewrite of laws governing the nation's banking, securities, and insurance industry. The Gramm-Leach-Bliley Act repealed key provisions of the Banking Act of 1933 and the Bank Holding Company Act of 1956, which prohibited affiliations between the banking and securities industries and affiliations between the banking and insurance industries, respectively. Enactment of the bill, which was sponsored by Sen. Phil Gramm of Texas, Rep. Jim Leach of Iowa, and Rep. Thomas J. Bliley Jr. of Virginia, was the culmination of several decades of efforts by the financial community to allow the banking, securities, and insurance industries to compete in each other's arena.

Congress completed work on a broad-ranging rewrite of laws governing a complicated class of financial investments known as derivatives—contracts that are bets on changes in the prices of financial instruments and commodities. The Commodity Futures Modernization Act of 2000 codified the unregulated status of certain derivatives, exempted many other regulated derivative contracts from oversight by the Commodity Futures Trading Commission, and legalized the trading of a new kind of futures contract based on the stock of an individual corporation. Treasury Secretary Lawrence H. Summers and Federal Reserve Board of Governors Chairman Alan Greenspan urged its passage in response to growing concern by U.S. commodity exchanges that uncertainty over the legal status of derivatives under U.S. law was driving business overseas, mostly to European exchanges.

Electronic commerce received a significant boost from legislation that allowed a broad array of business transactions for the first time to be completed with an electronic signature over the Internet. According an e-signature the same legal standing as a handwritten signature, it was argued, would expedite transactions and save the business community billions of dollars in administrative costs. Certain sensitive documents such as wills and court orders were excluded from the bill's coverage, which had bipartisan support. Critical to its passage was the inclusion of a series of consumer protections. The president saw the act as giving "fresh momentum to what is already the longest economic expansion in our history, an expansion driven largely by the phenomenal growth in information technologies, particularly the Internet."

Against the backdrop of a strong economy and a record low unemployment rate, technology companies successfully convinced Congress of the need for a dramatic increase in nonimmigrant visas available for highly skilled technical workers. Passage of the American Competitiveness in the Twenty-first Century Act of 2000 was seen by its supporters as critical for the United States to remain competitive in the world market. Many of the beneficiaries of the act, supporters argued, would be talented foreign students in mathematics, computer science, and engineering who had earned degrees at American universities and colleges. Opponents of the increase in H-1B visas stressed that no compelling evidence existed of a labor shortage that could not be met by qualified U.S. workers.

Enactment of the Trade and Development Act of 2000 ended nearly two decades of congressional debate on how to use trade incentives (instead of aid and loans) to promote economic growth and political stability in two of the world's poorer regions. Although the legislation was not as broad-ranging as some had hoped, focusing primarily on provisions designed to bolster the apparel industry in twenty-seven Central American and Caribbean nations and forty-eight sub-Saharan African nations, it was seen as an important step toward improving the economies of much of the third world. Also included in the act was language penalizing countries that imposed trade restrictions on certain items produced by other nations. In addition, the new law served as an important precursor to gaining approval for normalizing trade relations between the United States and China, which President Clinton supported.

The debate over changing China's trade status was accompanied by an intense lobbying campaign. Supporters argued that trade with the world's most populous nation offered huge economic benefits, while opponents saw any change as condoning Beijing's labor, human rights, and environmental policies. The bill ultimately approved by Congress included several mechanisms designed to hold China accountable for its actions on human rights. It also stipulated that the People's Republic would be granted permanent trade status only after it joined the World Trade Organization and significantly reformed its trade regime by eliminating or reducing a broad array of tariff and nontariff barriers on goods, services, and foreign investments.

Another lengthy struggle won for approximately eight million working-age individuals receiving Social Security Disability Insurance or Supplemental Security Income the right to retain Medicaid and Medicare benefits if they entered or reentered the work force. The Ticket to Work and Work Incentives Improvement Act of 1999 also provided for expanded vocational employment and rehabilitation services for the disabled. Advocates argued that a significant number of persons on federal disability rolls would take advantage of the measure. Critical to the measure's passage was the support of several members of Congress and congressional aides who had long championed expanded rights for the disabled. The disability community was able to mount a lobbying campaign on the Internet, which allowed much more convenient communication among members.

A dramatic increase in international trafficking of people (mostly women and girls) for prostitution or other forms of forced labor moved Congress to tighten penalties for those convicted of smuggling individuals into the United States. The Trafficking Victims Protection Act of 2000 allowed up to five thousand of an estimated fifty thousand trafficking victims to be granted a special U.S. nonimmigrant visa, with the possibility of permanent residency in three years. The act established programs to assist and protect trafficking victims and promote international assistance in eliminating trafficking. It also set up a process for cutting off nonhumanitarian aid to governments that tolerate or condone trafficking.

The Intercountry Adoption Act of 2000 sought to encourage more international adoptions, while protecting the rights of each of those involved in the adoption process. Procedures were established for joining the Hague Convention on Protection of Children and Cooperation in Respect of Intercountry Adoptions, and ratification of the treaty designed to regulate international adoptions was assured. Under the act, the Department of State assumed primary responsibility for implementation of the treaty. The intention of the implementing legislation was to hold intercountry adoption agencies in the United States accountable and ensure that they perform in an ethical manner.

Following several years of efforts to harmonize U.S. patent laws with those of the European Community and other major trading partners, Congress approved reforming legislation. Much of the impetus for the patent reform effort, the first since 1952, came from businesses that sought a better means for resolving disputes between inventors and companies over the ownership of new technology. The American Inventors Protection Act of 1999 also provided for the restructuring of the Patent and Trademark Office into a performance-based organization, giving it greater independence and flexibility to improve the quality and quantity of its work.

Through the establishment of House and Senate parliamentary point of order rules, Congress in 2000 ensured that all Airport and Airway Trust Fund revenues and interest would be used only for aviation programs. This enactment, which represented a compromise between those who sought to take the trust fund off budget and those who sought to create a fire wall around aviation programs, was achieved following several months of negotiations by House and Senate conferees. Much of the debate focused on whether to remove aviation programs from the appropriations process by making their funding mandatory. The law was named for former senator Wendell H. Ford of Kentucky, who had served as chairman of the Senate Rules and Administration Committee from 1987 to 1995.

The Religious Land Use and Institutionalized Persons Act was passed in the wake of the Supreme Court's decision in the *City of Boerne v. Flores*, 521 U.S. 507 (1997) that Congress had exceeded its authority in applying the Religious Freedom Restoration Act (1993) to state and local governments. Those portions of the law which applied to the federal government were upheld. The main purpose of the new act was to protect churches and religious organizations from zoning ordinances that targeted churches for different treatment, and strengthened the legal protections of religious practices among institutionalized persons.

The initial phase of what would become the largest and most expensive ecosystem restoration project in American history became law near the end of the One Hundred Sixth Congress. The Comprehensive Everglades Restoration Plan sought to reverse a 1948 U.S. Army Corps of Engineers project intended to control flooding and supply water to agricultural and urban areas and threatened estuaries. The project, however, had the unintended consequence of shrinking the rich South Florida ecosystem by almost half as it interrupted natural water flows. It was estimated that the plan's sixty-eight projects would take thirty-six years and $7.8 billion to complete.

The year 2000 brought the most protracted, closest, and most controversial presidential contest election in more than a century. Recounts and court challenges in Florida left unsettled for thirty-six days the status of the state's twenty-five electoral votes, the winner of which would become president. On December 12, 2000, the U.S. Supreme Court voted 5 to 4 in *Bush v. Gore* to reverse the Florida Supreme Court decision to proceed with a manual recount. The decision effectively declared the GOP candidate, Texas governor George W. Bush, and his running mate, former secretary of defense and U.S. representative from Wyoming Richard B. Cheney, the winners of the election with 271 electoral votes to 266 for the Democratic challengers—Vice President Al Gore Jr. and his running mate, Sen. Joseph I. Lieberman of Connecticut. The Democratic ticket, however, won the popular vote by 48.4 percent to 47.9 percent. Gore thus became the first presidential contender since 1888 to win the national popular vote but fall short in the Electoral College. George W. Bush, the son of George H. W. Bush, the forty-first president, joined John Adams, the second president, and John Quincy Adams, the sixth president, as the only other father-son set to serve as chief executive.

As a result of the November congressional elections, the Republicans retained control of the House. However, the Senate was left evenly divided for the first time since the Forty-seventh Congress convened in 1881.

Major Acts

Gramm-Leach-Bliley Act. Repealed provisions of the Banking Act of 1933, which restricted cross-ownership between the banking and securities industries, and the Bank Holding Act of 1956, which imposed barriers between banking and insurance activities. Required financial institutions to adhere to specific standards in sharing customer information, and mandated that standards be established to ensure information confidentiality. Authorized states to enact more stringent consumer privacy provisions than those established by federal law. Extended Securities and Exchange Commission regulation of securities to the securities activities of banks. Preempted state laws and rules that prevented or restricted affiliations between banks and insurance companies. Called upon the states to enact laws creating uniform state licensing standards for insurance companies. Made membership in the Federal Home Loan Bank System voluntary. Approved November 12, 1999 (P.L. 106–102; 113 Stat. 1338–1481). *(Banking Act of 1933 [Glass-Steagall Act], p. 243)*

American Inventors Protection Act of 1999. Required invention promoters to disclose specific information to customers in writing. Reduced certain patent fees, and provided for adjustment of trademark fees. Established a basic patent term of twenty years, and permitted extended terms for administrative delays. Provided infringement protection to inventors who developed and commercially used a patent for at least one year prior to the effective filing date of a patent. Required publication of a patent application within eighteen months after filing unless it was filed only in the United States or filed in a country that did not publish applications. Provided for an *inter partes* reexamination procedure. Established the Patent and Trademark Office (PTO) as an independent agency within the Department of Commerce. Authorized the secretary of commerce to appoint commissioners of patents and trademarks to serve as chief operating officers of the two PTO entities. Approved November 29, 1999 (P.L. 106–113, Title IV; 113 Stat. 1501A-552–1501A-591).

Ticket to Work and Work Incentives Improvement Act of 1999. Extended Medicare coverage to employed persons with disabilities, and created new optional categories of Medicaid eligibility for employed persons with disabilities. Created a Ticket to Work and Self-Sufficiency Program that offered individuals with disabilities a broader choice of vocational rehabilitation and employment service providers, and allowed them to purchase rehabilitation and employment services through state agencies or private providers. Established demonstration projects and studies to evaluate various work incentives for disabled individuals. Provided grants to states to significantly expand the Medicaid program. Approved December 17, 1999 (P.L. 106–170, Title I-IV; 113 Stat. 1860–1918).

Wendell H. Ford Aviation Investment and Reform Act for the 21st Century. Established House and Senate parliamentary point of order rules that ensured all receipts and interest in the Airport and Airway Trust Fund would be appropriated for aviation purposes, with a priority on capital needs in fiscal years 2001–2003. Created the position of chief executive officer for air traffic control at the Federal Aviation Administration with responsibility for setting overall policy and reaching "measurable goals." Granted the Department of Transportation inspector general authority to monitor airline industry voluntary plans to improve customer service. Provided for phasing out the restrictions on the number of flights at O'Hare International Airport (Chicago) and Kennedy and LaGuardia International Airports (New York). Allowed for increased flights at Ronald Reagan Washington National Airport. Approved April 5, 2000 (P.L. 106–181; 114 Stat. 61–197).

Trade and Development Act of 2000. Provided for expansion of U.S. trade with twenty-seven Central American and Caribbean basin nations and forty-eight sub-Saharan African nations by lowering import tariffs and removing quotas on certain types of goods—mainly apparel made from U.S. yarns and fabrics. Expanded duty-free treatment for almost all products from sub-Saharan Africa. Provided Caribbean Basin countries greater duty-free access and preferential tariff treatment for certain textile and apparel products made from U.S. fabrics. Authorized extension of permanent normal trade relations with Albania and Kyrgyzstan. Lowered tariffs on high-quality imported wools. Required the Office of the U.S. Trade Representative to rotate items on which it placed high tariffs when a country refused to comply with international trade rules. Approved May 18, 2000 (P.L. 106–200; 114 Stat. 251–306).

Electronic Signatures in Global and National Commerce Act. Gave financial transactions signed with a digital signature over the Internet the same legal standing as a written signature. Permitted a broad range of financial transactions to be conducted by e-mail, but retained the legal requirement that paper copies of sensitive documents involving wills, trusts, adoptions, divorces, court orders, and evictions be issued and retained. Required that consumers consent to receiving documents electronically; companies verify consumers were able, technologically, to receive documents; and new regulations be developed to ensure that stored electronic data were tamper proof. Required companies to inform consumers of their right to receive information in nonelectronic form and to opt out of such agreements at any time. Approved June 30, 2000 (P.L. 106–229; 114 Stat. 464–476).

Religious Land Use and Institutionalized Persons Act. Provided for the protection of the exercise of religion in two situations: (1) where state and local governments seek to impose or implement a zoning law on churches, mosques, and synagogues in a manner that imposes a substantial burden on religious exercise, and (2) where state and local governments seek to impose a substantial burden on the religious exercise of persons residing or confined to prisons, state hospitals, nursing homes, and similar institutions. Approved September 22, 2000 (P.L. 106–274; 114 Stat. 803–807).

Intercountry Adoption Act of 2000. Provided for implementation by the United States of the Hague Convention on Protection of Children and Cooperation in Respect of Intercountry Adoption to "protect the rights of, and prevent abuses against, children, birth families, and adoptive parents involved in adoptions (or prospective adoptions) subject to the Convention"; "ensure that such adoptions are in the children's best interest"; and "improve the ability of the Federal government to assist United States citizens seeking to adopt children from abroad and residents of other countries party to the Convention seeking to adopt children from the United States." Delegated to the Department of State responsibility for prescribing implementing regulations and, together with the attorney general, establishing a registry of immigration adoptions. Established accreditation requirements for immigration adoption agencies and persons involved in adoptions subject to the convention. Approved October 6, 2000 (P.L. 106–279; 114 Stat. 825–844).

United States-China Relations Act of 2000. Granted the People's Republic of China permanent normal trade relations status once it became a member of the World Trade Organization (WTO) and the president certified that the terms of China's membership were equivalent to the November 1999 U.S.-China WTO agreement. Urged that Taiwan's membership in the WTO be considered immediately after China's. Established a Congressional-Executive Commission on the People's Republic of China to monitor and report on China's actions on human rights, religious freedom, and the rule of law process. Required the U.S. trade representative to issue an annual report assessing China's compliance with its WTO obligations, and authorized funding to monitor and seek enforcement of China's WTO commitments. Established a government task force to halt Chinese imports suspected of being produced by prison labor. Approved October 10, 2000 (P.L. 106–286; 114 Stat. 880–908).

American Competitiveness in the Twenty-first Century Act of 2000. Increased H-1B visas (for temporary foreign workers in specialty occupations) by 297,500 for fiscal years 2000–2002. Excluded from the new ceiling H-1B nonimmigrants working for universities and nonprofit research facilities. Increased portability of H-1B status. Required the National Science Foundation (NSF) to "conduct a study of the divergence in access to high technology (commonly referred to as the 'digital divide') in the United States." Provided funding for the NSF "to carry out a direct or matching grant program to support private-public partnerships in K–12 education" in science, mathematics, and technology. Required the secretary of labor "to establish demonstration programs or projects to provide technical skills training for workers" covered by the act, and stipulated that a portion of Labor Department H-1B education and training fee funds be used to enhance skills in information technology shortage areas. Approved October 17, 2000 (P.L. 106–313; 114 Stat. 1251–1265).

Trafficking Victims Protection Act of 2000. Doubled the maximum penalty to twenty years for selling an individual into involuntary servitude or other similar crimes, and established a life sentence in cases involving kidnapping or attempted kidnapping, attempted or aggravated sexual abuse, or attempted murder or murder. Created a special nonimmigrant "T" visa for up to five thousand victims annually who assisted in trafficking investigations or prosecutions and would suffer retribution if returned to their native country. Made "T" visa victims eligible for permanent residency status after three years. Provided for establishment of programs in both the United States and other countries to assist and protect trafficking victims. Provided assistance to foreign countries developing programs and activities to eliminate trafficking, and withheld nonhumanitarian assistance to those that did not. Approved October 28, 2000 (P.L. 106–386, Div. A; 114 Stat. 1466–1491).

Comprehensive Everglades Restoration Plan. Authorized $1.4 billion for the first phase of a $7.8 billion, thirty-five-year plan to restore South Florida's ecosystem agreed to by federal, state, and local officials, Indian tribal leaders, agricultural groups, and environmentalists. Stipulated that the federal government pay half of the cost of the restoration effort and an array of state, local, and tribal agencies the other half. Authorized funding for ten construction projects, four pilot projects, and additional planning on how to restore the natural flow of water to the Everglades, control flooding, and supply water to South Florida. Mandated that House and Senate committees approve implementation reports before funds for the construction projects were appropriated. Required the president and governor of Florida to make a binding agreement ensuring that the state reserved a sufficient amount of the captured water from each project to sustain the ecosystem. Delegated to the U.S. Army Corps of Engineers the lead role in coordinating the implementation with local, state, and federal entities. Approved December 11, 2000 (P.L. 106–541, Title VI; 114 Stat. 2680–2693).

Commodity Futures Modernization Act of 2000. Excluded over-the-counter derivatives contracts (or swaps) from regulation under the Commodity Exchange Act of 1936 if traded in a market where access was limited to "eligible contract participants"; that is, market professionals, institutional investors, corporations, governments, and high-asset individuals. Required that trading involving small retail investors or that contracts based on farm commodities continue to be done on exchanges regulated by the Commodity Futures Trading Commission (CFTC). Authorized commodity exchanges to create two new markets, called "derivatives transactions execution facilities" and "exempt boards of trade." Repealed a ban on futures contracts based on the stock of individual corporations, and allowed new contracts called "security futures" to be traded on either securities or futures exchanges under the joint oversight of the Securities and Exchange Commission and CFTC. Approved December 21, 2000 (P.L. 106–554, Appendix E; 114 Stat. 2763A-365–2763A-461).

One Hundred Seventh Congress

January 3, 2001, to January 3, 2003

First session—January 3, 2001, to December 20, 2001
Second session—January 23, 2002, to November 22, 2002
(First administration of George W. Bush, 2001–2005)

Historical Background

During the One Hundred Seventh Congress, the nation's lawmakers wrestled with some of the most dramatic twists and turns in American history. Many of Congress's major accomplishments were not on the agenda of either party when Congress convened. Instead, members were forced to deal with acts of terrorism, a slowing economy, a series of financial scandals that rocked Wall Street, the loss of much of an unprecedented budget surplus, and political tumult. For a time, even normal, everyday operations were disrupted by terrorist assaults on America's financial and military centers and the discovery of anthrax contamination in congressional office buildings. Two letters containing anthrax were delivered to Senate members, one to majority leader Tom Daschle's (D-SD) office in October and a second to Democratic Sen. Patrick J. Leahy, of Vermont.

On Inauguration Day 2001, the Republican Party, for the first time in nearly half a century, controlled both the executive and legislative branches of government. Only the tie-breaking voting power of Vice President Richard B. Cheney gave the GOP an advantage in the Senate, where the two major parties were equally represented. Recognizing the potential for legislative gridlock, majority leader Trent Lott of Mississippi and minority leader Tom Daschle of South Dakota, in consultation with party colleagues, negotiated a historic power-sharing agreement to govern certain aspects of committee and floor activities and to determine the

chamber's legislative agenda. Then, in June 2001, Sen. James M. Jeffords of Vermont decided to leave the Republican Party and become an Independent and caucus with the Democrats. As a result, party control of the chamber, for the first time in history, switched in the middle of a session.

While the Republicans still controlled both houses, they were successful in securing passage of the largest tax cut in two decades. Three weeks after his inauguration, President George W. Bush sent Congress a tax proposal calling for tax cuts that over ten years would total $1.6 trillion. On Capitol Hill, the plan, which was the centerpiece of Bush's presidential campaign, was modified to provide more generous benefits to lower income taxpayers. By the time Congress finished its work on the Economic Growth and Tax Relief Reconciliation Act, the cost of the tax cut had been reduced to $1.34 trillion, but it still represented the most sweeping reduction since 1981.

An astonished and horrified nation watched on the morning of September 11, 2001, as two hijacked U.S. commercial airplanes were flown into the World Trade Center's 110-story twin towers in New York City; a third plunged into the Pentagon in Arlington, Virginia; and a fourth plane, apparently headed for another Washington landmark, crashed in Somerset County, Pennsylvania, after its passengers struggled with hijackers for control of the aircraft. The attacks left more than three thousand dead in New York, Washington, and Pennsylvania. Minutes after the second jet crashed into the World Trade Center, the Federal Aviation Administration, for the first time in history, grounded passenger and cargo air traffic within the United States. The White House, the Capitol, the Supreme Court, and all other federal buildings in Washington were evacuated soon after the Pentagon was hit, and senior congressional leaders were taken to a secret, secure location outside the city. Throughout the world, American military forces were placed on the highest level of alert.

When Congress reconvened at the Capitol, partisanship was set aside as attention shifted from economic issues to the need for a swift response to the terrorist attacks and an expression of solidarity with President Bush's effort to seek out the perpetrators. On September 14, the Senate, by a 98 to 0 vote, and the House, by a 420 to 1 vote, authorized the president "to use all necessary and appropriate force against those nations, organizations or persons" he determined were responsible for planning, executing, or aiding the terrorist attacks. On October 7, the United States began a military campaign in support of the Northern Alliance and other anti-Taliban forces in Afghanistan against the alleged mastermind of the terrorist attacks, Osama bin Laden and his al Qaeda network, as well as the Taliban regime that had sheltered the group. By mid-December 2001, the Taliban had been ousted from power and al Qaeda elements in Afghanistan largely defeated. While U.S. and coalition forces continued to conduct combat operations against the Taliban and al Qaeda in 2002, the major focus shifted to maintaining political stability and reconstruction of a post-Taliban Afghanistan.

Other important measures that emerged in the aftermath of September 11 illustrated how the terrorist assaults defined much of Congress's work. Congress in 2001 passed a $40 billion emergency supplemental appropriations act to aid in the recovery activities and cleanup efforts in New York, at the Pentagon, and in Pennsylvania; to repair damaged facilities; and to strengthen security and fight terrorism. The bill made $10 billion immediately available to the president and another $10 billion available fifteen days after Congress was notified of how the funds would be used. The final $20 billion was included in a 2002 defense appropriations act.

During consideration of the supplemental appropriations bill, members of the New York congressional delegation waged a campaign to include additional funding for the city. The final bill contained significantly less for defense than the president had requested and more for homeland security and recovery and rebuilding efforts in New York. Approximately 56 percent ($22.5 billion) of the total $40 billion emergency spending went for nondefense expenditures and 44 percent ($17.5 billion) went for defense.

The Air Transportation Safety and System Stabilization Act resulted in large part from the closure of U.S. airspace for three days following the terrorist attacks. At the time, the industry was in financial trouble and faced a future requiring large investments for tightened security, the prospect of insurers unwilling to cover further terrorist disasters, and a sudden drop in passengers. The act provided airlines $5 billion to cover their losses and $10 billion in loan guarantees, limited airline liability, established a victim compensation process, and allowed "war risk" insurance to be used to reimburse airlines for higher insurance premiums. Other legislation significantly expanded the federal security role at the more than four hundred commercial airports. The Aviation and Transportation Safety Act required the government to hire, train, and begin supervising some twenty-eight thousand airline passenger and baggage screeners within a year. A new, autonomous Transportation and Security Agency was given responsibility for the federalization of airport security and the security of all modes of transportation—air, ground, and sea—in the country.

An antiterrorism proposal by Attorney General John Ashcroft led Congress to adopt the USA PATRIOT Act, which granted law enforcement and intelligence agencies greater power to trace and intercept terrorists' communications, detain suspected terrorists, and obtain nationwide search warrants and wiretaps. Other provisions facilitated information sharing by federal officials, reinforced laws designed to deny terrorists financial resources, modified several terrorist-related laws, enhanced security along the U.S.-Canadian border, and limited possession of substances that could be used as biological or chemical weapons. Civil liberty advocates contended that the new surveillance powers were so broadly defined that innocent Americans would suffer and that its enforcement tools could be used in criminal cases unrelated to terrorism.

The Homeland Security Act launched the largest government restructuring since 1947. As the third largest federal employer, after the Departments of Defense and Veterans Affairs, Homeland Security absorbed all or major portions of twenty-two federal agencies and approximately 170,000 employees. Transferred functions included immigration, border and transportation security, emergency preparedness management, intelligence analysis, and presidential protection. Senate consideration of the measure was slowed by partisan and parliamentary factors, as well as a few highly contentious issues, such as the civil service protections and collective bargaining rights of department employees.

Passage of the Terrorism Risk Insurance Act was stalled for months, before President Bush urged adoption of the bill. In the aftermath of September 11, insurance claims exceeded $40 billion, and many commercial property and casualty insurers stopped offering terrorism coverage, which had been provided free prior to the attacks. Also, insurance companies told Congress that they could no longer insure large projects without the assistance of the federal government. Under the act, Congress agreed to have the U.S. government assume responsibility for 90 percent of the claims after insurer losses from terrorism surpassed established figures in 2003, 2004, and 2005, up to $100 billion annually.

The 2002 farm bill reversed a six-year market-oriented experiment intended to reduce federal intervention in the agricultural sector. In repudiating the Freedom to Farm Act of 1996, Congress increased federal payments by an estimated $82.8 billion over ten years. Ultimately the White House supported the bill, which was advocated in large part by farm-state lawmakers who demanded increases in federal support after several years of declining farm prices. Supporters argued the legislation was needed to offset years of low farm prices, provide farmers more flexibility in crop selection, and strengthen the U.S. position in negotiating trade reforms. Opponents contended that the bill was too expensive, reversed the market-orientation of the previous act, encouraged overproduction, increased the likelihood of depressed farm prices, and undermined foreign agricultural trade objectives. *(Federal Agriculture Improvement and Reform Act of 1996 [Freedom to Farm Act], p. 418)*

While some observers played down the economic effects of the U.S.-Jordan Free Trade Agreement Implementation Act of 2001, its provisions on labor and environmental standards as well as electronic commerce were precedent setting. The bilateral agreement, the first with an Arab nation, earned Jordan the distinction of becoming only the fourth nation—after Canada, Mexico, and Israel—to enjoy a virtually tariff-free relationship with the United States.

After a year and a half of debate, Congress granted the president broad authority to negotiate international trade agreements by renewing the fast-track procedure, which had lapsed in 1994. Fast track requires Congress to vote yea or nay on trade agreements negotiated by the president not more than ninety days after they were brought to Capitol Hill, with no amendments allowed. Approval of fast track was secured, however, only after its supporters linked it with expanded Trade Adjustment Assistance programs for trade-displaced workers.

Passage of the bipartisan No Child Left Behind Act marked the fulfillment of a Bush campaign promise. Some called the act the most far-reaching education legislation since the Elementary and Secondary Education Act of 1965. Congress used federal aid to education, for the first time, as leverage to force improvements in low-performing schools. The law mandated annual tests in reading and math for every pupil in grades three through eight, and it created accountability standards for schools with chronically low test scores and offered educational alternatives to students in those schools. *(Elementary and Secondary Education Act of 1965, p. 322)*

Enron Corporation, the seventh largest corporation in the United States, became the biggest business failure in American history when it collapsed in 2001 as a result of deceptive accounting practices. In the aftermath, both political parties, which had received large donations from Enron, moved to secure the first major overhaul of campaign finance laws in three decades. The Bipartisan Campaign Reform Act banned corporations, labor unions, and individuals from making unlimited, unregulated contributions known as soft money to national political party committees. Also barred, during certain periods, were broadcast advertisements funded by corporations, unions, and nonprofit groups advocating the election or defeat of specific federal candidates.

Amidst several corporate accounting scandals and a growing perception that the fall of the stock market in 2001–2002 stemmed from a loss in investor confidence, Congress passed the most sweeping securities legislation since the 1930s. At the heart of the Sarbanes-Oxley Act was a desire, the *New York Times* observed, to rid "Wall Street, the accounting industry, and corporate boardrooms of interest and greed-driven misconduct" that had previously gone largely unchecked. The act, sponsored by Sen. Paul S. Sarbanes of Maryland and

Rep. Michael G. Oxley of Ohio, made a broad overhaul of corporate fraud, accounting, and securities laws; established a new independent regulatory board to monitor the accounting industry and punish corrupt auditors; created new penalties for corporate wrongdoing; and developed new federal protection for corporate whistleblowers.

Passage of the Small Business Liability Relief and Brownfields Revitalization Act was the culmination of more than five years of congressional debate and negotiation regarding amendments to the Comprehensive Environmental Response Compensation and Liability Act (Superfund). The Brownfields Act provided important protections from Superfund liability to landowners who met certain statutory criteria, and significantly expanded federal grant authority for brownfields development.

Agreement was reached on legislation to improve the nation's voting procedures and provide the first substantial federal spending for that purpose. More than eighty election reform bills had been introduced in the One Hundred Seventh Congress, and nine congressional hearings were held. The new law represented a bipartisan effort to avoid another situation such as arose in Florida in 2000, which involved confusing ballots and incompetent elections administrators, among other things. While the act significantly expanded the federal role in regulating voter registration and elections, states retained primary responsibility. Federal funds were authorized to help them comply with the new requirements.

At the outset of the One Hundred Seventh Congress, the Congressional Budget Office (CBO) had projected a federal budget surplus of $281 billion in fiscal 2001 and $313 billion in fiscal 2002. It was estimated that by fiscal 2006, the surplus would be sufficient to pay off all the publicly held debt that was available for redemption. Within eighteen months, however, much of the projected surplus had declined sharply. A surplus of $127 billion was realized in fiscal 2001, a deficit of $159 billion was predicted for fiscal 2002, and deficits were projected through the following years, perhaps throughout the decade, with the result that publicly held debt would increase instead of being paid off. According to CBO, the projected surpluses fell victim to a weak economy, the June 2001 tax cut, the unanticipated spending approved in response to the September 11 terrorist attacks, and technical adjustments to its projections.

In September 2002 President Bush addressed the United Nations (UN) on the potential threat that Iraq represented and warned that the United States was prepared to take action against Iraq with or without Security Council sanction. Early in October, following a week of contentious debate, Congress authorized the president to take military action against Iraq, to remove Iraqi president Saddam Hussein from power, and to destroy Iraq's nuclear, chemical, and biological weaponry as deemed necessary. Not since the Vietnam-era Gulf of Tonkin Resolution (1964) had a president been granted such broad and flexible power to carry out an undefined military operation. Furthermore, Congress in essence endorsed the Bush administration's stated policy of allowing for a preemptive military strike against a foreign nation, perhaps for the first time in U.S. history.

The United Nations Security Council on November 8, 2002, voted unanimously for a resolution calling on Iraq to allow the UN unfettered access to search the country for weapons of mass destruction and demanding that Hussein give up such weapons voluntarily or a U.S.–led war would seek to force him to do so. The inspectors would report their findings to the Security Council on January 27, 2003, at which time President Bush would decide whether to go to war against Iraq with or without UN backing.

The 2002 midterm congressional elections saw the GOP regain control of the Senate and strengthen its hold on the House. Republican candidates benefited at the ballot box from the administration's focus on an impending war with Iraq. In the aftermath of the disappointing showing for Democrats in the election, Richard A. Gephardt of Missouri stepped down as minority leader and Nancy Pelosi of California became the first woman elected to the top party leadership post in either house of Congress. The One Hundred Seventh Congress closed with a shakeup in the Senate leadership. Majority leader Trent Lott, at a one hundredth birthday celebration for Sen. Strom Thurmond of South Carolina on December 5, 2002, publicly stated, "I want to say this about my state: When Strom Thurmond ran for president, we voted for him. We're proud of it. And if the rest of the country had followed our lead, we wouldn't have had all these problems over all these years, either." Thurmond had run for president in 1948 on a platform advocating racial segregation. Despite repeated apologies, Lott was unable to maintain the support of his fellow GOP senators and resigned as majority leader. Bill Frist of Tennessee, who was favored by the Bush administration, succeeded Lott.

Major Acts

Economic Growth and Tax Relief Reconciliation Act of 2001. Provided for a $1.35 trillion reduction in taxes through December 31, 2010. Called for a 2001 tax rebate of $300 for individual filers, $500 for heads of households, and $600 for couples filing jointly; a reduction in individual income tax rates to be phased in over six years (2001–2006); an increase in the standard deduction for married couples to be phased in over five years beginning in 2005; a doubling of the child tax credit to be phased in over ten years (2001–2010); a gradual phasing out of the federal estate tax between 2002 and 2010; several tax benefits for educational expenses; phased increases in the contribution limits of individual retirement accounts and pensions; and provisions designed to enhance pension benefits for women, increase the portability of pension savings, strengthen pension security and enforcement, and reduce the regulatory burdens placed on such accounts. Stipulated that all provisions of the act expired after December 31, 2010. Approved June 7, 2001 (P.L. 107–16; 115 Stat. 38–150).

2001 Emergency Supplemental Appropriations Act for Recovery from and Response to the Terrorist Attacks on the United States. Appropriated $40 billion for emergency expenses to respond to the September 11, 2001, terrorist attacks on the United States. Made $10 billion available immediately to the president to allocate for emergency relief, recovery, and rebuilding efforts; counterterrorism programs; airport, transportation centers, and public building security; investigating and prosecuting those involved in the attacks; and enhancements to national security. Made $10 billion available fifteen days after the Office of Management and Budget (OMB) submitted to the House and Senate Committees on Appropriations a plan for distributing the funds. Provided that $20 billion be "obligated only when enacted in subsequent emergency appropriations bill." Required the OMB director to provide quarterly reports to the Appropriations Committees on the use of the funds. Stipulated that no less than half of the $40 billion be allocated "for disaster recovery activities and assistance related to the terrorist acts in New York, Virginia, and Pennsylvania." Approved September 18, 2001 (P.L. 107–38; 115 Stat. 220–221).

Authorization of Use of Force Against Perpetrators of the September 11, 2001, Attacks. Authorized the president "to use all necessary and appropriate force against those nations, organizations, or persons he determines planned, authorized, committed or aided the terrorist attacks that occurred on September 11, 2001, or harbored such organizations or persons, in order to prevent future acts of international terrorism against the United States by such nations, organizations or persons." Stipulated that nothing in the resolution superseded any requirement in the War Powers Resolution of 1973. Approved September 18, 2001 (P.L. 107–40; 115 Stat. 224–225). *(War Powers Resolution, p. 351)*

Air Transportation Safety and System Stabilization Act. Provided the nation's troubled passenger airlines $4.5 billion and cargo carriers $500 million in direct aid for losses associated with the September 11, 2001, terrorist attacks. Provided up to $10 billion in guaranteed loans or other credit assistance to passenger airlines to be distributed by a four-member Air Transportation Stabilization Board (composed of the secretaries of the Treasury and transportation, chairman of the Federal Reserve, and the comptroller of the General Accounting Office) under regulations promulgated by the Office of Management and Budget. Extended war risk insurance to the industry for 180 days (a provision subsequently extended several times), and placed a limit on the liability of U.S. airlines. Established a process for victim compensation for those injured in the attacks and the families of those killed. Urged the secretary of transportation to protect essential air service to smaller communities. Approved September 22, 2001 (P.L. 107–42; 115 Stat. 230–242).

United States-Jordan Free Trade Area Implementation Act. Provided for the phasing out of duties on almost all goods (except for tobacco and tobacco-related products) traded between the United States and Jordan over a ten-year period. Committed the two nations to allowing access to various service sectors—such as business, communications, construction and engineering, distribution, education, environment, finance, health, tourism, recreation, and transportation—and not to impose customs duties on electronic transmissions or impose barriers to access digitized products or for services delivered electronically. Allowed for each nation to monitor the other's environmental and labor practices and, with the approval of a bi-national dispute panel, to impose trade sanctions if one of the trade partners is seen as gaining a commercial advantage by lowering standards. Approved September 28, 2001 (P.L. 107–43; 115 Stat. 243–252).

USA PATRIOT Act. Allowed agencies such as the Federal Bureau of Investigation to share grand jury and wiretap information with intelligence agencies, and allowed federal officials to obtain nationwide search warrants and "roving wiretaps" during terrorism investigations. Stipulated that surveillance and wiretap provisions would expire in 2005. Increased criminal penalties for committing terrorist acts or harboring or funding terrorists. Authorized the secretary of the Treasury to regulate the activities of U.S. financial institutions, particularly with respect to foreign individuals and entities, and to impose sanctions on foreign nations that refuse to provide information on depositors. Barred U.S. banks from doing business with offshore shell banks. Allowed the attorney general to detain foreigners suspected of terrorism for seven days without being charged. Made it illegal to possess substances that could be used as biological or chemical weapons except for peaceful purposes, and made it a federal crime to commit an act of terrorism against a mass transit system. Increased the number of federal agents monitoring the U.S.-Canadian border. Approved October 26, 2001 (P.L. 107–56; 115 Stat. 272–402).

Aviation and Transportation Security Act. Required that within one year all airport passenger and baggage screeners be federal employees who were U.S. citizens proficient in English and who had passed a background check. After three years, airports had the option of hiring private security firms, but they would remain under federal supervision. Required airlines to screen all checked baggage and all individuals, goods, and equipment entering secure airport areas, and to install stronger cockpit doors. Required flight schools to request background checks on all aliens seeking training in aircraft over a certain weight. Authorized a significant increase in air marshals. Established a Transportation Security Agency, headed by an undersecretary, to hire, train, and supervise airport screeners; develop uniform security procedures; and assure the security of all modes of transportation. Extended the liability protection provided airlines in the Air Transportation and Safety Stabilization Act of 2001 to aircraft manufacturers, state port authorities, airport owners and operators, and owners of the World Trade Center. Levied a surcharge on all passenger flights to cover the increased costs of security. Approved November 19, 2001 (P.L. 107–71; 115 Stat. 597–647).

No Child Left Behind Act of 2001. Required states to implement annual standards-based reading and mathematics assessments in third through eighth grades by the 2005–2006 school year and science tests at one grade each in elementary, middle school, and high school by the 2007–2008 school year. Required states to develop standards of adequate yearly progress (AYP). Stipulated that schools failing to meet AYP for two consecutive years were to receive additional federal aid. If scores still failed to improve, pupils from low-income families would be offered money for tutoring or transportation to other schools. Required that staff changes be made at schools where scores failed to improve after six years. Created a "teacher quality" program to hire new teachers, limit class sizes, train special education teachers and principals, and establish incentives to improve teachers. Provided for programs aimed at improving reading instruction, science and technology instruction, and bilingual education. Established new requirements regarding teacher qualifications. Approved January 8, 2002 (P.L. 107–110; 115 Stat. 1425–2094).

Department of Defense and Emergency Supplemental Appropriations for Recovery from and Response to Terrorist Attacks on the United States Act, 2002. Appropriated $8.3 billion for homeland security, including $2.84 billion for bioterrorism response programs, $2.1 billion in counterterrorism aid, and $1.3 billion for aviation and border security; $8.2 billion for disaster recovery in New York and other affected areas, including $4.36 billion for the Federal Emergency Management Agency (FEMA) and $2 billion in community development block grants to aid New York's economic recovery; and $3.5 billion for defense, including funds for the war in Afghanistan, repairing the Pentagon, and enhancing military readiness. Approved January 10, 2002 (P.L. 107–117; 115 Stat. 2230–2355).

Small Business Liability Relief and Brownfields Revitalization Act. Established Superfund liability exceptions for (1) businesses and others responsible for small quantities of contamination, (2) owners of property that became contaminated merely as a result of migration from a contiguous property owned by another person, and (3) "bona fide" prospective purchasers who otherwise might be hesitant to acquire property because of potential cleanup liability. Authorized federal grants to assist in the cleanup of "brownfields" properties (properties typically abandoned, underutilized, or idle sites where the known or suspected presence of contamination, and the potential for cleanup liability, could be viewed as a deterrent to the purchase of property for redevelopment). Approved January 11, 2002 (P.L. 107–118; 115 Stat. 2356–2381).

Bipartisan Campaign Reform Act of 2002 (McCain-Feingold Act). Barred corporations, unions, and individuals from making unlimited, unregulated contributions known as soft money to national political parties. Allowed contributions of up to $10,000 in soft money for state and local parties for get-out-the-vote drives and voter registration, but barred its use for broadcast advertisements for federal candidates. Doubled the amount individuals could contribute to House, Senate, and presidential candidates from $1,000 to $2,000, and increased the limit on total contributions to all federal candidates, political committees, and political action committees from $50,000 to $95,000, in each two-year election cycle. Barred unions, corporations, and nonprofit organizations from funding broadcast advertisements that referred to a federal candidate within sixty days of a general election or thirty days of a primary election. Provided that a court could strike down one provision of the law without invalidating the entire law. Approved March 27, 2002 (P.L. 107–155; 116 Stat. 81–116).

Farm Security and Rural Investment Act of 2002. Reestablished federal price support payments based on crop prices that had been abolished by the 1996 free-market Freedom to Farm Act (Federal Agriculture Improvement and Reform Act). Increased grain and cotton subsidies by 70 percent; restored price supports for wool, mohair, and honey; increased by 80 percent subsidies for farmers employing conservation and other environmental measures; extended new subsidies to peanut farmers; created a $1.3 billion dairy support initiative; and created new subsidies for sugar, dry peas, lentils, and chickpeas. Reduced the ceiling on annual payments to large agricultural corporations from $460,000 to $360,000. Expanded the food stamp program, and restored food stamp benefits to legal immigrants. Required the Department of Agriculture to establish guidelines for voluntary country-of-origin labeling for meat, fish, fruits, vegetables, and peanuts. Approved May 13, 2002 (P.L. 107–171; 116 Stat. 134–540).

Sarbanes-Oxley Act of 2002 (Corporate Fraud Accountability Act of 2002). Created a new independent Public Company Accounting Oversight Board under the Securities and Exchange Commission to investigate and discipline accounting firms and to establish auditing rules and standards. Prohibited auditors from offering a broad range of consulting services to publicly traded companies that they audit. Established new reporting and disclosure requirements for public companies. Increased penalties for corporate wrongdoing, and broadened the definition of document destruction. Required top corporate officials to personally attest to the accuracy of their firm's accounting. Required that stock trades by corporate insiders be made public within two days. Prohibited most loans by companies to their officers or executives. Established broad new protections for corporate whistleblowers. Approved July 30, 2002 (P.L. 107–204; 116 Stat. 745–810).

Trade Act of 2002. Renewed presidential fast-track trade negotiating authority to June 1, 2005, with an optional extension to June 1, 2007. Expanded the Trade Adjustment Assistance programs for workers who lost jobs because of foreign competition; extended the Generalized System of Preferences, which allows thousands of products from more than 140 nations to enter the United States duty-free; and reauthorized tariff preferences for Bolivia, Colombia, Ecuador, and Peru. Required the president to consult with Congress before negotiating agreements that would undermine U.S. trade laws. Approved August 6, 2002 (P.L. 107–210; 116 Stat. 933–1049).

Authorization for Use of Military Force Against Iraq Resolution of 2002. Authorized the president to use the armed forces of the United States to "(1) defend the national security of the United States against the continuing threat posed by Iraq, and (2) enforce all relevant United Nations Security Council resolutions regarding Iraq." Required the president to explain to Congress, within forty-eight hours after exercising this authority, why "further diplomatic or other peaceful means alone" would not "adequately protect the national security of the United States" or lead "to enforcement of all relevant United Nations Security Council resolutions regarding Iraq." Required the president to submit a report every sixty days on matters relevant to the resolution. Approved October 16, 2002 (P.L. 107–243; 116 Stat. 1498–1502).

Help America Vote Act of 2002. Authorized $3.86 billion over three years in grants to states to upgrade their election systems (replace punch-card and lever voting machines, train poll workers, establish state-wide voter registration lists, and make polling places more accessible to the disabled). Created an Election Assistance Commission to test voting equipment and to serve as a clearinghouse for information on election technology. Required each state to have a statewide, computerized voter registration list linked to its driver's license agency to assist verification. Allowed a voter whose registration was not in order to cast a "provisional ballot," which would be counted later if the voter's registration was confirmed, and required procedures to permit a voter to check for and correct any errors before ballots are cast. Required first-time voters to provide a valid identification when they vote. Allowed states to assign unique identifiers to voters who have neither a driver's license nor a Social Security number. Required that all mail-in registration forms include the question, "Are you a citizen of the United States of America?" Approved October 29, 2002 (P.L. 107–252; 116 Stat. 1666–1730).

Homeland Security Act of 2002. Provided for establishment of a Department of Homeland Security, headed by a cabinet-level secretary, and the transfer of all or major portions of twenty-two existing agencies to the new department. With the exception of the Coast Guard and Secret Service, which enjoy independent status within the department, all other transferred agencies were located within directorates for border and transportation security, emergency preparedness and response, science and technology, and information analysis and infrastructure protection. Transferred approximately 170,000 federal employees to the new department. Mandated a National Homeland Security Council, transferred the Bureau of Alcohol, Tobacco, and Firearms from the Treasury Department to the Justice Department, and authorized commercial airline pilots to carry firearms in the cockpit. Granted the president broad flexibility concerning human resource management for the new department. Approved November 25, 2002 (P.L. 107–296; 116 Stat. 2135–2321).

Terrorism Risk Insurance Act of 2002. Established a three-year federal program to assist insurers of commercial properties in covering the losses resulting from future terrorist attacks. Provided that the federal government would pay 90 percent of insurer claims after losses surpassed $10 billion in 2003, $12.5 billion in 2004, and $15 billion in 2003, until the annual insured losses reached $100 billion. Required that for lesser damages, insurance companies pay 7 percent of their premiums toward damages in 2003, 10 percent in 2004, and 15 percent in 2005, with the government covering the remainder of the cost. Established the Terrorism Insured Loss Shared Compensation Program in the Department of the Treasury to administer payment of the federal share of compensation for insured losses. Required that civil lawsuits stemming from a terrorist attack be consolidated in a single federal court for trial under the laws of the state where the attack took place. Approved November 26, 2002 (P.L. 107–297; 116 Stat. 2322–2341).

One Hundred Eighth Congress

January 7, 2003, to January 3, 2005

First Session—January 3, 2003, to December 9, 2003
Second Session—January 20, 2004, to December 8, 2004
(First administration of George W. Bush, 2001–2005)

Historical Background

Often during the final two years of President George W. Bush's first term, Congress became embroiled in bitter partisan battles. The rancor between Democrats and Republicans contributed to stalemates on welfare reform, Social Security, energy, highways, and an array of other issues. Even bills enjoying broad support often bogged down in intense partisan or regional standoffs. According to an analysis of party-unity votes by *Congressional Quarterly,* the One Hundred Eighth Congress was the most polarized in half a century. On most votes, only a handful of lawmakers sided with the opposition. Thomas E. Mann of the Brookings Institution ranked the second session of this Congress as "among the least productive and most contentious in modern legislative history."[1]

President Bush and his Republican allies were rebuffed on legislation to curb big awards from liability lawsuits and on a constitutional amendment to ban gay marriage. Democrats were thwarted in efforts to raise the minimum wage, extend unemployment benefits, overturn new overtime pay rules, and allow the importation of cheaper prescription drugs from abroad. Debate among Republicans was marked by discord as the Senate ignored legislation put forth by the House on tort reform and other traditionally conservative causes. House bills aimed at curbing class-action lawsuits and limiting medical malpractice damages suffered a similar fate.

The gridlock on Capitol Hill left many federal programs in "policy limbo because of Congress' inability to pass—and, in some cases, even to come to grips with—dozens of bills to reauthorize, update and continue a broad array of social policies, commercial regulations and government aid." This was not, however, a problem unique to this Congress. "The breakdown of the authorization process has been progressive," budget expert Allen Schick suggested at the time. "In other words, it is not a sudden development."[2] Without question, legislative accomplishment was limited in 2003–2004, but lawmakers on occasion did overcome partisanship to enact important measures.

Following six years of debate, Congress, in December 2003, passed the most comprehensive changes in the federal Medicare insurance program since its creation in 1965. The Medical Prescription Drug, Improvement and Modernization Act of 2003 provided Medicare recipients for the first time with non-hospital prescription drug coverage, and expanded the role played by private insurers. It also created a tax-free health savings plan for unreimbursed medical expenses.

With passage of the U.S. Leadership Against HIV/AIDS, Tuberculosis and Malaria Act of 2003, the stage was set for an unprecedented U.S. government investment in the fight against three serious global health challenges. The five-year, $15 billion initiative implemented President George W. Bush's Emergency Plan of AIDS Relief that he had proposed the previous January in his State of the Union Message. On signing the bill, the president called it the "largest, single up-front commitment in history for an international public health initiative involving a specific disease."[3]

The Bush administration's top domestic priority was achieved when Congress cleared a $350 billion budget reconciliation bill, which included the third largest tax cut in U.S. history. The economic stimulus package only reached the president's desk, however, after Vice President Dick Cheney bridged substantial differences among House and Senate Republicans and then cast the tie-breaking vote in the Senate on the bill. The centerpiece of the 2003 tax cut act was a six-year dividend and capital gains cut, aimed at sparking economic growth by encouraging an investor class representing roughly half of U.S. households to invest in stocks. Although the final bill was less than half the size of Bush's original $726 billion economic stimulus proposal, the bill was still seen as a major win for the president and handed him his biggest economic policy triumph of the year.

For the first time since the Supreme Court legalized abortion in its landmark 1973 *Roe v. Wade* decision, Congress passed a federal law restricting an abortion procedure. The new law banned a procedure called "partial birth" abortion except in instances when a woman's life was endangered "by a physical disorder, physical illness or physical injury." The law did not allow an exception for cases in which a woman's health was in jeopardy. Twice, in 1996 and 1997, bills outlawing the procedure had reached the White House but were vetoed by President Bill Clinton. Enactment of the Partial-Birth Abortion Ban Act was the culmination of an eight year pro-life struggle led by the National Right to Life Committee (NRLC) and congressional pro-life leaders.

Banks, credit card companies, retailers, and other businesses successfully pressed Congress for legislation reauthorizing the 1970 Fair Credit Reporting Act. The act blocked states from writing their own consumer credit reporting laws ensuring that businesses were covered by a single nationwide privacy standard. Other new provisions were designed to improve the accuracy and transparency of national credit reporting systems, and to enhance consumer rights in situations involving alleged identity theft, credit scoring, and claims of inaccurate information.

After September 11, 2001, and the subsequent anthrax attacks against Capitol Hill, Americans began to realize that the country was vulnerable to a large-scale biological attack. These events also highlighted the United States's lack of preparation for such an occurrence because of the inadequate amount of

medical and scientific products available to prevent or respond to such an attack. In his 2003 State of the Union message, President George W. Bush proposed Project BioShield, with the stated goals of speeding the development and availability of effective drugs, vaccines, and other countermeasures for use against a chemical, biological, or a radiological attack. A year-and-a-half later, Congress acknowledged that an inadequate private market existed for such products and accepted responsibility for creating such a market by providing incentives for the private pharmaceutical industry. The consensus was, as Representative Henry Waxman aptly observed, "When the market cannot foster the development of critical products by itself, the government must rise to the challenge."[4]

One of the major political battles of the One Hundred Eighth Congress was fought in reaching an agreement on the largest corporate tax overhaul since 1986. The impetus for the American Jobs Creation Act of 2004 was the need to respond to a January 2002 ruling by the World Trade Organization (WTO) that the U.S. tax code's extra-territorial income exclusion (ETI), which provided a tax benefit for U.S. companies exporting products abroad, was illegal. Subsequently, the WTO authorized the European Union (EU) to impose up to $4 billion a year in trade sanctions against the U.S. companies in retaliation for the $5 billion a year subsidy. While most lawmakers could agree on repealing the ETI, there was considerable disagreement over what should take its place. Some Members wanted to compensate the biggest users of the export tax, others sought to reduce taxes on the global business of U.S. multinationals, and still others wanted to reward domestic manufacturers who created jobs at home. The compromise finally reached gave something to each group.

Growing concern among tobacco farmers about their future livelihood prompted passage of the Fair and Equitable Tobacco Reform Act. The "tobacco buyout," as it is commonly called, significantly changed the production and marketing of U.S. tobacco by eliminating the complicated federal tobacco price support and production control system established by the Agricultural Adjustment Act of 1938. Over the years, federal tobacco regulations had artificially inflated the price of U.S. tobacco relative to foreign tobacco, causing the demand for U.S.-grown tobacco to decline. The resulting loss of revenue led to calls from tobacco states' lawmakers to terminate the federal tobacco program that led to the deregulation of the tobacco industry. To ease the transition to a free-market system, the act authorized a 10 year, $10 million compensation package to land owners and tobacco growers that was to be drawn from a Tobacco Trust Fund financed by assessments on tobacco product manufacturers and importers.

A nearly five year bipartisan effort by California's congressional delegation to obtain more federal funding for the California Bay-Delta (CalFed) project was realized late in 2004. (CalFed is a partnership of 25 California and federal agencies and representatives of the state's environmental, urban, and agricultural communities.) It is one of the nation's largest and most comprehensive efforts to improve water supplies, water quality, flood control, and environmental restoration. CalFed was created in 1996 to develop long-term solutions to problems in the San Francisco Bay and Sacramento-Joaquin River Delta region, which supplies water to the fertile farming fields in California's Central Valley. The Bay-Delta, one of the largest estuaries on the Pacific Coast, is the home of more than 750 species of plants and animals and is used by millions of recreationists. In 2004, the drinking water of more than 22 million Californians passed through the Delta.

Important tools and assistance to help state and local governments use DNA evidence to convict the guilty and exonerate the innocent were contained in the Justice for All Act of 2004, which was the result of more than four years of bipartisan negotiations. Prominent among the purposes of the act was a perceived need to create a new set of statutory victims' rights that were enforceable in a court of law and supported by increased funding for victims' assistance programs; eliminate a substantial backlog of unanalyzed DNA samples and biological evidence collected from crime scenes and convicted offenders; improve and expand the DNA testing capacity of federal, state, and local crime laboratories; stimulate new DNA research; develop new DNA testing technologies; and training about the collection and use of DNA.

With the passage of the Arizona Water Settlements Act in December 2004, Congress finalized one of the most far-reaching water settlements in U.S. history. More than a decade of negotiations between the federal government, the states of Arizona and New Mexico,

local governments, and the Gila River Native American Community and Tohono O'odham Nation preceded completion of the water settlement. The act allocated almost half of the 1.5 million acre-feet of water flowing through the Central Arizona Project canal to Indian tribes. This major milestone in Arizona's history contained significant funding to enable the tribes to build the water infrastructure needed to meet the needs of their reservations. It also resolved a long-running dispute over repayment fees that the state of Arizona owed the federal government for the construction of the Central Arizona Project in 1968.

Congress approved the most extensive overhaul of the U.S. intelligence community since World War II in response to the recommendations of the National Commission on Terrorist Attacks Upon the United States. Resolving differences in the Senate and House versions of the bill was only achieved after the House conferees agreed with the Senate's efforts to limit the power of the new Director of National Intelligence over military intelligence spending. This law represented the most far-reaching reform in U.S. intelligence operations in decades.

Several months earlier, blaming Senate Minority Leader Tom Daschle for what he called the Democrats' "obstructionism," Senate Majority Leader Bill Frist broke with Senate tradition by traveling to South Dakota in May 2004 to campaign against Daschle's reelection. Daschle lost his seat that fall, becoming the first Senate party leader to be ousted since 1952. The November 2, 2004 congressional elections increased the margin of Republican control in both chambers. The bitterly contested election also marked the end of a divisive year in which the parties in Congress—and the people of America—moved further apart.

Major Acts

United States Leadership Against HIV/AIDS, Tuberculosis, and Malaria Act of 2003. Required the president "to establish a comprehensive, integrated, five-year strategy to combat global HIV/AIDS that strengthens the capacity of the United States to be an effective leader of the international campaign against HIV/AIDS." Authorized $15 billion over five years for

U.S. global efforts to combat HIV/AIDS, tuberculosis, and malaria. Established within the U.S. Department of State a presidentially appointed coordinator of U.S. government activities to combat HIV/AIDS globally, and to oversee and coordinate U.S. efforts to combat HIV/AIDS internationally. Authorized participation in the Global Fund to Fight AIDS, Tuberculosis, and Malaria; programs for the placement of health care professionals in areas severely affected by AIDS, tuberculosis, and malaria; and grants to eligible organizations to expand activities to prevent the mother-to-child transmission of AIDS. Approved May 27, 2003 (P.L. 108–25; 117 Stat. 711–750).

Jobs and Growth Tax Relief Reconciliation Act of 2003. Provided for $330 billion in tax reductions and refundable tax credits over 11 years. Reduced the rates on dividends and capital gains to the 15 percent rate, and the rates on the four top income brackets. Increased the amount of income exempted under the alternative minimum tax (AMT), benefits for married couples filing jointly, the per-child tax credit, standard deduction, and business write-off on new equipment. Provided $20 billion in aid to states in 2003–2004— $10 billion for government services, and $10 billion earmarked for state-run Medicaid programs. Provided funding to allow low-income families to receive more payments under the child credit. Approved May 28, 2003 (P.L. 108–27; 117 Stat. 752–768).

Partial-Birth Abortion Ban Act of 2003. Prohibited physicians from performing a "partial-birth" abortion except when a pregnant woman's "life is endangered by a physical disorder, physical illness, or physical injury." Defined a partial-birth abortion as when "the person performing the abortion deliberately and intentionally vaginally delivers a living fetus . . . for the purpose of performing an overt act that the person knows will kill the partially delivered living fetus." (Procedure described in the act is usually used in the second trimester, from 18 to 26 weeks.) Allowed husbands and parents of a girl under 18 to file civil lawsuits seeking monetary damages for psychological or physical injuries. Approved November 5, 2003 (P.L. 108–105; 117 Stat. 1201–1208). On April 18, 2007, the Supreme Court upheld the Partial-Birth Abortion Ban Act in *Gonzales v. Carhart* (550 U.S. 124 [2007]).

Fair and Accurate Credit Transaction Act. Permanently prevented states from imposing new restrictions on how financial institutions share consumer information. Amended the Fair Credit Reporting Act to enhance the ability of consumers to combat identity theft, to increase the accuracy of consumer reports, and to allow consumers to exercise greater control regarding the type and amount of marketing solicitations they receive. Restricted the use and disclosure of sensitive medical information contained in a consumer report. Required financial regulatory agencies and the Federal Trade Commission to promulgate a coordinated rule designed to prevent unauthorized access to consumer report information by requiring reasonable procedures for the proper disposal of such information. Approved December 4, 2003 (P.L. 108–159; 117 Stat. 1952–2012).

Medical Prescription Drug, Improvement and Modernization Act of 2003. Created a voluntary prescription drug benefit program (Part D) to assist Medicare beneficiaries with the cost of outpatient prescriptions. Offered benefits either through stand-alone drug insurance plans, for seniors who wanted to remain in the fee-for-service Medicare program, or new private care networks, similar to PPOs. Required beneficiaries to pay a deductible and monthly premiums, and increased the Medicare Part B premium for some high-income beneficiaries. Contained provisions for combating Medicare fraud, waste, and abuse. Amended the Internal Revenue Code to allow qualifying taxpayers to make tax-free contributions to Health Savings Accounts for future medical expenses. Approved December 8, 2003 (P.L. 108–173; 117 Stat. 2066–2480).

Project BioShield Act of 2004. Authorized $5.6 billion for the government to purchase vaccines and other measures needed to counter biological terrorist agents such as smallpox, anthrax, and botulism toxin, as well as other pathogens such as Ebola and plague countermeasures for the National Strategic Stockpile. Granted the government additional flexibility in awarding grants for bioterrorism-related research. Allowed the Department of Health and Human Services to simplify the process for awarding research and development grants for biomedical countermeasures, and to distribute critically needed medicines and vaccines in an emergency, even if it had not been approved by the Food and Drug Administration. Approved July 21, 2004 (P.L. 108–276; 118 Stat. 835–864).

American Jobs Creation Act of 2004. Provided for $137 billion in tax cuts for American exporters over the next decade. Provided for a two-year phase out of an export subsidy known as the extra-territorial income exclusion (ETI) that the World Trade Organization had declared illegal. Lowered corporate income tax from 35 percent to 32 percent for domestic producers. Replaced the ETI with more than 20 new tax cuts, totaling $42.6 billion over 10 years, for overseas income of U.S.–based multinational corporations. Extended previously enacted increases in small business expensing allowance. Liberalized the rules governing S corporations (corporations that elect to pass corporate income, losses, deductions, and credit through to their shareholders for federal tax purposes). Permitted itemizers to deduct their state and local sales taxes instead of state and local income taxes. Eliminated a score of tax shelters and tax avoidance practices. Placed a limit on charitable contributions of motor vehicles, boats, and airplanes. Approved October 22, 2004 (P.L. 108–357; 118 Stat. 1418–1660).

Fair and Equitable Tobacco Reform Act of 2004. Terminated the federal government's tobacco support program, which used acreage allotments and marketing quotas to control supplies and prop up market prices. Provided a series of fixed installment payments to help eligible quota holders (landowners) and producers (farmers) transition to the free market. Created a Tobacco Trust Fund, financed by quarterly assessments on domestic tobacco manufacturers and importers, to pay an estimated $10.1 billion in equal annual payments over ten years. Allowed quota holders and producers to transfer or assign payments to a financial institution, such as the Tobacco Funding Advance, giving that institution the right to receive the contract payments in exchange for a lump sum or other payment. Approved October 22, 2004 (P.L. 108–357; 118 Stat. 1521–1536).

Water Supply, Reliability, and Environmental Improvement Act. Authorized $389 million in new funds over six years for the California Federal Bay-Delta (CalFed) project, $15 million for restoration of the Salton Sea in southern California, and $6 million for other water projects. Provided funds for increasing water supply through surface and ground water storage facilities, levee improvements, groundwater management projects, wastewater recycling efforts and other conservation programs; feasibility studies for projects aimed at expanding certain reservoirs and creating new ones; flood management programs; conservation projects; water recycling, and desalination projects; ecosystem restoration projects; water quality improvements; and projects that would improve water conveyance, and provide increased water to California's farms and cities. Required the federal government to develop a feasibility study regarding a preferred alternative for restoring the Salton Sea, which serves as an important stopping point for millions of migratory birds each year. Approved October 25, 2004 (P.L. 108–361; 118 Stat. 1681–1702).

Justice for All Act of 2004. Established procedures to ensure federal inmates could apply for DNA tests that could establish their innocence if an inmate asserted under penalty of perjury that he was innocent. Barred the destruction of DNA evidence in federal cases while a defendant remained incarcerated, with some exceptions. Authorized $151 million a year for five years to help states and localities improve DNA laboratories and speed up the processing of biological evidence. Authorized $150 million a year over five years for grants to state and local governments to improve the capacity of crime labs to handle DNA testing and evidence. Authorized $75 million a year over five years for grants to states for improving the quality of legal counsel and prosecutors in death penalty cases where a defendant was indigent. Codified eight specific rights for victims of federal crimes. Authorized more than $80 million over five years for victim assistance programs and other support services. Approved October 30, 2004 (P.L. 108–405; 118 Stat. 2260–2293).

Arizona Water Settlements Act. Provided a settlement of long-standing operational and financial issues on the Central Arizona Project (CAP), a 336-mile canal system that delivers water to the state's arid interior. Fixed Arizona's repayment obligation to the federal government for construction of the project at $1.65 billion. Settled the Gila River Native American Community's water right claims to the Gila River. Amended the Southern Arizona Water Settlements Act of 1982 with the Tohono O'odham Nation, so the settlement could be fully and finally implemented. Explicitly prohibited the out-of-state marketing of water allocated to the tribes, but allowed the tribes to transfer water to in-state non-Indian water users. Set aside money and Central Arizona Project water for use in future Native American water rights settlements in Arizona, and funded existing obligations of the United States as a result of past settlements. Approved December 10, 2004 (P.L. 108–451; 118 Stat. 3478–3574).

Intelligence Reform and Terrorism Prevention Act of 2004. Created a National Counterterrorism Center to plan intelligence missions and counterterrorism operations planning. Established a Director of National Intelligence to set the strategic direction of much of the intelligence community, to advise the president on foreign intelligence, to coordinate the U.S. intelligence operations, and to develop and determine the intelligence budget. Limited the director's influence over military intelligence spending. Established an independent Privacy and Civil Liberties Oversight Board to review all government counterterrorism policies and practices. Provided for enhanced border security and hiring of additional border patrol agents. Required states to ask for certain documents before issuing a driver's license. Authorized the Federal Bureau of Investigation to conduct surveillance and wiretaps of suspected terrorists who did not have ties to any foreign country or entity. Approved December 17, 2004 (P.L. 108, B458; 118 Stat. 3638–3872).

Notes

1. Quoted in Helen Dewar, "Congress Leaves Some Priority Bills Unfinished," *Washington Post,* October 14, 2004, A29.

2. Alex Wayne and Bill Swindell, "Capitol Hill Gridlock Leaves Programs in Limbo," *CQ Weekly,* v. 62, December 4, 2004, 2834.

3. U.S. Presidents (George W. Bush), *Public Papers of the Presidents of the United State: George W. Bush, 2003* (Washington, D.C.: U.S. Government Printing Office, 2006), I, 541.

4. "Project BioShield Act of 2004," *Congressional Record* v. 150, pt. 11, July 14, 2004, 15583.

One Hundred Ninth Congress

January 4, 2005, to January 3, 2007

First Session—January 4, 2005, to December 22, 2005
Second Session—January 3, 2006, to December 9, 2006
(Second administration of George W. Bush, 2005–2009)

Historical Background

As the One Hundred Ninth Congress came to a close, analysts and even some legislators lamented the lack of progress on key issues. "This Congress hit the ground stumbling and has not lifted itself into an upright position," concluded long-time congressional scholars Thomas E. Mann and Norman Ornstein. "The output of the 109th [Congress] is pathetic measured against its predecessors and considering its priorities." Several other commentators also labeled it a "Do Nothing Congress," a pejorative originally applied to the Eightieth Congress by Harry S. Truman during the 1948 presidential campaign. Noting the comparison, Ornstein said, "What would Harry Truman say about the 109th Congress? Harry Truman would apologize to the 80th Congress." "I would say the 109th went out of town not with a bang but a whimper," he added, "but that would be an insult to whimperers everywhere."[1]

A significant portion of the criticism leveled at the nation's legislators stemmed from the fact that during the One Hundred Ninth Congress the House met for the fewest days in more than 50 years. House lawmakers typically worked three-day weeks and took lots of time off. They worked 13 days less than the infamous Eightieth Congress—241 days vs. 254 days. The Senate by comparison in 2005–2006 was open for business 297 days. In 2006, the House was in session only 101 days, nine fewer days than the 1948 House that inspired Truman's campaign quip, which helped catapult him to a full term as president. During his successful quest for the White House, Truman ran as much against the "Do Nothing Congress" as against Thomas E. Dewey.

In 2006, leaders of the Republican majority in particular "faced a series of obstacles that only got worse as the year wore on; an unpopular president, a disrupted House leadership team and a nervous and increasingly independent rank and file."[2] President Bush's approval ratings plummeted, largely because of his prosecution of the Iraq War, and the House had to recover from the departure of majority leader Tom Delay, who resigned his leadership post after being indicted on charges that he had violated state Texas campaign finance laws.

Both parties agreed, upon reflection, that the One Hundred Ninth Congress did not do enough. Neither side was willing to either bargain or compromise. In yet another challenge left for the next Congress, work was finished on only two appropriations bills for the fiscal year beginning on October 1, 2006. Instead a temporary continuing resolution was passed that extended current spending levels for much of the federal government through mid-February 2007. Despite the often stinging criticism of the One Hundred Ninth Congress, it was far from devoid of achievement.

Legislation designed to limit class-action lawsuits was a major victory for business groups that in previous years had seen measures designed to overhaul the civil justice system stall in the Senate. The intent of the act was to ensure that interstate lawsuits having national importance were heard by federal courts rather than local state courts. Underlying this purpose was Congress's belief that state and local courts were "keeping cases of national importance out of Federal court," "sometimes acting in ways that demonstrated bias against out-of-State defendants," and "making judgments that imposed their view of the law on other States and bind the residents of those states."

A rewrite of the bankruptcy law, which had been sought for years by banks and credit card companies, made it more difficult for consumers to avoid repaying debts by filing for bankruptcy protection. This act represented the largest overhaul of the bankruptcy codes since 1978. Proponents of the act argued that its intent was to increase the fiscal responsibility of individuals and businesses, prevent abuse by wealthy filers who could pay their debts but use the bankruptcy system as a financial planning tool. Opponents believed the reform bill would adversely affect individuals who sought relief from debts caused by extenuating circumstances such as illness, divorce, or long-term unemployment. They also said it was a windfall for the credit card industry and faulted the bill for not addressing corporate bankruptcy.

Congress crafted a 1,724-page bill in making the first major overhaul of the nation's energy policy in 13 years. Beneficiaries of billions in tax breaks, and potentially billions in loan guarantees and other subsidies, included producers of oil, natural gas, coal, and nuclear power, as well as consumers who received tax credits for the purchase of hybrid-electric cars and tax breaks for making energy conservation improvements in their homes. The act also encouraged oil and gas drilling, improvements in natural gas and electric transmission lines, construction of new nuclear power reactors, and expansion of renewable energy sources, especially construction of wind turbines.

Reauthorization of federal highway, transit, and safety programs at $286.4 billion over five years (2005–2009) resulted in the largest infrastructure bill ever enacted. The appropriations contained in the Safe, Accountable, Flexible, Efficient, Transportation Equity Act: A Legacy for Users (SAFETEA-LU) represented about 10 percent of the domestic discretionary spending of the United States (not including defense or entitlement programs). The new law extended five so-called core programs—interstate maintenance, the national highway system, surface transportation, bridge and bridge maintenance, and congestion and air quality. It also added a new core program—highway safety improvement.

The Protection of Unlawful Commerce in Arms Act was passed at a time when shooting victims, as well as

municipalities with high incidences of firearms-related crimes, had filed numerous lawsuits that sought to blame the firearms industry for the criminal use of firearms. Successful lobbying by the National Rife Association and other advocates to stop these lawsuits resulted in legislation that prohibited civil liability cases in any state or federal court against manufacturers, distributors, dealers and importers of firearms and ammunition.

Controversial legislation designed to deter terrorism was enacted in May 2005, establishing standards for state-issued driver's licenses and identification cards. State and county governments joined in opposition to the bill because it would appreciably increase the work of state driver license issuers. Ten months later, following months of haggling and stalemate that resulted in two hard-fought short-term extensions of the USA PATRIOT Act, Congress passed the USA PATRIOT Improvement and Reauthorization Act of 2005. The original 2001 act dramatically expanded the authority of American law enforcement for the stated purpose of fighting terrorism in the United States and abroad. President George W. Bush, in signing the new bill, called the act "a piece of legislation that's vital to win the war on terror and to protect the American people." Critics argued that the broad authority the act gave the Federal Bureau of Investigation (FBI) and other law enforcement agencies jeopardized civil liberties.

The first significant savings in mandatory spending since 1997 was achieved by passage of the Deficit Reduction Act of 2005. Three-and-a-half months later, following lengthy negotiations, a tax reconciliation package containing $70 million in tax cuts over five years was signed into law.

With several provisions of the Voting Rights Act due to expire in 2007, the American Civil Liberties Union (ACLU) and several other civil rights organizations successfully argued that allowing those provisions to lapse would enable voting authorities to discriminate against certain categories of voters. The Fannie Lou Hamer, Rosa Parks, and Coretta Scott King Voting Rights Act Reauthorization and Amendments Act, named in honor of three historic figures who fought for equality at the polls, satisfied their concerns.

An important step forward in the nation's effort to protect children from sexual exploitation and violent crime, to prevent abuse and child pornography, and to make the Internet safer for children was realized with the passage of the Adam Walsh Child Protection and Safety Act of 2006. The act was named in memory of Adam Walsh, the slain son of John Walsh, a victims' rights advocate and host of the television show "America's Most Wanted."

After the Supreme Court ruled in *Hamdan v. Rumsfeld,* (548 U.S. 557 [2006]) that military tribunals at Guantanamo Bay, Cuba, violated U.S. and international law and needed to be authorized by Congress, legislation was passed revamping the rules for detainees. The Court had held that the military commissions set up by the Bush administration lacked "the power to proceed because its structures and procedures violate both the Uniform Code of Military Justice and the four Geneva Conventions signed in 1949."

Prompted by the default of several large defined benefit pension plans and an increasing Pension Benefit Guaranty Corporation (PBGC) deficit, the Bush Administration in January 2005 advanced a proposal for pension-funding reform. The proposal was designed to increase the minimum funding requirements for pension plans and strengthen the pension insurance system. Congress responded by passing the Pension Protection Act 2006, the most comprehensive reform of the nation's pension laws since the enactment of the Employee Retirement Income Security Act of 1974.

Shortly before adjourning for the 2006 election campaign, Congress completed work on the Federal Funding Accountability and Transparency Act. The purpose of the act was to increase transparency and accountability of federal expenditures by providing access to information on federal grants, loans, contracts, and other financial assistance in a single, regularly updated, user-friendly and searchable, publicly available Internet site. Previously, there had been no single way to search for the disposition of federal spending.

The future of the Federal Emergency Management Agency (FEMA) was the subject of much debate on Capitol Hill after the agency's widely criticized response to Hurricane Katrina in the fall of 2005. The central issue was whether to remove the once-independent agency from the Department of Homeland Security, which had absorbed it in March 2003. Ultimately, the decision was made to give FEMA more

autonomy but keep it within the Department of Homeland Security. The 2006 act called for some 300 changes in federal emergency management policy.

During the final days of the One Hundred Ninth Congress, legislation was enacted that allowed President George W. Bush to finalize negotiations on a nuclear cooperation treaty with India. Enactment was realized despite concerns of critics who believed it was a dangerous step toward sharing nuclear technology with nations (such as India) that refuse to sign the nuclear Non-Proliferation Treaty, and who felt it might fuel an arms race and help Iran.

When the One Hundred Ninth Congress adjourned at 5:00 a.m. on Saturday morning, December 9, 2006, it marked the end of 12 years of Republican control. Five weeks earlier, the congressional elections saw Democrats gain control of Congress for the first time since 1994, picking up 32 House seats and six Senate seats. The following January the mantle of leadership on Capitol Hill officially changed hands. Once again the cry to oust a "Do-Nothing Congress" had proven powerful at the polls.

Major Acts

Class Action Fairness Act of 2005. Granted federal courts jurisdiction over class action suits that had one hundred or more class members, sought damages of more than $5 million, and had at least one defendant who was a citizen of a different state from at least one member of the proposed class. Limited attorneys' fees in situations in which the plaintiffs received little or no financial benefit. Approved February 18, 2005 (P.L. 109-2; 119 Stat. 4–14).

Bankruptcy Abuse Prevention and Consumer Protection Act of 2005. Bolstered the legal rights of creditors, raised bankruptcy filing fees and paperwork requirements, and mandated that potential bankruptcy filers receive credit counseling in the six months prior to seeking bankruptcy protection. Provided a means test to determine which section of the Bankruptcy Code consumers could use. Those deemed to have sufficient assets were forced into Chapter 13 protection, which results in a court-ordered repayment plan.

Other filers fell under Title 7, which erases an individual's debts after certain assets are liquidated. Approved April 20, 2005 (P.L. 109–8; 119 Stat. 23–217).

REAL ID Act of 2005. Established national standards for state-issued driver's licenses and nondriver's identification cards. Set out extensive requirements for states to maintain copies of documentation provided to obtain licenses, use of technology and security features to stop tampering and fraud, facial imaging, ensuring the security of the location where licenses and identification documents are produced, security clearances for those who produce licenses and identification cards, and the sharing of information with other states. Waived laws that interfered with the construction of physical barriers at U.S. borders. Updated and tightened the laws on application of asylum and deportation of aliens involved in terrorist activity. Approved May 11, 2005 (P.L. 109–13, Div. B; 119 Stat. 302–323).

Energy Policy Act of 2005. Provided financial incentives for increased energy production, reduced the regulation of power companies, and encouraged but did not require more conservation. Provided $14.6 billion in tax breaks for the energy industry over the next decade, although provisions designed to increase revenue reduced the net cost to $11.6 billion. Contained an additional $1.6 billion in direct spending not subject to appropriations, and tens of billions of dollars more in authorized funds. Required refiners to ramp up the use of renewable fuels, starting at 4 billion gallons in 2006 and climbing to 7.5 billion gallons in 2012. Required an inventory of coastal oil and gas resources. Extended daylight savings time by a month in an attempt to conserve energy by retaining an extra hour of daylight in the evening. Approved August 8, 2005 (P.L. 109–58; 119 Stat. 594–1143).

Safe, Accountable, Flexible, Efficient Transportation Equity Act: A Legacy for Users (SAFETEA-LU). Reauthorized the nation's federal highway, transit, public transportation, and road safety programs. Guaranteed that in fiscal 2008, every state would receive at least 92 cents for federal highway projects for every dollar paid into the Highway Trust Fund. Created incentives for states to crack down on repeat drunken driving offenders and drivers who do not wear seat belts. Mandated tougher licensing standards for those hauling hazardous cargo. Allowed states to impose tolls on newly constructed roads and on some existing roads as part of a demonstration project. Contained provisions to encourage private sector road construction. Approved August 10, 2005 (P.L. 109–59; 119 Stat. 1144–1926).

Protection of Unlawful Commerce in Arms Act. Limited the legal liability of federally licensed manufacturers, dealers, and sellers of firearms or ammunition, as well as trade associations, from any civil action "resulting from the criminal or unlawful misuse" of firearms or ammunition. Required that civil lawsuits (with six exceptions) pending at the time of enactment, brought by shooting victims and municipalities "be immediately dismissed by the court in which the action was brought or is pending." The six exceptions included (1) an action against a manufacturer or seller who has been convicted of knowingly transferring a firearm with the knowledge that it will be used in a crime of violence or a drug trafficking crime, brought by a plaintiff who was directly harmed by the conduct of the manufacturer or seller; (2) an action brought against a seller for negligent entrustment or negligence per se; (3) an action in which a manufacturer or seller knowingly violated a federal or state statute applicable to the sale or marketing of firearms, where the violation was a proximate cause of the harm for which relief is sought; (4) an action for breach of contract or breach of warranty; (5) an action based on an alleged design or manufacturing defect; and (6) an action or proceeding commenced by the attorney general to enforce the federal firearms laws. Approved October 26, 2005 (P.L. 109–92; 120 Stat. 2095–2103).

Deficit Reduction Act of 2005. Provided for a $38.8 billion, five-year, budget-savings package that included reductions in student loan programs, Medicare, and Medicaid. Required higher premiums of the Pension Benefit Guaranty Corporation and counted on additional funds from an auction of portions of the radio spectrum—funds that were to be used to offset some additional mandatory spending increases. Reauthorized the Temporary Assistance for Needy Families (TANF) program. Approved February 8, 2006 (P.L. 109–171; 120 Stat. 4–184).

USA PATRIOT Improvement and Reauthorization Act of 2005. Reauthorized 16 provisions of the 2001 anti-terrorism PATRIOT Act. Approved March 9, 2006 (P.L. 109–177; 120 Stat. 192–246).

Tax Increase Prevention and Reconciliation Act of 2005. Provided $70 million in tax cuts and $20 million in revenue raises. Increased expensing allowance for depreciable business property from $25,000 to $100,000; increased threshold amount for determining reductions to the expensing allowance; and increased the period during which a taxpayer may revoke an election to expense depreciable business property through 2009. Extended through 2010 reductions in capital gains and dividend tax rates (5 percent for taxpayers in the 15 percent bracket and 15 percent for others) enacted in 2003. Accelerated the inflation adjustment to the exclusion amount for foreign earned income to 2008. Extended through 2008 certain exemptions for income of controlled foreign companies. Increased the alternative minimum tax (AMT) exemption, to $42,500 for single filers and $62,550 for married filers, through 2006. Allowed taxpayers to convert traditional IRA balances into Roth IRAs. Eliminated the income limit ($100,000) on Roth IRA conversions starting in 2010. Imposed an excise tax penalty on certain tax-exempt entities for participation in prohibited tax shelter activities. Approved May 17, 2006 (P.L. 109–222; 120 Stat. 345–373).

Fannie Lou Hamer, Rosa Parks, and Coretta Scott King Voting Rights Act Reauthorization and Amendments Act of 2006. Reauthorized the provisions of the Voting Rights Act of 1965, including those requiring jurisdictions with a history of adopting obstacles to minority voting participation to clear with the Justice Department any proposed changes in practices or procedures, and those requiring bilingual election materials and assistance for minorities with limited proficiency in the English language. Extended the Voting Rights Act for 25 years. Approved July 27, 2006 (P.L. 109–246; 120 Stat. 577–581).

Adam Walsh Child Protection and Safety Act of 2006. Established a comprehensive national register for sex offenders under which states were required to modify their registration systems in accordance with federal requirements at the risk of losing 10 percent of their Byrne program law enforcement assistance funds. Introduced amendments to federal criminal law and procedure, featuring, among other things, a federal procedure for the civil commitment of convicted sex offenders upon their release from prison, a random search authority over sex offenders on probation or supervised release, and a number of new mandatory minimum terms of imprisonment for various new and existing federal sex offenses. Created, amended, or revised several grant programs designed to reinforce private, state, local, tribal, and territorial prevention law enforcement, and treatment efforts in the case of crimes committed against children. Called for a variety of administrative or regulatory initiatives in the interest of child safety, such as the creation of the National Child Abuse Registry. Approved July 27, 2006 (P.L. 109–248; 120 Stat. 587–650).

Pension Protection Act of 2006. Made major revisions to the rules governing pension plans. Required companies to fully fund employee pension plans. Increased funding for the Pension Guaranty Corporation, which had been facing record deficits. Established new rules governing how companies funded benefits for their employees. Required "most pension plans to become fully funded over a seven-year period" starting in 2008. Allowed employers to deduct the cost of making additional contributions to fund the pension, provided strict funding guidelines, and imposed a 10 percent excise tax on companies that failed to correct their funding deficiencies. Approved August 17, 2006 (P.L. 109–280; 120 Stat. 780–1172).

Federal Funding and Accountability and Transparency Act of 2006. Required Office of Management and Budget (OMB) to establish, no later than January 1, 2008, a publicly accessible Web site containing data on all federal grants, cooperative agreements, subgrants, awards, loans, contracts, subcontracts, and other forms of funding awarded to public and private organizations in excess of $25,000. Exempted disclosure of personal information on federal employees and federal assistance recipients as well as information on credit card transactions until October 1, 2008, and subgrants or subcontracts until January 1, 2009. Authorized the OMB to issue guidance to federal agencies on reporting award data and instructed agencies to comply with that guidance. Approved September 26, 2006 (P.L. 109–282; 120 Stat. 1186–1190).

Post-Katrina Emergency Management Reform Act of 2006. Established the Federal Emergency Management Agency (FEMA) as an independent agency within the Department of Homeland Security (DHS), with the director of FEMA reporting directly to the secretary of Homeland Security. Gave the FEMA director more power to advise the president on disasters. Enhanced FEMA's responsibilities, stipulating that it was to lead and support the nation in a risk-based, emergency management based system of preparedness, response, recovery, and mitigation. Established new leadership positions and position requirements within FEMA. Called for FEMA to absorb many of the functions of DHS's Preparedness Directorate. Established a National Integration Center responsible for the National Incident Response Plan (NIMS) and National Preparedness Plan (NRP). Authorized a system of FEMA regional offices, "strike teams" to respond quickly to disasters, and created a National Advisory Council to allow state and local first-responders to advise FEMA. Approved October 4, 2006 (P.L. 109–295; Title VI, 120 Stat. 1394–1463).

Military Commissions Act of 2006. Established standards for the trial and treatment of accused terrorists, upheld indefinite detention of enemy combatants, and blocked prisoners from seeking court review of their detention and treatment. Granted the president broad latitude in defining mistreatment of detainees and allowed hearsay evidence and certain testimony obtained via coercion. Allowed people designated enemy combatants to obtain a court review of that status and, if they are convicted by a military tribunal, an avenue of appeal in a civilian court. Approved October 17, 2006 (P.L. 109–366; 120 Stat. 2600–2637).

Henry J. Hyde United States-India Peaceful Atomic Energy Cooperation Act of 2006. Allowed the president to waive parts of the Atomic Energy Act of 1954 to permit exports of nuclear materials, equipment, and technology to India. (In return, India promised to open its civilian nuclear sites to inspection by the International Atomic Energy Agency [IAEA] for the first time.) Stipulated that India must continue to negotiate with the United States on a fissile material cutoff treaty and sign a protocol with the IAEA governing inspections at civilian nuclear sites. Required a joint resolution of approval from Congress before the nuclear agreement can take effect. Contained a variety of reporting requirements and certifications aimed at keeping Congress abreast of each new development as the details of the agreement are worked out. Implemented a special agreement with the IAEA, called the Additional Protocol, which gave inspectors from the international agency carefully regulated access to U.S. nuclear sites. Approved December 18, 2006 (P.L. 109–401; 120 Stat. 2726–2753).

Notes

1. Quotes are found in: Norman J. Ornstein and Thomas Mann, "Our Do Nothing Congress," *Los Angeles Times,* September 27, 2006, 13; Scott Shepard, "109th Congress a Dud, Critics Say, 'Do Nothing:' Outgoing Congress is Pegged by Democrats and Republicans Alike as Ineffective," *The Atlantic Journal-Constitution,* December 10, 2006, A1.

2. David Nathan, "A Session Squandered," *CQ Weekly,* v. 64, December 18, 1962, 3324–3325. See also: "Resume of Congressional Activity: Eightieth Congress," *Congressional Record-Daily Digest,* v. 94, pt. 14, December 31, 1948, D537; "Final Resume of Congressional Activity: First Session of the One Hundred Ninth Congress," *Congressional Record-Daily Digest,* v. 151, pt. 24, March 2, 2006, D698; "Final Resume of Congressional Activity: Second Session of the One Hundred Ninth Congress," *Congressional Record-Daily Digest,* v. 152, pt. 20, December 27, 2006, D624.

One Hundred Tenth Congress

January 3, 2007, to January 3, 2009

First Session—January 4, 2007, to December 19, 2007
Second Session—January 3, 2008, to January 3, 2009
(Second administration of George W. Bush, 2005–2009)

Historical Background

At 2:08 p.m., on January 4, 2007, Nancy Pelosi, the first woman to be Speaker of the House, took the gavel from John A. Boehner, the Republican leader, whom she defeated by a vote of 233 to 202 in the election for speaker. "The floor and the packed galleries erupted in cheers when the vote was announced. Even Republicans grudgingly acknowledged the unprecedented nature of the day on which a woman ascended to power on Capitol Hill by rising as one to applaud her." As Representative Pelosi acknowledged in her first remarks as Speaker, it was "an historic moment for Congress," and "an historic moment for the women of America."[1] Earlier in the day, Democrat Harry Reid became Senate majority leader. Although both Reid and Pelosi promised a new era of cooperation, partisan jockeying continued in the narrowly divided One Hundred Tenth Congress. Among the biggest frustrations of the new Democratic majority in Congress was an inability to end or even set any sort of timetable for ending the Iraq War. Their only effective weapon was oversight over war policy and war expenditures. Standoffs between the parties continued to be commonplace, and *Congressional Quarterly's* annual review of party unity votes found the One Hundred Tenth Congress to be one of the most partisan in at least a half-century.

Two years of debate, which began in the previous Congress, preceded passage of legislation to strengthen the government's review of foreign investments in the United States. Impetus for the reform bill was prompted by several high-profile foreign transactions in 2005 and 2006 that raised considerable controversy and aroused congressional concern. This measure fundamentally altered the process by which the Committee on Foreign Investment in the United States (CFIUS) reviewed proposed acquisitions of U.S. businesses by foreign investors, and broadened the meaning of national security in such instances to include critical infrastructure and homeland security as areas of concern. Congress strengthened its own role in the process by enhancing its oversight of CFIUS.

Similarly, legislation implementing many of the recommendations of the independent 9/11 Commission took months of consideration. To fortify the nation's security against terrorism, provisions were included to significantly increase homeland security and emergency management grants, improve communications among first responders, enhance intelligence sharing, prevent terrorist travel, improve private-sector preparedness, and heighten critical infrastructure security, especially transportation. Lengthy negotiations also preceded an overhaul of lobbying and ethics rules. The Honest Leadership and Open Government Act placed new restrictions on members' ties to lobbyists and new rules regarding earmarks. The chief aim of the act was "to provide greater transparency in the legislative process," particularly on the activities of lobbyists.

Safety concerns about the arthritis drug Vioxx and other prescription pharmaceuticals prompted the largest expansion of Food and Drug Administration (FDA) regulatory powers in a decade. The FDA amendments bolstered the monitoring of prescription drugs and medical devices by broadening oversight of labeling, tightening the regulation of drug advertising, and providing consumers access to information on clinical trials for drugs and medical devices. Consumer advocates hailed the act "as the most significant drug safety legislation in more than 40 years."[2] Less than three months later, legislation hailed by some as the most sweeping energy efficiency legislation ever enacted passed after much partisan bickering and White House veto threats. For the first time in 32 years, the fuel economy standards for vehicle manufacturers were increased, and a mandated market for advanced renewable fuels was created. The new standards, which took almost a year of negotiations, represented a 40 percent increase in efficiency over existing requirements.

Near the end of 2007, legislation was sent to the White House to speed up the process for public access to government documents under the Freedom of Information Act (FOIA). The act provided a number of substantive and procedural reforms to FOIA that expanded the public's right to recover records and attorney's fees in litigation against the government, imposed stronger controls against agency delay and denial of FOIA requests, and enhanced the rights of individuals to sue under FOIA.

Although partisanship continued to be as high in 2008 as it had been in any recent year, the differences between the parties began to be overshadowed by increasingly dire economic news. As the year unfolded, the United States experienced a major financial crisis that ultimately led to the most serious recession since the Second World War. Frightened consumers watched as home foreclosures rose, job losses increased, the number of individuals seeking unemployment benefits climbed, and record high prices for gasoline prompted a growth in inflation. Early in 2008, House Speaker Pelosi, House Minority Leader Boehner, and Treasury Secretary Henry M. Paulson Jr. negotiated a $151.7 billion economic stimulus package in an effort to induce consumer and investment spending in the hopes of preventing a recession. The Economic Stimulus Act of 2008 included roughly $100 billion in tax rebates to low-income and middle-income taxpayers, and more than $50 billion of investment incentives for businesses. These incentives, it was hoped, would address the nation's declining economic growth and rising unemployment, as well as a collapse in the housing market.

When home foreclosures continued to rise, measures to assist local governments cope with one of the worst housing downturns in history were included in a mortgage relief bill that made it easier for troubled homeowners to refinance their loans. Other initiatives contained in the most sweeping housing bill in decades included incentives to improve confidence and stability in the housing market, to bolster financial giants Fannie Mae and Freddie Mac, to provide tax breaks for first-time home buyers as well as mortgage holders, and to modernize many aspects of Federal Housing Administration (FHA) regulations, so the agency would be more competitive.

Still, the economy continued to worsen. In mid-September congressional leaders were told at a closed-door Capitol Hill meeting with Treasury Secretary Henry M. Paulson Jr. and Federal Reserve Chairman Ben S. Bernanke that the losses on housing-related assets were about to cripple the economy. Already the government had taken control of two mortgage giants, and the nation's fourth largest investment house had gone bankrupt. The government had bailed out the country's largest insurance company, and banks were refusing to do business with each other. Global financial conditions deteriorated, and the stock market was faltering. Acting on Paulson and Bernanke's urgent request for action, Congress agreed to spend as much as $700 billion to stabilize the nation's battered financial sector. The Troubled Asset Relief Program (TARP), created by the Emergency Economic Stabilization Act, was the third broad effort in 2008 to address the faltering economy. The One Hundred Tenth Congress was indelibly shaped by its response to the financial crisis.

When Congress passed the Emergency Economic Stabilization Act, a massive reform in mental health parity laws was attached to the 2008 financial bailout. Passage of the Paul Wellstone and Pete Domenici Mental Health Parity and Addiction Equity Act of 2008 was the culmination of more than a decade of effort by mental health advocates for legislation requiring mental health and addiction benefits to be equal in cost and scope to traditional medical benefits. The law, which garnered bipartisan support, broadly outlawed health insurance discrimination against Americans with mental health and substance abuse conditions in employer-sponsored health plans.

Despite a preoccupation with the worst economic crisis since the Great Depression, several other important issues in addition to mental health captured attention in 2008. After stalling in Congress for 13 years, action was completed on a bill prohibiting employers and health insurers from discriminating on the basis of genetic information about workers and patients. The Genetic Information Nondiscrimination Act of 2008 was the first anti-discrimination law enacted to work proactively and prevent discrimination before it became entrenched in society. The intent was to encourage Americans to take advantage of genetic testing as part of their health care plans.

The Post-9/11 Veterans Educational Assistance Act of 2008—most commonly known as the Post-9/11 GI Bill—ushered in dramatic changes to educational benefits for veterans. The new GI Bill significantly increased the educational benefits offered to veterans of the Iraq and Afghanistan conflicts. Benefactors of the new law included activated reservists and National Guard.

Congress spent much of late 2007 and early 2008 considering a reform of the Foreign Intelligence Surveillance Act of 1978 (FISA), which established a statutory framework for the managerial structure of the United States intelligence community. Sparking this effort was a revelation by the *New York Times* on December 16, 2005, that President Bush, shortly after the 2001 terrorist attacks, had secretly authorized the National Security Agency (NSA) to begin intercepting telephone and email communications going to and from the United States, without a warrant. The amendments to the original act established new rules for the use of electronic surveillance to collect foreign intelligence, including monitoring communications involving parties on U.S. soil, and provided for the dismissal of lawsuits against companies that assisted in a warrantless surveillance program.

Headlines spotlighting a year of product recalls, particularly of toys and other products used by children, preceded passage of the Consumer Product Safety Improvement Act of 2008. The overhaul of product safety regulation affected an extremely broad array of products and dramatically changed the reporting, testing, and certification obligations of manufacturers, importers, distributors, and retailers of consumer products. This expanded mandate necessitated an increase in the staffing, funding, authority, and reach of the Consumer Product Safety Commission, as well as

enhancement of the ability of state attorneys general to enforce consumer product safety laws at the state level, and heightened consumer access to information about hazardous products.

Democrats, Republicans, and the White House were all in agreement on the need to revise the Americans with Disabilities Act (ADA), in response to a series of Supreme Court decisions that lawmakers said had narrowed the scope of protections under the act. The rewrite sought to "restore" the originally intended definition of disability, stating that it should be "construed broadly" so as to achieve the ADA's remedial purposes. Many conditions previously found not to be disabilities now garnered protection under the ADA. More than 220 national organizations, including the U.S. Chamber of Commerce, the American Society of Employees, disability organizations, veterans groups, church organizations, and the National Association of Manufacturers supported the measure.

Approval of a civilian nuclear cooperation agreement with India was reached after India, who had not signed the Nuclear Non-Proliferation Treaty, was granted needed exemptions from international nuclear regulations. Supporters, including leaders of both parties, said the U.S.-India deal would open business opportunities and strengthen ties with India, a key ally to enhanced U.S. security versus China and Iran. Others saw the agreement as providing increased security at nuclear power facilities within India, helping in the fight against global warming by providing a viable, cleaner alternative electric production over coal, and easing global demand of crude oil and natural gas.

The acting chairman of the National Transportation Safety Board praised passage of the Rail Safety Improvement Act of 2008 as helping to bring about safety improvements long sought by the board. The most comprehensive rail safety bill in more than 30 years, particular attention was paid to two long-standing issues, driver fatigue and positive train control.

On the evening of November 4, 2008, in the waning hours of the One Hundred Tenth Congress, the nation watched as Barack Obama became the first African American to capture the White House. Democrats also added to their majorities in both chambers of Congress. A lame duck session followed, but no major legislation resulted.

Major Acts

Foreign Investment and National Security Act of 2007. Codified the existence and role of the Committee on Foreign Investment in the United States (CFIUS). Expanded the scope of foreign investment transactions subject to national security reviews. Mandated second-stage investigations of transactions involving U.S. critical infrastructure and state-owned or -controlled foreign entities. Required CFIUS to enter into and enforce agreements with foreign buyers to mitigate national security concerns. Required CFIUS to report all transactions it reviewed to the chairman and ranking members of the congressional committees of jurisdiction. Required the director of national intelligence to provide an analysis to CFIUS of security implications of any transaction under review. Authorized the president to suspend or prohibit any transaction that threatened to impair national security. Approved July 26, 2007 (P.L. 110–49; 121 Stat. 246–260).

Implementing Recommendations of the 9/11 Commission Act of 2007. Required screening of all cargo on passenger airplanes within three years, and foreign maritime cargo bound for the United States within five years. Protected individuals who reported terrorist activity in and around airplanes, trains, and buses from lawsuits. Established a grant program to improve interoperability at local, state, and federal levels, and for states and high-risk urban areas to prevent, prepare for, respond to, and recover from terrorist attacks. Provided four years of grants for rail, transit, and bus security, airport checkpoint and baggage screening, and aviation security research and development. Mandated stronger security measures for Visa Waiver Program. Required the president to publicly disclose amount appropriated for the intelligence community. Established the Privacy and Civil Liberties Oversight Board "to ensure that liberty concerns are appropriately considered in . . . efforts to protect the Nation against terrorism." Approved August 3, 2007 (P.L. 110–53; 121 Stat. 266–550).

Honest Leadership and Open Government Act. Prohibited lobbyists and their employers from giving gifts (free meals, accommodations, flights, and tickets for entertainment and sporting events) to members of Congress or congressional staff, other than as permitted by House and Senate rules. Required lobbyists to file quarterly reports. Called for establishment of searchable public databases of lobbyist disclosure information, and member travel and personal financial disclosure forms. Increased civil and criminal liability of lobbyists, or organizations that employed or retained lobbyists who failed to comply with the Lobby Disclosure Act of 1995. Strengthened the "revolving-door rules." Changed Senate rules to establish temporary rules for congressional earmarks. Allowed certain provisions added to bills in conference to be challenged through points of order. Approved September 14, 2007 (P.L. 110–81; 121 Stat. 735–776).

Food and Drug Administration Amendments Act of 2007. Expanded the Food and Drug Administration's (FDA) authority to regulate the safety of prescription drugs and biologics, medical devices, and foods. Authorized the FDA to require post-approval clinical studies of new drugs, and impose new distribution and use restrictions. Called for the creation of a public Internet database where the results of clinical trials would be posted. Granted the FDA authority to levy higher fines on drug companies that violated its regulations. Required experts on FDA advisory panels to disclose financial conflicts of interest. Mandated regulations requiring food makers to report contaminated products within 24 hours. Approved September 27, 2007 (P.L. 110–85; 121 Stat. 823–978).

Energy Independence and Security Act of 2007. Directed the National Highway Traffic Safety Administration to set a fuel economy standard of 35 miles per gallon across a manufacturer's fleet of cars and light trucks by model year 2020. Established a fuel economy program for medium- and heavy-duty trucks, and a separate fuel economy standard for work trucks. Mandated that at least 36 billion gallons of ethanol and other biofuels be incorporated into gasoline by 2022. Increased funding for bioenergy research, and created new research and development programs for biofuel infrastructure and technology. Directed the Department of Energy (DOE) to set new efficiency standards for a variety of residential and commercial products and appliances, and standards for phasing-out conventional incandescent light bulbs in favor of energy-efficient lighting. Approved December 19, 2007 (P.L. 110–140; 121 Stat. 1492–1801).

Openness Promotes Effectiveness in Our National Government Act of 2007. Established a 20-day deadline for a government agency to determine how it would respond to a Freedom of Information Act (FOIA) request, and limited an agency's ability to claim exemptions. Allowed complainants litigating FOIA requests to recover attorney fees if a non-frivolous claim resulted in a government decision to comply with the request before the court had rendered a decision. Extended FOIA coverage to records "maintained for an agency by an entity under Government contract, for the purposes of records management." Established an Office of Government Information within the National Archives to review agency FOIA policies, procedures, and compliance; and to recommend policy changes to Congress and the president. Approved December 31, 2007 (P.L. 110–175; 121 Stat. 2524–2531).

Economic Stimulus Act of 2008. Provided for tax rebates of between $300 to $600 for individuals earning up to $75,000 in adjusted gross income and between $600 and $1,200 for married couples earning up to $150,000 in adjusted gross income. Provided a tax rebate of $300 for low-income taxpayers, disabled veterans, and the elderly, and an extra $300 rebate for each qualifying child claimed by the taxpayer. Provided tax incentives designed to promote business investment and to temporarily relieve the tax burden of business owners by significantly increasing the limits on expensive investment costs and accelerating depreciation of qualified investments. Increased the size of mortgages that Fannie Mae and Freddie Mac could purchase and that the Federal Housing Administration could insure. Approved February 13, 2008 (P.L. 110–185; 122 Stat. 613–622).

Genetic Information Nondiscrimination Act of 2008. Prohibited health insurers from basing coverage or premiums on the results of genetic tests. Prohibited employers from making employment or promotion decisions based on genetic information, or requiring genetic testing or purchasing genetic information,

except in certain instances. Created a "firewall" to protect employers from excessive lawsuits under the act. Allowed the military to collect genetic information in order to identify soldier's remains. Established a Genetic Nondiscrimination Study Commission charged with reviewing new developments in the field of genetics and advising Congress. Approved May 21, 2008 (P.L. 110–233; 122 Stat. 881–922).

Post-9/11 Veterans Educational Assistance Act of 2008. Established the Post-9/11 Veterans Educational Assistance program under which veterans and service members who served on active duty on or after September 11, 2001, were eligible for up to 36 months of tuition and fees assistance, a monthly housing allowance, and a stipend for books and supplies. Required individuals receiving benefits to serve at least 90 days on active duty (or who served at least 30 continuous days on active duty and were discharged with a service-connected disability). Required individuals discharged due to a service-connected disability to serve at least 30 continuous days on active duty. Allowed service members who met certain criteria to transfer unused veterans education benefits to family members after serving at least 10 years. Approved June 30, 2008 (P.L. 110–252, Title V; 122 Stat. 2357–2386).

Foreign Intelligence Surveillance Act of 1978 Amendments of 2008. Authorized warrantless surveillance of foreign targets who may be communicating with people in the United States as long as the government was not intentionally targeting U.S. citizens. Required the attorney general and Defense Intelligence Agency, before beginning a surveillance, to secure approval from the Foreign Intelligence Surveillance Court regarding the procedures to be used. Required approval of the Foreign Intelligence Surveillance Court for surveillance of anyone located in the United States. Called for federal and state courts to dismiss lawsuits against telecommunication companies that had participated in a warrantless wiretapping program conducted by the National Security Agency if there was "substantial evidence" the companies had received written assurances the program was legal and authorized by the president. Approved July 10, 2008 (PL. 110–261; 122 Stat. 2436–2478).

Housing and Economic Recovery Act of 2008. Granted the Treasury Department temporary emergency authority to purchase securities issued by Fannie Mae and Freddie Mac. Authorized the department to increase the already-existing line of credit to Fannie Mae and Freddie Mac. Established the Federal Housing Finance Agency (FHFA), with broad oversight over the government-sponsored housing enterprises (GSEs—Fannie Mae, Freddie Mac, and Federal Home Loan Banks). Created a five-member Housing Oversight Board to advise the FHFA director on overall strategy and policies. Increased FHA maximum loan limits for high-cost areas. Established a $300 billion trust fund for the Federal Housing Administration to help borrowers refinance loans using new government-backed mortgages. Provided $15.1 billion in tax incentives designed to support home ownership and affordable housing incentives. Approved July 30, 2008 (P.L. 110–289; 122 Stat. 2654–2913).

Consumer Product Safety Improvement Act of 2008. Expanded the staffing and funding authority of the Consumer Product Safety Commission (CPSC). Imposed more stringent safety standards for consumer products and stiffer penalties for violation of product safety regulations. Mandated independent testing of all products subject to juvenile and children's product safety rules, and new testing labels, registration requirements, and advertising rules for children's products. Banned lead and other harmful materials and chemicals in toys. Called for the creation of an online database of consumer reports and official accounts of product-related injuries and risks. Increased damage awards in product safety cases. Allowed state attorneys general to take enforcement actions. Provided whistleblower protections to private sector employees who reported product safety violations. Required the Consumer Product Safety Commission to review and adopt widely accepted product safety standards or write its own similar standards if the international standards were deemed inadequate. Approved August 14, 2008 (P.L. 110–314; 122 Stat. 3016–3077).

ADA Amendments Act of 2008. Expanded the coverage and definition of the American's with Disabilities Act (ADA) to ensure that protections were not withheld from everyone meeting those standards. Declared that a person's ability to mitigate the effects of a disability through means such as medication, prosthetics, or hearing aids did not affect his qualification under the ADA, and "an impairment that is episodic or in remission is a disability if it would substantially limit a major life activity when active." Directed the courts to adjudicate the merits of a disability claim and not the severity of the disability in cases involving clinically certified disabled people. Required a determination of disability to be made, except in the case of eyeglasses, without considering the impact of mitigating measures. Approved September 25, 2008 (P.L. 110–325; 122 Stat. 3553–3559).

Emergency Economic Stabilization Act of 2008. Authorized the Treasury Department to establish a program—the Troubled Asset Relief Program (TARP)—to purchase up to $700 billion in troubled assets from financial institutions. Required the Treasury to consult with the Federal Reserve Board, the Federal Deposit Insurance Corporation (FDIC), the Comptroller of the Currency, the Office of Thrift Supervision, and the Department of Housing and Urban Development in exercising its new authority. Required the Office of Management and Budget, in consultation with the Congressional Budget Office, to submit a report to Congress on the net amount in TARP. (If there was a shortfall, the president had to submit legislation to Congress to recoup the loss from the financial services industry.) Approved October 3, 2008 (P.L. 110–343; 122 Stat. 3765–3933).

Paul Wellstone and Pete Domenici Mental Health Parity and Addiction Equity Act of 2008. Required any group health plan (with 50 or more enrollees) and Medicaid managed-care plans that include mental health and substance abuse benefits along with standard medical and surgical coverage to treat them equally in terms of out-of-pocket costs, benefit limits, and practices such as prior authorization and utilization review. Preserved existing state parity and consumer protection laws while extending protection of mental health services to 82 million Americans not protected by state laws. Ensures mental health coverage for both in network and out-of-network services. Approved October 3, 2008 (P.L. 110–343; 122 Stat. 3881–3893, Title V, Subtitle B, Sec. 511–512).

United States-India Nuclear Cooperation Approval and Nonproliferation Enhancement Act. Granted approval to the United States-India Agreement for Cooperation on Peaceful Uses of Nuclear Energy, under which India agreed to separate its civil and military nuclear facilities and place civil facilities under International Atomic Energy Agency (IAEA) safeguards. Allowed for the transfer of nuclear information, material, equipment, and components for research and power production between the two countries. Allowed Congress to reject a presidential decision to resume nuclear trade with any country that detonated a nuclear explosive device by adopting a joint resolution of disapproval within 60 days. Approved October 8, 2008 (P.L. 110–369; 112 Stat. 4028–4034).

Rail Safety Improvement Act of 2008. Required railroads to install positive train control (PTC) technology on passenger and certain hazmat rail lines by 2015. Reduced the time train crews could work in a 30-day period, and increased the amount of rest time required between shifts. Prohibited railroads from interfering with or delaying medical treatment of injured workers. Established minimum training standards for railroad workers. Provided for increased federal safety inspections, risk-based safety programs, and improved safety at highway-rail grade crossings. Required the Federal Railroad Administration to study the use of personal electronic devices in locomotive cabs. Approved October 16, 2008 (P.L. 110–432, Title I-V; 122 Stat. 4848–4970).

Notes

1. John M. Broder and Robin Toner, "Jubilant Democrats Assume Control on Capitol Hill," *New York Times,* January 5, 2007, A1.

2. Michelle Andrews, "A New Law Should Ensure Safer Drugs," *U.S. News Health,* October 3, 2007, at http://health.usnews.com/health-news/articles/2007/10/03/a-new-law-should-ensure-safer-drugs

One Hundred Eleventh Congress
January 3, 2009, to January 3, 2011

First Session—January 6, 2009, to December 24, 2009
Second Session—January 5, 2010, to December 22, 2010
(First administration of Barack Obama, 2009–2013)

Historical Background

When the One Hundred Eleventh Congress convened on January 6, 2009, the United States was only two weeks away from the historic inauguration of Barack Obama. For the first time in eight years, Democrats would soon control the White House, and had already strengthened majorities in both houses. In capturing the White House, Mr. Obama gained the highest percentage of votes of any Democrat since Lyndon Johnson in 1964. It was also an impressive election for Democrats at the other end of Pennsylvania Avenue. With their victories in 2008, Democrats were in about the same position in Congress as when Bill Clinton moved into the White House 16 years earlier.

President Obama took office with an ambitious agenda and "settled on a legislative strategy that departed from those of his predecessors. He decided that rather than pursue big pieces of legislation one at a time, his administration would seek" several measures simultaneously.[1] At the time, experts questioned this approach. Congress did, however, during the first two years of the Obama presidency, produce an impressive list of big, bold initiatives, from a sweeping health care reform bill to major financial regulatory reform. These enactments, however, were only passed after contentious, drawn-out, partisan battles that left most Americans less than happy with the outcome. Somewhat less controversial was Senate confirmation of Sonia Sotomayor (2009) to become the Supreme Court's first

Hispanic justice, and only the third woman ever to serve on the Court; and justice Elena Kagan (2010), the Court's fourth woman justice. This Congress has the "odd distinction of being both historically busy and epically unpopular," one remembered for significant accomplishments as well as "endless filibuster threats, volcanic town hall meetings, and the rise of the tea party." The One Hundred Eleventh Congress functioned amid the "most dysfunctional political environment" ever seen by long-time congressional observer Norman Ornstein, and still was one of "the three most productive Congresses" since 1900.[2]

The American Reinvestment and Recovery Act was the first piece of legislation in the White House's multi-pronged approach to try to end the recession and help millions of Americans who had been affected by the worst economy since the Great Depression. While he was still president-elect, Mr. Obama was on Capitol Hill shortly after the One Hundred Eleventh Congress convened, meeting with leaders from both parties to push an economic package he said would create or save three million jobs and put an extra $500 into individual taxpayers' pockets. After less than a month in office, congressional Democrats handed President Obama his first significant legislative victory by agreeing to pump $787.2 billion into the economy, in order to keep it from sinking further into recession. The aim of the stimulus package was to increase employment and stimulate the economy through massive new investments in construction, energy, transportation, education, environmental cleanup, health care, and social safety-net programs.

Next, despite opposition from the credit card industry, significant limitations were placed on the ability of credit card companies to raise interest rates and charge hidden fees. During the previous two decades,

462

consumer credit had more than quadrupled, and credit card debt significantly increased as well. The intent of the Credit CARD Act of 2009 was to strengthen consumer protection in the credit card market by banning abusive credit card practices, enhancing consumer disclosures, and protecting underage consumers.

A longtime goal of civil rights and gay rights groups to expand application of hate crime laws to combat bias-motivated attacks was finally realized in October 2009. The act, enacted as a rider to the National Defense Authorization Act of 2010, expanded the definition of federal hate crimes to cover attacks based on gender, gender identity, sexual orientation, and disability, as well as race, color, religion or national origin. The bill honored the memory of Matthew Shepard, a gay Wyoming college student who was tied to a fence and beaten to death in 1988, and James Byrd Jr., an African American who was beaten, chained to the back of a pick-up truck, and dragged to his death in Jasper, Texas, the same year.

A week later, President Obama signed legislation that marked a dramatic shift in the federal government's approach to student lending and resulted in a consolidation of federal power over education financing. The Student Aid and Fiscal Responsibility Act (SAFRA) ended the federally guaranteed student loan program and created a new program that authorized the federal government to do 100 percent of the lending for student loans directly. The Congressional Budget Office (CBO) estimated the bill would generate $60 billion in savings over 10 years. SAFRA dedicated much of the savings to increased funding for Pell grants and other federal education programs awarding college students money based on financial need.

"With the stroke of 20 pens," President Obama on March 23, 2010, signed the Patient Protection and Affordable Care Act, the most sweeping piece of federal health care legislation since the passage of Medicare in 1965.[3] Democratic lawmakers in gaining approval for the act rode a year-long legislative roller coaster that saw Republican leaders attempt to block it at every stage, arguing that a vast majority of Americans opposed the changes being proposed. The act only passed "after an epic political battle that could define the differences between the parties for years."[4] Under the far-reaching health care overhaul, as modified by a budget reconciliation bill, the Congressional

Budget Office (CBO) estimated 32 million uninsured Americans could be expected to obtain health insurance coverage.

This would be done mainly through subsidized private insurance policies or expanded access to Medicaid. The cost of the combined bills—nearly $1 trillion over 10 years—was to be offset primarily through reductions in Medicare payment rates and new taxes, including a tax on high-cost employer-sponsored insurance plans and a tax on the investment income of the most affluent Americans. The health care available to veterans and their families was significantly enhanced with initiatives designed to devote more attention to caregivers, mental health needs, homeless veterans, and veterans in rural areas. To address the needs of the growing number of returning women soldiers, the bill also included improved health services for almost two million female veterans. Fifteen months later, in an historic 5–4 decision written by Chief Justice John G. Roberts Jr., the Supreme Court largely upheld President Obama's signature health care law. The decision protected provisions of the law already in effect and cleared the way, barring changes in the law, for a full implementation of the act. The Court did allow states to opt out of a provision that expanded the federal-state Medicaid program for the poor without losing all of their federal Medicaid funds.[5]

In the wake of the worst recession since the Great Depression, Congress completed a sweeping overhaul of a regulatory system that had failed to keep up with the expanding scope and complexity of modern finance. The most ambitious overhaul of banking and securities laws in generations established a comprehensive framework for monitoring and regulating systemic risk. While the central focus of the act was directed at financial institutions, it also included provisions addressing concerns associated with the securities and insurance industries. Lawmakers intended for the law to prevent future bailouts and eliminate the assumption that the government would step in to salvage huge financial companies because they were considered "too big to fail."

After months of debate and significant pressure from the White House, the most significant piece of small business legislation in over a decade created a $30 billion fund to expand the credit available to small businesses. In 2010, the small business sector employed just over half of all private sector employees and was responsible for creating approximately 65 percent of all new jobs between 1995 and 2010, yet little in earlier stimulus packages had persuaded risk-weary banks to lend to small businesses during the recession. To enable small business to grow in the future, the Small Business Jobs Act of 2010 expanded access to credit, provided tax incentives, and offered an incentive to assist states to increase the capital invested in small businesses.

With his wife, Michelle Obama, at his side, President Obama in December 2010 signed a child nutrition bill strongly pushed by the First Lady, who had made nutrition a key part of her campaign to help young people become more healthy. Public health advocates applauded the legislation which boosted funding for federal school meal and child nutrition programs by $4.5 billion over a decade, and gave the Agriculture Department authority to set nutritional standards for all foods sold in schools. It also authorized the first increase in reimbursements to schools for federally subsidized lunches in more than 30 years.

In his 2010 State of the Union message President Obama vowed to work with Congress to overturn the 17-year-old "Don't Ask, Don't Tell" policy, which barred openly gay people from serving in the military. In so doing, Obama repeated a pledge made during his 2008 presidential campaign. That goal was only realized, however, after a Republican filibuster led by Senator John McCain. In addition, the president confirmed that the Department of Defense had prepared the necessary policies and regulations to implement the repeal, and those policies and regulations were consistent with military standards for readiness, effectiveness, unit cohesion, and recruiting and retention.

Passage of the Food Safety Modernization Act represented the most significant change in U.S. food safety in more than 70 years. For the first time, the Food and Drug Administration (FDA) was given a mandate to require comprehensive, prevention-based controls across the food supply. This enabled the FDA to focus more on preventing food safety problems rather than primarily reacting to problems after they occur. It required food facilities to evaluate the hazards in their operations, implement and monitor effective measures to prevent contamination, and have a plan in place to take any necessary corrective actions. This ability to

hold food companies accountable for preventing contamination was a significant advance in the effort to modernize the food safety system.

As one of its last acts of the One Hundred Eleventh Congress, the Senate voted to approve ratification of a strategic arms reduction treaty with Russia known as New START. The treaty continued a long tradition of bilateral arms accords between the world's two preeminent nuclear powers—Russia and the United States. More than 20 hearings, and an intense effort by the Obama administration and Senate Majority Leader Harry Reid, preceded the 71–26 Senate vote. Supporters regarded the treaty as an important step forward in the global nonproliferation effort. Opponents worried that the treaty could have a negative impact on the nation's missile defenses and national security.

Historically, ambitious Congresses have managed to turn success on Capitol Hill into success at the ballot box. The November 2010 congressional elections, however, saw Republicans gain 63 House seats and four Senate seats amid widespread unhappiness with Congress. In December 2010, a Gallup poll found 83 percent of Americans disapproved of Congress, the highest number in more than three decades. Some observers blamed the Democratic electoral defeat on a bad economy while others viewed it as a message to Congress that it was out of control and focusing on the wrong priorities. Some even voiced the opinion that the most intractable problem Democrats faced was cynicism. In 2009–2010, both Congress and the Obama administration, Thomas E. Mann observed, "were beset by striking public skepticism of the value of these accomplishments, punctuated by the lowest rating of Congress by the public in polling history and the 'shellacking' the president's party took in the November midterm elections."[6]

Major Acts and Treaties

American Recovery and Reinvestment Act of 2009. Provided $575.3 billion in new funding over 11 years for a wide range of programs, including projects intended to save or create jobs, such as road construction, and energy initiatives; programs to assist the jobless, such as extended emergency unemployment benefits and food stamps; education programs; and initiatives to expand health information technology and the extension of broadband service to rural areas. Provided $211.9 billion in tax benefits over 11 years to individuals and businesses. Approved February 17, 2009 (P.L. 111–5; 123 Stat. 115–521).

Credit Card Accountability Responsibility and Disclosure Act of 2009 (Credit CARD Act of 2009). Increased supervision of credit card issuers, enhanced transparency of their practices, and included measures to shield consumers from misleading use of terms in credit card statements and solicitations. Prohibited interest rate increases any time in the first year an account is activated. Required a 45 day advance notice before any interest rate increase. Provided greater restrictions on "sub-prime" credit cards. Prohibited anyone under 18 from being approved for a credit card, unless they are fully emancipated under the law, anyone under 21 from getting a credit card limit greater than $500 or 20 percent of their income, and creditors from offering college students incentives to sign up for a credit card. Approved May 22, 2009 (P.L. 111–24; 123 Stat. 1734–1766).

Matthew Shepard and James Byrd Jr. Hate Crimes Prevention Act. Expanded the definition of federal hate crimes to cover attacks based on gender, gender identity, sexual orientation, and disability. (Previously, federal law had only made it a federal crime to use or threaten force against someone based on race, color, religion, or national origin.) Provided funding and technical assistance to state, local, and tribal jurisdictions to help them more effectively investigate and prosecute hate crimes. Authorized grants for local programs to combat hate crimes committed by juveniles, and programs to train local law enforcement officers in identifying, investigating, prosecuting, and preventing hate crimes. Approved October 28, 2009 (P.L. 111–84, Division E; 123 Stat. 2835–2844).

Patient Protection and Affordable Care Act. Required most U.S. citizens and legal residents to have health insurance by 2014. Placed a tax penalty on individuals who refused to purchase a government-approved health insurance plan. Required each state to establish an "American Health Benefit Exchange" to facilitate the purchase of federal qualifying health plans. Allowed families with incomes up to 400 percent of the poverty level to receive federal subsidies to help pay for premiums and out-of-pocket-expenses. Required employers with 50 or more employees to pay fees to help cover the cost of those employees who received subsidized coverage. Barred insurers from denying coverage because of pre-existing conditions. Allowed parents to keep their children on their policies until age 26. Phased out the requirement that Medicare recipients pay 100 percent of prescription drug costs above a certain level. Approved March 23, 2010 (P.L. 111–148; 124 Stat. 119–1024).

Health Care and Education Reconciliation Act of 2010. Made a number of health-related financing and revenue changes to the Patient Protection and Affordable Care Act (P.L. 111–148). Read together, P.L. 111–148 and the health care-related provisions of this act are commonly referred to as the Affordable Care Act. Approved March 30, 2010 (P.L. 111–152, Part I, Subtitles A–E; 124 Stat. 1029–1070).

Student Aid and Fiscal Responsibility Act (SAFRA Act). Eliminated federal guarantees for private student loans under the Federal Family Education Loan Program, and made the William D. Ford Federal Direct Loan Program the sole provider of the student loans. Allowed private lenders to continue servicing student loans under a competitive bidding system. Capped student loan repayments at no more than 10 percent of a borrower's salary. Provided for much of the anticipated savings in the act to be used to expand and enhance the Pell Grant program, increase funding for historically black colleges and universities, as well as other institutions of higher learning primarily serving minorities; increase funding for the College Access Grant Program; and create a competitive community college grant program to improve job training programs. Approved March 30, 2010 (P.L. 111–152, Title II, Parts I-II; 124 Stat. 1071–1081).

Caregivers and Veterans Omnibus Health Services Act of 2010. Authorized nearly $3 billion for veterans programs and construction projects for medical facilities. Focused increased attention on the Veterans Administration (VA) adapting to the needs of women veterans, providing better treatment for veterans suffering from mental health issues, expanding support services for homeless veterans, and improving access to care for veterans in rural areas. Provided veterans afflicted with traumatic brain injuries more access to private care. Provided nearly $1.6 billion for assistance to caregivers of disabled veterans. Approved May 5, 2010 (P.L. 111–163; 124 Stat. 1130–1183).

Dodd-Frank Wall Street Reform and Consumer Protection Act. Established a process to assess and reduce the risks of huge financial institutions whose failure could threaten the financial system. Created an orderly process for tightening restraints on faltering institutions and, if necessary, shutting down a business or financial institution. Created a Bureau of Consumer Financial Protection to enforce consumer protection laws and regulations for banks and credit unions, a Financial Stability Oversight Council to monitor broad financial economic risks to the financial system, and a Federal Insurance Office to monitor the insurance industry. Authorized the Federal Reserve, with the assent of two-thirds of the Oversight Council, to recommend the break up of large companies that pose a grave threat to the financial system. Granted the Federal Deposit Insurance Corporation power to dismantle large financial corporations. Subjected credit rating agencies to stiffer regulation by the Securities and Exchange Commission. Approved July 21, 2010 (P.L. 111–203; 124 Stat. 1376–2223).

Small Business Jobs Act of 2010. Authorized the secretary of the Treasury to create a $30 billion Small Business Lending Fund (SBLF) to encourage banks with less than $10 billion in assets to increase their lending to small businesses. Provided $1.5 billion in grants to state lending programs that in turn support loans to small businesses. Made numerous changes in Small Business Administration's loan guaranty and contracting programs. Provided $12 billion in tax incentives for small businesses. Increased the fines for companies that failed to file tax returns from $250,000 to up to $1.5 million. Approved September 27, 2010 (P.L. 111–240; 124 Stat. 2504–2604).

Healthy, Hunger-Free Kids Act of 2010. Reauthorized school lunch, school breakfast, and after-school feeding programs, and the Special Supplemental Nutrition Program for Women, Infants, and Children (WIC) as well as other programs. Authorized the Agriculture Department for the first time to set nutrition standards for foods sold in school vending machines, snack stores, and a la carte lines. Provided the first increase in meal reimbursements for schools since 1973. Tied the higher payments to schools meeting new nutrition standards that promoted more fresh foods on school menus. Expanded access to drinking water in schools. Provided for the cost of these programs to be offset by moving up the end date of a temporary increase in food stamp benefits enacted in the 2009 stimulus law (P.L. 111–5). Approved December 13, 2010 (P.L. 111–296; 124 Stat. 3183–3266).

Don't Ask, Don't Tell Repeal Act of 2010. Provided for the repeal of the Department of Defense policy concerning homosexuality known as "Don't Ask, Don't Tell Law," to be effective 60 days after the secretary of defense has received DOD's comprehensive review on the implementation of such repeal, and the president, secretary, and chairman of the Joint Chiefs of Staff (JCS) certify to the congressional defense committees that they have considered the report and proposed plan of action, that DOD has prepared the necessary policies and regulations to exercise the discretion provided by such repeal, and that implementation of such policies and regulations is consistent with the standards of military readiness and effectiveness, unit cohesion, and military recruiting and retention. Approved December 22, 2010 (P.L. 111–321; 124 Stat. 3515–3517).

New START Treaty. Extended the inspections framework of START I, which expired in December 2009, while seeking to reduce the strategic nuclear warheads of the United States and Russia by one-third. Allowed up to 18 short-notice on-site inspections per year. Required both nations to keep and exchange data on items limited by the treaty. Prohibited interference with the other's satellite observations. Concluded April 8, 2010. Ratification advised by the Senate December 22, 2010.[7]

FDA Food Safety Modernization Act (FSMA). Authorized the Food and Drug Administration (FDA) to issue mandatory recalls of suspected contaminated foods. Required the FDA to increase inspections of high-risk food facilities and to place greater focus on preventing outbreaks of food-borne illnesses that could stricken or kill. Required FDA to establish science-based standards for the safe production and harvesting of fruits and vegetables. Exempted small-scale farm and food-processing operations that sold directly to consumers and average less than $500,000 in annual sales. Provided for exemption to be withdrawn if a farm or facility had been involved in an outbreak of a food-borne illness. Approved January 4, 2011 (P.L. 111–353; 124 Stat. 3885–3973).

Notes

1. Scott Wilson, "Obama Lists Financial Rescue as 'Most Important Thing' of His First Year," *Washington Post*, December 23, 2009, A1.

2. David A. Fahrenthold, Philip Rucker, and Felicia Sonmez, "Stormy 111th Congress Was Still the Most Productive in Decades," *Washington Post*, December 23, 2010, A3.

3. Sheryl Gay Stolberg and Robert Pear, "A Stroke of a Pen, Make That 20, and It's Official," *New York Times*, March 24, 2010, A19.

4. Robert Pear and David M. Herszenhorn, "Congress Sends White House Landmark Health Overhaul," *New York Times*, March 22, 2010, A1.

5. *National Federation of Independent Business v. Sebelius, Secretary of Health and Human Services*, 567 U.S. ___ (2012), Case no. 11–393; *National Federation of Independent Business v. Sebelius, Secretary of Health and Human Services*, 132 Sup. Ct. 2566 (2012).

6. Thomas E. Mann, "Books Closed on the 111th Congress, What to Expect in the 112th," *Brookings: Up Front*, December 27, 2010, at http://www.brookings.edu/blogs/up-front/posts/2010/12/27–111th-congress-mann

7. *Journal of the Executive Proceedings of the Senate* (Washington, D.C.: U.S. Government Printing Office, 2010), 152: 633–645.

One Hundred Twelfth Congress

January 3, 2011, to January 3, 2013

First Session—January 5, 2011, to January 3, 2012
Second Session—January 3, 2012, to January 2, 2013
(First administration of Barack Obama, 2009–2013)

Historical Background

For the first time in more than more four decades, congressional lawmakers stayed at their desks past New Year's Eve on January 1, 2013, "ostensibly to find a way to avert the fiscal cliff." "Their reward . . . was almost-universal public scorn."[1] In the preceding days and weeks, a deeply concerned citizenry had anxiously watched as the nation moved ever closer to substantial tax hikes and large spending cuts that would affect nearly every aspect of American life. Many economists warned that unless the standoff between Congress and President Barack Obama on how to achieve long-term budget savings and tame the soaring national debt was resolved, the country would be plunged back into recession.

During the two years preceding the showdown over how to avoid the fiscal cliff, the One Hundred Twelfth Congress earned the dubious distinction of passing the fewest laws, considering the fewest bills, and holding the lowest number of conference committees of any since the end of World War II. Congressional observers quipped that it was as remarkable for its belligerent tone as for its lack of productivity. Some even went so far as to label it the "worst Congress ever."[2] Although there is no quantifiable measure for making such a judgment, most congressional observers portray the One Hundred Twelfth Congress as being among the most polarized, paralyzed, and least productive in history. Both parties spent more time focusing on blocking the other

party's agenda than on governing, and passed only 283 laws. Since the beginning of the Civil War, only the 44th Congress (1875–1877) passed fewer laws (278). Of the bills it did pass, 68 named post offices or other federal buildings, or otherwise honored individuals or organizations—going back to writer and orator Frederick Douglass, who died in 1895, and author and humorist Mark Twain, who died in 1910. Another 33 enactments extended existing laws—some for as little as a week—or provided continuing appropriations. Another 22 acts either amended, made technical corrections to, or reauthorized previously passed legislation.

Repeatedly, House Speaker John A. Boehner was caught between the imperative to govern and the need to satisfy restive conservatives in his conference. The most high-profile conflagrations, a 2011 fight over raising the debt limit and the sparring over the fiscal cliff, were eagerly sought by House Republicans, who wanted a showdown about the size and scope of government.

Some lawmakers, such as Senator Olympia J. Snowe (R-Maine), began the One Hundred Twelfth Congress "with a renewed sense of optimism for bipartisanship following a very productive lame duck session in November and December 2010," in which it had been "able to pass a number of high profile and significant pieces of legislation." In addition, many people, including Snowe, "believed that the challenges facing our nation were too great for us to resort to the partisanship of recent years." Unemployment remained high and the economy was still struggling. "The 2010 midterm election was viewed by many as a desire for change in Washington after two years of Democratic control of both the Executive and Legislative Branches of the Federal government."[3] In fact, little changed in Congress following an election which resulted in the "largest reshuffling of the House of Representatives in 50 years." Congress became even more polarized.[4]

Although this Congress left office with an 18 percent approval rating, the second lowest final score of any Congress, only a handful of lawmakers who sought reelection in November 2012 lost their seats.Interestingly, while the November 6, 2012, election maintained divided government in Washington, results left the picture in state capitals for their next legislative session starkly different. More than two-thirds of the states, as a result of the election, moved to single-party control, the largest number in 60 years. Only eight years earlier, only 30 states were divided between the parties.[5]

For much of the summer of 2011, the White House and congressional leaders worked at length on what became known as a "grand bargain," aimed at achieving more than $3 trillion in deficit reduction. The idea was ultimately torpedoed by a group of House Republicans, many of them freshmen, who identified themselves with the Tea Party movement and demanded bigger spending cuts with no tax increases. The long and bitter partisan debate over the debt limit and deficit reduction ended on August 2, 2011, with the signing of the Budget Control Act, but not before the prolonged standoff created widespread public disgust with Washington, especially Congress. Besides increasing the debt limit, the act contained a variety of measures intended to reduce the federal deficit by at least $2.1 trillion by FY2021. It also established a Joint Select Committee on Deficit Reduction, dubbed the "Super Committee" by observers, to identify further budgetary savings of at least $1.2 trillion over ten years. The joint committee's failure to produce a proposal to reduce the deficit by any amount before the deadline of Thanksgiving 2011 triggered an automatic spending reduction process, which was to begin in January 2013.

Congress had more than a year to agree on a way to reduce government spending or increase taxation in order to avoid the enforcement mechanism built into the Budget Control Act of 2011, but waited until the last possible minute to find an uneasy solution. Then it was left to Vice President Joseph R. Biden Jr. and Senate Minority Leader Mitch McConnell to work out a compromise Republicans and Democrats could live with. On New Year's Day 2013, a lame-duck session of Congress and President Obama endorsed the Biden/McConnell plan to keep the government from tumbling

over what Federal Reserve Chairman Ben S. Bernanke called the fiscal cliff. The American Taxpayer Relief Act of 2012 permanently extended an array of Bush-era tax cuts that were set to expire, raised taxes on the wealthiest Americans, and put off the painful, automatic across-the-board budget cuts required by the Budget Control Act of 2011 for two months.

With a lone exception, the other course-changing enactments of this Congress were long sought reforms previous Congresses had considered at length. After more than a decade of effort, Congress passed bipartisan legislation that made the most significant change to the U.S. patent system in more than 60 years. The Leahy-Smith America Invents Act (AIA) was enacted to create a first-inventor-to-file standard for patent approval, create a post-grant review system, and to address the backlog of patent applications at the U.S. Patent and Trademark Office. Supporters portrayed the legislation as a means of fostering innovation, creating jobs, and bolstering U.S. economic growth and global competitiveness. Authors of the bill unsuccessfully sought to allow the agency office to keep all of the revenue generated by patent fees to address its backlog. Instead, the distribution of revenue was left to appropriators.

Accusations of congressional insider stock trading became a hot topic after an exposé on the television show "60 Minutes," suggesting that members of Congress might have used knowledge gained in the course of their duties to profit in the stock market. President Obama joined those pushing for a rewrite of financial disclosure requirements applicable to members of Congress when he declared in his 2012 State of the Union address, "Send me a bill that bans insider trading by members of Congress; I will sign it tomorrow." That effort succeeded when a bipartisan group of lawmakers joined Obama at the White House to sign the Stop Trading on Congressional Knowledge Act of 2012. The STOCK Act contained many of the reforms sought by such watchdog groups as Citizens for Responsibility and Ethics in Washington and the Public Citizen.

The nation's legislators battled for more than a year before finally reaching agreement on the first major change to the legal framework that directs surface transportation funding since 2005. The Moving Ahead for Progress in the 21st Century Act (MAP-21 Act) reduced the number of federal highway programs, focused on national transportation goals, and increased accountability. In addition to providing funding for federal surface transportation programs, the act sought to address the need to improve safety, maintain infrastructure, reduce traffic congestion, improve the efficiency of the nation's transportation system and freight movement, protect the environment, and reduce delays in project delivery.

The conclusion of another multi-year battle over transportation-related funds resulted in legislation to provide long-term direction and funding for the Federal Aviation Administration (FAA). Since 2007, the FAA had relied on 23 temporary funding measures to continue its operations. A major focus of the law was the FAA's "NextGen" program, a variety of linked efforts to modernize navigation and communication technologies and switch air traffic control from current ground-based systems to satellite-based systems. Other parts of the law sought to improve airline safety standards and enhance passenger service. The bill, which was free of any user fee or fuel tax increases, was widely applauded by the airline industry.

For more than a decade, Senator Daniel K. Akaka championed legislation to strengthen the Whistleblower Protection Act to better protect federal employees who come forward to disclose government waste, fraud, abuse, and other wrongdoing. Just weeks before his retirement, Akaka's bill, after more than 13 years, reached the Oval Office. The bill reflected unequivocal bipartisan consensus, having received the vote of every member in the One Hundred Twelfth Congress, passing both the Senate and House of Representatives by unanimous consent. The act had nearly passed at the end of the previous four Congresses. During the waning days of the previous Congress, after passing both the Senate and House by unanimous consent in slightly different forms, it was killed by an anonymous Senator's "secret hold."

Although political wrangling in Washington is almost as old as the nation, it may have reached a new level in this Congress. But was the divisiveness just an issue at both ends of Pennsylvania Avenue? If the problem was simply with national policy makers, voters could elect different policy makers. If the cause was a more polarized population, solutions would be less clear. Interestingly, in the One Hundred Twelfth Congress, 17 states were represented by Senators from different parties. The Senators from the mixed-party states represented the same people, yet represented them in substantially different ways. During the decade prior to the national 2010 election, studies show state legislatures moving toward polarization similar to that which occurred in Congress over the same period. It is argued by some that state legislatures grew more polarized because state politicians, like those in Congress, increasingly developed views that were not in line with those of their constituents. At the same time, the American people may have become more divided in their views as well.

Major Acts

Budget Control Act of 2011. Authorized increases in the debt limit of at least $2.1 trillion, and up to a maximum of $2.4 trillion under certain conditions. Established caps on the amount of money that could be spent through the annual appropriations process for a 10-year period. Created a 12-member bipartisan Joint Select Committee on Deficit Reduction with instructions to develop a bill to reduce the federal deficit by at least $1.5 trillion over the 10-year period ending in FY2021. Provided that if a joint committee proposal cutting the deficit by at least $1.2 trillion was not enacted by January 15, 2013, or possibly enacted in other legislation, an automatic spending reduction process—known as sequestration—would be triggered in January 2013 to reduce the deficit by that amount. Approved August 2, 2011 (P.L. 112–25; 125 Stat. 240–267).

Leahy-Smith America Invents Act. Shifted the basis for awarding patents from a "first-to-invent" to "first-inventor-to-file" system. Authorized the U.S. Patent and Trademark Office to set and adjust its fees, a power previously exercised by Congress. Provided the opportunity for third parties to submit information regarding a pending patent application. Created a post-grant opposition proceeding to identify patents that should not have been granted. Allowed a patent application to be filed by the inventor's employer or other entity to which rights in the invention are assigned. Created a new procedure for inventors to challenge an earlier applicant's eligibility to receive a patent. Approved September 16, 2011 (P.L. 112–29; 125 Stat. 284–341).

FAA Modernization Act of 2012. Authorized $63.4 billion for the Federal Aviation Administration (FAA) through 2015, and $461 million over four years for the Essential Air Service program, which provides subsidies for airlines who fly to small, underserved airports. Enhanced aviation safety by promoting the sharing of safety data by airlines and airline employees with the FAA and established a risk-based inspection system for aircraft repair stations located overseas. Accelerated deployment of the FAA's proposed Next Generation ("NextGen") air traffic control system. Strengthened FAA research and development programs in the areas of alternative jet fuel and the use of advanced materials in aircraft. Limited the total resources available from the Airport and Airway Trust Fund to 90 percent of estimated revenue, and interest credited to the fund, and generally extended existing taxes used to finance the fund. Approved February 14, 2012 (P.L. 112–95; 126 Stat. 11–155).

Stop Trading on Congressional Knowledge Act of 2012 (STOCK Act). Prohibited members of Congress, judicial officers, congressional employees, and employees in the executive and judicial branches of the federal government from using nonpublic information derived from their employment or official responsibilities as a means of making a private profit. Affirmed that there was no exemption for members of Congress, congressional employees, or other federal officials from the "insider trading" prohibitions in federal securities laws and regulations. Required the president, vice president, members of Congress, congressional staff, and government officials subject to Senate confirmation to report stock or securities transactions exceeding $1,000 within 45 days. Approved April 4, 2012 (P.L. 112–105; 126 Stat. 291–305).

Moving Ahead for Progress in the 21st Century Act (MAP-21 Act). Reauthorized federal surface transportation programs through September 2014. Extended most Highway Trust Fund excess taxes through September 2016. Shortened the average review time for new projects from 15 years to seven.

Gave states more flexibility in spending funds set aside for "enhancements" such as highway beautification and bicycle paths. Provided for major program restructuring, which reduced the number of federal highway programs by two-thirds. Created a streamlined, performance-based, and multi-layered program to address the challenges facing the U.S. transportation system, and a new program to improve non-interstate roads and bridges deemed essential to the economy. Approved July 6, 2012 (P.L. 112–141; 126 Stat. 405–988).

Whistleblower Protection Enhancement Act of 2012. Clarified that any disclosure of gross waste or mismanagement, fraud, abuse, or illegal activity was protected, but disagreements over legitimate policy decisions were not. Established a whistleblower protection ombudsman in each agency. Declared that whistleblowers may disclose evidence of censorship of scientific or technical information under the same standards that apply to disclosures of other kinds of waste, fraud, and abuse. Established explicit whistleblower protections for Transportation Security Administration employees. Provided the office of special counsel with the independent right to file "friend of the court" briefs, or amicus briefs, with federal courts. Expanded the penalties imposed for violating whistleblower protections. Approved November 27, 2012 (P.L. 112–199; 126 Stat. 1465–1476).

American Taxpayer Relief Act of 2012. Permanently extended most of the tax cuts enacted in 2001 and 2003 for individuals with incomes below $400,000 and couples with incomes below $450,000. Raised the nominal tax rate on long-term capital gains and dividends from 15 percent to 20 percent for individuals with incomes above $400,000 and married couples with incomes over $450,000. Phased out personal exemptions and (partially) itemized deductions for individuals with incomes over $250,000 and couples with incomes over $300,000. Increased the tax rate for estates above $5 million to 45 percent. Extended for five years the tax credits in the 2009 stimulus law (P.L. 111–5). Postponed the automatic spending sequester required by the 2011 Budget Control Act until March 1, 2013, and reduced the $109.3 billion 2013 sequestration by $24 billion. Extended emergency unemployment compensation for one year. Deferred for a year a scheduled cut in reimbursement rates for doctors who serve Medicare patients. Approved January 2, 2013 (P.L. 112–240; 126 Stat. 2313–2371).

Notes

1. John Cranford, "Uncompromising Positions," *CQ Weekly,* v. 71, January 14, 2013, 66.

2. For example see Thomas E. Mann and Norman J. Ornstein, "5 Myths About the 112th Congress," *Washington Post*, January 6, 2013, B3; Ezra Klein, "14 Reasons Why This is the Worst Congress Ever," *Washington Post*, July 13, 2012, http://www.washingtonpost.com/blogs/ezra-klein/wp/2012/07/13/13-reasonswhy-this-is-the-worst-congress-ever;

Jonathan Allen, "112th Congress: The Worst Ever?" *Politico*, January 20, 2012, http://www.politico.com/news/stories/0112/71496html; and Norman Ornstein, "Worst Congress Ever," *Foreign Policy*, July 19, 2011, http://www.foreignpolicy.com/articles/2011/07/09/worst_congress_ever

3. Olympia J. Snowe, "The Effect of Modern Partisanship on Legislative Effectiveness in the 112th Congress," *Harvard Journal on Legislation,* v. 50, Winter 2013, 23–24.

4. Marjorie Connelly and Bill Marsh, "Rightward March: The Midterm Exit Polls," *New York Times,* November 7, 2010, WK3.

5. Lydia Saad, "Congress Approval at 18%, Struck in Long-term Low Streak," November 26, 2012, http://www.gallup.com/poll/158948/congress-approval-stuck-long-term-low-streak.aspx; and Monica Davey, "One Party Control Opens States to Partisan Rush," *New York Times*, November 23, 2012, A1, A14.

Sources for Further Study

General References

Adams, James Truslow, ed. *Dictionary of American History*. 2d ed. 6 vols. New York: Charles Scribner's Sons, 1951.

Bacon, Donald C., Roger H. Davidson, and Morton Keller, eds. *The Encyclopedia of the United States Congress*. 4 vols. New York: Simon and Schuster, 1995.

Bates, Christopher G., ed. *The Early Republic and Antebellum America: An Encyclopedia of Social, Political, Cultural, and Economic History*. 4 vols. Armonk, N.Y.: M.E. Sharpe, 2010.

Bates, Ernest Sutherland. *The Story of Congress, 1789-1935*. New York: Harper and Brothers, 1936.

Carruth, Gorton. *The Encyclopedia of American Facts and Dates*, 10th ed. New York: HarperCollins Publishers, 1997.

Carter, Susan B., Scott Sigmund Gartner, Michael R. Haines, Alan L. Olmstead, Richard Sutch, and Gavin Wright, eds. *Historical Statistics of the United States: Earliest Times to the Present*. Millennial ed. New York: Cambridge University Press, 2006.

Castel, Albert, and Scott L. Gibson. *The Yeas and the Nays: Key Congressional Decisions, 1774-1945*. Kalamazoo, Mich.: Western Michigan University, Institute of Public Affairs, New Issues Press, 1975.

Chamberlain, Lawrence H. *The President, Congress, and Legislation*. New York: AMS Press, 1967.

Chambers, John Whiteclay, II, ed. *The Oxford Companion to American Military History*. New York: Oxford University Press, 1999.

Christianson, Stephen G. *Facts about the Congress*. New York: H. W. Wilson Company, 1996.

Ciment, James, ed. *Encyclopedia of the Great Depression and the New Deal*. Armonk, N.Y.: Sharpe Reference, 2001.

Ciment, James, and Thaddeus Russell, eds. *The Home Front Encyclopedia: United States, Britain, and Canada in World Wars I and II*. 3 vols. Santa Barbara, Calif.: ABC-CLIO, 2007.

Commager, Henry Steele, ed. *Documents of American History*. 9th ed. New York: Appleton-Century-Crofts, 1973.

Congress and the Nation, 1945-2010. 12 vols. Washington, D.C.: Congressional Quarterly, 1965-2010.

Congressional Quarterly/Congressional Quarterly Weekly Report/ CQ Weekly. Vols. 1-71, 1945-2013.

Congressional Quarterly Almanac, 1945-2011. 63 vols. Washington, D.C.: Congressional Quarterly, 1948-2012.

Congressional Quarterly's Guide to Congress. 7th ed. 2 vols. Washington, D.C.: CQ Press, 2012.

Davidson, Roger H., Walter J. Oleszek, and Frances E. Lee. *Congress and Its Members*. 13th ed. Washington, D.C.: CQ Press, 2012.

DeGregorio, William A. *The Complete Book of U.S. Presidents*. 8th ed. Ft. Lee, N.J.: Barricade Books, 2013.

Dictionary of American History. Rev. ed. 8 vols. New York: Charles Scribner's Sons, 1976, 1978.

Dictionary of American History. 2 vol. supplement. New York: Charles Scribner's Sons Reference Books, 1996.

Faragher, John Mack, ed. *The American Heritage Encyclopedia of American History*. New York: Henry Holt and Company, 1998.

Finkelman, Paul, ed. *Encyclopedia of the New American Nation: The Emergence of the United States, 1754-1829*. 3 vols. Detroit: Charles Scribner's Sons: Thomson Gale, 2006.

Foley, Michael, and John E. Owens. *Congress and the Presidency: Institutional Politics in a Separated System*. Manchester, England: Manchester University Press, 1996.

Fredriksen, John C. *Chronology of American History*. New York: Facts on File, 2008.

Gale Encyclopedia of U.S. History: Government and Politics. 2 vols. Detroit: Gale, 2008.

Graham, Otis L., Jr., and Meghan Robinson Wander, eds. *Franklin D. Roosevelt: His Life and Times: An Encyclopedic View*. Boston: G. K. Hall, 1985.

Hall, Kermit L., James W. Ely Jr., and Joel B. Grossman, eds. *The Oxford Companion to the Supreme Court of the United States*. 2d ed. New York: Oxford University Press, 2005.

Johnson, Dennis W. *The Laws That Shaped America: Fifteen Acts of Congress and Their Lasting Impact*. New York: Routledge, 2009.

Josephy, Alvin M., Jr. *On the Hill: A History of the American Congress*. New York: Simon and Schuster, 1979.

Kane, Joseph Nathan, Steven Anzovin, and Janet Podell, eds. *Facts about the Presidents*. 8th ed. New York: H. W. Wilson, 2009.

Keller, Helen Rex. *The Dictionary of Dates*. 2 vols. New York: Macmillan, 1934.

Kirkendall, Richard S., ed. *The Harry S. Truman Encyclopedia*. Boston: G. K. Hall, 1989.

Kurian, George Thomas, ed. *A Historic Guide to the U.S. Government*. New York: Oxford University Press, 1998.

Kutler, Stanley I., ed. *Dictionary of American History*. 3d ed. 10 vols. New York: Charles Scribner's Sons, 2003.

Landsberg, Brian K., ed. *Major Acts of Congress*. 3 vols. New York: Macmillan Reference USA: Thomson/Gale, 2004.

Leab, Daniel, Kenneth J. Bindas, Allan Harris Stein, Justin Corfield, and Steven L. Danver, eds. *The Great Depression and the New Deal: A Thematic Encyclopedia*. 2 vols. Santa Barbara, Calif.: ABC-CLIO, 2010.

Lehman, Jeffrey and Shirelle Phelps, eds. *West's Encyclopedia of American Law*. 2d ed. 13 vols. Minneapolis/Saint Paul, Minn.: West Publishing Company, 2005.

Levy, Leonard W., and Kenneth L. Karst. *Encyclopedia of the American Constitution*. 2d ed. 6 vols. New York: Macmillan, 2000.

Levy, Leonard W., and Louis Fisher, eds. *Encyclopedia of the American Presidency*. 4 vols. New York: Simon and Schuster, 1994.

Levy, Peter B. *Encyclopedia of the Clinton Presidency*. Westport, Conn.: Greenwood Press, 2002.

———. *Encyclopedia of the Reagan-Bush Years*. Westport, Conn.: Greenwood Press, 1996.

Light, Paul Charles. *Government's Greatest Achievements: From Civil Rights to Homeland Defense*. Washington, D.C.: Brookings Institution Press, 2002.

Linton, Calvin D., ed. *American Headlines: Year by Year*. Nashville, Tenn.: Thomas Nelson Inc., Publishers, 1985.

Magill, Frank N., ed. *Great Events from History: American Series*. 3 vols. Englewood Cliffs, N.J.: Salem Press, 1975.

Morison, Samuel Eliot, Henry Steele Commager, and William E. Leuchtenburg. *The Growth of the American Republic*. 7th ed. 2 vols. New York: Oxford University Press, 1980.

Morris, Richard B., and Jeffrey B. Morris, eds. *Encyclopedia of American History*. 7th ed. New York: HarperCollins Publishers, 1996.

Nash, Gary B., ed. *Encyclopedia of American History*. 11 vols. New York: Facts on File, 2003.

Nelson, Michael, ed. *Guide to the Presidency and the Executive Branch*. 5th ed. 2 vols. Thousand Oaks, Calif.: CQ Press, 2013.

Olson, James S., ed. *Historical Dictionary of the Great Depression, 1929–1940*. Westport, Conn.: Greenwood Press, 2001.

Peterson, Mark A. *Legislating Together: The White House and Capitol Hill from Eisenhower to Reagan*. Cambridge, Mass.: Harvard University Press, 1990.

Peterson, Merrill D. *The Great Triumvirate: Webster, Clay, and Calhoun*. New York: Oxford University Press, 1987.

Remini, Robert Vincent. *The House: The History of the House of Representatives*. New York: Smithsonian Books in Association with HarperCollins, 2006.

Richter, William L. *Historical Dictionary of the Civil War and Reconstruction*. 2d ed. Lanham, Md.: Scarecrow Press, 2012.

Roller, David C., and Robert W. Twyman, eds. *The Encyclopedia of Southern History*. Baton Rouge, La.: Louisiana State University Press, 1979.

Roseboom, Eugene H., and Alfred E. Eckes Jr. *A History of Presidential Elections: From George Washington to Jimmy Carter*. 4th ed. New York: Macmillan, 1979.

Savage, David G., ed. *Guide to the U.S. Supreme Court*. 5th ed. 2 vols. Washington, D.C.: CQ Press, 2010.

Schlesinger, Arthur M., Jr., ed. *The Almanac of American History*. New York: Putnam Publishing Company, 1986.

Sisung, Kelle S. *Federal Agency Profiles for Students*. Detroit: Gale Group, 1999.

Sloan, Irving J., comp. and ed. *American Landmark Legislation: Primary Materials*. Dobbs Ferry, N.Y.: Oceana Publications, 1976–1977.

———. *American Landmark Legislation: Primary Materials*. Second series. Dobbs Ferry, N.Y.: Oceana Publications, 1984.

Stanley, Harold W., and Richard G. Niemi. *Vital Statistics on American Politics 2011–2012*. Washington, D.C.: CQ Press, 2011.

Tarr, David R, and Rhodes Cook, eds. *Congressional Quarterly's Guide to U.S. Elections*. 6th ed. Washington, D.C.: CQ Press, 2010.

Troy, Gil, Arthur M. Schlesinger Jr., and Fred L. Israel, eds. *History of American Presidential Elections, 1789–2008*. 4th ed. 3 vols. New York: Facts on File, 2012.

U.S. Congress. *Annals of Congress: Debates and Proceedings in the Congress of the United States*. 42 vols. Washington, D.C.: Gales and Seaton, 1834–1856. (1789, 1st Cong.–1824, 18th Cong., 1st sess.)

U.S. Congress. *Congressional Globe*. 46 vols. Washington, D.C.: Blair & Rives, 1834–1873. (1833, 23rd Cong.–1873, 42nd Cong.)

U.S. Congress. *Congressional Record*. 158 vols. Washington, D.C.: U.S. Government Printing Office, 1874–2012 (1873, 43rd Cong.–2012, 112th Cong.)

U.S. Congress. *Register of Debates in Congress*. 13 vols. Washington, D.C.: Gales & Seaton, 1825–1837. (1824, 18th Cong., 2d sess.–1837, 24th Cong.)

U.S. Senate. *Journal of the Executive Proceedings of the Senate of the United States of America*. Vols. 1–3 (Washington, D.C.: Duff Green, 1828), Vols. 3–154 (Washington, D.C.: U.S. Government Printing Office, 1887–2012).

United States Statutes at Large. Vols. 1–17 (Boston: Little, Brown, and Company, 1845–1873), Vols. 18–126 (Washington, D.C.: U.S. Government Printing Office, 1875–2012).

Whitnah, Donald R., ed. *Government Agencies*. Westport, Conn.: Greenwood Press, 1983.

Young, Roland. *Congressional Politics in the Second World War*. New York: Columbia University Press, 1956.

Agriculture

Benedict, Murray R. *Farm Policies of the United States, 1790–1950: A Study of Their Origins and Development*. New York: Twentieth Century Fund, 1953.

Bowers, Douglas E., Wayne D. Rasmussen, and Gladys L. Baker. *History of Agricultural Price-Support and Adjustment Programs, 1933–84*. Washington, D.C.: U.S. Department of Agriculture, Economic Research, 1984.

Cochrane, Willard W. *The Development of American Agriculture: A Historical Analysis*. 2d ed. Minneapolis, Minn.: University of Minnesota Press, 1993.

Harding, T. Swann, ed. *Some Landmarks in the History of the Department of Agriculture.* Agricultural History Series no. 2. Washington, D.C.: U.S. Department of Agriculture, rev. July 1948.

Hurt, R. Douglas. *American Agriculture: A Brief History.* Ames: Iowa State University Press, 1994.

Larson, Olaf F., Julie N. Zimmerman, and Edward O. Moe. *Sociology in Government: The Galpin-Taylor Years in the U.S. Department of Agriculture, 1919–1953.* University Park, Pa.: Pennsylvania State University Press, 2003.

Nordon, Dennis S., and Roy V. Scott. *From Prairie Farmer to Entrepreneur: The Transformation of Midwestern Agriculture.* Bloomington: Indiana University Press, 2005.

Rasmussen, Wayne D., ed. *Agriculture in the United States. A Documentary History.* 4 vols. New York: Random House, 1975.

Rasmussen, Wayne D., and Gladys L. Baker. *The Department of Agriculture.* New York: Praeger, 1972.

Schapsmeier, Edward L., and Frederick H. Schapsmeier. *Encyclopedia of American Agricultural History.* Westport, Conn.: Greenwood Press, 1975.

Smith, Maryann S., and Dennis Roth, comp. *Chronological Landmarks in American Agriculture.* Agriculture Information Bulletin 425. Washington, D.C.: U.S. Department of Agriculture, rev. November 1990.

U.S. House Committee on Agriculture. *United States House of Representatives Committee on Agriculture 150th Anniversary, 16th Congress, 1820 to 91st Congress, 1970.* 91st Cong., 2d sess. H. Doc. 91–350. Washington, D.C.: U.S. Government Printing Office, 1970.

U.S. Senate Committee on Agriculture, Nutrition, and Forestry. *A Brief History of the Committee on Agriculture, Nutrition, and Forestry: United States Senate and Landmark Agricultural Legislation 1825–1986.* Washington, D.C.: U.S. Government Printing Office, 1986.

U.S. Senate Committee on Agriculture, Nutrition, and Forestry. *The United States Senate Committee on Agriculture, Nutrition, and Forestry 1825–1998: Members, Jurisdiction, and History.* 105th Cong., lst sess. S. Doc. 105–24. Washington, D.C.: U.S. Government Printing Office, 1998.

Arms Control

Barnhart, Michael, ed. *Congress and United States Foreign Policy: Controlling the Use of Force in the Nuclear Age.* Albany, N.Y.: State University of New York Press, 1987.

Blacker, Coit D., and Gloria Duffy, eds. *International Arms Control: Issues and Agreements.* 2d ed. Stanford, Calif.: Stanford University Press, 1984.

Clarke, Duncan L. *Politics of Arms Control: The Role and Effectiveness of the U.S. Arms Control and Disarmament Agency.* New York: Free Press, 1979.

Dupuy, Trevor N., and Gay M. Hammerman, eds. *A Documentary History of Arms Control and Disarmament.* New York: R. R. Bowker Company, 1973.

Hyde, Harlow A. *Scraps of Paper: The Disarmament Treaties between the World Wars.* Lincoln, Neb.: Media Publishing, 1988.

Kaufman, Robert Gordon. *Arms Control during the Pre-Nuclear Era: The United States and Naval Limitation between the Two World Wars.* New York: Columbia University Press, 1990.

Krepon, Michael, and Dan Caldwell, eds. *The Politics of Arms Control Treaty Ratification.* New York: St. Martin's Press, 1991.

Platt, Alan, and Lawrence D. Weiler, eds. *Congress and Arms Control.* Boulder, Colo.: Westview Press, 1978.

U.S. House Committee on Foreign Affairs. Subcommittee on Arms Control, International Security, and Science. *Fundamentals of Nuclear Arms Control.* 99th Cong., 2d sess. Committee Print. Washington, D.C.: U.S. Government Printing Office, December 1986.

Arts and Culture

Bauerlein, Mark, with Ellen Grantham, eds. *National Endowment for the Arts: A History, 1965–2008.* Washington, D.C.: National Endowment for the Arts, 2009.

Benedict, Stephen, ed. *Public Money and the Muse: Essays on Government Funding for the Arts.* New York: W. W. Norton, 1991.

Cummings, Milton C., Jr., and Richard S. Katz, eds. *The Patron State: Government and the Arts in Europe, North America, and Japan.* New York: Oxford University Press, 1987.

Dubin, Steven C. *Bureaucratizing the Muse: Public Funds and the Cultural Worker.* Chicago: University of Chicago Press, 1987.

Larson, Gary O. *The Reluctant Patron: The United States Government and the Arts, 1943–1965.* Philadelphia, Pa.: University of Pennsylvania Press, 1983.

Levy, Alan Howard. *Government and the Arts: Debates Over Federal Support of the Arts in America from George Washington to Jesse Helms.* Lanham, Md.: University Press of America, 1997.

Mulcahy, Kevin V., and Harold F. Kendrick. "Congress and Culture: Legislative Reauthorization and the Arts Endowment." *Journal of Arts Management and Law* 17 (Winter 1988): 39–56.

Mulcahy, Kevin V., and Margaret Jane Wyszomirski, eds. *America's Commitment to Culture: Government and the Arts.* Boulder, Colo.: Westview Press, 1995.

Smith, David A. *Money for Art: The Tangled Web of Art and Politics in American Democracy.* Chicago: Ivan R. Dee, 2008.

Wyszomirski, Margaret Jane, ed. *Congress and the Arts: A Precarious Alliance?* New York: ACA Books, 1988.

———. "Congress, Presidents, and the Arts: Collaboration and Struggle." *The Annals of the American Academy of Political and Social Science* 499 (September 1988): 124–135.

Banking and Finance

Dewey, Davis Rich. *Financial History of the United States.* 12th ed. New York: Augustus M. Kelley Publishers, 1968.

Hammond, Bray. *Banks and Politics in America, from the Revolution to the Civil War.* Princeton, N.J.: Princeton University Press, 1957.

McCulley, Richard T. *Banks and Politics During the Progressive Era: The Origins of the Federal Reserve System, 1897–1913.* New York: Garland Publishers, 1992.

Moody, J. Carroll, and Gilbert C. Fite. *The Credit Union Movement: Origins and Development, 1850–1970.* 2d ed. Lincoln: University of Nebraska Press, 1984.

Munn, Glenn G., F. L. Garcia, and Charles J. Woelfel. *Encyclopedia of Banking and Finance.* 9th ed. 3 vols. Pasadena, Calif.: Salem Press, 1993.

Myers, Margaret G. *A Financial History of the United States.* New York: Columbia University Press, 1970.

Schweikart, Larry. *Banking and Finance to 1913.* New York: Facts on File, 1990.

———, ed. *Banking and Finance, 1913–1989.* New York: Facts on File, 1990.

Studenski, Paul, and Herman E. Krooss. *Financial History of the United States.* New York: McGraw-Hill Book Company, 1963.

U.S. House Committee on Banking, Finance, and Urban Affairs. *A Reference Guide to Banking and Finance,* 2d rev. ed. 98th Cong., 1st sess. Committee Print 98–1. Washington, D.C.: U.S. Government Printing Office, 1983.

U.S. House Committee on Financial Services. *Compilation of Basic Banking Laws within the Jurisdiction of the Committee on Financial Services.* Washington, D.C.: U.S. Government Printing Office, 2001.

U.S. House Committee on Commerce. *Compilation of Securities Laws within the Jurisdiction of the Committee on Commerce.* 106th Cong., 1st sess. Committee Print 106-B. Washington, D.C.: U.S. Government Printing Office, March 1999.

Woelfel, Charles J., ed. *Encyclopedia of Banking & Finance.* 10th ed. Chicago: Probus Publishing Co., 1994.

Bankruptcy

Coleman, Peter J. *Debtors and Creditors in America: Insolvency, Imprisonment for Debt, and Bankruptcy, 1607–1900.* Madison: State Historical Society of Wisconsin, 1974.

King, Lawrence P., ed. *Collier Bankruptcy Manual,* 3d ed. Vol. 1. New York: Matthew Bender and Company, 1999.

Mann, Bruce H. *Republic of Debtors: Bankruptcy in the Age of American Independence.* Cambridge, Mass.: Harvard University Press, 2002.

Noel, F. Regis. *A History of the Bankruptcy Law.* Washington, D.C.: C. H. Potter & Co., 1919.

Norton, William L., Jr., and William L. Norton III, eds. *Norton Bankruptcy Law and Practice.* 3d ed. St. Paul, Minn.: Thomson/West, 2008.

Sullivan, Teresa A., Elizabeth Warren, and Jay Lawrence Westbrook. *As We Forgive Our Debtors: Bankruptcy and Consumer Credit in America.* New York: Oxford University Press, 1989.

Tabb, Charles Jordan. "The History of the Bankruptcy Laws in the United States." *American Bankruptcy Institute Law Review* 3 (Spring 1995): 5–51.

Warren, Charles. *Bankruptcy in United States History.* Cambridge, Mass.: Harvard University Press, 1935.

Budget Process

Fisher, Louis. "The Authorization-Appropriation Process in Congress: Formal Rules and Informal Practices." *Catholic University Law Review* 29 (Fall 1979): 51–105.

———. *Presidential Spending Power.* Princeton, N.J.: Princeton University Press, 1975.

Ippolito, Dennis S. *Why Budgets Matter: Budget Policy and American Politics.* University Park, Penn.: Pennsylvania State University Press, 2003.

Joyce, Philip G. *The Congressional Budget Office: Honest Numbers, Power, and Policymaking.* Washington, D.C.: Georgetown University Press, 2011.

Joyce, Philip G., and Robert D. Reischauer. "Deficit Budgeting: The Federal Budget Process and Budget Reform." *Harvard Journal on Legislation* 29 (Summer 1992): 429–453.

Lee, Robert D., Jr., Ronald W. Johnson, and Philip G. Joyce. *Public Budgeting Systems.* 8th ed. Sudbury, Mass.: Jones and Bartlett Publishers, 2008.

Lynch, Thomas D. *Federal Budget and Financial Management Reform.* New York: Quorum Books, 1991.

McCaffery, Jerry, and L. R. Jones. *Budgeting and Financial Management in the Federal Government.* Greenwich, Conn.: Information Age, 2001.

Meyer, Annette E. *Evolution of United States Budgeting.* Rev. ed. Westport, Conn.: Praeger, 2002.

Penner, Rudolph G., and Alan J. Abramson. *Broken Purse Strings: Congressional Budgeting 1974 to 1988.* Ann Arbor, Mich.: Gerald R. Ford Foundation; Washington, D.C.: Urban Institute, 1988.

Powell, Fred Wilbur, comp. *Control of Federal Expenditures: A Documentary History, 1775–1894.* Washington, D.C.: The Brookings Institution, 1939.

Rubin, Irene. *The Politics of Public Budgeting: Getting and Spending, Borrowing and Balancing.* 6th ed. Washington, D.C.: CQ Press, 2010.

Schick, Allen. *The Capacity to Budget.* Washington, D.C.: Urban Institute Press, 1990.

———. *Congress and Money: Budgeting, Spending, and Taxing.* Washington, D.C.: Urban Institute, 1980.

———. *The Federal Budget: Politics, Policy, Process.* 3d ed. Washington, D.C.: Brookings Institution Press, 2007.

Sky, Theodore. *To Provide for the General Welfare: A History of the Federal Spending Power.* Newark: University of Delaware Press; London: Associated University Presses, 2003.

Smithies, Arthur. *The Budgetary Process in the United States.* New York: McGraw-Hill, 1955.

White, Joseph, and Aaron Wildavsky. *The Deficit and the Public Interest: The Search for Responsible Budgeting in the 1980s.* Berkeley: University of California Press, 1989.

Wildavsky, Aaron, and Naomi Caiden. *The New Politics of the Budgetary Process.* 5th ed. New York: Pearson/Longman, 2004.

Campaign Finance Reform

Alexander, Herbert E. *Money in Politics.* Washington, D.C.: Public Affairs Press, 1972.

Corrado, Anthony. "Money and Politics: A History of Federal Campaign Finance." In *Campaign Finance Reform: A Sourcebook,* edited by Anthony Corrado, Thomas E. Mann, Daniel R. Ortiz, Trevor Potter, and Frank J. Sorauf, 27–60. Washington, D.C.: Brookings Institution Press, 1997.

Corrado, Anthony, Thomas E. Mann, David R. Ortiz, and Trevor Potter. *The New Campaign Finance Sourcebook.* Washington, D.C.: Brookings Institution Press, 2005.

Hohenstein, Kurt. *Coining Corruption: The Making of the American Campaign Finance System.* DeKalb: Northern Illinois University Press, 2007.

Mutch, Robert E. *Campaigns, Congress, and Courts: The Making of Federal Campaign Finance Law.* New York: Praeger, 1988.

Overacker, Louise, and Victor J. West. *Money in Elections.* New York: Macmillan, 1932.

Pollock, James K. *Party Campaign Funds.* New York: Alfred A. Knopf, 1926.

Censorship and Freedom of Speech

Finan, Christopher M. *From the Palmer Raids to the Patriot Act: A History of the Fight for Free Speech in America.* Boston: Beacon Press, 2007.

Foerstel, Herbert N. *Free Expression and Censorship in America: An Encyclopedia.* Westport, Conn.: Greenwood Press, 1997.

Rasmussen, R. Kent. *Censorship.* 3 vols. Pasadena, Calif.: Salem Press, 1997.

Vile, John R., David L. Hudson Jr., and David Schultz. *Encyclopedia of the First Amendment.* 2 vols. Washington, D.C.: CQ Press, 2009.

Census

Alonso, William, and Paul Starr, eds. *The Politics of Numbers.* New York: Russell Sage Foundation, 1987.

Alterman, Hyman. *Counting People: The Census in History.* New York: Harcourt, Brace & World, 1969.

Anderson, Margo J. *The American Census: A Social History.* New Haven, Conn.: Yale University Press, 1988.

Anderson, Margo J., Constance F. Citro, and Joseph J. Salvo, eds. *Encyclopedia of the U.S. Census: From the Constitution to the American Community Survey.* 2d ed. Washington, D.C.: CQ Press, 2012.

U.S. Department of Commerce. *Measuring America: The Decennial Censuses From 1790 to 2000.* Washington, D.C.: U.S. Dept. of Commerce, Economics and Statistics Administration, U.S. Census Bureau, 2002.

Citizenship

Bredbenner, Candice Lewis. *A Nationality of Her Own: Women, Marriage, and the Law of Citizenship.* Berkeley: University of California Press, 1998.

Curran, Thomas J. *Xenophobia and Immigration, 1820–1930.* Boston: Twayne Publishers, 1975.

Franklin, Frank G. *The Legislative History of Naturalization in the United States: From the Revolutionary War to 1861.* New York: A. M. Kelley, 1971.

Karst, Kenneth L. *Belonging to America: Equal Citizenship and the Constitution.* New Haven, Conn.: Yale University Press, 1989.

Kettner, James H. *The Development of American Citizenship, 1608–1870.* Chapel Hill, N.C.: University of North Carolina Press, 1978.

Newman, John J. *American Naturalization Processes and Procedures, 1790–1985.* Indianapolis: Family History Section, Indiana Historical Society, 1985.

Smith, Rogers M. *Civic Ideals: Conflicting Visions of Citizenship in U.S. History.* New Haven, Conn.: Yale University Press, 1997.

Civil Liberties

Hall, Kermit L., ed. *Civil Liberties in American History: Major Historical Interpretations.* 2 vols. New York: Garland Publishing, 1987.

Lasswell, Harold Dwight. *National Security and Individual Freedom.* New York: McGraw-Hill, 1950.

Murphy, Paul L. *The Constitution in Crisis Times, 1918–1969.* New York: Harper and Row, 1971.

———. *World War I and the Origin of Civil Liberties in the United States.* New York: Norton, 1979.

Neely, Mark E., Jr. *The Fate of Liberty: Abraham Lincoln and Civil Liberties.* New York: Oxford University Press, 1991.

Preston, William, Jr. *Aliens and Dissenters: Federal Suppression of Radicals, 1903–1933.* 2d ed. Urbana: University of Illinois Press, 1994.

Regan, Priscilla M. *Legislating Privacy: Technology, Social Values, and Public Policy.* Chapel Hill: University of North Carolina Press, 1995.

Smith, James Morton. *Freedom's Fetters: The Alien and Sedition Laws and American Civil Liberties.* Ithaca, N.Y.: Cornell University Press, 1956.

Civil Rights

Bradley, David, and Shelley Fisher Fishkin, eds. *The Encyclopedia of Civil Rights in America.* 3 vols. Armonk, N.Y.: Sharpe Reference, 1998.

Carmines, Edward G., and James A. Stimson. *Issue Evolution: Race and the Transformation of American Politics.* Princeton, N.J.: Princeton University Press, 1989.

Graham, Hugh Davis. *The Civil Rights Era: Origins and Development of National Policy, 1960–1972.* New York: Oxford University Press, 1990.

Lowery, Charles D., and John F. Marszalek. *Encyclopedia of African-American Civil Rights: From Emancipation to the Present.* New York: Greenwood Press, 1992.

Lowery, Charles D., John F. Marszalek, and Thomas Adams Upchurch, eds. *The Greenwood Encyclopedia of African American Civil Rights: From Emancipation to the Twenty-first Century.* Westport, Conn.: Greenwood Press, 2003.

Martin, Waldo E., Jr., and Patricia Sullivan, eds. *Civil Rights in the United States.* 2 vols. New York: Macmillan Reference USA, 2000.

Orfield, Gary. *Congressional Power: Congress and Social Change.* New York: Harcourt Brace Jovanovich, 1975.

Sigler, Jay A. *Civil Rights in America: 1500 to the Present.* Detroit: Gale, 1998.

Civil Service

Fish, Carl Russell. *The Civil Service and Patronage.* New York: Russell and Russell, 1963.

Hartman, Robert W., and Arnold R. Weber, eds. *The Rewards of Public Service: Compensating Top Federal Officials.* Washington, D.C.: Brookings Institution, 1980.

Ingraham, Patricia W. *The Foundation of Merit: Public Service in American Democracy.* Baltimore: Johns Hopkins University Press, 1995.

Ingraham, Patricia W., and David H. Rosenbloom, eds. *The Promise and Paradox of Civil Service Reform.* Pittsburgh, Pa.: University of Pittsburgh Press, 1992.

Kettl, Donald F. *The Global Public Management Revolution.* 2d ed. Washington, D.C.: Brookings Institution Press, 2005.

Light, Paul C. *The Tides of Reform: Making Government Work, 1945–1995.* New Haven, Conn.: Yale University Press, 1997.

Shafritz, Jay M., Norma Riccucci, David H. Rosenbloom, and Albert Hyde. *Personnel Management in Government: Politics and Process.* 5th ed. New York: M. Dekker, 2001.

Stahl, O. Glenn. *Public Personnel Administration.* 8th ed. New York: Harper and Row, 1983.

U.S. Civil Service Commission. *Biography of an Ideal: A History of the Federal Civil Service.* Washington, D.C.: U.S. Civil Service Commission, Office of Public Affairs, December 1974.

U.S. Civil Service Commission. *History of the Federal Civil Service, 1789 to the Present.* Washington, D.C.: U.S. Government Printing Office, 1941.

U.S. House Committee on Post Office and Civil Service. *Legislative History of Civil Service Reform Act of 1978.* 2 vols. 96th Cong., 1st sess. Committee Print 96–2. Washington, D.C.: U.S. Government Printing Office, 1979.

U.S. House Committee on Post Office and Civil Service. Subcommittee on Manpower and Civil Service. *History of Civil Service Merit Systems of the United States and Selected Foreign Countries, Together with Executive Reorganization Studies and Personnel Recommendations.* 94th Cong., 2d sess. Committee Print 94–29. Washington, D.C.: U.S. Government Printing Office, 1976.

U.S. Office of Personnel Management. *Biography of an Ideal: A History of the Federal Civil Service.* Washington, D.C.: U.S. Office of Personnel Management, U.S. Civil Service Commission, 2003.

Van Riper, Paul P. *History of the United States Civil Service.* Evanston, Ill.: Row, Peterson and Company, 1958.

Communications and Telecommunications

Aufderheide, Patricia. *Communications Policy and the Public Interest: The Telecommunications Act of 1996.* New York: Guilford Press, 1999.

Bittner, John R. *Broadcasting and Telecommunication: An Introduction.* 3d ed. Englewood Cliffs, N.J.: Prentice Hall, 1991.

Brock, Gerald W. *Telecommunication Policy for the Information Age: From Monopoly to Competition.* Cambridge, Mass.: Harvard University Press, 1994.

Gordon, John Steele. *A Thread Across the Ocean: The Heroic Story of the Transatlantic Cable.* New York: Walker & Co., 2002.

Hearn, Chester G. *Circuits in the Sea: The Men, the Ships, and the Atlantic Cable.* Westport, Conn.: Praeger, 2004.

Horwitz, Robert Britt. *The Irony of Regulatory Reform: The Deregulation of American Telecommunications.* New York: Oxford University Press, 1989.

Shaw, James. *Telecommunications Deregulation and the Information Economy.* 2d ed. Boston: Artech House, 2001.

Starr, Paul. *The Creation of the Media: Political Origins of Modern Communications.* New York: Basic Books, 2004.

Stone, Alan. *Public Service Liberalism: Telecommunications and Transitions in Public Policy.* Princeton, N.J.: Princeton University Press, 1991.

Thompson, Robert Luther. *Wiring a Continent: The History of the Telegraph Industry in the United States, 1832–1866.* Princeton, N.J.: Princeton University Press, 1947.

Zarkin, Michael J. *Social Learning and the History of U.S. Telecommunications Policy, 1900–1996.* Lewiston, N.Y.: E. Mellen Press, 2003.

Congressional Oversight

Aberbach, Joel D. *Keeping a Watchful Eye: The Politics of Congressional Oversight.* Washington, D.C.: Brookings Institution Press, 1990.

Fisher, Louis. *The Politics of Shared Power: Congress and the Executive.* 4th ed. College Station: Texas A&M University Press, 1998.

Foreman, Christopher H., Jr. *Signals from the Hill: Congressional Oversight and the Challenge of Social Regulation.* New Haven, Conn.: Yale University Press, 1988.

Harris, Joseph P. *Congressional Control of Administration.* Washington, D.C.: Brookings Institution Press, 1964.

Lee, Mordecai. *Congress vs. the Bureaucracy: Muzzling Agency Public Relations.* Norman, Okla.: University of Oklahoma Press, 2011.

McKay, William, and Charles W. Johnson. *Parliament and Congress: Representation and Scrutiny in the Twenty-first Century.* Oxford; New York: Oxford University Press, 2010.

National Academy of Public Administration. Panel on Congress and the Executive. *Beyond Distrust: Building Bridges between Congress and the Executive.* Washington, D.C.: National Academy of Public Administration, 1992.

Ogul, Morris S. *Congress Oversees the Bureaucracy: Studies in Legislative Supervision.* Pittsburgh, Pa.: University of Pittsburgh Press, 1976.

Ripley, Randall B., and Grace A. Franklin. *Congress, the Bureaucracy, and Public Policy.* 5th ed. Pacific Grove, Calif.: Brooks/Cole Publishing Company, 1991.

Congressional Pay

Boeckel, Richard M. "Wages and Hours of Members of Congress." *Editorial Research Reports* 2 (October 13, 1937): 299–320.

Byrd, Robert C. *The Senate 1789–1989.* 4 vols. Edited by Wendy Wolff. 100th Cong., 1st sess. S. Doc. 100–20. Vol. 2, 347–359. Washington, D.C.: U.S. Government Printing Office, 1988.

Congressional Pay and Perquisites: History, Facts, and Controversy. Washington, D.C.: Congressional Quarterly, 1992.

Fisher, Louis. "History of Pay Adjustments for Members of Congress." In *The Rewards of Public Service: Compensating Top Federal Officials,* edited by Robert W. Hartman and Arnold R. Weber, 25–52. Washington, D.C.: Brookings Institution Press, 1980.

Congressional Reform

Davidson, Roger H., and Walter J. Oleszek. *Congress Against Itself.* Bloomington: Indiana University Press, 1977.

Galloway, George B. "The Operation of the Legislative Reorganization Act of 1946." *American Political Science Review* 45 (March 1951): 41–68.

Kravitz, Walter. "The Advent of the Modern Congress: The Legislative Reorganization Act of 1970." *Legislative Studies Quarterly* 15 (August 1990): 375–399.

McKay, William, and Charles W. Johnson. *Parliament and Congress: Representation and Scrutiny in the Twenty-first Century.* Oxford; New York: Oxford University Press, 2010.

Rieselbach, Leroy N. *Congressional Reform.* Washington, D.C.: CQ Press, 1994.

U.S. Joint Committee on the Organization of Congress. *Organization of the Congress, Final Report of the Joint Committee on the Organization of Congress: Organization of the Congress Pursuant to H. Con. Res. 192 (102d Congress).* 103d Cong., 1st sess. H. Rept. 103–413, Vol. 2; S. Rept. 103–215, Vol. 2. Washington, D.C.: U.S. Government Printing Office, 1993.

Wolfensberger, Donald R. *Congress and the People: Deliberative Democracy on Trial.* Washington, D.C.: Woodrow Wilson Center Press; Baltimore: Johns Hopkins University Press, 2000.

Zelizer, Julian E. *On Capitol Hill: The Struggle to Reform Congress and Its Consequences, 1948–2000.* Cambridge & New York: Cambridge University Press, 2004.

Conscription

Chambers, John Whiteclay, II. *To Raise an Army: The Draft Comes to Modern America.* New York: Free Press, 1987.

Flynn, George Q. *The Draft, 1940–1973.* Lawrence: University of Kansas Press, 1993.

Segal, David R. *Recruiting for Uncle Sam: Citizenship and Military Manpower Policy.* Lawrence: University Press of Kansas, 1989.

U.S. Selective Service System. *The Selective Service Act: Its Legislative History, Amendments, Appropriations, Cognates, and Prior Instruments of Security.* 5 vols. Washington, D.C.: U.S. Government Printing Office, 1954.

Constitutional Amendments

Ames, Herman Vandenburg. *The Proposed Amendments to the Constitution of the United States during the First Century of Its History.* New York: B. Franklin, 1970.

Bernstein, Richard B., with Jerome Agel. *Amending America: If We Love the Constitution So Much, Why Do We Keep Trying to Change It?* New York: Times Books, 1993.

Grimes, Alan P. *Democracy and the Amendments to the Constitution.* Lexington, Mass.: Lexington Books, 1987.

Kyvig, David E. *Explicit and Authentic Acts: Amending the U.S. Constitution, 1776–1995.* Lawrence: University Press of Kansas, 1996.

Levy, Leonard W., and Kenneth L. Karst, eds. *Encyclopedia of the American Constitution.* 6 vols. 2d ed. New York: Macmillan Reference USA, 2000.

Newman, Roger K., ed. *The Constitution and Its Amendments.* 4 vols. New York: Macmillan Reference USA, 1999.

Palmer, Kris E., ed. *Constitutional Amendments, 1789 to the Present.* Detroit, Mich.: Gale Group, 2000.

U.S. Congress. Senate. *The Constitution of the United States of America: Analysis and Interpretation: Analysis of Cases*

Decided by the Supreme Court of the United States to June 28, 2002. Prepared by the Congressional Research Service, Library of Congress; Johnny H. Killian, George A. Costello, Kenneth R. Thomas, co-eds. David M. Ackerman, Henry Cohen, Robert Meltz, contributors. 108th Cong., 2d sess., S. Doc. 108–17. Washington, D.C.: U.S. Government Printing Office, 2004.

Vile, John R. *A Companion to the United States Constitution and Its Amendments.* 5th ed. Santa Barbara, Calif.: Praeger, 2010.

———. *Encyclopedia of Constitutional Amendments, Proposed Amendments, and Amending Issues, 1789–2010.* 3d ed. Santa Barbara, Calif.: ABC-CLIO, 2010.

———. *Rewriting the United States Constitution: An Examination of Proposals from Reconstruction to the Present.* New York: Praeger, 1991.

Consumer Protection

Asch, Peter. *Consumer Safety Regulation: Putting a Price on Life and Limb.* New York: Oxford University Press, 1988.

Brobeck, Stephen, Robert N. Mayer, and Robert O. Herrmann, eds. *Encyclopedia of the Consumer Movement.* Santa Barbara, Calif.: ABC-CLIO, 1997.

Burda, Joan M. *An Overview of Federal Consumer Law.* Chicago: American Bar Association, Solo and Small Firm Section, General Practice, 1998.

Frank, Dana. *Buy American: The Untold Story of Economic Nationalism.* Boston: Beacon Press, 1999.

Goodwin, Lorine Swainston. *The Pure Food, Drink, and Drug Crusaders, 1879–1914.* Jefferson, N.C.: McFarland, 1999.

Hasin, Bernice Rothman. *Consumers, Commissions, and Congress: Law, Theory, and the Federal Trade Commission, 1968–1985.* New Brunswick, N.J.: Transaction Books, 1987.

Krohn, Lauren. *Consumer Protection and the Law: A Dictionary.* Santa Barbara, Calif.: ABC-CLIO, 1995.

Maney, Ardith, and Loree Bykerk. *Consumer Politics: Protecting Public Interests on Capitol Hill.* Westport, Conn.: Greenwood Press, 1994.

Marsh, Gene A. *Consumer Protection Law in a Nutshell,* 3d ed. St. Paul, Minn.: West Group, 1999.

Meier, Kenneth J., E. Thomas Garman, and Lael R. Keiser. *Regulation and Consumer Protection: Politics, Bureaucracy and Economics,* 3d ed. Houston, Tex. Dame Publications, 1998.

The Continental Congress

Boatner, Mark Mayo, III. *Encyclopedia of the American Revolution.* Bicentennial ed. [rev. and expanded]. New York: D. McKay Co., 1974.

Burnett, Edmund Cody. *The Continental Congress.* Westport, Conn.: Greenwood Press, 1975, c1941.

Ford, Worthington Chauncey, and Roscoe R. Hill, eds. *Journals of the Continental Congress: 1774–1789.* 34 vols. Washington, D.C.: U.S. Government Printing Office, 1904–1936.

Fremont-Barnes, Gregory, Richard Alan Ryerson, James Arnold, and Roberta Wiener, eds. *The Encyclopedia of the American Revolutionary War: A Political, Social, and Military History.* 5 vols. Santa Barbara, Calif.: ABC-CLIO, 2006.

Henderson, H. James. *Party Politics in the Continental Congress.* New York: McGraw-Hill, 1974.

Jensen, Merrill. *The Articles of Confederation.* Madison: The University of Wisconsin Press, 1953.

Jillson, Calvin, and Rick K. Wilson. *Congressional Dynamics: Structure, Coordination, and Choice in the First American Congress, 1774–1789.* Stanford, Calif.: Stanford University Press, 1994.

Montross, Lynn. *The Reluctant Rebels: The Story of the Continental Congress, 1774–1789.* New York: Barnes & Noble, 1970.

Rakove, Jack N. *The Beginnings of National Politics: An Interpretive History of the Continental Congress.* Baltimore, Md.: Johns Hopkins University Press, 1982, c1979.

Sanders, Jennings B. *Evolution of Executive Departments of the Continental Congress, 1774–1789.* Chapel Hill: The University of North Carolina Press, 1935.

Selesky, Harold E., ed. *Encyclopedia of the American Revolution.* 2d ed. 2 vols. Detroit: Charles Scribner's Sons, 2006.

Copyrights, Trademarks, Patents, and Intellectual Property Rights

Bowker, Richard Rogers. *Copyright: Its history and Its Law.* Boston and New York: Houghton Mifflin Company, 1912.

Calvert, Robert, ed. *The Encyclopedia of Patent Practice and Invention Management.* Huntington, N.Y.: Robert E. Krieger Publishing Company, 1974, 1964.

Campbell, Levin H. *The Patent System of the United States so Far as It Relates to the Granting of Patents: A History.* Washington, D.C.: Press of McGill & Wallace, 1891.

Goldman, Abe A. *The History of U.S.A. Copyright Law Revision, 1901–1954.* Washington, D.C.: Library of Congress, Copyright Office, 1955.

Joyce, Craig, William Patry, Marshall Leaffer, and Peter Jaszi. *Copyright Law.* 8th ed. New Providence, N.J.: LEXIS Publishers, 2010.

Klitzke, Ramon A. "History of Patents—U.S." In *The Encyclopedia of Patent Practice and Invention Management,* edited by Robert Calvert, 392–404. Huntington, N.Y.: R. E. Krieger Publishing Company, 1974.

McCarthy, J. Thomas. "Historical Basis of Trademarks and Legislative History." Chap. 5 in *McCarthy on Trademarks and Unfair Competition.* 4th ed. 6 vols. St. Paul, Minn.: West Group, 1996.

Outline of the History of the United States Patent Office. Washington, D.C.: Patent Office Society, 1936.

Patry, William F. Introduction to *Latman's the Copyright Law.* 6th ed., 1–15. Washington, D.C.: Bureau of National Affairs, 1986.

Solberg, Thorvald. *Copyright in Congress, 1789–1904: A Bibliography and Chronological Record of All Proceedings in Congress in Relation to Copyright from April 15, 1789, to April 28, 1904, First Congress, 1st Session, to Fifty-Eighth Congress, 2d Session.* Westport, Conn.: Greenwood Press, 1976.

U.S. House Committee on the Judiciary. Subcommittee on Courts, Civil Liberties, and the Administration of Justice. *The History of Private Patent Legislation in the House of Representatives.* Prepared by Christine P. Benagh. 96th Cong., 1st sess. Committee Print 1. Washington, D.C.: U.S. Government Printing Office, 1979.

U.S. Patent and Trademark Office. *The Story of the U.S. Patent and Trademark Office.* Washington, D.C.: U.S. Department of Commerce, Patent and Trademark Office, 1988.

Walterscheid, Edward C. *To Promote the Progress of Useful Arts: American Patent Law and Administration, 1798–1836.* Littleton, Colo.: F. B. Rothman, 1998.

Weber, Gustavus Adolphus. *The Patent Office: Its History, Activities and Organization.* Baltimore, Md.: John Hopkins Press, 1924.

Criminal Justice

Beale, Sara Sun. "Federal Criminal Jurisdiction." In *Encyclopedia of Crime and Justice,* edited by Sanford H. Kadish. 4 vols. Vol. 1, 775–779. New York: Free Press, 1993.

Chernoff, Harry A., Christopher M. Kelly, and John R. Kroger. "The Politics of Crime." *Harvard Journal on Legislation* 33 (Summer 1996): 527–584.

Conboy, Martin. "Federal Criminal Law." In *Law: A Century of Progress, 1835–1935,* edited by Alison Reppy. 3 vols. Vol. 1, 295–346. New York: New York University Press, 1937.

"Extending Federal Powers Over Crime." *Law and Contemporary Problems* 1 (October 1934): 399–508.

Friedman, Lawrence. *Crime and Punishment in American History.* New York: Basic Books, 1993.

Henderson, Dwight F. *Congress, Courts, and Criminals: The Development of Federal Criminal Law, 1801–1829.* Westport, Conn.: Greenwood Press, 1985.

Marion, Nancy E. *A History of Federal Crime Control Initiatives, 1960–1993.* Westport, Conn.: Praeger, 1994.

Oliver, Willard M., and Nancy E. Marion, eds. *The Making of Criminal Justice Policy in the United States: Essays on the Role of the President, the Congress, and the Public.* Lewiston, N.Y.: Edwin Mellen, 2008.

Strazzella, James A. *The Federalization of Criminal Law.* Washington, D.C.: American Bar Association, Criminal Justice Section, Task Force on the Federalization of Criminal Law, 1998.

Debt Limit

Robinson, Marshall A. *The National Debt Ceiling: An Experiment in Fiscal Policy.* Washington, D.C.: Brookings Institution Press, 1959.

Shuman, Howard E. *Politics and the Budget: The Struggle between the President and the Congress.* 3d ed. Englewood Cliffs, N.J.: Prentice Hall, 1992.

Stabile, Donald R., and Jeffrey A. Cantor. *The Public Debt of the United States: An Historical Perspective, 1775–1990.* New York: Praeger, 1991.

U.S. Congress. Congressional Budget Office. "Debt Subject to Limit." Chap. 4 in *Federal Debt and Interest Costs.* Washington, D.C.: Congressional Budget Office, 1993.

Defense

Allison, William Thomas, Jeffrey G. Grey, and Janet G. Valentine. *American Military History: A Survey from Colonial Times to the Present.* 2d ed. Boston: Pearson, 2012.

Bauer, K. Jack. "Naval Shipbuilding Programs, 1794–1860," *Military Affairs,* v, 29 (Spring 1965), 29–40.

Blechman, Barry M., with the assistance of W. Philip Ellis. *The Politics of National Security: Congress and U.S. Defense Policy.* New York: Oxford University Press, 1990.

Borklund, C. W. *The Department of Defense.* New York: Frederick A. Praeger, Publishers, 1968.

Brown, Jerold E., ed. *Historical Dictionary of the U.S. Army.* Westport, Conn.: Greenwood Press, 2001.

Ekirch, Arthur Alphonse. *The Civilian and the Military: A History of the American Antimilitarist Tradition.* Oakland, Calif.: Independent Institute, 2010.

Hagan, Kenneth J. *This People's Navy: The Making of American Sea Power.* New York: Free Press; Toronto: Collier Macmillan, 1991.

Hagan, Kenneth J., and Michael T. McMaster, eds. *In Peace and War: Interpretations of American Naval History.* Westport, Conn.: Praeger Security International, 2008.

Hewes, James E., Jr. *From Root to McNamara: Army Organization and Administration, 1900–1963.* Washington, D.C.: Center of Military History, U.S. Army, 1975.

Huntington, Samuel P. *The Soldier and the State: The Theory and Politics of Civil-Military Relations.* Cambridge, Mass.: Belknap Press of Harvard University Press, 1957.

Inouye, Daniel K. "Congress and the Military." In *Encyclopedia of the American Military: Studies of the History, Traditions, Policies, Institutions, and Roles of the Armed Forces in War and Peace,* edited by John E. Jessup and Louise B. Ketz. 3 vols. Vol. 3, 235–278. New York: Charles Scribner's Sons, 1994.

Jessup, John E., and Louise B. Ketz, eds. *Encyclopedia of the American Military: Studies of the History, Traditions, Policies, Institutions, and Roles of the Armed Forces in War and Peace.* 3 vols. New York: Charles Scribner's Sons, 1994.

Kolodziej, Edward A. *The Uncommon Defense and Congress, 1945–1963.* Columbus: Ohio State University Press, 1966.

Legere, Laurence J. *Unification of the Armed Forces.* New York: Garland Publishing, 1988.

Millett, Allan R., and Peter Maslowski. *For the Common Defense: A Military History of the United States of America.* New York: Free Press, 1994.

Smith, Louis. *American Democracy and Military Power: A Study of Civil Control of the Military Power in the United States.* Chicago: University of Chicago Press, 1951.

Snow, Donald M., and Dennis M. Drew. *From Lexington to Baghdad and Beyond: War and Politics in the American Experience.* 3d ed. Armonk, N.Y.: M. E. Sharpe, 2010.

Stewart, Richard W., ed. *American Military History.* 2 vols. 2d ed. Washington, D.C.: Center of Military History, United States Army, 2009–2010.

Symonds, Craig L. *Navalists and Antinavalists: The Naval Policy Debate in the United States, 1785–1827.* Newark: University of Delaware Press, 1980.

Weigley, Russell F. *History of the United States Army.* Enl. ed. Bloomington: Indiana University Press, 1984.

Young, Roland. *Congressional Politics in the Second World War.* New York: Columbia University Press, 1956.

Diplomacy and Foreign Affairs

Bailey, Thomas A. *A Diplomatic History of the American People.* 10th ed. Englewood Cliffs, N.J.: Prentice Hall, 1980.

Barnes, William, and John Heath Morgan. *The Foreign Service of the United States: Origins, Development, and Functions.* Washington, D.C.: Department of State, Bureau of Public Affairs, Historic Office, 1961.

DeConde, Alexander, ed. *Encyclopedia of American Foreign Policy: Studies of the Principal Movements and Ideas.* 2d ed. 3 vols. New York: Charles Scribner's Sons, 2002.

———. *A History of American Foreign Policy.* 3d ed. New York: Charles Scribner's Sons, 1978.

Findling, John E. *Dictionary of American Diplomatic History.* 2d ed. New York: Greenwood Press, 1989.

Flanders, Stephen A., and Carl N. Flanders. *Dictionary of American Foreign Affairs.* New York: Macmillan, 1993.

Hodge, Carl C., and Cathal J. Nolan, eds. *U.S. Presidents and Foreign Policy: From 1789 to the Present.* Santa Barbara, Calif.: ABC-CLIO, 2007.

Jentleson, Bruce W., and Thomas G. Peterson. *Encyclopedia of U.S. Foreign Relations.* 4 vols. New York: Oxford University Press, 1997.

Plischke, Elmer. *U.S. Department of State: A Reference History.* Westport, Conn.: Greenwood Press, 1999.

Smith, Joseph. *Historical Dictionary of United States-Latin American Relations.* Lanham, Md.: Scarecrow Press, 2007.

Steigman, Andrew L. *The Foreign Service of the United States: First Line of Defense.* Boulder, Colo.: Westview Press, 1985.

Tuch, Hans N. *Communicating with the World: U.S. Public Diplomacy Overseas.* New York: St. Martin's Press, 1990.

Westerfield, Bradford. *Foreign Policy and Party Politics: Pearl Harbor to Korea.* New York: Octagon Books, 1972.

Disabled and Handicapped

Berkowitz, Edward D. *Disabled Policy: America's Programs for the Handicapped.* New York: Cambridge University Press, 1987.

Colker, Ruth, and Adam A. Milani. *Federal Disability Law in a Nutshell.* 4th ed. St. Paul, Minn.: West/Thomson, 2010.

Nielsen, Kim E. *A Disability History of the United States.* Boston: Beacon Press, 2012.

Rothstein, Laura F. *Disabilities and the Law.* 4th ed. Egan, Minn.: West Group, 2012.

Schweik, Susan M. *The Ugly Laws: Disability in Public.* New York: New York University, 2009.

Scotch, Richard K. *From Good Will to Civil Rights: Transforming Federal Disability Policy.* 2d ed. Philadelphia, Pa.: Temple University Press, 2001.

Stone, Deborah A. *The Disabled State.* Philadelphia, Pa.: Temple University Press, 1984.

Van Etten, C. Angela. *Americans with Disabilities Act: Analysis and Implications.* Rochester, N.Y.: Lawyers Cooperative Pubishers, 1993.

District of Columbia

Green, Constance McLaughlin. *Washington: Village and Capital, 1800–1950.* 2 vols. Princeton, N.J.: Princeton University Press, 1962–1963.

Harris, Charles Wesley. *Congress and the Governance of the Nation's Capital: The Conflict of Federal and Local Interests.* Washington, D.C.: Georgetown University Press, 1995.

U.S. Congress. House. *Governance of the Nation's Capital: A Summary History of the Forms and Powers of Local Government for the District of Columbia, 1790 to 1973.* 100th Cong., 2d sess. Committee Print. Serial No. S-2. Washington, D.C.: Government Printing Office, 1990.

Economic Policy and Business

Carson, Thomas, and Mary Bonk, eds. *Gale Encyclopedia of U.S. Economic History.* 2 vols. Detroit: Gale Group, 1999.

Clark, Cynthia L., ed. *The American Economy: A Historical Encyclopedia.* 2 vols. Santa Barbara, Calif.: ABC-CLIO, 2011.

Dubofsky, Melvyn, ed. *The Oxford Encyclopedia of American Business, Labor, and Economic History.* 2 vols. New York: Oxford University Press, 2013.

Fainsod, Merle, Lincoln Gordon, and Joseph C. Palamountain Jr. *Government and the American Economy,* 3d ed. New York: W. W. Norton and Company, 1959.

Landmarks in Modern American Business. Edited by the editors of Salem Press. Pasadena, Calif.: Salem Press, 2000.

Newman, Peter, ed. *The New Palgrave Dictionary of Economics and the Law.* 3 vols. London: Macmillan Reference; New York: Stockton Press, 1998.

Northrup, Cynthia Clark, ed. *The American Economy: A Historical Encyclopedia.* Santa Barbara, Calif.: ABC-CLIO, 2003.

Porter, Glenn, ed. *Encyclopedia of American Economic History: Studies of the Principal Movements and Ideas.* 3 vols. New York: Charles Scribner's Sons, 1980.

Pusateri, C. Joseph. *A History of American Business.* 2d ed. Arlington Heights, Ill.: Harlan Davidson, 1988.

Puth, Robert C. *American Economic History.* 3d ed. Fort Worth, Tex. Dryden Press, Harcourt Brace Jovanovich College Publishers, 1993.

Robinson, Richard, comp. *United States Business History, 1602–1988: A Chronology.* New York: Greenwood Press, 1990.

Scheiber, Harry N., Harold G. Vatter, and Harold Underwood Faulkner. *American Economic History.* New York: Harper and Row Publishers, 1976.

Schweikart, Larry. *The Entrepreneurial Adventure: A History of Business in the United States.* Fort Worth, Tex. Harcourt College Publishers, 2000.

Walton, Gary M., and Hugh Rockoff. *History of the American Economy.* 12th ed. Mason, Ohio: Cengage, 2013.

Education

Blanchfield, Deirdre S. *Environmental Encyclopedia.* 2 vols. 4th ed. Detroit: Cengage Learning, 2011.

Carleton, David. *Landmark Congressional Laws on Education.* Westport, Conn.: Greenwood Press, 2002.

Cross, Christopher T. *Political Education: National Policy Comes of Age.* New York: Teachers College Press, Teachers College, Columbia University, 2004.

Eidenberg, Eugene, and Roy D. Morey. *An Act of Congress: The Legislative Process and the Making of Education Policy.* New York: W. W. Norton and Company, 1969.

Gladieux, Lawrence E., and Thomas R. Wolanin. *Congress and the Colleges: The National Politics of Higher Education.* Lexington, Mass.: Lexington Books, 1976.

Graham, Hugh Davis. *The Uncertain Triumph: Federal Education Policy in the Kennedy and Johnson Years.* Chapel Hill, N.C.: University of North Carolina Press, 1984.

Hill, David Spencer, and William Alfred Fisher. *Federal Relations to Education: Report of the National Advisory Committee on Education.* Vol. 2. Washington, D.C.: National Capital Press, 1931.

Lapati, Americo D. *Education and the Federal Government: A Historical Record.* New York: Mason/Charter Publishers, 1975.

Lu, Hsien. *Federal Role in Education: A Comprehensive Study of Federal Relations to Education in the United States—Their Past, Present, and Future.* New York: American Press, 1968, 1965.

Milazzo, Paul Charles. *Unlikely Environmentalists: Congress and Clean Water, 1945 1972.* Lawrence: University Press of Kansas, 2006.

Reutter, E. Edmund, Jr. *The Law of Public Education.* 4th ed. Westbury, N.Y.: Foundation Press, 1994.

Rudy, Willis. *Building America's Schools and Colleges: The Federal Contribution.* Cranbury, N.J.: Cornwall Books, 2003.

Russo, Charles J., ed. *Encyclopedia of Education Law.* Thousand Oaks, Calif.: Sage, 2008.

———. *Encyclopedia of Law and Higher Education.* Thousand Oaks, Calif.: SAGE, 2010.

Sears, William P., Jr. *The Roots of Vocational Education.* New York: John Wiley and Sons, 1931.

Emergency Powers

Lehman, John F. *Making War. The 200-Year-Old Battle Between the President and Congress Over How America Goes to War.* New York: Charles Scribner's Sons, 1992.

Relyea, Harold C. "Stretch Points of the Constitution: National Emergency Powers." In *Renewing the Dream: National Archives Bicentennial '87 Lectures on Contemporary Constitutional Issues,* edited by Ralph S. Pollock. Lanham, Md.: University Press of America; Washington, D.C.: National Archives Volunteers Constitution Study Group, 1986.

Tap, Bruce. *Over Lincoln's Shoulder: The Committee on the Conduct of the War.* Lawrence: University Press of Kansas, 1998.

U.S. Senate Committee on Government Operations and U.S. Senate Special Committee on National Emergencies and Delegated Emergency Powers. *The National Emergencies Act (Public Law 94–412): Source Book: Legislative History, Texts, and Other Documents.* 94th Cong., 2d sess. Committee Print. Washington, D.C.: U.S. Government Printing Office, 1976.

U.S. Senate Special Committee on National Emergency Powers and Delegated Emergency Powers. *A Brief History of Emergency Powers in the United States: A Working Paper, Prepared for the Special Committee on National Emergencies and Delegated Emergency Powers, United States Senate.* Prepared by Harold C. Relyea. 93d Cong., 2d sess. Committee Print. Washington, D.C.: U.S. Government Printing Office, 1974.

Zeisberg, Mariah Ananda. *War Powers: The Politics of Constitutional Authority.* Princeton, N.J.: Princeton University Press, 2013.

Energy and Natural Resources

Clark, John G. *Energy and the Federal Government: Fossil Fuel Policies, 1900–1946.* Urbana: University of Illinois Press, 1987.

Davis, David Howard. *Energy Politics.* 4th ed. New York: St. Martin's Press, 1993.

Energy Policy. 2d ed. Washington, D.C.: Congressional Quarterly, 1981.

Fehner, Terrence R., and Jack M. Holl. *Department of Energy, 1977–1994: A Summary History.* Washington, D.C.: U.S. Department of Energy, November 1994.

Kash, Don E., and Robert W. Rycroft. *U.S. Energy Policy: Crisis and Complacency.* Norman: University of Oklahoma Press, 1984.

Katz, James Everett. *Congress and National Energy Policy.* New Brunswick, N.J.: Transaction Books, 1984.

Rabbitt, Mary C. *The United States Geological Survey, 1879–1989.* U.S. Geological Survey Circular 1050. Washington, D.C.: U.S. Government Printing Office, 1989.

U.S. Congress. Senate. *History of the Committee on Energy and Natural Resources United States Senate as of the 100th Congress, 1816–1988.* 100th Cong., 2d sess. S. Doc. 100–46. Washington, D.C.: U.S. Government Printing Office, 1989.

Vietor, Richard H. K. *Energy Policy in America since 1945: A Study of Business Government Relations.* Cambridge, Mass.: Cambridge University Press, 1984.

Environment and Conservation

Bailey, Christopher J. *Congress and Air Pollution: Environmental Policies in the USA.* New York: Manchester University Press, 1998.

Bean, Michael J., and Melanie J. Rowland. *The Evolution of National Wildlife Law.* 3d ed. Westport, Conn.: Praeger, 1997.

Brooks, Karl Boyd. *Before Earth Day: The Origins of American Environmental Law, 1945–1970.* Lawrence: University Press of Kansas, 2009.

Clark, Ray, and Larry Canter, eds. *Environmental Policy and NEPA: Past, Present, and Future.* Boca Raton, Fla.: St. Lucie Press, 1997.

Cooley, Richard A., and Geoffrey Wandesforde-Smith, eds. *Congress and the Environment.* Seattle: University of Washington Press, 1970.

Cunningham, William P., Terence Ball, Terence H. Cooper, Eville Gorham, Malcolm T. Hepworth, and Alfred A. Marcus, eds. *Environmental Encyclopedia.* 2d ed. Detroit: Gale, 1998.

Hays, Samuel P. *Explorations in Environmental History: Essays by Samuel P. Hays.* Pittsburgh, Pa.: University of Pittsburgh Press, 1998.

Lindstrom, Matthew, ed. *Encyclopedia of the U.S. Government and the Environment: History, Policy, and Politics.* 2 vols. Santa Barbara, Calif.: ABC-CLIO, 2011.

MacDonnell, Lawrence J., and Sarah F. Bates, eds. *The Evolution of Natural Resources Law and Policy.* Boulder, Colo.: Natural Resources Law Center, University of Colorado School of Law, 2010.

Meier, Kenneth J., E. Thomas Garman, and Lael R. Keiser. *Regulation and Consumer Protection: Politics, Bureaucracy and Economics.* 3d ed. Houston, Tex. Dame Publications, 1998.

Petulla, Joseph M. *American Environmental History.* 2d ed. Columbus, Ohio: Merrill Publishing Company, 1988.

Rosenbaum, Walter A. *Environmental Politics and Policy.* 8th ed. Washington, D.C.: CQ Press, 2011.

Smith, Frank E. *The Politics of Conservation.* New York: Pantheon Books, 1966.

U.S. Senate Committee on Environment and Public Works. *History of the Committee on Environment and Public Works, United States Senate.* 100th Cong., 2d sess. S. Doc. 100–45. Washington, D.C.: U.S. Government Printing Office, 1988.

Vig, Norman J., and Michael E. Kraft, eds. *Environmental Policy: New Directions for the Twenty-first Century.* 8th ed. Washington, D.C.: CQ Press, 2013.

Executive Branch

Arnold, Peri E. *Making the Managerial Presidency: Comprehensive Reorganization Planning, 1905–1996.* 2d ed. Lawrence: University of Kansas, 1998.

Carpenter, Daniel P. *The Forging of Bureaucratic Autonomy: Reputations, Networks, and Policy Innovation in Executive Agencies, 1862–1928.* Princeton, N.J.: Princeton University Press, 2001.

Emmerich, Herbert. *Federal Organization and Administrative Management.* Tuscaloosa: University of Alabama Press, 1971.

Fisher, Louis. *The Politics of Shared Power: Congress and the Executive.* 4th ed. College Station: Texas A&M University Press, 1998.

Fisher, Louis, and Ronald Moe. "Presidential Reorganization Authority: Is It Worth the Cost?" *Political Science Quarterly* 96 (Summer 1981): 301–318.

Levy, Leonard W., and Louis Fisher, eds. *Encyclopedia of the American Presidency.* 4 vols. New York: Simon and Schuster, 1994.

Seidman, Harold. *Politics, Position, and Power: The Dynamics of Federal Organization.* 5th ed. New York: Oxford University Press, 1998.

Skowronek, Stephen. *Building a New American State: The Expansion of National Administrative Capacities, 1877–1920.* New York: Cambridge University Press, 1982.

Sundquist, James L. "Congress as Public Administrator." In *A Centennial History of the American Administrative State,* edited by Ralph Clark Chandler, 261–289. New York: Free Press, 1987.

White, Leonard Dupee. *The Federalists: A Study in Administrative History.* New York: Macmillan, 1948.

———. *The Jacksonians: A Study in Administrative History, 1829–1861.* New York: Macmillan, 1954.

———. *The Jeffersonians: A Study in Administrative History, 1801–1829.* New York: Macmillan, 1951.

———. *The Republican Era, 1869–1901: A Study in Administrative History.* New York: Macmillan, 1958.

Exploration

Dupree, A. Hunter. *Science in the Federal Government: A History of Policies and Activities to 1940.* Cambridge, Mass.: Belknap Press of Harvard University Press, 1957.

Goetzmann, William H. *New Lands, New Men: America and the Second Great Age of Discovery.* Austin: Texas State Historical Society, 1995.

Hechler, Ken. *Toward the Endless Frontier: History of the Committee on Science and Technology, 1959–79.* U.S. Congress. House of Representatives. 99th Cong., 2d sess. Committee Print. Washington, D.C.: U.S. Government Printing Office, 1980.

Logsdon, John M. *The Decision to Go to the Moon: Project Apollo and the National Interest.* Cambridge, Mass.: MIT Press, 1970.

Manning, Thomas G. *Government in Science: The U.S. Geological Survey, 1867–1894.* Lexington, Ky.: University of Kentucky Press, 1967.

McCurdy, Howard E. *The Space Station Decision: Incremental Politics and Technological Choice.* Baltimore, Md.: Johns Hopkins University Press, 1990.

Family Policies

Jacobs, Francine H., and Margery W. Davies, eds. *More Than Kissing Babies? Current Child and Family Policy in the United States.* Westport, Conn.: Auburn House, 1994.

Michel, Sonya. *Children's Interests/Mothers' Rights: The Shaping of America's Child Care Policy.* New Haven, Conn.: Yale University Press, 1999.

Steiner, Gilbert Y. *The Futility of Family Policy.* Washington, D.C.: Brookings Institution Press, 1981.

U.S. House Select Committee on Children, Youth, and Families. *Federal Programs Affecting Children and Their Families, 1992: A Report of the Select Committee on Children, Youth, and Families.* 102d Cong., 2d sess. H. Rept. 102–1075. Washington, D.C.: U.S. Government Printing Office, 1992.

Zigler, Edward F., Sharon Lynn Kagan, and Nancy W. Hall, eds. *Children, Families, and Government: Preparing for the Twenty-first Century.* New York: Cambridge University Press, 1996.

Federalism

Conlan, Timothy. *From New Federalism to Devolution: Twenty-five Years of Intergovernmental Reform.* Washington, D.C.: Brookings Institution Press, 1998.

Dilger, Robert Jay, ed. *American Intergovernmental Relations Today: Perspectives and Controversies.* Englewood Cliffs, N.J.: Prentice Hall, 1986.

Elazar, Daniel J. *The American Partnership.* Chicago: University of Chicago Press, 1962.

Graves, W. Brooke. *American Intergovernmental Relations: Their Origins, Historical Development, and Current Status.* New York: Charles Scribner's Sons, 1964.

Grodzins, Morton, ed. *The American System: A New View of Government in the United States.* Chicago: Rand McNally and Company, 1966.

Marbach, Joseph R., Ellis Katz, and Troy E. Smith. *Federalism in America: An encyclopedia.* 2 vols. Westport, Conn.: Greenwood Press, 2006.

Riker, William H. *The Development of American Federalism.* Boston: Kluwer Academic Publishers, 1987.

Walker, David B. *The Rebirth of Federalism: Slouching toward Washington.* 2d ed. Chappaqua, N.Y.: Chatham House Publishers, 2000.

Wright, Deil S. *Understanding Intergovernmental Relations.* 3d ed. Pacific Grove, Calif.: Brooks/Cole Publishing Company, 1988.

Zimmerman, Joseph F. *Contemporary American Federalism: The Growth of National Power.* Albany, N.Y.: State University of New York Press, 2002.

Foreign Aid

Guess, George M. *The Politics of United States Foreign Aid.* New York: St. Martin's Press, 1987.

Meyer, Jeffrey A. "Congressional Control of Foreign Assistance." *Yale Journal of International Law* 13 (Winter 1988): 69–110.

Obey, David R., and Carol Lancaster. "Funding Foreign Aid." *Foreign Policy* 71 (Summer 1988): 141–155.

Payaslian, Simon. *U.S. Foreign Economic and Military Aid: The Reagan and Bush Administrations.* Lanham, Md.: University Press of America, 1996.

Ruttan, Vernon W. *United States Development Assistance Policy: The Domestic Politics of Foreign Economic Aid.* Baltimore, Md.: Johns Hopkins University Press, 1996.

Sewell, John W., and Christine E. Contee. "Foreign Aid and Gramm-Rudman." *Foreign Affairs* 65 (Summer 1986): 1015–1036.

Tarnoff, Curt, and Larry Q. Nowels. *U.S. Foreign Assistance: The Rationale, the Record, and the Challenges in the Post-Cold War Era.* Washington, D.C.: National Planning Association, 1994.

U.S. Agency for International Development. *Development and the National Interest: U.S. Economic Assistance into the Twenty-first Century.* Washington, D.C.: Agency for International Development, 1989.

U.S. House Committee on Foreign Affairs. *Background Materials on Foreign Assistance: Report of the Task Force on Foreign Assistance to the Committee on Foreign Affairs, U.S. House of Representatives.* 101st Cong., 1st sess. Committee Print. Washington, D.C.: U.S. Government Printing Office, 1989.

U.S. House Committee on Foreign Affairs. *Report of the Task Force on Foreign Assistance to the Committee on Foreign Affairs, U.S. House of Representatives.* 101st Cong., 1st sess. Committee Print. Washington, D.C.: U.S. Government Printing Office, 1989.

Government Ethics

Association of the Bar of the City of New York. Special Committee on Congressional Ethics. *Congress and the Public Trust: Report.* New York: Atheneum, 1970.

———. Special Committee on the Federal Conflict of Interest Laws. *Conflict of Interest and Federal Service*. Cambridge, Mass.: Harvard University Press, 1960.

Thompson, Dennis F. *Ethics in Congress: From Individual to Institutional Corruption*. Washington, D.C.: Brookings Institution Press, 1995.

Government Printing and Publishing

Huston, John Alexander. *Historical Sketch of the Government Printing Office, 1861–1916*. Washington, D.C.: The Forston Press, 1916.

Kling, Robert E. *The Government Printing Office*. New York: Praeger, 1970.

Schmeckebier, Laurence F. *The Government Printing Office: Its History, Activities, and Organization*. Baltimore, Md.: The Johns Hopkins Press, 1925.

Stathis, Stephen W. "The Evolution of Government Printing and Publishing in America." *Government Publications Review* 7 (1980): 377–390.

U.S. Government Printing Office. *Keeping America Informed: The U.S. Government Printing Office: 150 Years of Service to the Nation*. Washington, D.C.: U.S. Government Printing Office, 2011.

U.S. Government Printing Office. *100 GPO Years, 1861–1961: A History of United States Public Printing*. Washington, D.C.: U.S. Government Printing Office, 1961.

Walters, John S. *U.S. Government Publication: Ideological Development and Institutional Politics from the Founding to 1970*. Lanham, Md.: Scarecrow Press, 2005.

Gun Control

Carter, Gregg Lee. *The Gun Control Movement*. New York: Twayne Publishers, 1997.

Carter, Gregg Lee, ed. *Guns in American Society: An Encyclopedia of History, Politics, Culture, and the Law*. 2d ed. 3 vols. Santa Barbara, Calif.: ABC-CLIO, 2012.

Henderson, Harry. *Gun Control*. New York: Facts on File, 2000.

Kruschke, Earl R. *Gun Control: A Reference Handbook*. Santa Barbara, Calif.: ABC-CLIO, 1995.

Patterson, Samuel C., and Keith R. Eakins. "Congress and Gun Control." In *The Changing Politics of Gun Control*, edited by John M. Bruce and Clyde Wilcox, 45–73. Lanham, Md.: Rowman and Littlefield, 1998.

Spitzer, Robert J. *The Politics of Gun Control*. 5th ed. Boulder, Colo.: Paradigm Publishers, 2012.

Utter, Glenn H., and Robert J. Spitzer. *Encyclopedia of Gun Control and Gun Rights*. 2d ed. Amenia, N.Y.: Grey House Publishers, 2011.

Wilson, Harry L. *Guns, Gun Control, and Elections: The Politics and Policy of Firearms*. Lanham, Md.: Rowman & Littlefield, 2007.

Health and Medicine

Anderson, Odin W. *Health Services as a Growth Enterprise in the United States since 1875*. 2d ed. Ann Arbor, Mich.: Health Administration Press, 1990.

Cooper, Richard M., ed. *Food and Drug Law*. Washington, D.C.: Food and Drug Law Institute, 1991.

Feldstein, Paul J. *Health Policy Issues: An Economic Perspective on Health Reform*. 5th ed. Chicago: Health Administration Press, 2011.

Fox, Daniel M. *Health Policies, Health Politics: The British and American Experience, 1911–1965*. Princeton, N.J.: Princeton University Press, 1986.

Goodman, Richard A., Richard E. Hoffman, Wilfredo Lopez, Gene W. Matthews, Mark A. Rothstein, and Karen L. Foster, eds. *Law in Public Health Practice*. New York: Oxford University Press, 2007.

Mann, Thomas E., and Norman J. Ornstein. *Intensive Care: How Congress Shapes Health Policy*. Washington, D.C.: American Enterprise Institute and Brookings Institution Press, 1995.

Marmor, Theodore R. *The Politics of Medicare*. 2d ed. New York: Aldine de Gruyter, 2000.

Morone, James A., Theodor J. Litman, and Leonard S. Robins, eds. *Health Politics and Policy*. 4th ed. Clifton Park, N.Y.: Delmar Cengage Learning, 2008.

Shonick, William. *Government and Health Services: Government's Role in the Development of U.S. Health Services, 1930–1980*. New York: Oxford University Press, 1995.

Starr, Paul. *Remedy and Reaction: The Peculiar American Struggle Over Health Care Reform*. Rev. ed. New Haven, Conn.: Yale University Press, 2013.

———. *The Social Transformation of American Medicine*. New York: Basic Books, 1982.

Strickland, Stephen P. *Politics, Science, and Dread Disease: A Short History of United States Medical Research Policy*. Cambridge, Mass.: Harvard University Press, 1972.

Temin, Peter. *Taking Your Medicine: Drug Regulation in the United States*. Cambridge, Mass.: Harvard University Press, 1980.

Housing, Subsidized Housing, and Housing Finance

Fish, Gertrude Sipperly, ed. *The Story of Housing*. New York: Macmillan, 1979.

Hays, R. Allen. *The Federal Government and Urban Housing: Ideology and Change in Public Policy*. 3d ed. Albany, N.Y.: State University of New York Press, 2012.

Mitchell, J. Paul, ed. *Federal Housing Policy and Programs*. New Brunswick, N.J.: Center for Urban Policy Research, 1985.

U.S. House Committee on Banking, Housing, and Urban Affairs. Subcommittee on Housing and Community Development. *Housing—A Reader*. 98th Cong., 1st sess. Committee Print 98–5. Washington, D.C.: U.S. Government Printing Office, 1993.

U.S. House Committee on Financial Services. *A Chronology of Housing Legislation and Selected Executive Actions, 1892–2003.* 108th Cong., 2d sess. Committee Print 108-D. Washington, D.C.: U.S. Government Printing Office, 2003

U.S. House Committee on Financial Services. *Compilation of Basic Laws on Housing and Community Development: Revised through December 31, 2002 (End of the 107th Congress).* 108th Cong., 1st sess. Committee Print 108-C. Washington, D.C.: U.S. Government Printing Office, 2003.

U.S. Senate Committee on Banking and Currency. Subcommittee on Housing and Urban Affairs. *Congress and American Housing 1892–1967.* 90th Cong., 2d sess. Committee Print. Washington, D.C.: U.S. Government Printing Office, 1968.

Immigration Policy

Bankston, Carl L., III, ed. *Encyclopedia of American Immigration.* Pasadena, Calif.: Salem Press, 2010.

Bernard, William S. "Immigration: History of U.S. Policy." In *Harvard Encyclopedia of American Ethnic Groups,* edited by Stephan Thernstrom, Ann Orlov, and Oscar Handlin, 486–495. Cambridge, Mass.: Belknap Press of Harvard University, 1980.

Cose, Ellis. *A Nation of Strangers: Prejudice, Politics, and the Populating of America.* New York: William Morrow and Company, 1992.

Dinnerstein, Leonard, and David M. Reimers. *Ethnic Americans: A History of Immigration.* 5th ed. New York: Columbia University Press, 2009.

Fitzgerald, Keith. *The Face of the Nation: Immigration, the State, and the National Identity.* Stanford, Calif.: Stanford University Press, 1996.

Gold, Martin. *Forbidden Citizens: Chinese Exclusion and the U.S. Congress: A Legislative History.* Alexandria, Va.: TheCapital.Net, 2012.

Hutchinson, E. P. *Legislative History of American Immigration Policy, 1798–1965.* Philadelphia, Pa.: University of Pennsylvania Press, 1981.

Jones, Maldwyn Allen. *American Immigration.* 2d ed. Chicago: University of Chicago Press, 1992.

LeMay, Michael C., ed. *Transforming America: Perspectives on U.S. Immigration.* 3 vols. Santa Barbara, Calif.: Praeger, 2013.

LeMay, Michael C. *U.S. Immigration: A Reference Handbook.* Santa Barbara, Calif.: ABC-CLIO, 2004.

LeMay, Michael, and Elliott Robert Barkan, eds. *U.S. Immigration and Naturalization Laws and Issues: A Documentary History.* Westport, Conn.: Greenwood Press, 1999.

U.S. Senate Committee on the Judiciary. *History of the Immigration and Naturalizaton Service.* 96th Cong., 1st sess. Committee Print. Washington, D.C.: U.S. Government Printing Office, 1980.

———. *The Immigration and Naturalization Systems of the United States.* 81st Cong., 2d sess. S. Rept. 1515. Washington, D.C.: U.S. Government Printing Office, 1950.

Indian Policy

Bee, Robert L. *The Politics of American Indian Policy.* Cambridge, Mass.: Schenkman Publishing Company, 1982.

Davis, Mary B., ed. *Native America in the Twentieth Century: An Encyclopedia.* New York: Garland Publishing, 1996.

Harmon, George Dewey. *Sixty Years of Indian Affairs: Political, Economic, and Diplomatic, 1789–1850.* Chapel Hill, N.C.: University of North Carolina Press, 1941.

Henriksson, Markku. *The Indian on Capitol Hill: Indian Legislation and the United States Congress, 1862–1907.* Helsinki: Societas Historica Finlandiae, 1988.

Hoxie, Frederick E. *A Final Promise: The Campaign to Assimilate the Indians, 1880–1920.* Lincoln: University of Nebraska Press, 2001.

Johansen, Bruce E., and Barry M. Pritzker, eds. *Encyclopedia of American Indian History.* 4 vols. Santa Barbara, Calif.: ABC-CLIO, 2008.

Kappler, Charles J., comp. and ed. *Indian Affairs. Laws and Treaties.* 7 vols. Washington, D.C.: U.S. Government Printing Office, 1903.

Newton, Nell Jessup, ed. *Cohen's Handbook of Federal Indian Law.* New Providence, N.J.: LexisNexis, 2012.

Prucha, Francis Paul. *American Indian Treaties: The History of a Political Anomaly.* Berkeley: University of California Press, 1994.

———. *The Great Father: The United States Government and the American Indians.* 2 vols. Lincoln: University of Nebraska Press, 1984.

Rockwell, Stephen J. *Indian Affairs and the Administrative State in the Nineteenth Century.* Cambridge; New York: Cambridge University Press, 2010.

Schmeckebier, Laurence F. *The Office of Indian Affairs: Its History, Activities, and Organization.* Baltimore, Md.: Johns Hopkins University Press, 1927.

Stuart, Paul. *The Indian Office: Growth and Development of the American Institution, 1865–1900.* Ann Arbor, Mich.: UMI Research Press, 1979.

Taylor, Theodore W. *The Bureau of Indian Affairs.* Boulder, Colo.: Westview Press, 1984.

Tyler, S. Lyman. *A History of Indian Policy.* Washington, D.C.: U.S. Department of Interior, Bureau of Indian Affairs, 1973.

Intelligence Policy

Fain, Tyrus G., with Katharine C. Plant and Ross Milloy, eds. *The Intelligence Community: History, Organization, and Issues.* New York: R. R. Bowker Company, 1977.

Jeffreys-Jones, Rhodri. *The CIA and American Democracy.* 3d ed. New Haven, Conn.: Yale University Press, 2003.

Johnson, Loch K. *A Season of Inquiry: Congress and Intelligence.* Chicago: Dorsey Press, 1988.

Koh, Harold Hongju. *The National Security Constitution: Sharing Power after the Iran-Contra Affair.* New Haven, Conn.: Yale University Press, 1990.

Lowenthal, Mark M. *Intelligence: From Secrets to Policy.* 5th ed. Washington, D.C.: CQ Press, 2012.

Smist, Frank J., Jr. *Congress Oversees the United States Intelligence Community, 1947–1994.* 2d ed. Knoxville: University of Tennessee Press, 1994.

U.S. Senate Select Committee on Intelligence. *Legislative Oversight of Intelligence Activities: The U.S. Experience.* 103d Cong., 2d sess. S. Print 103-88. Washington, D.C.: U.S. Government Printing Office, 1994.

Watson, Bruce W., Susan M. Watson, and Gerald W. Hopple, eds. *United States Intelligence: An Encyclopedia.* New York: Garland Publishing, 1990.

Internal Improvements

Albjerg, Victor J. "Federal Policy toward Internal Improvements, 1789–1861." PhD diss., University of Wisconsin, 1927.

———. "Internal Improvements without a Policy (1789–1860)." *Indiana Magazine of History* 28 (September 1932): 168–179.

Armstrong, Ellis L., Michael C. Robinson, and Suellen M. Hoy, eds. *History of Public Works in the United States, 1776–1976.* Chicago: American Public Works Association, 1976.

Goodrich, Carter. *Government Promotion of American Canals and Railroads, 1800–1890.* New York: Columbia University Press, 1960.

Harrison, Joseph H., Jr. "The Internal Improvement Issue in the Politics of the Union, 1783–1825." PhD diss., University of Virginia, 1954.

Hill, Forest Garrett. *Roads, Rails and Waterways: The Army Engineers and Early Transportation.* Norman: University of Oklahoma Press, 1957.

Jackson, W. Turrentine. *Wagon Roads West: A Study of Federal Road Surveys and Construction in the Trans-Mississippi West, 1846–1869.* New Haven, Conn.: Yale University Press, 1965.

Larson, John Lauritz. " 'Bind the Republic Together': The National Union and the Struggle for Internal Improvements." *Journal of American History* 74 (September 1987): 363–387.

Rae, John Bell. "Federal Land Grants in Aid of Canals." *Journal of Economic History* 4 (November 1944): 167–177.

Internal Security

Carr, Robert K. *The House Committee on Un-American Activities, 1945–1950.* Ithaca, N.Y.: Cornell University Press, 1952.

Goodman, Walter. *The Committee: The Extraordinary Career of the House Committee on Un-American Activities.* New York: Farrar, Straus, and Giroux, 1968.

Herman, Arthur. *Joseph McCarthy: Reexamining the Life and Legacy of America's Most Hated Senator.* New York: Free Press, 2000.

Irons, Peter. *Justice at War.* Berkeley: University of California Press, 1993.

Latham, Earl. *The Communist Controversy in Washington: From the New Deal to McCarthy.* Cambridge, Mass.: Harvard University Press, 1966.

Schrecker, Ellen. *The Age of McCarthyism: A Brief History with Documents.* 2d ed. Boston: Bedford St. Martin's, 2001.

U.S. Senate Committee on the Judiciary. Subcommittee to Investigate the Administration of the Internal Security Act and Other Internal Security Laws. *Administration of the Internal Security Act of 1950.* Prepared by A. Warren Littman. 94th Cong., 1st sess. Committee Print. Washington, D.C.: U.S. Government Printing Office, 1975.

———. *Internal Security Manual, Revised to July 1973: Provisions of Federal Statutes, Executive Orders, and Congressional Resolutions Relating to the Internal Security of the United States.* 2 vols. 93d Cong., 2d sess. Committee Print. Washington, D.C.: U.S. Government Printing Office, 1974.

Judiciary and Judicial Review

Carp, Robert A., and Ronald Stidham. *The Federal Courts.* 4th ed. Washington, D.C.: CQ Press, 2001.

Crowe, Justin. *Building the Judiciary: Law, Courts, and the Politics of Institutional Development.* Princeton, N.J.: Princeton University Press, 2012.

Lehman, Jeffrey, and Shirelle Phelps, eds. *West's Encyclopedia of American Law.* 2d ed. 13 vols. Minneapolis/Saint Paul, Minn.: West Publishing Company, 2005.

Marcus, Maeva, ed. *Origins of the Federal Judiciary: Essays on the Judiciary Act of 1789.* New York: Oxford University Press, 1992.

Posner, Richard A. *The Federal Courts: Challenge and Reform.* Cambridge, Mass.: Harvard University Press, 1996.

Ritz, Wilfred J. *Rewriting the History of the Judiciary Act of 1789.* Norman: University of Oklahoma Press, 1990.

Savage, David G., ed. *Guide to the U.S. Supreme Court.* 5th ed. 2 vols. Washington, D.C.: CQ Press, 2010.

Surrency, Erwin C. *History of the Federal Courts.* 2d ed. Dobbs Ferry, N.Y.: Oceana Publications, 2002.

Wheeler, Russell R., and Cynthia Harrison. *Creating the Federal Judicial System.* 3d ed. Washington, D.C.: Federal Judicial Center, 2005.

Wilson, Steven Harmon, ed. *The U.S. Justice System: An Encyclopedia.* 3 vols. Santa Barbara, Calif.: ABC-CLIO, 2012.

Labor

Ashford, Nicholas Askounes. *Crisis in the Workplace: Occupational Disease and Injury, A Report to the Ford Foundation.* Cambridge, Mass.: MIT Press, 1976.

Cihon, Patrick J., and James Ottavio Castagnera. *Employment & Labor Law.* 7th ed. Mason, Ohio: South-Western Cengage Learning, 2011.

Commons, John R., and John B. Andrews. *Principles of Labor Legislation*. 2d ed. Holmes Beach, Fla.: Gaunt Inc., 2001.

Derber, Milton, and Edwin Young, ed. *Labor and the New Deal*. Madison: University of Wisconsin Press, 1957.

Fields, C. Kerry, and Henry R. Cheeseman. *Contemporary Employment Law*. New York: Aspen Publishers, 2010.

Forbath, William E. *Law and the Shaping of the American Labor Movement*. Cambridge, Mass.: Harvard University Press, 1991.

Gregory, Charles O., and Harold A. Katz. *Labor and the Law*. 3d ed. New York: W. W. Norton and Company, 1979.

Kaps, Robert W., J. Scott Hamilton, and Timm J. Bliss. *Labor Relations in the Aviation and Aerospace Industries*. Carbondale: Southern Illinois University Press, 2012.

McNaughton, Wayne L., and Joseph Lazar. *Industrial Relations and the Government*. New York: McGraw-Hill Book Company, 1954.

Moss, David A. *Socializing Security: Progressive-Era Economists and the Origins of American Social Policy*. Cambridge, Mass.: Harvard University Press, 1996.

Nordlund, Willis J. *The Quest for a Living Wage: The History of the Federal Minimum Wage Program*. Westport, Conn.: Greenwood Press, 1997.

Rehmus, Charles M. "Evolution of Legislation Affecting Collective Bargaining in the Railroad and Airline Industries." In *The Railway Labor Act at Fifty: Collective Bargaining in the Railroad and Airline Industries*, edited by Benjamin Vaaron, Beatrice M. Brugoon, Donald E. Cullen, Dana E. Eischen, Mark L. Kahn, Charles M. Rehmus, and Jacob Seidenberg, 1–22. Washington, D.C.: National Mediation Board, 1977.

Van Horn, Carl E. and Herbert A. Schaffner, eds. *Work in America: An Encyclopedia of History, Policy, and Society*. 2 vols. Santa Barbara, Calif.: ABC-CLIO, 2003.

Lobbying

Mulhollan, Daniel P. "An Overview of Lobbying by Organizations." In U.S. Congress. Commission on the Operation of the Senate. *Senators, Offices, Ethics, and Pressures*, 157–192. Washington, D.C.: U.S. Government Printing Office, 1977.

Ornstein, Norman J., and Shirley Elder. *Interest Groups, Lobbying, and Policymaking*. Washington, D.C.: CQ Press, 1978.

Schriftgiesser, Karl. *The Lobbyists: The Art and Business of Influencing Lawmakers*. Boston: Little, Brown, 1951.

Susman, Thomas M., ed. "Introduction to Federal Regulation of Lobbying Act." Chap. 1 in *The Lobbying Manual: A Compliance Guide for Lawyers and Lobbyists*. Chicago: American Bar Association, Section of Administrative Law and Regulatory Practice, 1993.

U.S. Senate Committee on Governmental Affairs. Subcommittee on Intergovernmental Relations. *Congress and Pressure Groups: Lobbying in a Modern Democracy*. 99th Cong., 2d sess. S. Print 99–161. Washington, D.C.: U.S. Government Printing Office, 1986.

Maritime Policy

Gibson, Andrew and Arthur Donovan. *The Abandoned Ocean: A History of United States Maritime Policy*. Columbia: University of South Carolina Press, 2000.

Labaree, Benjamin W., William M. Fowler, Jr., Edward W. Sloan, John B. Hattendorf, Jeffrey J. Safford, and Andrew W. German. *America and the Sea: A Maritime History*. Mystic, Conn.: Mystic Seaport, 1998.

Lawrence, Samuel A. *United States Merchant Shipping Policies and Politics*. Washington, D.C.: Brookings Institution Press, 1966.

Noble, Dennis L. *Lighthouses & Keepers: The U.S. Lighthouse Service and Its Legacy*. Annapolis, Md.: Naval Institute Press, 1997.

Money and Monetary Policy

Allen, Larry. *The Encyclopedia of Money*. 2d ed. Santa Barbara, Calif.: ABC-CLIO, 2009.

Doty, Richard G. *America's Money, America's Story: A Chronicle of American Numismatic History*. 2d ed. Atlanta, Ga.: Whitman Publishing, 2008.

Lange, David W. *History of the United States Mint and Its Coinage*. Atlanta, Ga. Whitman Publishing, 2006.

Schwarz, Ted. *A History of United States Coinage*. San Diego, Calif.: A.S. Barnes; London: Tantivy Press, 1980.

Taxay, Don. *The United States Mint and Coinage: An Illustrated History from 1776 to the Present*. New York: Arco Publishing Company, 1966.

Narcotics and Other Dangerous Drugs

Belenko, Steven R., ed. *Drugs and Drug Policy in America*. Westport, Conn.: Greenwood Press, 2000.

Greenberg, Martin Alan. *Prohibition Enforcement: Charting a New Mission*. Springfield, Ill.: Charles C. Thomas, 1999.

Inciardi, James A., ed. *Handbook of Drug Control in the United States*. New York: Greenwood Press, 1990.

Maisto, Stephen A., Mark Galizio, and Gerard J. Connors. *Drug Use and Abuse*. 6th ed. Belmont, Calif.: Thomson/Wadsworth, 2011.

McWilliams, John C. "Through the Past Darkly: The Politics and Policies of America's Drug War." In *Drug Control Policy: Essays in Historical and Comparative Perspective*, edited by William O. Walker III. University Park: Pennsylvania State University Press, 1992.

Morgan, H. Wayne. *Drugs in America: A Social History, 1800–1980*. Syracuse, N.Y.: Syracuse University Press, 1981.

Musto, David F. *The American Disease: Origins of Narcotic Control*. 3d ed. New York: Oxford University Press, 1999.

Musto, David F., and Pamela Korsmeyer. *The Quest for Drug Control: Politics and Federal Policy in a Period of Increasing Substance Abuse, 1963–1981*. New Haven, Conn.: Yale University Press, 2002.

Temin, Peter. *Taking Your Medicine: Drug Regulation in the United States.* Cambridge, Mass.: Harvard University Press, 1980.

Walker, William O., III. *Drug Control in the Americas.* Rev. ed. Albuquerque: University of New Mexico Press, 1989.

National Parks and Forests

Dilsaver, Lary M., ed. *America's National Park System: The Critical Documents.* Lanham, Md.: Rowan and Littlefield Publishers, 1994.

Frome, Michael. *The Forest Service.* 2d ed. Boulder, Colo.: Westview Press, 1984.

Ise, John. *Our National Park Policy: A Critical History.* Baltimore, Md.: Published for Resources for the Future by Johns Hopkins University Press, 1961.

Runte, Alfred. *National Parks: The American Experience.* 4th ed. Lanham, Md.: Taylor Trade Publishers, 2010.

Sellars, Richard West. *Preserving Nature in the National Parks: A History.* New Haven, Conn.: Yale University Press, 2009.

Smith, Darrell Hevenor. *The Forest Service: Its History, Activities and Organization.* Washington, D.C.: The Brookings Institution, 1930.

U.S. Office of Technology Assessment. *Forest Service Planning: Accommodating Uses, Producing Outputs, and Sustaining Ecosystems.* Washington, D.C.: U.S. Office of Technology Assessment, 1992.

U.S. Senate Committee on Energy and Natural Resources. *History of the Committee on Energy and Natural Resources, United States Senate, as of the 100th Congress, 1816–1988.* 100th Cong., 2d sess. S. Doc. 100–46. Washington, D.C.: U.S. Government Printing Office, 1989.

Wilkinson, Charles F., and H. Michael Anderson. *Land and Resource Planning in the National Forests.* Washington, D.C.: Island Press, 1987.

Williams, Gerald W. *The Forest Service: Fighting for Public Lands.* Westport, Conn.: Greenwood Press, 2007.

Older Americans

Achenbaum, W. Andrew. *Shades of Gray: Old Age, American Values, and Federal Policies since 1920.* Boston: Little, Brown, 1983.

Estes, Carroll L. *The Aging Enterprise.* San Francisco, Calif.: Jossey-Bass Publishers, 1980.

Hudson, Robert B. *The Aging in Politics: Process and Policy.* Springfield, Ill.: C. C. Thomas, 1981.

Hudson, Robert B., ed. *The New Politics of Old Age Policy.* 2d ed. Baltimore, Md.: Johns Hopkins University Press, 2010.

Koff, Theodore H., and Richard W. Park. *Aging Public Policy: Bonding the Generations.* 2d ed. Amityville, N.Y.: Baywood Publishing Company, 1999.

Pratt, Henry J. *The Gray Lobby.* Chicago: University of Chicago Press, 1976.

Torres-Gil, Fernando M. *The New Aging: Politics and Change in America.* New York: Auburn House, 1992.

U.S. Social Security Administration. *History of the Provisions of Old-Age, Survivors, Disability, and Health Insurance, 1935–1996.* Washington, D.C.: U.S. Social Security Administration, 1997.

Postal Service

Baxter, Vern K. *Labor and Politics in the U.S. Postal Service.* New York: Plenum Press, 1994.

Cullinan, Gerald. *The United States Postal Service.* New York: Praeger Publishers, 1973.

Fowler, Dorothy Ganfield. *Unmailable: Congress and the Post Office.* Athens, Ga.: University of Georgia Press, 1977.

Fuller, Wayne Edison. *The American Mail; Enlarger of the Common Life.* Chicago: University of Chicago Press, 1972.

John, Richard R. *Spreading the News: The American Postal System from Franklin to Morse.* Cambridge, Mass.: Harvard University Press, 1995.

Kielbowicz, Richard Burket. *News in the Mail: The Press, Post Office, and Public Information, 1700–1860s.* New York: Greenwood Press, 1989.

Mayton, William Ty. "The Missions and Methods of the Postal Power." In *Governing the Postal Service,* edited by J. Gregory Sidak, 60–113. Washington, D.C.: AEI Press, 1994.

Scheele, Carl H. *A Short History of the Mail Service.* Washington, D.C.: Smithsonian Institution Press, 1970.

Presidential Disability, Succession, and Tenure

Bayh, Birch. *One Heartbeat Away: Presidential Disability and Succession.* Indianapolis, Ind.: Bobbs-Merrill Company, 1968.

Engdahl, Sylvia, ed. *Amendment XXV: Presidential Disability and Succession.* Detroit: Gale Cengage Learning, 2010.

Feerick, John D. *The Twenty-fifth Amendment: Its Complete History and Applications.* 3d ed. New York: Fordham University Press, 2013.

Silva, Ruth. *Presidential Succession.* Ann Arbor: University of Michigan Press, 1951.

Stathis, Stephen W. "The Twenty-second Amendment: A Practical Remedy or Partisan Maneuver?" *Constitutional Commentary* 7 (Winter 1990): 61–88.

U.S. Senate Committee on the Judiciary. Subcommittee on Constitutional Amendments. *Selected Materials on the Twenty-fifth Amendment.* 93d Cong., 1st sess. S. Doc. 93–42. Washington, D.C.: U.S. Government Printing Office, 1973.

Privacy

Cate, Fred H. *Privacy in the Information Age.* Washington, D.C.: Brookings Institution Press, 1997.

Hanus, Jerome J., and Harold C. Relyea. "A Policy Assessment of the Privacy Act." *American University Law Review* 25 (Spring 1976): 555–593.

Personal Privacy in an Information Society: The Report of the Privacy Protection Study Commission. Washington, D.C.: Privacy Protection Study Commission, July 1977.

Regan, Priscilla M. *Legislating Privacy: Technology, Social Values, and Public Policy.* Chapel Hill: University of North Carolina Press, 1995.

Smith, Robert Ellis. *Ben Franklin's Web Site: Privacy and Curiosity from Plymouth Rock to the Internet.* Providence, R.I.: Privacy Journal, 2000.

Swire, Peter P., and Robert E. Litan. *None of Your Business: World Data Flows, Electronic Commerce, and the European Privacy Directive.* Washington, D.C.: Brookings Institution Press, 1998.

U.S. Senate Committee on Government Operations and U.S. House Committee on Government Operations, Subcommittee on Government Information and Individual Rights. *Legislative History of the Privacy Act of 1974, S. 3418 (Public Law 93–579): Source Book on Privacy.* 94th Cong., 2d sess. Joint Committee Print. Washington, D.C.: U.S. Government Printing Office, 1976.

Westin, Alan F. *Privacy and Freedom.* New York: Atheneum, 1967.

Public Lands

America 200: The Legacy of Our Lands. Special bicentennial ed. Washington, D.C.: U.S. Department of the Interior, 1976.

Cawley, R. McGreggor. *Federal Land, Western Anger: The Sagebrush Rebellion and Environmental Politics.* Lawrence: University Press of Kansas, 1993.

Foss, Phillip O. *Politics and Grass: The Administration of Grazing on the Public Domain.* Seattle: University of Washington Press, 1960.

Gates, Paul W. *History of Public Land Law Development.* Washington, D.C.: U.S. Government Printing Office, 1968.

Hibbard, Benjamin Horace. *A History of the Public Land Policies.* Madison: University of Wisconsin Press, 1965.

Oberly, James W. *Sixty Million Acres: American Veterans and the Public Lands before the Civil War.* Kent, Ohio: Kent State University Press, 1990.

Robbins, Roy M. *Our Landed Heritage: The Public Domain, 1776–1936.* Lincoln: University of Nebraska Press, 1942.

Rohrbough, Malcolm J. *The Land Office Business: The Settlement and Administration of American Public Lands, 1789–1837.* New York: Oxford University Press, 1968.

Stegner, Wallace. *Beyond the Hundredth Meridian: John Wesley Powell and the Second Opening of the West.* Lincoln: University of Nebraska Press, 1954.

Utley, Robert M., and Barry Mackintosh. *The Department of Everything Else: Highlights of Interior History.* Washington, D.C.: U.S. Department of the Interior, 1988.

Wilkinson, Charles F. *Crossing the Next Meridian: Land, Water, and the Future of the West.* Washington, D.C.: Island Press, 1992.

Public Works

Armstrong, Ellis L., Michael C. Robinson, and Suellen M. Hoy, eds. *History of Public Works in the United States, 1776–1976.* Chicago: American Public Works Association, 1976.

Hill, Forest G. *Roads, Rails and Waterways: The Army Engineers and Early Transportation.* Westport, Conn.: Greenwood Press, 1977.

Hoy, Suellen M., and Michael C. Robinson, comp. *Public Works History in the United States: A Guide to the Literature.* Nashville, Tenn.: American Association for State and Local History, 1982.

Maass, Arthur. *Congress and the Common Good.* New York: Basic Books, 1983.

———. *Muddy Waters: The Army Engineers and the Nation's Rivers.* Cambridge, Mass.: Harvard University Press, 1951.

Pross, Edward L. "History of Rivers and Harbors Appropriations Bills, 1866–1933." PhD diss., Ohio State University, 1938.

U.S. Federal Highway Administration. *America's Highways, 1776–1976: A History of the Federal-Aid Program.* Washington, D.C.: U.S. Department of Transportation, Federal Highway Administration, 1977.

U.S. Senate Committee on Environment and Public Works. *History of the Committee on Environment and Public Works, United States Senate.* 100th Cong., 2d sess. S. Doc. 100–45. Washington, D.C.: U.S. Government Printing Office, 1988.

Regulation and Deregulation

Cushman, Robert T. *The Independent Regulatory Commissions.* New York: Octagon Books, 1972.

Derthick, Martha, and Paul J. Quirk. *The Politics of Deregulation.* Washington, D.C.: Brookings Institution Press, 1985.

Funk, William F., Jeffrey S. Lubbers, and Charles Pou Jr., eds. *Federal Administrative Procedure Sourcebook.* 4th ed. Chicago: American Bar Association, Section of Administrative and Regulatory Practice, 2008.

Koch, Charles H., Jr. *Administrative Law and Practice.* 3d ed. 5 vols. Egan, Minn.: West/Thomson, 2010.

Lubbers, Jeffrey S. *A Guide to Federal Agency Rulemaking.* 5th ed. Chicago: American Bar Association, 2012.

Meier, Kenneth J. E., Thomas Garman, and Lael R. Keiser. *Regulation and Consumer Protection: Politics, Bureaucracy and Economics.* 3d ed. Houston, Tex. Dame Publications, 1998.

Vietor, Richard H. K. *Contrived Competition: Regulation and Deregulation in America.* Cambridge, Mass.: Belknap Press of Harvard University Press, 1994.

Weidenbaum, Murray L. *Business, Government, and the Public.* 7th ed. Upper Saddle River, N.J.: Pearson/Prentice Hall, 2004.

Religion

Ahlstrom, Sydney E. *A Religious History of the American People.* 2d ed. 2 vols. New Haven, Conn.: Yale University Press, 2004.

Benson, Peter L., and Dorothy L. Williams. *Religion on Capitol Hill: Myths and Realities.* New York: Oxford University Press, 1986.

Cookson, Catharine, ed. *Encyclopedia of Religious Freedom.* New York: Routledge, 2003.

Djupe, Paul A., and Laura R. Olson. *Encyclopedia of American Religion and Politics.* New York: Facts on File, 2003.

Edel, Wilbur. *Defenders of the Faith: Religion and Politics from the Pilgrim Fathers to Ronald Reagan.* New York: Praeger, 1987.

Fowler, Robert Booth, Allen D. Hertzke, and Laura R. Olson. *Religion and Politics in America: Faith, Culture, and Strategic Choices.* 2d ed. Boulder, Colo.: Westview Press, 1998.

Queen, Edward L., Stephen R. Prothero, and Gardiner H. Shattuck, Jr. *Encyclopedia of American Religious History.* 3d ed. New York: Facts on File, 2009.

Reichley, A. James. *Religion in American Public Life.* Washington, D.C.: Brookings Institution Press, 1985.

Stokes, Anson Phelps. *Church and State in the United States.* 3 vols. New York: Harper and Row, 1950.

Woods, James E., Jr., and Derek Davis, eds. *The Role of Religion in the Making of Public Policy.* Waco, Tex. Baylor University, J. M. Dawson Institute of Church-State Studies, 1991.

Science and Technology

Barke, Richard. *Science, Technology, and Public Policy.* Washington, D.C.: CQ Press, 1986.

Blanpied, William A. *A History of Federal Science Policy from the New Deal to the Present.* Houston: Rice University Press, 2010.

Del Sesto, Steven L. *Science, Politics, and Controversy: Civilian Nuclear Power in the United States, 1946–1974.* Boulder, Colo.: Westview Press, 1979.

Dupree, A. Hunter. *Science in the Federal Government: A History of Policies and Activities.* Baltimore, Md.: Johns Hopkins University Press, 1986.

Kleinman, Daniel Lee. *Politics on the Endless Frontier: Postwar Research Policy in the United States.* Durham, N.C.: Duke University Press, 1995.

National Academy of Sciences. Committee on Science and Public Policy. *Federal Support of Basic Research in Institutions of Higher Learning.* Washington, D.C.: National Academy of Sciences–National Research Council, 1964.

Penick, James L., Jr., Carroll W. Pursell Jr., Morgan B. Sherwood, and Donald C. Swain. *The Politics of American Science, 1939 to the Present.* Rev. ed. Cambridge, Mass.: MIT Press, 1972.

U.S. House Committee on Science and Technology. *A History of Science Policy in the United States, 1940–1985.* 99th Cong., 2d sess. Committee Print. Serial R. Washington, D.C.: U.S. Government Printing Office, 1986.

Slavery

Alexander, Thomas B. *Sectional Stress and Party Strength: A Study of Roll-Call Voting Patterns in the United States House of Representatives, 1836–1860.* Nashville, Tenn.: Vanderbilt University, 1967.

Franklin, John Hope, and Evelyn Higginbotham. *From Slavery to Freedom: A History of African Americans.* 9th ed. New York: McGraw-Hill, 2011.

Freehling, William W. *The Road to Disunion.* 2 vols. New York: Oxford University Press, 1990.

Hamilton, Holman. *Prologue to Conflict: The Crisis and Compromise of 1850.* Lexington: University of Kentucky Press, 1964.

Knupfer, Peter B. *The Union as It Is: Constitutional Unionism and Sectional Compromise, 1787–1861.* Chapel Hill, N.C.: University of North Carolina Press, 1991.

Miller, William Lee. *Arguing about Slavery: The Great Battle in the United States Congress.* New York: Alfred A. Knopf, 1996.

Potter, David M. *The Impending Crisis, 1848–1861.* New York: Harper and Row, Publishers, 1976

Small Business

Anglund, Sandra M. *Small Business Policy and the American Creed.* Westport, Conn.: Praeger, 2000.

Aoyama, Yuko, and Michael B. Teitz. *Small Business Policy in Japan and the United States: A Comparative Analysis of Objectives and Outcomes.* Berkeley, Calif.: University of California, Berkeley, Institute of International Studies, International and Area Studies, 1996.

Bean, Jonathan J. *Beyond the Broker State: Federal Policies toward Small Business, 1936–1961.* Chapel Hill: University of North Carolina Press, 1996.

Blackford, Mansel G. *A History of Small Business in America.* 2d ed. Chapel Hill, N.C.: University of North Carolina Press, 2003.

Parris, Addison W. *The Small Business Administration.* New York: F. A. Praeger, 1968.

Phillips, Joseph Dexter. *Little Business in the American Economy.* Urbana: University of Illinois Press, 1958.

Social Security

Achenbaum, W. Andrew. *Social Security: Visions and Revisions.* New York: Cambridge University Press, 1986.

Altmeyer, Arthur J. *The Formative Years of Social Security.* Madison: University of Wisconsin Press, 1966.

Coll, Blanche D. *Safety Net: Welfare and Social Security, 1929–1979.* New Brunswick, N.J.: Rutgers University Press, 1995.

Derthick, Martha. *Policymaking for Social Security.* Washington, D.C.: Brookings Institution Press, 1979.

Lubove, Roy. *The Struggle for Social Security, 1900–1935.* 2d ed. Pittsburgh, Pa.: University of Pittsburgh Press, 1986.

Nash, Gerald D., Noel H. Pugach, and Richard F. Tomasson, eds. *Social Security: The First Half-Century.* Albuquerque: University of New Mexico Press, 1988.

Schieber, Sylvester J., and John B. Shoven. *The Real Deal: The History and Future of Social Security.* New Haven, Conn.: Yale University Press, 1999.

U.S. Senate Select Committee on Aging. *Fifty Years of Social Security: Past Achievements and Future Challenges.* 99th Cong., 1st sess. S. Print 99–70. Washington, D.C.: U.S. Government Printing Office, 1985.

Witte, Edwin Emil. *The Development of the Social Security Act: A Memorandum on the History of the Committee on Economic Security and Drafting and Legislative History of the Social Security Act.* Madison: University of Wisconsin Press, 1962.

Social Welfare and Poverty

Abramovitz, Mimi. *Regulating the Lives of Women: Social Welfare Policy from Colonial Times to the Present.* Rev. ed. Boston: South End Press, 1996.

Amenta, Edwin. *Bold Relief: Institutional Politics and the Origins of Modern American Social Policy.* Boston: Allyn and Bacon, 2001.

Axinn, June, and Mark J. Stern. *Social Welfare: A History of the American Response to Need.* 7th ed. Boston: Pearson/Allyn and Bacon, 2008.

Day, Phyllis J. *A New History of Social Welfare.* 6th ed. Boston: Pearson/Allyn and Bacon, 2009.

Gordon, Linda. *Pitied but Not Entitled: Single Mothers and the History of Welfare, 1890–1935.* New York: Free Press, 1994.

Quadagno, Jill S. *The Color of Welfare: How Racism Undermined the War on Poverty.* New York: Oxford University Press, 1994.

Skocpol, Theda. *Protecting Soldiers and Mothers: The Political Origins of Social Policy in the United States.* Cambridge, Mass.: Belknap Press of Harvard University Press, 1992.

Weir, Margaret, Ann Shola Orloff, and Theda Skocpol, eds. *The Politics of Social Policy in the United States.* Princeton, N.J.: Princeton University Press, 1988.

Statehood

The Concept of Statehood within the American Federal System: A Report for the Alaska Statehood Commission. Prepared by Birch, Horton, Bittner, and Monroe, PC, for the Alaska Statehood Commission. Fairbanks, Alaska, April 15, 1981.

Dávila-Colón, Luis R. "Equal Citizenship, Self-Determination, and the U.S. Statehood Process: A Constitutional and Historical Analysis." *Case Western Reserve Journal of International Law* 13 (Spring 1981): 315–374.

Grupo de Investigadores Puertorriquenos. *Breakthrough from Colonialism: An Interdisciplinary Study of Statehood.* 2 vols. Río Piedras, Puerto Rico: Editorial de la Universidad de Puerto Rico, 1984.

Murphy, Russell D. *Strategic Calculations and the Admission of New States into the Union, 1789–1960: Congress and the Politics of Statehood.* Lewiston, N.Y.: Edwin Mellen Press, 2008.

U.S. Congress. Senate. *Organic Acts for the United States.* 56th Cong. 1st sess. S. Doc. 148. Washington, D.C.: U.S. Government Printing Office, 1900.

Taxation

Blakey, Roy G., and Gladys C. Blakey. *The Federal Income Tax.* London: Longmans, Green and Company, 1940.

Blank, Steven A., Kirk J. Stark, and Joseph J. Thorndike. *War and Taxes.* Washington, D.C.: Urban Institute Press, 2008.

Brownlee, W. Elliot. *Federal Taxation in America: A Short History.* 2d ed. Washington, D.C.: Woodrow Wilson Center Press; Cambridge, UK; New York: Cambridge University Press, 2004.

Cordes, Joseph J., Robert D. Ebel, and Jane G. Gravelle, eds. 2d ed. *The Encyclopedia of Taxation and Tax Policy.* Washington, D.C.: Urban Institute Press, 2005.

Doris, Lillian, ed. *The American Way in Taxation: Internal Revenue, 1862–1963.* Englewood Cliffs, N.J.: Prentice Hall, 1963.

IRS Historical Fact Book: A Chronology, 1646–1992. Washington, D.C.: U.S. Department of the Treasury, Internal Revenue Service, 1993.

Kimmel, Lewis H. *Federal Budget and Fiscal Policy, 1789–1958.* Washington, D.C.: Brookings Institution Press, 1959.

Paul, Randolph Evernghim. *Taxation in the United States.* Boston: Little, Brown and Company, 1954.

Pechman, Joseph A. *Federal Tax Policy.* 5th ed. Washington, D.C.: Brookings Institution Press, 1987.

Ratner, Sidney. *American Taxation, Its History as a Social Force in Democracy.* New York: W. W. Norton & Company, Inc., 1942.

Stanley, Robert. *Dimensions of Law in the Service of Order: Origins of the Federal Income Tax, 1861–1913.* New York: Oxford University Press, 1993.

Verdier, James M. "The President, Congress, and Tax Reform: Patterns Over Three Decades." *Annals of the American Academy of Political Science* 499 (September 1988): 114–123.

Willan, Robert M. *Income Taxes: Concise History and Primer.* Baton Rouge, La.: Claitor's Publishing Division, 1994.

Witte, John F. *The Politics and Development of the Federal Income Tax.* Madison: University of Wisconsin Press, 1985.

Territories and Possessions

Laughlin, Stanley K., Jr. *The Law of United States Territories and Affiliated Jurisdictions.* Rochester, N.Y.: Lawyers Cooperative Publishing, 1995.

Leibowitz, Arnold H. *Defining Status: A Comprehensive Analysis of United States Territorial Relations.* Dordrecht, The Netherlands: Martinus Nijhoff Publishers, 1989.

Pomeroy, Earl S. *The Territories and the United States, 1861–1890: Studies in Colonial Administration.* Seattle: University of Washington Press, 1969.

Pratt, Julius W. *America's Colonial Experiment: How the United States Gained, Governed, and in Part Gave Away a Colonial Empire.* New York: Prentice Hall, 1950.

Stuart, Peter C. *Isles of Empire: The United States and Its Overseas Possessions.* Lanham, Md.: University Press of America, 1999.

U.S. Senate Committee on Energy and Natural Resources. *History of the Committee on Energy and Natural Resources, United States Senate, as of the 100th Congress, 1816–1988.* 100th Cong., 2d sess. S. Doc. 100–46. Washington, D.C.: U.S. Government Printing Office, 1989.

Trade and Tariffs

Aaronson, Susan Ariel. *Trade and the American Dream: A Social History of Postwar Trade Policy.* Lexington: University Press of Kentucky, 1996.

Destler, I. M. *American Trade Politics.* 4th ed. Washington, D.C.: Institute for International Economics; New York: Twentieth Century Fund, 2005.

Dobson, John M. *Two Centuries of Tariffs: The Background and Emergence of the U.S. International Trade Commission.* Washington, D.C.: U.S. International Trade Commission, December 1976.

Eckes, Alfred E., Jr. *Opening America's Market: U.S. Foreign Trade Policy since 1776.* Chapel Hill: University of North Carolina Press, 1995.

Northrup, Cynthia Clark, and Elaine C. Prange Turney. *Encyclopedia of Tariffs and Trade in U.S. History.* 3 vols. Westport, Conn.: Greenwood Press, 2003.

Pastor, Robert A. *Congress and the Politics of U.S. Foreign Economic Policy, 1929–1976.* Berkeley: University of California Press, 1980.

Ratner, Sidney. *The Tariff in American History.* New York: Van Nostrand, 1972.

Taussig, F. W. *The Tariff History of the United States.* 8th ed. New York: G. P. Putnam's Sons, 1936.

Transportation

Goodrich, Carter. *Government Promotion of American Canals and Railroads, 1800–1890.* New York: Columbia University Press, 1960.

Haney, Lewis H. *A Congressional History of Railways in the United States.* 2 vols. Madison, Wis.: Democratic Printing Company, State Printer, 1910.

Kane, Robert M., and Allan D. Vose. *Air Transportation.* 16th ed. Dubuque, Iowa: Kendall/Hunt Publishing Company, 2012.

Lawrence, Harry. *Aviation and the Role of Government.* Dubuque, Iowa: Kendall/Hunt Pub., 2004.

Locklin, D. Philip. *Economics of Transportation.* 7th ed. Homewood, Ill.: Richard D. Irwin, 1972.

Mauch, Christof, and Thomas Zeller, eds. *The World Beyond the Windshield: Roads and Landscapes in the United States and Europe.* Athens Ohio University Press; Stuttgart: Franz Steiner Verlag, 2008.

Rose, Mark H., Bruce E. Seely, and Paul F. Barrett. *The Best Transportation System in the World: Railroads, Trucks, Airlines, and American Public Policy in the Twentieth Century.* Columbus: Ohio State University Press, 2006.

Rose, Mark H., and Raymond A. Mohl. *Interstate: Highway Politics and Policy Since 1939.* 3d ed. Knoxville: University of Tennessee Press, 2012.

Smerk, George M. *The Federal Role in Urban Mass Transportation.* Bloomington: Indiana University Press, 1991.

Swift, Earl. *The Big Roads: The Untold Story of the Engineers, Visionaries, and Trailblazers Who Created the American Superhighways.* Boston, Mass.: Houghton Mifflin Harcourt, 2011.

U.S. Department of Transportation. Office of Environmental Affairs. *A Nation in Motion: Historic American Transportation Sites.* Washington, D.C.: U.S. Government Printing Office, 1976.

U.S. Federal Highway Administration. *America's Highways, 1776–1976: A History of the Federal-Aid Program.* Washington, D.C.: U.S. Department of Transportation, Federal Highway Administration, 1977.

U.S. Office of Federal Coordinator of Transportation. *Public Aids to Transportation.* 4 vols. Washington, D.C.: U.S. Government Printing Office, 1938–1940.

Witnah, Donald R. *U.S. Department of Transportation: A Reference History.* Westport, Conn.: Greenwood Press, 1998.

Treaties

Axelrod, Alan. *American Treaties and Alliances.* Washington, D.C.: CQ Press, 2000.

Bevans, Charles I., comp. *Treaties and Other Agreements of the United States of America, 1776–1949.* 13 vols. Washington, D.C.: U.S. Department of State, 1968–1976.

Dangerfield, Royden J. *In Defense of the Senate: A Study in Treaty Making.* Norman: University of Oklahoma Press, 1933.

Fleming, Denna Frank. *The Treaty Veto of the American Senate.* New York: G. P. Putnam's Sons, 1930.

Glennon, Michael J. "The Senate Role in Treaty Ratification." *American Journal of International Law* 77 (April 1983): 257–280.

Hayden, Joseph Ralston. *The Senate and Treaties, 1789–1817: The Development of the Treaty-Making Functions of the United States Senate during Their Formative Period.* New York: Macmillan, 1920.

Holt, W. Stull. *Treaties Defeated by the Senate: A Study of the Struggle between President and Senate Over the Conduct of Foreign Relations.* Union, N.J.: Lawbook Exchange, 1999.

U.S. Department of State. *United States Treaties and Other International Agreements.* Washington, D.C.: U.S. Government Printing Office, 1952–.

———. Office of Legal Adviser. *Treaties in Force: A List of Treaties and Other International Agreements of the United States in Force on January 1, 1999.* Department of State Publication 9434. Washington, D.C.: U.S. Government Printing Office, 1999.

U.S. Senate Committee on Foreign Relations. *Treaties and Other International Agreements: The Role of the United States Senate.* 106th Cong., 2d sess. S. Print 106–7. Washington, D.C.: U.S. Government Printing Office, 2001.

Wiktor, Christian L. *Treaties Submitted to the United States Senate: Legislative History, 1989–2004.* Leiden; Boston: Martinus Nijhoff, 2006.

Urban Policy

Biles, Roger. *The Fate of Cities: Urban America and the Federal Government, 1945–2000.* Lawrence: University Press of Kansas, 2011.

Cleaveland, Frederic N., Royce Hanson, M. Kent Jennings, John E. Moore, Judith Heimlich Parris, and Randall B. Ripley. *Congress and Urban Problems: A Casebook on the Legislative Process.* Washington, D.C.: Brookings Institution Press, 1969.

Fox, Kenneth. *Metropolitan America: Urban Life and Urban Policy in the United States, 1940–1980.* New Brunswick, N.J.: Rutgers University Press, 1990.

Gelfand Mark I. *A Nation of Cities: The Federal Government and Urban America, 1933–1965.* New York: Oxford University Press, 1975.

Hays, R. Allen. *The Federal Government and Urban Housing.* 3d ed. Albany, N.Y.: State University of New York Press, 2012.

Judd, Dennis R., and Todd Swanstrom. *City Politics: Private Power and Public Policy.* 8th ed. Boston: Longman, 2012.

Kaplan, Marshall, and Franklin James, eds. *The Future of National Urban Policy.* Durham, N.C.: Duke University Press, 1990.

Kleinberg, Benjamin. *Urban America in Transformation: Perspectives on Urban Policy and Development.* Thousand Oaks, Calif.: Sage, 1995.

Martin, Roscoe C. *The Cities and the Federal System.* New York: Atherton Press, 1965.

Peterson, Paul E. *City Limits.* Chicago: University of Chicago Press, 1981.

Teaford, Jon C. *The Twentieth-Century American City.* 2d ed. Baltimore, Md.: Johns Hopkins University Press, 1993.

Veterans

Dearing, Mary. *Veterans in Politics: The Story of the G.A.R.* Baton Rouge: Louisiana State University Press, 1952.

Dillingham, William Pyrle. *Federal Aid to Veterans, 1917–1941.* Gainesville: University of Florida Press, 1952.

Glasson, William Henry. *History of Military Pension Legislation in the United States.* New York: Columbia University Press, 1900.

Levitan, Sar A., and Karen A. Cleary. *Old Wars Remain Unfinished: The Veteran Benefits System.* Baltimore, Md.: Johns Hopkins University Press, 1973.

Pencak, William, ed. *Encyclopedia of the Veteran in America.* 2 vols. Santa Barbara, Calif.: ABC-CLIO, 2009.

Skocpol, Theda. *Protecting Soldiers and Mothers: The Political Origins of Social Policy in the United States.* Cambridge, Mass.: Belknap Press of Harvard University Press, 1992.

U.S. Department of Veterans Affairs. *The Veterans Benefits Administration: An Organizational History, 1776–1994.* Washington, D.C.: Veterans Benefits Administration, 1995.

U.S. House Committee on Veterans' Affairs. *The Provision of Federal Benefits for Veterans: An Historical Analysis of Major Veterans' Legislation, 1862–1954.* 84th Cong., 1st sess. House Committee Print 171. Washington, D.C.: U.S. Government Printing Office, 1955.

Voting and Suffrage

Chute, Marchette. *The First Liberty: A History of the Right to Vote in America, 1619–1850.* New York: Dutton, 1969.

Flexner, Eleanor, and Ellen Fitzpatrick. *Century of Struggle: The Woman's Rights Movement in the United States.* Enl. ed. Cambridge, Mass.: Belknap Press of Harvard University Press, 1996.

Foster, Lorn S., ed. *The Voting Rights Act: Consequences and Implications.* New York: Praeger Publishers, 1985.

Keyssar, Alexander. *The Right to Vote: The Contested History of Democracy in the United States.* Rev. ed. New York: Basic Books, 2009.

Peirce, Neal R., and Lawrence D. Longley. "The Right to Vote in America." Chap. 5 in *The People's President: The Electoral College in American History and the Direct Vote Alternative.* Rev. ed. New York: Simon and Schuster, 1968.

Porter, Kirk H. A *History of Suffrage in the United States.* Chicago: University of Chicago Press, 1918.

Rogers, Donald W., and Christine Scriabine, eds. *Voting and the Spirit of American Democracy: Essays on the History of Voting and Voting Rights in America.* Urbana: University of Illinois Press, 1992.

Women's Issues and Rights

Cullen-DuPont, Kathryn. *Encyclopedia of Women's History in America.* 2d ed. New York: Facts on File, 2000.

Davis, Flora. *Moving the Mountain: The Women's Movement in America since 1960.* Rev. ed. Urbana: University of Illinois Press, 1999.

Flexner, Eleanor, and Ellen Fitzpatrick. *Century of Struggle: The Woman's Rights Movement in the United States.* Cambridge, Mass.: Belknap Press of Harvard University Press, 1996.

Freeman, Jo. *The Politics of Women's Liberation: A Case Study of an Emerging Social Movement and Its Relation to the Policy Process.* New York: McKay, 1975.

Gelb, Joyce, and Marian Lief Palley. *Women and Public Policies: Reassessing Gender Politics.* Charlottesville: University Press of Virginia, 1996.

Harrison, Cynthia. *On Account of Sex: The Politics of Women's Issues, 1945–1968.* Berkeley: University of California Press, 1988.

Hartmann, Susan M. *From Margin to Mainstream: American Women and Politics since 1960.* New York: McGraw-Hill, 1996.

McGlen, Nancy E., Karen O'Connor, Laura van Assendelft, Wendy Gunther-Canada. *Women, Politics, and American Society.* 5th ed. Boston: Longman, 2011.

Mink, Gwendolyn, and Alice O'Connor, ed. *Poverty in the United States: An Encyclopedia of History, Politics, and Policy.* Santa Barbara, Calif.: ABC-CLIO, 2004.

Index

Page numbers in **bold** refer to Major Acts and Treaties entries.

SAGE research**methods**

The essential online tool for researchers from the world's leading methods publisher

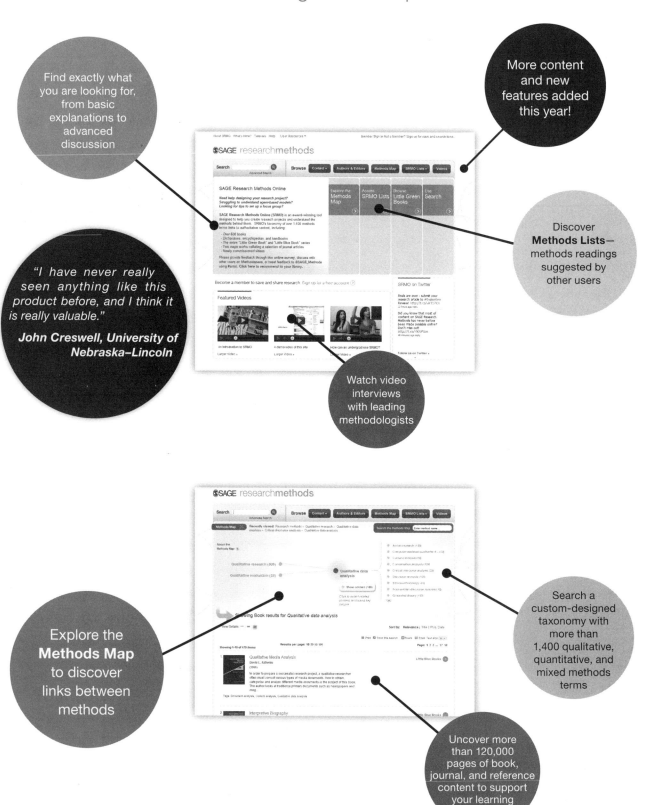

Find exactly what you are looking for, from basic explanations to advanced discussion

More content and new features added this year!

"I have never really seen anything like this product before, and I think it is really valuable."

John Creswell, University of Nebraska–Lincoln

Discover **Methods Lists**—methods readings suggested by other users

Watch video interviews with leading methodologists

Explore the **Methods Map** to discover links between methods

Search a custom-designed taxonomy with more than 1,400 qualitative, quantitative, and mixed methods terms

Uncover more than 120,000 pages of book, journal, and reference content to support your learning

Find out more at
www.sageresearchmethods.com